An early baptism near Philadelphia — th...
Edwards, *Materials Toward a History of the* ...

The Brethren
in Colonial America

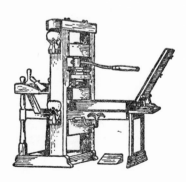

The Brethren
in Colonial America

A Source Book on the Transplantation and Development of the

Church of the Brethren in the Eighteenth Century

Edited by
Donald F. Durnbaugh

THE BRETHREN PRESS

ELGIN, ILLINOIS

BOOK DESIGN BY PAUL DAILEY

Printed in the United States of America

DEDICATED

TO

GLADDYS E. MUIR

who showed what concerned Christian teaching can be

Table of Contents

PREFACE 9

INTRODUCTION 11

I. TRANSPLANTATION
  1. Arrival and Settlement 23
  2. Expansion and Schism 61
  3. Contemporary Accounts 112
  4. On the Frontier 141

II. CONGREGATIONS
  5. Colonial Congregations 171
  6. Germantown 192
  7. Mack Correspondence 232

III. RELATIONS
  8. Brethren and Moravians 267
  9. Brethren and Universalists 321

IV. REVOLUTION
  10. The Brethren Response 341
  11. The Sauer Family 377

V. PUBLICATIONS
  12. Doctrinal Writings 425
  13. Devotional Writings 548

  APPENDIXES 597

  NOTES 609

  INDEX 635

Preface

This book is a sequel to *European Origins of the Brethren* (1958) and follows much the same pattern. It is a collection of original sources (mostly translated from the German) so organized as to attempt to tell the story of the colonial Brethren. The close of the Revolutionary War is the general cut-off date, although this has been breached when the topic made it seem wise to do so.

The bulk of existing documents pertaining to the Church of the Brethren in the colonial period is preserved in the collection of the modest antiquarian, Abraham Harley Cassel, which is now located at Juniata College (Huntingdon, Pennsylvania). The pioneer Brethren historian, Martin Grove Brumbaugh, recognized this when he dedicated his *History of the German Baptist Brethren in Europe and America* (1899) to Cassel, "whose life-long devotion to the history of the church, and whose unequaled collection of original manuscripts [made] this volume possible."

It was possible in the present volume to include many other sources not tapped by Brumbaugh, in addition to those documents from the Cassel Collection which he employed. The Cassel items have all been freshly translated for this source book. An additional emphasis has been the effort to relate the Brethren to other religious movements and general historical developments, rather than telling the story in isolation.

Because of the nature of the book as a source collection, it has been impossible to cover adequately all aspects of early Brethren history in

America, even all important aspects. Some areas will need to await attention in the already-projected comprehensive history of the Church of the Brethren.

Acknowledgments

In the years since 1958 when serious work was begun in gathering, translating, and editing the materials here presented, a sizable number of people have aided its preparation — too large, in fact, to be named here in entirety. The following persons, however, must be named because of their contributions.

The Christian Education Commission of the General Brotherhood Board, through the Historical Committee, made available grants for photo-duplication of data and for travel. It is largely owing to the initiative of Ora W. Garber, secretary of the Historical Committee and book editor of the Brethren Press, that the book was undertaken. Dr. Calvert N. Ellis, president of Juniata College, graciously furthered the project while the writer was on the college faculty from 1958 to 1962 and found a donor, who remains anonymous, to subsidize a research trip in the summer of 1961.

The staffs of the libraries and archives visited were uniformly helpful. Their willingness to allow materials in their care to be published is appreciated. Other individuals who provided assistance were Miss Grace E. Smith, Quincy, Pennsylvania; Lee H. Dierdorff, Greeley, Colorado; Lawrence W. Shultz, North Manchester, Indiana; and Vernard Eller, La Verne, California.

My wife, Hedda, has been of the greatest assistance in completing this project. She checked my translations, typed the several drafts involved, and generally provided critically sympathetic support.

The letters on pages 24-39 were first published in *The Pennsylvania Magazine of History and Biography*. Excerpts from the *Journals of Henry Melchior Muhlenberg* are used with the permission of the Muhlenberg Press. All quotations from the Old and New Testaments are from the Revised Standard Version, copyright 1952 and 1946 by the Division of Christian Education of the National Council of Churches of Christ in the United States of America.

Donald F. Durnbaugh
Lombard, Illinois
August 1966

Introduction

THE RELIGIOUS SETTING

Just as the climate, natural resources, and topography of America shaped the lives of those Europeans who migrated to North America, so the religious setting played its role in shaping their future. The story of religion in America is primarily one of the interaction between the European heritage and innovations brought on by life in the Western Hemisphere.

Most of the major religious movements present in America are offshoots of European church bodies. The very diversity of religious expression, so striking to visitors to this country then and now, stems primarily from the theological, doctrinal, and ethnic differences imported from the Old World. Because of the tight control by governmental authority upon the churches there, many young religious plants in European soil needed the freer air of North America in order to grow and flourish. But their roots stretched across the Atlantic.

A recent history of religion in America illustrates this vividly: "The religious heritage which links us to Europe is immediately apparent to any visitor to the British Isles. When an American walks down the street of an English city, he will be reminded of home as he passes Anglican (Protestant Episcopal), Presbyterian, Congregational, Baptist, Methodist, and Roman Catholic churches. He may be handed a Plymouth Brethren tract, encounter a Salvation Army lassie, or find a Quaker meetinghouse or Jewish synagogue half hidden in a side street.

. . . But it is not from the British Isles only that our churches have come, for there are German, Swedish, Danish, Norwegian, and Finnish Lutheran churches; German, Dutch, and Hungarian Reformed churches; Mennonite, Moravian, Dunker, and Schwenkfelder communities. . . . "[1]

Until the Revolution, the ties linking American church bodies with Europe were very close. "For half of American history, the churches were in fact but minor deposits of European Christendom."[2] Anglicans were under the episcopal tutelage of the Bishop of London, the Reformed looked to the Dutch church authorities, the Lutherans to Germany, the young Methodist movement to England. "Weighty" representatives of the Society of Friends journeyed to America repeatedly, and some American Quakers, such as John Woolman, repaid the visits. Even those groups such as the Brethren, who came virtually as one body, remained in surprisingly close touch with coreligionists in Europe. The Moravians, whose missionary zeal was exemplary, maintained their own sailing vessels to care for the continual coming and going across the Atlantic.

One corollary of the European rootage was the transplantation of the state or established church system in the young colonies along the Atlantic seaboard. To modern Americans unburdened by historical knowledge, separation of church and state seems completely natural. In the seventeenth and eighteenth centuries, the idea seemed radical in the extreme, propounded only by subversive revolutionary sects. The eras of bloody religious wars in Europe had been brought to a close only by the universal adoption of the Westphalian principle that "the prince determines the religion," *i.e.,* one official faith per territory. In the words of an eminent church historian: "Each of these groups [Anglican, Lutheran, Reformed, Roman Catholic] claimed within its territory religious absolutism. All the dominant groups believed in and demanded religious uniformity within their civil commonwealth enforced by the civil power."[3]

A typical statement of the advantages of establishment was penned by William Smith, an Anglican divine in colonial Pennsylvania (who himself had ambitions of becoming an American prelate):

"As to the political uses of national establishments, he must indeed be a very shallow politician who does not see them. The statesman has always found it necessary for the purposes of government, to raise some one denomination or religion above the rest to a certain degree; this favored denomination, by these means, becomes as it were the creature of the government, which is thus enabled to turn the balance and keep all in subjection. For as such establishments may be made in favor of one party as well as another, the party that is uppermost becomes a balance for all the tolerated sects; and these last, in hopes of that preference in their turn, are always tractable. But let a government once give away the powers of bestowing its own favors, and let all sects and persuasions be equally favored, equally independent of the constitution, how shall they be influenced or how ruled?"[4]

It is quite well known that the Puritans who came to New England for religious freedom had no intention of extending that privilege to others. Their understanding of religious liberty was well expressed by the Reverend Mr. Nathaniel Ward, who wrote: "I dare take upon me, to be the herald of New England so far as to proclaim to the world, in the name of our colony, that all Familists, Antinomians, Anabaptists, and other Enthusiasts, shall have free liberty to keep away from us, and such as will come to be gone as fast as they can, the sooner the better."[5]

Virginia's first charter in 1606 provided for the setting up of a church "according to the doctrine, rights, and religion now professed and established within our realm of England," and early laws threatened ferocious penalties for lack of respect for the minister or absence from church services. Nine of the colonies instituted church establishments, with only Rhode Island from Baptist influence, New Jersey and Pennsylvania from Quaker influence, and New York from practical necessity allowing religious freedom. It should be said that, very early, the legal establishment was in practice tempered by varying degrees of accommodation to dissenting groups, but the principle of the state-church tie remained unshaken.[6]

There were many forces which broke down the principle of establishment and led to the enthroning of religious liberty in post-Revolutionary America — the chief American religious innovation. First, the basic principles of the Reformation — Scripture as sole authority, justification by faith, priesthood of all believers — provided the groundwork for religious freedom even though the "right-wing" Reformation churches persisted in the traditional state-church pattern. Second, the beliefs of the "left-wing" of the Reformation — Baptists, Quakers,

German sectarian groups — were given a practical test in America and found to be not only workable but actually better suited to local conditions than the older system. Third, the economic and political self-interest of the colonial proprietors and the English government dictated a tolerant religious policy in order to attract and preserve dissenting colonists. Fourth, the availability of inexpensive land on the frontier made strict regimentation impossible, owing to the ease of evading control by movement west. Fifth, the sheer necessity of dealing with the diversity of religious opinions present in America made establishment unfeasible. Sixth, the deistic and social-contract leanings of the framers of the Constitution made them more friendly to the democratic and tolerant principles of religious liberty than to the monarchial and rigid characteristics of a state church. Seventh, the effect of the Pietistic background of many American churchmen of various bodies and the impact of the Great Awakening were to stress the importance of the personal religious experience of the individual. "Here was an intimation that the essence of a church was the voluntary association of individuals who had had the experience."[7]

All of these played their role in creating the setting for the promulgation of religious freedom, so that "Congress was shut up to this course by the previous history of the American Colonies and the actual condition of things at the time of the formation of the national government."[8]

It was in this period of change that the Brethren came to America. In some ways, the history of the Brethren — a small, Germanic, sectarian group of Reformed parentage, shaped by the religious movements known as Pietism and Anabaptism — in their transplantation to America is symbolic of the experience of many other religious bodies. How they adapted to the new environment, the internal stresses they experienced, their pioneering on the frontiers, their relationships to other faiths, the impact upon them of war and revolution — these make up the story of the Brethren in colonial America.

THE BRETHREN IN EUROPE AND AMERICA

An eighteenth-century account of the Brethren by the Quaker author Samuel Smith will provide an appropriate bridge between the beginnings of the movement in Europe and the early history in

America. Smith (1720-1776) began the writing of a history of the province of Pennsylvania about 1765, the year in which he published his history of New Jersey. He did not live to see the work into print, but the manuscript was preserved and was published in 1913.[8]

A letter from the prominent Quaker Anthony Benezet to Smith on October 17, 1765, indicates the reason for the substantial space given to the Brethren in the history:

" . . . I have acquainted Owen James and James Pemberton, [and] Robert Proud with thy intention of proceeding in the publication of the history which is extremely agreeable to them, time calling loudly for something of that nature from Friends, which may answer many good ends, particularly as it may prevent a publication under the same name, which might give us exceeding great pain and trouble. . . . I would just remark, lest I should hereafter forget it, that in making mention of our testimony against war, as it is so momentous a subject, it will be well in a particular manner to enforce on the mind of the reader, that from the beginning of the promulgation of the Gospel, some in all ages have bor[n]e that testimony, but particularly since the Reformation, not only the Quakers, but the Mennonites . . . have since Luther's time bor[n]e that testimony, and many, very many of them laid down their lives in the fire for the support of it. The followers of Caspar S[ch]wenkfeld have also from the same time, in great numbers and much simplicity and truth bor[n]e the same testimony in Silesia and Moravia. And besides about the end of the last century and the beginning of this, several other smaller sects [such] as the Dumplers [Dunkers] and Pietists, a people coming mostly from Germany, etc., who have many meetings for worship both in Germany and here, besides a great part of the Moravians."[10]

The Robert Proud mentioned also published a history of Pennsylvania, utilizing the Smith manuscript.[11] The account of the Brethren found in Smith's history is quite accurate, with the exception of mistakes in the spelling of proper names, which have been corrected, where possible, in the following. It bears evidence of being based on firsthand information from Brethren living in Pennsylvania. The author says of his writing:

"The merit of this collection (if any) must . . . principally rest upon materials left by others: such of these as I have here and appeared to me sufficiently founded, and worthy of credit, either from

public notoriety or undisputed memorials, original settlers, and records;
... And nothing depending barely upon the memory of any man we
adopted without caution. The last however was but a small part."[12]

Of the German Baptists Commonly Known by the Name of Dunkards or Dumplers

"Some of these people came over to Pennsylvania in the year 1719,
others in 1729, and others afterward. They hold it not becoming a
follower of Jesus Christ to bear arms or fight, since their true Master
has forbid His disciples *to resist evil*. And because He has also told
them not to swear at all, they will by no means take an oath, but stick
in this respect close to His advice to affirm with yea what is yea, and
by nay what is nay. As to their origin they will allow of no other
than that which was made by Jesus himself, when He was baptized of
John in Jordan. They have a great esteem for the New Testament,
valuing it higher than all other books; and if they are asked about
the articles of their faith, they know of no other than what is contained
in this book, and therefore can give none.

"They declare that the most ancient among them were awakened
here and there in Europe from their profound sleep of sin by the voice
of God in and about the year 1705, that being a time of many awakenings in that part of the world. Being then quickened by the light of
Christ to a sense of their degenerate evil condition, they began to see
a reformation necessary. Many of them being taught by the Calvinists
from their youth out of the Heidelberg Confession had given them high
notions of the purity that ought to be in those who were converted to
God, with the sense of their own evil condition. . . . In consequence of
it they began to see that the ministers themselves were not yet converted, and although they were freely admitted to the communion
table, they say they observed them to be a covetous people, and often
worse. For these reasons, they determined to depart from under their
tuition, and daily searching the Holy Scriptures, after the practices of
the first and best Christian, they became in time to have a particular
gift of prayer. After they could no longer say the prayers which before
they had learned by heart, they went into the fields and prayed by
themselves. When they met together, [they] bowed their knees in
fellowship, praying and prophesying as they thought the spirit gave
them utterance.

"After some time the clergy began to oppose them, but to little effect, and at length growing inveterate excited the magistrates to persecute them. This occasioned their being banished from many places of their former abode, and made them choose an asylum in a few places where they had liberty of meeting without being disturbed, to wit Schwarzenau in the county of Wittgenstein and Krefeld in the duchy of Cleves belonging to the king of Prussia. In these two places they gathered themselves together from many parts, namely Switzerland, Strasbourg, out of the Palatinate, from Silesia, the duchy of Württemberg, Saxony, from Hall, Harburg and many other places besides. Some indeed were allowed for a while to keep undisturbed meetings at the Ronneburg, an old castle in the county of Büdingen and at Marienborn in the county of Ysenburg where they had taken refuge, but at last were also at different times persecuted there, and obliged to flee from thence and join their brethren, some at Schwarzenau, others at Krefeld.

"Having chosen the New Testament for their rule or canon, eight persons among them met to endeavor to agree upon and establish the right use of externals in religion at Schwarzenau aforesaid, and agreed that in conformity to the example of their true Master, they should among other things establish baptism by way of immersion or plunging in water. That was the meaning in the original Greek in the place, which does not signify to sprinkle or pour water upon any one but to dip or immerse him into the water, as also most agreeable to the comparison the apostle Paul makes (Rom. 5:7) where he calls baptism a *burying*. In consequence of this conclusion, in the year 1708 they were baptized into the water. To these eight persons a number was soon added here and there, and wherever they went, they were called Baptists.

"The learned sometimes endeavored to controvert this point with them, but were, they say, obliged to acknowledge that the first Christians had been baptized in this manner. They alleged the climate, as being [originally] in warm eastern countries, and that in the cold northern parts of the world, it was not advisable because it might impair people's health. To this they replied that Christ had ordered His gospel to be preached not only in warm but also in cold climates without any exception at all, that it is no where found that in cold countries He would have people only to be sprinkled.

"The Scripture says all things are possible to him that believes; if therefore people believe [that] their being dipped in cold water upon such faith would not hurt them [it would not]. In this belief they had been powerfully strengthened, and many occasions had afforded them so many instances of God's power in preserving those who in simplicity of heart keep to His command, that in the midst of winter they have sometimes cleared the water by cutting off the thick ice, and baptized without any hurt. Nay, women that were brought up so delicately that they could not bear to wet their feet, without being made sick by it, when through faith in the Lord Jesus, they had suffered themselves to be quite immersed into the water it had not only not hurt them, but [had] been a means for their recovery from bad states of health, of which they give the following as an instance.

"There lived on the banks of the Rhine an ancient matron, who had been sick for a considerable time, in such a manner that all hopes for her recovery and life were vanished, as well with herself as those who attended her. This woman desired to be baptized, but her friends endeavored to dissuade the baptist [baptizer] from it, telling him that she would doubtless die in the water. Whereupon the baptist asked her whether she had faith, that this might yet be done to her. She replied: 'Yea, I have, and were I to die in the water, I will be baptized.' Upon this, two healthy persons took her between them and carried her to the large river Rhine, the baptist immersed her into the water in the name of the Father, of the Son, and of the Holy Ghost, and she was whole, from that very same hour and [had] no need of anybody's leading her, but went before them all, and coming home, served them.[18]

"This much for baptism. They hold what they call the Eucharist, in commemoration of the sufferings of Christ at night, as they say, Christ himself kept it, washing at the same time one another's feet, agreeable to His example, and command. They meet together to worship on the first day of the week, in confidence of His promise, who said [that] 'where two or three are gathered together in my name, there am I in the midst of them.'

"They have from time to time suffered a great deal in Europe, not only [having] been banished from their native country, but often and in many places [being] fettered and imprisoned. They have been put to the wheelbarrows, and as prisoners made to work at the fortifications. One of them was pilloried in the city of Basel in Switzerland; another was made a galley slave and obliged to row with an iron about his neck like the convicts with whom he worked. Six of them were imprisoned at and near Düsseldorf in the Lower Palatinate for four years together, and obliged to work at the fortifications for a long time. They were sometimes visited by the clergy who endeavored to draw them from their confessions, and make them return to their religion, which they had forsaken, but their labor was in vain. They were then condemned as stubborn and incorrigible, and threatened with death, which being told them in prison, one of them for himself and the rest, wrote the following farewell letter to their brethren. [There follows a letter from John Lobach, May 1, 1717, here omitted.]

"During the confinement of those just mentioned, many went over to Pennsylvania. Those who stayed behind in Germany are said to have been many times badly treated, robbed and imprisoned. Once sixteen of them at a religious meeting at a brother's house near the castle of Hartenburg, on the mountain Rutemburg, surrounded by a sergeant and his men, were bound two and two together, and so carried to Hartenburg castle, where a large sum of money was demanded of them and not having so much about them, they were obliged to deliver what they had. The brother at whose house they had been, was driven from house and home, and went afterwards to Schwarzenau.

"Soon after this some of them were put in prison at Düsseldorf through the cunning of a treacherous clergyman called Ruebel who, pretending he should be glad of a friendly interview with those people, persuaded a simple man to bring them in good confidence to him. But as they were come there, the priest sent for a clerk, who took down what, upon examination by the clergyman, they declared about the baptism of infants, going to church, taking oaths, etc. When everything was set down he said: 'Now, you heretics, get you gone out of the country, as fast as you can, or you will be told of something else.' They left him, but the same night were taken, and by his contrivance as they thought, confined for seven weeks, till the father confessor of the old elector, a discreet Catholic, heard in what an unfair manner they had been trapanned [trapped], [and] spoke with the elector about the affair, who sent orders to release them.

"This imprisonment was in the year 1703 [?]. During these persecutions the king of Prussia had granted a general liberty of conscience, but his press-gangs or soldiers on recruiting parties vexed them sorely several times. One John Fisher from Hall, who had been baptized, they [sought to] force against his conscience to [en]list in the king's service, and tormented him terribly for ten days together [in] different ways, because he would not comply with their wills. They tied his hands and feet together and by them hung him up, thrusting and beating him with sticks and pricking his body with pins to such a degree that his shirt became stiff with blood. When he was quite faint and could stand no longer on his legs, they put him near a deep water and he tumbling into it, they pulled him out again by his legs. But at last when they had tired themselves with tormenting of him, and he still refusing to swear to the colors and take arms, they threw him into a hole. The prince of Dessau . . . seeing him in such a sad condition told them to let him go, for he had suffered his torment.[14]

"Those of the Dumplers who had made Schwarzenau in the county of Wittgenstein (a very poor country, where people are put hard to it for a livelihood) their place of refuge, went from thence to Friesland, where some of them died, and the rest, some after five, others after nine years' abode there, did almost all of them come over to Pennsylvania, the latter in the year 1729. But those who had fixed their residence at Krefeld for the most part came over in the year 1719. The few that were left came to Pennsylvania in 1733.

"When at first these people were banished from their homes and relations, and obliged to emigrate, some to one place, others to another, the goods and effects of some were taken from them, but to others part [was] left which afterwards served them to live upon, and when it was consumed, some of them commemorate that in great poverty they frequently experienced the special providence of God. But since they could never gain strength enough in Europe to eat their own bread, although in Holland good friends were moved to assist them and actually did show them great love, they were continually longing for a place, where by the blessing of God they might be able to maintain themselves by the labor of their hands and to pass the rest of their time in perfect liberty of conscience, which nowhere in Europe they could enjoy together. In their native country they had not full liberty of conscience nor in Holland. Besides there, many could not maintain themselves, but were helped by others, which made them all come over by degrees, except some few, who are still at Krefeld [and] in Friesland.

"Since they have been here they have considerably increased in numbers and wealth, and have enjoyed a complete liberty of conscience, and [have] been able both to maintain themselves and their own poor. They are a quiet inoffensive people. . . . "[15]

It was, then, according to Smith's informants, a combination of religious suppression and economic necessity which motivated the Brethren to turn their faces toward America as a refuge. A natural destination, given the enlightened religious policies of the Quaker proprietors and the Brethren contacts with other Dissenters from the Continent who had already migrated, was the colony of Pennsylvania.

The first part of the story of the Brethren in colonial America, therefore, deals with the uncertainties and hardships of the Atlantic passage, the problems of settlement in unfamiliar locations, the re-actions of earlier settlers to these newcomers, and the ways in which necessary relationships with the homeland were maintained. Sub-stantial, though by no means complete, insights into these matters can be gleaned from contemporary letters and writings.

I. Transplantation

1. Arrival and Settlement

As had some hundreds of religiously and economically oppressed Germans before them and many thousands were to after them, the Brethren looked to the New World as a haven. Their homeland — dominated ecclesiastically by religious establishments, convulsed militarily by continual warfare, and thwarted economically by a surfeit of petty principalities — seemed a poor second to the advantages of America. Books and tracts, private correspondence from immigrant friends, persuasion by the so-called "Newlanders" (agents of shipping firms) — all combined to extol the extensive freedom and economic opportunity abroad.

Of the several possible destinations in America, the colony of Pennsylvania became the preferred, even the single, choice of the German immigrants. Harsh experiences in New England and New York, together with failures of colonization in the Carolinas, pointed the Rhinelanders to the middle colony under Quaker proprietorship. The first major group of immigrants from the Lower Rhine, the Mennonite-Quakers of the *Concord* (1683), had established Germantown near Philadelphia as the center for German immigration. Newcomers found there countrymen who spoke their language and were willing to help them in the often-difficult task of settlement.

Migration had its real dangers, given the perils of ocean passage of the time. Increasingly, however, the dangers of human greed outweighed the uncertainties of the sea. Unscrupulous shipowners and agents packed ships from bilge to scupper to wrest more profit from each voyage. Overcrowding, compounded by poor diet, resulted in shocking numbers of deaths at sea, particularly if unfavorable winds caused the voyage to last longer than anticipated. Concerned colonials of German extraction were soon active in warning their fellows of the dangers involved in migrating.[1]

Thus it was no light decision when the early Brethren determined to establish themselves in the American colonies. The first group migration was from Krefeld in 1719, and the departure of a larger group from Friesland under the leadership of Alexander Mack, first minister of the Brethren, took place in 1729. These have been previously described. Other migrations in the 1730's virtually completed the Brethren exodus.[2]

TRAVEL DESCRIPTIONS

The best contemporary description of the experiences of the Brethren in crossing the ocean is found in the letter written by John Naas to Germany in 1733. This has been published in English translation.[3] Three other early letters supplement Naas's account, and, moreover, provide valuable information on the conditions in America found by the Brethren upon their arrival.

John George Käsebier to Count Casimir

A party of immigrants arrived in Pennsylvania in 1724 from the county of Wittgenstein in west-central Germany, where the Brethren originated in 1708. Among them were John George Käsebier and his wife, who were taken into the home of John Gumre (Gumrie, also Gomorry), early Brethren leader in Pennsylvania. Käsebier, formerly in the service of the Pietist Count Reusz in Vogtland, died within two months after setting foot on American soil.[4]

Count Casimir (1687-1741) was the ruler of Sayn-Wittgenstein-Berleburg, which adjoined the territory Sayn-Wittgenstein-Hohenstein in which Schwarzenau was located. He was noted for his favor shown to religious dissenters and his personal leanings toward Pietism. Under his regimen, religious freedom was guaranteed for several decades after the death of Count Henry Albert in 1723 marked the close of the halcyon days of toleration in the Schwarzenau area. The publication of the so-called "Berleburg Bible" (1726-1742) by religious dissenters favored by Count Casimir is considered to be the highmark of Radical Pietist activity.[5]

> Roxborough, November 7, 1724
> A half-hour from Germantown and four
> hours from Philadelphia

Honorable Count: Gracious Count and Lord:

I report herewith to Your Grace that we departed from Rotterdam on August 3, left from Helfer Sluice [Hellevoet Sluis] to cross the sea to England on August 14 at four o'clock in the afternoon, and arrived off Dover at about ten or eleven o'clock on the forenoon of August 15. Of the 170 people aboard, only a few were not violently seasick. We remained off Dover for eight days and had continuously strong winds so that many became sick from the great rocking. Two small children from the Palatine group and an unmarried man died. We stayed so long off Dover because they loaded still more provisions, and inspected the commercial goods and put them through customs, though none of the passengers had to take his goods through customs no matter how much commercial goods he might have had. This has certainly not happened before to any other ship, though there was a great deal of commercial goods among the passengers — at least 100,000 sewing needles, not to mention other things.

From Dover, we went back along the coast to Tihlen [Deal?] because of the heavy winds. The captain feared that the wind might snap the anchor rope and drive the ship up on a sandbank. It took a long time in Tihlen and no one was allowed to go ashore, as had been the case in Dover, because they said that the King had forbidden it. The Palatines became very indignant at the captain for this and suspected him of having contrived this in the city. They wanted to make a complaint against him, but it was not done because they could not go ashore. As he gave them very poor victuals, they suffered considerably.

We departed from Tihlen on September 6, and had a rather favorable wind for sailing. Soon, however, it shifted so that it came directly against us, and they had to tack continually until toward the evening of the 9th when the northeast wind arose. Then we sailed very rapidly. We went past a tower which is built in the ocean four hours from land on a small, round rock. A family live on it who have to make a light in the evening after sunset so that the sailors can see it and not sail into the rock.

At five o'clock early Sunday morning, the 10th, we left land behind us with an especially favorable wind. During the night from Sunday to Monday a young unmarried woman who had had seasickness died. She had been bled by an English doctor who opened such a large hole in her vein that it burst during the second night. She bled severely and died the following night. She was wrapped in a cloth, stones were tied to her feet, and she was cast overboard from a plank in the morning.

On the 11th we had a good wind and on the 12th also. Toward evening we saw entire schools of large fish close to the ship. We had seen them already at Rotterdam but not so close to the ship. When they show themselves, a strong wind is generally to be expected.

On the 13th we had a strong wind and sailed eight English miles in one hour. Six English miles make one German mile. From coast to coast there are 1,100 or eleven hundred German hours according to the sailors' reckoning. If, however, the distance is reckoned which is traveled along the English coast and the similar distance up the river in Pennsylvania, then there are thirty-four hours in England and fifty hours in Pennsylvania, which make eleven hundred and eighty-four hours from the first departure in England.

My wife and Sauer were very ill, although at times worse than others. When she was unable to eat, it so happened that a bird which was tired from flying over the ocean landed on the ship. The Palatines chased it across the ship for a long time. It ran past me and I seized it by its long legs. In this way I got a roast fowl for my sick wife. I cannot describe how sick you get if you are sick at sea. Although I experienced it but a little, it greatly weakened my constitution.

On the 14th we had a mild southeast wind and very pleasant weather along with it. We sailed three and four E[nglish] m[iles] per hour. Toward evening, however, we got a strong south wind which lasted all night, and we sailed eight and nine E. m. per hour. During the night two small children of the Palatines died, and were buried as described above. Toward evening on the 15th, the wind shifted to the west and we got a strong contrary wind. Nevertheless, in those five days at sea, we had sailed over two hundred hours.

On the 16th my wife was deathly sick the whole night and thought she was going to die. God, however, heard the prayer and, suddenly, her illness subsided.

On the 17th, still a strong west wind. On the 18th, still strong gales, but it seemed as if it would become better. We were driven far to the north by them. On the 19th, the contrary wind still continued with considerable waves on the ocean, until about three o'clock in the afternoon. We then met a ship from the West Indies. Its captain spoke with our captain in English. One minute before they spoke the wind shifted to the north and we sailed more comfortably.

On the 20th the same wind. Sauer and my wife were still sick. I cannot describe how difficult it is for both sick and well when there are contrary winds at sea. Even if there is still something to cook and great care is taken, the rocking of the ship can spill it in an instant. When the most skillful thinks that he is standing on one side of the ship, lo and behold, he finds himself on his behind on the other side of the ship. I fell myself very little, whether standing, sitting, or lying.

The victuals on board the ship, after we put to sea, included meat, which had been in barrels about six or seven years and had returned from the East Indies, peas and barley cooked in putrid water, and butter and Dutch cheese, which was the best.

On the 21st considerable wind.

On the 22nd toward evening we sailed rather fast, but we got a gale wind at midnight which continued.

On the 23rd — [left blank].

During the night of the 24th, an unmarried woman, who had fallen into the ship's hold with an iron kettle of soup about four weeks before, died. She lay sick about fourteen days, then got up again, but several days later she took to her bed once more and died. She was sent to the bottom with coal tied to her feet.

On the 25th a north wind and comfortable sailing.

On the 26th in the evening when it was dark we saw a terribly large fish. As it sped through the water it looked to us as if it were a [illegible], and it spouted with its nose.

On the 27th we had an east wind, but very mild and good weather.

On the 28th a north wind, but we did not sail fast.

On the 29th we had clear weather and a good wind.

On the 30th clear weather and an east wind. On October 1 we had clear weather with a south wind and saw a large school of fish which leaped from the water like a herd of swine.

On the 2nd, we had a warm day — it hardly gets this warm in your summers — and the ocean was completely calm. On the 3rd we had directly contrary winds, but we tacked ahead. Very far away to the south we saw a ship which was the third that we had seen so far.

During the night from the 3rd to the 4th we got a strong north wind which was rather good for us. A man from among the Palatines, who had severe nosebleeding but had not lain sick very long, died and was buried as the others had been. On the 4th [the wind] shifted northeast and we sailed eight E. m. in one hour. We saw fish which flew a bit above the water like swallows. They had four wings; the front ones were exactly like swallows' wings, but the rear ones were much shorter.

On the 5th we had a strong east wind and sailed rapidly, but toward evening [came] a west wind.

On the 6th we still had a west wind which was almost like a storm.

On the 7th, it continued until toward evening, then it shifted to the southwest.

On the 8th, we also had a contrary wind. On the 9th and 10th forenoon. In the afternoon we got a north wind and sailed eight E. m. in one hour. During the night from the 9th to the 10th, an old unmarried Swiss man, who had been ill three or four weeks, died, was placed in an old sack and sunk.

On the 11th, the weather was fair, and we also had a favorable wind. We saw a school of medium-sized fish hopping along the water like mice because a fish of prey could be seen chasing them.

On the 12th we had a south wind in the forenoon but it developed into quite a storm. In the afternoon it shifted suddenly to the north. We also saw a sloop and spoke with her.

On the 13th the same wind, but more agreeable.

On the 14th [an] east wind and warm weather, also on the 15th.

On the 16th also warm and a gentle east wind. Toward noon, however, it shifted and came from the south and continued through the night until four o'clock in the morning.

On the 17th a storm from the north. We gathered much rainwater in our great scarcity of water as it was a heavy rainstorm.

On the 18th a mild west wind.

On the 19th a mild southwest wind, but during the night it shifted to the east and blew so strongly that we sailed 153 E. m. in twenty-four hours on the 20th. On the 21st, 154 E. m. with the same wind.

On the 22nd, still east wind, favorable for us.

On the 23rd, a northwest wind but not strong. On the 24th still a north wind. We saw land birds and from this we noticed that we were not far from land. Also great flocks of wild ducks. In the evening at seven o'clock we sounded bottom. On the 25th toward evening we approached land which is called South Island [*Süder Eyland*]. It was twenty-two hours to the south on our left. That same evening and night we sailed along its coast quite a distance. On the morning of the 26th we again got a good wind which drove us so strongly ahead that by the evening at dusk we reached the mouth of the river which leads inland to Philadelphia. However, the captain sailed too far from shore and the terribly large and heavily-laden ship ran onto a sandbank. The ship took a great jolt and then another. We all thought that the ship had burst open.

This lasted for over a quarter of an hour as if the ship were scraping over sharp rocks. The earnest prayers and cries to God in the highest, that were uttered in the open air, were indescribable. We had thought that we had evaded all danger, but God showed us that He could bring ruin to us and our property close to land as well. Yes, my legs shook so that I could hardly stand, but in my heart I heard a voice saying that there was no danger. I called upon His mercy that He might spare us, and He heard it and helped. When we had sailed away from the sandbank a distance, they cast anchor and remained there overnight. If there had been a strong wind, however, the ship would have been smashed to pieces.

On the 27th the sailors began their game, for they had a custom that whoever had never traveled on the river had to donate a quantity of brandy. All of the crew who had not traveled on it gave something except one Scotchman who would not pay. He was tied, hauled a good twelve feet high with a ship's pulley, and suddenly released so that he fell head over heels into the water. This was done three times, and the first time a shot was fired. When they had finished with the crew, then it was the turn of the Palatines. They all gave something. If someone refused they set about tying him until he promised to give something.

About nine o'clock we took on board two pilots, one from Loisz-taun [Lewes-town?] and the other from Philadelphia. They had to guide the ship in the river. It was full of sandbanks, but they knew the river. On the 28th we sailed up the river and arrived at Phila-delphia safely on the noon of the 29th. Twenty shots were fired. It is a beautiful town because all of the streets are laid out at right angles. Many say that there are at least two thousand houses there. The ship lay for three more days in the river.

We disembarked on November 2, but did not receive our things until November 3. On the fourth, one of the Brethren congregation [*Täuffer Gemeinde*], Gumrie by name, took us into his home in heartfelt love and evidenced brotherly love to us with plenty to eat and to drink, and also a place to sleep to this hour. He wants to shelter us until we find a place somewhere else. John Henry Traut from Germantown, another of the Brethren, hauled our things a distance of four hours to this place without taking pay. (This is written and refers to me and Nicholas [Wolff], for Sauer lives in Germantown.)

As far as this country is concerned, it is a precious land with the finest wheat, as well as unusual corn, fine broomcorn, maize, and white beets of such quality as I never saw in Germany, apart from that which I have not yet seen. There are apples in great quantities from trees which grow up wild without being grafted, so delicate to look at that I have not seen the like in Germany. I saw in Germantown so many spoiled apples in various piles in a garden, that a wagon loaded with them could not be budged by four horses. Many trees are full of apples which are frozen, because there is a shortage of workers.

A reaper earns a *Florin* a day in the summer plus "wedding meals" along with it, and the work is not nearly so hard as in Germany. A day laborer earns ordinarily a half-*Florin* in the winter, and twenty *Albus* in the summer. Food is cheap compared to Germany. The freedom of the inhabitants is indescribable. They let their sows, cows, and horses run without a keeper.

The man in our house came to this country in 1719 and did not bring much with him. Now he has a property worth at least one thousand *Florins,* three horses, cows and sheep, hens and sows. (He slaughtered three of these today which were as big as donkeys.) There are more people like him who came here in 1719 and now have properties worth two to three thousand *Florins,* and livestock in quantity.

The trees which grow in the forests are cedar, two kinds of nut trees, chestnut, and many young oaks. It is, however, so easy to be cleared that it is hard to believe. Deer, rabbits (but not so many of these two as of others), pheasants, wild partridge, and pigeons are plentiful, and all can be shot without limit.

One can, to be sure, obtain land in the city, which is more expensive. Ten and twelve hours distant from the city it is much cheaper. Whoever is willing to work can become rich in a short time through God's blessing. Goods, however, which can be brought from Germany, are expensive. For example, gunpowder — for one pound, one *Florin;* a thousand sewing needles, nine, ten, or eleven *Kopfstück.* Silk and lace are four times as expensive, also shoe nails and other nails.

Tailors, smiths, and shoemakers, also weavers, are the best-paid artisans. It costs ten *Florins* in the city for a dress, in the country, six *Florins* and twenty *Albus.* A pair of men's shoes costs seven *Kopfstück.* It is possible, though, to earn enough, if one just has a will to work. A day laborer does not like to take on two days' work, but rather for a quarter of a year, or half a year. I now close, and commend Your Grace, the Count, to the protection of the Most High, and remain, Your Grace, with warm greetings to all the servants,

> Your dear friend
> John George Käsebier.

I ask Your Grace, the Count, to deal paternally in your country, so that God may deal paternally with you.

P.S. I would like to remind Your Grace that if someone wishes to come and appeals for a travel subsidy in order to come to this country, you would "open your hand" and share with him according to your ability. People who are willing to work can thus in truth be helped. God is indeed a rewarder of all goodness.

Something else remarkable has come to my mind, that the day in summer here is two hours shorter, and in winter two hours longer, and also that it is so safe from thieves here that it is not necessary to lock the door at night. My host told me that often they all went away from the house and had often left it unlocked.

There are horses here in great numbers. Some have one hundred; some have sixty; some have thirty. They are all English riding horses. The women here ride sidesaddle despite a man and also small boys [?].

There is so much that could be written that it is impossible to write everything. Today we saw more than ten wild partridge in the field of our host, but we could not get to them to shoot because they were wary from much shooting.

Käsebier

(After this letter was written my dear husband became ill. He still went threshing for a day with Nicholas despite of it. The illness grew worse so that he could not do it the next day. He had chills, and fever and this lasted at least eight days. After this the fever prevailed and my dear husband became delirious. He kept on working until the illness became so bad that he could not walk any more. He lay in bed five weeks having to be lifted and carried, and died on December 19, 1724.)[6]

Christopher Sauer I to Wittgenstein Friends

Some of the qualities which were later to make Christopher Sauer I (1695-1758) one of the most influential leaders of the German element in America are noticeable in his early letter to friends in his former homeland. His searching observations of economic and religious conditions in Pennsylvania reveal alertness and acumen.

This and other letters of Sauer found wide circulation in Germany and resulted in the immigration of many. In 1755 Sauer asserted in a letter to the governor of Pennsylvania that

> when I came to this province and found everything to the contrary from where I came from, I wrote largely to all my friends and acquaintances of the civil, and religious liberty, privileges, etc., and of the goodness I have heard and seen, and my letters were printed and reprinted, and provoked many a thousand people to come to this province, and many thanked the Lord for it, and desired their friends also again to come here.[7]

This is corroborated by a comment of a resident of Wittgenstein, Count De Marsay, who wrote in 1725 of the impact of Sauer's letters:

> These letters contained a description of Pennsylvania that

it was like an earthly paradise. . . . The country had abundance and was fruitful in all necessary things. There was complete freedom. One could live there as a good Christian in solitude, as one pleased, and if one wanted to work a little, especially craftsmen . . . then one could earn his livelihood with abundance. . . . Other families decided the same [to migrate], at least one hundred persons from this area, all people whom we knew.[8]

Although Sauer had very close dealings with the Brethren, and was sympathetic to many of their concerns, he never joined them formally. His like-named son did become a Brethren leader, which has occasioned considerable confusion by later writers.

> Germantown, two hours from Philadelphia,
> in America
> August 1, 1725

To all good friends and acquaintances at Schwarzenau, Berleburg, Laasphe, and Christianseck:

May the grace of God which has been given to you in great measure remain and increase among you all. Amen!

As I was asked by most of you to write how we were getting along, and to report about the character of this country, I sent a long letter to you shortly after my arrival.[9] I do not know, however, whether it arrived safely or not. I therefore do not want to waste the present opportunity to report briefly to you again what I previously wrote in detail, as a good friend is sailing with his own ship to Germany, to Hamburg and Berlin, to be specific.

As far as I am concerned, I crossed the ocean safely along with my wife and child, and also Nicholas and Käsebier with all of their families. The ship voyage is as one takes it. For my part, I maintain that it is a comfortable trip if one carries along victuals to which one is accustomed and controls his imagination. The laziest person can endure several weeks of idleness, sitting, lying down, strolling, eating, drinking, and sleeping. Even the smallest children are used to being rocked to and fro occasionally. During the worst storm we experienced, we cooked biscuits on the deck. We do not know any one on the ship who showed the least fear. Rather, the worse the storm, the more people came out on deck to see the proud waves. However, when we came a half-hour's distance from land, the ship ran onto a sandbank, and it looked a little dangerous for the cargo. The people, however, could have been taken to the shore by small boats, because it was very calm weather. We passed safely over it, and in about twenty-four hours we sailed one hundred miles upstream to Philadelphia, after being on the ocean for six-and-a-half weeks. We sailed from Holland to England with favoring winds in sixteen hours, which sometimes takes eight days.

Now we are here in a well-blessed land. There are neither guilds nor burdens from the authorities. My host has a well-built house, and is a cooper by trade. He has fifty acres of fields and forest, for which he must pay the governor one and a half *Reichstaler* yearly. Others pay twenty *Reichstaler* for one hundred acres, others more. Mr. Gülte has about nine hundred acres, with a rent of two *Reichstaler*. It is not an uninhabited country, but rather has been and is being well settled. Philadelphia was a wilderness forty years ago, and now there live there at least eight hundred important merchants and shopkeepers according to my estimate. It is handsomely built. The straight streets are laid out at right angles. It lies on a large river called the Delaware. A strict government using English law opposes godless men. In the press there is weekly news from Germany, France, England, Holland, and Sweden.

Every sixteen weeks small ships sail to England. They supposedly often cross the ocean in seven days. They are small and there are often only three or four men in them. Whoever wishes to cross with them must pay more than [on] the large ships, but it is very safe. There has never been a report of one of them suffering shipwreck. They escape pirate ships in times of danger by their speed. Many ships from neighboring lands call here with merchandise. Foodstuffs are usually cheaper than over there, but not much is being raised yet. All vegetables and fruit grow the same as over there, except for plums and pears. Wine grapes also grow well, but are little planted. The people do not bother because here there are other nice beverages. Whoever wants to drink wine must pay one *Florin* for one German quart. It comes from a neighboring island called Madeira.

All labor is well paid. A man's suit, like I made in Laasphe, sells in the city for ten to twelve *Florins*. The usual costume, however, has the coat without pockets, no buttons and buttonholes on the pockets, no pleats in the jacket, and no more buttonholes than buttons. For such a suit one earns four, five, or six *Florins;* for a pair of trousers with pockets and buttonholes on the sides, two *Florins.* The tailors in the country work mostly in people's homes. They earn two *Kopfstück* a day and board.

Leather is cheap, but a pair of shoes costs seven *Kopfstück.* A linen-weaver earns at least ten, eleven, or twelve *Reichstaler* for an ell of woven shirt material. A day laborer receives his board and forty to fifty *Reichstaler* a day, a carpenter on a ship four to five *Kopfstück.*

A mason earns five to six *Kopfstück* and board; a farm hand, one hundred *Florins* a year; a hired girl, forty to fifty *Florins;* a journeyman tailor earns four *Florins* a week and board in the city, and in the country three *Florins.* I do not know that any rope-makers are here, and there are many ships built here. There is a great shortage of day laborers, farmhands, hired girls, and artisans. A shoe-last costs four *Batzen.* A spinning wheel of the poorest quality, fifteen to sixteen *Kopfstück.* A poor-quality bucket with wooden handle and hoops costs thirty *Reichstaler.* In sum, whoever can and will work here will not suffer much want.

The spirit of this world promises her admirers a great fortune weekly. When a day laborer or artisan arrives here without debts, then in two or three years he can buy property of one hundred acres of fields, and forests, with wheat, trees, and other gardens, as well as a soundly built stone house. This is more independent than a nobleman's estate in Germany. "For 999 years" is written in the land contract by the authorities. Such people know no limits in their pleasure, as they do not know how many horses or cattle they have. Some have one hundred horses. It is then a minor item that the wife has a lady's saddle costing sixty *Florins.*

In order that I describe this country briefly and objectively, you should know that it is a good and free country, as everyone can live according to his will and knowledge. The children of God find a Pella therein, where they are secure from outward persecution. The hermits have the best opportunity; the greedy find fodder in abundance; the hard workers find enough to do. Those who are content with little easily attain outward peace of mind.

It is also especially a gathering place for many hundreds of restless and eccentric people. It seems also as if the constellation of our horizon greatly favors the artful. The place is filled with so many scheming people that one can hardly believe what intrigues are here thought of. One must certainly not imagine that this is a paradise. It is rather Babel just as much as across the water. One hears with horror what luxury prevails in Philadelphia, and it only lacks licensing the houses of prostitution, then things would have reached the limit. The rapidly approaching judgment day will hardly spare our borders.

The all-too-great abundance to which everyone can easily attain has, it seems to me, brought many sincere souls to great spiritual danger. There are still, to be sure, many souls who have a pleasing understanding. Most, however, have barricaded themselves into sects and groups. The Brethren have erected a fence around themselves; they admit and expel, and are jealous of and quarrelsome with others. The Mennonites conduct things somewhat more honorably. In the meantime may God help us to the true insight of our Savior. The Quaker Society is the largest. There may well be several thousand, but they [also] say, "Here is the temple of the Lord." I have very little knowledge where quiet souls exist, here and there, but God knows well. Whoever wants to be very secluded can remain hidden here his entire life.

Dear friends, I do not know anything else that is necessary to write you. If, as it seems, some of you plan to migrate here, it is hard for me to advise you. The country is very good, to be sure, but if a person is discontented he is badly off no matter where he is. Wherever one communes within himself, and seeks heaven in himself, he has made the right move. On the other hand, when he retains the world within himself and seeks still more outside himself, he loses God and Christ, heaven and salvation. If I had known the goodness and love of God before, and about the world, myself, and what all lives within me and is capable of living there, I would not have moved one step away in order to have a better life, until I was persecuted. I do not regret, nevertheless, that I migrated here, now that I am here.

In the meantime, dear friends, let us concentrate all our efforts on being more and more united with God. It is certainly worth the effort, and indeed good to live under Him, and have Him as a friend, as otherwise one has only trouble, dissatisfaction, fear, and trials in oneself and in the world. God help us all to this end.

Should, however, someone migrate here, which I would like to leave to each person's judgment, he should take care that he stock himself with food to which he is accustomed, so that if he cannot stand the ship diet, the poor body need not suffer. A little wine is good for refreshment, as can be seen among other things in Käsebier's letter. When one sails here from Holland, one can bring along, of course, much merchandise, as all goods here cost twice as much as over there, especially yellow, white, brown, and red sewing and quilting threads. If examined by customs in England, it will be confiscated, because the merchants of England do not tolerate it. They are not supposed to check in the bedsteads, however.

No one should indenture himself to the captain, but rather promise to repay on this side if he has no money or little money. One can borrow the money here and repay in cash. Many of the Palatines paid the captain nothing, although they had money. Instead, they bought knives, combs of ivory and horn, steel and nails, and paid only after they had come here. Everyone should act according to his own best judgment. The children of this world are very clever in their kind. Whoever is guided by God goes safely.

Käsebier died, as you can see from his wife's letter. Nicholas and his family are in good health. Käsebier's widow can earn a good living by spinning. I live near her in Germantown. The rent seems high, to be sure, but when one figures, on the other hand, that all wages are two, three, or four times as high, then it is not expensive. I live in a house where I have as large a room as at Laasphe, a kitchen, attic, garden, cellar, stable, a cow and two pigs, as well as a large orchard with thirty-six apple trees, many peaches and cherries. When the cow and the pigs are fattened from the peaches and apples, I hope to have fifty measures of apples left to shake down. I also have free split firewood on the farm. For this I pay twenty-seven *Florins* a year.

I have done little tailor work so far, because one must work so far away in the houses round about, if one does not live in the city. I have therefore made clocks up to now. I sell a new clock, which I can make in three or four weeks, for forty, fifty, sixty, seventy, or eighty *Florins*. I have made three clocks during the three quarters of a year that I have been here. As there is no tinker here, I do much of that kind of work. The rest of the time I make clocks. My wife combs wool, and earns three *Batzen,* fifteen to sixteen *Reichstaler* a pound. She has several hundred pounds to comb.

I wish that if someone comes over here, he might bring me some brass plates, about one eighth of an inch thick. I would be glad to pay double for it, even if it were forty to fifty pounds. In case I died in the meantime, there are others requesting it. I wish that I had a cutting tool with which to cut gears, such as Mr. Marsay has. They are, however, not to be had where you are, otherwise I would ask someone to bring one for me. Whoever brings with him a copper brandy kettle [still] has good merchandise. Recently one of eighty gallons was sold here for two hundred *Florins,* Frankfurt currency.

This serves as further information. Whoever brings silver money with him has its full value here. Whoever brings gold coins [*Pistolen*] earns half a *Reichstaler* on each *Florin.* One loses with ducats. Whoever exchanges for English crowns in England and receives for them copper money in England profits one hundred with one hundred. All silver and gold is weighed. The gold coins and ducats are cut so small that one can buy a pound of butter with a small piece. They are not as readily accepted, however, for paper money is preferred. I maintain that as long as this natural kingdom lasts, one must spend and earn money, be it paper or gold.

Now, then, I close, commending you to the grace of God, and I remain,

your loyal fellow pilgrim
John Christopher Saur.

P.S. If anyone wants to send a letter by mail, he must pay fifteen *Reichstaler* to Rotterdam or Amsterdam. Then the letter goes without fail overseas to Philadelphia. I can pay for it from Holland. The letters from Holland go without fail, because there are only two stations. Please do not think unkindly of me for not writing a separate letter to each one who desired it. I must write in haste, because the ship will sail soon with the flood tide. I hope you have received my lengthy letter of half a year ago. Enclosed are several letters, one written by Käsebier before his death. Mrs. Käsebier asks Mr. Seebach to send her letter to Halle. If my first letter has not arrived, Käsebier's letter should give all the information you might want. I ask the dear sister Juliane to send this letter of mine to Alzey by mail via Marburg. My wife is getting very fat; if she continues like this, she will soon look like Sophie-Liz. Christopher seems to be developing a good character.

He does not pay attention to other children and their games, is very serious, eager to learn and obedient. He likes to be with us and at home. Adieu.[10]

Andrew Boni to a German Relative

Some excerpts have been preserved from a letter written by Andrew Boni (1673-1741) to a cousin named Martin in Germany. Boni, one of the first eight Brethren in 1708, had arrived on the *Allen* with Alexander Mack in 1729. His comments on travel arrangements are quite informative.

The reference to the helpfulness of Christian Liebe (1679-1757) is of interest in light of the earlier difficulties involving Liebe in Krefeld, which disrupted the active Brethren congregation. The Peter De Koker mentioned in the letter was a wealthy merchant affiliated with the Dutch Collegiants. While in The Netherlands (from 1720 to 1729) the Brethren had close connections with the family, and some of the De Kokers seem to have become members of the Brotherhood. The family played a key role in religious and mercantile transactions between Europe and America and between England and the Continent.[11]

[Kingsessing]
October 16, 1736

I wish grace, love, peace, and mercy to all those who read or hear this.

The dear Lord, He it is who sends all help that is given on earth, whether men deign to believe it or not.

Dear Cousin Martin:

You write that you also wish very much to come over here if you had the money for the passage. In the first place, the best thing to do is what I have already pointed out to you, whether you decide to come or not, for I can hardly encourage someone to come because of the great, long, and difficult journey. For those who wish to venture out in the name of God (as should be done in everything) I thought I would write my opinion.

First, regarding young and industrious persons: they need less for the journey. They could travel to Rotterdam on foot, if they do not have the fare. Little money is needed at sea. The passage is six doubloons, and the skipper provides the victuals, food and drink.

Whoever can buy some things in addition at Rotterdam is well off — especially a whole ham for every one or two persons and a jug of vinegar. This I found to be the best. Furthermore, perhaps some bedding, a pillow or a blanket. Boat freight down the Rhine River is so high that the money [could be used to] buy more at Rotterdam.

As for the old people without means, I can but commend them to God. All is possible to faith and love. Here, young and industrious people are welcome. Whatever work they can do — including spinning of wool, flax, or cotton — is well paid, so that many can make a good living with it. A good day laborer earns two shillings in the summer, and a shilling is equal to a *Florin*. Bread, meat, and butter, as long as I have been here, have been available either to buy or sell. So if it please God, I would certainly wish you here.

Here they make wine from apples. Pears are scarce, but peaches plentiful. Weaving also [pays well] and even better in the New York area. Coming here from there is quite easy. In case someone decided to come it would be better for him to go with a New York ship. Merchants' goods are [duty] free there, as well as whatever one happens to buy new for oneself. Here, everything that a newcomer has brought is taken from him. Whoever lacks his six doubloons must indenture himself.

For the information of those who come, whether they come on foot or by ship, at Krefeld, ten hours below [*i.e.*, north of] Cologne, one hour from Urdingen (where the ship usually lands) they might go on land and inquire for Christian Liebe. He will be able to advise you well. Those who go to Rotterdam, ask for the Kornmarkt, and there inquire for Peter De Koker, but do not demand anything from him. Occasionally it takes a long time until the ship is ready. In that case ask Peter De Koker whether he, as a good friend, could not give you some work or arrange for it. He will do so.

Those who come to Philadelphia or New York will arrive well. In New York it is even better, especially for those who have bought new things. But according to many people it is very bad in South Carolina, as I have myself talked to trustworthy people of whom there are many here. They say it is a hot, sandy land, where only wild corn and rice grow. Good bread is so expensive that poor people cannot buy it. Jacob Bohni is said to have migrated there with many others from the Basel area, which saddens me very much. May the good

Lord grant them to use it for their conversion and humility. There is
no good drinking water there. Here, however, it is rather hilly so that
there are plenty of brooks and wells. The same is true for New
York. . . .

Your obliging friend,
Andrew Boni

P.S. There are kidnappers in Rotterdam. They come especially
in the evenings to where young men or journeymen are staying
overnight. Then they use their practices of gently luring them away
to sell them. But in all things it is well done to put one's trust in
God and to ask Him for wisdom.[12]

WARNING TO IMMIGRANTS

Among the flood of literature portraying the advantages of migration
to the New World appeared in 1739 a now-little-known publication which
painted quite a different picture. It was signed by fourteen prominent
German leaders in the Philadelphia area, who were concerned about the
staggering loss of life on incoming passenger ships. The year 1738 had
been especially bad in this respect, and this led to the issuance of the
tract which warned their former countrymen against hasty and ill-pre-
pared immigration. While not completely discouraging Germans from
coming, the authors provided a sobering description of actual conditions.[13]

At least two of the signers were Brethren — Lawrence Schweitzer and
John Henry Kalcklöszer — and others were closely associated with them,
including Sauer, Gruber, and Mackinet[h]. This publication seems to
have gone unnoticed by writers on German immigration in America.

The recipient of the letter is unknown. A possibility would be Dr.
Henry Ehrenfried Luther (1700-1770), typefounder and influential Frankfurt citizen, with whom Christopher Sauer I had connections. Luther's
active concern about migration was well known at that time.[14]

Authentic OPEN LETTER from Pennsylvania in America,
wherein are contained several thorough accounts of (1) the nature of
the land; (2) the migration, sea voyage, and arrivals of the European
passengers in general; and (3) in particular some conscientious and
authenticated accounts of the last and numerous but also miserable
and pitiful migration of the year 1738, etc. Written out of ardent love
and sympathy as a warning to their European, and especially to their
German, countrymen, and attested to with their own seals by some

right-minded persons there, etc. . . . . Frankfurt-Main, 1739, [to be had] at Just[us] Heinr[ich] Wigand's, bookbinder on the market place at the Three Romans.

Pennsylvania, November 25, 1738

Very esteemed Sir and Friend:

Although not all of those of us undersigned know you personally — in fact, only a very few do — we have yet been led by various good reports of your kindness to take the liberty of addressing to you this following communication to our countrymen who are filled with such an overwhelming desire to migrate to this land and are still being stirred up to do so. We also ask you kindly to publish this communication, as it is for the benefit of the public, as early as possible, so that the poor people are at least well informed, challenged, and brought to a more mature consideration of their outward undertaking and plans.

We, the undersigned, along with many of like mind, herewith write to you, our European and, especially German, countrymen, who have been filled with such a strong desire to migrate to this land. We send you first of all our friendly greetings and ask you herewith to consider very seriously what kind of intention or spirit it is that moves you to such a general commotion and to undertake such an indescribably difficult move with your families. Is it really divine providence and will that motivates you? If it is, then this very hand of God would aid you in all situations, and would help bring you to your desired end and goal. (But alas!) is it not perhaps rather a long-lived and fearful secret desire to escape because of fear, and from waiting for events to come, and judgments, which really ought to cause repentance and betterment of heart? Or is it an imagined hope for an earthly paradise which may be attained? Or whether, as is well known and true, [is it] the exaggerated letters of praise and unauthenticated accounts by a few moneybag brethren [*Reichmanns Brüder*] and the generally greedy and selfish decoy birds [*Lock-Vögel*] and so-called Newlanders who are a special divine judgment and the real agitators in these troubled times, which were caused by the heavy pressure of the authorities through the very same divine verdict?

Whichever of these latter causes it might be, we are all compelled and feel obligated, for your own good, to give you a thorough account of the nature of this country, of the migration, sea voyage, and arrival of the German passengers in general and also, in particular, a conscientious and authenticated account of the indeed numerous but also miserable migrations of this year. Whether you believe it or not, time and experience of the historical truth will testify that we have not withheld such from you.

Fifty years ago the country of Pennsylvania, by an especially beneficial providence of God, was opened and offered to the foreigners and refugees persecuted here and there in Europe and in Old England who would gladly support themselves by their hands and diligence under divine protection and blessing. Our dear forefathers as the first inhabitants of this land consisted of Swedes, Englishmen, Germans, and Dutch. After breaking the ice and enduring many a difficulty, they lived a long time in considerable fear of God, righteousness, and genuine neighborly love as well as untiring industry, so that in some of their old people still living a rather exemplary pattern of their first love and unpartisan mutual friendship toward all nationalities, especially toward right-minded people, can still be seen.

However, since there were not many of them at that time, and the news spread, little by little many others arrived, of whom the majority acted against the very aim of the esteemed founder. They sought to gain much property and land and at the same time accumulated great wealth. Thus, along with other nationalities, many Germans who heard of this were enticed and persuaded and have migrated here and are still doing so every year because of ungodly purposes in order to become rich and grand. However, already several times — and it seems to be so again this year — the stars in their courses have crossed them through divine judgment, and hundreds, yes, even thousands, of them have been buried at sea without seeing the imagined promised land.

To be true, the country has until now had its generous blessings for hearts and stomachs, timber and water, bread and meat, flax and wool enough to satiation and shelter and beyond. Yet, it has become so crowded with people that, since it is very fruitful and for many years now large numbers of English, Irish, Scots, Germans, not to mention the slaves, have immigrated annually, it will see in perhaps twenty years hence more people than in the most populous countries over there.

Yet, on the other hand, there is less trade, commerce, and provisions than there, for in this country there is a shortage of money (even though it is only paper money which, however, has a certain fixed amount as high [as], yes, even higher than, over there) because of the great numbers of people who are already here. This is the reason for borrowing being so common here, among farmers and craftsmen, among great and small, so much so that hardly a place could be found in the old country, where the borrowing and frequent failure to repay is as common as here. It has been increasing continually, so that in the twelve, fifteen, to twenty years that we here can remember, it has become worse every year.

Also, because of the number of people who have immigrated and the increase in population, the good land has become so rare that it is to be considered good fortune when someone finds a good piece of land with all of the necessities provided, for which, accordingly, he must pay a high enough price even if it is far from Philadelphia, the only large city in the country. That which twenty or thirty years ago cost sixty or ninety guilders is now worth four hundred, six hundred, indeed, even one to two thousand guilders, namely for uncultivated and untilled land. There is, to be sure, still good and cheap land in Virginia and Maryland where many migrate, including old residents from here. However, the distance from this city is all the more difficult [to travel] when one has to travel two, three, or four weeks by horse and wagon in order to sell his crops and buy other necessities. Land here near the city is so expensive that a single acre costs sixty, one hundred to two hundred guilders, yes, even much more, without buildings, depending on its location.

The majority of those who are not long-time, wealthy, debt-free residents or very rich newcomers, must work strenuously and are hard put to earn a living, for there is neither baker nor butcher, salt nor spices, wine nor brandy, physician nor barber, medicines nor schools to be found for miles around. Also, because of the lack of money they cannot very well live there, so that almost everything must be brought from and secured in the city under great difficulties. This is the reason why even wealthy people who are immigrating these days have regretted their move and wish themselves back over there once again. There are said to be many who would not hesitate to return again if it were not for the difficult journey. Some have already done this and are content with poorer circumstances than they once had. As was mentioned, land near the city being extremely expensive and wood and rent very high, it requires a real pouchful of money or a good income in order to rent for any length of time. So much for the country.

Now to report about the migration generally; as is well known, there are so many recruiting agents over there, all for their own profit, that no one who has a slight inclination toward change can miss them. In the first place, there are some braggarts, or those who came into a fat, wealthy man's kitchen (of whom, however, there are no longer very many) who send letters with exaggerated praises of their supposedly good positions to their relatives and acquaintances over there. Yes, when those immigration agents or Newlanders, as they actually do, open the letters that were sent along with them, and which had been properly and dearly paid for, and find that everything is not described in grand enough terms, they make large numbers out of small, and add that they are to be paid so much more per letter over there. This has happened to us more than once, and even this year letters which had been sent a year ago and were falsified on the way have been returned. Then these Newlanders (the majority if not all) make a deal with the shipping people of the Rhine and Neckar rivers and stir the people up out of selfish and greedy motives and fan more and more excitement. The latter [do this] in order to profit from the people traveling down the Rhine, the former, in order to receive an even fatter commission from the sea captain and to have free passage with their goods. In addition, they go so far as to conceal from the people what provisions, spices, wine, and brandy they should take with them for their benefit and use. At the same time they and the captains take along quantities of these and then at sea force their business upon the poor people and thereby cause them to run up greater debts than they already have, all to increase their greedy profits the more. However, especially this year, many [Newlanders] have paid dearly enough with their lives through illness and had to leave their ill-gotten goods to others. Those who are still living may perhaps be called before a greater court one day, if they do not honestly repent in time.

Now, [traveling] down the Rhine the poor emigrants are in hope of occupying in prosperity a Canaan all prepared for them, as they had been falsely informed. They dance themselves silly, fiddle, scuffle, guzzle, and fight. In other words, they prepare a sure foundation and treasure for the inevitable illnesses at sea by their intemperance and irregular life. They allow swinish filth of lice and dirty clothes on themselves and their families to become an ill preparation for the almost unavoidable uncleanliness at sea. When they arrive at the border of Holland, the big agents and the sea captains are ready to meet them and allow the little agents to drive the poor people under the guise of the best counsel and frankness into their hands, yes, even into caves and dens of murder. They say, this one is a good captain, he has already been in America, and has good references from famous people he has transported over there (often these have been forged and the people whose names are written there know nothing of it). What is even worse, a few have arranged that other captains cannot take any passengers until they have one thousand "freights" on their ships. And that is where the promises of mountains of gold often begin and the poor, deluded, drunken, yes, captive, people are loaded together with their things with great swearing, quarreling, cursing, and fighting.

They are packed in almost like herring, so that many a man whose family numbers eight or more has hardly a space six feet long and wide and three feet high. There he and his family with their bedding, linens, cooking utensils, and victuals are imprisoned for six weeks (as it is said, but actually it usually turns out to be fifteen to twenty and more weeks). If he has many crates and quite a bit of furniture, he must either abandon or destroy several or at least one. If it is sent later, it will be half-rotten and ruined, as is also the case in the ship where he is. As the captains and the immigration agents have much goods themselves and wish to have many people on board, the other passengers can have so much the less. It is true that some of the latter take along more than they absolutely need and require in order to gain a profit. In this way they lack room for victuals and water for which they will pay dearly later. Besides, merchandise which they brought cannot be sold as dearly by far as they had counted on, inasmuch as there is already a surplus of all merchandise which is imported frequently. Often they barely get their money out of it.

The major evil with the crowding [comes] when the slightest illness spreads. With such numbers and their continual and unchanged air and exhalation (inasmuch as they have to lie two or three levels high) such illnesses can easily change into a contagious epidemic, which sweeps away the poor people in large numbers, especially the small children. Very few of them have survived the trip this year; they are always taken first.

From Holland, then, the voyage goes toward England, where the misery begins. Then the excessive meals that had been eaten are violently vomited. It is soon quiet on the ship, especially when a small gale rises. Then those people who had previously quarreled a bit with the captain and the sailors are even worse off, for they are in their hands. They can make their lives miserable for them in many ways, as many, even good-natured, men have already experienced. When they arrive in England, they pass through customs. Even for those who have had a great loss going through customs, which is often the case, after having refreshed themselves a bit, a new hope arises that in six weeks they will be across. But usually this misses the mark by far.

After sailing for two months (for out of twenty ships hardly one arrives after two months and many a one has fallen victim to the sea amidst great remorse, need, and misery), then they begin to speak of only the first half of the distance or somewhat more. By that time the provisions of the people are usually gone because they had eaten and wasted them as if there would be no end to them and often, for example during a stiff wind, vomited them again. Also, the captain must reduce a bit the ration of water and all other victuals, which the people up to that time had often contemptuously and disdainfully thrown overboard instead of saving them carefully. When people are still quite healthy, their stomachs get hungry. . . .

If in a gale the ship is blown off the course, the rations are reduced even more. Then comes a miserable crying, lamenting, regret, and hunger, and especially thirst, but to no avail. Then envy and enmity arise openly if perhaps one still has provisions and his neighbor has nothing. The best of friends and neighbors become the bitterest enemies. Providence is blasphemed and despised. The wind, as earlier the belly, is their god, to which alone they look. Finally, after ten, twelve, even up to sixteen, weeks, land and bottom are found. After much sailing about, healthy or (usually) ill, they sail into the river and up toward land. Then there is jubilation and joy and plenty until they arrive at Philadelphia.

Then all of a sudden the tone changes once more when it is time to be redeemed. If families perhaps still have small children or old people, they must go begging — and that even in fear of the captain, something which they had never in their lives thought of, much less done. It takes a long time for feeble people to find a place and often they are not taken at all. Then they have to sell themselves as the captain is able and wills. Those who still have some means boast and swagger about the land with their rifles acting as if everything ought to fall at their feet and welcome them. This does not last long. There begins cursing and damning of the land and of those who advised them to the move (especially when they still have to pay), if they do not find it to their taste (no vineyards or German ways in the cities and the villages, etc.). Those who have no [money for the] passage are torn from each other — parents from children, man from wife, one here, the other there — and sold for several years [as indentured servants]. Often much is promised in words but not put in writing or kept.

Those coming from the ships smell and stink, are full of lice, filth, and dirt (especially those who were ill or still are) so that no one will touch their clothing out of disgust except good friends or relatives who take care of some. Then all, stranger and native, bewail the money and the deceased parents, children, and friends.

Here, then, is the truth about the migration and arrival of the Europeans, briefly described, when all goes well. From this you, our countrymen, whose thoughts are full of travel ideas, can decide and judge for yourselves whether the rich and prosperous are doing right — even if all goes well — to spend such a large sum as this journey requires during a half-year with great privations and difficulty, and then to come into a strange land where, after considerable time and paying dearly for their lessons, they finally find out things. And whether it is profitable for the poor, elderly, those burdened with small children (for young, strong, single people, if they are healthy, get jobs more easily) to bind themselves and their children into years of servitude after such a difficult journey (for it is seldom, if all goes well, that a family arrives without loss, either at sea or here). Or whether both parties would not do better, if the former consumed their wealth in peace, and the latter performed their work in the sweat of their brow (which they have to do here as well as there) trusting in the Lord faithfully and giving the authorities what is theirs. There is still a God who knows how to govern the hearts of men and who will not let them starve who trust in Him.

Now we wish to report as promised about the miserable migration of this year and its consequences. It is perhaps known to you that on a ship four years ago, two thirds of the Palatines on board starved to death on the voyage which lasted three fourths of a year, and they had to buy rats and mice for dear money. Also, a year ago a ship with rich Englishmen aboard was shipwrecked off New England with over one hundred drowned at once. However, this year the sea has reaped quite a different harvest. By moderate reckoning, of fourteen ships which have so far arrived, and two are still missing (of which one has reason to believe that hardly anyone will survive inasmuch as they have been at sea for over twenty-four weeks), more than eighteen hundred have died at sea and here in Philadelphia.

To begin with Holland — as we have unanimous reports from about one hundred eyewitnesses of the following as well as all other circumstances — the captains and their *factors* or merchants went to meet [the travelers] up the Rhine and Maas rivers as far as the borders. The two leading figures of sea-voyagers, from the *Hope* and Stedman's ship, carefully picked the people who still had some means and baggage, enticed them and signed them up for themselves. Later, after the Rhine vessels had gone partly to Rotterdam and partly to Amsterdam, they set up tents at the former place and stayed there for some time. However, already there a tendency to dysentery and high fever was noticeable owing to the great irregularity, partly to the many cold rains followed by great heat in Holland at that time. About eighty infants died there within that short time.

Then the people were parceled out to the different ships, over two hundred in some, in others over three hundred, in others four hundred or more. Then they were packed in so tightly and crowded into each other that throughout at least one third too many were lodged on the ships. Everywhere the bedsteads were double-deckers, in some indeed they were triple-decked above each other. The crates of many were either smashed, and the people had to store their goods as well as they could (because the captains and the Newlanders had themselves so many crates and goods . . .) or were left behind and sent along on other ships. Much clothing and linens became rotten and moth-eaten.

The convoy now proceeded to sea, where they generally spent three to five weeks, until they arrived at the English port. The harbingers of suffering could be seen on several ships even on this short voyage, but it was not yet general, despite the fact that some had already been buried at sea, and also at Corves [Cowes], the place of customs. They had to stay there seven weeks until their departure. From there the poor people were taken to the great ocean where illness, suffering, and misery soon became general. In one ship the captain and the first mate died after three weeks; [they] were followed by the sailors along with a large number of Germans, so that during the fourteen-week-long sea voyage almost two thirds of them died.

The stinking water had to be the refreshment of the ill, for most of the captains were very merciless. Butter was soon gone, so that whoever had not provided enough victuals for himself and used his food sparingly had to suffer need and want enough in sick conditions. The two Stedmans, who up to that time had been famous for their transporting of the Germans and wanted to retain this reputation, had to suffer along with the others, inasmuch as the one lost almost 120 before he reached land, among them a party from the *Hope* who are among the roughest and hardiest people. Even so they, too, finally succumbed to the illness and death. The other [Stedman] lost probably five sixths of his passengers for hardly sixty were left of three hundred. He lost his mates and some of his sailors as well, and he himself lay near death.

This is the way it went generally. According to reliable reports, six, eight and more died daily at sea. Only two ships of so many arrived on land fairly safe and sound. Yet even there the small children were hit hard. On one, ninety died, on another 104, on another, 180, and so forth. The smallest number of deaths was forty, and many more are dying each day quickly and suddenly, even those who arrived here healthy. Entire families of six to eight persons have been wiped out. Indeed, of nine families who came from a Palatine village, only two men and several children survived. Many fathers and mothers of children [are dead]. On a ship with sickness it is a rarity to see a small child of two to three years, regardless of the number who were aboard originally. On one ship that recently arrived, only thirteen were in good health. It is also known reliably that when the ship stopped in the river near the city and many people were still dying, the sailors by night pitched six to eight of them over-board at a time, just like at sea. In sum, it was just as bad as a plague.

To be true, many houses outside of the city have been rented by the captains on order of the authorities to accommodate the sick, who have been brought there. But in reality it is easy to guess how this goes. The burden rests mostly on those Germans who still have some love for their countrymen, and often collections and charitable distributions are made by the latter to the starving, miserable people. In this connection it is most remarkable that jealousy, envy and malice on the part of the survivors is so much in evidence that the poor receive a contribution of food from the rich and vice versa.

Also, the ships with sickness on them must halt a distance from the city (for fear of contagion). Indeed, those in the city as well as in the country, who have taken sick [immigrants] into their houses or had contact with them, caught the very same illnesses and already several have died very suddenly. It looks indeed as if the illness would spread throughout the country. The stench on the ships and around these people who come from them is so terrible that it makes anyone who is somewhat sensitive sick right away. Therefore the inhabitants rather shy away from the sick people. Generally, the illness ends in apoplexy so that there is grief, misery and lamenting, begging and [looking for] shelter, that those who live close to the docks can hardly endure it.

Despite the fact that so many have fallen victim to death through the divine judgment, because of the large number this time, a large portion, especially elderly and feeble people who even had to pay up for their dead, were not redeemed. This is a time of money shortage among the farmers and the captains want their money or at least some security. It also happened to many a man who redeemed a servant who seemed healthy that the latter died within a few days or weeks and his master had paid his sixty to ninety guilders for nothing. This has made the people hesitant. Eight to ten cases of this are known.

You see, dear countrymen, the misery and suffering this year was so great among us and your fellows who had immigrated from over there that it can hardly be described or related. Thus, God's judgments are visited on those who had traveled down the Rhine with fiddling and whistling, dancing and jumping, cursing and swearing, swilling, guzzling and luxury, and supposed good living, in pursuit of their hoped-for earthly paradise. Oh, how many rich and poor alike, with few exceptions, regret it, what tears one sees of widows and orphans, lengthy chest illnesses and quinsy, swollen bodies, scorbutic boils, swollen lame legs — these are the least relics which accompany the ill and those who had otherwise been well.

In case none of this discourages you from undertaking your journey so carelessly, thoughtlessly, obeying your own will in defiance, against the wishes and protests of your authorities, we do not tell you to stay at home. On the other hand, we do not recommend that to anyone either, lest you think that we do not want anyone else to enjoy the glory which we possess. Not so at all. We are always gratefully content with what divine providence has given us, but things are far from what you there allow yourselves to be persuaded of. We find ourselves duty bound to lay before your eyes for your warning this authentic historical report. Despite this, so that those among you, who still have some fear of the Lord and who are either for conscience' sake or actual outward necessity forced to migrate, may not remain entirely without advice, we therefore remind you in a well-meaning way to make sure that your cause is right and divinely intended, whether it is God's will that speaks to you as He did to Abraham: "Go from your family and your kindred," etc.

If you have secondary motives such as escaping pressure and suffering or accumulating wealth or wanting an easier life, then you will certainly not succeed. Not only will you not reach your goal but inasmuch as you have a better understanding, you will be all the more severely punished. But if some among you are motivated by the finger of God himself, and are moved to migrate, then He will accompany you with His angels, will prepare the way and regulate the outward things to your wonder, and turn other people's hearts to you in love. He will help you bear in patience the sufferings and difficulties of the journey in such a way that you and others shall have reason to praise His holy name. You shall be confident in suffering and death, whereas others who, following their perverted, thoughtless minds, undertake such things in the name of their god, will perish with confused and heavy consciences frightened by their sins and the destroying angel of righteousness. Since they themselves were the cause for the deaths of several or even many among their number or among their families, [they will perish] as people who, as it were, already have the verdict of the great Judge before their eyes.

May the great God save you from this and keep you from such an ungodly, stubborn mind and from rejecting good counsel and admonition. It is our warm and loyal wish that this year's great judgment might make a real impression upon us as well as upon the survivors and upon you who remained behind, and cause earnest soul searching and the true fruits of change of mind. They have not been the only sinners before us or others. The Lord has still other [means] to do justice if one does not take it to heart. If one will not be converted, then He sharpens His spiritual, physical, and eternal sword and bends His bow and aims (Psalm 7, v. 13). May He, the great Savior, redeem all who at this opportunity will let themselves be saved, softened, frightened, awakened, and converted to Him, for His name's sake. Amen.

Finally, we report that the above-related things and events are of such a nature that we have sufficient cause and reason to set our names, places of residence, and seals as a witness to the truth of this letter, for as many as told us to do so, as follows:

(seal)   Henry Graff in Amwell
          Christopher Sauer in Germantown
          John Bechtel in Germantown
          John Adam Gruber in Germantown
          Lawrence Schweitzer in Germantown
          John Eckstein in Germantown
          Jacob Baumann in Germantown
          David Deschler in Philadelphia
          John Wüster in Philadelphia
          Christopher Meng in Germantown
          John Henry Kalcklöszer in Germantown
          Blasius Daniel Mackineth in Germantown
          Anthony Benezet in Philadelphia
          John Benedict Müntz in Falkner's Swamp.[15]

LATER COMMUNICATIONS WITH EUROPE

Maria Naas and the Inheritance From Europe

Two long letters from John Theobald Endt, a Germantown merchant affiliated with the Brethren, to Arnold Goyen in Krefeld, Germany, although dealing with the administration of an estate, provide much information about the process of communication abroad and about the John Naas family. Endt was writing on behalf of the daughter-in-law of Naas, the sister of the recipient of the letters. Her father was Gossen Goyen, prominent Mennonite leader in Krefeld.[16]

Germantown, May 10, 1758

Esteemed and beloved friend Arnold Goyen:

First, our affectionate greetings to your entire worthy family. [I] hope these few lines will find you all in good health. As regards ourselves, including your dear sister Maria and her daughter along with your brother-in-law Jacob William Naas, praise God, all are still well. I did not receive your letter of January 7, 1757, until this winter, that is, in March 1758, and learned from it what I am to do for your sister Maria Naas. I therefore report that I immediately paid the forty *Reichstaler* and she sent me two drafts, that you, dear friend Arnold Goyen, are to pay the forty *Reichstaler* to Christian Liebe, for I owe him eighty *Reichstaler*. I wrote twice last summer concerning this, but it seems that neither [letter] arrived.

As it is, I again paid you eighty *Reichstaler* last summer, that you, by virtue of your letter to me, pay Christian Liebe the eighty *Reichstaler* in cash, for I paid them here in all honesty. Now friend Christian Liebe wrote me a very sharp letter as if I were a dishonest man, and [I] am really innocent since I had clearly written in the previous letter that you were to pay the eighty *Reichstaler* to Christian Liebe. I ask you not to be lax but to pay friend Christian Liebe immediately and have him give a receipt for it, upon life or death, since I have not only paid these eighty *Reichstaler* but more than four hundred *Reichstaler* besides.

For during the five years that your brother-in-law was over there [in Europe], the mother, that is your sister, with her daughter, was not able to earn anything, yet they had to live and have the most necessary clothes. Consequently she ran up a debt of more than one hundred pounds in our money in the hope that Jacob William Naas would bring the entire inheritance back with him, so that everything might be properly repaid. But when your brother-in-law returned and brought nothing back, the creditors came and demanded to be paid. It went so far that he was to go to jail or prison and he was actually arrested by the authorities. So the daughter came and entreated me to help lest her father be dishonored. So I said to her, that if her uncle Henry Landes gave bail with me, each for half of it, we would try to borrow one hundred pounds. Thus we freed him from these difficulties.

In return he promised us, together with the mother and the daughter, that, if the money were forwarded here we should receive and be paid these one hundred pounds, and in case this would not be done the interests were to be accumulated and saved until the one hundred pounds were paid. But as [interests] are six percent a year in our part of the country and in Amwell, where Naas lives, seven percent, you can imagine how much she, that is the child, would lose each year since with you in Krefeld they are only four percent. For that reason I would like to request of you, esteemed friend, to send the child her inheritance and to put it under the trusteeship of two or three guardians here, for example Mr. John Wister [Wüster] of Philadelphia and Christopher Sauer, printer in Germantown, and David Däschler, merchant in Philadelphia. These are three trustworthy men who will see to it that whatever is left after the death of her parents will be turned over to the child.

Furthermore, the daughter ought to have at least enough from the capital to buy about two hundred acres of land and to purchase some [livestock] for raising cattle, which is necessary for a farmer. The remainder ought afterwards to be transferred to the above three men, that they might invest it for interest and pay the two old parents the interests every year as long as they live and then they should be able to make do.

Furthermore, I have to report that the daughter is a grown, adult, marriageable person and will perhaps really marry this summer, for she is being courted by quite a few, but only one can marry her, of course. The reason is that it has been rumored that she has come into an inheritance from her cousin in Maastrich. Also, she is almost twenty-one years old, but I am not sure when. According to the law here, all children are entitled to their inheritance at the age of twenty-one. I do not know how it is in Krefeld. However, my beloved friend Arnold Goyen, it would be only fair to forward her inheritance to the child. For you, as guardian and uncle besides, it would be but reasonable to take care that the child receive what is due her since, after all, it is hers and has come to her according to divine providence.

You are justly obligated to have her inheritance transferred to the child for two reasons. First, because they could receive higher interests on it here than in Krefeld, and because there would not be all the correspondence every year, especially in this dangerous time of war which, moreover, is expensive. Secondly, because she is almost of age and will actually enter into matrimony. You also know that they are poor people who call nothing their own, no household goods, no bedding, for everything was worn out during the long years, and your dear sister Maria has become senile because of all the many and difficult hardships and trials which she had had to endure while Naas was away, so that she is unable to do housework. Moreover, she is old and frail so that she can neither sew nor spin. Now if the daughter leaves the home, the good old Naas will have to do all the housework and with patience to seek to endure and overcome everything, which is not an easy matter for the head of a house.

. . . . .

Therefore, if it pleases you to do so, the money can be properly forwarded here through a bill of exchange via London or Rotterdam, in care of John Wister, an honest merchant, who is worth more than eighty thousand *Reichstaler,* and who is a man of good repute for his honesty. If it could be sent via London, [it is to be addressed] to Mr. Israel Pemberton's or Mr. Philip Benezet's correspondent, whose name I shall add as an address for you. They have regular people in London, where the money will be properly paid on the same day that the exchange calls for even if it were twice the amount. . . . Since I must close for this time, I commend you to the protection of the eternal love and to its gracious mercy revealed in Christ Jesus as the Savior of the world, who gave himself as an eternal sacrifice for all men in order to reconcile the world with God, the unfathomably highest gift, who wills that all men be helped and no one be lost who loves the innocent, strangled Lamb in the time of grace, and obediently follows all His blessed commandments according to His holy gospel brought from heaven.

This great high priest whom God has elevated, who is exalted above all heavens, whose kingdom has no end, make us all able to live according to the faith, whose originator and perfecter He is. No one can help himself except He, who is the man provided by God, who can secure eternal salvation. To Him be the honor through the Father, for willingly letting himself be strangled, as a lamb on the wood of the cross, and for pouring out the Holy Spirit over all the plants which His Father has planted and will yet plant until the end of the world. Magnified be the glorious name of the most high in all eternity of eternities. Amen. I am and remain my very esteemed sir and friend's sincere friend,

John Theobald Endt.

P.S. I must remind you and urgently request of you to be sure to write again soon and to send it to us by mail via London, for your dear sister is very much in need of a quick answer. The name of the merchant in London is: Richard Neave, merchant in London. To him you may make out the address or salutation, then to Mr. Philip Benezet or Israel Pemberton, both important merchants in Philadelphia. This Richard Neave in London has a brother in Philadelphia named Samuel Neave. I did not know this before, but he is a rich merchant here. His brother Richard in London exports more than 100,000 pounds sterling worth of merchandise here every year, for he supplies very many merchants here in Philadelphia.[17]

Germantown, February 10, 1759

Beloved and very esteemed friend Arnold Goyen:

First, my affection and greeting with all due respect to your dear ones and to all the Goyen family and kin. Your letters of this past August 11, 1758, which I received in good order via Mr. Nathaniel Voht in London, arrived safely on January 15, 1759. There were three letters, one to William Naas, one to me written in your hand, and the third from Arnold Liebe. I wrote four times during the past year of 1758, but it seems that only one [letter] arrived, namely the one which was dated May 10, 1758. I mailed one to you as early as January 1758; though I was told it had not arrived, it may perhaps have arrived by now. Later on I wrote you two more letters, one via London in care of Mr. Richard Neave, local merchant, the other via Mr. Zacharias Hopp in Rotterdam. Presumably these letters will yet arrive. Should they not arrive, the one will suffice. Only this should be mentioned that I wrote that she, namely the daughter [of Maria Naas] would be married this past summer, which did occur.

She has already given birth to a young daughter who is well and healthy.

Therefore, it would be no more than just that you send her the money — which she inherited from her dear grandfather's brother, who lived in Maastrich and who in his will left part of his estate to her — without delay according to the proposal submitted to you after it has been in your hands for so long. The money [is to be sent] to the honorable Mr. Richard Neave, a distinguished merchant in London, who will produce a power of attorney from us first in copy, later the genuine original upon receipt of money. The final receipt is to follow later in full by the heirs and by both of us authorized agents, namely, Mr. Philip Benezet, merchant in Philadelphia, and myself, John Theobald Endt. The two of us are authorized to receive the money and shall take care in every way that it remains in safe keeping. That, however, which is to be deducted from the capital for the purchase of a piece of land, they will receive immediately, and later on the debts, which your sister and the daughter made during the absence of Jacob William Naas, will have to be paid, to which [the daughter] and her husband, John Severens, are completely agreed. The remainder, however, is to be invested for interest for your dear old sister Maria Goyen, now Naas, so that she may have a livelihood for the rest of her life. Later on [the daughter and her husband] are to receive everything and may use it as they please.

．．．．．

The condition of your sister is poor at the present, but she is content. She has mastered self-denial better than I or you. She can get along with poor clothing and meager food and out of conscientiousness desires nothing beyond the bare necessities. But the child had to be a little presentable and therefore, after your letter to me, I have always given as needed. I also wish to mention that when the drafts arrive and the money is being transferred, it will not be necessary to pay more on my account except for the forty *Reichstaler* to Arnold Liebe, which must properly and honestly be paid to the dear friend in Wesel, because you run the risk of his collecting it through the power of the authorities; thus the charges would be saved. You may then forward the remaining sum.

I assume that you have already paid friend Arent Hassert. There is nothing else of which I need to remind you except that you would do in love as written above and, in closing, to remind you once more to make every effort to forward to the child her rightful inheritance from her beloved cousin, which he bequeathed to her out of his good and loving heart for her use and to support her parents with the interests, which the child is willing to do with all her heart, as long as the old parents are living, especially her dear mother Maria. Further, there needs to be remembered that the power of attorney, which she and her husband signed together with her father and mother, has been turned over to us, namely, Mr. Philip Benezet and myself, Theobald Endt, and that our authorized agent in London, of the name of Richard Neave, local merchant, is to receive all these sums of money from your hand. [This can be done] through a bill of exchange or in cash, whichever seems best to you, although exchange is better.

The power of attorney is signed by the governing mayor of the city of Philadelphia, named Thomas Lawrence, and has been registered by the notary public in the minutes of the city of Philadelphia and sealed with the common city seal. [This was done] so that in case this our original power of attorney is lost through shipwreck, another might be sent without great expense. May the Lord and ruler over everything preserve it that it may no longer be necessary to write, for I am very burdened by correspondence. I close therefore and commend you to the divine grace and His eternal mercy, and remain your loyal, sincere, and devoted friend.

John Theobald Endt

P.S. I shall soon write another letter, so that in case this one does not arrive, the other may get there. The ship which takes this letter was built in Philadelphia by the merchant Philip Benezet for Mr. Richard Neave in London.

[P.S.] Esteemed friend Arnold Goyen. This letter is not in my own handwriting; I want you to know that I had it copied. I do not have a very neat hand. I have therefore wanted to add this here, lest you become suspicious of me, for there are so many letters in my handwriting at Krefeld, where my name can be seen and how I write. I call this to your attention as a precaution lest you think that I was not the author. My own signature can be found in Krefeld with Liebe and others, perhaps even with you. I kept my own draft as a copy.

Just as I finished writing this, my friend Christian Laasche, who is my nextdoor neighbor, about thirty steps away, came to me and asked me to request you to pay to Henry or Herman von Laasche fifty *Reichstaler* from the sum which you are sending over. It will be alright, if you please to do so. The money is very good, for Christian Laasche is prosperous enough to pay and everything [is] alright. Herewith I close once more asking you to take care of everything without further delay. I remain your friend John Theobald Endt.

Note: Do not forget to pay the forty *Taler* to Arnold.

To my very esteemed and beloved friend Arnold Goyen, merchant in Krefeld.[18]

2. Expansion and Schism

Christmas Day, 1723, marked the reorganization and renewal of the Church of the Brethren in America. The first large migration had taken place in 1719. What is the explanation for the four-year gap? The Ephrata chroniclers, upon whom we are dependent for most of our knowledge about the earliest Brethren beginnings in America, attribute the delay to disunity created by the differences within the Krefeld congregation about church policy and marriage. Others have pointed out the inevitable difficulties in getting established in a new and largely unsettled land and the scattering which took place as the Brethren looked for available land.[1]

Although these explanations have basis in fact, there is reason to believe that a sharp break or discontinuity did not occur. In the absence of contemporary data, it is difficult to state precisely what did happen. A valuable clue demonstrating continuity of Brethren religious concern is found in the fact that in 1719-1720, immediately after arrival, John Gumre bought a plot of land in Germantown along the Wissahickon in his name and the name of the "congregation of the Brethren." It was on this property that the first baptisms took place.[2]

In 1722 Peter Becker (1687-1758) and other Brethren made a concerted effort to bring together in close fellowship those Brethren who lived in diaspora. Meetings were begun that winter, alternating between the homes of Becker and Gumre. In 1723 the rumor of the arrival in Philadelphia of Christian Liebe brought a number of those living along the Schuylkill River to the city to hear the famed one-time galley slave and noted speaker. Although the rumor proved to be false, the visitors stayed to attend the Brethren services in Germantown. This led to a closer bond of unity and resulted later in a request of six to join the Germantown Brethren.

Though often described as the beginning of the church in America, the Christmas Day baptisms of these "first fruits" should more accurately be considered to be the beginning of a period of renewal or revival, akin to the Great Awakening of colonial America spearheaded by Frelinghuysen, Whitefield, and Edwards.[3]

THE FIRST BAPTISMS AND LOVE FEAST

The events of December 25, 1723, have been often described, important as they are for the early history of the Brethren in America. All of them are fundamentally based on the contemporary record in the *Ephrata Chronicle*. Probably the most dramatic narrative is found in Julius Sachse, *The German Sectarians of Pennsylvania,*[4] but this is marred by the author's taste for the legendary. Martin G. Brumbaugh, major Brethren historian, described the day graphically and with imagination, but with greater conformity to the facts.

Doubly memorable Christmas Day, 1723! Christ's anniversary and the date of the birth of His church in America! There is an activity at Peter Becker's house in Germantown. The spindles are still; and the voice of praise is raised. Six persons, Martin Urner, his wife Catherine, Henry Landis, his wife, Frederick Lang, and John Mayle, all from what is now the Coventry district, were in the midst of seventeen members, and they were preparing to hold the first immersion in the church in America. There was no ordained minister this side of the Atlantic.

The members hold a council. Peter Becker is chosen to act as elder. The preliminary examination is held, prayer is offered, and then these twenty-three souls walk out into the winter afternoon, in single file, headed by Peter Becker. They journey to the Wissahickon Creek. The group kneels. Overhead the solemn sentinels of the forest fastness — the pines and hemlock — are stilled. The icebound stream utters strangely solemn music. Curious eyes from the Kelpianites rest reverently upon the group.[5] Peter Becker's voice breaks the stillness. The prayer is ended. The six candidates for membership in God's family are led one by one into the water and are baptized by trine immersion. The procession returns to Germantown.

They assembled in the house of John Gomorry [Gumre]. It is evening now. The old-time tallow-dips are lighted. They gather about a long table, a hymn is sung, and in the silent evening hour, with no witness but God, and curious children, these people begin the observance of the ordinances of God's house on Christmas evening, 1723. The sisters on one side, the brethren on the other, arise and wash one another's feet. Then they eat the Lord's Supper, pass the kiss of charity with the right hand of fellowship, partake of the holy communion, sing a hymn, and go out.

It is night! But under God's guidance their acts have been repeated in a thousand twilights, in all parts of this country in all the years that have come and gone; and please God, we will repeat them again and again until He shall say, "It is enough. Come up higher."

Let us look yet more closely at this company. Who are they? Six are already named. They are babes in Christ. But the other seventeen are warriors of two continents. They had a remarkable career. At the head sat Peter Becker, pioneer preacher in America. He could have told of blessed meetings in Kreyfeld and of sermons by Elders Mack, Li[e]be, and Naas. He is not a gifted preacher, but he leads the sacred music that fills the dimly-lighted room with echoes of heaven's choir. His prayers are eloquent and overmastering. He loved God and talked with Him in the full faith of an expectant child of the King.

To his right sat John Jacob Price, who had prayed and preached in the Rhine Valley with Elder Naas. He was not large in body, but fervent in spirit. There was Stephen Koch, John Hildebrand, Henry Traut and Henry Holsapple. . . . They were rich in experiences with God's people in Germany. There was John Gomorry, in whose house they sat. Near him were Jeremiah and Balser Traut, Daniel Ritter, John Kempfer, Jacob Koch, and George Balser Gans, all sterling men of God.

To the left of Peter Becker sat Maria Hildebrand, whose daughter was destined to wed a son of founder Mack. By her side sat Magdalene Traut, Anna Gomorry, and Johanna Gans. Seated in their midst were the six new members — twenty-three in all. Who can lift the veil and record this hour's holy service? What thoughts, what emotions, what religious experiences, what covenanted pledges, what rejoicings, moved lips and heart and head! To God only is known the ecstasy of that communion. "Ye know not now; but ye shall know hereafter." Blessed beginning of the church in America; may her latter days be like her first![8]

COVENTRY AND CONESTOGA

Following the first baptisms in America, we are told by the *Chronicle,* the Brethren experienced "great blessing and edification" so that in the spring of 1724 "the whole region round about was moved thereby."

Young people especially "began to walk in the fear of the Lord and to love the brethren" to the "great gratification of their elders." As news of the awakening spread, "there was such an increase at their meetings that the room could hold only a fraction of them." The Brethren then decided to expand the revival by visiting the "bush" or back country.

The gratifyingly complete and detailed account of Brethren extension inland stems from the fact that the emergence of Conrad Beissel as a religious leader occurred at this time. This background is the beginning of the movement which crystallized as the Ephrata Community. For the same reason, however, the *Chronicle* account poses problems in interpretation. It was written to justify Beissel's break from the Brethren, after he had been placed in a position of leadership by them; in order to enhance his status, the Brethren must be belittled. Despite this, there is reason to believe that events are reported faithfully, even if their interpretation is often distorted.

To balance the bias of the *Chronicle's* authors, and also to provide portions of the original journal of the community (from which the published chronicle was taken and edited), excerpts from the autobiography of Henry Sangmeister are interspersed (in italicized type) within the following account. Sangmeister (1723-1785?), a former member of the Ephrata Community, was Beissel's harshest critic. In the early parts of his four-volume life history (projected as six volumes), Sangmeister quoted from the early manuscript *Chronicle,* often with his own comments added parenthetically. The writer's bias against, if not outright hatred for, the community leader must be kept in mind. Here, too, narrative material, apart from interpretation, seems to be trustworthy.

Sangmeister's own assessment of the point of view of the Chroniclers, especially in relation to the Brethren, was:

> I can assure [you] most certainly that arrogance and self-praise obtained exceedingly in this work from the very beginning. Especially did they traduce and treat as petty and poor the old Brethren congregation, which had begun in Germany amidst much persecution, poverty and misery. They tramped under foot, so to speak, the old faithful and sincere men. Despite the repeated attempts of the latter, they refused to enter into any reconciliation with them, even though the latter intended it most warmly and sincerely. Therefore, they have had to depart this life saddened, without having been able to reconcile themselves; this, even though Conrad Beissel was baptized by them and afterward left them on his own initiative.

A portion of a Frisian map drawn about the time of the Brethren residence in Surhuisterveen (spelled *Suyr Huys ter Veen* on the map). The illustration depicts the digging of peat, the major local occupation. In the upper-center is seen an area called *Kort-Wolde* where the Brethren performed their baptisms.

A Germantown surveyor's sketch including land of John Gomry (Gumre) on the Wissahickon Creek, where the first Brethren baptisms in America took place on December 25, 1723. Courtesy of the Historical Society of Pennsylvania.

The present appearance of the Wissahickon site of the early Brethren baptisms.

Conrad Beissel (1690-1768), the leading figure of the Ephrata movement and still a controversial personality, was born in Eberbach on the Neckar, not far from the birthplace of Alexander Mack. Beissel's father died before the son was born, and his mother, too, died eight years later. Trained as a baker, the young Beissel led a dissolute life, as he later portrayed it, before his conversion in Heidelberg after joining a Pietist circle there. His Pietist beliefs caused him to be exiled.

In the areas of Büdingen and Schwarzenau — two of the rare areas of religious freedom of the time — he came into contact with the several current strands of religious dissent, including the Brethren. They seemed to him, "as a strict separatist, entirely too sectarian." For a time he was associated with the Community of True Inspiration (later to become the Amana Community in Iowa), but parted with them because they did not sufficiently recognize his spiritual talents.

In 1720 he came to Pennsylvania, and was apprenticed as a weaver with Peter Becker, Brethren minister and leader. In the autumn of 1721 he left Becker's house and settled in the wilderness of the Conestoga area along Mill Creek. There he and some friends lived as hermits, though failing in an experiment of communal living. Beissel built a new house at a place called the "Swede's Spring" and was joined there by Michael Wohlfahrt (known among the English speaking as Michael Welfare). It was shortly after this that Beissel encountered the Brethren in their evangelistic tour in the back country. The account of the *Ephrata Chronicle* relates the meeting in considerable detail. (Beissel is always referred to as the "Superintendent.")[7]

The Brethren Visitation

Now after God had so manifestly blessed their labors, they sought to work forward to meet the awakening, and resolved to undertake a general visitation to all their brethren in the whole country. They fixed upon the twenty-third day of October of the year 1724, as the time for starting on their visitation from Germantown. They first went to Skippack; from there they traveled to Falckner's Swamp, where a meeting with breaking of bread was held with great blessing at the house of a brother named Albertus. From there they journeyed to Oley, where a similar work was done with similar blessing. Finally they came to their newly baptized Brethren on the Schuylkill, where they held a meeting and bread-breaking, and also baptized two persons.

Here they agreed to travel up the country toward Conestoga, for they had heard that there were several awakened persons here. But as some of them were on horseback and some on foot, they divided, and those on foot spent the following night, November 9, with John Graff, and the riders with Jacob Weber. The following day the party united again at Rudolph Nägele's, at that time a Mennonite minister [*Lehrer*], but afterwards a faithful follower of the Superintendent, who at that time lived with Michael Wohlfahrt in isolation. The following night, that is November 10, they lodged with Stephen Galliond, and from there continued on their journey to Henry Höhn's, after they had sent two Brethren on ahead to announce their coming. In this fruitful wilderness there lived at that time partly Mennonites, and partly Separatists. . . .

A meeting was held at Höhn's on the following day, November 12, at which the Superintendent was present. At this meeting extraordinary revival powers were manifested. The Brethren spoke with such power concerning baptism and the divine purpose concerning fallen man involved therein, that after the close of the meeting five persons applied for baptism, namely the before-mentioned Höhn, his wife, John Mayer and his wife, and Joseph Shäfer, who were at once baptized in apostolic fashion by Peter Becker in the Pequea stream. Soon a sixth one followed these, namely Veronica, the wife of Isaac Frederick.

Now the Superintendent fell into great perplexity. For, to withstand this ordinance of God seemed to him great presumption; at the same time, the calling of these people was not deemed important enough by him, for he had been the recipient of a weighty testimony from God, and feared that if he associated with them he might lose all the good that he had attained through so much pain. Suddenly, however, his heart was enlightened by a bright ray from the gospel, in whose light the whole purpose of God was revealed to him, namely, that Christ had permitted himself to be baptized by one who was less than himself, and had said thereof: "Thus it becomes us to fulfill all righteousness," and that, in order to make this work easier for us, God himself had thus gone before, and first sought out the field in which he would sow His grain of wheat.

Consequently, after the sister referred to before came out of the water, he came down from his spiritual pride, humbled himself before his friend Peter Becker, and was baptized by him on the same day in apostolic fashion, under the water. It was thus that Wisdom brought him into her net: he received the seed of his heavenly virginity at his first awakening, but now a field was prepared for him in America into which he might sow his seed again. Now we will resume our narrative.

In 1724 Conrad Beissel had himself baptized by Peter Becker in the Pequea (which is described with great detail, especially that before this he had baptized himself to satisfy his own conscience, but to no avail; therefore, he had to humble himself and be baptized by someone else. Although he had experienced himself that this self-baptism was not sufficient, he later baptized himself many times.)

After the baptism they spent the rest of the day in edifying conversation unto the praise of God, until evening, when a love feast was held at Höhn's, the first ever held in Conestoga since the country began to be cleansed from its pagan inhabitants; it was held on November 12, 1724. The following day they made a visit to Isaac Frederick's mill, when disagreement sprang up among them, because some of them so vehemently insisted on returning home. Peter Becker and the majority, however, insisted upon holding another meeting, which was then done on the following Sunday at Sigmund Landert's.

But this meeting was not at all like the previous ones in power and spirit, and it was remarked that from that day on their power declined. First of all the women began a quarrel; and then Simon König, Michael Wohlfahrt, and others, joined to assail the Brethren on account of their controversies across the sea [in Europe]. Simon König made the attack, but as he acted very injudiciously, the rest were ashamed of him and left him in the lurch. Consequently, the meeting passed over fruitlessly, as did the baptism of Sigmund Landert and his wife which followed; for they baptized them in such unclean water that they ought to have had a bath afterwards.

On this occasion Peter Becker made the following address to the people: "These two persons have applied to us for baptism; but as they are unknown to us in their walk and conversation, we make this announcement of the fact to all men here present, especially their neighbors. If you can bear favorable witness concerning their lives, it is well, and we can baptize them with the greater assurance; but if you have any complaints to bring against them, we will not do it." It appears from this that he required candidates to have led an honorable life before he would baptize them. Whether this is apostolic we will not stop to discuss; baptism contains in itself the forgiveness of all past sins.

We will now proceed to their departure. Before they left this newly planted congregation, they, especially Peter Becker and Henry Traut, conferred much with the newly baptized with reference to the organization of their household, and said among other things: "You can now arrange your affairs among yourselves to the best of your ability; the better you do it, the better we will be pleased, since you constitute together a small congregation. You are in no way to be bound to us, as we are at too great a distance from you. We therefore advise you to arrange your affairs among yourselves, according to your daily circumstances. Neither do we recognize any pope who would rule over you, but we commend you to the grace of God, which must accomplish everything, etc."

Later they directed him [Beissel] and the newly baptized that they were now to stand on their own feet, and support one another, and extend the hand to each other, because they [the Germantown group] were too far away from them. It was this opportunity and reason which Conrad Beissel and his small group of followers knew very well to exploit for their own purpose. (This event then is discussed lengthily as a great guilt and error on the part of the Brethren.)[8]

Beginning of the Tension

Afterwards they were very sorry for these words, and they themselves regarded what they had done as unwise, because they had let this new congregation pass out of their hands. They thought they should not have entrusted so much to beginners, and that now they would have to tolerate everything, no matter how strangely these newly converted might act toward them. However, they were entirely mistaken, at least as regards the Superintendent, who at that time had already spent eight years in his calling, and had been well trained therein. After they had given the kiss of peace to one another, they began their homeward journey.

A sensible person, acquainted with the counsels and plans discussed by them on their homeward journey, as they are described by a brother among them, J[ohn] M[eyle], must soon become aware that they gave entirely too much room to their suspicion against this new congregation, from which of a necessity such a schism had to follow. They indeed considered it a blessing that they now already had planted two congregations in the land, namely, one on the Schuylkill and the other in Conestoga; but concerning the latter they were in perplexity, and thought they ought to send a brother there as superintendent, for which they proposed Kemper, as being both edifying and having the gift of prayer.

But what troubled them most was that they heard that the Superintendent and two others observed the Sabbath. Most of them insisted that rules should be proscribed for the Brethren in Conestoga, that they might observe the Sabbath for themselves, but should not preach its observance to anyone else, so that whoever wished to do so might observe Sunday. Thereupon another one said: "If they intend to observe the Sabbath, they might observe the whole law; for he who ordained the Sabbath ordained also circumcision."

Others said it was a strange thing that the Brethren in Conestoga had so firmly settled upon the Sabbath, and yet would not preach it; for if it was ordained to be observed, it must also be preached. This they said because the Superintendent had declared that he had received no command to preach it to others, but only to observe it himself. At last, however, they all became agreed that as long as the Brethren in Conestoga were so few in numbers they might grant liberty to others, but that if they increased they would probably make the attempt to bring others also under this Jewish ordinance. Finally, they charged Peter Becker with having left too much in the hands of these newly converted souls.

After this the Brethren began to consider very seriously their new congregation in Conestoga, whom they should send there, in order to maintain and support them. Inasmuch as Conrad Beissel and his following were already observing the Sabbath, they feared not without reason that some lambs might be taken from their hands and torn from them; which, in fact, soon happened. Then the Brethren were at a great loss to know whom to send, since it seemed to them improper to accept the Sabbath and observe it on Conrad Beissel's account. In that case they would have to place themselves as novices under him. It did not seem possible to observe the Lord's Day and reside with them. They feared that in the end almost all of the congregation would break away and join the Sabbatarians; this did happen on the sixteenth day of the ninth month of 1724.

All these matters deserve closer investigation. Whoever considers this journey, together with the great blessing accompanying it, must confess that God was with them, at least up to the time when that man was found whom He had destined for a more important work. It is also certain that the Superintendent dealt with them in sincerity, and entered into communion with them with his whole heart. Had they not in the beginning permitted their suspicion against him to overmaster them, but had they condescended to him as he had done to them, he would have been the man through whom they would have recovered again their first vocation received at Schwarzenau, for he had a higher witness than they. Such an unpleasant division would not have taken place, but on the contrary, they might have received into their fold many virgin spirits in future times.

The Superintendent visited Peter Becker yet on his deathbed, and said to him among other things: "What a pity it is that there were no wise men among you when the awakening in Conestoga commenced; how we could now live in your fold!" Whereupon the latter wept. [See pages 104-111.] Of all this, honest Henry Kalckgläser, one of their ministers and founders, who ended his days at Ephrata, may be accepted as a witness; for he gave as the reason why he left them and joined the new congregation that at Ephrata he had found again his first revival spirit.

However, they had at that time already strayed so far away from the bounds of the spirit that they could not live under so sharp a testimony. Defection from God takes place first of all within the heart, even while outwardly there may often still be a great deal of ado made about Him, especially in some forms of worship; but its fruits at last will be brought to light. Accordingly, as they failed in God's trial of them, His choice passed from them, and with the election all blessing also, unto the person of the Superintendent, of which Peter Becker must have had a consciousness, for he confessed that on the journey to Conestoga they had lost something which they never afterward recovered. Even if the Superintendent had been a deceiver, as many of them called him, they did not follow the right method to reclaim him. They ought to have come down to him in humble faith, then he would have stood by them; or if he had not been the right man, God would have released them. This was done by many others who would have had more right to withstand his testimony, since they had been under his leadership for many years, which certainly was a stern and strange one; but these made it a matter of conscience to do so, as being convinced of his being divinely sent.

Whether or not such trials will come again, time will show; certain it is that nothing can be bypassed in the divine Providence's leading. The Superintendent, shortly before his death, met some of them on a journey, when he asked a brother what kind of people they were, being so reserved toward him. The brother answered: "They are Brethren." "Well, well," said he, "I shall yet become their prince in eternity." These circumstances have a certain likeness to the history of Jacob and Esau; for to these good people belonged indeed, as to the older son, the rights of the first-born; but they lost them through the younger one, and therefore, like Esau and Jacob, they conceived a strong dislike against him, which later they handed down to their descendants.[9]

The Conestoga Congregation Expands

After the Superintendent had now ratified his covenant with God in the water, in which he gave himself unconditionally to Him, Providence brought it about that those who had been baptized with him elected him their teacher.

We would like to report further how the congregation at Conestoga began. There were twelve in number, whose names follow: the first brother is our God-approved patriarch [Beissel] who alone was honored by God, who placed His witness in him for the edification and propagation of the new congregation of the church; the second, Brother Joseph Schäffer; third, John Meyer; fourth, Henry Höhn; fifth, Sealtiel [Landert]; sixth, Jonadab [H. Höcker]; the sisters: first, Migtonia; second, Christina; third, Veronica; fourth, Maria; fifth, Elizabeth; sixth, Franzina.

In this [election] John Mayer was mainly instrumental. And thus, without seeking it himself, Beissel was thrust into the vineyard. His ordination to this office was received from the same one who had bestowed it upon Elijah, John the Baptist, and other reformers, who were awakened especially and directly in order to come to the help of a church fallen asunder. Experience has shown that as soon as he assumed the office, a large measure of the Spirit rested upon him. For this reason, as soon as he began to hold meetings, contention arose against him throughout the whole land, which has not ceased even after his death.

Many of his former friends, when they became aware of the sudden change in him, declared that he had gone out of his mind. Thus Henry Zimmermann once said to him: "Conrad, Conrad! You have taken upon you a sore load; you will become a fool. I have known such people in Germany." He conducted all meetings, however, with astonishing strength of spirit, and used so little reflection over it, that even in the beginning he was not suffered to use a Bible, so that the testimony in its delivery might not be weakened by written knowledge. He began his discourse with closed eyes, before a large crowd of hearers, and when he opened his eyes again, most of them were gone, not being able to endure the Spirit's keenness. On such occasions wonderful mysteries of eternity were often revealed through him of which he himself had before been ignorant. But these were soon sealed up again, and then he would say: "The Spirit retires into His secret chamber."

Whenever he felt that persons were present who sought to catch and confine his discourse in the meshes of reason, he would suddenly be moved to hold a discourse directly contradictory to his former one, and that too with equally strong reasoning, so that his listeners were thrown into a holy confusion. . . . He was a born orator, and could carry out a proposition to great length, especially if he had rationalistic persons before him, for which his opponents blamed him very much. In his delivery, however, he was too fast, because he had to hurry after the Spirit, when he often concerned himself but little about the rules of language.

To return to the history. The congregation went on, and in December 1724 held its first love feast with Brother Sigmund Landert, at which the Superintendent officiated for the first time.

As our father [Beissel] had for nearly ten years experienced and learned much about the ways of God, he was thus able to instruct others in their [spiritual] beginnings. In addition to this, our church father had received unusual gifts from God for the edification of the congregation, so that they increased from day to day. And after a period of three to four weeks, after the older brethren had returned home to Germantown, a love feast, breaking of bread, and feetwashing were held. (The poor Baptist Brethren were left out.) This was the first one held in Sigmund's house, in the tenth month of the year 1724.

At the beginning of the next year he made a journey to the Schuylkill and Germantown, to the Brethren, for at that time they were still united. He had for companions two Judaizing brethren, who were very burdensome to him and [to those] at the places where they lodged, for they had such a fear of pork that they would not eat out of any vessel that was not quite clean. It is true that the Superintendent had a deep insight into the secrets of nature. From the nature of the food he knew how it would affect the unclean members, and from this the suspicion against pork and unclean food first arose; the first Christians, as is well known, also avoided them.

His followers, deeply enamored with his pure life, imitated him not only in this, but went still further and raised scruples against geese also, because they supply man with their feathers for his luxurious indulgence. Consequently both these creatures were banished from the housekeeping of the Sabbatarians. At this circumstance the Brethren were not a little offended, for they had already before suspected the new congregation of intending to revive Judaism. To this was added another circumstance, that also pained them much, in that in the year 1725 one of their proselytes, John Meyle, went over to the new congregation, whom later many followed.

The beginning was made of no longer eating pork, nor eating any food from utensils in which it had been cooked without a special scouring and cleaning. (In which they proceeded in a peculiarly extremist manner.) In 1725 Brother Lamech [Jacob Gass?] joined the congregation, who had previously been with the Brethren. . . . In the beginning of the third month, 1725, the Superintendent baptized seven at one time: Meyle and his wife, John Landes and his wife, Johnny Landes and his wife; and Brother Agonius [Michael Wohlfahrt].

In the beginning of May 1725, a meeting was held at John Landes's, where the Superintendent for the first time held a baptism, baptizing seven, of whom the most important were Michael Wohlfahrt and Rudolph Nägele. The former had lived with him, and it seems that the divine wisdom had given him to the Superintendent that the latter might be exercised in his holy walk, for they were both of choleric disposition.

Concerning Brother Agonius, he has been very burdensome for Father Friedsam and the congregation up to the present, because of his constant teaching and preaching in the meetings. He has felt himself superior before as well as after baptism, as in his mind he has always placed himself alongside Father Friedsam, acting as if he were to be a co-laborer in the work of God. (Naturally, Conrad Beissel was not pleased by this.) Shortly thereafter he was placed in the ban by Beissel and the congregation because of a minor incident; it was not actually because of this insignificant cause, but because he would not subordinate himself. He was, therefore, the first to be placed in the ban. The reason for the ban was the word "I," which he, however, denied and said that he had used the plural, namely, "We." He was banned because of this. (If one had applied this to Beissel as well, he would have had to be banned several times a day; but this was not the point. Beissel wanted to be the only one in everything.) At this time the congregation numbered twenty-two persons.

Soon after this man's [Wohlfahrt's] baptism, these two traveled about the country, and announced to men the counsels of God concerning future salvation, whereby many became greatly exercised, and some few were awakened, but most of them disregarded it. Several tried to hide themselves from the truth behind the law of Moses, for soon after, A[dam] W[eidner] of Oley, and D[avid] C[aufmann], circumcised each other after the Jewish manner, and then blasphemed much against Paul because he did away with circumcision. On this account the Superintendent wrote them an emphatic letter, in which he speaks thus: "I counsel you, for the sake of the mediator J[esus] C[hrist], leave off your folly, lest you lose thereby even the grace and promises of the New Covenant. You have not a single witness among all the apostles upon going among the gentiles with the gospel that circumcision was even so much as thought of at a single place."[10]

The Tension Heightens

Circumstances now demanded that they must sacrifice to God their beloved solitude in the wilderness for the good of their neighbor.

For this reason they moved apart, and a little house was erected for the Superintendent on the land of the before-mentioned Nägele.

Here is reported that Conrad Beissel moved from his residence to the old Nägele [house], and left his house to Stumpf. He remained at Nägele's over the winter, and secretly built a new house for himself on Nägele's land, and moved into it in the spring. Brother Agonius, who lived with Conrad, also moved out, to Caspar Walter, and also built [a house].

And here these spiritual Israelites had their first settlement, after they came out of Egypt, passing through the Red Sea, that is, the water of baptism. Soon others joined him and then there could be seen in their little houses an edifying picture of the huts of the holy fathers in the Egyptian wilderness. In this region wonderful influences came down upon them from eternity, of which hardly anything ever became known. . . .

Now, however, the time drew nigh when God remembered Rachel in her long barrenness so that she became pregnant. For it was resolved in the council of the Watchers that in the sixth period, as being the Philadelphian church season, a virgin should be made ready as the bride of the high priest, and for this Pennsylvania was specially chosen. And now the Spirit awakened many free souls of both sexes, who began to strive for the knightly crown. Among the female sex the first were two natural sisters, A[nna] and M[aria] E[icher]. They fled from their father's house in the year 1726 and put themselves under the Superintendent's guidance, which caused much talk in the country, especially since he had to be with them very much. The congregation built them a house on Mill Creek, in which they lived for four years.

In the same year, at Easter, R[udolph] N[ägele] held a love feast at which two Brethren from the Schuylkill, H[enry] L[andes] and D[aniel] E[icher], were present, and at which a controversy arose between H. L. and the Superintendent. The former asked how it could be consistent with the righteousness of God that so many innocent children had to suffer along with the rest in the general courts of justice. The Superintendent answered: "They have indeed not sinned as yet; but they are not on that account innocent, for the evil nature is in them, which plainly shows itself with the increase in years." *Question:* "Do you not believe that they will be saved if they died thus?" *Answer:* "That we do not say, but we hold that they must be purged from their inherited sin by means of a kind of purgatory." Their [Brethren] purpose was to elevate the natural married estate into a holy estate, in order thus to give the right of salvation to children; but when they failed in this, they both became offended and did not hold to the congregation any more. One of them afterwards took his child up in his arms, and, kissing it, said: "Oh, thou poor child! Art thou to be damned if thou wert now to die? That would be a horrible thing, since thou hast not yet sinned."

Many were deeply offended by this discussion and much trouble came of it, especially from John Meyer and Landes, who were very much put off by these curious expressions, and who stirred up the Brethren so that considerable enmity arose.

And because this man [Henry Landes] afterwards passed into eternity in his offended mood, the rumor was brought to the Brethren that the Superintendent had permitted a brother to die without being reconciled to him. Yes, and that he had spread a new heresy in Conestoga, namely, that innocent children are damned when they die. These people, as is apparent in some of their hymns, agree with the Mennonite Church in this that they think that infants are born pure and innocent. And because the Superintendent recognized the advantage flesh and blood sought to gain over these people, his opposition caused him to be called a forbidder of wedlock.

Now follows a letter written with great severity by the Superintendent to Henry Landes, by which he provoked him still more. In the course of these events the Brethren rose up in a body and opposed the Ephrata group and the latter in turn opposed the former. This continued until the Ephrata group completely separated themselves from them. In 1726 Henry Landes died in the Schuylkill area. He had been in opposition to the congregation, and they to him.

Meanwhile, amidst these differences, the work of revival went on. About seven weeks after these occurrences, a brother on the Schuylkill of the name of [Martin] Urner, held a love feast on Whitsuntide, to which both congregations were invited, for apparently at least, they were as yet undivided; and because the regular minister, P[eter] B[ecker], was not present, the Superintendent was obliged to officiate. On this occasion quite extraordinary powers of eternity manifested themselves, such as were never known before or after, so that it was called the congregation's Pentecost. On the first day of the festival everybody in the meetings was as though drunk with wine, and it was noticed that several who had engaged in prayer, soon afterward married, and thus dragged the gifts of the Spirit into the flesh. The Superintendent bore himself calmly in the matter as if it did not concern him at all, for he had then already learned enough in the school of the Spirit to treat the good without any self-assumption, which is the worst of sins. After the meeting he baptized eleven in the Schuylkill.

Through this occurrence the Brethren were confounded in the person of the Superintendent. On the one hand, they had to admire the extraordinary gifts of the man; on the other, they knew that he had the reputation of being a seducer and a destroyer of wedlock. They put their heads together and took counsel, but knew not what judgment to form. Meanwhile on the following night the love feast went off with blessing. At the same time it was announced that on the following Whitmonday another meeting would be held.

This meeting threw the good Brethren into the greatest amazement, for the powers of the new world were again poured out like a river, the singing was Pentecostal and heavenly, yes, some declared that they heard angel voices mingling with it, of which the reader has liberty to judge for himself. Certain it is that in the time following it pleased the Spirit to bring revivals to men by means of song, so that at last there was developed such singing among the Solitary as has never been equaled by any party of the Christian Church from the days of Ignatius on, to whom first was made known by revelation the antiphonal style of singing of the holy angels.

As the suspicion against the Superintendent had notably increased after the close of the meeting, many thought that he must be a sorcerer, and were in fear lest their wives be seduced. One otherwise upright brother, M[artin] U[rner], embraced his wife and exclaimed, "Oh, my dear wife! I pray you for God's sake, do not leave me!" Such is the effect when God reaches forth into the church of Adam.

In the summer of 1726 Brother Hildebrand also traveled to Conestoga. There he let himself be extraordinarily taken in by the attractive appearance of the congregation, and said that the Brethren had only an empty form and structure. He then bought a lot near the congregation and later moved there. . . .

On the 25th day of the 10th month, Brother Hildebrand held a love feast in his house, and invited the congregation to it. On this day B[eissel] baptized again three b[rethren] and three s[isters]; two of the [sisters] were Brother Daniel's daughters, Anna and Maria [Eicher].

Brother Hildebrand was extremely attached to the congregation. This did not last long, however, and he came into great temptation through his own works and deeds. In the spring of 1727 Brother Daniel Eicher also joined the congregation. Shortly after this, Brother Hildebrand got rather in the way with his preaching and talking, and they directed him to his own house, that he might set that right first. But he opposed the congregation from time to time and raised all kinds of complaints against the congregation. If we were to report all of the events which passed between him and the congregation it would amount to a fair-sized book. (For he was a continual witness against their strange beliefs.)

His interest at this time consisted in that they remain quiet on the Sabbath day, and not be in such continual hustle and bustle, but that they should rather immerse themselves and retreat into God, and hold their meetings on Sunday. (Of course, this made no impression on the restless Father.)

In August 1727, a grand visit was made by the Brethren of Germantown to the congregation in Conestoga. On the way Henry Traut and Stephen Koch left the party and visited one named J[ohn] S[tumpf], who had been with the Superintendent when he was still a pioneer settler, and his whole house had been drawn to him; at this time, however, he was under a ban for having married too near a relation, and was possessed of satanic powers. Him they loosed from his ban and brought him to Henry Höhn, where there was a general gathering. There he began to rave and imitated the cries of various animals, mostly, however, of ducks, so that no one could imitate him. As the two Brethren had loosed him from his ban on their own responsibility they were put under discipline; wherein the Superintendent had to adapt himself to the circumstances of the time, otherwise the ban was something contrary to his convictions.

After this a meeting was held and following it these two above-mentioned Brethren along with Stumpf were placed in the ban, because they had taken him into their full fellowship and defended him.

At this time in the fall, the Brethren came from Germantown to visit the congregation. As they were thus together, the Superintendent showed his magnanimity, and testified that it was an injustice to keep servants or apprentices, because it was against the New Testament, etc.

These statements so affected Peter Becker that he became quite upset and went to Brother Daniel Eicher's house, and took sick over it. Brother Hildebrand took him to his house and cared for him for eight days, and after he was improved they accompanied him home. The cause for this quarrel may have been that the Father at one time had been an apprentice with Peter Becker and had not completely freed himself from him.

From this time on temptations overwhelmed Brother Hildebrand completely and altogether lured him away from the congregation. And as he had left, he united himself again with the Brethren and renewed his previous brotherhood. (For, as these blinded people say, man cannot live without community.) After this, he finally left his house and stayed away for ten years.[11]

The Falckner's Swamp Controversy

The growing antagonism between the Brethren in Germantown and the group led by Beissel is clearly depicted in the controversies centering in Falckner's Swamp. This area played an important role in the religious history of the Pennsylvania colony, especially after the arrival of the Lutheran patriarch, Henry Melchior Muhlenberg. It is located near the present town of Pottstown. The following passages from Sangmeister's book are taken largely from the early manuscript *Chronicle* and contain interpolated comments by the disgruntled monk.

At this time Brother Agonius [Michael Wohlfahrt] made a visit in Falckner's Swamp and visited the awakened souls all by himself. After the Superintendent had learned from him that there were some serious-minded people there and he could thus do some fishing, he went there with three other brethren. On this trip they also got hold of Andrew Frey, and gave him leave to offer baptism to the others in [Falckner's] Swamp, for they were open to it. (This he did, because he wanted to be something special, thus placing a noose around his neck with his own hand; later he was to rue this enough.) [The baptism was to be held] when they came back from their trip to Oley. Brother Andrew Frey then did what they had instructed him to do, and thus Conrad Beissel baptized eleven in number on the return trip at [Falckner's] Swamp, on the eighth day of the first month of 1728. This was a good catch of fish. . . .

At the end of the second or third month five more brethren and sisters were baptized in the Swamp. At this time Brother Hildebrand traveled alone to the Swamp, giving the impression that he was still completely in unity with the congregation, but Andrew Frey was quite aware of his standing. He must also have known that he was in the ban and yet he received him with welcome. Then, in the Swamp, they went together from house to house to visit, at which Brother Andrew was of great use because the Conestoga brethren had placed responsibility in his hands. Afterwards he [Hildebrand] went down to Germantown and related everything that he had found there, which set the Brethren into motion in order to make a catch of fish too, if it were possible.

After the Brethren in and around Germantown had received such good information about the Swamp from Brother Hildebrand, they set out to visit the Swamp, and did this and held a meeting there. (According to the Ephrata group's story.) This resulted in blinding the eyes of the poor people. They professed a genuine love toward the Ephrata group, saying they were positively not holding the slightest grudge against them. With all their sugar-coated talk they stole the hearts of these poor people. After having thrown these poor souls into greatest confusion and robbing them of their love for the brethren, they returned home once again. After Brother Hildebrand had returned home he said the souls in the Swamp felt extremely friendly toward him, and that the Brethren had visited them. . . .

After the congregation had learned that the Brethren had visited the Swamp and held a meeting there, they held counsel to see what should be done (for if the matter is left to take its course, we would lose these people) and how this trouble could best be dealt with and eliminated altogether. After this, it came to the Father, that it would be best to write a sharp letter to the Brethren pointing out to them what bad people they were, etc., which was done.

After they had received the letter and read it well, they got together and traveled once more to the Swamp. They took the letter along and called upon these simple souls in the Swamp as witnesses, read them the letter, and then asked them if that of which they were

Chronicon Ephratenſe,

Enthaltend den Lebens=Lauf des ehrwürdigen Vaters in Chriſto

Friedſam Gottrecht,

Weyland Stiffters und Vorstehers des geistl. Ordens der Einsamen in Ephrata in der Grafschaft Lancaſter in PENNSYLVANIA.

Zuſammen getragen von Br. Lamech u. Agrippa.

Er iſt wie das Feuer eines Goldschmieds, und wie die Seiffe der Wäscher: Er wird die Kinder Levi reinigen wie Gold und Silber. Malach. 3, 2. 3.

Es iſt die Zeit, daß anfahe das Gericht am Hauße Gottes, ſo aber zuerſt an uns, was will vor ein Ende werden mit denen, die dem Evangelio Gottes nicht glauben. Und ſo der Gerechte kümmerlich erhalten wird, wie will der Gottloſe und Sünder erscheinen 1. Petr. 4, 17. 18.

EPHRATA: Gedruckt Anno M D C C L XXXVI.

The title page of the *Ephrata Chronicle* (1786). This copy, now in the Historical Society of Pennsylvania, was given to Alexander Mack, Jr., by Peter Miller.

Two recent views of the restored Ephrata Cloister.

*accused in the letter was the truth, and whether they were the kind
of people that the letter accused them of being, for they could actually
prove the opposite. "You are our witnesses, that we said nothing
suspicious or unkind about them to you, but rather only spoke in love
and respect to them, along with wishes for every good thing as you
well know." etc. etc. (This is the Ephrata group's own testimony.)*

*Then they held a meeting, and decided that they would hold
another in four weeks at Brother William Frey's house. The brethren
in Conestoga were also to be invited to attend and prove whether
we were the kind of people they claimed us to be or not. "The
meeting is to be a trial and you are to receive testimony as impartial
judges and judge which side, Conestoga or we, is in the right. This
will stand, be it they or we. For this reason you must stand in the
middle, between us and them. Therefore remain impartial. In the
meantime and even when the meeting begins, you are not to receive
them or us either with handclasp or kiss, so that you can make a pure
and impartial judgment." (This was honorable enough.) The matter
was thus arranged and communicated to the Conestoga congregation.
(Which procedure would not agree with Conrad Beissel, as we shall
see.)*

*After our congregation had heard this true message and learned
of the invitation, we were not a little amazed, especially about this
curious meeting and about that political trick by which they had so
blinded the poor souls in the country; and that they had the audacity
to invite our community to their show. Hereupon counsel was held
once more, and two weeks prior to the time announced for the meeting
to be held, five brethren were sent to the Swamp: Brother Agonius,
Brother Onesimus [Israel Eckerlin], Brother Jonadab [H. Höcker],
Brother Daniel [Eicher] and Brother Höhn. They went there to save
(according to their view) the small flock and agreed to visit first the
house of Henry Hageman, which they did. They were received with
handclasp and kiss, which greatly annoyed the others in the Swamp,
as this was so completely against their agreement. They were all
dismayed at this unexpected visit, because it came too early for them.
Those who were not (according to their story) basically and intention-
ally wicked, were content with the visit, and they received grace and
were freed from those false spirits.*

But the others who (according to their impression) were wicked in their hearts, were angered by this visit, especially as they had heard that the six brethren who had come treated the affair with mockery and laughter (because of the meeting, which was a disorderly thing to do). These were the ones who took the greatest offense: Andrew Frey and William Frey and his wife. They did, indeed, return to the community in the fall, but on account of their offended eyes, did not remain and strayed once more.

In 1731 the mentioned angry ones returned to the community once more but again did not stay long, but took offense for the third time and turned away to Sodom in Egypt. Let this be enough of this affair.

P. S. I personally saw the mentioned Andrew Frey in his old age. He was stone blind; he praised and thanked God for his misery. He also told me how the Herrnhuters [Moravians] had dealt with him, and also the Sabbatarians — how they both tormented him with their magic. He said that the Herrnhuters were more violent in this matter than the Sabbatarians, because there were so many of them; but the latter were more persistent, and had tormented him the most; for they never give up.[12]

The Final Separation

The sharp differences between Germantown and Conestoga, worsened by the arbitrary manner of Beissel, led to the inevitable rupture. This came late in 1728. Some of those at Conestoga remained loyal to the Germantown Brethren and constituted a separate congregation.

It appears that the Superintendent at that time was much indebted in his divine work to the Brethren of Germantown, which came from the fact that he had received his baptism from them. They boasted that they had given birth to the new congregation out of the elements, thus priding themselves in fleshly things. On this account we must make some allowance for the Superintendent's vehemence against them. They interfered with the way of that Spirit under whose dominion he stood, so that, in the hymns he wrote at that time, he used terrible expressions about them. Consequently, when he noticed that their power of opposition was owing to his baptism, the resolve was finally reached to give these people their baptism back again, which was then done in December of the year 1728. For then Brother Amos [J. Meyle] first rebaptized the Superintendent, who then rebaptized him, another brother and four sisters, so that once more the Sabbatic number of seven became the foundation of the rebaptism of the congregation. This transaction not only provoked the Brethren anew, but also caused a great disturbance in the congregation itself; for some halted between two opinions, and secretly held to the Brethren, because they hankered after worship in which flesh and blood could be redeemed.

Here follows a long explanation about the poor Brethren, namely how they never with all their own strivings and business dealt with themselves and were quite unaware of what this prophecy had effected. On the contrary, they were continually battling against what was good and against the witness of God (Beissel is meant), and repressing and subduing, early and late, God's community with all their might.

Thus it is noteworthy that from the hour and time on, when the Conestoga congregation began, the old Brethren were under judgment, which was born out of the opposition to the congregation of Ephrata. It was therefore within the divine wisdom of God and still is, that the beginning of the Conestoga congregation was to have been incorporated into this new brotherhood. If these good people had understood this mystery, they would have given up their previous economy, destroyed it, and turned it over completely to the new one (and to Conrad Beissel), etc., etc.

Since their ears were stopped and they would not hear it, God continued with His new economy and removed all His blessings and all good things from the old Brethren and placed them upon this new economy, etc., leaving them nothing but an empty and mere appearance, and a completely powerless and empty worship among them.

And yet they would not relinquish and give God the glory, but heaped judgment upon judgment etc., etc. (so much has been written about these old Brethren that it makes one ill).

It is known that the congregation in Conestoga had acted very contrary to the Brethren and had cut off all fellowship with them for over a year already, and avoided them to the sharpest degree, in an attempt to take from their hands the claim which they held against the congregation in Conestoga. Yes, the more they separated themselves from each other, the more they raged and ranted, and it got worse and worse as time went on. After the cause for this had been more and more investigated, it became clear that their power consisted in this — that they had baptized the first in the Conestoga congregation, etc. In order to eliminate this claim, Beissel set about to have himself baptized by Amos, then he, in turn, baptized Amos, and so on until all around were baptized who had been baptized by the Brethren (and according to them [Ephrata] this baptizing of everyone around had resulted in great blessing).

Just at that time the little tract on the Sabbath came from the press which caused great commotion, and so all who belonged to the congregation near and far, began to celebrate the Sabbath. . . .

Just during that summer there was a meeting at John Landes's, at which V[ater] F[riedsam] spoke about matrimony, how the people presumed too many rights therein, and therefore lived against the order of God, especially in the unclean lust. That and similar speeches greatly angered Brother Daniel Eicher and others, who attacked him and the congregation, and therefore turned their backs on the congregation, in that they were not worthy to be in the congregation. Thus Brother Daniel stayed away for four years for this reason. . . .

All those who left the congregation during that year of 1728 and later went to the old Brethren in Germantown and made the congregation suspect in their eyes as people who had broken the covenant. All of them the Brethren received as dear and faithful brothers and sisters.

During that fall all the apostates and oathbreakers in Conestoga came together in a pack and held meeting. The first day at John Landes's, then at Hildebrand's, at Daniel Eicher's in Roland's house and at Luis'; there they expounded great things to each other. Daniel Eicher and Hildebrand religiously visited and presided over these meetings. The group of the apostates was almost as strong as the true congregation. Brother Agonius and Brother Joel [Peter Bucher] also went to the meeting of the disloyal and testified against it. Daniel Eicher's two daughters, Maria and Anna, suffered much from their parents at that time (according to their story) because they did not wish to become disloyal and breakers of the covenant (along with him); rather, they became ever more firm, and testified against their parents and the company of the godless. As, however, they did not dare to continue for a long time, they moved out during that year of 1728 in the eighth or ninth month [October or

November] and moved in with Brother Lamech. These two were therefore the first sisters who began the solitary life in Ephrata. (It is no wonder that they were against their parents, for Conrad Beissel was much and often alone with these two sisters and exercised his priestly office with them, which he has regretted many times as he himself has told me.)

The two mentioned sisters had lived with Lamech for a while during which time they had a house built for them, where they lived together for four years. . . .

In the 10th month [December 1728] Brother Joel went to Germantown to the meeting of the Brethren (and in his ignorance allowed his zeal against them to show) and said, "You have become Irrhere," which is a desolated city. He said to Peter Becker, "Thus speaks the Lord, how dare you proclaim my rights, and take my covenant in your mouth," etc., etc. After this, he rose and went out the door.

During the 11th and 12th months [January and February 1729], Brother Joel was moved to go to Brother Hildebrand's house to the meeting of the apostates to deliver a testimony. He spoke thus: "To you, John Hildebrand, I have to announce a word from the Lord. Thus says the Lord, 'You are not to go out any more and teach other men; rather, you must first convert yourself and your household. When you have done this, then you can go out and teach other people.' If you do not obey this voice, the judgment of the Lord will visit you, because you have not acted according to His words. It shall also be revealed this day whether it is you or we who are the congregation of God. For today God will perform a miracle on me. If I fall down before your eyes as a dead man, pray to God for me that I might rise again. If God answers your prayer, then God did not send me to you, and you are the congregation of the Lord. If, however, I do not fall dead before your eyes, but can go in health and vigor from you, you shall know that God has sent me to you, and that you are not the congregation of the Lord." Eight days ago he looked Daniel Eicher, John Landes, Hildebrand and Henry Höhn so long and so penetratingly in the eyes that one after the other cast down their eyes and he called them wolves in their meeting, etc.

In the spring of the year 1729 Brother Amos [J. Meyle] and Brother Onesimus [Israel Eckerlin] went with the Superintendent's fellowship to the Swamp and placed Andrew Frey in the ban.[13]

BRETHREN ATTEMPTS AT RECONCILIATION

It was clear from the tension between the group around Beissel at Conestoga and the Germantown Brethren, which had come to a head in 1728, that fundamental differences of belief existed. Despite a common origin in Radical Pietism, the Brethren could not accept the Conestoga emphasis upon personal revelation above Scripture, celibacy above marriage, Judaizing tendencies above Christian, and adulation of a human leader above reverence for Christ.[14]

Nevertheless, repeated efforts were made to attempt to reconcile the two groups. These were usually avoided by Beissel and his followers, or were rebuffed. The most important attempt came shortly after the arrival in Pennsylvania of Alexander Mack, Sr. (1679-1735), the leader of the original movement. Although its effort failed, it did show the Brethren concern for peace within their ranks. Both accounts are given, as the difference in some details is enlightening.

Mack and Beissel

In the year 1729 Alexander Mack, the founder of the Brethren, with the rest of the brotherhood mentioned, left Friesland and came to Pennsylvania. This venerable man would have well deserved to have been received with arms of love by all the devout in common, after all that he had had to suffer in Germany, especially from his own people. But he had no sooner arrived among his brethren than they filled his ears with heavy accusations against those at Conestoga, namely how they had separated from them, had written abusive letters, and had treated them very unkindly with judgments and condemnations; yes, and over and above all this, they had yet done a terrible thing whereby not only they, but even their dead, had been condemned and put into the ban. When he asked what this was, the reply was, that they had all had themselves rebaptized and had withdrawn from the B[rethren].

In 1729 Alexander Mack came with his congregation from Friesland to this country. He immediately became involved in the strife between the Conestoga congregation and the Brethren, and the Conestoga congregation gave him quite a bit of trouble. After Alexander Mack had heard so many strange things about the congregation in Conestoga, he went with several of his brethren to speak to Conrad Beissel. However, the latter escaped him, and did not let them speak with him. (Once again there follows a very long interpretation which

I did not consider worth reporting, insofar as everything is interpreted only for the benefit and honor of Conrad Beissel.)

Now the good man should have suspended all judgment at least until he had made himself thoroughly acquainted with the matter. But prejudice so overpowered his mind that he was not capable of passing a sound judgment, nor of reconciling the separation. Nevertheless, he made an attempt, and in October, 1730, undertook a visit to Falckner's Swamp with several of his brethren. The Superintendent knew nothing of this, but made a journey there at the same time, and held a meeting at Brother John Senseman's, to which also, quite unexpectedly, the visitors from Germantown came.

Alexander Mack addressed them and said: "The peace of the Lord be with you!" The Superintendent replied: "We have this peace." Thereupon Alexander Mack asked why they had put them under the ban and proposed that both parties pray that God might reveal to them who was guilty of the separation. It would, of course, have been better for them to take upon themselves both known and unknown sins than to compel divine righteousness; however, judgment lay so heavily upon them that they had not the ability to do so.

They accordingly fell upon their knees, and after making their complaints to God, they arose, and A[lexander] M[ack] asked: "Where is Conrad Beissel?" They pointed toward him and said: "There he stands." He answered: "I am a stranger to him; I do not see him unless he speaks." It seems that his eyes were held that he could not see him. This happened several times to the Superintendent, as even to Christ himself and other holy persons. Thereupon the Superintendent answered: "I am the man after whom you ask." A. M. then began asking the reasons why such things had been done. The Superintendent answered asking why they had come here in such improper manner to disturb the meeting; they should have chosen a different time for this matter; and then spoke not a word more. Then things became lively.

One brother from Conestoga said: "A. M., I regard you as a servant of God." Peter Becker replied: "What kind of a servant do you consider him? A servant of His righteousness?" It was noticed that all of those from Conestoga who, at that time and afterwards, became involved with the Brethren in judgment, as Jacob Weiss, Valentine Leslie, David Gmähle, etc., afterwards themselves fell away from their calling. Yes, good M[ichael] W[ohlfahrt] had to suffer for it even on his death bed, and would have certainly fallen into the hands of the avenger of blood, if the faithfulness of the Superintendent had not saved him.

In the same year [1730], in the eighth month [October], we had a meeting in the Swamp, at Senseman's house; after we had been together in our worship for a time, the old Brethren also came into our meeting, in a very disorderly manner. As soon as they had entered through the door of the room Alexander Mack greeted us with peace saying: "The peace of the Lord be with you." (There was nothing disorderly in that, as they pretend; they seem to have forgotten how often they had treated the poor Baptist Brethren with much more rudeness.)

Alexander Mack asked for Brother Friedsam right away and why we [Ephrata] had put them in the ban, and what the . . . reason for the ban was? At the same time he insisted that we join them in prayer before God, so that He might reveal to us upon which side the guilt lay. After this they kneeled down holding their staffs in both hands, and laid their heads on their hands. They began to pray loudly, complaining about the congregation in their prayer. (I was told that Brother Agonius mocked them greatly during their prayer saying: "Call loudly, call loudly, perhaps your God is asleep." The writer of the Chronicle had known better than to record that.)

After the prayer Alexander Mack asked for Conrad Beissel. When he answered: "I am the man," Alexander [Mack] began to ask him why they had done thus and so to them. To which Brother Friedsam countered: why had they come here, in such an immodest and unmannerly fashion, only to disturb the meeting? If there was some business to take care of, they could have met in a different manner.

After this V[ater] F[riedsam] said not one more word to them. Brother Agonius, however disputed with them at length, etc.

Jacob Weisz also let himself be heard in a most rash way, so that Gantz said: "He is a mocker." On the other hand, one of our brethren said to A. Mack: "I consider you to be a servant of God," etc. On both sides words were uttered which are better not repeated. After they had failed to accomplish anything they went out through the door and left.

With the Superintendent, however, the matter was quite different, for he had to stand up for the charge entrusted to him by God, wherein it was not by any means allowed anyone else to imitate his zeal, and to mix up his own passions with it. Those who know how the affairs stood between the two congregations know also that a close union between them was impossible; for they were born of diverse causes, since the one had the letter as its foundation, and the other the spirit; and while both had the same Father, they had different mothers.

Here it is also to be remarked that, according to law, the rank is always inherited from the mother, so that if a king lies with a slave woman, the child must also be a slave. On the part of God, indeed, the seed of the new birth is always one and the same; but the great diversity among the awakened arises from their varied susceptibility, by reason of which the word of life penetrates more deeply into one than into another, on which account as great a difference of tribes and families arises under the new covenant as existed under the old, which indeed cannot be changed, and should not diminish their love. As at Schwarzenau the Separatists and others sought to enter the congregations of the Brethren without becoming subject to their ordinances, the good Alexander Mack felt constrained to write a little tract, in which he showed them that each tribe must hold to its own standard.

The Superintendent referred to this difference in his letters to P[eter] B[ecker]. In one of them he also mentions what displeased him in them [the Brethren], where he writes: "I am well disposed toward you all in those matters in which the spirits can unite in God; but in those which concern your mode of divine worship I can take no part." (See his seventeenth printed epistle.) It is easy to understand that in succeeding years this breach must have greatly pained them. And they made several attempts to mend it, but effected nothing, because they would not recognize the fault in themselves.

At one time they undertook a visit to him; but before they arrived, he was impelled to go out. Then they imagined that he had run away from them, and had no good conscience. At another time both parties met on a visit. The Superintendent saw that something would happen, and called his people aside, where they agreed to offer them peace in Christ, and to forget everything that had happened. But they would not accept this, but wanted to have matters investigated and judgment passed upon them.[15]

EXODUS FROM GERMANTOWN

The death of Alexander Mack, Sr., in 1735, combined with a religious awakening in the Germantown congregation, provided the opening for further proselyting from among the Brethren by the Beissel group. The loss of Mack's hand on the helm, which had been turned over to him by Peter Becker in 1729, left the leadership among several Brethren who did not always agree on church policy. The writer of the manuscript *Chronicle* asserted that "in the 11th month of the year 1734 [February 1735], Alexander Mack passed over from this life into eternity. . . . From this time on the Brethren congregation stood without a foundation, because they had lost their leader. Therefore seventeen brothers and sisters from the congregation came to ours."[16]

Among those who left in 1738-1739 were some of the most active and capable members of the congregation, including the late Alexander Mack's own son, Sander Mack (Alexander Mack, Jr.). The best insights into the causes of the departure are found in the account of Stephen Koch (1695-1763), who had come to Pennsylvania in 1719 with the Peter Becker party. Reputed for his mystical gifts, Koch was best known for his "Vision," first published by the Sauer press in America, beginning in 1744. Koch found the Ephrata Community more to his liking than the more evangelical Brethren at Germantown. His description was included in the printed *Chronicle,* whose editors wrote of him: "At the same time there was among the Brethren at Germantown an old experienced Solitary brother, Stephen Koch by name, who ended his holy walk in the Settlement."[17] Sangmeister wrote of Koch:

> About this time it happened that Brother Agabus [Koch] came again to live at Ephrata. They seated me next to him, at the table as well as in the service of worship. This annoyed me very much, as he was deaf and a poor cripple, and had such curious expressions and mannerisms that I often could not refrain from laughing. I complained about this, and a certain brother said to me: "You don't know him yet; I would rather sit beside him than by any of the others." This made me reconsider, and I visited him. Because I occasionally expressed myself in oral prayer, he directed to me the rhyme of Gerhard Tersteegen: "You always run around the tangent like an enthusiast, and yet pray yourself poorer and poorer." [*Stets läufst du draussen, wie ein Schwärmer, und betest dich doch immer ärmer.*][18]

Tersteegen was one of the Pietists with whom Koch corresponded.

Koch's Account

It is known that the Schwarzenau Brethren at first were an awakened people, among whom the spirit of virginity had his abode, and the way of holiness was trodden. It was noticed, however, that after they had become a people by covenant and thereby were joined together into an external brotherhood, the revival spirit gradually was extinguished among them, and they instead fell back upon mere external forms of divine worship as that upon which flesh and blood depended for redemption. Though these were instituted by God himself, yet they were never meant to be the end itself, as though everything were fulfilled if one met once every week and heard something talked about which, after all, no one intends to carry out, and then devoted the remaining days of the week to the world. For this cause God kept the worship of the Jews in constant disturbance, and often destroyed their temple, so that it might not become the essential thing for them.

In this, however, they did not succeed any better than the other parties in the Christian church; for each one has inculcated a form of service peculiar to its own people, whereby it is distinguished from every other people, until so many religious hedges have come into being that it is hardly possible to count them any longer. Thus among these good people the outer forms of service, which should have helped them in their awakening, became their lord and master, and they all became bondsmen to them. It is, therefore, no wonder that the spirit of awakening, in its virgin strictness, had to leave them and place their ordering into the hands of that man who everywhere builds up again the church of Adam. Wherefore among them as among other parties the claim is made: "Come here! We have the true church; here one baptizes into the faith in Jesus," etc.

As they have been sold into bonds under their forms of worship, so also with their water baptism; for they recognize no one as a brother who has not been baptized, even though he should surpass them in knowledge and experience; such a one has to be satisfied with the title of "friend." They went even further in this literal and narrow manner, and committed the teaching office mostly into the hands of married men. Thereby they brought matrimony into high favor, and finally cast off the estate of virginity, which before their baptism they had rated so high. Young people, when they saw that

the married state was so highly honored, lusted after it; but as long
as they were unbaptized they were regarded as heathen, for according
to their principles, marriage is consummated only between two believers. If, therefore, they wished to marry, they first had to have
themselves baptized; which at last opened a wide door for carnal
presumption.

Under such circumstances, when there were still many who had
witnessed the awakening in Schwarzenau, it is no wonder that the
fire still smoldering under its ashes should have been rekindled.
About this time, however, an important brother, Henry Traut, by
name, passed out of time into eternity, on January 4, 1753. When
with sorrowful heart and deeply grieved I saw him pass into eternity,
it made so deep an impression on me that I continually sighed unto
God whether it were not possible that in this life yet I might attain
unto health of conscience. For I might do what I would, yet I always
lacked that which was best, because it appeared to me that I had
never in my heart been converted to God, which indeed also I experienced to be the case. The deeper I searched, the more I became aware
that in my deepest nature I was still lacking that true change of
heart, without which the peace of God, which passes all understanding, could not reveal itself to me. From this I could well see
that there was nothing else for me to do than repent anew and be
sincerely converted to God. . . .

For this repentance and conversion, however, I had no power
within me. A long while I went about in grief and sighing, and I
was even as it is written: "The children are come to the birth and
there is no strength to bear them." But at length the power of darkness so revolted within me that for the life of me I had no resource
left; and I now was able to realize in what grievous condition the
deceased brother, Henry Traut, had been when at times he had so
sorely wept, for I was in like condition. But I did not feel free to
tell anyone of it. To God, however, I often said: "Must I then forever
be cast off from Thee? Alas, must I now become the prey of unclean
spirits! Was it in vain that so many years I have shed so many tears,
and poured out unto Thee, my God, so many heart-sighings? Have
mercy upon me, lest I perish, for my uncleanness is become so great
that it ever hangs over my head, and my enemies rejoice over me,
and say, "'Aha! Aha! This we gladly see! When once he is down,

he shall not rise again!'" (Psalm 35). And this I had to hear continually.

But with all this I found no salvation; instead, it grew ever worse, so that at last I became very fearful and thought: "Now it will continue that my poor life is consumed, and what will happen after that, God knows." In this way I spent several years, and had, besides, great pain from stones in the bladder, so that I often lay two or three days in the greatest extremity, and had death ever before me, until I was again relieved from it for a time. But God finally regarded my misery and came to my help in a wonderful manner. On May 3, 1735, at Germantown, as late at night I went behind the house into the orchard, there being bright moonlight, there came to me a delightful fragrance, partly from the blossoms of the trees, partly from the flowers in the garden, upon which I, sobbing, spoke to God: "Oh, my God, everything is in its order and contributes to Thy glory and honor, save I alone! For I am created and called by a holy calling to love Thee above everything, and to become a pleasant savor unto the glorification of Thy name. Now, however, I behold the contradiction; for not only do I not love Thee as I ought, but I am also become an evil smell in Thy nostrils. Alas, unfortunate that I am! Must I then pass my days in such misery? I gladly would love God, the highest good, but I cannot. The world with all its glories cannot satisfy my sad spirit, for I ever see before my eyes spiritual and bodily death."

While I lamented thus to God it seemed to me as though suddenly a flame of God's voice struck into me, which entirely illumined me inside, and I heard a voice say to me: "Yet one thing thou lackest." I asked: "What is it then?" The answer was: "You do not know God, and never have really known Him." I said: "Yes, that is so; but how shall I attain it?" Then it seemed as though I were beside myself. But when I came to again, I felt an inexpressibly pleasing love to God in my heart; and on the other hand, all anxiety, with all the temptations of the unclean spirits, had vanished. Yes, it seemed as if all my transgressions were pardoned and sealed, and day and night there was nothing else in my heart but joy, love, and praise to God.

After several days I went to my intimate brother, the young Alexander Mack, who told me that he was in so sorrowful a state that he believed he would soon die. Therefore he had made his last will, wherein he made several his heirs, whom he mentioned to me by name. I told him how I, too, had made a testament that I would belong wholly to my God. He asked me how that had happened. I said that he probably had noticed that for several years already I had been in a sorrowful condition. Thereupon I recounted the whole matter to him, what had happened to me, and how God had saved me from all my misery in a wonderful manner, and that I now felt in my heart such a love to God that I could not express it. He said: "Oh, if you are really such as you say, then you are happy indeed! I believe you will remain thus, and will come to quite a different estate from what you were before. I feel from what you say that something marvelous has happened to you, and I rejoice greatly therein."

We often had similar conversations with each other and it was not long before he also came to an awakened state. As he was a ready speaker, he began to speak in the meeting so powerfully that it was a marvel to hear him, and this aroused much notice in the congregation. Some were well pleased at it; but others could not comprehend it. At that time we had a meeting for the unmarried every Sunday afternoon, where we also spoke together as related above. At last the spirit of revival came upon all who were assembled, so that one often heard with astonishment how they praised God; however, with many it did not last long.

In the meantime it happened that the people in the house in which I had lived so long were no longer satisfied with me; for the life I now led was a witness against their life. Accordingly, the above-mentioned A. Mack received me into his house; but he lived together with another brother, Henry Höcker, in half the house, while the other half was occupied by his brother after the flesh, Valentine Mack. At this time, Henry Kalckglässer, then the oldest minister of the congregation at Germantown, who afterwards ended his course at Ephrata, came to us in the house, and said: "I hear so much said about you among the people, Stephen Koch. Tell me the truth: in what estate were you? How did you come to another condition? And how are you now?"

I told him first of all in what a sad state I had been; how marvelously God had brought me out of it; and that I now, day and night, felt such a love to God in my heart that no tongue could express it. Thereupon he answered: "Oh, I know your condition very well, for I was in the same state a long while; but through the various occurrences one meets therein I fell away from it again. Now I will learn anew to walk before God." He rejoiced greatly that the good old way shown him at the beginning of his conversion was again revealed to him; in everything of which we had spoken he agreed with us. For we spoke yet much more concerning the celibate estate, and a life of virginity, of which he said that all this had been revealed to him at his first conversion.

Thus, this old brother was quickened again, and spoke openly at the meeting concerning such things with much impressiveness, remarking also that he believed that if he had died in the condition in which he had been he would have been found to be a foolish virgin. Many of the congregation, however, took this amiss of him, and said that he had been a minister so long and had baptized so many, and yet spoke now of himself so doubtfully. But he insisted that such had been his experience.

At another time the other minister, Peter Becker, also came to us. During the night we spoke much together, so that in the morning he tearfully bade us farewell. He said to us that he also would begin anew to walk before God; but this was so far reversed in him again that he at last declared himself against us.

Before I came to live with Brother A. Mack, I saw in a vision a beautiful virgin come into our meeting, who preached wonderfully concerning sanctification and a life of virginity. At this I was so glad that in the morning I said to the Brethren that I had seen a most beautiful virgin come into our meeting, who had delivered an extraordinary address concerning purity and the life of virginity; whereupon they rejoiced with me. At the time when I saw this vision, V. Mack saw me go to his brother Alexander very often, and said to me: "You come to the house so often, yet you never come to see me." I answered: "Perhaps your house-sister [wife] would not like it." From that time on I frequently visited them and spoke with them of the way of holiness, and she always listened with devout attention. . . .

On April 12, 1736, therefore, I moved in with Brother A. Mack, and for a time the three of us lived together. In the year 1737 we built a house in a valley, a mile from Germantown, into which we moved on October 14 of the same year. There another Solitary brother, named John Reisman, besides a pious married couple, came to live with us. But on March 21, 1738, my three brethren, Alexander Mack, Henry Höcker, and John Reisman, removed to the Solitary at Ephrata, and the housefather, mentioned before, went back to his own piece of land. Thereupon another pious housefather, Lewis Hoecker by name, came to live with me; but we did not live together any longer than until March 27, 1739, when I also removed to the Solitary at Ephrata. Thus my first call came back to me again, and thus I found again the piece of silver I had lost, about which I greatly rejoice. May God comfort all the sorrowing in Zion, and redeem Israel from the rod of the oppressor. Amen.[19]

A Letter of Koch to Lobach About Germantown and Ephrata

Stephen Koch, as did many of the Germans in Pennsylvania, corresponded frequently with Brethren in Germany. In 1738 he wrote to John Lobach (1683-1750),[20] Pietist and Brethren leader, providing news about the Quakers and slavery (omitted here), but especially about developments in Germantown and the Ephrata Community. It is one of the best early descriptions of the Cloister. Koch's reference to the loss of life of migrants is another echo of the tragedy told in detail in the *Open Letter* previously.

> In the valley near Germantown
> November 13, 1738

Dear Brother J[ohn] L[obach]:

I greet you in friendship, along with all of your dear household and wish you, and myself, grace from God, that we might learn really and in truth to pray: "Lord, thy will be done now and forever!" Amen.

Dear brother, I duly received your dear letter. It truly seemed to me an echo which sounded across the great ocean to me and resounded in my heart with "Yea" and "Amen." May the Lord increase in us more as time goes on the uniting of the spirit that we may be one with Him and His children, and so remain now and in eternity! It also pleases me greatly to learn that in Germany the grace of God still reveals itself in many souls. In this country there is also a great awakening, and some of the previously awakened souls begin again to strive for the first love as well as many newly awakened people.

Those who are [members] of congregations cause strife and conflict within their congregations. . . .

I wrote you, furthermore, last year, that some souls were being awakened who stress a true life, even among the Brethren. This occasioned great strife among them, and still continues to do so. Christ is indeed come to bring peace, but not for the old life. That is why He says: "For from henceforth there shall be five in one house divided, three against two, and two against three" [Luke 12:52]. For life born of God cannot be reconciled with a fellowship that [only] appears to be good and is founded on the letter and governed according to outward truth. On the contrary, there must be spirit and life along with it without which, in the New Covenant, nothing is acceptable before God. As the people so easily are concerned with external things, thinking that now they had got hold of what is right, God again causes souls to be awakened, who then are compelled to witness in great earnest that outward ceremonies without spirit and an inner life count for nothing before God. This, then, often causes much dispute and trouble within a congregation.

The dear Father, however, derives this advantage from it, that due to this agitation many souls often begin to dig more deeply in their search and are thus brought to an inner spiritual life, of which I have experienced a bit myself. Oh, how incomprehensible are the ways of the Lord! And who can determine the wonderful ways in which the Lord works with souls, until He brings them to knowledge of themselves and of their God? And this will continue in all eternity. Yes, often, when I have this insight as at a glance, I prostrate myself in my spirit before Him, with great amazement at His great love for poor, fallen man. Oh, that a deep impression of it might constantly remain in our hearts!

I also wrote you last year that we brethren, as mentioned previously, have started a communal life with one another. You should know that last March these brethren moved together to Conestoga, about twenty hours distance in the wilderness, where about forty unmarried people have been living a communal life for several years now. They have everything in common, and live very secluded from the world. The place where they live is called Ephrata. Sometimes two or three live in one house; however, each has his separate lodging. Now they have built two large houses; in one there are only single women; in the other, some distance away, there are only brethren who are unmarried, and each has a small room to himself. They all help one another build their own houses. They have neither horses nor cows. Whatever they sow and plant in the fields, they till by hoeing. They insist very much on an austere life. Their clothing and food are humble. They also think highly of continence and of the unmarried state. Therefore they are very despised and many lies are told about them. They also observe the seventh day, but not to the letter, as I have seen and also heard from them. They also observe baptism, the love feast, and feetwashing like the other Brethren whom you know.

There is also a very large congregation of householders, who belong to them. They, however, live each on his own land together with his family. They only participate in the spiritual life of the community. As regards keeping house, etc., they take care of themselves. They have their own cows and horses, and sow and plant each on his own land as he thinks best, still, in such a manner that they all strive for a humble life, and even continence.

As for me, I still live in my small room. One of the brethren has bought the house and he and his wife live with me.

The two brethren J[ohn] N[aas] and P[eter] B[ecker] are very active in leading the work of the congregation of the old Brethren, although in serious confusion. Though I cannot go along with them, I do wish them all those good things that I wish for myself and all God-fearing souls. The dear friend Sp[angenberg][21] lives about six hours from here at a friend's, in the country. He does farm work, like chopping wood, hoeing, and digging. It is amazing how this dear friend has humbled himself, for he was such a great scholar, yes, even professor, in H[alle]. Oh, what can the love of Jesus not do, if it is the right kind! It makes of great scholars small schoolboys of Jesus, who are studying in order to forget what they have learned, as the dear friend G[erhard] T[er] St[eegen][22] says in a hymn, that great men will become children and small children will be called great in this school. Oh, Jesus, you were the greatest and made yourself the least in order to give us an example to follow after you. You are the master of that school in which one can learn to be a child who enters the Kingdom of God. Oh, teach us through Thy Spirit to become truly small. Amen.

Oh, dear brother, in this school one can learn to escape the selfishness and self-will of which you write. For here is one taught to hate and part from oneself. May the Lord grant us the power to be true disciples of Jesus. I also greet the dear and worthy friend G. T. St.

Concerning Brother G[umre], you should know that he and his wife departed from this world last spring after a feverish illness. On the day he was buried, his wife died also. I visited him three days before his death, when I heard that both of them were ill. He had not been ill very long; she somewhat longer. When I came to him he was very glad that I had walked all that distance to visit him. I asked him in what state of mind he was in his condition, as it could easily be that the Lord might call him. He answered that he had been secretly longing for that for some time, and yearned for it in order to learn to be content with that which God would do with him in this time and in eternity. It was the same with him now, and therefore he had no freedom to wish for this or that, but only to give himself over to the will of God in tranquility. Thus it was his innermost longing that God might grant him the grace to praise Him in everything regardless of what He might do with him. Everything he said was in this manner. As I took leave of him, I wished him a steadfastness in this wish. He then asked me to help him pray the Lord to strengthen his faith. I did not see them after that.

Concerning friend G[ruber?] and his sending the excerpt about the strange awakenings in New England that occurred there too, I also heard about this a year ago, and nothing further since. Nor can he give me any further news about it, as he lives over one hundred German hours from here. He sends you friendly greetings. The man who takes these letters also lost his wife during the sea voyage. This year many hundred people died at sea and during the journey here. According to another letter, about fifteen hundred people died, mostly from dysentery, and daily others have died of it on land, so that the misery of these people is great and indeed indescribable. May God have mercy on them!

I also greet your brother who sent greetings to us, as well as all the dear friends there with you. What is our friend H[ubert] R[ahr][23] doing? I have not heard from him for a long time. Finally, I remain your true and loyal friend and brother.

S[tephen] K[och][24]

THE EPHRATA BRETHREN VISIT NEW JERSEY

Late in 1738 a substantial number of the Sabbatarians led by Beissel himself visited the Brethren at Amwell, with whom they had close and cordial relationships. One of the Eckerlins was delegated to work with them, and several of the congregation there did move to Ephrata and joined the Community. One of these was Jacob Mohr, to whom Beissel addressed a long letter in 1755.

The Chronicle Account

In December of the year mentioned, the Superintendent, with many of the Solitary, made a lengthy visit to the Brethren at Amwell, in Jersey. These people, from the time of their first awakening, had a great love for the work of the Lord in the Settlement. This visit opened the door for the breaking of bread together, which otherwise, because they were united with a congregation of Brethren in Germantown, would not have been looked upon with approval. When the Superintendent returned home, he called together a church council, and related with what love they had been received in those regions by the children of God (may this be recorded in their favor in the book of holy remembrance before God!). At the same time he announced how concerned he was for those poor people and that they would have to be helped out with a brother from Ephrata.

These good people in Amwell specially availed themselves of this open Philadelphian church door, and made many a visit of more than a hundred English miles to the Settlement, and built themselves up in the unity of the Spirit on the death of Jesus Christ. Thereby the Superintendent was induced to undertake another visit, on which he was accompanied only by solitary brethren. As many of the Brethren there stood in judgment against the work of God in the Settlement, some feared that the two parties might get into each other's hair, whereby the general edification might be hindered. Yes, some sought to take the visitors to the then-Brethren minister, Bechtelsheimer by name, in the hope that matters might occur over which they might gloat; but they were disappointed in this.

The Superintendent, who bore in his heart the seal of the redemption of the whole world, started on his visit, and was received with all affection by the minister referred to and his helpmate. They sat down with him and listened to him for more than an hour, during which there flowed from him in a flood all that the Spirit gave him. And at the very time when everybody thought the visitors might now be dismissed in peace, these good people showed forth their particular love by treating him to a rich collation. May God reward them on the day of reckoning! So likewise the whole congregation helped the visitors across the river again at their own expense. This is mentioned here with the intent that if any of these dear people should still be living and read this, they might know that their faithfulness shown toward the work of God has been held in hallowed remembrance.

Meanwhile some among them were eager that there might be established among them a household, such as they had seen at the Settlement, for they had well-brought-up young people and hoped something useful might be accomplished among them. It would indeed have been easy to introduce the form among them, but to fill this effigy with the Spirit was not a human work. At that time there was among the brethren at the Settlement one by the name of Elimelech, one of the Eckerlins [Emanuel], whom the stars had formed for a priest and redeemer of the bodily life, so that while other brethren spent their time in hard labor, he sought his own pastures and imposed his priesthood upon people. . . .

After the Superintendent had ordained Brother Elimelech to be teacher at Amwell, he publicly consecrated him to this office by the laying on of hands, on account of which many maintained that he would become the Superintendent's successor in his office, as the former was already his right hand. . . .

This letter Elimelech took along to Amwell, where he showed it to everyone as his credentials which he had received from the Superintendent. His people indeed sought to sustain him in his office, but when they noticed that it was an imitated affair and not inborn they lost courage so that when he wanted to institute midnight meetings like those in the Settlement, and invited their daughters to the same, they feared that offense might occur and dismissed him. Whereupon he returned to the Settlement in disgrace. Thereupon several families left Amwell and removed to the Settlement, namely Dietrich Fahnstock, Conrad Boldhausen, John Mohr, Bernhard Gitter, etc., which added several solitary ones to the sisters' house, though none of them remained steadfast save one Armella [Fahnestock] by name, who ended her days among them.[25]

Conrad Beissel to Jacob Mohr

Ephrata, October 12, 1755

To Jacob Mohr, Sr., in Amwell

May the Lamb elevated by God bless you along with your whole household and family in order that the divine success bless what you have plowed that it may flourish in the new life of grace and that your grain may stand you in good stead when your sheaves are heaped up on the day of God's harvest in the joyful or blessed eternity. The holy and divine power of love from above impels me to address this letter to you because of this very good opportunity, for it seems to me that you are all woven into the loom of the heavenly wisdom's loveplay, in which, however, God's language has at times not been understood to our fullest instruction, as something that helps us grow in holiness and live in God and His love. . . .

Beloved Brother Jacob. I have not yet completely forgotten the conversation which we had with each other when you visited me, which, however, consisted more of the power of love than of words. It did seem to me to some extent that you had not achieved your full purpose in everything, for a portion of the full love of God was lacking which would have been also bestowed upon you. Yet, I remember the essence or the kernel of our conversation, which has moved me to address this letter to you. If this pleases you, my purpose has been met. Otherwise I do not know of anything except that a certain love has impelled me to write to you and the dear souls among you, without my knowing about what matters. . . .

Beloved Brother Jacob, do not let my letter appear strange in your eyes. It was a certain love given by God from heaven which urged me to it, which is stronger than I in all things. This is not surprising, for this love has been my commander for many a year, by which it has achieved such a power over me, that it can do with me just as it pleases. Thus there has developed such a close kinship between us that it has become as my mother and I as its child. It is in this childlike spirit that this letter has been written.

Now, as it generally happens that children fail despite their good intentions, it might well have happened that in this letter the childlike intent might have been erring here or there. If, in that case, just as it is customary for parents to close one eye at the folly of their children, the same is done about these errors; everything is alright and I am and remain your well-wisher for salvation. I also wish for all of you the peace of God from heaven in order that the blessing of Abraham might descend upon all of you, and that you might be and become a true man of God who rules his household in a divine manner and according to the will of his Savior. And for her, who is your partner in marriage, that she might walk as is appropriate for holy women, that is, modest, discreet, reserved, temperate, not given to sensuality, devout, chaste, not quarrelsome but gentle in all things, etc.

Neither must I forget the dear friend and brother Daniel, to whom I wish the joy of heaven as his dowry, so that his marriage or wedding day might be saved until the wedding of the Lamb. Then they will drink the wine from the best vineyard. Oh, how blessed are thus those who here preserve their bodies and souls in purity until that time, for such will partake of it at that time when God judges the souls. He will give them a better lot for their inheritance and a share in the temple of the Lord. Likewise, I must remember the dear married couple, Jacob Mohr and his wife Christina, for whom I wish especially abundant salvation and blessing from God and His love. . . .

The beloved brother Peter Wirtz and his dear sister must not be forgotten either, to whom I wish especially abundant salvation and blessing from God and His bounteous Spirit. Also, I wish that Sister Christina's untimely widowhood might be a cause for her to become God's own property, because that is the way God works in the counsels of His love that He calls home whatever is lost and abandoned, and that He seeks that which is lost, and in doing so restores what has been neglected and rescues him who has no helper. Oh, blessed is he who does not turn to any alien comfort in his desolation and who diligently awaits help from the hand of the Lord only. To him the Lord must and indeed shall be and remain an eternal comfort! There is no more blessed state than when a man is left to the wings of divine mercy and abides in that bosom until the end of his days. He will find his inheritance in the land of the living. Both of you be therefore blessed and beloved by me unto eternity.

Ought I then not also to remember the beloved old Sister Naas? She is still written into my holy remembrance. Oh, how happy I would be if I could see her face once again. Yet, love is an invisible power of the Almighty, and is close to and present with all spirits who are akin to it, and is not limited by boundaries. Let this same all-pervading presence speak. I want to tell this sister that the love which I still bear for her and the entire divine race is quite without measure, and that it must therefore certainly be an unquenchable fountain and remain so in eternity.

Likewise, Sister von Laskin has not been quite forgotten either, because her name has also been written into the book of the saints. May the Lord bless her hope and grant it increase so that it might blossom forth in the world to come. Otherwise and finally, all of you be once again kissed, beloved, and greeted by me. I am and remain who I am, namely, a poor and sorrowful stranger and pilgrim here on earth,

> Friedsam,
> one who possesses nothing here on earth.[26]

LATER BEISSEL-BECKER CORRESPONDENCE

Shortly before the death of Peter Becker, the Germantown leader was visited by, and received several letters from, Conrad Beissel. Brumbaugh claimed the correspondence as a vindication of Becker and as a "plea of forgiveness" from Beissel.[27] Although they do indicate considerable veneration still cherished by Beissel for his former employer and host, there is no indication that they amount to an apology. First and last for Beissel, there was but one live option for the Brethren — to join his movement under his spiritual leadership.

Conrad Beissel to Peter Becker

April 12, 1755

To Brother Peter Becker

I greet and kiss you in the love of Jesus, and in the blood of the New Covenant. My very dear and worthy [brother] in the Lord.

A certain love constrains me somehow to send you another brief message, although I have no outward reason for doing so; yet the urgings of my spirit will not allow me to be completely silent. I have to become no other person than what the kindness of God taught me when it revealed itself to me thirty-six years ago. It taught me godliness, piety, and through it to despise all bliss and glory of this world, according to the saying of our dear and worthy Mediator of the New Covenant (when He says): "If anyone will follow me, he must deny himself, and take up his cross, and follow after me." Also: "He who will keep his life will lose it and whoever hates his life in this world, he will receive eternal life, etc."

This was then my actual rule at the beginning of my conversion. However, at that time I did not know that I had no right yet to follow Jesus, for I was still a foreigner and had not yet been brought under the testament of promise. For this reason, I always lacked the true piety, so that my awakened conscience, instead of being healed, became poorer and poorer every day and was plunged into even greater misery, until finally the helper awakened and taught me the way of denial and humility (which had been hidden from me up to that time) and opened to me the covenant of God in the water of baptism, for it is only there that the true and narrow way to heaven can be found. In this covenant through faith in the hope for something better, all life of vanity is planted into the death of Jesus and surrendered. Through grace I have succeeded in this covenant to this very day.

During the times and days of God's merciful visitation of this country, this very sincere desire on my part to attain to joy in the Lord with a pure heart and a good conscience was all the more able to penetrate [to God] and that in a simple, childlike manner, whereby I did not hesitate to surrender what I deemed my most precious possession and all that for the sake of the love of Jesus which brought Him from heaven for our salvation. Oh, how happy I am that my ever-yearning spirit has been brought to its purpose, goal, and end after so much longing.

My dear and beloved one in the Lord! You do realize and sense that which is still a problem. Godliness and an innocent life before God and man I have loved, and as I realized that I could not achieve it without being embodied in Christ through the New Covenant of grace in the water of baptism, such did happen. Thus the spirit of filiation was attained, which with sighing pleads for us before God in everything.

My dear! It has pleased God from the beginning of my conversion on, to lead me on a very sad and troubled path and often in such a manner that I have always remained rather hidden from men. All divine comfort which has been offered me during this time unavoidably has been coupled with sorrow at all times. For this reason I have never remained completely hidden from men, which to some degree you yourself have perhaps noticed in me when I came to you in this country thirty years ago. At that time I was not yet a child of the New Covenant, but stood in the fearful birth in the current of waters. And even though the childlike relationship has indeed been attained, one's body still stands here in this turbulent world, where, it is true, a great many and sometimes raw winds blow over it, before it reaches its full maturity and age.

This I faithfully learned from the time on when I entered into the covenant, since I have been faithfully supplied with it up to this time, as with a spiritual traveling rod on my sad pilgrimage to the goal of blessed eternity. If I were to describe to you how many dismal waves have washed over this little vessel you would hardly be able to read it without sorrowful sympathy and tears. Yet, the time of comfort before the countenance of the Lord makes one forget all of this and the happy harvest in the New World will surely reward our sad time of sowing with great joy.

My attempt at communicating is poor, for what is really the nature of my spirit I can neither say nor write. Just remember this — that there is a certain power of love with which we are filled from above. When this happens you will realize that a hidden blessing has been added to it which duly follows the basic rules of the New Covenant; especially when it says: "Bless and curse not, for to this you are called that you go and inherit the blessing."

I must admit I wish one could kiss each other in spirit in the blessing as it is given from above, and that one could participate in it in the same measure as heaven pours it out. For I can say that this has been the real test for me at all times, namely, communicating God and His love, without which all of our works are lost. We know nothing and understand not how His spirit communicates in grace. This it is that we must understand, namely, that we know nothing and understand nothing. Thus we praise God's goodness as it reigns over us in grace and mercy, teaching us a new way in which we learn to keep the rules and ways of our God through which we shall always be made pleasing and acceptable in His sight. It is done in and through Him himself out of whose fullness we all receive grace upon grace, which makes us rich in poverty and strong in weakness and thus our glory is in our abasement.

Oh, how well he has fared who has once entered the tent of the New Covenant! For there is found eternal freedom, where one is safe from the hellish avenger. It is bound to happen that we are led to praise the mercy of God, by which we are made holy through faith in Jesus in the spirit and water and blood of the New Covenant. Moreover, this remains my only task, that I may be made holy for the Lord and be found immaculate and in peace before Him in order that I may have joy on the day of judgment, and not perish at His advent.

It is, of course, not known whether your labor is also directed to this, in which case our spirits would indeed be rejoicing and embracing each other. As far as I know, our labors have at all times been directed to this, and as it is likely that your course in this warring world will soon be completed, I thank God from my heart, who has granted such blessing, that I was able once more to write a letter to you. Should this be the last time, and we will not be able to talk to each other anymore, and should it come to the point where I would be left behind, I wish you a blessed parting that you might receive for all your toil and sorrow here on earth a joyful harvest toward the day of the revelation of God and His advent.

I greet and kiss you once again most warmly in the spirit of the purest love of Jesus, into whose holy wounds I am faithfully commending you. In Him we are made holy through the blood which He shed on the cross. May His spirit, which restores in us the true life and the image of immortality, be in you and us all, surrounding and inspiring us now and forevermore. Amen.

Please extend my greeting in the faith to Sister Anna Dorothea [Becker], to whom I desire my sincere regards to be conveyed. I send her my blessing; may she live eternally and receive her reward with the righteous made perfect in heaven and may her inheritance come to no other. And thus I am and remain your well-wisher for the future joy of the blessed eternity.

Written by me, Brother Friedsam, one who owns nothing on this earth.[28]

Conrad Beissel to Peter Becker

Ephrata, May 20, 1756

Patient in suffering, innocent in loving, consumed in misery, thus a soul is proved to be in God.

May heaven rain justice and may the dew of God spread itself over the whole earth, so that all that is hard may be softened, all that is stony and harsh be made mild, so that God's field may be prepared for the last evening rain long promised by God, that it may fall on the entire church of God for the glorious sprouting and growing into the new life of grace, so that soon the fulfilment of the people of God may become reality. The whole creation waits with groaning and moaning for its completion, that it, too, may be made free from the servitude of the vanity of the mortal existence.

As to my own moaning and longing in all this time and many years, my pen will indeed not be able to describe it, for it is known to God alone. Oh, in what miraculous ways the spark of eternity, or that new life of grace which is hidden in God, must twist and turn through this bodily dwelling — or mortal life — until it can be brought to sprout and grow. Oh, how many winds of tribulation roar over this plant, if it has even before in its roots brought forth many heartrending blooms. Oh, dear friend, had it but been granted to me to embrace you more often in this precious life of grace, what a God-pleasing joy it would have caused me. Yet, sorrowful regret must be my solace even to this hour.

You can hardly imagine, my dear friend, the kind of God-melting emotions my heart and spirit evidenced when we left your house after our visit. Although no one to this hour has been permitted to say it or has said it, my pen does now bring it to light and I must open my heart to you: the idea came into my mind and gave me much to think about, that the harvest of the matter when I lived with you thirty-five years ago was still not brought in and neither you nor I understood what it meant, for there was something good contained therein which has remained. I have been the debtor, for none of you have taken pleasure for all that you have done to me. Oh, how great is the ignorance! The Lord of heaven has to be your reward and repay you, for I cannot bring it back anymore.

Of course, it should and could have been done in the times thereafter, when a kiss of love was exchanged in the water of baptism, if one had not been so blind. Yet, may the good God be eternally praised who forgives sins and misdeeds and has pleasure in mercy and not in judgment. Meanwhile, I remain your debtor and well-wisher. Perhaps the balsam of life and heavenly dew of grace may heal this sick one [Beissel], if he is clothed in faith and love with the patience of God.

As for the rest of our journey, this is what we found. There was a beautiful harvest of faithful souls in Amwell, but the best is not yet; if some spirits among them were drenched completely with the sacred oil of anointment of the high-priestly spirit, which flows over one's entire body until it reaches the hem of the robe, then it might well create a plant whose sheaves would be harvested in the New World. To this I wish much divine blessing. In addition, I can say that we enjoyed great blessing there, and in almost all the homes that we visited. This moved me to a warmly loving compassion, for I recognized their faithful and loyal disposition. Still I did not yet see the right door opened with the Philadelphian church key, where a church may be built after the manner of the new Jerusalem where all the gates are open into all four parts of the world night and day to all peoples, generations, tongues, and languages, and yet nothing enters that is impure. For eventually, at the very last call to the supper of our great God, all those lying by the fence must be called up and away so that the number or the house of the Lord might be full.

It is true, I pass my days in great pain and tribulation about the loss of the children of my people. Yet what is to be done? It is written: "The patience of God take for your salvation." The Lord will know at the end how to gather His own and pluck them from all their misery. For it is certain that the divine and heavenly work of deliverance is at this time in a fearful groaning, because the heavenly "Magia" is rather closed up, whereas the worldly one has opened wide instead. Therefore, the entire earth is in upheaval for the devout and the worldly alike. This is to make the saints raise their heads in faith, for all of these are the signs that the day of their salvation is near.

As regards myself, otherwise and what I have been doing since my return from the journey, I can report that the journey has made me very quiet. I have left the house very seldom and have even inwardly been very withdrawn so that I could have hardly kept my promise had not old Brother König come to me and said that he was about to start his journey. Immediately I felt the urge to write, but whether I shall be able to restore myself I do not know, for I have been relieved of that which lay upon my heart.

To return again to the two of us, I can say that in those things in which I have realized to be your debtor, I have felt in my spirit once and for all such a power of blessing that it surpasses all comprehension. Is [the reason] that my spirit can touch you as a spirit? Then I think it is as it should be. As I do not know any better counsel I shall pledge the love given by God from heaven, for I do not have any other goods in my possession. I hope that the sharing love of God will make itself so felt that all frailty can be discarded in time and eternity.

Allow me, my dear friend, to take delight in thee. This will happen when you allow yourself to be loved in the spirit only as much as it desires. Because of our old age we will both have to rest satisfied with caresses only. But could one, however, proceed to embracing and kissing, and from there into the chaste marital bed in spirit, where one would be united with all the pure spirits of the righteous who have been made perfect, who are constantly in the presence of God in united harmony, where I, too, long to be and which I fervently anticipate until the glory of the great God will reveal itself to all heavens among His saints, then one will drink from the vineyard which has no dregs in it.

If I have expressed myself clearly to you, my dear friend, as I do not doubt, it is as it should be. I remain one who lies at the feet of all those who pass by, until God takes pity and raises the miserable from the dust, and humbles those who sat in high places for the pride of their hearts. Be then blessed by God and His abundant Spirit with the abounding plenty of His grace, that you may be strengthened inwardly and be made strong to the blessing of your tired and faint spirit. May your withered bones be made to sprout with might to the ever-blooming priesthood, that they may be brought to the lot in which the entire human race is reconciled. Thus may the lot of all of the saints remain your inheritance for ever and ever. Amen.

Here, at long last, you have perhaps another letter; may the Lord bless it, with an eternal blessing, that your pilgrimage from time to eternity may blossom in the eternal world, into which I hope also to be included for ever and ever. Amen.

I remain, then, your faithful friend,
Friedsam, otherwise known as Conrad Beissel,
one who possesses nothing on this earth.

P.S. Greet and kiss Anna Dorothea for me most warmly, along with her daughter and son-in-law. Farewell.[29]

3. Contemporary Accounts

The movement led by Conrad Beissel at Conestoga (which took on monastic characteristics in the 1730's) and its relationships with the Brethren at Germantown and elsewhere attracted a great deal of attention. An entire book has been compiled under the title *Ephrata, As Seen by Contemporaries* (1952), printing the more important accounts of travelers, theologians, and others fascinated by the unusual movement. Even Voltaire took notice of the Ephrata community, calling them the "most inimitable Christians" current.[1]

Here follow some of the more significant observations by contemporaries dealing with the mainline Brethren and the Sabbatarians at Ephrata. They are from a variety of denominational backgrounds, and range in time from 1730 to 1792. Some are taken from manuscript materials and have never before been published; others have appeared in print, but are here freshly translated. Those appearing originally in English are here published as they first appeared, with the exception of slight editorial changes for the sake of easier reading. Less-than-careful observers often failed to make the necessary distinction between the Brethren and Ephrata. In these cases editorial comments are added for clarity.

EARLY DESCRIPTIONS

Morgan Edwards on Ephrata

The Baptist historian Morgan Edwards included a description of Ephrata in his account of the Brethren in Pennsylvania (1770). It is quite a balanced treatment, with but minor inaccuracies, and will help in putting other accounts into perspective. Special attention is called to the long list of names, containing as it does many who were at one time affiliated with the Brethren.

Ephrata

This church is distinguished by the above name which is the name of the village where it exists, in Cocolico Township and Lancaster County, sixty miles WNWbW from Philadelphia. The same village is frequently called *Tunkerstown*. It consists of between thirty and forty buildings, and stands on a parcel of land containing 155 acres. The land is formed into a triangle by the crossings of the Paxton and Lancaster roads and Cocolico River. The places of worship in the village are three: one (called *Sharon*) adjoins the sisters' apartments by way of [the] chapel; the other, called *Bethany*, is a chapel belonging to the apartments of the brethren, where they resort to worship morning and evening, and sometimes in the night, as the sisters also do in the other chapel; the third is a common church called *Zion*, built on the summit of a little hill, about two hundred yards distant from the other. Here the single brethren and [the] single sisters and the married people and their children meet once a week for public worship.

The brethren have adopted the dress of the white friars with some alteration, and the sisters that of the nuns; and both, like them, have taken the vow of celibacy. But some break through the vow. Then they quit their cells and go to the neighborhood among the married people. All the fraternity wear their beards.

Their livelihood they get by cultivating the land, by a printing office, by a grist mill, a paper mill, an oil mill, etc.; and the sisters by spinning, weaving, sewing, etc. They slept at first on board couches with blocks for pillows, but now sleep on beds; and have otherwise abated much of the severity of their order. They keep the seventh day of the week for Sabbath, to which their founder had been proselyted by the remains of the Keithian Baptists, particularly Rev. Thomas Rutter, who in this affair was the disciple of Abel Noble.[2] From the uncouth dress, the recluse and ascetic life of these people, sour aspects and rough manners might be expected; but on the contrary, a smiling innocence and meekness grace their countenances, and a softness of tone and accent adorn[s] their conversation, and make[s] their deportment gentle and obliging. Their singing is charming; partly owing to the pleasantness of their voices, the variety of parts they carry on together and the devout manner of performance.

The families belonging to the society are about forty whereof about 135*) persons (including the single brethren and sisters) are baptized and in communion.

---

*) The number of single brethren is only fourteen. Their names are Rev. Peter Miller, John Mayle, Jacob Moyer, Mark Graff, John Huple, John Reisman, Christian

Reb, Jacob Eiker, Samuel Funk, George Miller, Jacob Kimmel, William Lebrecht, Henry Bendle, Jacob Funk.

The number of single sisters is twenty-eight, Barbara Moyer and Elizabeth Eckstone, *matrons,* Catherine Hegeman, Mary Landert, Catherine Volzin, Elizabeth Zinn, Barbara Bream, Elizabeth Heafly, Anna Maria Gramar, Hannah Leighty, Catherine Gardner, Rosina Good, Christiana Funk, Maria Miller, Elizabeth Mack, Catherine Henrick, Veronica Funk, Christiana Lessley, Mariah Henrick, Susanna Stedtler, Louisa Beissel, Barbara Kimmel, Maria Hecker, Maria Eiker, Maria Graff, Dorothy Monshour.

The married members and their offspring are John Hoffman, John Miller and wife, Mrs. Pethkoffer, John Pethkoffer, Isaac Pethcoffer, Mrs. Heuple, Henry Heuple and wife, Magdalene Leshar, Jacob Seibers and wife and son and daughter, Godfreid Scusinger and wife, Elon Miller and wife, Jacob Kellar and wife, Sebastian Keller, Joseph Keller and wife, Frederick Keller and wife, Joseph Heafly, John Heafly and wife, Magdalene Gitter, Jacob Martin, Maria Martin, Jacob Spregle and wife and daughter, Mrs. Hahn, Jacob Graff and wife, Joseph Graff, Daniel Good and wife, James Anguis and wife and daughter, Jacob Senseman and wife, Mrs. Senseman, Mrs. Shreid, Jacob Gorgas and wife, Adam Kenickmaker, Jacob Neagley and wife and maid, Catherine Jansin, Herman Zinn and wife, Conrad Beldhauson, Peter Fahnstick and wife, John Garber and wife, Benjamin Bowman and wife, John Bowman, Laurence Double and wife, Martha Simeon and daughter, John Huber, Jeremiah Miller and wife, Lodowich Hecker, Susanna Hartman, Barbara Rorback, Geo. Zinn and wife, And. Hook and wife, Lod. Bender and wife, Gertrude Mellinger, An. Thommin, Ann Lessley, Jacob Rohrer and wife and son and daughter, John Fahnstick and wife.

This was their state in 1770. They had their existence as a society on November 12, 1724, when Conrad Beissel, Joseph Shaffer, John Moyer and wife, Henrick Hehn and wife and Veronica Frederick were baptized in [the] Pequea River by [the] Rev. Peter Baker [Becker]. The same day these seven incorporated into a church and chose Conrad Beissel to be their minister. After this they continued some time at Mill Creek; and then, removing about three miles northward, pitched on the land of Rudolph Neagley, in Earl Township.

Here they continued about seven years; and here resorted many to see them, some of which joined the society. Here they began their economy, the men living by themselves on the fore-mentioned lands, and the women also by themselves on the adjoining lands of John Moyly. Here Conrad Beissel appointed two elders and a matron to preside over his church in the wilderness, binding them by a solemn promise (and at the same time giving to each a testament) to govern according to the rules of that book.

Then he withdrew, and made as though they should see him no more. This was done in the year 1733. He traveled northward till he came to the spot where Ephrata or Tunkerstown now stands, and with his hoe planted Indian corn and roots for his subsistence. But he had not been long in the place before the society found him out and repaired to his little cot[tage]; the brethren settling with him on the west banks of Cocolico, and the sisters on the east, all in sight of one another with the river running between them. The next year they set about building their village, beginning with a place of worship. The village is inclosed with a large ditch, and fortified with posts and rails and quicksets. The founder of this people and their minister was

Rev. Conrad Beissel

This was his real name; but when he became a Baptist [Brethren], he assumed the name of *Freidsam* [Friedsam] *Gottrecht,* and gave new names to all the brethren and sisters. He was born in 1690 at Eberback [Eberbach] in Germany. Bred a Presbyterian. Arrived in Boston in 1720. From there he and his two companions, Stunts and Steiffel, travelled westward to Pennsylvania, and lived as hermits about Mill Creek and the Swedes Spring in Lancaster County. He embraced the principles of the Baptists [Brethren] in 1724. Died July 6, 1768, and was buried at Ephrata. As for his character I give it in the words of one who knew him well: "He was very strict in his morals and practiced self-denial and mortification to an uncommon degree. Enthusiastic and whimsical he certainly was, but an apparent devoutness and sincerity ran through all his oddities. He was not an adept in any of the liberal arts and sciences except music, in which he excelled. He composed and set to music (in three, four, six and eight parts) a folio volume of hymns, and another of anthems. He published a dissertation on the fall of man in the mysterious strain, also a volume of letters. He left behind several books in manuscripts curiously written and embellished." It is expected his life will be published by his successor and the present minister of Ephrata

Rev. Peter Miller

He was born in 1709 in the bailiwick of Kaiser[s]lautern in Germany. Had his education in the university of Heildeberg [Heidelberg]. Came to this country in 1730 and settled with the Dutch Presbyterians in Philadelphia. There he was ordained by Rev.

Messieurs Tennent, Boyd and Andrews the same year. He embraced the principles of the Baptists [Brethren] in 1735; and in 1744 received another ordination from Rev. Conrad Beissel to be *prior* of the society, over which he still presides. Dr. Douglas (in his history of the provinces) says that he is a good scholar and writes fine Latin.

No very remarkable event has happened in this society, which has now existed for forty-six years, except a confederacy which Eckerlin (their first prior) had formed to supplant the founder. He had seduced the brethren to his purpose, and began to tamper with the sisters; but they, perceiving his design, opposed and defeated it. He has since caused uneasiness by reason of the power he has as trustee for the land. But the society are meditating to have their grievances redressed by a bill of assembly. The number of single brethren and sisters is much reduced; nor is it likely that young people will join them to keep up a succession.[3]

European Publication Describes Defection

In a three-volume work published against the Moravians by an active Lutheran pastor and theologian in Frankfurt, there is a long description entitled "American Reports of Herrnhuter Matters," which mentions the Brethren and the Sabbatarians quite often. The anonymous author referred to the awakening in Germantown of 1738 and the problems of the Brethren leadership leading to the exodus to Ephrata.

And now the so lovely, warm, spring-like glances, which had been exchanged for a while among the friends of all religious parties and opinions, began to change again into something cooler, all the more so because — as mentioned — a certain pride, self-will and peculiarity began to creep in among some of the young, talented people who had been awakened and stirred up by them. They would not be advised and warned against it. Now there was one party, the Sabbatarians, who have always been passionately seeking loyal young minds. To this was added an especial dissension, which had arisen because of the stubbornness of the leader (J[ohn] N[aas]) of yet another party, and which was not easily solved. Consequently, the others, who are called Sabbatarians, used this to their advantage and succeeded in insinuating themselves in such a way that they caused quite a schism. They enticed and brought into their fold dear young and old friends, which caused much regret among the others.[4]

SEPARATISTS REPORT TO GERMANY

John Adam Gruber to Friends in Berleburg

A quiet but influential Pennsylvania religionist was John Adam Gruber (1693-1763), son of a leader of the Community of the True Inspiration in Germany, Eberhard Lewis Gruber, and a leader of the Inspired in his own right. After his migration to Germantown in 1726, he lived as a neighbor of Christopher Sauer, emerging into prominence only with the coming of Count Zinzendorf in 1741-1742. Gruber was an active correspondent with friends in Germany.[5]

One of his letters, describing religious conditions in Pennsylvania, was published in the Radical Pietist publication, *Geistliche Fama*. He was in an excellent position to observe the Brethren, although not sympathetic with their views.

Germantown, October 28, 1730
(Received, February 12, 1731)

[Berleburg Friends:]

. . . In this region, everything is as if dead, and the good spark of the initiated is completely smothered in the worldly tumult. About our well-known fellow passengers, one could fill a veritable register of serious sins and offenses. May the Lord have mercy and save whosoever will let himself be saved and those who sigh and moan under this corruption so that the Enemy might not devour everything completely.

At Conestoga, some twenty miles from here, there has arisen a new awakening among some of the Brethren. Their leader is the well-known baker, Conrad Binsel [Beissel]. They find a great response among the people. They insist upon renunciation of the world and one's self. Their life, in clothing and nourishment, is limited to the bare necessities. They discard superfluous property and livestock. They greet no one whom they meet in the street, but walk straight ahead. To outward appearance they live in great harmony. Both sexes hold services and communion almost daily. They observe the seventh day and claim in general that it is their goal to achieve a perfect life and continual union with God, and this with great power and zeal.

In their meeting houses here, they have given very sharp testimonies for a re-awakening of their former brethren, namely the

Schw[arzenau] Brethren (from whom they had seceded, and from whom they have received much resistance) and also against the deteriorated Quaker sect. Time will tell how they will get along further. I wish them true sincerity, life and assistance from the Lord. At least, many in these places and this country consider it one of the signs of the times. A[lexander] Mack has a written dispute with them concerning the observance of the Sabbath.

Socinianism, Naturalism, and Atheism are expanding greatly here and there. For that reason, I often wish that one or the other of the older brethren from abroad were here, or that I were there, in order to exhort ourselves together in the Lord. However, my wife will not consent to that. So I must remain patient, until God arranges otherwise. . . . The best-intentioned of the friends, who came along, want to go to the new B[eissel?] congregation. They desire hymnals; if some friends want to render us a service in that way, which is pleasing to God, they may send several hundred here.[6]

Christopher Sauer Writes to Germany on Ephrata

Of those inhabitants of Pennsylvania who kept in contact with the Old Country, none was more active than the Germantown printer, Christopher Sauer. After the establishment of his printing press in 1738, he made it his business to keep up on affairs on the Continent, and was in continuous touch with friends and commercial agents in several European countries.[7]

One of his letters of 1750, likely written to Andrew Gross, a book dealer in Frankfurt/Main, found publication in one of the major journals devoted to religious and ecclesiastical history, the *Acta historico ecclesiastica,* published in Weimar in 1751. An introduction to Sauer's letter provides information about the Sabbatarians at Ephrata, albeit in somewhat garbled form, and a description of the versatile Germantown printer himself.

Reference is made in Sauer's letter to the exodus of the Eckerlins and Alexander Mack, Jr., from Ephrata and their travel to the frontier, which will be more fully covered in the next chapter.

Copy of a noteworthy letter from Mr. Sauer in America, concerning the conversion of the savages and other unique things, which he sent to one of his acquaintances in Frankfurt. . . .

The so-called Zionitic Brotherhood which has been established for many years (about forty) at Ephrata and Kedar in Pennsylvania is a peculiar sect. As they celebrate the Sabbath and consider the true peace of mind and quiet of the same as the greatest happiness and the best way to unite here in this world with the Supreme Being, they are called Sabbatarians or Seventh-Dayers. This church organization is constituted in such a way that those who chose the unmarried state (inasmuch as they generally look down upon the married state and prefer celibacy) live together in a cloister. This is a very spacious and rambling building, with the men living on the one side and the unmarried women on the other. The men as well as the women have their superiors. After the manner of the convents here, the superior of the men might be called "superintendent" [*Oberbischof*] and the superior for the women, "abbess." Yes, the superintendent as well as the abbess may well differ very much from those in Europe, because they reject pomp, finery and splendor, and to the contrary orient their religion and way of life according to mysticism and live very meagerly. Then, too, all of the brothers as well as sisters are common people. They are artisans and unlearned, from the superintendent down to the most lowly. And yet, in their way, they do write, partly in sermons, partly in books.

They surpass with their clever inventions many who are especially trained in that, for they are well versed in mechanical skills. Witnessing to this are their mechanical works of all types, such as mills, etc., in which they surpass the best mechanics of England. In the center of the cloisters there are the quarters of the superintendent, whose name is Beissel, and who is also a craftsman by trade. This Beissel directs the entire establishment from there, the economy as well as spiritual matters.

This Brotherhood violently opposed Count Zinzendorf or the so-called Herrnhuters, who, several years ago, were eager to move in there. In so doing, the former exposed the weaknesses of the latter in doctrine and conduct.

The married brothers and sisters live around the cloister. They gather on the regular meeting days in the beautiful chapel that was built inside the cloister. This chapel has been adorned with most beautiful sculptures, many ornaments and signatures, the most artistic organs, etc., which the brethren made all by themselves. Some time ago, Superintendent Beissel turned the economy of the cloister over to the Prior [*Obervater*] or, as he is called by them, Father Friedsam [actually Brother Onesimus], whose name is Eckerlin, and who is a mason by trade. But as he [Eckerlin] did not want to comply in everything with the ideas of the former, he [Beissel] appealed so to his conscience, or (as Mr. Sauer put it) so oppressed him with his magic, that he lost almost all his respect among his brethren and removed himself about four hundred miles away into the wilderness in order to live the life of a hermit, in a kind of hermitage.

Mr. Sauer gives further details of these events in his [hereafter] appended report. There is noted — among other things — the very strange report about the spirits of the deceased brethren partaking of bread and meals with them even after their death. Thus it is not hard to understand how the pagans put food and drink on their altars in the belief that they [the spirits] would partake of the food. (This we let pass in its truth or error.) This Mr. Sauer does not himself belong to the brotherhood, but his wife has spent a long time in the cloister, and is to this date separated from her husband from bed and board. Thus he, his son and his wife have their own separate households. He is a very ingenious man, a Separatist, who has mastered nearly thirty trades without a teacher. He went to America as a tailor, and has become printer, apothecary, surgeon, botanist, maker of small and large clocks, cabinetmaker, bookbinder, editor of newspapers (who made all of his book-printing tools himself), maker [of] lead and wire, paper-maker, etc.

Note. Here follows the report of Mr. Sauer of America about this Zionitic Community [c. 1750]

The community at Ephrata, of which Conrad Beissel is head and bishop, is diminishing; it seems that God is not supporting it. In my last shipment of Bibles I sent you [Andrew Gross] a book in which Beissel expresses himself and portrays his personality. But recently it nearly verged on popery: whoever has begotten children after his spirit must be called father. The weaker souls were unbelievably domineered over and oppressed and tormented with magic powers, so that I doubt if there ever was a pope who held everything so completely under his body and soul, life and mind as does Conrad Beissel. In order that it might not appear so, he turned the government over to the Eckerlin brothers in the hope that they would not take any action without him. However, Israel Eckerlin ruled dictatorially, preached six to seven hours without stopping, ordered large buildings erected, and did not ask Conrad for permission first. Then Beissel bestirred himself, placed him [Eckerlin] in the ban, pressed him so that he virtually lost his soul, until he left Ephrata and Zion and went four hundred miles into the wilderness, together with two of his brothers, Samuel and Gabriel Eckerlin, and Alexander Mack, and also a little dog. The two last, that is, Mack, returned to Germantown and is now the leading minister among the Old Brethren who moved from Schwarzenau to Friesland and here.

Otherwise, it is certainly true that the souls at Ephrata, who bound themselves to celibacy and this brotherhood, very much adhere together as far as they have received the spirit. Even in death they do not part and so far all the deceased have reappeared and were very visible, of whom my wife (who was with them, that is the brethren in Ephrata, for a long time) saw and even talked to many. Indeed, Conrad Beissel was offended by the Prior Israel Eckerlin. For after he had moved into Beissel's lodging and the spirits (according to their habit) appeared to keep Beissel company and to partake of the communion, Israel drove them away and bade them depart rather than break bread with them as if they were alive, in accord with his office which had placed responsibility upon him for the souls.

Otherwise the poor souls labor under a hard yoke. They sleep only three hours out of twenty-four, eat once — seldom twice — a day, and besides, from the superintendent to the novice, they have to do very hard work. In addition to the hard daily labor, they must sing from notes very precisely, and not only in four-part harmony but in six, and only melodies which Beissel has composed. For this they all have very large hand-written books, and those who know something about music say that they have never heard such beautiful music.

There are [now] about forty single brethren and about forty single sisters, but one would think with all of the daily building that they had hopes of having one thousand more. Yet they keep decreasing in number. They have erected three chapels; one has now been torn down and the fourth built. Therefore one of them, who is still in the brotherhood, wrote a testimonial against all the great outward activity which will not let one soul come to peace and quiet. He gave it to Conrad who accepted it and promised to print it. But as their printshop and paper mill are to stand idle for a year, it will have to wait that long. However, the author, by the name of Hildebrand, was very anxious about it and urged me until I promised him to print it. So it is now finished.[8] For this reason I am sending you copies to give away, since it is not likely that all of the copies can be sold here. It is not to everyone's liking.

Note. *The enclosed copy is one of them.*
Note. *These were Mr. Sauer's own words.* . . . [9]

The Description by "J.B.S."

About the year 1750 a group of Pietists known only as the "Quiet Ones in the Land" [*Die Stillen im Lande*], arrived in Pennsylvania under the leadership of a certain "J.B.S.," a learnéd scholar born in Altona, Germany. Driven from his position as a pastor because of Radical Pietist views, he sought a haven in the New World. Arriving without money or contacts, he soon found friends around Philadelphia, Germantown, and Conestoga. Funds were provided for the group to rent a small plantation in Leacock Township.

Unfortunately, none of the group were real farmers, and the enterprise failed financially. Their benefactors rescued them, paid their debts, and were about to provide the group with a large house when the leader died. According to Sangmeister, the son of John Adam Gruber tried to carry on the enterprise, but failed. Most of the followers returned to Germany.[10]

This Pietist leader wrote a book in Germantown in 1761, called *The Alert Traveller through Europe and America.* First published in Altona, Germany, in 1777, it was reprinted in Philadelphia in 1784. A free translation of portions of the booklet was published in Ephrata in 1793 under the title *Anonimus' Travels through Europe and America.*[11]

In this writing, the author narrates a vision in which an angel took him to a city, readily to be identified as Philadelphia. The city square had meetinghouses on all four corners (a circumstance which later European visitors to North America would also remark upon) respectively, Society of Friends, Brethren, Mennonites, and Sabbatarian (Ephrata Community). Although critical in tone, the descriptions are quite informative.

In this confusion I travelled from Europe to America expecting to find something better there. However, I found myself disappointed which I took very much to heart. I often sighed secretly and wished for enough enlightenment so that I could put everything in its place, in order that I might not be misled but rather surrender myself to the omniscient, supreme truth. After I had long remained in such affliction, it [enlightenment] came all of a sudden. I was at the time on a journey through this land, for I had to travel across a large portion of it just as if my desire for travel should be repaid with a vengeance.

As I lay down under a tree because of great weariness, it seemed to me that I saw a man standing before me who said to me: "Arise, and go with me; I will show you what you have long wished to know." I went with him and he took me to a pleasant place, a large and populous city, surrounded by a wall. Its four large gates stood open day and night; trade from all four corners of the earth was directed there. I was amazed at the size and beauty of this city, for it was beautifully laid out. I asked my guide what kind of a city this was, and what was its name. He said that it was the world-renowned spiritual Babylon.

As we passed through the city gate, there was written above it:

Whoever comes naked into the city cannot be a citizen of me. Not substance, but show do I admit as citizens.

After we had walked into the city for half a day, we came upon a large, rectangular square, which was the center of the city. On each corner stood a building in which divine exercises were held. On the corner at the right there stood the largest and best-constructed building. When the people who belonged inside entered, we also went inside. They conducted their meetings in great quiet, without outward ceremony. They were very modest and kind to one another. They do not preach anything unless they are led to do so by the spirit, [including] women as well as men. They go in and out quietly, speak familiarly to everyone, do not remove their hats for anyone. Their clothing is modest, neat and of the best material. In their teaching they place great emphasis on the inner substance. As we left, we noticed two sculptured swords above the door, which crossed each other. They had this inscription:

Simplicity declines;
Humility sinks into its grave.

These people are the most powerful and the richest in the city.

On the left across from this house there stood the second house, not as large, to be true, but it struck the eye because of its beautiful paint. Above the door was a lamp which had been overturned, with this inscription:

> We sing and preach with great outcry;
> If only the Spirit could be thereby.

These people seem rather peaceful and modest in their conduct. Their clothing is middle-class [*bürgerlich*]. Most of the men wear beards. They do not tolerate infant baptism. When they become adults, and wish to be baptized, they go to where there is water and are immersed three times. They hold communion or love feast often. Their meetings are zealous and their preaching and praying often take place with great clamor, as if their God were hard of hearing. One hymn chases another as if they lacked [inner] silence. They teach their cherished truths after the letter.

The house on the third corner was not very striking because it seemed to be rather old, being patched in many places. Above the door there were two men, one of them blind-folded; he was leading the sighted one by a staff. Above, there was written:

> Because we lack the power of the Word
> We are content with the dead letter.

These people were no less modest than the previous ones, and upright in their conduct. They wear plain clothing; proud colors may not be worn by them. Most of the men wear beards. When they are grown up they are baptized and a little water is poured over their heads. Their meetings are often very sleepy affairs.

On the fourth corner a new house had recently been erected, which was in no way inferior to the other three. Above the door there was a man painted wearing a long white garment. On his back he carried a heavy cross. Beneath this there was written:

> Our light even the blind can see,
> If only they from Babel flee.

These people are very earnest in the outward discipleship of Christ. Like the Jews, they celebrate the seventh day. ([Footnote:] They are called Sabbatarians, of whom there are many in Pennsylvania.) Their clock must strike according to the old time. ([Footnote:] Galatians 4:9-10.) They baptize adults in and under water and even more than once depending on what they consider necessary. They do not readily greet anyone [on the street]. The men wear beards and have purposed to remain single, likewise the women. Marriage is too inferior for them. They have completely renounced worldly trade and business. They strive to increase their congregation. In their meetings they often speak about deep mysteries which often they themselves do not understand.[12]

GERMAN LUTHERANS REPORT TO HALLE AND LONDON

The most important figure among colonial Lutheranism was Henry Melchior Muhlenberg (1711-1787), who succeeded in establishing order among Lutheran congregations plagued by disreputable and vagabond pastors. His multifold activities on behalf of his church, from arrival in America in 1742 until his death, have earned him the title "patriarch of American Lutheranism."

One of the reasons for his success was the support he enjoyed from the "fathers" at Halle, the citadel of churchly Pietism, to which American Lutherans looked for guidance and material aid. Muhlenberg forwarded a steady flow of dispatches and reports, which, supplemented by reports from other laborers in the American vineyard, appeared as the *Halle Reports* [*Hallische Nachrichte*]. Primarily designed to inform European readers of the progress of Lutheranism in the New World, the reports now provide an excellent source for the history of colonial America.[13]

Muhlenberg, accustomed to the state church pattern of Germany, was dismayed by activities of the free churches in Pennsylvania. The dissenting groups had pioneered in migration to the Quaker colony, and their "gathered church" concept, with a self-supporting ministry, was suited to the conditions obtaining in America. Muhlenberg's criticism took the form of a rather heavy sarcasm in referring to the Brethren, whom he called "Sunday Baptists," and the Ephrata group or "Seventh Day Baptists."

In explaining to Halle the reasons for the poverty of Lutherans in America, Muhlenberg noted:

> . . . there are also to be found among the Germans in Pennsylvania wealthy people, but most of those who possess the goods of this world have joined the Anabaptists, Quakers, or other sects. This is not surprising when one considers that this poor folk had no respectable pastors for so many years. These groups had the upper hand, because from the beginning the Quakers were the proprietors of this land. Whoever wishes to

have prestige can find no better opportunity than to go over to their side. . . . Most of our German Lutheran inhabitants in Pennsylvania came as the last to this country. The English and German Quakers, Inspired, Mennonites, Separatists, and similar smaller denominations arrived in the beginning, when land was still very cheap. They selected the best and richest areas and are now profiting from them. When, however, in the latter years the poor Lutherans found the spoor, and migrated to this country, only a few of them found some of the rich soil here and there. Most of them, however, have to labor as maids and hired men for several years to pay for their passage, and then get along as best they can with the poor land, and eat their bread in the sweat of their brows.[14]

It must be noted, however, that whereas the sectarian groups came to the New World primarily to find religious freedom, the later Lutheran migrants of the eighteenth century were motivated by economic interests. As members of one of the established confessions in Germany, Lutherans were not expelled or oppressed to any degree on religious grounds.

Muhlenberg Describes the Brethren and the Sabbatarians

If melancholy personalities are found, who would be happy to be completely out of the world, there is a comfortable organization prepared by cunning men, which is called the organization of the Seventh Day Baptists [Siebentäger Tauchsgesinnten]. There a beautiful rich piece of land was purchased, and large community houses for single men and women and the like, also mills, breweries, bakeries, were built by the sweat and blood of the members living in self-denial. What remarkable institutions and converts are found there! One should, according to them, not consider Christ as anything more than an example, but rather pay attention to men who became equal to Christ in holiness, and who attained the state of being able to produce virgins by the process of rebirth. There one hears nothing of justification by faith. If one effects justification by life through fasting, self-mortification, hard work, and ridiculous costumes, places his property and possessions into the common treasury, is baptized into their community, and allows himself to be governed for life by the chief drillmaster in body and soul — then one is a convert, and is sorry for all others who do not wish to have things as well. . . .

If one wants to be master of his own property and land, and still become something special, which has a better appearance than the usual church system [*gemeines Kirchenwesen*], then one can be converted to the belief of the so-called Sunday Baptists [*Sonntags-Taufgesinnte*]. All one needs to do is to memorize several verses from the Revelation of John about Babel, the Beast and the Harlot, present along with this a good outward appearance, and be publicly baptized by them by immersion. Their lessons are very comfortably and easily learned. All that is necessary is to mock infant baptism, and condemn all others who do not agree with them, especially the clergy and church people. Also, one must believe, among other things, that the Devil and the damned will be again redeemed from Hell. The conversion to the Mennonites is also very easy, comfortable, and advantageous, and is one of the most quiet.[15]

Muhlenberg Writes on Immigration

Toward the end of this period [1708-1720], a large number of High Germans also appeared, who were either actually Separatists bringing with them a deeply rooted hatred of and aversion to the doctrine and organization of our church, or who were Baptists (Dunkers, as they are here called), Mennonites, Schwenkfelders, and generally of this sort, to name all of which would take too long to mention here. These were primarily concerned with deepening their own opinions, and with inducing into their midst by all kinds of seemingly good reasons, others who arrived later and who still maintained a concept of our Lutheran doctrine. This could happen all the more easily because there were no pastors here, and each man principally fixed his gaze on how to buy land, build houses, till the soil, plant crops, and support his family in this way. No one thought about the continuation of our all-hallowed doctrine. . . . [16]

Muhlenberg Depicts Lutheran Turned Anabaptist

Before my time a married couple, N. H., [N. Housteter?] had arrived, who were of the Lutheran faith. The husband had a stronger will than he had sense, but despite this sought to save his soul. The German Lutherans had either no preachers at all, or had only disreputable preachers, who had appointed themselves and conducted themselves offensively. On the other hand, the smaller denominations were much in evidence and sought to entice the seeking souls into their sects. Therefore, this husband thought he would do better to abandon his evangelical doctrine and church, and to join the Anabaptists. He had himself baptized again in their society, and learned their manner of speaking and reading. He was very zealous, but without understanding.[17]

Muhlenberg and the Anabaptists in the Coventry Area

Near the Coventry congregation were several Lutheran congregations. Scattered references to "Anabaptists" may be found in the diaries and reports of Henry Melchior Muhlenberg. As others than Brethren may be referred to as Anabaptists, we cannot be sure that all such references do in fact pertain to Brethren. The general orientation of the "church people" to the "plain people," however, can be learned from such remarks.

[January 16, 1743. Providence.]

Today I announced to the congregation that they should not give me any money at baptisms or the Lord's Supper. After the Holy Communion, we also had a baptism. The Anabaptists are quite numerous in attendance and thus they hear what is declared at the baptism of infants. . . .

[April-May, 1747. New Hannover and Providence.]

As long as the "church people," as the Lutherans and Reformed are called, are unenlightened and unconverted, the sects throw it up to us and say, "You have so many worthless and dead members. Your preaching and your churchgoing do no good." They will not give us time, though God shows His long-suffering and patience toward them as well as toward us all, and He has His own times and seasons. Whenever they see that some souls are improving, they try to lure them away from their simplicity by all sorts of tricks and ruses and draw them into their sectarian net. But the Lord preserveth the simple! . . .

[October-November, 1748. New Hannover.]

In the months of October and November, Mr. Weygand and I instructed twenty young persons in New Hannover who purposed to come to the Lord's Supper for the first time. Among them was a young married man, whose father had gone over from the Lutheran faith to the Anabaptists, but was now dead. The father had permitted the son to learn to read and write, but he was not allowed to learn the Catechism because the father said that it was a book of the devil and of witchcraft with which (the Lutheran parsons) cast a spell over the children. The Anabaptists let their children read the New Testament, but will not permit them to learn anything by heart. The children are supposed to grow up to the age of understanding and then wait until they themselves feel an impulse to believe and be baptized. . . .

[January, 1749. New Hannover.]

I supplied the New Hannover congregation with another young married man who had taught school in the neighborhood for several years and with whom I was acquainted. This man . . . had come to this country when he was young and had been sold to a prominent Quaker until he came of age. The little he had grasped concerning the Lutheran faith in Germany had prevented him from espousing the views of the Quakers despite the fact that he worked among them for many years, attended their meetings, and had many temptations [to go over to them], especially since he had no opportunity to attend his own church and further establish his faith. Besides, the few German people who lived thereabouts were adherents of the new Anabaptist denomination. . . .

[June 27, 1757. Providence.]

Rode with my wife to Mr. Bickel's, seven miles from home. Spoke to him at great length of God's word, examined his son Heinrich's wife, Elizabeth, and baptized her after she had made her profession of faith. Her parents, her father in particular, were reared in the Lutheran faith in Germany, but in this country he had many years ago joined the Baptist persuasion and consequently allowed his children to grow up without being baptized. I found the whole family, and especially the old man, very eager and happy to hear and speak of divine things. . . .

[May 11, 1763. Providence.]

On the way we stopped in at the home of a schoolmaster whose wife, twenty years old, I had to examine and baptize in the presence of several witnesses, because she was born in this country of Anabaptist parents and had not been baptized in her infancy. . . .

[August 29, 1764. Providence.]

During my absence my wife bought some flour from an Ana-baptist from the country. He began to dispute with her about infant baptism and called it a superficial sprinkling which the children know nothing about when they grow up, etc. She replied that David knew very well when he was grown up that he had been circumcised in infancy, and he also knew that Goliath, the blasphemous Philistine, was uncircumcised, I Samuel 17. This put the disputant to confusion and he made himself scarce. . . . [18]

Handschuh and the Brethren

The German Lutheran clergyman, John Frederick Handschuh (1714-1764) pursued his labors in the Germantown area, and related in his account of his work his efforts with a sick "Tumpler," that is, a Brethren person. He also mentioned the baptism of the daughter of a Brethren family.

[September 14, 1751.]

On the return trip through Germantown I had the opportunity to visit a Tumpler who had been ill for a long time, whom I led to a serious examination of himself and to the free grace of God in Christ, the universal Savior of the world, and closed with prayer.

[September 16, 1751]

. . . I visited the above-mentioned sick . . . and also the Tumpler.

[November 11, 1751.]

. . . Among others I visited a Separatist, who had formerly been Reformed and later joined the Tumplers. This man expressed with great gratitude, how pleasant and comforting my visit was, and how he together with his wife, had already several times considered having themselves and their children baptized by me.

On December 8, [1751], Mr. Heinzelmann and I went about three to four miles from here to visit several sick persons. One of them was the former Tumpler mentioned several times, who is preparing himself for his blessed end.

On December 17, 1751, I also visited this evening the sick former Tumpler who is becoming more simple and honest from day to day.

On December 19, . . . after this we visited our neighbor by the church, the sick Tumpler, with whom Pastor Muhlenberg spoke separately and very edifyingly prayed.

[January 2, 1752.]

... [I received] a greeting from the oft-mentioned sick Tumpler, whom I had visited frequently during his illness, and had worked on his soul according to the wisdom which God had given me, with a fervent request to visit him just once more; he had such a great longing for me, for he was very near the end and looked forward to it with anticipation.

[1757] ... Among the large number of baptized children this year which is already great, I baptized not only six members three to five years old, but also a twelve-year-old girl, whose parents are Tumplers. ... [19]

GERMAN REFORMED CLERGY
WRITE TO THE NETHERLANDS

Ministers from those Protestant churches used to state support in their home countries found the voluntaryistic arrangement in the American colonies a source of continual trouble. They looked to church bodies in Europe for direction, for the sending of ministers, and especially for financial support. The German Reformed attachment was with the Dutch Reformed, because of the relative weakness of the Reformed in the Germanies.

Some of the reports submitted by Reformed clergy to the Classis (Synod) of The Netherlands describe the activities of the Brethren and the Sabbatarians. They complained that these groups were active in proselyting among those Reformed without church connection and, on occasion, among those with church affiliation. The following excerpts are typical of their concern.

John Philip Boehm (1683-1749) was one of the most active of the Reformed leaders, and was for that denomination what Muhlenberg meant for the Lutherans.[20]

Boehm to the Classis

November 12, 1730

Very Reverend Classis:

... Desiring to transmit to the Reverend Classis for their gracious consideration the blasphemies which the New Baptist [Ephrata] sect (or "Tumplers," as they call themselves) have published, we are doing so herewith. Is it not the all-too-great liberty [in this country] which causes such brazen insolence? An appalling number of people have been misled by this pernicious sect and even married couples here and there have been separated when one party went over to them. The two chief heretics who have been expelled from every other place, and who are the authors of the two pamphlets live in this country, where they engage in a blasphemous business (especially at Conestoga and Falckner's Swamp). They observe Saturday [as the Sabbath] and do all kinds of work on Sunday without shame! But when they are called on to account with regard to this, they say that Saturday was instituted by God himself, hence it is their Sabbath, whereas Sunday was appointed by the popes, and hence it is idolatry. . . .

However, the above-mentioned Tumplers, although they are divided and hold conflicting opinions, mainly about the Sabbath or seventh day, still have a large following everywhere, which is the result of nothing else but this great liberty. No certain prediction can be made about them, however, except that their breakup will not fail to come, for their kingdom is altogether divided.

Meanwhile it is to be feared that if they are not checked, many poor people will be misled by them and exposed to great danger of their souls, for they are constantly traveling through the whole country trying to recruit as many as they possibly can. We hear all the time, often with great astonishment, that such or such a one has gone over to them, even several Reformed people, which compels me to make a humble report concerning it. This is done in the hope that the merciful God will enable the Reverend Classis to find a way of checking these and other likewise most dangerous errors. Nothing can be done here; everything is accepted, because of this liberty.

I remain, as long as I live, Very Reverend Classis, your most submissive, most obedient and humble fellow servant in Christ,

John Philip Boehm.[21]

Boehm to the Dutch Deputy Vellinguis

October 23, 1734

Right and Very Reverend, Pious, and Very Learnéd Sir:

. . . The decline of true religion in this country is indeed deplorable, and whence does it derive but from a lack of faithful and orthodox ministers? The three ministers who arrived here at different times have introduced dissension and division even in the three regularly established congregations of D[omine] Boehm and, in addition, by their free thinking have plunged the simple people into doubt with regard to the true Reformed religion, so that through these and other quarrels the number of those who since that time have gone over to the Tumplers, Sabbatarians, Mennonites and others is so large that it cannot be stated without tears in one's eyes. Who knows how many there are yet in this widely-extended country, who are unknown to us. May the good God have mercy upon His own and preserve them from such men. . . .

With reference to the members of the Reformed [Church] reported to you as being fifteen thousand to sixteen thousand, we look upon that report with horror and are exceedingly surprised at such a scandalous falsehood to the Christian Synod. It is indeed true that there are many Germans in this country, but if they could all be counted (which, however, is impossible to do very easily), the total would not reach that number by far. Most of them are Mennonites. There are also more Lutheran than Reformed people. All Tumplers are Germans, with whom the whole land is filled, also the Sabbatarians and other sects besides.

There is also a large number who live here and there and keep themselves altogether aloof from everyone, since they can see no means by which our church can be established in this country, among whom the Lord will preserve His own until His time comes. Hence, we expect that, when through God's grace we shall have obtained Christian support, many of these will come forward.

The ministers and elders of the German Reformed
congregation in Philadelphia,
John Philip Boehm [and consistory][22]

Boehm and Others to the Dutch Synods

March 8, 1744

Very Reverend Sirs of the Two Christian Synods of South and North Holland, Devout Church Fathers:

. . . Now our souls, sad before because we seemed to be entirely abandoned, have been gladdened inasmuch as we have seen in your gracious letter that the Messrs. Deputies take much interest in the welfare of our churches and are willing to contribute as much as possible. This, we believe, would already have taken place, if a true and clear report had not been lacking. May God forgive him who has kept it back. For, since the founding of our churches here, there have been many people who, though they were of Reformed antecedents, kept aloof, because there were no Reformed church services here, and they joined no religion or sect. They were of the opinion that our cause could not be maintained in this country, principally because of our inability to support ministers.

They were, now, within the last few years, scattered here and there, mostly among the Mennonites (who may be in the majority), the Tumplers (Seventh-Day as well as Eighth-Day Tumplers), and the like. Especially Count Zinzendorf (who arrived here at the end of December 1741) and his brood of false apostles, brought along or made many converts here, some under the name of one religion, others under the name of another. . . . In this they succeeded because they came in sheep's clothing and with smooth hypocritical words offered their services to all people and without cost. All this would surely have gone differently, if some assistance and help (especially in the sending of faithful ministers) had come from our richly blessed fellow brethren. . . .

[Your] humble and most submissive brethren and children in the Lord, members of the consistories, now in service in the German Reformed churches in Pennsylvania, in whose name we sign,

John Philip Boehm, minister. . . . [23]

Amwell Presbytery to the Dutch Synod

Amwell [New Jersey], October 29, 1762

Right Reverend Sirs:

If we did not most obediently thank Your Reverences on behalf of the whole congregation for the calling and sending of our dear preacher, the Rev. Stapel, we would be the most ungrateful people, for God is with him and through him has turned our disgrace into joy in the face of many congregations. We are — praise God! — no longer the barren one, but a blessed mother before many, even without

equal who, together with her spiritual husband, her Stapel, has brought
forth in so short a time eighty-four souls. They are all of age, partly
married, partly former Dumplers or Anabaptists. He instructed them
— since we had but English schools — free of charge and led them
to the Lord's table. Thereby he destroyed at once all hopes that New
Jersey would soon have to recognize the English Presbyterian Church
as her own. We have already three German schoolteachers under
his supervision and various Dumplers have their children — grown as
well as young ones — baptized by us; others move away from this
area. . . .

Your Reverences' most obedient servants

Peter Hoffman   (

elders[24]

Matthew Hauschilt   (

Monocacy Elders to Schlatter

Many of the German Reformed congregations in the colonies were
without pastors. This often led to the turning of Reformed members to
other groups to satisfy their religious needs. The elders of the congregation in Monocacy (Maryland) demonstrate this process in an appeal written to Michael Schlatter (1716-1790), the leading German Reformed
churchman following Boehm. In the course of one of his many trips,
Schlatter visited the Maryland congregations in May 1748.

Managuasey Congregation [Monocacy]
March 1, 1748

[Rev. Michael Schlatter]

You are probably aware of the fact that ten months have passed
already since you preached and held Holy Communion here at the
Reformed church in Managuasey. During this time several have left
the church and joined the Dunker sect, namely Nicholas Pink and
Henry Rotts, who are also making every effort to lead even more
astray. Therefore, we elders and some members of the congregation
thought it good to write to you, sir, and at the same time request to
please consider with us how we might check these sects with God's
help and assistance, and preserve our churches in good order as
behooves Christians. Therefore do grant us the kindness and come
here as soon as is convenient to hold Holy Communion with us and

to establish a good Christian order in our congregation. But please
send us exact information of your arrival beforehand, so that we
might send several [persons] with horses to meet you and be able
to provide what else is needed.

We hope that this communication finds you well, and fervently
commend you to divine protection. Anticipating your reply we remain, dear sir, your faithful and most devoted elders of the congregation at Managuasey.

[Signatures of six elders][25]

LATER EIGHTEENTH-CENTURY REPORTS

Two of the many accounts dealing with the Ephrata Community
and the Brethren are included here, selected from the many which might
be chosen. These are less well-known and are more informative than
others, which tend to repeat essentially the same information found in a
few early sources.

Caspipina and His Corrector

One of the best accounts of the Ephrata Community in the eighteenth
century was written by Jacob Duché (1738-1798), an Anglican curate of
St. Peter's in Philadelphia. His letter (1771) describing Ephrata was contained in a volume of essays, *Caspipina's Letters: Containing Observations on a Variety of Subjects* (London: 1777). A review of this work
appeared in a British journal, the *Monthly Review,* in October of the
same year.

An American reader responded to what he thought incorrect statements in the book in a letter printed in the *Review* for February 1778. His
information on the Community, while none too friendly in tone, seems
to be based on some firsthand knowledge. The letter does not seem to
have been noticed by writers on Ephrata.[26]

> *To the Monthly Reviewers.*
> Gentlemen:
>
> I beg leave, under the character of a correspondent, to correct
> some glaring mistakes, in a volume of letters, entitled *Caspipina's,*
> noted in your review for October last. As Englishmen it was as little
> your province to detect such errors as it is mine to point out the
> other blemishes of the book as a critic. I have further to assure you,

that my information on this subject is certainly true, inasmuch as I shall communicate to you only what I myself have seen and known.

The author of these letters is the Rev. Mr. Jacob Duché; the gentleman who has lately engaged the attention of the public, by a published and pretty singular letter to General Washington. He is a native of Philadelphia; and, at the time these letters were written, was *curate at St. Peter's in Philadelphia in North America:* the initial letters of the words printed in italics forming the anagram, Caspipina. He is a man of some learning, and more piety; but both deeply tinged with the nonsense and mysticism of Behmen [Jacob Boehme] and the Methodists. As a preacher he is much admired, and not altogether without reason; for his voice is mellow and musical, his countenance pleasing, and his person graceful. His discourses he delivers without notes; and, as the Bishop of Gloucester said of Fester, "acts a sermon" very notably — but therein consists the whole merit; for by transfusion through the press, all the spirit evaporates.

His account of the Dunkers is at once very defective, and very erroneous. The reverse of what he says is the truth. They did as a sect emigrate from Holland. The writer of this was at their settlement in 1752, and saw the founder of the sect, a venerable, old man, of eighty or upwards. A particular friend of mine, the late Col. [Thomas] C[olvill], was a fellow passenger with him and some of his followers from Rotterdam to Philadelphia, and thirty or forty years afterwards, being one of the Commissioners upon a treaty with the Indians, held at Lancaster, he went to see his old acquaintance, the father of the Dunkers and was recognized by him. He had been a baker at Rotterdam, and was perfectly illiterate. They live in a collegiate way, and meet at their meals in a common hall, or refectory (the men I mean) and are precisely seventy in number. They are under no tie or vow of celibacy, and marry when they please; but must in that case leave the Society of the Seventy Brethren, as they call themselves. The reason for their pitching on this number is obvious. You meet with them scattered through the provinces of Pennsylvania and Maryland; your correspondent has two of them for tenants on his own land.

A most untoward accident has befallen them, just before I was at Ephrata in 1752. One of their girls was delivered of no less than three children at a birth, and this previous to marriage. As they make high pretensions to chastity, it is not to be wondered at that this should have drawn down great ridicule and disgrace upon them, so that contrary to what the author of those letters says, it appears that they do sometimes find means to come together, if *not at their devotions.* But this is a mistake too; for the two sexes do *come together* at their devotions, and that at midnight. The women, however, are concealed by a grate or curtain, in the manner of the nuns in the monasteries abroad.

Though they occupy no more than 150 acres of land, they are known to be wealthy. They have two very fine grist mills, a paper mill, and a printing press, and carry on several works in great perfection. The town of Lancaster is supplied with vegetables in great abundance by them. There was a work in their press, when I was there, which they told me was an historical account of the German Protestant martyrs; for which they were to be paid two thousand pounds on the delivery of so many copies. This shows that they are not wholly above the interests and concerns of this lower world.

I heard of one person among them of some learning [John Peter Miller]; and from him I hoped to have learned their distinguished [——ing] religious tenets; but unluckily he was absent when I visited them. It is probable their creed differs but little, if at all, from that of the Mennonists or German Anabaptists, save in some very few particulars, which the peculiarity of their situation may seem to have recommended to them (together with some things borrowed from the Romanists). They hold with our Quakers the unlawfulness of oaths in the matter of testimony.

I am no connoisseur in music, but their singing appeared to me to be exquisitely fine. I went into their chapel, to hear some of the girls sing, who were concealed behind a curtain. We were first entertained with a solo which I and every other person who had not been there before took for a wind instrument of some sort; I could almost have sworn that it had been the lute-stop of an organ, and could not be satisfied that it was not, till the curtain was drawn, and I was shown the performer. The old man, their founder, was present, and seemed highly enraptured; his countenance was the most strongly marked with enthusiasm that I ever beheld. Some of the girls were very beautiful, but pale and emaciated, owing, as I imagined, to their vegetable diet.

The neatness and cleanliness which prevails in their houses and furniture are most remarkable. In a country which abounds with flies and insects, with them there is not one to be seen. But with respect to this last mentioned instance, it is not peculiar to them; it is common to all the Germans settled in America, and is effected by means of a chemical preparation they have, much resembling crude antimony which they call *Fly-Stone* and which is almost instantly fatal to these insects. It requires great caution in the use of it, for it is very poisonous, if taken into the stomach. The common method of using it is to sweeten a little water in a plate, and infuse in some of the fly-stone, [and] to suspend it to the ceiling.

For the rest, not having seen the book in England, and having also formerly run through it, perhaps very blameably, in a hasty manner, as a flimsy production, unworthy of any stricter attention, you will, I hope, excuse me for having confined my remarks to the single extract with which you have furnished me.

I am, gentlemen, your humble servant

a Pennsylvanian.[27]

Benjamin Rush on the German Sectarians

One of the most notable figures around post-Revolutionary Philadelphia was the physician, writer, professor, and reformer Benjamin Rush (1745-1813). Among his many interests were the Germans of Pennsylvania, who, it seemed to Rush, were not sufficiently appreciated. In an essay, "An Account of the Manners of the German Inhabitants of Pennsylvania," published first in the *Columbian Magazine* (January 1789), Rush described the various denominations and had several favorable things to say about them. An excerpt on the German churches follows.

The freedom and toleration of the government has produced a variety of sects among the Germans in Pennsylvania. The Lutherans compose a great proportion of the German citizens of the state. Many of their churches are large and splendid. The German Presbyterians are the next to them in numbers. Their churches are likewise large and furnished, in many places, with organs. The clergy, belonging to these churches, have moderate salaries, but they are punctually and justly paid. In the country they have glebes which are stocked and occasionally worked by their congregations. The extra expenses of their ministers . . . are borne by their respective congregations. . . .

The German Lutherans and Presbyterians live in great harmony with each other, insomuch as that they often preach in each other's churches, and in some instances unite in building a church in which they both worship at different times. This harmony between two sects, once so much opposed to each other, is owing to the relaxation of the Presbyterians in some of the peculiar doctrines of Calvinism. I have called them Presbyterians, because most of them object to being designated by the name of Calvinists.

The Mennonists, the Moravians, the Swingfelders [Schwenk-felders], and the Catholics, compose the other sects of the German inhabitants of Pennsylvania. The Mennonists hold war and oaths to be unlawful. They admit the sacraments of baptism, by *sprinkling,* and the supper.

From them a sect has arisen, who hold, with the above principles and ceremonies, the necessity of *immersion* baptism; hence they are called *Dunkers,* or Baptists. Previously to their partaking of the sacrament of the supper, they wash each other's feet, and sit down to a love feast. They practice these ceremonies of their religion with great humility and solemnity. They, moreover, hold the doctrine of universal salvation.

From this sect there have been several seceders, some of whom devoted themselves to perpetual celibacy. They have exhibited for many years a curious spectacle of pious mortification at a village called Ephrata, in Lancaster County. They are at present reduced to fourteen or fifteen members. The *Separatists,* who likewise dissented from the Dunkers, reject the ordinances of baptism and the sacraments; and hold the doctrine of the *Friends,* concerning the internal revelation of the gospel. They hold, with the Dunkers, the doctrine of universal salvation. The singular piety, and exemplary morality of these sects, have been urged, by the advocates for the salvation of all mankind, as a proof that the belief of their doctrine is not so unfriendly to morals, and the order of society, as has been supposed. The Dunkers and Separatists agree in taking no interest upon money, and in not applying to law to recover their debts. . . .

Perhaps those German sects of Christians who refuse to bear arms for the shedding of human blood may be preserved by Divine Providence as the center of a circle which shall gradually embrace all nations of the earth in a perpetual treaty of friendship and peace.[28]

4. On the Frontier

Although the Brethren were by no means the first Germans to arrive in America, they were at times among the earliest pioneers in frontier areas of the Middle Colonies. Their later arrival from Europe meant that they had to go farther inland in order to find the fertile soil that they sought. Thus we find Brethren moving beyond the Susquehanna River, and later beyond the Allegheny Mountains.

Pioneering does not make for accurate record-keeping, and much of the early process of settlement is lost in the mists of time. Yet, a few episodes have been preserved which shed some light on situations met by Brethren attempting to wrest a living from the wilderness. Indian raids, boundary disputes, unfriendly churchmen — all added to the difficulties of life on the frontier.

THE PENNSYLVANIA FRONTIER

Michael Danner and the Border Dispute

Settlers in the interior lands of the colonies often had the problem of securing valid titles to property located in areas claimed by competing interests. For many years the provinces of Pennsylvania and Maryland disputed land in what is now middle and western Pennsylvania, until the establishment of the famous Mason and Dixon line in 1767.

The progenitor of an influential Brethren family was a key figure in such a border clash in 1736. Michael Danner (1706-c.1780), who arrived in the province from his native Palatinate in September 1727, settled on a tract of two hundred acres just west of the Susquehanna River in 1734. He and three others were the first German residents on land originally developed by the Quaker James Hendricks in present-day York County.[1]

A year later an adventurer who called himself "Colonel" Thomas Cresaps resurveyed the land, claiming authority from the Maryland government. He then proceeded to sell the land, terrorizing the original settlers in the course of his activities. Some of the leading residents were captured and taken as prisoners to Maryland.[2]

The following documents, excerpted from the records printed in the *Pennsylvania Archives* series, relate to Michael Danner's involvement. Danner was one of the foremost figures in that area. As one of the king's commissioners for highways, he helped to lay out the road from the Susquehanna to Frederick, and the one from York to Maryland. He was active also in school affairs. A historian of York County asserted that "Michael Danner and his two sons were the three most intelligent Germans west of the Susquehanna River and figured conspicuously in their day."[3]

In the documents the term *Dutch* is used to indicate settlers of German ancestry.

[King's Surveyor to Governor Denny]   1732

We had given repeated orders to the Dutch to keep together and stand on their defence. It so happened that on the 28th last, the wives of those Dutch men who are in our prison heard that one Henry Smith was to bury a child the next morning in a burying place in the woods forty or fifty perches from my house, of which they gave notice to Higgenbotham in the morning on the 29th. As six men were getting the grave made and keeping watch while others worked, the graveyard being just below a hill, Higgenbotham and his company came directly upon them all and carried them immediately through the woods without stopping at any place. 'Tis said that they were to deliver them to other hands at Rigby's to be conveyed to Annapolis.

The persons taken are Michael Danner, Conrad Strickler, Henry Bacon, Jacob Welshaver, Charles Jones, and Joseph Evans. This unhappy incident has so terrified the rest that they have all left their houses and are come over the river. . . .

Before this happened, if the Sheriff had gone over he might have had thirty or forty Dutch to assist him.

Samuel Blunston (Seal)[4]

[Danner and Hendricks to Governor Denny]

Whereas we, the subscribers, are informed it has been asserted that the late resolution of Dutch inhabitants on the west side of Susquehanna River to put themselves under the protection of the government of Pennsylvania and submit to the laws thereof, was occasioned by the prevalency and influence of the magistrate of Lancaster County, do voluntarily and solemnly declare that we were chosen and appointed by the aforesaid Dutch inhabitants on [the] west side of Susquehanna River opposite to Hempfield to apply in our own, and their behalf to the magistrates of said County that we believed in our consciences it was our duty. And we do further solemnly declare and affirm that this association and return was made of others on our own mere notions and free will without any previous persuasion, threatening or compulsion from the magistrates of said County or any other person in their behalf as far as we know; and that the letter signed by the inhabitants of aforesaid County to be communicated to the governor of Maryland was written at their own request and according to instruction given.

Subscribed the 13 day September 1736
Henry Hendricks
Michael Danner[5]

Deposition of Michael Danner 1736

Michael Tanner, late of Germany but now of the County of Lancaster and Province of Pennsylvania, aged about thirty years, upon his solemn affirmation according to law, saith that by virtue of a grant from the proprietors of Pennsylvania, bearing date the seventeenth day of September, 1734, this affirmant went and settled on a tract of two hundred acres of land on the west side of Susquehanna River, about six miles southwesterly from John Hendricks and built and improved upon the same; that in the latter part [of] the said year and the year following one Thomas Cresaps, pretending to have an order from the governor of Maryland to survey lands came into the neighborhood of this affirmant and sold his building with all his improved lands unto one Daniel Law. This affirmant further says that although in, or about, the month of September, 1735, the governor of Maryland and one Thomas White of Baltimore County, said to be surveyor general, told this affirmant that the said Thomas Cresaps had no authority to survey lands and all his surveys were invalid, yet nevertheless the said Daniel Law with his family came and dwelt in the affirmant's house.

And this affirmant could have no redress but was obliged to pay the said Law eight pounds for the house which this affirmant at his own proper cost had built or otherwise must wholly lose his said buildings and improvements of a considerable value and himself and family be exposed to the open air without shelter or means whereby to earn their bread.

Michael Tanner (Seal)[6]

John Martin and the Indian Raids

The earliest permanent settlers in that rich valley in middle Pennsylvania known as Morrison's Cove were Brethren. According to James Sell, the most knowledgeable writer on Brethren in that area, "about 1755 a colony of Brethren entered the Cove through Loy's Gap and gradually worked their way northward and became residents of the territory now [1924] embraced in the Clover Creek and Albright congregations." Sell also described later developments:

> A colony of Scotch-Irish settled here as early as 1749, but they were considered squatters and were expelled as the land belonged to the Indians. The Penns made a new purchase in 1754 and when the Brethren came they secured title to lands they purchased, and by 1790 all the desirable lands passed into private ownership. The Brethren secured the greater part of the land. Some of them purchased large tracts, as much as fifteen hundred acres. They were the pioneer settlers and did the first preaching.[7]

During the Indian wars of 1762 the nonresistant Brethren suffered at the hands of the raiders. A glimpse of the tragedy often experienced in those days is found in the petition of the Brethren member, John Martin, who wrote to the provincial authorities, asking for aid in recovering those of his family who had been seized by the Indians.

The historians of Bedford and Somerset counties consider the following excerpt from a letter of a contemporary to refer to the raid which resulted in the capture of Martin's family:

> On the 13th inst. we have had, in a place in this county called "Great Cove" five persons killed and six missing. Whether taken prisoner or killed is not known; two of the dead are soldiers. The enemy were followed as far as Sideling Hill, where they had killed a child not able to travel, which they had taken from the Cove.[8]

The journey mentioned in the petition would have involved a trip deep into wilderness territory in present-day Ohio. Of the names mentioned, Colonel "Bucquits" is Henry Boquet, Pennsylvania military leader, and Croghan was an Indian agent. King Beaver and Shingas were well-known Indian chieftains.

August 13, 1762

[Petition of John Martin]

The humble petition of your most obedient servant sheweth, sir, may it please your excellency, hearing me in your clemency a few words. I, one of the bereaved of my wife and five children, by savage war at the captivity of the Great Cove, after many and long journeys, I lately went to an Indian town, viz., Tuskaroways, 150 miles beyond Fort Pitt, and entreated in Col. Bucquits and Col. Croghan's favor, so as to bear their letters to King Beaver and Capt. Shingas, desiring them to give up one of my daughters to me, while I have yet two sons and one other daughter, if alive, among them. After seeing my daughter with Shingas he refused to give her up, and after some expostulating with him, but all in vain, he promised to deliver her up, with other captives to your excellency.

Sir, your excellency's most humble servant, humbly and passionately beseeches your benign compassion to interpose your excellencies [*sic*] beneficent influence in favor of your excellencies [*sic*] most obedient and dutiful servant.

John Martin[9]

The Cove in the Revolutionary War

Again in the 1770's Indian raiders made their dread visitations among the peaceful inhabitants of Morrison's Cove. The fullest account of the tragedy is given by U. J. Jones in his *History of the Early Settlement of the Juniata Valley* (1889), written in 1855.[10] The evident bias in Jones' book probably reflects the views of most of the contemporaries of the colonial Brethren regarding the peace position. Noteworthy is the effect even on the savages who committed the killings.

. . . The greater portion of the beautiful valley [Morrison's Cove], however, was almost unexplored until the Penns made the new purchase. About 1755, a colony of Dunkards took up the southern portion of the Cove, and their descendants hold possession of it to this day. They have unquestionably the finest farms, as well as the most fertile land, in the State; and right glad should we be to end *their* portion of the chapter by saying so, or even by adding that for thrift and economy they stand unsurpassed; but a sense of candor compels us to speak of them as they are, — "nothing extenuate, nor set down aught in malice."

In the first place, let it be understood that we are in no particle indebted to them for one iota of the blessings of government we enjoy. They are strict non-resistants; and in the predatory incursions of the French and Indians, in 1756-1763, and in fact, during all the savage warfare, they not only refused to take up arms to repel the savage marauders and prevent the inhuman slaughter of women and children, but they refused in the most positive manner to pay a dollar to support those who were willing to take up arms to defend their homes and their firesides, until wrung from them by the stern mandates of the law, from which there was no appeal.

They did the same thing when the Revolution broke out. There was a scarcity of men. Sixty able-bodied ones among them might readily have formed a cordon of frontier defence, which could have prevented many of the Indian massacres which took place between 1777 and 1780, and more especially among their own people in the Cove. But not a man would shoulder his rifle; they were *non-resistants!* They might, at least, have furnished money, for they always had an abundance of that, the hoarding of which seemed to be the sole aim and object of life with them. But, no; not a dollar! They occupied neutral ground, and wished to make no resistance. Again, they might have furnished supplies. And they *did* furnish supplies to those who were risking their lives to repel the invaders — but it was only when the almighty dollar accompanied the demand.

After the massacre of thirty of them, in less than forty-eight hours, Colonel Piper, the lieutenant-colonel of Bedford County, made a stirring appeal to them. But it was of no avail; they were non-resistants, and evidently determined to remain such.

Of the peculiar religious tenets of these primitive people we do not profess to know anything; hence our remarks are unbiased. We are solely recording historical facts. . . .

The alarm was spread among the inhabitants [November 1777] and they fled to the nearest forts with all dispatch; and on this first expedition they [the Indians] would have had few scalps to grace their belts, had the Dunkards taken the advice of the more sagacious people, and fled too; this, however, they would not do. They would follow

but half of Cromwell's advice: — They were willing to put their
"trust in God," but they would not "keep their powder dry." In short,
it was a compound they did not use at all.

The savages swept down through the Cove with all the ferocity
with which a pack of wolves would descend from the mountains upon
a flock of sheep. Some few of the Dunkards, who evidently had a latent
spark of love of life, hid themselves away; but by far the most of them
stood by and witnessed the butchery of their wives and children,
merely saying, "Gottes Wille sei gethan."* How many Dunkard scalps

---

[Note]* "God's will be done." This sentence was so frequently repeated by the
Dunkards during the massacre, that the Indians must have retained a vivid recollection of it. During the late war with Great Britain [1812-1815] the older Indians
on the frontier were anxious to know of the Huntingdon volunteers whether the
"Gotswiltahns" still resided in the Cove. Of course our people could not satisfy
them on such a vague point.

---

they carried to Detroit cannot now be, and probably never has been,
clearly ascertained, — not less than thirty, according to the best authority. In addition to this, they loaded themselves with plunder, stole a
number of horses, and under cover of night the triumphant warriors
marched bravely away. . . .

The band of Indians, after the Dunkard massacre, worked their
way toward the Kittaning war-path, leaving behind them some few
stragglers of their party whose appetite for blood and treasure had
not been satiated. Among others, an old and a young Indian stopped
at Neff's Mill. Neff was a Dunkard; but he was a single exception so
far as resistance was concerned. He had constantly in his mill his loaded
rifle, and was ready for any emergency. He had gone to his mill in
morning without any knowledge of Indians being in the neighborhood,
and had just set the water-wheel in motion, when he discovered the
two Indians lurking, within a hundred yards, in a small wood below the
mill.

Without taking much time to deliberate how to act, he aimed
through the window, and deliberately shot the old Indian. In an instant the young Indian came toward the mill, and Neff ran out of the
back door and up the hill. The quick eye of the savage detected him,
and he fired, but missed his aim. Nothing daunted by the mishap,
the savage followed up the cleared patch, when both, as if by instinct,
commenced reloading their rifles.

They stood face to face, not forty yards apart, on open ground, where there was no possible chance of concealment. The chances were equal: he that loaded first would be victor in the strife, the other doomed to certain death. They both rammed home the bullet at the same time — with what haste may well be conjectured. This was a critical juncture, for, while loading, neither took his eye off the other. They both drew their ramrods at the same instant, but the intense excitement of the moment caused the Indian to balk in drawing his, and the error or mishap proved fatal, because Neff took advantage of it, and succeeded in priming, and aiming before the Indian. The latter, now finding the muzzle of Neff's rifle bearing upon him, commenced a series of very cunning gyrations and contortions to destroy his aim or to confuse him, so that he might miss him or enable him to prime. To this end, he first threw himself upon his face; then, suddenly rising up again, he jumped first to the right, then to the left, then fell down again. Neff, not the least put off his guard, waited until the Indian rose again, when he shot him through the head.

Neff, fearing that others might be about, left the mill and started to the nearest settlement. A force was raised and the mill revisited; but it was found a heap of smoldering cinders and ashes, and the dead bodies of the Indians had been removed. It is altogether likely that the rear of the savage party came up shortly after Neff had left, fired the mill and carried away their slain companions.

For the part Neff took in the matter he was excommunicated from the Dunkard society. Nevertheless, he rebuilt his mill; but the Dunkards, who were his main support previously, refused any longer to patronize him, and he was eventually compelled to abandon the business.[11]

Correction of the Neff Anecdote

James Sell, writing in the history of the Middle District of Pennsylvania, corrects the previous account by Jones concerning the incident involving Jacob Neff.

Daniel Ullery was the original owner of Roaring Spring. He built the first mill. Jacob Neff was his miller. During the Indian massacre he shot an Indian. He was counseled by the church for his violation of her peace principles. He did not plead justification. He admitted that it was wrong to take human life but said his deed was done under strong temptation and excitement. He was excused, but required not to speak of his act in company in a boasting or justifying way. This restriction he frequently violated and he was expelled from the church.

This story has been repeated and exaggerated and the church through it misrepresented so that we take this opportunity to tell the story as we have it from our own tradition. The history of Juniata Valley says that when Neff rebuilt his mill the Brethren refused to patronize him. This is not correct.

The chain, or abstract of title shows that Neff never owned the mill, did not build it in the first place, did not in the second place. Ullery built it and rebuilt it. It was a necessity in the new settlement.[12]

THE VIRGINIA FRONTIER

Martin G. Brumbaugh once wrote "An Outline for Historical Romance" in which he stated:

> If I were a romancer, gifted and leisured, I would weave out of this unique society on the Cocalico [the Ephrata Community] a story — mostly supported by historic record and only in a small way supported by the easiest of imaginative processes — that for pathos, beauty and graphic situations has few if any equals. The outline of this, hastily sketched, may, I trust will, stir some sympathetic soul to give to the world a volume which may with some propriety be entitled "Bon Chretien."[13]

He then proceeded to relate the fascinating story of the Eckerlin family, which originated in the Alsatian city of Strassburg. The head of the family, Michael Eckerlin (1643-c.1720), was a responsible burgher and master craftsman who became active in Pietist conventicles. His widow and four sons migrated in 1725 to Pennsylvania, where the sons later became involved in the Sabbatarian movement.[14]

The Eckerlin brothers — Israel, Samuel, Emanuel, and Gabriel — held positions of authority in the Community, and indeed rivaled Conrad Beissel for dominance. It was owing to the administrative genius of the Eckerlins that Ephrata flourished as a center of manufacture and agriculture. Beissel felt that economic success would eventually cause spiritual failure, and was able to regain control. Thereupon three of the Eckerlins left Ephrata, settling more than four hundred miles west and south within Indian territory. They established friendly relationships with the Indians, and prospered in the wilderness until widespread frontier warfare led to the tragedy related in the following original sources.

The romance to which Brumbaugh refers — that of the "White Lily" (Regina Hartman, a white woman held captive for years by the Indians) with one of the Eckerlins seized by the French and their Indian allies — is not supported by evidence, yet the fact that two of the Eckerlins died on the way to or in France not far from their ancestral home is in itself a truth stranger than fiction.

Early History of the Eckerlin Family in Pennsylvania

Sangmeister included in his autobiography the account written by Israel Eckerlin of the circumstances relating to the arrival of his mother, himself, and his brothers in this country and their association with the Beissel-led Ephrata Community. This is similar to the account in the published *Ephrata Chronicle* but provides some interesting details not included when the manuscript *Chronicon* was edited for publication.

In the fall of 1725 the widow of Michael Eckerlin with her four sons arrived in this country. Abraham Devon [DuBois] and Luy, and the old widow Becker with her children were their travel companions. Luy moved immediately to our congregation, and V[ater] F[riedsam], or Conrad Beissel, and Brother Amos [John Meyle] built him a house. This Luy caused the congregation a great deal of trouble with his objectionable conduct and way of life.

In regard to the old widow Becker and her children, they were even worse in their way of life and conduct than Luy. For that reason the Father [Beissel] grew very tired of these people and discouraged of ever accepting any more of the old Brethren. It was a completely perverted sect; these people could hardly be brought to the right path for they would not be dissuaded from their old concepts.

The following words are taken directly from Brother Onesimus (Israel Eckerlin, whose fraternal name was Onesimus): As we were on our voyage to Pennsylvania, I became deathly sick. While I was so hard pressed I fervently sighed and prayed to God to restore me to health and not to let me die. I also promised God that if I came to land I would repent and begin a new life. God heard my prayer and I was restored. As we approached land I wished I could stay on the water forever. In so doing I realized that I had not meant my promise to God. After we had gone ashore I was not very faithful in keeping my promise to God, as I lapsed quite a bit into vanity again, especially pride.

Upon arrival in this country with her children, my mother was advised by everyone to buy a plantation and settle down there with her children. Because of all this advice she bought one near Germantown, and moved onto it the very same autumn. However, things did not seem to work out in that location, for everything seemed to go at a snail's pace. Therefore my mother was obliged to sell the plantation again, and to buy that of Brother Hildebrand as a widow's residence. She moved there in the fall of 1726.

There is one more thing to be mentioned especially. While we were still living on the plantation, Brother Agonius [Michael Wohlfahrt] visited us while my mother and I were alone at home. He stayed over night with us. He spoke with great fervor to my mother about true Christianity until late at night. Those words pleased me very much and I kept them in my heart. Thus the spirit of the Conestoga Community was kindled in me and from that time I have had a yearning to be with them.

At the new residence there was very much that needed repair, which we now had to bring in order, especially the cellar. For that reason we had to find a mason and happened to hit on Brother Henry Miller. I then asked him if I might be apprenticed to him. He took me on for two years, without making a written contract. I was much better off there than my brother Jotham [Gabriel] who had a very strict apprenticeship with Brother Gumre; Brother Jotham had a much stricter and more exacting master than I. After this I went with Henry Miller to Conrad Matthe, who was our good friend, and for whom I had a special liking. He dissuaded me from Germantown and advised Conestoga, for there were very simple people there, almost like the Swiss [Amish]. This appealed to me and to Brother Henry very much and we traveled there in the sixth month of the year 1727. We went first to the Mennonite congregation, but in their doctrine they did not appeal to us as much as in their dress.

We were told subsequently that the Sabbatarian congregation lived in whoredom and lewdness. This we could not believe. We therefore went there together and happened to arrive when the old Brethren were visiting in their meeting. Brother Deboy [DuBois] was also there. In that meeting I was greatly encouraged by V. F.'s words. After the meeting Brother A. Deboy turned me over to V. F. and Agonius to look after me, lest I became spoiled by neglect. Thus I became acquainted with the congregation. The next year I went once again with Brother H. Miller to the congregation at Ephrata and was baptized, along with Br[other] H. [Miller] and Brother Jethro [J. Gass].

In 1730 Brother Jephune [Samuel Eckerlin] came here to Conestoga in response to Brother Onesimus' [Israel Eckerlin's] letter, and became so enamored of Beissel and his fellowship that he had himself baptized immediately. After he had returned home and told his wife about it, she also became inflamed, and came at the first opportunity and was baptized.[15]

The Eckerlins and Mack Leave the Community

By the early autumn of 1745 relationships between the Eckerlins — especially the Prior, Israel Eckerlin — and the rest of the Community had reached such a point that a radical break occurred. Eckerlin and his brother Samuel, accompanied by Alexander Mack, Jr. (Sander Mack), later joined by two others, left the Community, going far "toward the setting of the sun." The departure created a whirlpool of curious speculation, which was partially clarified by the accounts printed by Christopher Sauer in his newspaper.

Their destination, New River, lies in what is now southwestern Virginia, between Christiansburg and Newbern, at the juncture of Montgomery and Pulaski counties. These pilgrims gave it the name Mahanaim, taken from Genesis 32:1-2: "Jacob went on his way and the angels of God met him; and when Jacob saw them he said, 'This is God's army!' So he called the name of that place Mahanaim." The site is referred to by early travelers as "Dunker's Bottom." The New River takes its origin in North Carolina east of the mountains, flows northward into Virginia, and then breaks westward through the Alleghenies, joining the Great Kanawha, which runs eventually into the Mississippi.[16]

The *Chronicle* reported the following description of the departure from Ephrata, subsequent to an ultimatum delivered to Israel Eckerlin by the faction loyal to Conrad Beissel.

When this resolution was communicated to Onesimus [Israel Eckerlin], he by no means objected but promised to move next day into the fulling-mill, and was greatly rejoiced, because he perceived that the severe judgment, which was the result of his administration, would soon reach its end. But, good God! it was a short-lived joy, for when his oldest brother [Samuel], to whose advice he had always paid more obedience than to that of his faithful spiritual Father, came home and heard the resolve of his brother, he said to him that it was time again to turn to a hermit's life, and that he should escape with him into the desert. He should leave misfortune to the Community; they would not carry on matters for any length of time, for they had not intelligence enough to conduct a household.

This proposition pleased the Prior, therefore he left the Settlement on the following day, September 4, 1745, with his above-mentioned brother Jephune [Samuel], and another, Timotheus [A. Mack, Jr.] by name, and moved toward the wilderness, after having administered the office of prior for not much longer than four years. They fled about four hundred English miles toward the setting of the sun, as if someone were chasing them, for justice pursued them on account of the spiritual debts which they had contracted in the Settlement, until, beyond all Christian governments, they reached a stream which runs toward the Mississippi, New River by name. Here they settled, in the midst of a pack of nothing but tramps, the dregs of human society, who spent their time in murdering wild beasts. These they had to take into their companionship instead of the brethren they had left behind. . . .

It was necessary to give a clear record of these matters, because nearly everyone had the suspicion that the Superintendent had persecuted the Prior and his brothers. No one can be blamed for it, because many in the Community were not cognizant of the condition of the household in the Settlement. . . .

As soon as the office of prior became vacant by the departure of the Prior, his youngest brother Jotham [Gabriel] successfully worked himself into this position, for the Eckerlins had the delusion that the office was hereditary in their family. The Prior was once heard to say: "The Community is mine," to which his brother Jotham answered: "Then the Brotherhood belongs to me," which the third, Elimilech [Emanuel], heard, and said, replying: "By God, brothers, both of you are mistaken," for in his opinion both belonged to him! . . .

Soon after Brother Jotham assumed the office, the spirits of judgment, which had overthrown his brother, took possession of him also, for he began to make arbitrary reforms. . . .

The brethren, however, did not allow him to get warm in his seat before they declared against him; they did not want to have an Eckerlin again as their prior. They wanted him to move into the house which the Eckerlins had in the Settlement, and to let them reform the Brotherhood; after that he might again dwell with the brethren.

He, however, did not wait that long, for in the following winter his brother Jephune [Samuel] came for him and took him to the New River. Thus all the Eckerlins lost their right in the inheritance of the Lord, for which they had to thank their carnal connection alone, which had helped them to bring everything, even the Superintendent, under their sway. But the scandal of this schism spread through the whole country, and just as formerly this small Community had by its harmony brought everything close together, so did this disunion now dissolve everything.

The merchants of Philadelphia, who had traded with them, were displeased at this loss. They had expected to find indulgence for their worldly life from these supposed saints, and if the government had been able to interfere the affair would have been brought before the courts. But the sins were not against the government but against God. Everybody wished them well, for it was hoped that they would discover a road closer to the Kingdom of God than the one the Solitary in the Settlement had walked thus far.

The pious of the country were the most beguiled by this deception toward God. Separatist friends in Germantown were all ready to follow them [Eckerlins], but were prevented by the subsequent Indian war, for nothing is sweeter in the world than to desert God again after having lived for some time nearer to Him. . . .

A man of note [Dr. Henry Ehrenfried Luther?] wrote from Frankfurt: "The flight of the Eckerlins into the wilderness is a great marvel; let me know the result of it." And now a pilgrimage was undertaken to those regions, for whoever became troubled about his salvation took refuge with them, and they understood how to cure him. Others hoped to find out some of the sins and infamies which, as was supposed, were carried on in the Settlement. A famous doctor was most likely induced thereby to undertake his long journey to them.[17]

A young brother in the Settlement, Henry Zinn by name, also longed at last for such a life of license; he begged the brethren to accompany him thither, and promised in return to love them all his life long. He and the whole family of Bingeman were killed there by the Indians.[18]

Christopher Sauer Reports the Departure

Two news items were published in Sauer's Germantown newspaper to provide accurate information about the much-talked-about exodus.

October 16, 1745

The reports about the departure of divers Brethren from Zion vary. That both brothers, Samuel and Israel Eckerlin together with Alexander Mack, in order to completely escape from the turmoil of the world and to follow their calling and desire, did journey into the distant wilderness after they had taken a proper farewell, is certain. That they secretly went to Bethlehem for the purpose of having wives given to them is either a misunderstanding or circulated to injure both institutions.[19]

May 10, 1746

To satisfy the many requests about the Brotherhood at Ephrata we can report this much in brief. There were not seventy but five fathers and brothers who left the Cloister. [They went] not to Bethlehem but rather four hundred miles into Virginia on the New River in order to lead a solitary life there, each in his hut according to his needs. [They] never again [wish] to rule over souls. According to their testimony, they did not part in anger but in love. The change resulted from their ordering a bell without prior knowledge of the father of fathers, and from their wishing to place a tower on a new Cloister.

Otherwise, things of secondary importance have increased to such an extent that in a short time there was a ringing and sounding, tinkling, banging, and jangling at Zion, Ephrata, Kedar, Peniel and Saron just as in Rome, Jerusalem, Bethlehem, Nazareth and Babylon. The Cloister has not been sold. Those remaining wish to correct what mistakes had been made and no one is to be forced to remain. That which a person has brought or demands back, he may take with him [when he leaves]. They were accused of being traders and merchants, therefore they will buy no more wheat or linseed to sell. They have disposed of cows, oxen, horses, wagons, clocks and bells. The saw mill will be sold. The same goes for the paper mill and for this reason temporarily no wood will be taken on for cutting, nor any rags. In the future the brethren will be more careful about asking the father first. Human institutions must be dependent on their leaders, otherwise they cannot exist.[20]

Mack and Höhnly Return to the East

Not all of the small band of pioneers remained in the New River area, according to the *Chronicle* account. First, Alexander Mack, Jr., and then Jacob Höhnly, returned to Pennsylvania. The latter soon died, but Mack lived an active life until his death in 1803, becoming the leading Brethren churchman and a prolific poet and writer.

After the former Prior, together with his own brother and two other brethren, namely Timotheus [Alexander Mack, Jr.] and Ephraim [Jacob Höhnly], had left their place in the Settlement of the Solitary, and had moved toward the wilderness, they built their lonely huts on the banks of the New River on very fertile soil, and called the place Mahanaim. When they began to live in their huts it was revealed to Brother Timotheus at night, in a dream, that the Indians were about to lay waste their hermitage. Since Indians actually did arrive after a few days and destroyed their corn, he revealed his dream to the Eckerlins, who answered him that if he had no faith in this way of living, they would not object to his leaving them again. He, therefore, turned his hut over to them, said good-bye to the solitary life and returned to his people in Germantown from whom he had come. The other brother, called Ephraim, soon followed him and ended his life at the house of a merchant of Philadelphia.

These were two important proofs that a life chosen by one's own will, even if it appears to be ever so holy, finds no acceptance with God. Thus the three brothers were left alone, each of whom chose a special mode of making a livelihood. Jephune [Samuel], the oldest, applied himself to medicine, and spent his time among the people on the border. The other, the former Prior [Israel], occupied himself with writing, of which we will speak hereafter. But the youngest, Jotham [Gabriel], became a hunter, an employment unfit for a Solitary, which was looked upon with much suspicion in the Settlement.[21]

Soon they all became aware of their mistake, but the Prior, under whose influence the two other brothers stood, was a venturesome fellow and still hoped to bring the Community in the Settlement to bow down before him, as the sons of Jacob did before Joseph. We are assured that Jotham shed so many tears that it was feared he might lose his sight, for the Superintendent loved him so dearly on account of his innocent youth that, as already mentioned, he once omitted all divine service in the Settlement until he had freed him from the snares of the tempter. His brother also testified of him that it would have been impossible for them to remain on the New River another day, such was his hunger for their mother-church. They had little or nothing to do with anything relating to divine worship, because they soon fell into the fetters of freethinking. Besides, they thought meanly of the church ordinances in the Settlement, such as the Sabbath, baptism, breaking of bread, etc., for they pretended to honor God in a more important way.[22]

An interesting answer by Mack to his brother Valentine, a resident at Ephrata, indicates that the Community was eager to have their former Brother Timotheus return. Mack's response was a kindly but quite firm refusal.

Germantown, August 27, 1748

[Alexander Mack, Jr., to Valentine Mack]

In Christ Jesus, our only High Priest and Redeemer.

Beloved Brother Valentine:

May the eternal covenant of grace and peace, which God has created with us in the blood of the Lamb through the water bath in the Word of Salvation, live and be verdant in your soul and mine to eternal life, and may it make you and me healthy in the faith and in the love of Jesus and His members. Amen.

I received your letter dated June 27 in good order and accepted in love the upwelling of your love which was expressed in this letter. Yet, until now I could not bring myself to answer it. For when a poor man gambles with a rich man, the rich man will and can take care that the poor man wins nothing from him. If I were to begin today to learn from the loss I have suffered, it would indeed be none too early. For nearly twenty years I have been tried in all kinds of manners in the ways of the heavenly calling. I have given many an example of my childlike lack of understanding. It is about high time for me to study better the tenth commandment in order that even spiritually I should not covet my neighbor's goods. Even though I can claim nothing and extreme poverty is my lot, such ought to be more desirable for me than to plume myself with what belongs to others.

Yet, I do wish from my heart that this simple letter might cheer you as a pleasing answer. Even though I can do nothing and own nothing, the spark of love for you does urge me to answer with a simple heart. In the first place, Brother Samuel Eckerlin did not understand me correctly, for I have no intention to move again to the New River, unless Divine Providence obviously ordered me to do so and convinced me of it more emphatically to make a change than I have ever been persuaded.

Secondly, it is no great wonder that now Brother Henry Miller despises the life of the brethren at the New River. It does not change my ideas about it from those I had before. To the extent that he had over-praised it, just so must he now despise it to excess. Should he yet hit the right mark, it would be reason for him to ascribe it to the infinite mercy of God and not to his own understanding. For humans easily err, now through praise, now through scorn. When, however, we begin to know ourselves, we are glad to let each matter rest as it is, because we know that we cannot make it better or worse.

Thirdly, out of love you wish to take me into your house. This would be a great help for anyone who has need of lodging. In Germantown one has to pay if one needs lodging. Yet God cares even for those who have nothing. However, I — praise God — have so far been able to eat my own bread, under the blessing of God.

Finally, you write that I have nothing to fear from the brethren in Ephrata, because every day they center more and more into the divine humility and childlikeness. I rejoice to hear this. If, as you report, all judging and self-seeking melts like the "frost in the sun," I shall have nothing to fear from them here in Germantown either, for here I am even farther from them than if I were living with you. Indeed, perfect love casts out fear, and he who still has fear has not come to love perfectly.

You wrote that the pent-up stream of the grace and love of God will soon cover the entire earth like the waters of the ocean. I join you in this expectation and heartfelt desire.

Your humble fellow pilgrim,

Sander Mack

Written in haste because of the present opportunity. To be delivered near Ephrata to the dear Brother Valentine Mack.[28]

New River — Visited by Travelers

Despite the remote location of the Eckerlin home, there were early visitors, or near-visitors, who make reference to the "Dunkers." Some of the practices of the former Ephrata dwellers, who kept up certain monastic characteristics, were so unusual as to be thought noteworthy.

That complete isolation was not found along the New River is attested to by the decision of the authorities in August 1746 that inhabitants of the area were to be held to roadmaking duty. Residents ordered to road work in the New River territory were mentioned by name, except "all the Dunkers."

One often-quoted early account, given below, is Dr. Thomas Walker's "Journal of an Exploration in the Spring of the Year 1750." Other references are found in the diaries of the Moravian missionaries Schnell and Brandmueller, for example, this cryptic notation of Sunday, November 26, 1749: "We were only a few miles from the Sabbatarians who live here at the New River. But we had enough of the description which the people gave of them."[24]

[Excerpts from Dr. Walker's Journal]

March 16 [1750]. We kept up the Staunton [River] to William Englishes. He lives on a small branch, and was not much hurt by the fresh [flood]. He has a mill, which is the furthest back except one lately built by the sect of people, who call themselves of the Brotherhood of Euphrates [Ephrata], and are commonly called the Duncards, who are the upper inhabitants on the New River, which is about four hundred yards wide at this place. They live on the west side, and we were obliged to swim our horses over. The Duncards are an odd set of people, who make it a matter of religion not to shave their beards, lie on beds, or eat flesh, though at present, in this last, they transgress, being constrained to it, as they say, by the want of a sufficiency of grain and roots, they having not long been settled here. I doubt [not] the plenty and deliciousness of the venison and turkeys has contributed a little to this. The unmarried have no private property, but live on a common stock. They don't baptize either young or old. They keep their Sabbath on Saturday, and hold that all men shall be happy hereafter, but must first pass through punishment according to their sins. They are very hospitable. . . .

March 20. We went very early to the track of our horses. After following them six or seven miles, we found them all together. We returned to the Duncards about ten o'clock, and having purchased half a bushel of meal and as much small hominy, we set off and lodged on a small run between Peak Creek and Reedy Creek.[25]

Eckerlins Return to Ephrata and Relocate

In 1750 Israel and Gabriel Eckerlin returned to Ephrata, where they found feelings toward them to be good again, so good, in fact, that they seriously spoke of rejoining the Community. They returned to the interior (after also visiting the Brethren in Germantown) to arrange for removal to Ephrata. Two Ephrata brethren went with them to demonstrate the restored friendly relationships.

However, after the former Prior, Israel Eckerlin, had come back to Ephrata and lived there for five months, some of the old antipathies arose once more so that he persuaded his brothers upon their subsequent arrival in the fall of 1750 to turn around and go back.

This time they relocated in what is now Greene County, Pennsylvania, along "Dunkard Creek." They arranged with the Delaware Indians for their stay in that area, and remained on good terms with them. Samuel Eckerlin was a gifted physician, and was respected by the Indians for his medicinal talents.[26]

Yet, this was a time of Indian uprising, and the Delawares soon conducted the Eckerlins to a secluded site in the mountains along the Cheat River, near present-day Kingwood, West Virginia. Here they flourished unharmed by raiding Indian bands.[27]

The entrepreneurial gifts of the Eckerlins were not idle; along with their trapping and hunting they planned a large settlement of their friends from Germantown and elsewhere in that area. Surveys and land records reveal that Samuel Eckerlin claimed large tracts of land, having sold land on the New River to Garret Zinn. Frontier unrest kept these plans from materializing.[28]

After the brethren in the Settlement had become aware that the rod of the taskmaster was broken, and that they were no longer kept captive under the rule of the Eckerlins, they dropped their violent opposition to them. So also the Eckerlins, who had obtained all their power in the Settlement from the opposition of the brethren — when they perceived that this had subsided — thought it a favorable opportunity to visit the Settlement; and on February 23, 1750, the two brothers, Onesimus and Jotham, arrived in the neighborhood of the Settlement. As soon as this became known to the brethren they assembled in their meeting hall, with their Superintendent, and sent two delegates to them to welcome and offer them shelter in the convent, which these two brethren gratefully accepted. Then both parties embraced each other in the brethren's meeting hall, which was so edifying to behold that it was not done without tears, because the Philadelphia brotherly spirit was then revived among brethren who for many a year had eaten the bread of misery together.

The Eckerlins were astonished at such kind behavior on the part of the brethren, and offered not only to live with the brethren again, as regards their own persons, but also to deposit all their acquired property in the treasury of the brethren. The Superintendent answered that they must bear patiently with us, as we had become a bad people after their departure, which gave them the more courage. Thereafter they attended the evening meeting of the brethren, and as many housefathers as were present at the time, these too, received them with special love and admonished them to return again to the brethren.

After this they resolved to visit their friends here and there in the country, but because the opinion was everywhere prevalent that they were inimical to the Solitary in the Settlement, they requested the Superintendent to give them a traveling companion. He appointed one who had formerly been the best friend of the Prior, but who had separated from him on account of his rebellion. At every place to which they came the people were astonished at the sudden change, and many worked up the old lies again, namely, that the Superintendent was a sorcerer and had drawn these two brothers into the Settlement by witchcraft.

Since the Prior, during his administration, had greatly wronged the Brethren [at Germantown] by his judgments, he now tried to make amends. This he did with Peter Becker and Gantz near Germantown, the latter of whom was a particular enemy of the Superintendent and commonly called him an arch-heretic. But even if the good Onesimus had in some measure been guilty, this recantation would not have been necessary. But herein lies the reason why God cannot get any more witnesses to condemn the sins of men, for when the sin and wickedness of men come upon them they recant, and thus God loses His honor through them, as happened to Traut, Tennhard and several others in our fatherland.[29]

When they returned to the Settlement after this visit, they again prepared for their departure. . . . After the Eckerlins had taken such an edifying farewell, they went back to their lonely homes. Thereupon two brethren of the Settlement, Nathaniel [Eicher] and Manasse [Martin Funk], were sent after them, who were instructed to assist them in properly arranging their affairs. . . .

After he [Israel Eckerlin] had brought his brothers over to his side they took their Indian wares to market and traded them for other goods and prepared for their return to the wilderness; but because winter was at the door the brethren offered them shelter until the weather was milder, which they modestly declined and started on their journey. However, when they came to the Allegheny Mountains they met with such masses of snow that it was with great danger that they crossed these fearful mountains and came to inhabited regions. Then they directed their journey toward the Ohio River into the neighborhood of the place where the French were building a fort at the time, named Duquesne. Here they placed themselves under the protection of the Delaware Indians who showed them great friendship. . . .

About this time a bloody war commenced between England and France, in which all the Indians sided with the French. The Delawares, therefore, told the Eckerlins that they could no longer guarantee them safety, for the French savages would overrun those regions. They, therefore, led them to a region which the Indians believed would seldom be visited by their people and said at the same time that they would warn them whenever danger approached. This place was high up in the mountains, on a stream called Cheat River, which empties into the Monongahela River. There they built a well-arranged hermitage for themselves, kept servants, horses, etc., as if they had to supply a large household. . . .

At that time two brethren, Henry Sangmeister and Anthony Höllenthal, left the Settlement and settled as hermits on the river Schannedor [Shenandoah] in Virginia. But as they preferred an unfettered life to the discipline of God, which still reigned in the Settlement, they joined the Eckerlins, for like joins like. They thereby became participants in the judgment which rested on the latter, although they had not yet committed as many offenses in the Settlement. This Sangmeister once brought a large manuscript of the Prior to the printer in the Settlement, which contained an account of the falling away at Ephrata, and desired to have it printed. The printer sent him the reply that the first writings which he had produced in the Settlement he had brought from the starry sky, but this last from that dark region where brother-hate reigned, and that he did not want to have anything to do with such things. The messenger was ill-pleased with this; he would have it printed at some other place, for the country should now realize that the Prior was a prophet. But it was not done; nor was his prophecy fulfilled, that the Indians would come to take vengeance on the Settlement, because the brethren had resisted them, and had sought to trample under foot an innocent man and witness of God. That this same judgment should soon overtake them themselves was at this time hidden from them. . . . [30]

Sangmeister's Account

Other Ephrata brethren followed the Eckerlins' precedent, as mentioned in the *Chronicle,* but contented themselves with settling around Strasbourg, Virginia.[31] One of them, Sangmeister, visited the Eckerlin location and left a picturesque description of the way of life of the Eckerlins and their redemptioner servants at this time.

. . . after we had arrived at their home where Brother Gabriel was, he was very happy and they did everything in their power for me. Yet, I had to change my entire nature, for as I was used to bread and they had almost nothing but meat, I was often ill, but I did not show it. I framed their windows, even made a plow for them among other things. I had to endure much at the time, because the insects were so bad that I said to Brother Israel that even if he were to give me the entire land as far as the Mississippi, I would not accept it to live on, because of the gnats and other vermin. Their way of life and their actions were so curious as I had never heard or seen in my life about people who lived solitary lives. But that was not all.

After I had lived with them for a time, I saw their great unrest and also the killing of animals. Brother Israel was busy day and night with writing concerning the Ephrata group, and Brother Gabriel with hunting and taking the lives of the poor creatures and skinning them for the hides. Samuel then helped with the scraping and caring for them. They lay in such heaps that we slept on piles which could not have been purchased for one hundred pounds or more. On one side behind the chimney were hanging so many dead bears that it horrified one to look at them. They had at least one hundred bushels of corn [*Welschkorn*] and the new crop was just about ripe, about six acres. As I counted the horses, there were twenty-eight head; during the day the large flies plagued them so that they galloped around until the earth shook. The servant [redemptioner], John Schilling, had just completed his service, and would have gladly traveled home with me, but Gabriel ordered me to talk him out of it, and by no means to give him reason to leave, for they needed him so much in the terrible land that they had. . . .

They had a restless old man with them, Daniel Hendricks, who was the cook and although he was a stubborn creature, he did customarily tell them the straight truth from time to time and criticized them for their life and actions. But his words had very little effect. They had the impression that they were above everything, and that they thought they could own everything in the world without [spiritual] harm. They also talked much about buying all of the land between their house where they now were and Peterson's Creek (two days' travel away), and to settle devout people there, so that they would always have places to stay on their own land with pious people when they traveled back and forth. . . . [32]

Tragedy Strikes the Eckerlins

The increasing tide of frontier conflict in the mid-1750's did not spare the peaceful eremites. Their Delaware Indian friends were themselves unable to protect them. Farther south in the New River area, where the Eckerlins had first settled, Dunker families suffered from Indian depredations. Some of them took refuge in North Carolina with the Moravians. The Wachovia community diary for July 22, 1755, noted:

> A so-called Dunkard or Bearded Man came to the smithy. He had just come from New River with his entire family, fearing to remain there longer because of the Indians, who are wandering about. Although his home was only about seventy miles from here the journey had taken them three weeks, as they had no other road to take than to the Roanoke. The man told us that some ten weeks ago a man named Stahlnecker, living on Holston River, about one hundred miles from the New River Settlement, had been captured by the Indians, and his entire family murdered. A few days before the Dunkard left, several families had been

attacked, and part murdered, part captured; and the last night before his flight the family of one of his nearest neighbors had been murdered, only three miles from him. So far as the man knew, twenty-eight persons had been killed or taken prisoner. When the man reached the Roanoke he found other refugees from New River, but it was no place to stay, for the settlers there were much alarmed by the news they brought . . . . [33]

Finally, in 1756-57, during the absence of Samuel Eckerlin, who had gone east for needed supplies, a small band of Indians led by a French officer ravaged the settlement on the Cheat River. Their plantation was destroyed, the livestock killed, and the inhabitants dragged off into captivity.

These developments, described often with conflicting details, are based largely on the account in the *Ephrata Chronicle* given below, embellished by imagination and local lore.[34] A more detailed account is given by Sangmeister, and is reputedly derived from the eyewitness narrative of Schilling, a servant of the Eckerlins, who escaped from Indian captivity after a period of three years.

The sole survivor, Samuel, retired farther east in the Strasburg, Virginia, area, later returning to eastern Pennsylvania, where he died. His attempts to secure information about his brothers are indicated by his letter to Benjamin Franklin, then in France.

In their seclusion they lived in the greatest security in the midst of war; they raised horses, cleared land, and made good use of the chase and other advantages of the country. At one time the Iroquois went to war against the northern Indians; it was winter, and they were so unlucky that they had to flee in their nakedness. So they took all their clothes and rugs from the Eckerlins and then left. This should have been a warning to them. The Delaware Indians also sent word that they would no longer be secure at that place. But they took it to be a fable.

They sometimes went to Virginia, which created the suspicion that the Eckerlins were spies, on which account the Prior was at one time kept captive in a fort. But when the Virginians did not want to let them stay there [at their home] any longer, Samuel Eckerlin tried to get permission to do so from the governor of Virginia; but it was refused, and a company of soldiers went with him in order to take his brothers safely into inhabited regions. They were not very far from their hermitage when seven hostile Mohawk Indians, under the command of a Frenchman, attacked it. The servant gave the alarm, but the Prior [Israel] did not allow himself to be disturbed in his writing until they bound his hands on his back; they packed all their property on horses, of which the hermits possessed a great number, set the house on fire and decamped with their prisoners. Meanwhile Samuel Eckerlin arrived with the soldiers, while the fire was still glowing under the ashes. This distressing sight brought tears to his eyes; he stepped aside and allowed them to flow. An Indian who was concealed there, lying in wait according to their custom, to see whether anyone was looking for them, was moved by his tears to save his life.

Now let us lay before the reader the further fortunes and misfortunes of the above-mentioned Prior and of his brother Jotham [Gabriel] to their end, following the account obtained from their fellow prisoners. Because an English army, under General Forbes, was at the time on its march to besiege Fort Duquesne, the Indians made a wide detour to that fort to avoid the English. It took them eight days to make this journey, on which their captives were sorely maltreated by the Indians, who cut off the beard of one of them in such a fashion that part of the cheek went with it. At the said fort they sold the two brothers to the French; but kept their servant, Schilling by name, for themselves. During a severe season the French took their prisoners across the lakes to Montreal, where they were lodged for some time in the Jesuit College.

From there they were sent to Quebec, where they had to endure a hard winter on poor fare. Yet the Canadians had so much respect for a hermit's life that they permitted them at times to go begging in the town, and thus they became an object of pity to many; may God reward their kindness. They wished to leave this unfriendly region during the coming spring, but there were no flags of truce there, such as used to go from here to Halifax with prisoners. They therefore resolved to let themselves be transported to France along with other prisoners. They did arrive there but both of them were stricken with fever, which proved fatal. The Prior, when he felt his end approaching, was received as a member of an order of monks of the Roman Church which is the more credible as he had always entertained a particular esteem for friars. They gave him the tonsure and afterwards called him *Bon Chrètien*. Soon thereafter both brothers departed this life."[35]

Sangmeister's Description of the Captivity

The following is the news which I heard from the lips of John Schilling and which I wrote down about the Eckerlin brothers and their capture in the Alleghenies.

After the mentioned brethren had lived in the Allegheny Mountains for some time and had been warned by both devout and worldly people to leave there, God allowed a party of Cherokee Indians to come to them, which scared them very much. Yet, since they were on the side of the English, they did them no harm, but robbed them as they left. Now this should have served as a warning to them, but they did not take it seriously; instead they felt more important, and became more reckless.

After they had lived there about two years it happened about harvest time in 1757, that the servant glimpsed several Indians on the mountains, which he told the brothers at once. They then immediately said that they must be hostile but there was no other alternative except to leave everything up to the will of God or to pray, because they were too few. After they had made this decision there must have been about seven Indians and one Frenchman who came to the house with utmost speed, making a simply terrible noise. They seized the two brothers along with the servant. Then they searched the whole house and whatever they thought worthwhile they took out and loaded it on two horses and the other things that they did not want to take or load up they shot at once. After this they set the house on fire and within two hours everything was in ashes.

They then set out on their trip again toward Fort Duquesne. However, they took a long detour out of fear that the English might be following them and overtake them. They were thus seven days on the journey. The two brothers received little to eat during this time and were bound. As the captors immediately chose the servant [Schilling] to take the place of an Indian who had been shot, he was unbound and given more to eat than the two brothers. When he secretly gave the brothers some of his food, the Indians were angry with him. The brothers were able to gather from these events that the Indians did not have very good intentions toward them. They were therefore both very sorrowful and spoke little with each other. They did ask the servant to forgive them, for they acknowledged that they were the cause of his being captured. . . .

After they had arrived on the seventh day at the above-mentioned fort on this side of the river, the Indians demanded of the brothers that they should cut off their beards, but they would not do it. Then all of their clothes were stripped off except their shirts and trousers and he [Schilling] was taken in a canoe to lead the two brothers. When they were several steps from land, they were both thrown into the water. When they crawled to land as best they could there was a quarrel among the Frenchmen as some did not want them to be beaten whereas others favored it. Finally the latter won and the French then began, along with the Indians, to beat them with pieces of wood and with stones. One Indian stepped forward with a club and struck Brother Israel on the head so that he fell to the ground as if dead. Brother Gabriel tried to lift him up and the Indian did the same thing to him. After they had recovered themselves a bit and stood up they were knocked down again. This happened six or seven times. In the midst of this misery they gradually came to the top of a small hill close to the fort. An Indian took his knife and leaped on Brother Gabriel and slashed a piece of flesh with beard adhering from his cheek. After Gabriel had recovered a bit from the shock, he asked the above-mentioned servant who had done that? He pointed the perpetrator out to him, but the latter immediately threatened that he would do worse if Gabriel were not content.

Hereupon the head officers came quickly from the fort and ordered that they be freed since they had already been treated miserably enough. They were then led into the fort. In the meantime the servant was led by an Indian to the fort and was not harmed. Then the Indians sold the two brothers to the French for a new rug and a pair of leggings each. The servant, however, was taken by the Indians to the area where they lived with their nation.

After the two brothers had come under French authority, they were spoken to through interpreters. The French began then to gain a different impression of them, considered them religious men and clothed them in white. The servant remained with them for only two days in the fort and then he was taken away again by the Indians. He was with the Indians for three years and several months, and then finally escaped. . . .

The remaining news which we have received of the brothers is this that they were sent from the fort to Montreal and from there to

Quebec, where they suffered great dearth and hunger in a hospital. From there they went to Rochelle in old France with two other prisoners. Some have it that they died at sea, others, that they died in France in a hospital in great misery. We were able to learn nothing further about them.[36]

Philadelphia, November 5, 1764

[Samuel Eckerlin to Benjamin Franklin]
Esteemed Friend:

My brethren Israel and Gabriel Eckerlin were taken by the French and Indians from the Aligany [sic] Mountains in the month of August, 1757, and some time after went to Rochelle in France, where I am informed they died in the hospital. [I] shall esteem it a particular favour if you will enquire whether my information be true or not.

Please to let me know by a few lines directed to me to be left at Thomas Say's in Philadelphia, the result of your enquiry. All charges that may accrue thereon shall be thankfully repaid by

your affectionate friend,
Samuel Eckerlin.[37]

To Benjamin Franklin.

A Late Reference to the Eckerlins

A letter of April 19, 1788, from Brother Obed [Lewis Höcker] at Ephrata to Alexander Mack, Jr., concerning the settlement of Samuel Eckerlin's estate, contains some interesting detail.

. . . Israel and Gabriel were (as you know) captured by the Indians; their house and property were burned. Samuel had property which he disposed of in his will. . . . He left the land in Virginia to Ezechiel [Sangmeister] and also willing something to the two brothers. . . . The reason why the Eckerlins were considered such wealthy people was that they had claimed a large district of land in the area where Israel and Gabriel lived at the last. After the war, though, others took possession of it.[38]

II. Congregations

5. Colonial Congregations

The strains and stresses of the division between the mainline Brethren and the Ephrata movement or the dangers and hardships of the frontier make up only a part of the early history of the Brethren in America. In less dramatic, but in more lasting, manner, a steady establishment of congregations in the several colonies (with the exception of New York and New England) took place. An anonymous writer in an 1810 edition (first English translation) of Mack's *Rights and Ordinances* and *Basic Questions* provides a thumbnail account of the process of Brethren expansion from the Germantown origins:

> In the year 1729, a number of the society emigrated from different parts of Germany and Holland to North America, where persecuted virtue found an asylum under the government of William Penn. The emigrants settled first at Germantown, a small village about six miles north from Philadelphia, where they soon formed themselves into a society, which through the kind providence of God continues unto this day, not withstanding re-

peated removals into different parts of the continent, where societies have since been formed, namely, in the interior of this state,
in New Jersey, in Maryland, Virginia, North Carolina, Kentucky,
and in the state of Ohio, where instead of the fathers are the
children, who are risen up as their successors to bear witness to
the truth of those principles, in which many of their predecessors
lived joyfully and died triumphantly.[1]

For a more nearly complete description of the congregations it is
necessary to turn to a Baptist writer of the latter part of the eighteenth
century. An authority on American letters said of his efforts: "A noteworthy example of the true historic spirit then at work among us — at
work after the right method even when expressing itself in the crudest
form. . . . "[2] No other contemporary source, with the possible exception
of the *Ephrata Chronicle,* provides such a mine of information on the
Brethren in colonial America as does Morgan Edwards' multivolume
*Materials Toward a History of the American Baptists both British and
German* (1770ff.). Here are found detailed accounts of the early histories of Brethren congregations, brief biographies of leading churchmen,
and data on names and numbers of members around 1770.

The Baptist pastor and writer Edwards (1722-1795) noted three motives for his lengthy travels and researches on Baptist groups from New
England to Georgia: he wanted, first, "to know the American Baptists";
second, "to make them known one to another"; and third, in what he
called a "grand motive," to bring them "together and to settle some
useful means of intercourse and familiarity between their churches,
whereof there are on this continent about three hundred including the
German Baptists."

As a historian, rather than in his capacity as a churchman, he was
further concerned to "preserve some anecdotes, chronologies, and facts
which otherwise would have perished with the loose papers from which
many were taken, or with the death of ancient people who communicated
[other details] from memory." The fact that he understood believer's baptism to be a root principle of Christianity enabled him to include in his
accounts the Brethren and the Mennonites, although he noted those beliefs which these groups held which were not shared by Baptists.[3]

Because of Edwards' unfamiliarity with the German language, many
of the names of families are given an English spelling. It was thought
better to leave the names as given by the author, because of the possibility
of error in substituting the likely German originals.

MORGAN EDWARDS
ON PENNSYLVANIA CONGREGATIONS

Treats of the Germans in Pennsylvania who are commonly called "Tunkers," to distinguish them from the Mennonists; for both are styled "Die Täufer" or "Baptists."

They are called *Tunkers* in derision which is as much as to say *Sops,* from *tunken,* to "put a morsel into sauce;" but as the term signifies *Dippers* they may rest content with the nick-name, since it is the fate of Baptists in all countries to bear some cross or other. They are also called *Tumblers,* from the manner in which they perform baptism, which is by putting the party's head forward under water (while kneeling) so as to resemble the motion of the body in the action of tumbling. The Germans sound the letters *t* and *b* like *d* and *p*; hence the words *Tunkers* and *Tumblers* have been corruptly written *Dunkers* and *Dumplers.*

The first appearing of these people in America was in the fall of the year 1719 when about twenty families landed in Philadelphia, and dispersed themselves, some to Germantown, some to Skippeck, some to Oley, some to Connestogo and elsewhere. This dispersion incapacitated them to meet for public worship; and therefore they soon began to grow lukewarm in religion. But in the year 1722 Messieurs Baker, Gantz, Gomery and the Trautzs visited their scattered brethren which was attended with a great revival, in so much that societies were formed wherever a number of families were within reach one of another. But this lasted not above three years.

They settled on their lees again, till about thirty families more of their persecuted brethren arrived in the fall of the year 1729, which both quickened them again and increased their number every where. These two companies had been members of one and the same church, which originated at Schwardzenau in the year 1708. The first constituents were Alexander Mack and wife, John Kipin and wife, George Grevy, Andreas Bhoney, Lucas Fetter and Joanna Nethigeim. These had been Presbyterians, except Kipin who was a Lutheran; and, being neighbours, they consorted together to read the Bible, and edify one another in the way they had been brought up; for as yet they did not know that there were any Baptists in the world. However, believer's baptism and a congregational church soon gained upon them, in so much that they were determined to obey the gospel in these matters.

They desired Alexander Mack to baptize them; but he deeming himself in reality unbaptized, refused, upon which they cast lots to find who should be administrator. On whom the lot fell has been carefully concealed. However, baptized they were in the River Eder by Schwardzenau; and then formed themselves into a church; choosing Alexander Mack to be their minister. They increased fast; and began to spread their branches to Merienborn and Epstein, having John Naass and Christian Levy to their ministers in those places. But persecution quickly drove them from there, some to Holland, and some to Creyfelt.

Soon after the mother church voluntarily removed from Schwardzenau to Serustervin in Frizland, and from there migrated towards America in 1719. And in 1729 those of Creyfelt and Holland followed their brethren. Thus we see that all the Tunker churches in America sprang from the church of Schwardzenau in Germany; that that church began in 1708 with only seven souls, and that in a place where no Baptists had been . . . nor any now are. In sixty-two years that "little one is become a thousand, and that small one a great nation."

It is very hard to give a true account of the principles of these Tunkers as they have not published any system or creed, except what two individuals have put forth; which have not been publicly avowed. However, I may assert the following things concerning them from my own knowledge. They are *General Baptists* in the sense which that phrase bears in Great Britain; but not *Arians* nor *Socinians,* as most of their brethren in Holland are. General redemption they certainly hold; and, withall, general salvation; which tenets though wrong are consistent. They use great plainness of language and dress, like the Quakers; and like them will neither swear nor fight. They will not go to law; nor take interest for the money they lend. They commonly wear their beards; and keep the first day sabbath, except one congregation. They have the Lord's supper with its ancient attendents of *love-feasts, washing feet, kiss of charity, and right hand of fellowship.* They anoint the sick with oil for recovery; and use the *trine immersion* with *laying on of hands* and prayer, even while the person baptized is in the water; which may easily be done as the party kneels down to be baptized; and continues in that posture till both prayer and imposition of hands be performed. But though their baptism be well contrived for trine immersion, yet it loses the resemblance of a *burial*.

Their church government and discipline are the same with those of the English Baptists; except that every brother is allowed to stand up in the congregation to speak in a way of exhortation and expounding; and when by these means they find a man eminent for *knowledge* and *aptness* to teach, they choose him to be a minister, and ordain him with imposition of hands, attended with fasting and prayer and giving the right hand of fellowship. They also have *deacons;* and ancient widows for *deaconesses;* and *exhorters;* who are licenced to use their gifts statedly. They pay not their ministers unless it be in a way of presents, though they admit their right to pay; neither do the ministers assert the right, esteeming it *more blessed to give than to receive.* Their acquaintance with the Bible is admirable. In a word, they are meet and pious Christians; and have justly acquired the character of the *Harmless Tunkers.* Of these there are, in Pennsylvania, several congregations. Here follow some accounts of them, and of their preachers. Those in other provinces shall be spoken of hereafter. The first society of this people is that at

Beggarstown.

This takes its distinction from a little village of the above name, in the township of Germantown, eight miles NW from the city. The meeting house is of stone, thirty feet square, erected this year, on a lot of eighty rods, the gift of one Peter Shilbert. On the same lot stands their old building erected by one John Pettikoffer for his dwelling house in 1731; and because it was the first house in the place, and erected by a beggar, the village assumed the name of Beggarstown.[4] The families . . . are about thirty, whereof fifty-seven*) persons are baptized and in the communion of the church. This was their state in 1770.

---

*) Alexander Mack, *minist*[er] with his wife and daughter, Christopher Sower *exh*[orter] with his wife and son, Margaret Boyer *deac*[oness], George Shriber and wife, Henry Slingluff and two daughters, Philip Weaver and wife, Peter Lybert and wife, John Slingluff and wife, Henry Slingluff, Anthony Snyder and wife, Richard Roob, Michael Keyser, Peter Keyser and wife, Jacob Bowman and wife, Justus Fox and wife, John Kime, Conrad Good, Conrad Stamm and wife, Hannah Stamm, Mary Baker, Sarah Baker, Susannah Baker, Eve Fith, Elizabeth Boyer, Mary Bossert, Margaret Hertzback, Magdalen Mellinger, Elizabeth Roob, Christian de Lashet and wife, William Spyra and wife, Nathaniel Shryber, Katherine Shryber, Henry Sharpneck and wife, Mary Nyse, Rudolph Harly and wife, Mary Fend, Sybella Ent.

For their beginning we have no further back to look than December 25, 1723, when the following persons (some baptized in Germany and some in this country) formed themselves into a society, having Mr. Peter Baker [Becker] to their minister; and had the Lord's supper and love feast, etc., for the first time; and the first time they were celebrated by them in the province. Their names were Mr. Peter Baker, Henrick Traut, Henry Holzapfel, Johannes Gomery, Jeremiah Traut, Balser Traut, Stephen Koch, John Preis, John Kempfer, Magdalina Traut, Ann Gomery, Maria Hildebrand, and Joanna Gans. From this final beginning with sixteen persons they have in forty-seven years increased to the number of fifty-seven. No other remarkable event had happened in this congregation. The minister they first had was

Rev. Peter Baker

He was born in 1687 at Dilsheim in Germany. Educated a Presbyterian. Embraced the principles of the Baptists in 1714. Arrived in this country in 1719. Settled with the church of Beggarstown in 1723. Went to Skippek in 1747 where he died and was buried March 19, 1758. He married Dorothy Partman by whom he had two daughters, Mary and Elizabeth who married into the Heerly and Stump families and have raised him fifteen grand children. Whatever his real character was, yet this may be said of him, he laboured more abundantly than all his contemporaries.[5] His successor who had been also his colleague was

Rev. Alexander Mack

He was born in the year 1680 at Schrisheim in Germany. Was educated a Calvinist. Embraced the Baptist principles in 1708. Arrived to this country with many of his congregation in 1729, and became a minister of Beggarstown the same year. Died in 1735 and was buried at Germantown. He married Anna Margareta Kling by whom he had children, Valentine, John, Alexander (now minister of Beggarstown) who married into the Hildebrand, Sneider and Nise families and have raised him many grand children. His fourth child was Anna, now a single sister at Ephrata. Mr. Mack was a man of real piety. He had a handsome patrimony at Schrisheim, with a profitable mill and vineyards thereon, but spent all in raising and maintaining his church at Schwardzenau whereof he was father, and the father of all the Tunkers.[6] His successor is his own son

Rev. Alexander Mack

He was born at Schwardzenau, January 28, 1712. Baptized in 1728. Arrived to America in 1729. Ordained in 1749, at which time he took on him the care of the church. He married Elizabeth Nise, by whom he has children, William, Sarah, Hannah, Lydia, Elizabeth, Margaret. Mr. Mack is a sincere good man.[7] Assistant to him is

Rev. Christopher Sower

He was born, September 26, 1721, at Lasphe in Witgeinstein. Bred a Presbyterian. Came to this country in 1724. Baptized in 1737. Ordained June 10, 1753. He married Catherine Sharpneck by whom he has children, Christopher, Daniel, Peter, Catherine, Esther, David, Samuel.[8] The next church to this is

Greatswamp

This society is distinguished by the above name, which is the name of a tract of land called the Great Swamp. The meeting is kept at the house of Mr. John Frick in Upper Milford township, in the county of Bucks, about forty miles NW from Philadelphia. The families belonging to the society are about twenty whereof twenty-eight*) persons are baptized. Thus stood things with them in 1770.

---

*) John Frick *exhor*[ter] and wife, Lawrence Erboch and wife, Andrew Meinzinger, John Demud and wife, John Sleifer and wife, Henry Kun, Philip Goodman and wife, Philip Deal, Frederick Deal, John Redroch and wife, Egite Christian and wife, Lodowick Christian and wife, Jacob Staut and wife, Mary Christian, Widow Rinker, Catherine Rinker, Widow Olinger, Widow Crayling, Freny Triffel.

Their beginning was in this manner. In the year 1733 one Salome Miller and Joseph Miller her brother, John Brech and wife, Peter Longanacre and Peter Rhode were baptized by Mr. John Naass. In 1735 were baptized, by Mr. Peter Baker and Mr. Martin Urner, one Hanse Zuk and wife, John Sleifer, and John Frick and wife; and the same time had the Lord's supper administered to them by Mr. Peter Baker. This was the period of their existence as a society; and eleven their number. They have existed for thirty-five years without any remarkable event, except that Count Zinzendorf took away some of them in the year 1752 [1742]. At first they were visited by ministers from other parts, and increased fast. Several of the Mennonists joined them. But since that time the increase has been inconsiderable. The first settled minister they had was

Rev. Abraham Duboy

He was born in 1679 at Epstein in Germany. Bred a Presbyterian. Embraced the principles of the Baptists in 1712. Came to America in 1728. Settled at Perkiomen; and from thence went to the Great Swamp in 1738, where he died and was buried March 21, 1748.[9] Since that time Mr. John Frick hath preached to them; but is not ordained. The next church is

Coventry

This takes its distinction from the township where most of the members reside, in the county of Chester, thirty-seven miles NWhW from Philadelphia. Coventry is on the banks of Schuylkill, opposite to Potsgrove. These people have no public place of worship, but hold their meetings in a kind of rotation at five private houses. The present minister is Mr. Martin Urner, who has to his assistant Mr. Peter Reinhart. The families belonging to them are about twenty-two, whereof forty*) persons are baptized. This was their state in 1770.

---

*) Martin Urner *minist*[er] and wife, Peter Reinhart *exhor*[ter], Owen Reinhart, Henry Dasker and wife, Nicholas Harwick and wife, Abraham Grub and wife, Christian Monsieur, Barbara Miller, Barbara Welty, Frederick Reinhart and wife, Barbara Urner, Elizabeth Ingles, Catherine Grumbacker, Catherine Boch, John Eiker, Jacob Pfauts and wife, Abraham Boch, Andrew Woolf, Esther Switser, Wendle Danfelser, Henry Bear and wife, Jacob Sweitser and wife, Maud Reinharth, Jacob Light and wife, Philip Waggoner and wife, Elizabeth Holderman, Anthony Bernard and daughter, John Light and wife.

For their original [*sic*] we must look back to 1724 when one Daniel Eiker and wife, Henry Landis and wife, Peter Heffly, Martin Urner, Owen Langanacre and Andrew Sell (who had been baptized before) did unite to celebrate the Lord's supper and to walk together in love, having Rev. Peter Baker to their assistance. They increased fast, and would now be a very large society had not so many families gone away to Virginia, Carolina and other parts. The first minister they had was

Rev. Peter [Martin] Urner

He was born in Alsace about the year 1695, and was bred a Presbyterian. He came to America in 1715. Embraced the principles of the Baptists in 1722. Was ordained by Rev. Alexander Mack in 1729, at which time he took on him the oversight of the church. He died in 1755 and was buried in the grave yard at Coventry. His wife was Catherine Reist by whom he had children Mary, Martin, Jacob.

These married into the Woolf, Edis and Light families.[10] Assistant to Mr. Urner was one Casper Ingles. The next and present minister is

Rev. Martin Urner

He is nephew to the fore-mentioned Martin Urner. Was born in 1725 in New Hanover township and county of Philadelphia. Ordained in 1756, at which time he took on him the care of the congregation. His assistant is Mr. Peter Reinharth. Mr. Urner married Barbara Sweitser by whom he has children Mary, Joseph, Martin, Elizabeth.[11] The next society is

Ephrata [see pages 112-116]

Oley

This society takes its distinction from the township where most of the people reside, in the county of Berks, fifty-four miles NW from Philadelphia. The present preachers are Mess[rs]. Martin Gaby and Jacob Joder, but not ordained. The families belonging to the place are about twelve whereof twenty*) persons are baptized. This is their present state.

---

*) Martin Gaby exhor[ter] and wife, John Joder exhor[ter] and wife, Conrad Price and wife, David Price and wife, David Kinsey and wife, Jacob Baker and wife, Christian Kinsey and wife, Peter Kleine, Liss Ellis, Margaret Harpine, Catherine Plank, Daniel Kleine and wife.

They had their beginnings about 1732 when one Ritters, Shilbert, Blansh, and others did unite for communion of saints, having Peter Baker to their assistance. Since this time they have had no ordained minister, but are visited by Rev. George Kleine. This church is much reduced by reason of removals of families to other parts, particularly to Conecocheague in 1743.

Cocolico

This society is distinguished by the above name which is the name of a little river near to which the people reside, in Cocolico township and county of Lancaster, sixty miles WNWhW from Philadelphia. The minister is Rev. Jacob Sonday, who has Mr. John Landis to his assistance. Mr. Sonday was born in Germany in 1700. Came to this country in 1733. Was ordained in 1763, at which time he took on him the oversight of the church. He married Mary Landis by whom he has one son.[12] The families belonging to the society are about fifty-three whereof eighty-six*) persons are baptized. This is their present state.

*) Rev. Jacob Sonday and wife, John Landis, *exhor*[ter] and wife, John Rosh and wife, Peter Eychelberger and wife, Michael Frantz and wife, Henry Mohler and wife, Peter Reyer and wife, Tobias Miller and wife, Christopher Becker and wife, Elizabeth Lessley, Catherine Harlacher, Ann Mohler, Magdalene Millenger, Daniel Ballinger and wife, Daniel Reyer and wife, John Reyer and wife, Martin Meyer and wife, Jeremiah Woolf and wife, George Schwarts and wife, Jacob Landis and wife, David Landis, Christopher Westenberger and wife, Jacob Sponhauer and wife, Christopher Widder and wife, Jacob Knodel and wife, Salome Harlacher, Barbara Frantz, Catherine Reyer, Margaret Landis, Barbara Steiner, Barbara Schob, Henry Schneider and wife, Daniel Hollinger and wife, Christopher Reyer and wife, John Meyer and wife, Samuel Good and wife, Eva Sychrist, Jeremiah Woolf, Jr. and wife, Jonas Joner and wife, Jacob Heller and wife, Mrs. Histant, Mrs. Moser, Mrs. Behr, Christian Haas and wife, Jacob Harnly and wife, Magdalene Landis, Mary Frantz, Magdalene Bellenger, Mary Koch, Barbara Koch, Henry Schneider, Jr., and wife, Susannah Landis, Catherine Landis.

They originated about the year 1735 when the following persons separated from the church of Ephrata and became a distinct society, viz. Michael Pffauts, Rant Woolf, John Frantz, Emick Reyer, George Reyer, John Landis, Samuel Good, Henry Sneider, Philip Rouland and others, having Rev. Peter Baker to their assistance. — The first minister they had was Rev. Michael Frantz, a native of Switzerland. He was ordained in 1734 and the next year took on him the oversight of the church. He died in 1748 and was buried at Cocolico.[13] After his death Rev. Michael Pffautz and others preached to them until their present minister was ordained.

White Oak Land

This society is distinguished as above from a tract of land so called, in the parish of Warwick, Lancaster County, seventy-five miles WbN from Philadelphia, and two miles from Letitz. They hold their meeting at private houses. The minister is Rev. Christian Langanacre, who was born November 11, 1732 in Raffo Township. Ordained May 15, 1769 at which time he took on him the care of the church. He married Margaret Geib by whom he has six children. The families . . . are about thirty-nine, whereof sixty-five*) persons are baptized. . . .

*) Rev. Christian Langanacre and wife, John Zug and wife, John Langanacre and wife, Christian Zug and wife, John Pffautz and wife, Henry Kuensing, Jacob Kuensing and wife, Christian Krabiel and wife, Jacob Zug and wife, Widow Huber, Catherine Bitner, Elizabeth Rein, Abraham Flohry and wife, Conrad Gingle, George Mohler and wife, Elizabeth Huft, Martin Schuh and wife, Jacob Hershy and wife,

Andrew Eby and wife, Henry Giebel and wife, Barbara Eby and four daughters, Henry Eter and wife, Elizabeth Langanacre, Henry Langanacre and wife, Ulrick Langanacre, John Hackman and wife, Henry Stohler and wife, John Lautermilch and wife, George Kleine and wife, Catherine Gish, John Frantz and wife, Ann Huber, Fronica ...., Catherine Reyer, Salome Borghart, Mrs. Kratzer, Conrad Hausser and wife, and George Stohler and wife.

They began in this manner. About the year 1729 one George Reyer, John Langanacre and others came from Germany and settled in this neighborhood. After them came several more from other places who in the year 1736 united together and had the Lord's supper administered to them by Rev. Michael Pffautz. He was their first minister but lived at Cocolico. He married Catherine Schlauch by whom he had four children. Was ordained in the year 1735. Died May 21, 1769 leaving behind him a good character.[14]

Great Swataro

This church is so distinguished from a river near to which the people dwell; and sometimes by the name of *East Conewago* which is another river that runs through the neighbourhood. The meeting is held chiefly at private houses in the township of Mountjoy, county of Lancaster, twenty miles from Lancaster and eighty-six miles WbN from Philadelphia. Their preachers are Mess[rs]. George Miller and Adam Hammaker, but not ordained. The families belonging to the congregation are about twenty whereof thirty-nine*) persons are baptized. This is their present state.

*) George Miller *exhor*[ter] and wife and daughter, Adam Hammacker *exhor*[ter] and wife and daughter, Peter Ertzstone and wife, Philip Roemer and wife, John Buck and wife, John Eter and wife, Jacob Metsegar and wife, Henry Thomas and wife, Christopher Branser and wife, Margaret Thomas, Philip Reicker and wife, Peter Bersh and wife, Henry Stohner and wife, Jacob Eter and wife, George Balshbach and wife, George Henry and wife, Barbara Henry, Freny Cass.

They began in this manner. In the year 1752 the said George Miller embraced the principles of the Baptists, and soon after, his wife. Others removed hither from White Oak Land, and in the year 1756 united into a society, having Rev. Michael Pffauts to their assistance. He continued to visit them while he lived; and after him, others. They purpose soon to ordain Mr. Miller to be their minister.

Little Swataro

This church also takes its distinction from a river of the above name, in the township of Tulpehokon and county of Berks, twenty-five miles from Reading and eighty-one miles NWbW from Philadelphia. Some of the people live in Bether Township in Lancaster County. They hold their worship in private houses. Their preacher is Mr. Peter Heckman, but he is not ordained. The families belonging to the society are about nineteen whereof forty-five*) persons are baptized. This is their present state.

*) Peter Heckman, *exhor*[ter] and wife, Jacob Heckman and wife, Michael Frantz and wife, Nicholas Gerst and wife, Jacob Moyer and wife, George Beasher, David Marge and wife, Simon Menich and wife, John Frantz and wife, Christian Frantz and wife, Rose Shnables, Jacob Smith and wife, Liss Kentzel, Adam Henrich, Mrs. Cyder, Philip Zeigler and wife, Jacob Breneisen and wife, David Kleine and wife, Widow Benedict, Elizabeth Benedict, Sophy Kish, Leonard Sebalt and wife, John Grove, Jacob Baker and wife, John Deal and wife, Hans Stohler and wife, Jacob Beshor and wife.

Their beginning was in this manner. About the year 1745 one George Besher settled in this neighbourhood, and one Michael Frantz, Peter Heckman, John Frantz, and others. These were baptized by Rev. George Kleine, and in 1757 coalesced into a church having the said Kleine to their assistance. He has ministered the Lord's supper to them ever since; but they purpose soon to ordain Mr. Peter Heckman.

Northkill

This little society is distinguished as above from a small river called Northkill, in the townships of Tulpehokon and Bern, county of Berks, fifteen miles from Reading and seventy-one miles NWbW from Philadelphia. The minister is Rev. George Kleine. He was born at Zweinbrecken in Germany, October 9, 1715. Came to America in 1738. Was baptized in 1739 by Mr. Naas of Amwell in the Jersey. Ordained in 1757 by Rev. Michael Pffautz and Martin Urner. He married Dorothy Repman by whom he has seven children.[15] The families belonging to them are seven, whereof eleven*) persons are baptized and in fellowship. This is their present state.

*) Rev. George Kleine and wife, Valentine Lang, Elizabeth Reiler, Elizabeth Stump, Sarah Solenberger, John Stohner and wife, Mary Stohner, Susanna Mackley, Elizabeth Brandel.

They began to be a church about the year 1748 when one John Stump and sister, Frederick Moyer and wife, with a few more, had the Lord's supper administered to them by the Rev. Michael Pffautz.

About two years after, their present minister settled among them. The society was reduced to its now low estate, by the removal of families to other parts.

Codorus

This society is distinguished as above from a river, that is called Codorus, in a township of the same name in the county of York, eleven miles from the town of York, and ninety-nine miles WhS from Philadelphia. The preacher is Mr. Henry Neff, but he is not ordained. The families belonging to the place are about twenty whereof thirty-five*) persons are baptized and members of the church. This is their present state.

---

*) Henry Neff *exhor*[ter] and wife, Jacob Tilman and wife and daughter, Jacob Spitler and wife and two daughters, Peter Brilharth and wife, Jacob Neiswanger and wife, Ann Neiswanger, Catherine Beightley, Elizabeth Leip, George Beary and wife, John Harold and wife, Rudy Yunt and wife, William Spitler and wife, Christian Eby and wife, Wendel Baker and wife, Michael Berkey and wife, George Ettor and son, Mathias Sitler and wife, Susanna Weltner.

They began to be a church about the year 1758 when one Rudy Yunt, Peter Brilharth, John Brilharth and others, united for communion of saints, having Rev. Jacob Tanner to their assistance. This Tanner left them to go to Monocasy; since, they have been supplied from other places. Mr. Neff will soon be ordained.

Little Conewago

This society is so distinguished from a branch of the river Conewago near to which the people made their settlements, in the township of Hanover and county of York, twenty miles from the town of York and 107 miles WhS from Philadelphia. The preachers are Mess[rs]. Jacob Moyer and James Henrick, but are not ordained. The families belonging to the place are about forty, whereof fifty-two*) persons are baptized.

---

*) Jacob Moyer, *exhor*[ter] and wife, James Henrick, *exhor*[ter] and wife, Hans Adam Sneider and wife, Barbara Sneider, George Wine and wife, John Geiny, Daniel Woods and wife, Henry Geiny and wife, Joseph Moyer and wife, Nicholas Housteter and wife, Christian Housteter, Rudy Brown and wife, Mrs. Moyer, Stephen Peter, wife and daughter, Maud Powser, George Peter, Henry Tanner and wife, Michael Tanner and wife, John Moyer and wife, Jacob Souder and wife, Henry Hoeff and wife, Hesther Weise, Christian Etor, John Peter Weaver, Barbara Bear, John Swarts and wife, Liss Bearing, Great Hymen.

Their beginning was in 1738 when one Eldrick, Dierdorff, Bigler, Gripe, Studsman and others united into a church, having Rev. Daniel Leatherman to their assistance. He left them and went to Monocasy. After him they had Rev. Nicholas Martin who also quitted them to go to Conecocheague, of both [of] which we shall speak when we come to the Baptists in Maryland. Their successors are the present ministers, before mentioned.

Conewago

This society also takes its distinction from a river of the above name near to which the people reside, in the township of Reading, county of York, fourteen miles from the town of York and 101 miles W from Philadelphia. Their preacher is Mr. George Brown, who is not ordained. The families are about forty-five whereof seventy-seven*) persons are baptized.

---

*) George Brown, *exhor*[ter], and wife, Peter Werds, John Heiner and wife, Peter Fox and wife, Anthony Dierdorff and wife, John Dierdorff and wife, Nicholas Moyer and wife, Manass Bruch and wife, Michael Basserman and wife, David Erhard and wife, Ann Mummard, Daniel Baker and wife, Abraham Stauffer and wife, Henry Dierdorff and wife, John Burckholter and wife, Christian Fray, Andrew Trimmer and wife, Ustace Reinsel and wife, Samuel Arnold, Peter Dierdorff and wife, Barnet Achenbach and wife, Mary Latzcho, Catherine Studybaker, John Neagley and wife, Michael Brissel and wife, Velte Brissel and wife, Mathias Bonser and wife and daughter, Laurence Bakener and wife, Nicholas Bakener, Philip Snell and wife, Nicholas Bakener, Jr. and wife, Adam Sower and wife and two daughters, Adam Dick and wife, Marilis Baker, Henry Brissel and wife, David Brissel and wife, Sarah Brissel, Henry Raudibush and wife, George Waggoner and wife, Jacob Miller, Mrs. Martsh, Rudolph Brown, George Reesop and wife.

Their beginning as a society, was in the year 1741 when John Neagley, Adam Sower, Jacob Sweigard, Peter Neiper, Joseph Latzcho, etc., did unite for communion of saints, having to their assistance Rev. George Adam Martin, of whom more hereafter. Next to him were Rev. Daniel Leatherman and Nicholas Martin, of whom we shall speak when we come to Maryland.

Bermudian

This society also is distinguished by the above name of a little river, in the township of Warrington and county of York, fifteen miles from the town of York and 102 miles WhN from Philadelphia. Most of these people observe the seventh day of the week for sabbath, and are to be considered as the offspring of [the] Ephrata church. Their preacher is Mr. Henry Lowman, who is not ordained. The families are about forty, whereof fifty-eight*) persons are baptized.

*) Henry Lowman, *exhor*[ter] and wife, Frederick Reuter wife and daughter, Daniel Fahnstick and wife, Peter Henry, wife and mother, Diertick Fahnstick and wife, Paul Traub and wife, Sebastian Shalles and wife, John Cook and wife and son, Peter Bender and wife, Melchior Webber and wife, John Bence wife and daughter and four sons, ... Frick, John Lehn and wife, John Messerbach and wife, John Miller, wife and two sons, George Reiss, George Neiss and wife, Benjamin Gebel and wife, Philip Gebel, Peter Beussel wife and son and daughter, Philip Beussel and wife, Belzar Smith and wife, Adam Weyley and wife, Mrs. Dorothy, ... Stauffer, Elizabeth Foltz.

They began to be a church in 1758 when Philip Gebel, Peter Beissel, Henry Lowman and others united for communion of saints, having Rev. Conrad Beissel to their assistance. Afterwards Rev. Mess[rs]. Peter Miller and George Adam Martin and others officiated among them.

Stony Creek

This is also denominated from a little river of the above name, in the township of Bruederthal (alias Brotherstown) in the county of Bedford, thirty miles from Bedford and 245 miles WhN from Philadelphia. The minister is Rev. George Adam Martin of whom mention has been made before. He was born near Landstuhl in Germany in the year 1751. Was bred a Presbyterian. Embraced the principles of the Baptists in 1737, and was ordained by Peter Baker in 1739. Afterwards he resided at Little Conewago where some misunderstanding arose between him and the people and occasioned him to remove to Antitum. In the year 1762 he adopted the sentiments of the Seventh Day Baptists, and preached at Bermudian. From there he went to Stonycreek this year. He married one of the Knippers and has many children.[16] The families belonging to the place are twelve whereof seventeen persons are baptized and may be considered as the constituents of the church, viz. Rev. George Adam Martin and wife, Henry Roth and wife and daughter, Henry Roth, Jr., and wife, George Newmoyer, Philip Oswald and wife and daughter, Abraham Gebel and wife, Philip Kimmel and wife, Mr. Widdebarger and wife. This church also is the offspring of Ephrata where (for the most part) the seventh-day sabbath is kept.

Thus we see that there are in this province fifteen churches of

Tunker-Baptists; to which appertain eight ordained ministers, and thirteen exhorters or probationers, and four meeting houses; the reason of their having no more places of worship is that they choose rather to meet *from house to house* in imitation of the primitive Christians. We see also that their families are about 419, which contain about 2095 souls (allowing five to a family); whereof 763 persons are baptized and in communion. There are more Tunkers about Conecocheague, Antitum, etc., but they border on Maryland and belong to churches in that province.[17]

MORGAN EDWARDS ON THE NEW JERSEY CONGREGATION

Treats of the Tunker Baptists[18]

The word *Tunker* in German, and the word *Baptists* in Greek, and the word *Dippers* in English, are exactly of the same significance. The Germans sound the letter *T* soft, like the *D*: hence these Baptists are called *Dunkers.* Had Dr. Douglas attended to this, he would not say that they should be called *Dunkards.* The first appearance of these people in America was in the fall of 1719, when twenty families arrived in Philadelphia. In 1722 about ten families more arrived. In 1729, other thirty families arrived at the same place, which was the last division of the *Tunker* church which originated with eight souls at Schwartdzenau in Germany, in 1708. (See my account of them in Vol. I, p. 64; or in Morse, under the word *Tunker,* where the same account is transcribed.)[19]

Among the last division were Rev. John Naas, Anthony Deerdorf, Jacob More, Rudolph Harley, and John Peter Laushe. These five persons, and their families, crossed the Delaware in 1733, and settled at Amwell, in Hunterdon County, about thirty-eight miles NbEhE from Philadelphia. The present number of families is twenty-eight; whereof forty-six persons are baptized and in the communion, here administered at no set time; but as often as a brother finds himself disposed to give the feast of charity, then the church is invited to meet at his house (for they have no meeting house): and when washing feet is over, and the right hand of fellowship and kiss of charity is given, the Lord's supper is administered, with the usual elements and singing of hymns.

Remarkables

[1] It is the only Tunker church in the Jersey, and the only church which statedly uses the eight Christian rites. In Pennsylvania there are fifteen Tunker churches; in Maryland seven, and in the more southern states ten. (2) Their church government was purely republican, as I observed in my first volume, but in Maryland (and I suppose in other states) they have a superintendent, whose name is Daniel Leatherman. To him is referred the decision of variances among the ministers, or between the ministers and the people; and as the Tunkers call all their ordained ministers *bishops,* it follows that Leatherman holds the rank of *archbishop.* (3) The Tunker church in Jersey has existed for fifty-seven years, and has increased from five to forty-six.

Ministry

The first minister was Rev. John Naas. He was born in Germany, and emigrated here with the last division of the church of Schwartdzenau. I am sorry I could not come at more of this good man's history (for these people keep no records) and all his contemporaries are dead.[20] His successor was Rev. John Bechleshammer, who had one Gideon Rouser to his assistant. Some of Bechleshammer's children are alive; but for want of understanding their Dutch, and they my English, nothing could be done in a way of history. His successors in the ministry, but not in the episcopate, are Mess[rs]. William Housel and Abraham Laushe. The first was born at Neuvitt in Germany in 1728; the other in 1732 at Crayfelt in the Prussian dominion. The first has a wife, but no issue; the other's wife is Margaret Bechleshammer, by whom he has children John, Henry, Jacob, Abraham, Ann, and Margaret. The above is the present state of the Tunker church at Amwell, February 2, 1790.

MORGAN EDWARDS ON MARYLAND CONGREGATIONS

Treats of the Tunker-Baptists in Maryland[21]

These with respect to faith and order, are the same with their brethren in Pennsylvania, from which they originated; and therefore the account which we have given (Vol. I, p. 64) of them will serve for our account of these. Here follows a short view of their present state.

Connecocheague

So distinguished from the river near to which the people reside, in Frederick County, fifty-four miles NW from Anapolis, and 120 SW from Philadelphia. The families about forty whereof 130 baptized and in communion. The minister is Rev. Nicholas Martin,[22] who has to his assistants Mess[rs]. John Titer and Stephen Waller. They had their beginnings as a society in 1743. The next is

Monocacy

So distinguished from the neighboring river, in Frederick County, eighty miles NW from Anapolis and 130 SW from Philadelphia. The families about twenty-nine, whereof seventy-nine persons are baptized. The minister is Rev. Daniel Leathermann,[23] who has John Carver to his assistant. They originated as a society in 1749 by means of ———— Albach who removed here from Jersey. The next is

Middle Creek

So called from a brook which runs into Monocacy between the mountains, in Frederick County ninety-two miles NW from Anapolis, and 142 SW from Philadelphia. The families about forty, whereof eighty-two persons are baptized. The minister is Mr. Jacob Tanner[24] who has Anthony Hartman to his assistant. These originated as a church about 1747. The next is

Antitam

So called from a creek of the same name in Frederick County, 120 miles NW from Anapolis and 130 SW from Philadelphia. The families about forty, whereof ninety-one persons are baptized. The minister, Rev. William Stober.[25] They originated in 1750. The next is

Piper Creek

In Frederick County, seventy-five miles NW from Anapolis and 120 miles SW from Philadelphia. The families about thirty-five whereof seventy persons are baptized. The minister is Wollery Grumbacker,[26] but not ordained. They originated in 1751. It is to be remarked that there is no meeting house in any of these places; they preferring to assemble in each other's private dwellings in imitation of primitive Christians.

MORGAN EDWARDS ON VIRGINIA CONGREGATIONS

Treats of the Tunkers in Virginia[27]

The account which we gave of the Tunkers in Pennsylvania (Vol. I, p. 64) serves for the history of them in Virginia, as far as faith and order are concerned. They emigrated here (some from said Pennsylvania and some from Maryland), about the year 1752, and settled on the water of *Shandore* [Shenandoah], and have increased to about thirty-six families, whereof thirty-six persons are baptized. Their ministers are Rev. Jos. Creyfelt, Joh. Chiefly, [and] Christopher Guss.[28] Some of them keep the seventh day sabbath by means of their connection with the Tunkers of Ephrata. These have also been much harassed by reason of their militia law and their scrupling to take an oath.

MORGAN EDWARDS ON NORTH CAROLINA CONGREGATIONS

Treats of the Tunker-Baptists in the Province of North Carolina[29]

These are the same with their brethren in Pennsylvania with respect to faith and order, and therefore we need not repeat what has been said in Vol. I, p. 64. In this province there are three societies; one at

Catawba

the north branch of Peedee, —— miles WbS from Newburn and —— SW from Philadelphia. The families about forty whereof thirty persons are baptized. The minister Samuel Saunder,[30] another at

Yadkin on the Atkin

the same branch of Peedee further from the forks, —— miles SbW from Newburn, and —— SW from Philadelphia. The ministers Hans and Conrad Kearn.[31] The families about twenty-nine whereof forty persons are baptized. The third at

Ewarry

one of the waters of the north branch of Peedee, —— miles from Newburn, and —— SW from Philadelphia. The minister Jacob Studeman.[32] The families about nineteen whereof thirty persons are baptized. These all came to the province about thirty years ago [1742] having Rev. Dan[iel] Leatherman at their head.

MORGAN EDWARDS ON
SOUTH CAROLINA CONGREGATIONS

Treats of the Tunker-Baptists in South Carolina[33]

These (with respect to faith and order) are the same with their brethren in Pennsylvania, of which a large account has been given in our first volume. . . . There are three societies of them in South Carolina. The first is that at

Beaver Creek

which is a little brook running into Broad River on the north side on the edge of Craven County, about 180 miles SSW from Charlestown and 759 miles SW from Philadelphia. They hold their worship from house to house. The families about twenty-five whereof fifty persons are baptized. They had their beginning in this manner. About the year 1748, Michael Millers, Jacob Canomore, Lawrence Free, with their wives, arrived here from Connecocheague; after them came Rev. George Martin and wife, and Hans Waggoner and wife. These united in communion in the month of July, 1759, and increased fast. Their minister is

Rev. David Martin

He was born October 8, 1737, at Connestoga. Came to this country in 1754. Ordained September 28, 1770 by Rev. Messrs. Daniel Leatherman and Nicholas Martin. He married Ann Lessley by whom he has children, Esther, Catherine, David. He bears an excellent character, and has John Pearson to his assistant.[34] Mr. Martin has the happy cast of mind that he is facetious and devout at the same time.[35] The next society is that at

Clouds Creek

A small brook running into Edesto River, near to which the people are settled, in Berkeley County, 109 miles NW from Charlestown, and 862 SSW from Philadelphia. No meeting house. No minister except James Warren who exhorts among them. The families about thirty whereof forty-two persons are baptized. They had their beginning as a society in 1768 when Mr. Martin administered the Lord's supper to Snowden Kirkland and wife with some others. Soon afterwards the Seventh-Day Baptists in the neighborhood joined them with such as

Mr. Martin baptized. All this society is English, some keeping the first day and some the seventh for Sabbath. The next is

Edesto

So distinguished from the river about which the people have settled, in Osangebury parish and county of Berkeley, one hundred miles SW from Charlestown, and 885 miles SSW from Philadelphia. No meeting house. The families eight, whereof sixteen persons are baptized. Their preacher is Elijah Patchet, but not ordained. They began in this manner. In the month of January, 1770, Rev. David Martin preached in these parts, and baptized the said Patchet and wife and mother of two of their negroes; also Mrs. Taylor and her sons; the father (Mr. Thomas Taylor) joined them. These, the fourteenth of the same month, were formed into a church, and all are English, some keeping the first day and some the seventh for Sabbath. . . .

Thus we see that there are in the province (1) three churches of the Tunker-Baptists. (2) eighty-two communicants. (3) sixty-three families which contain about 315 souls. (4) one minister, and two exhorters. (5) no meeting houses.

GEORGIA

Although Morgan Edwards does not mention any Brethren congregations in Georgia in his compilation of Baptist churches there, there is some evidence of Brethren activity there in the colonial period. A letter in 1737 to Moravians in Germany from recent immigrants to Pennsylvania in describing the various German groups mentions the "Tumplers" or Brethren, "who have here and in Georgia several congregations where more is to be found than with the others." It is known that several of the early colonizing attempts in Georgia failed because of the climate and the poor soil. Perhaps something similar occurred with the early Brethren settlement.[36]

6. Germantown

"The name of Germantown has a universal charm and interest to all those who have any knowledge of or taste for the historical accounts of the settlement of Pennsylvania," asserted George N. Falkenstein, in devoting a chapter of his study of the Church of the Brethren to the Germantown congregation.[1] For the thousands of German immigrants to the American colonies, whether of the "plain" or "church" people, Germantown held the same significance that Plymouth or Massachusetts Bay held for the English settlers.

"Mother Church" is a term often used to designate the Germantown Brethren congregation, although there are those who point out that greater growth and more influence have come from other early meetings. Yet, Germantown holds priority of place and time, and much attention has rightly been accorded its early history.[2]

The beginnings of the Brethren in America coincide with the beginnings of Germantown, and have already been related. Also noted was the exodus of many of the leading members from Germantown in the latter part of the 1730's as they followed the siren call of Christian perfection at Ephrata. Shaken for a time, the congregation slowly recovered its poise and outreach, and flourished in the second half of the century. Two men bearing the names of prominent fathers — Alexander Mack, Jr., and Christopher Sauer II — rose to prominence themselves, and led the Germantown congregation in its religious, intellectual, and charitable life.

Problems there were, and some record has been preserved of the manner in which the congregation set about to solve them in faithful obedience to Christ's commandments as they understood them. Other records relate the baptism of new members and the observances of church ordinances, which give a more nearly complete portrait of a Brethren congregation during the colonial and early national periods than is otherwise available.

THE GERMANTOWN MEETINGHOUSE

Typical of many local traditions about the establishment of a place of

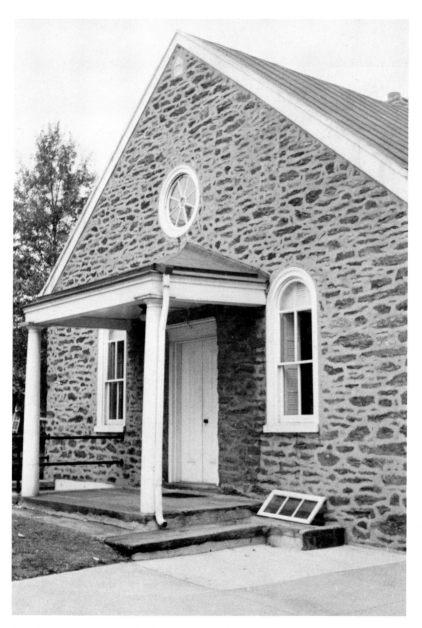

The Germantown meetinghouse erected in 1770.

A fragment of a document dealing with the Germantown congregation. The text reads: ". . . to be helpful in establishing residence with her children.

Sander Mack	Justus Fuchs	John Weber
Peter Leibert	Peter Keiser	Peter Keiser, Jr.
Carl Hobs	Michael Keiser	Gerhard Clemens

Signed in the name of the Brotherhood of Baptists in Germantown on September 10, 1797."

meeting for the congregation at Germantown is the following excerpt from the pen of Benjamin Lehman. In 1824 Lehman copied the careful survey of Germantown prepared by his grandfather Christian Lehman (d. 1774), early surveyor and scribe, adding historical notations about personalities and institutions of the town. Although Lehman's account is defective in many particulars, it does preserve local lore of interest. Lehman may be following the lead of Morgan Edwards (see page 175) in his reference to "Beggarstown" and the origin of the name.[3]

Traditional Account

In 1719 the Dunkards from Germany and Holland migrated to Pennsylvania and settled first at Germantown. Their first collected meetings were held in the log house in front of their present stone church in Beggar's Town. Alexander Mack, Sen., was then their principal religious leader who was a very rich miller in Cresheim and gave all his property in common and came with eight or ten to Germantown in 1708. He died old, and his son Alexander Mack lived to be ninety-one years of age (died 1803). The aforesaid log house was built in 1731 by John Pettikoffer for his dwelling, who procured his funds by asking gifts therefor from the inhabitants. Because it was the first house in the place and procured by begging, it was therefore called Beggar's Town. The stone church on the same premises was built in 1770. Alexander Mack succeeded his father as a minister, and Peter Baker had been their minister as early as 1723. The Rev. Morgan Edwards' history of the Babtists [*sic*] in Penn[sylvani]a confirms several of the above facts and so does the *Ephrata Chronicle*.

The original Dunkers here, from Ephrata, used to dress all alike and without hats and covered their heads with the hoods of their cloaks, which were a kind of grey surtout, like [that of] the Dominican Friars, also girt about the waist and bare-footed or with sandals. Old persons now living [1824] remember when forty or fifty of them would come thus attired on a religious visit (from Ephrata near Lancaster).[4]

GERMANTOWN DEEDS

In Falkenstein's history of the Germantown congregation is a sharp attack on the tradition noted by Edwards and Lehman, which was also followed by Brumbaugh in his standard history.[5] Instead, the former demonstrated from the actual land records that there exists a complete pedigree of transferral of title from Peter Shoemaker, one of the very earliest landholders in Germantown. Because of the clarification of this record, and because of interesting sidelights on the congregation, excerpts from the deeds and indentures are here included.

Shoemaker transferred ownership in 1731 to John Pettikoffer, having previously disposed of a parcel of land contiguous to it to the south to John Mack. In 1739 Mack acquired with Andrew Boni the Pettikoffer lot. Following Boni's death (1741) Mack sold the property to Peter Schilpert, who decided to give the land to the Germantown congregation. He died before carrying this out, but in 1760 the transfer was made to four trustees of the congregation — Alexander Mack, Jr., Christopher Sauer II, Peter Leibert, and George Schreiber. These men executed a declaration of trust establishing the conditions for the trusteeship.

It was on this land that in 1770 the first meetinghouse of the Brethren was constructed, a well-proportioned structure which still stands in good, albeit changed, condition. In 1783 the church through its trustees entered into an agreement with Philip Weber, one of the members of the church, for a friendly exchange of property for mutual advantage.

Shoemaker Issues Indenture to Pettikoffer

This indenture made the fourth day of August in the year of our Lord, 1731, between Peter Shoemaker of Germantown in the county of Philadelphia in the province of Pennsylvania, turner, and Margrett his wife of the one part, and John Pettenkoven [Pettikoffer] of Germantown aforesaid, stocking-knitter, of the other part, witnesseth that the said Peter Shoemaker and Margret his wife, for and in consideration of the sum of five pounds and five shillings lawful money of Pennsylvania to them in hand paid by the said John Pettenkoven, the receipt whereof they do hereby acknowledge and thereof do fully acquit and forever discharge the said John Pettenkoven, his heirs and assigns by these presents have granted, bargained, sold, aliened, enfeoffed, released and confirmed and by these present do grant, bargain, sell, alien, enfeoff, release and confirm unto the said John Pettenkoven (in his actual possession now being by virtue of one Indenture of Bargain and Sale to him thereof made by them the said Peter Shoemaker and Margret his wife for one whole year bearing date the day before the date hereof and by force of the statute made for transfering uses into possession) and to his heirs and assigns a certain piece parcel of land situate lying and being in the adjacent side-land of the said Germantown be-

ginning at a stone by the north east side of the highway leading from
the said Germantown to North Wales being also a corner of John
Mock's land thence by the same and other land north east forty perches
to a post set for a corner, thence north west two perches eight foot, and
three inches to a post set for a corner, thence by the said Peter Shoemaker his land south west forty perches to a stone set for a corner by the
said highway and by the said highway south fifteen degrees east two
perches eight foot and five inches to the place of beginning, containing a
half acre and twenty perches of land, together with all and singular the
buildings, woods, fowlings, hawkings, huntings, rights, liberties, privileges, improvements and profits thereof to have and to hold the said
piece or parcel of land, hereditaments and premises hereby granted and
released or mentioned so to be with their appurtenances unto the said
John Pettenkoven, his heirs and assigns to the only proper use and be-
hoof of him and said John Pettenkoven, his heirs and assigns forever.[6]

Mack and Schilbert Deed Issued
    This indenture made the twentieth day of July in the year of our
Lord, 1742, between John Mack of Germantown and the county of
Philadelphia, stocking-weaver, and Margrett his wife of the one part,
and Peter Shilbert of Germantown aforesaid, yeoman of the other part,
whereas an indenture made the twenty-second day of August, 1739, between John Petenkoven of Germantown aforesaid, stocking-knitter and
Ann Elizabeth his wife of the one part, and the said John Mack and
one Andreas Bonney [Boni] of the other part, the said John Petenkoven
and Ann Elizabeth his wife, for the consideration therein mentioned,
and grant release and confirm unto the said John Mack and Andreas
Bonney a certain messuage or tenement and piece or parcel of land
thereunto belonging situate in the adjacent side land of Germantown
aforesaid containing by computation half an acre and twenty perches
of land, to hold the one full equal and undivided moiety thereof unto
the said John Mack his heirs and assigns forever and to hold the other
full equal and undivided moiety thereof unto the said Andreas Bonney,
his heirs and assigns forever, under the yearly rent of one half-penny
lawful money of Pennsylvania payable to Peter Shoemaker, his heirs
and assigns as in and by the said recited indenture, relation thereunto
had appears; and whereas the said Andreas Bonney did make his last
will and testament in writing bearing date on or about the sixth day of

October 1741 and therein and thereby devised in these words or to the
effect following viz.: And I leave unto the said John Mack and to his
heirs forever the house and lot whereon I now dwell (being the same
messuage) for the consideration of twenty-nine pounds, ten shillings
money of Pennsylvania with full powers to keep or sell the same at his
pleasure, and if the same John Mack should sell the same house and lot
to any person or persons I give him full power and authority to sign,
seal and deliver deed or deeds of sale to the purchaser for the same according to law, as in and by the same last will and testament duly
proved and entered in the Register General's office at Philadelphia, relation thereunto had appears now this indenture witnesseth that the said
John Mack and Margrett his wife for and in consideration of the sum
of seventy-three pounds lawful money of Pennsylvania to them in hand
paid by said Peter Shilbert have granted, bargained, sold, released, and
confirmed, and by these present do grant, bargain, sell, release, and confirm unto the said Peter Shilbert . . . and to his heirs and assigns,
etc. . . . [7]

Schilbert Property Deeded to Congregation

. . . And whereas the said Peter Shilbert dying (in effect) intestate
possessed of the said messuage and three pieces of land and premises
(he having made only a non-occupative will) the right of the inheritance of his said possessions depending legally unto Johanna Hoech,
the wife of Bastian Hoech, which Johanna being the only issue and
heir of Abraham Shilbert who was the brother and heir at law of the
said Peter Shilbert and the said Bastian Hoech and Johanna his wife in
and by a certain deed, roll or writing under their hands and seals
bearing date the twenty-sixth day of August A. D., 1746, did for the
consideration therein mentioned (among other lands of which the said
Peter Shilbert died possessed of), grant, and convey the said messuage
and three pieces of land (by the name of the little place and house near
Germantown) unto the said Theobald Endt and Henry Slingloff in
fee, now this indenture witnesseth that the said Theobald Endt and
Henry Slingloff, for and in consideration of the sum of ten pound [sic]
lawful money of Pennsylvania to them in hand paid by the said
Alexander Mack, Christopher Sower, Peter Leibert, and George
Schreiber the receipt whereof is hereby acknowledged, have granted,
bargained, sold, released, and confirmed and by these presents do grant,

bargain, sell, release, and confirm unto the said Alexander Mack, Christopher Sower, Peter Leibert and George Schreiber and to their heirs and assigns the said messuage and above described three pieces or parcels of land thereunto belonging, etc. . . . [8]

Trustees Execute a Declaration of Trust

In the opening part of this declaration, Alexander Mack, Christopher Sauer, Peter Leibert and George Schreiber formally acknowledge having received the property from Theobald Endt and Henry Slingloff; and then the important document continues as follows:

Now know ye that the said Alexander Mack, Christopher Sower, Peter Leibert, and George Schreiber do hereby acknowledge and declare that the said messuage or tenement and three pieces of land or ground was so as aforesaid granted unto them in trust nevertheless by the direction and at the appointment of the persons who are members of the Religious Society or Community of the people called Dutch [*i.e.,* German] Baptists and belonging to the meeting of that people in or near Germantown aforesaid to the intent only that they the said Alexander Mack, Christopher Sower, Peter Leibert and George Schreiber and such or so many of them as shall be and continue in unity and religious fellowship with the said people and remain members of said meeting whereunto they do now belong, shall stand and be seized of the said messuage or tenement three pieces or parcels of land or ground and premises so conveyed to them as before recited to the use and intents hereinafter mentioned and declared and under the conditions and restrictions hereinafter limited and restricted and to no other use or purpose whatsoever, that is to say, one room in the said messuage to be made use of for a meeting place of the said people living at or near Germantown aforesaid and for such other as the said community may think proper to admit thereto the which room may be improved or enlarged for the better convenience of the said meeting at the discretion of the said community in such manner as they may think and one room and kitchen of the said messuage to be made use of for a dwelling place for some widow woman of the said society or community to live in rent-free, and that the said society or community shall and do keep the said messuage or tenement and pieces or parcels of land or ground in repair from time to time towards the charge of which they are to have the use, rents, issues and profits which may accrue or arise

yearly from the remaining part of the premises, provided always nevertheless that if it should so happen that a regular society and community
of the said people should cease to be kept up at and near Germantown
and that they should decline holding up their said meeting, that then
and in such case it shall and may be lawful for the said Alexander
Mack, Christopher Sower, Peter Leibert and George Schreiber, or the
survivors or survivor of them in the said trust to sell and dispose of the
said messuage or tenement three pieces or parcels of land or ground and
premises and to make and execute a fee simple deed of conveyance for
the same to the purchaser, and the money arising by such sale to distribute (chiefly or mostly) to and among the poor belonging to the
said society in or near Germantown aforesaid (not exempting the poor
of other societies from some part thereof) and to be assisted in making
the said distribution by and with the advice and consent of the elders
and other discreet persons of the same society holding community and
keeping a regular meeting at the next or nearest place to Germantown
aforesaid, to which meeting the accounts of such distribution shall be
made and submitted; provided also that neither the said Alexander
Mack, Christopher Sower, Peter Leibert and George Schreiber nor any
of them, nor any person or persons succeeding them in this trust who
shall be declared by the members of the said society for the time being
to be out of unity or church fellowship with them shall be capable to
execute this trust or stand seized thereof to the uses aforesaid, nor have
any right or interest in the premises or any part thereof whilst they or
any of them shall so remain, but that in all such cases as also when any
of them or others succeeding them in the trust aforesaid shall happen to depart this life then it shall and may be lawful to and for the
said members as often as occasion shall require to make choice of others
to manage the said trust and to execute the same instead of those or
such as shall so fall away and be out of unity with the said people
called Dutch Baptists or depart this life, etc. . . . [9]

Congregational Exchange With Weber

Germantown, September 2, 1783

Agreement of Exchange

It is hereby made known and set forth to any one who reads this
or hears it read an agreement and exchange hereby attested between
Alexander Mack, Christopher Saur, and Peter Leibert as trustees on

the one side, and Philip Weber on the other: the congregation of the
Baptists [*Tauffs-gesinnte*] in Germantown has agreed to give a letter
of assurance to Brother Philip Weber and his heirs in reference to the
free passage in and out between his house and the piece of land belonging to the meeting house through the legacy of the deceased Brother
Peter Schilbert and through the further conveyance of his two executors. Said free passage in and out (between his house and between
the wall which was made in the place of a riding block) he has enjoyed
with common consent for some years, because half of the said passage
does belong to the land which is his property. As the other half, however, is part of the land belonging to the congregation, he and his heirs
have demanded a letter of assurance from the congregation in case of
possible changes.

In return he promises the congregation free passage in and out by
horse and cart between his stable and the building which was designated
as a widow's residence by the before-mentioned Brother Peter Schilbert
and his executors, so that wood may be brought without hindrance by
horse and wagon to the door of the meeting house. To this end he
promises to move back the wall of his stable far enough and to sign
over to the congregation as much land as the congregation signed
over to him as described above so that it will be a fair exchange. He
has also volunteered to have a piece of wall erected at his own expense
next to his entrance for the convenience of both parties.

This document is meant to state that the congregation completely
agrees to this exchange and herewith attests such for him and his heirs.
If after he has moved the wall of his stable according to his promise
for the free passage in and out of the congregation and feels that he
needs a more complete document according to the laws of this country
regarding this exchange, such shall also be signed for him in the name
of the congregation, provided it is in compliance with this document
and done at his own cost or the cost of his heirs. For future assurance
that this document shall be honored as an agreement and exchange
properly transacted between both sides, both parties have signed their
own names and sealed it with their own seals, in the name of the
congregation of the Baptists of Germantown.

Philip Weber   Alexander Mack   Christopher Saur   Peter Leibert
Signed in the presence of us,
Justus Fox   Henry Sharpnack   Christian v. Laaschet[10]

CHURCH DISCIPLINE

Concern for the diligent observance of high ethical standards was essential for the early Brethren. How this worked out in actual life is seen in the cases of those involved in real estate problems, moral lapse, commercial activity found not to be consistent with the Brethren doctrinal position, and involvement with slavery. The impression is given of firm but brotherly action designed to correct the errors, while conserving the unity of the Brotherhood. Great respect for individual personality was paired with keen criticism of dubious action and improper attitude.

The pattern set forth in the eighteenth chapter of the gospel according to Matthew was taken as the appropriate procedure for solving problems that came up within the Brotherhood. Important matters could finally be brought before the combined elders of the Brotherhood for final disposition at what became known as "Annual Conference."

Brethren to Brother Schwartz and Brother Peter

Evidence of the way church discipline was exercised can be obtained from the following communication signed by prominent members of the Germantown congregation. Specific steps for the resolution of the difficulty are outlined in the expectation of compliance and restoration of unity. In 1770 George Schwartz and his wife are listed as members of the Conestoga church. The identity of "Brother Peter" is not clear.

December 28, 1758

This day, December 28, 1758, we, the undersigned brethren, have consulted together in the fear of the Lord concerning the unreconciled difficulties between Brother Schwartz and Brother Peter, and have deemed it right and just, that Brother Peter should give to Brother Schwartz in money six pounds ten shillings, because it so happened that Brother Schwartz could not keep his share in the contract about land which they had purchased together, and he had been a party concerned from the beginning. Afterwards it turned out that the advantage of the cheap bargain slipped from his hand, and he had to pay for his field, compared to the other, too dearly, and Brother Peter has not been quite guiltless, as he himself confesses. But in order that we may be satisfied with his acknowledgement, we have laid the above upon him, and give him time for reflection. If he can do it, and will then be at peace and reconciled with us and with Brother Schwartz, all shall be forgotten . . . , and no man shall have a right to remember it again.

Until then we shall give him in hope the [salutation of the] kiss, but cannot break bread [*i.e.,* commune] with him. But if he does as stated above, then we can also break the bread of communion with him, if nothing else should be made manifest that would make him unfit for it. Yet with this proviso, that if it would go too long (before said Peter will do what is laid upon him), we will upon counsel with the church make again inquiry about this matter. On the other hand we have concluded that, if Brother Schwartz will be able to be at peace with us, and make no [further] complaint or demand on Brother Peter concerning those old matters, we will be satisfied with him also.

(Signed) Sander Mack, Lorentz Schweitzer, Christopher Sauer, Henry Slingluff, Philip Weber, Anthony Schneider, George Schreiber, Justus Fuchs, Philip Diehl, Henry Danner, John Steiner[11]

Christopher Adam Böbel to the Germantown Congregation

An unspecified moral lapse seems to be the crux of the problem facing the writer of the following letter. Repentance followed by willingness to accept direction from the church characterizes the brief letter.

January 1, 1763

Dearest brethren, along with the whole congregation:

I cannot help reporting to you my present condition at this opportunity. I admit and confess that I have deeply offended the Divine Majesty, as well as the entire congregation. I have caused the enemies of God to blaspheme because of the evil deed, and I have also been the object of it unceasingly. I was surprised at an evil time, for I did not want to listen at all to the voice of my God. Consequently it has happened to me as it is written in the Psalm: "Be not like a horse or a mule . . . " [32:9].

All the darts of the devil pierced my soul; the chains of hell encircled me. God in the Lord Jesus can indeed make the high mountains level. It would be better to lose all of the favor and glory of the world than to lose the kingdom of God. Oh, this is the way it goes where knowledge does not have a firm foundation! Indeed, it is not possible for the tongue to express what heavy temptations have taken place. Be it as it may, I cannot help it.

May God have mercy on me. I await an answer via Brother

Alexander Mack. I will gladly submit to the counsel of God. Your unworthy brother,

Christopher Adam Böbel

[P.S.] I am willing, with divine assistance, to live my life in quietness, for I am weary of the irregular way of life. I thank God for His long suffering that I was not converted as were Sodom and Gomorrah. I ask God for forgiveness of sins, and the entire congregation, for having offended them. I know of no other righteousness — should there be enough mercy left for me — than that which is in Christ Jesus the crucified who has died for us all. Amen.[12]

The Brethren to Christopher Sauer II

In some accounts of the early publishing activity of the Church of the Brethren, the famous Sauer press is spoken of as if it were the organ of the Brotherhood. That such was not the case is evident from an incident in which kindly but firm pressure was brought to bear by members of the Germantown congregation upon Sauer II and his colleagues for printing doctrinal treatises of another denomination, in this case the *Heidelberg Catechism* of the German Reformed tradition. Again the concern for the preservation of the fellowship is seen in the postscript which reaffirmed the determination to "seek peace," lest "strife and dissension" result.

August —, 1764

In Jesus Christ our only and true Lord and Saviour dearly beloved Brother Christopher Sauer:

The love to the salvation of all of us in Christ causes us many inward afflictions in these dangerous times and days. May the eternally merciful God take loving care of our souls, lest we stray from the true path, lest we take the road to ruin through secret approval of the commandments of men. Our souls are justly prostrated in the dust appealing for divine mercy: "Oh Lord, spare, spare your inheritance, and have mercy on your lost lambs."

Dear brother, it seems to us as if hidden but very strategic powers of the spirit of the world have laid a secret trap for your soul, and seek to catch you in a net by your well-meant printing of catechisms. May God Himself grant your soul strength that you may become young again as an eagle among those who hope in the name of the Lord and place their trust in the Lord of Lords, who can save from death.

Yes, dear brother, may the Lord Jesus Christ make you healthy in faith and in love of your weak fellow-members. May He make your feet like the feet of the hart, that you may flee from all the snares of the Enemy. Oh how happy our soul will be when we arrive with a good conscience at the end of our pilgrimage and hear the blessed and glorious words: "Well done, good and faithful servant; you have been faithful over a little, I will set you over much; enter into the joy of your master" [Matthew 25:21]. And the Lord still calls to us: "Be faithful unto death, and I will give you the crown of life" [Revelation 2:10].

Dear brother, it seems to us that you have already committed an error, or rather have been overtaken by an error, which can happen often before one is aware of it unless one pays close attention to the wonderful and completely perfect example of doctrine. According to our understanding this was already an error that you ever printed a single copy of the *Heidelberg Catechism*. For he who wants to teach the commandment of God must not teach any commandments of men, lest because of the commandments of men all his worshiping of God becomes a vain worship, even your printing business. If it is to honor God, it must not honor man's commandments, for God's commandments and man's commandments do not go together.

Indeed, some time ago we had reason to hope that grace had healed and corrected this error even in the testimony of your conscience. Especially, since you so willingly promised the [church] members not to print the catechism any more. As, however, we now see with regret that the dear Brother Justus Fuchs has also been overtaken along with you by the same error, and that you say you could not promise any longer what you were once so ready to promise, the matter has therefore become very serious and questionable for us. We find ourselves compelled for the sake of our own consciences to lay the matter before both of you dear brethren, for a more considered judgment, hoping to God and His grace that He might awaken your consciences once again in order to consider and, as it were, to say to yourselves: "Whatever are we doing!"

Christ commanded us to teach all nations and then to baptize them. You print that one should baptize young children. Christ said we should not swear at all. You print that one should or could swear an oath upon the name of God and still be blessed. Christ says: "If you love me, you will keep my commandments" [John 14:15]. You print that not even a converted man can keep God's commandments. Christ says: "Not everyone who says to me: 'Lord, Lord,' shall enter the kingdom of heaven, but he who does the will of my Father who is in heaven" [Matthew 7:21]. You print that to him who has never kept any of God's commandments and is still inclined to all that is evil, the merits of Christ shall be imputed as if he had himself fulfilled all obedience, as long as he accepts this with a believing heart.

Dearly beloved brother, the more we consider these things, the more they appear inconsistent to us. Do consider with us that which James says: "But above all, my brethren, do not swear . . . that you may not fall under condemnation" [5:12]. Do consider, what hypocrisy this idolatrous booklet brings with it. It teaches that one may indeed swear in a blessed fashion, although He who alone can save has commanded that one must not swear. What kind of godliness has ever been found in disobedience?

Christ, the eternal truth, calls those hypocrites who annul God's commandments, in order that they may observe their own traditions. Both repentance and baptism are here annuled by this miserable sprinkling of infants. To be true, it is not our purpose to indicate here in particular each instance of hypocrisy which is sown by this booklet as a fertile seed into the hearts of tender youth. Yet we believe that, just as once hypocrisy spread from the prophets in Jerusalem, over the entire land, even hypocrisy spreads from the seed of the commandments of men in Babel and grows and blossoms among the large mass of those who call themselves Christians.

Oh, if we might only separate ourselves from all hypocrisy! You have naturally not received this impression from this booklet, or else you could not possibly have printed it. We wish, however, that neither of you, dear brethren, may have offended his own conscience in this matter. Also, that you might realize with us that you have not even achieved your well-intended purpose in printing this booklet. As far as we have understood from you, Brother Christopher, you cannot give any more important reason [for printing it] than that one should not be an offense to anyone. Actually, if this were the case, it would not be surprising if you [two] considered this catechism a useful book. But oh, how far this is from being true! You have already offended your fellow members by it, and the offense which the rough world has taken is of varying nature. Some say that their catechism must be correct because Sauer prints it. Others say that Sauer will print anything for money.

And oh, how easily we can cause young babes in the truth to take offense when they learn that we are quarreling over the catechism. It is only to peace[making] that we have been called by God and this we must pursue, and holiness, without which no one can see the Lord.

Therefore, do understand, dear brethren, that we do not expect you to make a specific promise of something against your own will, but we do wish that whenever in the future one of you should intend to print the booklet, you would let us know about it in love. This would enable us to call a large council meeting of all the elders in the entire country, in order to learn the opinion of them all on whether we have done well or ill in reminding you of this matter, and whether it is possible for a disciple of Christ to print such a book or not after a reminder such as this one. Furthermore, we have understood from your speaking to us, that you would appreciate knowing whether we could wish you well in your good undertaking to be of use among all kinds of people with your printing business. As far as we are concerned, we wish you well from our hearts, namely that the word of God may dwell richly in your hearts, and in your printing business. As regards the word of the serpent, however, which will have man's commandments honored instead of God's, we also wish you well that the Lord might save you from it and that your printing business might also be cleansed of it. It is written that whatsoever a man sows, that he shall reap. If you will sow good seed with your printing business, your children and your fellow members will wish you well and they can expect a good harvest from it, according to the saying, one sowed, and another reaped.

Thus it is the will of the Lord that our harvest become complete in truth and righteousness, so that both may rejoice together, he who sows and he who reaps.

Written in August, 1764.

Henry Schlingluff, Anthony Schneider, Alexander Mack, Philip Weber, George Schreiber

Note. In consideration of my mortal nature, I testify that although

I still stand with everything in the judgment as expressed above, I did not intend this to mean that I have given or ever will give my consent for the sake of this matter to endorse or call in our name a great meeting, lest we, in our good intention to seek peace, cause strife and dissension.

May 17, 1767   Sander Mack

P.S. That we are united with the sentiments expressed above is herewith testified to by our signatures.

George Schreiber, Philip Weber, Henry Schlingluff
May 17, 1767[13]

Christopher Sauer II to a Brother
The spirit in which the Germantown Dunker publisher took criticism such as the above is indicated in his response to what must have been a similar correction, this time at the hand of John Preisz (Price).

Germantown, December 13, 1775

In Jesus dearly beloved Brother John Preisz:

I greet and kiss you warmly in the spirit of true brotherly love, and report to you briefly (because I have little time) that I have indeed received your dear note. I was very pleased with your frankness and loving concern for me. I wish everyone would take this way and reveal their difficulties, instead of talking behind one's back, as [is] so commonly practiced, which is a destructive plague and has yet to set anybody straight.

You wrote that one should chide no one but rather pray for one's enemies. I agree completely, as with all your other ideas. Also, I concur with all that you mention in your letter about how things should be practiced.

I cannot write at length about it, but would only like to say in brief that I did indeed err in that I did not delete the offensive words in reading the proofs. This happened because I was swamped with business, for it was market day; there were constantly many people here and the one wanted this and the other that. The newspaper deadline was also due and in the confusion the matter was overlooked.

I must, however, tell you that you are mistaken in thinking that this was my work, because it is set within brackets. That is not the

case. It read like this in all the English newspapers, and as I did not
have the time to translate it myself, my son gave Henry Miller's newspaper to the apprentices. He had not deleted the words. Thus the
error happened because of an oversight, and not because of intention.
I cannot say other than that I shall attempt to be more careful another
time. And yet there will always be mistakes because we humans can
do nothing other than make mistakes.

I remain your faithful brother,

Christopher Sauer

To John Preisz in Skippack[14]

THE BRETHREN ON SLAVERY

Unlike the Quakers, many of whose members owned slaves until their
consciences were awakened by such Friends as John Woolman and Anthony Benezet, the Brethren from the first took a strong stand against
the institution of human bondage. In this they were completely in agreement with the strong protest against slaveholding drafted in the Germantown Quaker meeting of 1688 (with its strong Mennonite background),
which has rightly achieved widespread notice as the first public declaration of the evils of slavery in North America.[15]

Christopher Sauer II followed his father in combatting slavery, writing strong editorials in his publications to influence public opinion
against it. In 1761 he attacked the practice in his newspaper, *Pennsylvanische Berichte,* and added editorial comment after an advertisement for
the recovery of a runaway slave which showed his position clearly.

Editorial Statement of Christopher Sauer II

February 15, 1761

It is with the utmost regret that we learn that Germans are to
engage in the nefarious slave traffic. Though they are well paid for
everything they sell, they still begrudge laborers, servants, or maid-
servants their pay. This godless traffic could find, up to the present, no
safe footing in Pennsylvania, owing to the abhorrence the Germans
still have for it. But, for some years now, even some of them have
begun to take part in this great injustice. For, as merchants learn that
these "black goods" find a ready market they engage in it. Thus we
are assured that three ships have been sent from Philadelphia to the
African coast to steal these poor creatures, though this has never hap-

pened before. May God be merciful to our country before its measure
of iniquity is full and the vials of His wrath are poured out upon it![16]

The advertiser had mentioned tattered clothing in describing the
runaway slave.

July 31, 1761

One has to wonder why the Negro was so senseless as to run away
barefoot and wearing old clothes. He should have put on new ones!
If masters often did right and properly to their employees and remembered that they have a Lord in heaven (Col. 4:1), many would
not run away. But money is the root of all evil.[17]

John van Laschet to the Germantown Congregation

John van Laschet, of the Conestoga congregation, erred against the
discipline of the church on slaveholding, which became a matter of concern for Germantown. The Annual Meeting of 1782 spoke out on the
same issue with due deliberation over appropriate forms of freedom
without causing hardship to the former chattel.

June 24, 1775

A warm greeting to the dear and beloved congregation in Germantown.

I wish you peace from God, the Father, from whom all good comes.
I have found that I must make peace with God and therefore wish to
exert every energy to reconcile myself with Christ Jesus, as long as I
remain in this life.

Thus I find myself needing to beg you, all together, brethren and
sisters, in anything where I may have sinned against you or angered
you, be it in words or works, or otherwise in my conduct. I fervently
beg your forgiveness and hope in the future with the help of God to
conduct myself better and more carefully.

As far as I know, the greatest complaint was about a Negro
woman, that I should let her go. That I have done, both her and
her son. She wanted two of her children to be kept until they have
earned some money, lest they become the wards of the township when
they are old or ailing. And now I request you, dear brethren and
sisters, to pray for me that God may forgive me, for I have strayed
from the faith and caused myself great pain. However, through the

The home of Christopher Sauer I and II. It formerly stood on 4645-4653 Germantown Avenue.

An eighteenth-century view of the Germantown market square.

The Indian Creek meetinghouse near Harleysville, Pennsylvania.

help of God I will flee from such and will run after righteousness and faith.

If you wish to take the trouble, send a brief letter to me or to the congregation in Conestoga, that they might know how to conduct themselves toward me. I have not yet been in the congregation in Conestoga. Otherwise, when I go some will receive me as a brother, and some will not know where they stand. Thus I would upset them, until they knew how to treat me.

I commend myself to your corporate prayers. Written by your sincere well-wisher and fellow brother,

John van Lasche[t].

To the dear brethren and congregation in Germantown[18]

Annual Meeting of 1782

Concerning the unchristian negro slave trade, it has been unanimously considered that it cannot be permitted in any way by the church, that a member should or could purchase negroes, or keep them as slaves. But concerning Brother John van L[aschet], who had bought a considerable time ago a negro woman, and the same has given birth already, during that time, to four children by fornication, it is the united and earnest counsel of the brethren that the said Brother L. shall let the old negro woman go free from this time on, and shall tell her that she is free; but if she will not leave him after he has given her liberty, then he may enter with her into a contract for her wages. But this setting free or emancipation shall be done before some brethren, as witnesses of the transaction. Concerning the children, it is also unitedly considered that he is to free the children at the age of twenty-one years, and is to have them schooled and provided with [food], clothing, and bedding during the time, as it is just and proper; and when they are twenty-one years old he is to give them free [new] outfits of clothing. Still it is our sincere desire and counsel that if the old negro woman would not like to go away, he [who was her master] should use all diligence to prevent such unchaste life, and lay it before her earnestly, and if she would be free to give her her manumission, etc.[19]

CONGREGATIONAL RECORDS

Several old records of congregational activity have been preserved at

Germantown which give real insight into the life and actions of this early church group.

Care for the poorer members of the congregation marked the Germantown congregation, which used part of the meetinghouse from the first for the housing of widows. Excerpts from the poor-book indicate the type of care afforded widows and other members of the congregation in need of assistance.

Excerpts From the Poor-Book

£ -s-d

1759, December 3, I distributed a quarter-beef between Margaret Baker and Sophia Fischer. It weighed 68 pounds at 2½ pence a pound 0-14-2

1760, April, when I visited Sister Anna Dorothea, I gave her in money one pair of stockings and wine 0-14-0

Soon afterwards to Sister Margaret in tea, saffran and wine ... 0- 5-0

On July 24, to Sister Margaret in tea 0- 5-0

November, 1760, sent to Sister Margaret, a widow, somewhat more than a half of a quarter-beef and the other part to Sophia Fischer. Together it weighed 70 pounds, at 2½ pence per pound, makes 0-14-7

December 1, 1760, to Widow Bayer 100 pounds of wheat flour at 16 shillings 0-16-0

The same to Sophia Fischer, 100 pounds, of the same 0-16-0

June 15, 1761, paid Bastian Müller for wood for Sophia Fischer 1- 2-6

June 27, transferred to Bro. Henry Landes for Widow Naas to alleviate her weakness 2-19-6

In the month of March, gave Widow Rünckel in cash 1- 0-0

To Sister Bayer 300 pounds of rye flour, at 10 shillings 10 pence per 100 pounds, makes 1-11-6

To Sister Sophia Fischer 100 pounds [of flour] 1-10-6

Also to Sister Sophia in cash 1- 0-0

On July 21, paid Veronica from the Madetschi [Methacton] for caring for Widow Zittels 0-10-0

December 16, took to Sophia Fischer 72 pounds of pork, at 3½ pence a pound, makes 1- 1-0

and to Sister Margaret Bayer 75 pounds of the same pork, makes 1- 8-8

1761, the same winter, one pair of three-ply stockings and one
pair of mittens makes 0- 8-8
One more pair of stockings for her daughter's son 0- 4-0
One more pair of two-ply mittens 0- 2-0
February 5 gave Betty Du[i]ck one pair of three-ply stockings .. 0- 5-0
1760, March 17, paid Peter Leibert for wood for Sophia Fischer 0-10-0
1760, gave to Rudolph Lap for Sister Gundis 1- 8-0
Gave Sister Bayer for the second time .... 1- 0-0[20]

Leibert's List of Germantown Members

A record of baptisms from 1766 to 1797 kept by John Leibert provides invaluable information on those individuals and families who joined
the church in the latter half of the eighteenth century. A somewhat
parallel record from the pen of Alexander Mack, Jr., is drawn upon for
indication of the holding of communions and love feasts.

"A record of the members of the society of German Baptists who
have been baptized into the Church and became members since the
year 1766. This is translation of the German record by J. Leibert"
[note by Abraham H. Cassel].

1766

May 15	Margaret Hertzbach	by Alexander Mack
October 3	Nathaniel Schreiber	d[itt]o
" 17	Henry Schlingluff	do
" "	Catharine Schlingluff	do
" "	Dorothea Fox	do

1767

July 12	Charles Lang	do
August 7	Anna B. van Lashett	do
" "	Elizabeth Schlingluff	do
" 16	Jacob Bowman and	do
" "	Anna Barbary Schlingluff his wife	do

1768

March 27	Christian Schlingluff Jr.	do
September 25	Hannah Stamm	do

1769

May 14	Sarah Baker by A[lexander] M[ack]

July 29	Christopher Saur Jr. A. M.	
September 3	Michael Keyser	do
" "	Sarah Mack	do
" "	Susan Baker	do
October 5	Peter Keyser and	do
" "	Hannah Keyser his wife	do
" "	Henry Sharpneck and	do
" "	Sarah Sharpneck his wife	do
" "	John Schlingluff	do
" "	Conrad Stamm	do
1770	Maria Fendt by A. M.	
	Elizabeth Raab	**do**
1770		
July 8	The Brethren congregated for the first time in their new meeting house in Germantown.	
September 2	John Weaber	by Alexander Mack
" "	William Leiber[t]	do
" "	Derick Keyser and	do
" "	Rachel Keyser his wife	do
" 30	Julius Roberly and	do
" "	Appollonia Roberly his wife	do
1771		
May 19	Thomas Langstroth and	
	Catharine Langstroth his wife	
	Hannah Mack by	do
September 8	Johannes Kaempfer by A. M.	
November 10	Rudolph Harley, Jr. and	do
	Barbara Harley his wife	do
	John Harley and	do
	Margaret Harley his wife	do
	Ulrich Stauffer and	do
	Hannah Stauffer his wife	do
1772		
April 19	Michael Corbitt	by Christopher Sauer
	Garehart Clemens	do
	Gertrude Clemens his wife	do

1773		
January 4	Jacob Landes and	by Christopher Sauer
	Maria Landes his wife	do
	John Preiss	Alexander Mack
20	Phillippina Werner	do

1774		
March 27	Edmond Langstroth	by Christopher Sauer
July 3	Cornelius Neisz	do
	William Heisler	do
	David Meredith	do
	Jacob Raab	do
	George Duke	do
	John Leibert and	do
	Anna Leibert	do
	Susanna Henkle	do
	Conrad Stamm's maid	do
	Hanna Knorr	do
	Lydia Keyser	do
	Catharine Bauman	do
October 16	William Preisz	do
	Susanna Knorr	do
	Edmond Bright and	do
	Elizabeth Bright his wife	do

1774		
May 12	Edward Bright and	C. Sauer
	————— Bright his wife	do
	Ruth Silence	do
	Elizabeth Painter Bowman's wife's sister	do

1781		
April 8	David Sauer and his sister	by Martin Urner
	Esther Sauer	do
	Jacob Seydel	do
	Elizabeth Dettery	do
July 15	George Becker and	by Christopher Sauer
	Catherine Becker, his wife, and	do
	Nancy Becker their daughter	do

Catherine Stamm,
Fred. Stamm's daughter — do

1783

October 20 — Susanna Weaver,
wife of John Weaver — by A. M.
Catherine Keyser,
wife of Michael Keyser — by A. M.
November 6 — Adam Weaber — by Martin Urner
[or Chr. Sauer?]

1784

August 15 — Derick Keyser, and — do
Elizabeth Keyser his wife — do
Susan Weaver, Philip's daughter — do

1785

March 6 — Emanuel Fox, and — Alexander Mack
Margaret Fox his wife — do
Jacob Ziegler — do
Lydia Kulp — do
September 25 — Nicholas Oliver — by Martin Urner
Benjamin Lehman — do
Peter Keyser, Jr. — do

1786

September 14 — Henry Rinker — do
William Keyser, and — do
Barbara Keyser his wife — do
Elizabeth Lehman — do
Mary Heisler — do

1788

September 4 — Charles Hubbs, and — by Martin Urner
Mary Hubbs his wife — do
Catherine Clemens — do
Hannah Keyser,
daughter of Derick Keyser — do

1789

June 1 — Sibilla Duick — by Peter Leibert

	Margaret Duick	do
November 12	George Righter, and	do
	———— Righter his wife	do
November 15	Elizabeth Weaver, John Weaver's wife	do
17	Christian van Lashet and	do
	———— van Lashet his wife	do
	Ann Rose	
	Frederick Haas and	by A. van Lashet
	Widow Righter	by A. van Lashet

1790
| January 8 | Elizabeth Dull | by Peter Leibert |
| | John Clemens | by Peter Leibert |

1792
| May 6 | Elizabeth Pastorius | do |
| | Margaret Gorgas | do |

1793
October 17	Benjamin Gorgas, and	
	Julia Gorgas his wife	
	Thomas Keyser	
	Charles Adams	
	Catherine Wood	
	Sarah Gorgas	by Peter Leibert
20	John Wood	do

1794
| August 14 | Barbara Drukel | do |

1796
October 23	William Tysen and	
	[crossed out in original]	do
	Elizabeth Tysen	do
	William Ziegler	do
	Elizabeth Ziegler	do

1797
| September 12 | John Zellers | by P. Leibert |

1799
| July 28 | Mary Sperry | do |

1800

October 12	Sarah Gorgas	by Jonas Urner
	Sibilla Lehman	do
	Rachel Gorgas	do

1803

August 7	Elizabeth Leibert (John's wife)	
	Hannah Keyser	by Peter Keyser, Jr.
	Catherine Lynd	do
	George Smith and	do
	Susanna Smith his wife	do
	Mary Keyser Peter's wife	do
September 11	James Lynd	do
	Widow Sarets	do
	Eve Carter	do

1805

| July 7 | Hezekiah Huntsman and | do |
| | ———— Huntzman his wife | do[21] |

Excerpts From the Germantown Congregational Diary
by Alexander Mack, Jr.

1769, September 3, three persons were baptized, namely Michael Keyser, Sarah Mack and Susanna Bäcker.

1769, in the month of October, eight persons were baptized namely, Peter Keyser and his wife Hannah Keyser, Henry Sharpnack and his wife Sarah Sharpnack, John Schlingluff, Conrad Stamm, Elizabeth Kolb, and Sister Fend.

1770, September 2 on Elisa Day, four persons were baptized, namely D. Keyser and his wife Rachel Keyser, John Weber and William Leibert.

1770, September 30, Julius Reubey and his wife Apolonia Reubey were baptized.

1785, September 5, three persons were baptized namely, Nicholas Oliver, Benjamin Lehman and Peter Keyser, Jr.

1785, October 16, the [above] three baptized persons were present for the first time at the communal breaking of bread.

1792, August 2, a communal breaking of bread with the Lord's supper once again was held at Germantown after an interval of fourteen months and six days.

1793, December 14, the Lord gave us another blessed love feast here at Germantown along with a communal breaking of bread, after an interval of fifteen months and seventeen days. Eight persons were present who had just recently been baptized.

1794, October 9, the bread of community was broken once again at the Lord's supper, after an interval of ten days less than ten months. Barbara Dänckel was there for the first time.

1795, December 24, once again at the Lord's supper the bread of community was broken at Germantown after an interval of fourteen months and fifteen days.

1797, January 22, once again a love feast and breaking of bread were held at Germantown after an interval of one year and nineteen days.

1797, December 28, once again a love feast and communal breaking of bread were held at Germantown after an interval of eleven months and sixteen days. At this time the young Brother Haas and the young Brother William Ziegler were present for the first time for they had been baptized during this past year.

1799, March 21, once again a love feast and communal breaking of bread were held at Germantown after an interval of an entire year, two months and twenty days.

1800, October 7, the Lord's supper was held with blessing at Germantown. The following week three persons were baptized. There had been no holy breaking of bread for eighteen months in the congregation of the Brethren at Germantown.

1801, November 10, once again the Lord's supper was held in the Brethren congregation at Germantown, at which the bread of the Lord was broken in community for the proclamation and the memory of the death of Jesus Christ, after there had been none at Germantown for one year, one month and eighteen days.[22]

Excerpts from the Congregational Book

Mack also described the organization of the burial ground in the rear of the meetinghouse, made necessary by the many deaths of the virulent epidemic of yellow fever in Philadelphia in 1793. In narrating

the grim incidents accompanying the outbreak, a historian of Germantown noted:

> An incident that tended to divert thought from the distress
> caused by epidemic was a baptism which the Church of the
> Brethren conducted in Wissahickon Creek on October 17 [1793]
> when seven converts were immersed. A great assemblage witnessed
> the ceremony.

The congregational book of the brethren of the meeting of the
Brethren in Germantown.

(Wherein the servants of the congregation propose to write down
the receipts and expenditures of the money for the poor. Also, how
they will account for this annually in the monthly meeting.

However, they are also to have room and liberty to indicate to
good benefit in our monthly meeting various noteworthy happenings
old and new; and finally, with everyone's permission, to record in this
book that which has been found worthy in our monthly meetings.
Written April 29, 1793, by a pilgrim who was born into this world
in the year 1712 on the twenty-eighth of January, has therefore lived
eighty-one years and three months in this mortal state, and is now
expecting at any time his transformation and the release from the body
of this death in order to enter completely into his true fatherland.)

Alexander Mack

In the year 1793 it pleased the almighty God for divine reasons to
visit the city of Philadelphia with a severe and fatal illness (called the
yellow fever), especially in the three months of August, September and
October, in which time many thousands have been taken. Mere observation of the cemeteries in Germantown brought us to the realiza-
tion, as early as the spring before, that they were all so full of the dead
that burial places were becoming very scarce. Inasmuch as the love of
God and neighbor has given us through our late blessed brother Peter
Schilbert a piece of land for the use and benefit of the Brethren congregation (in which he had served for many years as a faithful servant
until his death), upon which after unanimous agreement there was
built a meeting house at the expense of the congregation, which they
indeed carried out alone without any assistance from outside.

Now, upon urgent necessity, they unanimously agreed also to lay
out a burial place there, where from time to time the said congregation

could bury their dead without inconvenience to our neighbors or fellow pilgrims. The burial place is to be fenced in with a good board fence and red-cedar posts.

We therefore hope in love that our dear fellow members in later years will always be concerned to preserve the said burial place in this condition, and never to prohibit a member of the congregation from burying his dead there without cost (unless he desires to give a voluntary contribution towards the upkeep of the burial place).

It has been agreed unanimously to record the names of all the members together with their subscriptions, namely:

	s d
Bro. Sander Mack	10-0
Bro. Emanuel Fox	10-0
Sis. Catherine Schneider	3-9
Bro. Peter Keyser	15-0
Bro. Geret Clementz	15-0
Bro. Justus Fox	10-0
Bro. Michael Keyser	15-0
Bro. Dirck Keyser	10-0
Bro. Christian Laaschet	15-0
Bro. Bauman Jr.	10-0
Bro. William Leibert	7-6
Bro. John Weber	7-6
Bro. Peter Keyser, Jr.	11-3
Bro. Adam Weber	11-3
Bro. William Keyser	10-0
Bro. Benj. Lehman	11-3
Bro. Dirck Keyser	11-3
Bro. Nicholas Oliver	7-6
Bro. Philip Weber	5-0
Bro. Charles Hubbs	3-9
Bro. Daniel Lichte	4-8
Bro. George Reiter	15-0
Bro. Thos. Longstroth	1-00-0
Bro. Peter Leibert	15-0
Bro. Frederick Haas	7-6
Bro. Jacob Ziegler	7-6
Bro. Benj. Gorgas	12-0

In the monthly meeting held on February 13, 1794, the brethren Peter Keyser and Christian Laaschet, deacons of this congregation, turned in their account which was audited by the brethren listed below and found correct. The balance in cash on hand amounts to £27-10-7½. Included in this sum are ten pounds which came as a legacy from the dear deceased Brother Peter Wertz, which money was paid to this congregation by Brother Michael Frantz as executor of the above. This we attest,

Peter Leibert, Justus Fox, Charles Hubbs, Philip Weaver.

Today, that is January 1, 1798, the brethren unanimously agreed that Brother William Leibert as one of the present trustees should supervise the meeting grounds (lots), land as well as residences, and to rent them, to collect the rents and to take care also that the houses and land are kept in good repair, and to pay the costs from the rents which are received. He is always to keep an accurate account of the income and expenses and enter them into this book. Whenever requested he is to present his account from time to time in the customary manner to the congregation.

At the present, the houses are rented, the one in front for six pounds and the one in back for five pounds, yearly.

1798		£ s d
May 28	Bro. Peter Keyser, Sr., turned over to me money received from rents in the sum of	5-17-2
October 6	Rent received from Widow Erb	1-17-6
November 12	Rent from Widow Haas	4-00-0
December 20	Rent in full from Widow Haas	2-00-0[23]

CHRISTOPHER SAUER II: PROMINENT LEADER

By all odds the best known and the most influential member of the congregation was the Germantown publisher, Christopher Sauer (1721-1784).[24] Examples of his stands on controversial issues have already been cited. Of interest here are more personal references to his life in Germantown and responsibilities with the congregation. In his diary are included brief sketches of his life history and that of his family. Though terse, they are informative. Mention is made of his imprisonment as a Tory in the Revolutionary period, which will be dealt with in more detail later.[25]

Sauer was described by contemporaries as being a heavy man (250 pounds), of patriarchal mien, with a long white beard. Like other

Brethren he allowed his beard to grow but shaved his upper lip, because the wearing of a moustache was associated with the military.[26]

Some noteworthy happenings which have occurred during my — Christopher Sauer's — life.

I was born on September 26, 1721, in the town of Laasphe in the county of Wittgenstein, six hours distant from Marburg. I came to Pennsylvania in the fall of 1724, and lived in Germantown until the spring of 1726 and then resided in Lancaster County along Mill Creek until April, 1731, and then moved back once more to Germantown. I was reborn through holy baptism on February 24, 1737.

My father began his printing business in the summer of 1738.

I began my hermitage [*Einsiedler Stand*] in the fall of 1743.

My mother moved in with me in mid-November, 1744. Brother George Schreiber moved in with me on May 18, 1745. My mother resumed my father's housekeeping on June 20, 1745.[27] Brother Philip Weber moved in with me on February 24, 1746.

In May, 1747, the brethren made me overseer of the poor.

On June 1, 1748, I was among the four brethren elected to minister to the congregation.

On June 7, 1748, Sander Mack and I were given the supervision of the congregation, on trial.

On November 3, 1748, I baptized for the first time.

On July 7, 1749, Brother George Schreiber moved out.

On November 24, 1749, Brother Henry Weber moved in with me.

On June 7, 1751, Brother Henry Weber moved out.

On December 14, 1752, my dear mother passed away in the Lord.

On June 10, 1753, Brother Sander Mack, Brother Henry Schlingluff and I were ordained by the laying on of hands.

On September 25, 1758, my dear father passed away in the Lord, aged sixty-four years.

On January 8, 1777, my dear wife Catherine passed away in the Lord, aged forty-one [?] years, nine months.

On October 19, 1777, I moved to Philadelphia.

On May 23, 1778, I went back to Germantown and

On May 24, around ten o'clock in the evening, I was arrested.

On [May] 26, taken to the Provost [Marshal].

On [May] 29, released again.

On [May] 30, arrived at Methacton and

On June 23, returned home.

On July 27, 1778, they began to make lists of my belongings.

On [July] 28, they ordered me out of my house, and

On July 30, I moved with four children into Brother Henry Sharpnack's house.

On April 7, 1780, I moved to Methacton.

On August 9, 1780, I traveled to the Schuylkill, on the 10th with Brother Martin Urner to Little Swatara, and on the 12th, held a meeting there and ordained the following brethren, namely Brother Martin Gaby [Gaube] as elder, and Brother David Kintzey as minister in Oley, and Brother Michael Frantz as elder, and the brethren George Büszhaar and Jacob Mayer as ministers in Little Swatara. On August 15, we confirmed Brother George Müller as elder at Great Swatara and held a meeting. On the 16th at [White Oak] we ordained Brother John Zug as elder under Brother Christian Langenecker. If, however, Brother Langenecker dies, becomes ill, is abroad or moves away, he is to perform the office of elder entirely. With the exception of these circumstances he is to undertake nothing important without the counsel of Brother Langenecker.[28] Held a large meeting there with good attendance. On the 17th held a meeting at Brother ─────────── Royer's. On the 18th, held a meeting at Michael Rank's and on the 19th I arrived home safe and sound. On the 20th held a meeting in Skippack at Brother Kemper's.

On October 20, 1781, my David went to live with Henry Sharpnack.

On December 5, 1781, my Samuel went to live with Brother Peter Reinhart.[29]

.   .   .   .   .

A list of all my children and when they were born.

On April 21, 1751 (Old Style), I married Catherine Scharpnack.

October 12, 1752, my daughter Christiana was born.

On January 27, 1754, my son Christopher was born at half past twelve.

On October 14, 1755, my son Daniel was born at 11:45 in the morning.

On December 17, 1757, my son Samuel was born, and died on December 23.

On January 8, 1759, my son Peter was born at a quarter to seven in the evening.

On February 25, 1761, my daughter Catherine was born at half past four in the morning.

On August 30, 1762, my daughter Esther was born at half past seven in the evening.

On November 6, 1764, my son David was born forty-five minutes after six o'clock in the morning.

On March 20, 1767, my son Samuel was born at half past three in the afternoon.[30]

Christopher Sauer II to Justus Fuchs

Two letters to his friend and publishing colleague Justus Fuchs shed light both on Sauer's printing enterprise, one of the most important in all the colonies, and his concern for his fellows. Fuchs, also called Fox (1736-1805), achieved considerable fame as a master type-founder or typecaster, although his early occupation was making lampblack. His mechanical ingenuity was of considerable aid to his employer, Sauer.[31]

Philadelphia, March 20, 1777

Dear Brother Justus Fuchs:

I greet you along with your dear wife most warmly and wish you both the grace of God and all health and happiness of body and soul. Amen!

The reason for this letter is as follows: After the dear sister, your wife, had left me yesterday, it suddenly occurred to me that in these hard times you would no doubt like to keep your cow and yet you do not have any hay for it. So I thought that my swampland which is leased to Dirck Keyser would be just right for you. You have your two boys who could dig a ditch along the road, and I would show you how to do this in the easiest manner. This way you could get enough hay for more than one cow and your boys could plant potatoes and maize in the field which belongs to it.

Joseph Free or George Schäffer could show you how to direct the water in the most useful way. As for the price, we shall come to an agreement, so that you will not come off on the short end. If you like this suggestion, go at once to Thomas Duick and tell him that he need not come into town. The next time you come into town I will make a proper agreement with you about this, how it could be done in the easiest way, how much timber you should take, etc.

If you are inclined to accept this offer, let me know a day ahead when you want to come into town, so that I might stay home. Otherwise, I might perhaps stroll down to the Schuylkill and you would not find me at home. If you are not interested in this, let me know soon also, so that I shall know what to do.

I remain your loyal brother,

Christopher Sauer.

Justus Fox, Germantown, Pa.[32]

Philadelphia, May 14, 1778

Dear Brother Justus Fuchs:

I greet you sincerely and wish you all health and happiness in body and soul and report to you that a typecaster has come here from Nuremberg as a soldier. However, he is in a very sickly, and, if I am not mistaken, consumptive state.

He seems very willing to reveal all kinds of improvements in his craft. He claims he can melt and make ready eight large crucibles full of stuff in one day. He can make the forms himself, strike matrices and adjust them, make forms for squares and such forms that allow all kinds of title letters to be poured in one form — not only entire words and lines but many lines at the same time, for example, a whole week in a calendar, Sunday, Monday, Tuesday, etc. In brief, he says that he has perfected the art to such a degree that he has met only one man in all of Europe who could match him. As his health is so poor, it might perhaps not be unwise for you to try to talk to him soon.

I greet your dear wife cordially and commend you all to the protection of God and remain your loyal brother,

Christopher Sauer.

Justus Fuchs in Germantown, Pa.[33]

ALEXANDER MACK, JR.: PROMINENT LEADER

While possessing neither the wealth nor the prestige of Christopher Sauer II, Alexander (Sander) Mack, Jr. (1712-1803), in his own way emerges as the leading personality among the Brethren in the later colonial period. After a religiously turbulent young adulthood with his brief association with Ephrata and the Eckerlins on the New River, Mack spent a quiet life at Krefeld near Germantown, earning his bread as a weaver of stockings. The oversight of the Germantown congregation was placed in his hands, and he remained active until an advanced age.[34]

Mack had a definite gift for writing and produced much. Although fragmentary, the collection of his preserved poetry, manuscript prose, and publications is sizable. Some of these will be included in this volume.[35]

An indefatigable letter-writer, Mack it is to whom we owe much of our current knowledge of the inner life of the Brethren of the eighteenth-century period. It is in his letters to others and their correspondence with him that the best insight is gained into Brethren life and thought in colonial America (see chapter seven).

The Brethren recognized Mack's stature and entrusted him with leadership responsibilities in the church. His name is found at the head of most major pronouncements of the time, and he was usually the one who was called on to draft the statements.

In his personal life Mack had perhaps more than his share of problems, especially in relationship with his children. Unfortunate family differences over the estate of his father-in-law darkened his latter years, and caused criticism by non-Brethren. Never financially prosperous, Mack listed several debts, which, however, he was careful to retire before his demise at the age of ninety-one — an event which he predicted almost to the month. His self-composed epitaph is fitting judgment of his worthy life.

Mack's Account Book

Excerpts from the Account Book; account with Christopher Sauer.
1770. Bro. Chr. Sauer lent me 20 shillings
    and again .... 40 shillings

60

On May 1, 1772, Bro. Christopher brought me yarn which I dyed for him

15 lbs of linen yarn, makes	30 shillings
and 8 lbs of cotton	16 shillings
also about 5/4 half blue	1-6
and earlier gave him cotton for	5-6

53-0

On November 28 made Bro. Christopher a pair of three-
ply stockings 6-0
On December 15 a pair for his [son] David 2-6
On December 20 a pair with white insert for his little
Catherine 3-6
"   one pair for his Esther 3-6
"   one pair for his Samuel 2-0
"   one pair for his Nanni 3-6
"   one pair of men's stockings for his servant 4-6

                         25-6
                  above   53-0

                         78-6 = 3-18-6

1773 November, acquired a new loom [for stockings];
Bro. Christopher lent me in order to advance to the
mechanic before the loom was finished 4- 0-0
then made for Bro. Christopher a pair of large
stockings for himself 5-0
a pair for his man servant 4-6
another pair, somewhat smaller 4-0
another pair for his maid servant 4-0

1774, January 8, one pair for the young Bro. Christopher 4-6
one pair for Daniel Sauer 4-6
another pair for his man servant 4-6

                         31-0

1774, October 23, [I] took Bro. Christopher Sauer three
pairs of stockings for his men servants, makes 13-6
December 25, one pair of three-ply [stockings] for himself 6-0

1775, January 12, one pair for the sister [Sauer], his wife 5-0
One pair linen stockings for him, woven from his
own yarn 3-0

June 12, 2 pairs of mittens for his children 3-0
One pair of stockings for his Esther 2-6

                         33-0

from the preceeding page 31-0

$$64-0 = 3-4-0^{36}$$

October 25, 1785, I talked to the dear Brother Gerhard Clemens, my executor, in the presence of my dear wife, and the brother promised me to act according to my will as follows: If the Lord should take me away through my temporal death before I have repaid Brother Keyser the fifteen pounds, my loom (for weaving stockings) is to be sold as soon as possible and otherwise as many "moveables" to pay the fifteen pounds together with the compounded interests (pertaining thereto) for it is my serious intention that this note which I gave him should be properly resolved. The note was already due New Year's Day past, because it should have been paid January 1, 1785. I borrowed the money for my daughter Lydia and gave it to her. As the dear Brother Gerhard Clemens promised me in the presence of my dear wife [to do so], I do hope and believe that it will be done. In addition I must only call to attention that the loom must be offered first to the dear Brother William Duschong according to a promise I gave him, for whatever he wants to pay for it. If he does not want to buy it himself, he will probably advise how it can best be sold.

Sander Mack

Note. On November 1 of this year, 1785, I paid back to the dear Brother Peter Keyser the above-mentioned fifteen pounds, and therefore the above-mentioned is not to be taken into special consideration excepting that which pertains to my loom, namely, that after my death it ought first to be offered to the dear Brother William Duschong as directed above. This is still my intention.

Sander Mack

January 2, 1766, I have here compiled my debts as follows:

To Christopher Sauer .... 10 pounds
" Henry Weber .... 10 ditto
" Betty Ox .... 27 ditto
" Sarah Wister .... 60 ditto, of which is paid 30
" Ulrich Reinhardt .... 30 ditto, of which is paid 10
September 22, 1774, the last of these debts was paid.

Sander Mack[37]

The Death of a Grandchild

The sixth child of Alexander Mack, Jr., was Lydia. Her first husband, Dielman Kolb, died in 1785. She married Jacob Lentz, a baker in Philadelphia, in 1788. The following undated letter tells of the death of Mack's grandchild.

Esteemed Father-in-Law, as well as other esteemed friends:

I must report to you in great sorrow that last evening about ten o'clock the Lord removed our small daughter from this world of misery and took her to Him into eternal rest. He has left us behind here in this miserable world of grief to struggle and strive a bit longer. The Lord has rescued our dear child from this cruel turmoil of the world and led her while still innocent with His loving arms into the eternal joy, after she had lived to be only ten months and ten days. If it is possible that she be buried in a new grave we will make arrangements to leave with the body here tomorrow about one or two o'clock so that we would arrive with the body at the meetinghouse, the Lord willing, about four o'clock. The other arrangements I shall leave to you and hope that you will take steps to let some of the friends know, if they will make the effort to attend.

It might perhaps also be worthwhile for someone to say a few words. It would certainly not be without blessing. I wish, however, to leave it up to others as to who should do it.

There is just this to be said yet. Once, when the child felt better I thought that God would give her to us for a while longer. Therefore I drew a verse in order to see what the Lord had decided about the child. This then came to hand: "The Lord gave, and the Lord has taken away; blessed be the name of the Lord." Thus I contented myself in that the Lord wished to have her back.

This much from me, your sorrowful son-in-law

Jacob Lentz.

This to Alexander Mack, Chestnuthill[38]

Articles of Agreement

1799 the thirteenth of November. (I, Alexander Mack, now aged eighty-seven years, nine months and fifteen days, am writing upon request the following memorandum of a trial agreement between my wife Elizabeth Mack on the one hand and friend Philip Jacobs on the other.) If he consents to farm my land for me for half of the crops in the coming year of 1800, from the first day of April until the first day of April 1801, he shall be welcome to live in the front part of my house facing the street in the room downstairs and the one above, as well as the kitchen in the courtyard where the baking oven is, and also above the kitchen. I will dispose of my livestock and make room for him in the barn, the stables and the spring house. He shall therefore share the whole house with me, with the exception of the room where my husband sleeps and the small room where I sleep, which I desire to reserve for myself.

He shall have half of all the crops which land and garden yield. But he must take everything to market and divide the money with me. The maize, rye, wheat, and buckwheat shall be half mine and half his, and whatever profit he gets from the asparagus, currants, grapes and other garden produce shall be half his and half mine after every market [day].

The meadow and the pasture land shall be his to feed his livestock. In return, he shall give me a pound of butter every week and a pint of fresh milk every morning. All manure must remain in and on the land. He shall also have freedom to cut as much wood from my forest land as he and I need, but not from the green timber which is still growing, but rather from the dead wood. But he must not sell any wood.

After we have made this beginning and each has given it a try, and if both live to see the new year in 1802, we can discuss with each other any improvements or whether we should give it another try, or give up, so that everything might proceed peaceably and in good order.

[Signed]   Elizabeth Mack   Philip Jacobs[39]

Mack's Last Letter

According to M. G. Brumbaugh the last letter of Alexander Mack, Jr., was the one written to the Germantown congregation on behalf of an elderly widow.[40]

An aged stranger and pilgrim on this earth finds himself compelled in love to commend himself before his departure as much as possible to the brotherhood in Germantown, dearly beloved in God, with the following words:

Christ says — give to him who asks of you.

The dear brethren will not have completely forgotten that somewhat more than a quarter of a year ago the old widow Stierli from Philadelphia was here with us and asked to be fully accepted again. However, this was hardly possible because of her unstable character and because of her all-too-great lack of recognition of her weakness. It was to be feared that she would derive more harm than benefit from it. At the same time she was indeed, and still is, a widow lying at our door, poor, needy, weak and suffering badly from many boils on her head, who seeks to nourish herself with the crumbs which fall from our table.

Now it is true that several brethren at one of the Thursday meetings out of love for the words of Christ: "Give to him who asks of you," did deem it good in these dear times to give her a quarter of flour every month. I would have preferred it if they had decided to add a pound of butter along with it. I could not assume then that I would live to see the next New Year's Day, about four months hence. I did, however, have every right to assume that when the mortal shell of mine is buried, the New Testament is not buried with it. And it is there that the Lord speaks and says: "It is more blessed to give than to receive!" This gave good grounds for hope. When on New Year's Day more dear brethren will meet to investigate the need and the concern of the poor begging widow, the brethren will, out of love to the word of the Lord, rather add a pound of butter, and experience indeed that it is more blessed to give than to receive.

But when on New Year's Eve I learned that the brethren had taken away from her [even] the quarter of flour, my senses stood still and I did not know what to say or think. Jesus, the son of Sirach, says in his thirty-fifth chapter, verse twenty-five: "The poor man has nothing except a little bread; whoever deprives him of it, is a murderer."

Many a testimony can be found of verses which come quite close to this, in the Holy Bible, but especially where he speaks further about the tears of widows, namely, that although they run down the cheeks, they nevertheless rise up to God against him who caused them.

The contemplation of these matters has more and more virtually baptized my soul in sorrow in this new year. In the beginning I knew fairly well what to do [about it]. I made a good bed for myself in the denial of my will and sought to cover myself with the will of God as best I could. After I had rested for a while it seemed as if someone said to me: "What are you doing? It seems as if you wish to make yourself comfortable. But what good does it do to the poor widow?"

Then the sorrows of my heart and conscience returned and even much more so than before. Love only comforted me and some few members here. They refreshed my spirit, so that, for the time being, we have collected enough so that next Saturday a quarter of good flour or a quarter of wood, depending on her need, will be bought and given to her along with a pound of good butter. That brother who is convinced in his own mind that the widow belongs in the poorhouse, will — we hope — be given enough wisdom by God to persuade her to request admission there. Until then, dear brethren, she lies at our door.

Sander Mack[41]

7. Mack Correspondence

In the previous chapter on the Germantown congregation, considerable attention was given to Alexander Mack, Jr., as an articulate leader
and prolific writer among the Brethren. Documents from his pen, along
with some of the answers from his correspondents, give us a good idea
of both the personalities and the church issues of his day. His own rich
background and long life spanned the beginnings on the European continent, removal to Friesland, migration to America, the Ephrata troubles,
up through the Revolutionary War and the early national period of American history.

M. G. Brumbaugh, whose history of the Brethren incorporates many
of Mack's letters although in somewhat inadequate translation, wrote of
Mack:

> Perhaps no man in the early church had as wide a circle of
> correspondents as Alexander Mack. In my own collection of his
> MS [manuscript] remains, secured from Abraham H. Cassel,
> are at least thirteen letters written by him and an equal num-
> ber written to him by such well known members as Catharine
> Hummer, Martin Urner. . . , Jacob Mack, Jacob Stoll, Ludwig
> Hoecker, Jacob Donner, Michael Pfautz, Daniel Letterman . . . ,
> Charles Horlacher, and Rudolph Harley. In all of these there
> breathes the spirit of Christian love and confidence, stamping
> Elder Mack as a counsellor and a leader among them.
> Among the number are six to Elder John Price of Indian
> Creek. . . . To him Alexander Mack pours out his heart in full
> sympathy. The love between them was like that between David
> and Jonathan. . . .[1]

Two of the letters, dealing with Ephrata matters, have already been
included (see pages 157-158; 169). Most of the rest of the extant Mack
correspondence is given in the following, with little editorial introduction.

MACK-PREISZ CORRESPONDENCE

As noted by Brumbaugh, an especially close bond united Mack with John Preisz or Price (1752-1829), who was for a long period the elder of the Indian Creek congregation around Skippack. Preisz was in the fourth generation of a noted Brethren family. The scion of the American Prices was John Jacob Preisz (died c. 1742), who arrived in Pennsylvania in 1719. A son, John, a poet who died at the age of twenty-two, is said to have taken an Indian girl as his wife, who bore him two sons, the second born after his father's premature death. One of the sons, Daniel Preisz, became the father of the John Preisz who was the intimate of Alexander Mack.[2]

The brotherly ties between the two were maintained by visits and by warm notes and letters, in which their deepest thoughts, doctrinal points, family and marital perplexities, and church matters all were shared in an open fashion. Mild but definite reproof, if felt necessary, was also not lacking.

The Lord's Supper

In Jesus Christ, who is our hope both in this world and in the one to come, dearly beloved Brother John Preisz:

After I had safely returned home to my dear ones by the mercy of God and the protection of the Highest through the intercession of the innocent Lamb, I looked once again diligently into the witness which the holy evangelists have left us through the inspiration of the Holy Spirit about the last night, in which our Lord Jesus Christ blessed the bread and the wine and ordained them for His followers as a memorial of His suffering. Thus I discovered in the accounts of Matthew and Mark that the good master offered indeed separate blessings of the cup and bread, but as both of them describe the matter somewhat briefly, the Spirit of God awakened and blessed the diligence of Luke that we might have certain ground for the doctrine in which we are instructed. So I looked it up also in the testimony which he gives of it.

There I find in the seventeenth verse of the twenty-second chapter that the cup over which the good Master gave separate thanks concluded the Passover [*Osterlamm*]. It seems to me and is my understanding that it was a true expression of thanksgiving wherein He not only [gave thanks] for the partaken nourishment that His mortal body had ever received from the fruit of the natural grape vine according to the will of His Father. He gave thanks and at the same time, after this thanksgiving, took leave from the fruit of this vine as may be seen in verse eighteen; this seems edifying to me. Thus it might well be that it was here where He delivered the emphatic sermon which the holy evangelist John describes in his fifteenth chapter, namely, "I am the true vine," and so forth. Now Luke says in verse nineteen: "And he took bread, and when he had given thanks he broke it," etc. He also [took] the cup after the supper and said: "This is the cup, the new covenant in my blood," etc.; and finally: "Do this in remembrance of me." Here is an explicit commandment, not only that one should keep it, but also why and for what reason one should keep it, namely, in His remembrance.

In just this way St. Paul writes in his [first] letter to the Corinthians, verses twenty-three, twenty-four, twenty-five and twenty-six. Of the cup then, of which Jesus said: "This is the cup, the new covenant in my blood, which is poured out for you," neither Luke nor Paul states that He gave *separate* thanks over it, but it seems to me instead that the giving of thanks over the cup was here included in the giving of thanks over the bread.

In the same way, according to my humble understanding, the giving of thanks over the partaken Paschal Lamb was included in the giving of thanks over the cup, which He had drunk after the Paschal Lamb and shared with His disciples. It is, however, not very surprising for us that the two holy evangelists Matthew and Mark recorded [this] in such a manner that the witness of the holy evangelist Luke had to divide the word for greater clarity and indicate to us what kind of cup it was over which the Lord pronounced a separate public thanksgiving; this is not surprising when we consider that even St. Luke says [only] one word here in verse twenty-one: "But behold the hand of him who betrays me is on the table."

If St. John, the fourth evangelist, had not told us specifically how long the hand of the traitor had been with Him on the table, namely, until Jesus had dipped the morsel and given it to him (John 13:26-30), if [in other words] we did not have this report from John, we would be led to think and almost believe along with many others that Judas Iscariot partook of the bread and the cup of communion along with the other eleven apostles. Thus the Holy Spirit through the words of the one had made clear the words of another evangelist and confirmed them according to the words of Christ when He said, whoever will do the will of the one who sent me, will understand it.

That is why it happened that our brethren in Schwarzenau found in their diligent study in the witness of John that Christ our Lord, the last night before the supper, washed the feet of His disciples and also commanded that they too should wash one another's feet, even though St. Mark and St. Luke record nothing about the feetwashing. And, by contrast, St. John records nothing about the bread and the wine and thus only supplements what the others report also, namely, what glorious messages the Lord Jesus delivered during that last night. All of which evolves into a glorious harmony for a believing soul and gives testimony at the same time of how the Holy Spirit has avoided in [the writings of] the holy evangelists all unnecessary repetition of words. Thus the Spirit of God has been a steward of the entire holy Bible so that the divine harmony has to be found through prayer and diligent reading, etc.

I remain, therefore, your humble brother and fellow pilgrim toward the land of eternal rest, along with warm greetings to you and your dear loved ones.

Sander Mack

To the dearly beloved Brother John Preisz on the Indian Creek in Lower Salford Township.[3]

No Greater Joy

Krefeld, November 24, 1772

The name of the Lord is a poured-out salve. In the name of this lovely and gracious Jesus I wish peace and salvation to my dear brother John Preisz.

I have received and read your letter, and rejoiced that the Lord is so gracious and has invited you so lovingly to His heavenly wedding. Oh, my beloved in the Lord, do not consider the punishment of the Lord to be slight, especially since He has looked upon you so graciously and reveals your misery of sin to you and at the same time comforts your heart with a good intention to lead a better life through the grace of the Lord. I may well say that I have no greater joy than when I see and hear that people were drawn [to Him] in their youth. Oh what glory! But if one then really comes [to Him] and becomes faithful through the grace of God, the glory will be all the greater.

I have read the lines from your hand with tears of joy and I wish from my heart that when the Lord completely lifts you again and restores your health, your resolution may be made anew and renewed with your restored heart. Yet much more do I wish and pray that the Lord might complete the work which He has begun in you for your own joy and that of your parents, and to the joy and comfort of all those who esteem the work of the Lord.

I do not intend to write much this time, until another time when you perhaps again write a few lines. Or perhaps I will visit you soon, when we — the Lord willing and we live — can personally talk with each other.

In the meantime, I wish you from my heart God's blessing and a blessed outpouring of His divine power to your intention, along with a warm greeting to you. Please greet your dear parents from me also. I am your humble brother and fellow pilgrim,

Sander Mack.

NB. My dear wife and my two children also send their greetings. This was written in haste and with a broken quill. You will probably have some difficulty reading it.[4]

A Single-Minded Walk

Krefeld, December 29, 1772

In Jesus, the crucified, much beloved brother [John Preisz]!

In Him, our Immanuel, I wish you from my heart all the consolation of love, according to the pleasure of the mercy of our God in the knowledge of our Savior, who died for our sins and who was raised for the sake of our righteousness.

I have received your dear letter and read it in sympathetic love. In it I found first of all the concern of your love that none of us should ever be found to have been an unfaithful servant, for as you well remarked, the day is approaching when all of us shall be revealed before the judgment chair of Jesus Christ. To escape this great misfortune, we have much reason to pray to Jesus, the true light of the world, to give us an artless eye that our body be light and that we might follow Him, the true light of the world, lest we walk in darkness. For whoever has a wicked eye, his body will be in darkness, says the mouth of truth, and in such darkness man loses his trust in God, and can find no pleasure or delight in the denial of himself, from which all spiritual growth and advance in what is good is derived. Therefore the Lord says, He who will be my disciple, let him deny himself and take his cross upon himself daily and follow me.

Oh my dear brother, he who thus walks in single-mindedness, he walks safely. May the Lord enlighten the eyes of our understanding, that we may miss in nothing the footsteps of our good shepherd. As regards your further remarks that you have no assurance yet that your sins are forgiven — this is not a bad sign, for God reserves this right for Himself, in His own very wise power of love, when, how, and where He will grant the repenting sinner the certainty that his sins are completely forgiven. This is already a sure sign that God wishes to forgive our sins when He grants us profound repentance of everything with which we have offended the eyes of His exalted Majesty — especially when such repentance is accompanied by a loathing of evil and a fervent desire to do the will of God. I consider this a better sign than if a visible angel came from heaven and announced to one who had not yet tasted the bitterness of sins: "Your sins are forgiven." We may, however, thankfully assume that when the Lord through the inward joyful voice of strength and comfort of the good shepherd gives a soul a certain assurance which penetrates to the very marrow, his sins are forgiven and his name is now recorded in heaven.

Yet, it seems to me that our prayer ought to be directed more [toward asking] the Lord to keep us from sin and to guide us into the pleasure of His will, so that our will, our desire and all our pleasure may become a daily burnt offering to the pure love of God. After Saul had been converted and had fasted and prayed for three days, Ananias said to him: "Dear Brother Saul, why do you delay? Arise and be baptized and let your sins be washed away," etc. Now if the Lord were to give you no total assurance of the forgiveness of your sins until you, too, were likewise baptized, it would be nothing new and unusual, but rather a matter that many before you and me have also experienced.

Nevertheless, the good hand of God is not bound to anything, but He takes and gives as it benefits His children and serves to their improvement. For our part, let us but seek to become faithful to God. It surprised me somewhat that you have postponed baptism until spring when you do not know if you will live that long.

Be warmly greeted and kissed in the spirit and commended to the mercy of God. My wife and children send their greetings also. Greet also your dear parents from me and whoever of your relatives might receive a greeting. I am your humble fellow brother

Alexander Mack.

To the dear brother John Preisz to be opened at his convenience.[5]

Mack's Family and Church Discipline

Krefeld in Germantown Township

February 14, 1776

Dearly beloved Brother John Preisz:

Although at present I find my greatest pleasure in a quiet contemplation of the great love of my faithful shepherd who let His noble and pure blood be poured out so freely and generously on the trunk of the cross for me and all penitent sinners, I do feel obligated to write you briefly in answer to your beloved and sympathetic letter. First, I wish you all beneficial comfort of the eternal salvation for your immortal soul to the strengthening of your faith in these quite miserable times. Although it moved me very much that you were made so sorrowful on account of me and my children, I do recognize in this your loyal, sympathetic heart and it cheers me in my misery that you, along with the originator and perfecter of our faith, love justice and hate unrighteousness.

I can therefore not very well avoid telling you a bit about the present situation of my children. It is true, my Hannah had thought at first that her sin was not so great because they had been engaged never to leave each other, and both she and her husband [Adam Weaver] indeed intend to prove this. However, she realizes her error and recognizes her misdeed. She wants me to ask you especially for your forgiveness as she has always held a special love for you, because she believed that you feared the Lord. She would be especially grateful if you prayed to the Lord for her that He might have mercy on her in her condition and request, for she does not want to remain behind completely.

My Sarah thinks that she has done quite well, because she has rejected many and finally accepted the one she loves. She has indeed been spared the kind of shame my Hannah bears. Her husband is

Jacob Ziegler, a tanner, who lives not far from you. She has been excluded from the kiss [of love] and the communion for three reasons. First, because she married outside of the brotherhood; secondly, because [the marriage] was performed with a license; and thirdly, because her husband had not quite completed [his apprenticeship] and his master knew nothing about [the marriage]. My Hannah, however, has been disciplined even more severely, so that we do not even eat with her. Yet most of the members said that they would be more willing to accept her again if she returned in repentance, in fact they would be more willing to accept her again than they were ready to expel her. Her husband's name is Adam Weber. These two young men used to come to the meeting for some time and I suspected no evil to come from them.

As far as I am concerned, I publicly asked the brethren whether they had anything against me but they testified that they were satisfied with me and really did not wish to place any blame on me.

Yet before God I cannot declare myself entirely blameless, even though I did certainly think that I had used great diligence and sent up many sighs to the Eternal Love for these two poor children. I owe it only to the goodness of God that it is not completely over with us and that I can still hope that everything will serve to our best through the intercession of Jesus Christ.

I then commend myself once again to your brotherly intercession and remain, along with repeated warm greetings, your sorrowing fellow-pilgrim to the land of the quiet eternity.

Sander Mack

P.S. My dear wife and children send their kind greetings as far as it is possible and acceptable.

To the much beloved brother John Preisz in Lower Salford. To be opened at his convenience.[6]

Mack's Reproach to a Mennonite

Mack's letter to the Mennonite leader Lazarus Weidner has often been reprinted.[7] The Mennonites, just as did the Brethren, had strict rules about a member marrying outside of the brotherhood. It was to the exclusive quality of this principle that Mack is here addressing himself.

[December, 1780]

Dear Friend:

I have been told that you have expelled your sister from the congregation because she married my dear brother John Preisz. In the hope that you may be willing to account to anyone who calls on you to account for the hope that is in you, I find myself compelled to lay before you several questions in childlike love.

First question: Is it possible that you could do this and still be a preacher of the gospel? Second question: Do you perhaps consider my brother John Preisz to be an unbeliever? And why would John the apostle say: "We know that we have passed out of death into life, because we love the brethren. He who does not love the brethren remains in death" [1 John 4:14]?

Much beloved friend, should you prefer not to answer my questions, I hope that you will seek to answer them in some measure to your own conscience. I shall strive to remain your kind friend and well-wisher.

Sander Mack[8]

Mack on Baptism

Krefeld, April 24, 1788

May the love of Christ encourage us lest we through all-too-great indolence forfeit our greatest happiness, for it is written: "Hold fast to what you have, so that no one may seize your crown" [Revelation 3:11].

My dearly beloved brother John Preisz:

Our last conversation has raised many questions in my mind. We talked with each other about several mistakes in wording made at a human baptismal ceremony by a friend who is unknown to me. After you had left, however, and I had regained my composure in my solitude, the spirit of my conscience spoke to me: "How does this concern you?" It is God's old way that He marks all human works, especially in matters of worship, with many mistakes. To be true, we poor men embellish our actions so that God might be merciful to us. But the Lord casts His net over us and captures us in His hunt. And if we humble ourselves, He saves us out of His infinite grace.

That the dear friend said that Jesus was baptized *at* the Jordan is, of course, not according to the truth, for the holy evangelist Matthew testifies that Jesus came up out of the water (Matthew 3:16); Mark testifies that Jesus was baptized in the Jordan by John (Mark 1:9) and in verse ten he says: "And when he came up out of the water, immediately he saw the heavens opened. . . ." Just as Matthew testifies that Jesus came up out of the water, Mark testifies that also John came up out of the water. From this it may be proved incontestably that both were in the water of the Jordan when Jesus was baptized. Whoever insists then that Jesus was baptized at the Jordan says either nothing with these words or a secret untruth. Yet he who wants to sell his wares for more than they are worth must not be so scrupulous about the truth.

If such a friend came to me and wanted to begin a discussion with me about his baptismal ceremony, I believe it would be my duty to be ready to account to anyone who demands of me the reason for the hope that is in me. However, with such a person, who has not published anything in writing by which the truth might be abused, I personally do not feel called upon to involve myself in a written controversy.[9]

That, accordingly, these our dear friends who have borrowed their baptismal ceremony from the spirit of this world must be ashamed of the truth when they practice the same, is not surprising. For, if they witnessed too freely to the truth, they would lose their credit with the world and even with their own brethren and sisters. Yet we, who have publicly and voluntarily promised to be and to remain faithful to the teachings of Christ even unto death, have we not good reason to examine ourselves to see whether we are not sometimes still all too ashamed of the precious words of Christ with no reason?

Dear brother, did you perhaps deal fairly with your dear sister? And did you show her in a brotherly fashion the great danger which faces everyone who subjects himself to the commandments of men, bows before them, and receives them on his knees just as if Jesus had commanded it? See, my very dear brother, if you have done this, *you* have done, as far as I can see, what it was your duty to do. But if you did not do it, one almost ought to ask you why you neglected this duty. Were you perhaps still ashamed of the truth yourself?

In the meantime be warmly commended to God and His word of grace. And I remain your faithful brother, also, along with warm greetings and the kiss of love, your humble fellow pilgrim

Sander Mack.

P.S. Greet from me also your dear wife, the sister, and the dear brother Rudolph Harley and his dear wife, sister Maria.

To the much-beloved brother John Preisz at Indian Creek, to be opened by him personally.[10]

The Heavenly Calling

Written at Krefeld in our hut on the first day of June 1798.

May the innocent Lamb have mercy on us, and grant and keep us in His peace. Amen.

My much-beloved brother John Preisz:

I have read all the words which you have written to me several times with care and deliberation. So far I have found nothing therein which might be a reason for me to change the opinion which I have of this matter. But this I will confess to you that I hate no opinion as much as that of the Sadducees. Should the question arise in you why I hate this opinion so much, I would wish that you read with love and deliberation the first and second verses of the fourth chapter of the Acts of the Apostles and especially the seventeenth verse of the fifth chapter, and also the eighteenth verse of the same. Then you will discover why I hate this opinion so much.

Wherever this opinion is able to gain the upper hand in a heart, it extinguishes all the little sparks of the love of God and makes a swine out of a man! Oh Lord, mercifully save for your own sake all souls who still have a tiny spark of Christian love in their hearts from this swinish manner. In the epistle of St. Jude, in the twenty-first verse, I find these words: "Keep yourselves in the love of God; wait for the mercy of the Lord Jesus Christ unto eternal life."

Oh my dear brother, do not be surprised that I cannot accept anything which threatens to distract me from the heavenly calling. As to the parables, concepts, and interpretations in your letter, I do find several that I cannot praise with a good conscience; I think, however, that I am well advised to leave them completely alone, for the only good and only wise God alone knows why you had to write the way you did.

To this God, who alone is powerful, be honor and praise in eternity. Amen. Be warmly commended to the father of all mercy and God of all comfort, by your little worm hungering after grace, your otherwise familiar and humble brother,

Sander Mack.[11]

The Harmonious Flowers

[October 23, 1798]

Tenderly beloved brother, dear and respected fellow-pilgrim John Preisz:

Along with a warm greeting and kiss in the spirit of honest fraternal love, I herewith send you your letter according to your wish. Although I have diligently read your letter several times in the fear of the Lord, I still cannot say that all of the Scripture texts which you quote make the same impression on me as I understand they have made on you. What am I to say? The flowers in the gardens are quiet and peaceful even though one is embellished in blue, another in red and still another in white. They peacefully praise their creator and laud in complete harmony the manifold wisdom of the being of all beings. One praises thee, God, in the quiet of Zion!

During the past night the youngest child of my youngest daughter left this mortal body and passed from the land of the mortal across the river which has no bridge into the land of life. This child completed its entire journey in thirteen months and I have already journeyed eighty-six years and seven months and still have not crossed over Jordan. Yet, whatever God does is well done. It really does not depend on one's running or racing, but rather on God's mercy!

P.S. I have not told any person in our area that there has been a dispute between you and me, and I have not let anyone see your letter.

The Lord has called me to peace. The same peace which passes all understanding keep our hearts and minds in Christ Jesus. Amen. Amen. Written at Krefeld in my hut, on October 23, 1798; from your weak brother and humble fellow-pilgrim,

Sander Mack.

To the beloved brother John Preisz on Indian Creek.[12]

MACK-LETTERMAN CORRESPONDENCE

Usually considered as the outstanding churchman in Maryland is Daniel Letterman, or Leatherman (1706?-1798). Morgan Edwards referred to him as the "superintendent" in Maryland, and added: "As the Dunkers call all their ordained ministers bishops, it follows that Leatherman holds the rank of archbishop."[13]

We have earlier seen that Letterman was active in the leadership of the congregations of Little Conewago and Conewago in Pennsylvania, before moving to Maryland in 1756. His home was on the plateau of the Blue Ridge near Garfield in Frederick County. The relatively poor soil found there led to the area's being known as the Sand Hills *(Sandbergen)*.

The exchange of letters between Mack and Letterman is noteworthy for the information it reveals about several congregations, as well as matters of concern to these leading churchmen.

A Mutual Concern

[1785]

This sheet you might wish to read for yourself only; if you wish to read the enclosed two sheets to the congregation, I have no objections.

Beloved Brother Daniel:

Warm greetings to you and your dear children from my dear children, namely, Brother Adam Weber and his wife, my eldest daughter, sister Hannah; likewise from Brother Jacob Ziegler and my daughter, sister Sarah, his wife; as well as from Brother Manuel Fox and his wife, sister Anna Margaret, my youngest daughter. If my very youngest daughter Lydia, who is also baptized and likewise has become our dear sister, were here, I know she would also send her greetings to you, but she lives in Schippack. She is very fond of you.

Besides, she has a special cross to bear. Her husband is a Mennonite [Dielman Kolb] and has been ill now for over a year. It is very doubtful that he will recover [died December 14, 1785]. You have probably heard already that the dear Brother Michael Keyser's wife and Brother Philip Weber's daughter have been baptized and become dear sisters. But likely you have not yet heard that the dear Brother Christopher Sauer's daughter [Catherine] was baptized here in Germantown after her father's death [1784].[14]

Now I would like to report to you something confidential, which I ask you and other likeminded persons to keep in confidence and to offer it up to the Lord as a mutual concern with sighs and compassionate supplications. Our dear sister, the dear Brother John Weber's wife, of whom I have written you that she has been baptized, has a mother, Elizabeth Keisser by name, who is a daughter of the dear old sister Regina Rincker, who was baptized about fifty years ago in Germantown, by our dear Brother Peter Becker, I believe. This sister Regina passed away more than thirty years ago.

And now this daughter of hers, Elizabeth Keisser, about seventeen
years ago had an urge to be baptized, but was ailing. She desired that
her husband, John Keisser, who is a stubborn Mennonite, send word
to me that I might visit her. She did it several times and finally he
said; "Don't you see that he does not want to come?" But he had
never told me about it. Soon thereafter she had a breakdown and became very confused in her mind and ailing. Finally they persuaded
this troubled person and performed baptism on her in the manner
customary now with the so-called Mennonites. I say, they performed
this baptismal ceremony on this person in her bed and sought to convince her that she was now baptized, etc.

Now after she had regained her health, she became quite frivolous
and vain and allowed herself to be misled to mock the true baptismal
ordinance and those who held to it in their absence. However, after
her daughter (who had received the same baptism as her mother) had
broken through and was baptized in the true faith in the Son of God
and had also found refuge in Jesus after leaving that previous vain life
and beginning a new one, she [the mother] fell into deep melancholy
about a quarter of a year ago, bitterly accusing herself on account of
her great vanity, mockery and hypocrisy. At the same time, the Enemy
tried her thoughts very much saying that she had committed the sin
against the Holy Spirit; she also complained that she was not "baptized." But she encountered much opposition from the so-called Mennonites, so that she became completely confused, and finally refused to
eat so that they even thought she would die. I, however, had always
commended her to God in warm sympathetic concern, yet never visited
her openly lest her misery be increased by the strange opposition from
the Mennonites.

It is true, she is somewhat better now; she has started to work and
to eat regularly again. She has asked her son-in-law John Weber's forgiveness for what she had spoken against him. He had really never
held anything against her and wishes very much for her full redemption. Her husband, however, vowed that during his lifetime she could
never be baptized in the manner she desired. She wishes from her
heart to be in the same state as her daughter, disciplines severely the
members of her household for their idle words, but does not have
enough faith for a complete breakthrough. Although I cannot inform

you about this need and concern as completely as I would like, I do have the deep confidence in you that you will be willing to join me in supplication to God for this miserable, imprisoned, confused, tempted person of little faith, and that you will not reveal this to anyone except those who have something of the spirit of testing and could have sympathy for an afflicted person. You might tell the dear brother Nicholas Martin of it along with my warm greeting. I remain herewith your brother united with you in the love of Jesus.

Sander Mack

To my much-beloved Brother Daniel Letterman to be opened by him.

In the Sand Hills in Frederick County in Maryland.[15]

Church Conditions and George Adam Martin

Sandbergen, Frederick County, Maryland
August 26, 1787

May the sweet love of Jesus pour into, greet and embrace itself in our hearts.

My very dearly beloved in God Brother Sander Mack:

I cannot refrain from letting you know that I did not receive your dear letter until today. I rejoice that the Lord has brought you safely from the great meeting to your dear ones and that you found them well also, for I have been wondering whether you have returned safely. You wrote me of several whom the Lord has called home. I think very often that the hour is soon coming when the Lord will call me. My heart's desire and longing is that God through grace might completely purify and prepare me, if it be His holy will.

As far as I and mine are concerned, we are all rather well physically and all the [church] members appear to be in good health. I received and read your letter in the meeting. Your letter moved their hearts and they were happy to hear how you were; they warmly greet you and your dear ones and all of the members. Also the dear Brother Daniel Arnold of Redstone [sends greetings] and he reports that all the members there are well with the exception of the sister, the wife of Brother George Krafft. Claus Grebielen's daughter is still in her old afflicted condition. You have no doubt heard that she has become feeble-minded. The brother also says that there is powerful shouting and preaching by the Methodists and English Baptists there, but the Lord gives the brethren grace so that people are moved and convinced to believe in the truth; twenty were baptized this summer.

You wrote that you read in the *Chronicon* which Brother Jabetz [Peter Miller] sent you about George Adam Martin, that he had written a letter in which he called the Old Brethren "cursers." After a conscientious examination I can say with a sincere heart and a good conscience before God, who examines hearts and livers, that I have never cursed him or his followers, but rather on the contrary prayed for mercy for them and that God might give them grace; however, I have not done this as much as I realize that I should. I have never wished him nor his following any evil, but rather that which I wish for my own soul, namely true salvation and preparation in this life. But it is true that insofar as their shining forth and, as what seems to me their opinion that they have found a way other than the path of salvation to lead them to peace, for this soul-corrupting knowledge I cannot wish them success but rather that God may lead them through repentance and penitence onto the path of betterment and salvation.

Herewith I will close and I, my wife, and children, greet you, your dear wife and children most warmly. Greet also warmly for me all of the members there. Herewith be warmly commended to God and to the word of His grace, by me, your weak fellow-pilgrim.

Daniel Letterman

Dear brother, pray for me, that I might achieve complete purification and salvation. My dear brother, do write me again soon — about two weeks ago two persons were baptized in Baltimore.

To the dear brother Alexander Mack at Chestnut Hill near Germantown to be opened at his convenience.[16]

Self-Examination

Sandbergen, Frederick County, Maryland
May 23, 1794

First, my greeting of love along with wishes for all health and happiness for soul and body, especially salvation and blessing from the abundant riches of Jesus — inward comfort through His presence in the heart — through the ardent feeling of His warm love as a comfort and joy in your old age.

My in God much beloved Brother Sander Mack:

I received your dear note of April 1 on May 4, in good order, together with Samuel Sauer's letter, and I rejoiced very much to receive something from your hand. The greeting of love from your dear wife, the dear sister, and your dear children was very pleasing to me, and comforting, that they still remember poor me. May God remember them according to the richness of His mercy in Jesus. Amen. What you report about how the sufferings or pains in the body mortal are bearable and, as I notice, that you bear them willingly in patience and tranquility, and that you were able to walk ten miles in one day, all this is grace and gives me another reason to thank God for His great goodness, because He is so very merciful and bestows so much on His children. Yes, praised be His great name forever.

You spoke of what gives you pain — to this I say, yes, my dearly beloved brother, yes, oh might the children of God believe and love the poor world-despising Jesus-life and remember the word of Jesus: "You will have fear in the world," etc. and turn their backs on the world and from their hearts seek and find the highest good and the immeasurable riches: the precious pearl and the precious treasure — Jesus: God within them. Oh, how peacefully and happily would they be able to walk the pilgrim path if only they left the worldly burdens behind. Oh may my God grant His dear children anointed eyes that they might see what serves in this time for their eternal peace.

My dear brother, you write that you wish to know whether Brother David Martin is still living and whether he still stands entirely before God who is the truth himself. I can only say what I learned from the brethren who saw him last autumn and spoke with him and have also heard him speak. They say that he was very kind. But the dear brother Jacob Danner and his brother will visit you and then you can ask them; they can give you better information about how his conduct and speech were. The dear Henry Danner will tell you personally how things are going in Morrison's Cove. I should like to have your opinion on what one might do so that things would be right and good. I hear a very good testimony about the dear Brother Kögie [Kagi] in the Glade, that he is greatly increasing in or through grace. Of the other two brethren who were ordained during my last journey to Redstone I have not heard for considerable time.

My dear brother, I am not aware of ever praying in my family devotions without my spirit being drawn before God remembering you in my feeble prayer. You write that you have such great need of the prayers of the believers; when I reflect upon myself I need it much more. The weakness of my body and my spirit or soul reminds me daily of the brevity of my life and when I look back — even the best that I have done, it was all done in imperfection — with mistakes and shortcomings — with weakness and frailty. And if God did give me grace, it happened to me exactly as Gottfried Arnold says in his little verse:

> The ever-tender love of God
> must surely fall to flesh a prey
> unless the mighty work of God
> leads us to ever watch and pray.

My own, or personal, life or self-love took too great a part in it whereas I ought to have died to everything and lived alone to God. And, because I ought to see much evil in myself, I often think: "Oh God, whoever is able to recognize how often he fails?" so that I often think like this at first: "If my God will only count me among the lowliest of the saints — I would consider it an immeasurable grace and give infinite praise and thanks for it to my God." But then I would think: "What can one do? You must hold still and patiently surrender yourself to your God and be content, however He may be dealing with you now or later. But [always] in hope — for God is love and Jesus shows that He alone is good — that He will turn everything with me for the good, for I cannot even hope for and believe this unless God gives me grace thereto." Oh my dearly beloved brother, therefore pray for me that God might give me such grace, that I might die to myself and live unto Him and expect in hope every good thing from Him, and all this through Jesus Christ, our so faithful Savior. Amen. Oh my dearly beloved brother, for writing so much and imposing on you do bear with my weakness; I do not know why I must write so much and why my heart is so open toward you. Perhaps this is the last time that I may communicate with you in writing. If my God makes me worthy I hope to see you soon in the dwelling place of the saints, where we shall praise God together forever (and rejoice without end).

I must conclude now and greet and kiss you warmly in the spirit of the true brotherly love. Greet for me warmly your dear wife, the dear sister, and also your dear children, especially those who have sent greetings to me. I was very happy that they still remember poor me. May God bless them and give them grace that they might take root in the true foundation of God below them, and grow above themselves and bear much fruit to the praise of God. Give my greetings when convenient to all of the members there. Commending myself herewith warmly to God, I remain in love your loyal brother and fellow-pilgrim in meekness.

Daniel Letterman

Remember me in your prayer before God, for I have great need of it.

To the dear brother Alexander Mack near Germantown.[17]

LETTERS TO MACK FROM SEVERAL CORRESPONDENTS

The following letters range over a wide number of topics, from bushels of grain being sent to requests for guidance on involved problems of church polity. One theme running through them is the love and esteem in which Mack's contemporaries held him. Although Mack's responses are not available, we may assume that the replies were couched in much the same way as seen earlier in the several letters to John Preisz.

Martin Urner to Alexander Mack, Jr.

The younger Martin Urner (1725-1799) was an intimate friend of Mack. Of their correspondence two letters have been preserved. They give some idea of the economic arrangements common at that time. Urner was a noted preacher and often journeyed into other provinces on preaching missions.[18]

Coventry on the Schuylkill
October 30, 1766

My dear Brother Alexander Mack:

May God give you much grace, peace, and blessing, along with your dear loved ones. Yes, the Lord greet you all with His peace and make himself known through revelation of His power and love in your hearts. Amen.

Also, I am sending you thirty-five bushels of ground [rye] and three bushels of wheat and ten pounds of butter in the hope that it will be faithfully turned over to you by the bearer. I am not quite sure any more how much grain you wish to have. If you wish more rye, tell it to the bearer. I imagine that it should have been twenty bushels of wheat and so I hope to deliver to you soon the remaining seventeen bushels and some more butter. If it were convenient for you to send back some instructions as to how much butter and grain it is to be, it would be very helpful.

I report further that the dear brother Michael Pfautz visited me and delivered the letter to me in person, and further, he gave me twenty shillings in money from Cousin Guthmann for you, which, it seems, Cousin Guthmann had borrowed from you. He wants you to have it back. I am told that we are said not to have a good conscience, but for my part I can well believe that He who is alone good can cleanse our consciences through the blood of the Lamb from the dead works to serve the living God. And such I hope also of you, my dear brother.

I rejoice that in the new Jerusalem none but children of peace increase the glory of the Prince of Peace where all sorrow and noise, yes, hammering, sawing, and filing, will come to an end, where the building will fit together above our own understanding. Be greeted and kissed, dear brother and sister, by us poor unworthy worms, who yet live in the hope that He is faithful who loved us.

Martin Urner

A warm greeting from my dear housemother [wife] Barbara Urner.[19]

Coventry on the Schuylkill
October 31, 1770

Dear Brother Alexander Mack:

The God of peace greet you and your dear wife and children with His love in Jesus, His dear son, our faithful shepherd, whose beloved voice has called us poor worms to life, when we were still dead in sins and misdeeds. Yes, may He live in us, may He live and work in us that which will serve to His honor. Amen.

I am sending you through the service of the dear bearer, Andrew Wolf, twenty bushels of ground rye and fifteen bushels of ground wheat if you can use it. The price is to be as usual, four shillings a bushel for the rye and five shillings for the wheat.

When our stockings are done and the cloth is dyed, draw the balance of the amount in the bill and send it. If it is not finished, it is alright, too,

I would have liked to visit you, but it does not suit now. I do hope, however, that we will see each other at Brother Rudolph Herli's by November 10, if we live and the Lord wills it. Then I can perhaps tell you personally about our journey and the dear [church] members whom we saw. Be greeted once again and kissed in spirit by me and my dear housemother [wife] as your fellow travelers to the city of peace.

Martin Urner, Barbara Urner

Written in haste with a broken quill.

Note. I think, dear brother, that the last account was twelve pounds, nineteen shillings, but I will gladly be corrected if there is something else which I do not know. I hope that you will not misinterpret my simple letter or intent. Do not worry if it is not convenient for you to pay the old bill.

To my dear Brother Alexander Mack in Krefeld to be opened by him only.[20]

Charles Harlacker to Alexander Mack, Jr.

An undated letter from the Cumberland Valley area, written by a Charles Harlacker, contains not only an account of the writer's spiritual state but also information on Mack's son William (1749-1813), who had traveled to the "Antietam Country" in the company of Henry Schlingluff, also of Germantown.

[Antietam, c. 1770]

May the holy will of our dear heavenly Father be done in us always through Jesus Christ according to His pleasure. Amen.

In the same name, tenderly beloved brother, I greet and kiss you in the spirit, in genuine brotherly love. I have perceived from your esteemed letter that all of you have been well, about which I rejoice and for which I give heartfelt thanks to the dear Lord. As far as I am concerned, physically, I am as I desire, for I never wish to be better than I am. Yet, from time to time, I do taste the sweet fruits of the light yoke of the bridegroom of my soul, in the midst of my harsh denials. However, as regards my inner state, it has been subject to strange changes most of the time, and is now in a good and then in a sorry condition. This causes fear, joy and sadness in my soul in continual alternation. I am often overcome with thoughts that my submission to God's will could be much rather called a carelessness, for I find in myself many flaws, weaknesses, and real faults, of which I am convinced that they are sinful. These are heavy and almost unbearable crosses for the will that governs my soul and it would rather be freed from them today than tomorrow.

Then often such thoughts arise in me, that my sluggishness or carelessness [is] to blame and that I ought to fight them with a more courageous spirit. But I find little strength for this battle on my part and fear the shadowy valley of my egotism and my deeds — of which you also wrote me — in which I have already spent many a troubled hour but unfortunately without benefit. Therefore it appears to me that, when called to fight, I do too much and when called to be calm, I am too indolent. It is very difficult for me, therefore, to find the middle road, which I would so gladly take. It often occurs to me that if my submission were right and pleasing to the Lord, He would have cleansed me from the above-mentioned sinful imperfections long ago.

On the other hand I think that I ought to learn to have patience with myself and, as you wrote me, to deny and sell my own and to wait upon the help of the Lord until He chooses His own time. Oh, if I only knew that it were according to the will of my dear heavenly Father to bear this, I would suffer, endure and wait with a happy spirit, for His will is dearer to me than my soul and salvation. And I would gladly, if He so wished, let myself be counted among the condemned. But as I fear and cannot believe otherwise than that I displease my God through the above-mentioned sinful faults, it then happens that often severe and difficult hours of misery overwhelm me and all joyfulness seems to be banned from my vicinity. God's plan with me is quite hidden from me and most of the time I must tread the dark paths of faith, albeit with weak faith. Often I wish to know whether my way is right and pleasing to God.

Again, at other times I am content, even if God's plan with me should be hidden from me until that last day. I ask you, pray with me to the Lord that He might, out of grace, bestow upon me the spirit of Jesus Christ, that it might lead me in the right path and guide me into all truths, for I wish very much to belong completely to my

God and, through Jesus Christ, to live according to His merciful will, in humility and wholly for our love. If anything in this brief letter seems unclear or unintelligible to you, I ask you to forgive it in love, for I have written it in simplicity according to my inner foundation, as well as it has been given me.

I remain your fellow-yearner for the revelation of the children of God and a poor pilgrim who is wishing for and doing battle with you.

Charles [Harlacker]

Greet for me your dear ones and all the members in Germantown.

N.B. As far as your son William is concerned, he arrived here safely with Brother Schlingluff and is minded, I understand, to remain here this winter. He works at his trade at David Steiner's. I believe your brother John has written you a detailed report.

Please deliver this letter to the dear Brother Sander Mack to be opened by him.

Krefeld.

Through a dear brother, whom the angels of the Lord may accompany.[21]

Nicholas Martin to Alexander Mack, Jr.

Nicholas Martin, minister of the early Conococheague congregation, had previously been an elder of the Little Conewago church, beginning about 1757. His letter to Alexander Mack, Jr., gives good insight into the way church leaders visited other congregations to preach and preside at love feasts. Also current practices of church order are seen in the statements about ordination. The "Brother Stephen" referred to is doubtless Stephen Waller, listed by Morgan Edwards as Martin's assistant.[22]

Conococheague, May 24, 1772

First, my kind and warm greeting with wishes for health and happiness in soul and body to you, much beloved and esteemed brother in the Lord, Alexander Mack, along with your dear wife and children. Yes, I wish that it may be well with your soul, as I also hope that He is with you in your daily tasks.

As far as I and my family are concerned, we are, praise God, still rather healthy and well physically. For good health in the faith we are still indefatigably called by God's grace and His good Spirit to remain faithful unto death in order finally to obtain or inherit the crown of righteousness and glory through grace.

I received your dear letter in good order, but only after the dear Brother Martin Urner had been with us. Furthermore, we must not deny that the grace of God has been poured out in large measure, for the number of disciples has considerably increased, and several of them seem to be truly awakened souls and it seems almost as if the last will be the first, and the first will be last. May the Lord yet add ten thousand times as many and increase the number of His disciples daily for His own sake and for the honor of His holy name.

You will perhaps know that the dear Brother Michael Miller died a year ago. Brother Jacob Stutzman is again quite improved; he was very feeble this past winter.

As far as the brethren are concerned who were to be ordained, they did not come, nor did Brother Daniel Letterman and Brother Jacob Donner [Danner]. I believe there were twenty in number who were baptized at that time. I was told this by Brother Daniel Letterman and I am to greet you warmly for him in my letter and to report to you that there was much opposition against Brother Donner so that he could not be ordained with unanimity of the congregation. As regards Brother Stephen, I believe there would not have been much opposition to him at that same time. However, he has now become more reluctant because he thinks that he has become estranged to the brethren throughout the country because he became naturalized. Now I learned recently that he wishes to move and go away because his brother has already moved away.

Dear brother, do not think ill of me for being so slow in answering, for I have waited a long time for a good opportunity. Greet for me also the dear Brother Christopher Sauer and the dear Brother George Schreiber whenever it is convenient for you. My wife sends you her warm greetings. I commend myself to your prayer and may you be warmly commended to God and the word of His grace.

Written in haste by me, your very humble brother.

Nicholas Martin

This is for the dear friend Sander Mack near Germantown.
This letter is to be delivered to Christopher Sauer in Germantown.[23]

Jacob Mack to Alexander Mack, Jr.

Antietam, November 3, 1774

Dearly beloved Brother and esteemed Cousin:

I greet you warmly and wish that these few lines might find you and your dear ones in good health. Your dear note of September 10 reached me safely via Brother Jacob Niederer. I cannot deny that it was very comforting and pleasing to me to hear from you and that all of you are in good health and well. May the gracious God look upon us all in kindness, strengthen and comfort us so that we might persevere in the love until a blessed end.

Dear cousin, at present I have nothing special to write to you. As far as I am concerned, I am healthy in body but very changeably so for I am often afflicted with a weak stomach and headaches. As far as my inner life is concerned, that too is very variable and I must lie captive, as it were, upon hope and wait for my deliverer.

I do realize that I am in need of a strong deliverer. Although I remain as quiet as I can outwardly, I must nevertheless walk a very thorny path. I am still in the desert of temptation. Dear cousin, I can hardly write you otherwise than how I feel. I can well quote the hymn: "The time is not yet when Zion triumphs."

Dear cousin, I greet you again most warmly. Remember us for our well-being. From your humble yet faithful brother,

Jacob Mack.

Note. I passed on the love-greetings to my dear brother and sister. They were well and greet all of you warmly in return. My dear wife and children also send their warm greetings to you. Also greet warmly for me your dear wife, the dear sister, and all of your children. Greet warmly also the dear cousin Lewis Engelhard and cousin Jacob Schneider, my mother's brother. We also send warm greetings to our old friend, Sister Bayer, and the dear brother George Schreiber and his dear wife. May the Lord grant him patience in his illness. It would please me to hear that all of you are well. I commend you to the grace of God.

I would also appreciate it very much if you wrote upon this very good opportunity, namely, [by sending it] with your son William.

To my dear brother and cousin Alexander Mack in Krefeld.[24]

Jacob Danner and His Wife to Alexander Mack, Jr.

An informative letter from Jacob Danner which he sent to Alexander Mack, Jr., in 1789, has been preserved. It is a good example of the way members of the various congregations were concerned to keep informed of both the spiritual and the physical health of their brethren in other churches. The son of Michael Danner (referred to on pages 141-144), Danner was a hymnwriter and poet, and a well-known church leader.[25]

Lieginohr [Linganore], Frederick County, the eleventh day of March in the year of our Lord and Savior and Redeemer Jesus Christ, the Son of God, who remains the comfort of all believers, 1789.

Dearly beloved and esteemed Brother Alexander Mack:

I greet and kiss you in the spirit out of brotherly love, as well as your dear wife and your daughters and sons-in-law. I also greet warmly all brethren and sisters and their children in all of Germantown and in your household. I especially greet your ministers and elders as many as are known to me: Brother Peter Leibert, Brother Peter Keyser, Brother Daniel Weber, Brother Langstrath, and anyone else who might have been chosen to this office among you. May God grant you, my dearly beloved brethren, that you may remain faithful in your service through the grace of God, wherein the Lord has placed and called you as watchmen and fellow-workers in the vineyard of the Lord, to tend His flock as sheep of Jesus Christ, under your sovereign, chief shepherd and bishop, Jesus Christ.

Do not despise an old man, much less rebuke him, but honor the aged men and admonish them as your fathers, and the aged women as your mothers, the young men as your brothers, the young women as your sisters, the youths and maidens with all modesty as your dear children. And in this service each of you will gain a considerable advance toward the day of the coming of the Lord Jesus Christ. I do hope, my dear brethren, even though you know this already, that you will not take it amiss when I remind you of your reward and compensation from God, namely, when you will bless yourselves and those who hear you. And likewise, my very dear brethren and sisters and cousins, I have not forgotten you; even though I do not know you very well yet, I do rejoice greatly in your earnestness and zeal in what is good. I should have liked to be more often in your company if I could have arranged it. However, since it cannot be, I nevertheless wish all of you well and wish that you, like obedient sheep, will let yourselves be led and guided by your good shepherd, and by His good Spirit into all truth. Then you will gladly obey your ministers and follow them faithfully, because they watch over your souls as those who will have to account for them, so that they might do this with joy and not with sighing. It would be bad for you otherwise.

I do hope, however, my beloved, that you will instead out of love for God and them, pray for them to God, as well as for me and all the saints, so that the Lord might make known the secret of His truth and the door of His word in His blessed gospel to all His servants and witnesses of His truth, so that our comfort might always be that we have a good conscience and are diligently striving to lead a good life with everyone.

However, to write you this, my beloved, may well be very superfluous; therefore I intend to make it short.

Yet, my dearly beloved brother Sander Mack, I would like you to know that I have very often remembered you in love, and the members of your congregation, since the time I was with you, and have wished for you, if it be God's will, good health, for when we were with you you were not well, which made me sad. I do hope, my dear brother, that this my letter will find you in good health, which would please me greatly. Let me also inform you that I and my family as well as all of the brethren in this area are still in good health and well, as long as the Lord wills it. However, how long this will continue is known to the Lord alone. As far as the youth are concerned, many have the pox and even many adults have been vaccinated, but none of the Brethren, who commend their children to God their creator, who has given them and who will turn everything to their and their children's good and welfare.

Dearly beloved brother, I heard day before yesterday from the dear Brother Daniel Letterman that he is still not well. For after I left you I visited him and he was ailing then, but it seems that his illness is mostly an infirmity of the body. He could hardly stand the cold and, as I understand, he is still in rather the same condition. As regards his family, however, they were all still well. I also told him about you and extended warm greetings of love from you and the dear Brother Peter Leibert, because we had made our final departure from your house, although most of the brethren had asked me to extend their corporate greetings from your area.

Now then, my dear brother, I intend to conclude. I hope that you will bear my imperfection with patience and overlook my weakness. Should it please God that we see each other in this life again, it would please me. But the Lord's will be done. I wish for myself through the grace of God the love of Jesus Christ into my heart — to remember you before God — in like manner I desire your remembrance of me. It is the good God who can equip us for this. To Him I warmly commend you all. Also, greet for me warmly the dear Brother Justus Fox and his dear wife, the sister, and also all those whom you love. I do not know all of their names, but greet warmly also your brother-in-law and his dear wife, the sister, your sister, who was ill at the time. I trust the Lord will have had mercy on her, as on all of us, and even on your unworthy friend and brother, who along with his wife greets you warmly.

Jacob Danner
Elizabeth Danner

To the dear brother Alexander Mack at Chestnut Hill near the city of Germantown.[26]

CATHERINE HUMMER'S VISIONS

Among the more unusual letters received by Mack were those concerning visions and signs. Not surprisingly, these occurrences created considerable excitement. The Pennsylvania-Germans seem to have shared with their contemporaries intense interest in such happenings, as is attested to by the popularity of the publications of Christopher Sauer I and others describing these phenomena.

Most noteworthy of the early history of the White Oak congregation was the Catherine Hummer incident. Catherine was the daughter of Peter Hummer (d. 1784), the first minister to live within the bounds of what became later the White Oak district. The *Ephrata Chronicle* gives the story of the visions seen over a period of years by Catherine Hummer, compatible as this activity was with the Ephrata spirit. A considerable awakening resulted from the visions, which the father rated highly. She accompanied him on meetings and testified about her heavenly visitations. The Germantown Separatist and former Inspired leader, John Adam Gruber, reported the Hummer visions to Europe in 1763, noting that she saw "many hundred persons baptizing in eternity" in Paradise.[27]

The notoriety of the Hummer affair disquieted some in the Brotherhood, especially when it transpired that during the trances no one was allowed in her presence except one young man (whom she later married). After the nuptials the visions abruptly ceased. The Ephrata explanation saw the marriage as a lapse from spiritual virtue, in their Böhmist way of thinking, but the Brethren tended to think more practically. Catherine Hummer explained in a letter to Alexander Mack in 1763 that she was being persecuted for her faith. The judgment of Annual Meeting, held before the above denouement of the marriage, counseled both sides to brotherliness and cautioned against division and a judging spirit.

Excerpts From the Chronicle

The history and revelations of Catherine Hummer follow now in order of time. . . . The account, however, is taken from her own confession and is as follows:

While sitting in the kitchen near the fire on the night of October 3, 1762, between ten and eleven o'clock, there was a knock at the door. I looked out, but nobody was there. Again, there was knocking and I again went out but found nobody. At last there was knocking for the third time, and going out and looking about I saw an angel standing at my right hand who said: "Yes, my friend, it is midnight and late; the hour of midnight is approaching. Alas, what shall I say? Love has grown cold among the members. Oh that this were not so among those who are brethren in the faith!" Then he sang, so that it echoed through the skies, and I thought it must be heard far and wide.

When he had ceased, I said: "Shall I go in and tell my friends that they may rejoice with me?" He said: "No; they have retired." I said: "They are not asleep." He said: "Yes, they are sleeping." Then I kept silence and thought, how well I feel, how well I feel! Thereupon the angel began to sing: "How well I feel, how well I feel, when our God doth show himself in spirit to my soul, so that within I leap and jump for joy, and bring all praise and honor to the Lord, although the tongue oft silence keeps."

In the middle of the verse he told me to join in the singing; then he knelt down and I with him. He prayed fervently and beautifully for the salvation of believers. Now I wept for joy, and he dried my tears; but I dared not touch him. Then I said: "Shall I go and tell my friends?" He laid his hands upon my shoulders and answered: "My

dear child, they are asleep." I said: "My dear friend, they just now
lay down; they do not sleep." After this we again began to sing: "The
children of God indeed sow in sorrow and in tears; but at last the
year yieldeth what they long for. For the time of the harvest cometh,
when they gather the sheaves, and all their grief and pain is turned to
pure joy and laughter." Then I again said: "Shall I go in and tell my
father that he may rejoice with me?" He said: "No, all your friends
are asleep, and their hearts also want to sleep."

Then I wept bitterly, and the angel asked: "Why do you weep?"
I answered: "I have committed many sins and often grieved my
Savior." He said: "Do not weep. Your Savior forgave you your sins,
for He knows that you have gladly listened to the good and that you
did not delight in the greatness of this world, that you have no pride
in your heart, and that you have kept lowly company with the believers." Then the angel and I began to sing: "Who knows what shall
come, what shall be our lot, when the Lord one day will take His own,
His chaste bride so full of honor? He hath already known her in His
own mind. She follows well His guiding hand and much augments
His honor." Then we knelt and prayed again, and he prayed for the
sinners. Then I asked for the fourth time: "Shall I go in and call my
friends?" He said: "This is asked once too often; do you not know
that the Savior awakened His disciples three times?" I said: "This
is too much," and I wept. He said: "Weep not," and I kept silent.

Then we began to sing: "Oh blessed he will be who shall enter
with me into the realms of bliss; it surely is but right that we should
here below always well prepare ourselves." Then the angel began to
speak and said: "My dear child, did you ever see such ungodly display?
Did you notice the daughters of Jerusalem walking about in gay calico,
of which things they have much on earth. They will be sent down
to the wicked if they do not turn back, for they will not enter the Kingdom of God; and there is still a great deal of this godless display upon
earth. They will be shown into hell. Then the Lord will say: Depart
from me, you sinners! I know you not! And then you will burn to
all eternity and will be tormented from everlasting to everlasting."

Then he ceased to speak of these things, and we again began to
sing: "They all will see suddenly with pleasure and joy the beauties
of the heavenly realm, and the beautiful throng will walk two by two
on Zion's meadows." Then, for the third time, we knelt down on the

ground and he prayed about the sufferings and the death of the Savior, and then we got up. Now he said to me: "Go in and lie down;" and said: "Hallelujah! Hallelujah in Christ Jesus! Amen." Then he ascended toward heaven and spoke in a loud voice, so that it reached to heaven: "Father, Father, faithful Father!" and called out three times in a loud voice saying: "I ascend into heaven." I looked after him until he disappeared from my sight; then I went in and lay down.

After this I lay in a trance for the greater part of seven days and nights, so that my spirit was separated from my body. In this state I was led through strange conditions and dwelling places of spirits, and saw such wonderful things that I greatly hesitate to reveal them. After this it became quite customary for me to talk with good spirits and angels and also to be transferred in spirit out of my visible body into the heavenly principalities, just as if it had happened bodily. The almighty God in His mercy also allowed me to translate myself in spirit into eternity as often as I wished, either by day or night, and there to see, hear, and touch the divine wonders. My body was always as if asleep until my spirit returned. I wandered through indescribable habitations of the blessed, and saw innumerable hosts. Once I was told their number, but I could not remember it. Oh what joy and happiness did I there behold! There you feel a bliss that is inexpressible and indescribable. . . . [There follow extended descriptions of the visit of her spirit to heaven.]

I find that these visions continued at least till April, 1765. The father of this person was a respected Brethren preacher. He, because he also had a great desire to build churches, made use of this circumstance and traveled through the country with his daughter, baptizing and preaching God's kingdom, whereby many were awakened from their spiritual sleep, some of whom he baptized in the stream Codorus, at Yorktown. It is beyond description how quickly this awakening spread through the country. People came from a distance of more than sixty miles to the house of the above-mentioned Hummer, so that the too-numerous visitors emptied these good people's house and barn of their provisions. Night services were then arranged, to which people came every night. But if some tried to steal in from impure motives, the Instrument [Catherine Hummer] was so keen as to find it out that they were exposed and excluded from the service. . . .

But it appears that after the above-mentioned person had changed her state and married, the spirit retired into its chambers again and the whole work stopped and fell into decay, which is usually the case with angelic visions and revelations. May God grant that it may turn into a plentiful harvest in eternity.[28]

Catherine Hummer to Alexander Mack, Jr.

White Oak Country, November 6, 1763

Glory to God in the highest for His great love, kindness and mercy, for He is continually merciful, kind, and full of love, and does not forsake those who believe in Him, but awakens them from the indolence of the world and their lusts and desires. I wish from all my heart and all my soul that I, too, may be lifted up to God's honor together with all of His faithful and may join in crying: "Glory to God in the highest, peace on earth and good will toward men." Peace has been taken from the earth, from the entire world, and from most of those who call themselves believers and each one acts according to his own pleasure.

Dear Brother Sander Mack! I thank you warmly for your love and loving admonitions and for your warm greeting. I, Catherine Hummer, your lowliest fellow-sister, my heart and my soul wish you health and happiness of body and soul. I will be patient in the paths of tribulation, for the dear Savior has said that one must pass through many tribulations in entering the Kingdom of God. Therefore I will prepare myself for it as far as the Lord provides grace that I might be found worthy to enter into the Kingdom of God, for the winter of persecution is here.

Contempt and persecution are great, but I comfort myself with the dear Savior and with the small herd of Zion, which has been gathered from all peoples. I am not only persecuted by the world but also hated by those who call themselves believers. They say that what has happened through me is idolatry. They blaspheme about something that they know nothing about. May the Lord have mercy on them and not punish them according to their merits.

Dear Brother Sander, you wrote me that in the end the weightiest will weigh less than nothing, once they are weighed on the right scales. I am indeed imperfect, but may the Lord put His good spirit into my heart so that when I am weighed I might have the correct weight and be taken out of this sorrowful world into eternal rest, where no enemy can trouble me any more. Let everything be commended to the Lord and may He deal with me as He wishes. His will be done now and in eternity. Amen.

I firmly believe that the day of the Lord is much nearer than is believed. Then all mockers will be afraid, and it will be night and dark in their hearts, so that they cannot see the bright light. My heart and my soul wish from the bottom of my heart that the light which has been lit in all those who call themselves believers may not be extinguished again but rather be more and more illuminated. Oh, love has been extinguished by the enemies; hatred has been increasing. . . .

If I were as forsaken by God as I am by most of those who call themselves believers, there would be no grace left for me, nor any hope for salvation. I confess that I am a great sinner, and that I was born in sin, so that I must say with the poor publican: "God be merciful to me a poor sinner." He will do it, because He is merciful, but men are not.

May God forgive them this shame, contempt, and scorn. The poet says: "Let them mock, let them laugh. God, my salvation, will quickly put them to shame." May the Lord have mercy on us and our enemies and let none perish. May He have mercy on us all and not punish as we deserve.

Oh God, fill all our hearts with Thy Holy Spirit so that we might pray from our whole hearts for divine peace, that it might be planted in all hearts who call themselves believers, that peace might be planted in this time of grace, that we might be as one heart and soul in eternity.

Dear brother, I am writing this in great meekness and imperfection. I hope, however, you will not reject it but rather consider and read it in love. When and wherever I may have erred I will be gladly reminded of it by you and accept it from you in love. Dear Brother Sander, I greet you most warmly along with your wife, the dear sister. My father and mother and sisters and all good friends send you all their warm greetings.

I commend all of you to the protection of God.

I remain your most humble sister and fellow-traveler,

Catherine Hummer.

This letter is to go to Brother Sander Mack in Krefeld near Germantown. . . . [29]

Minutes of Annual Meeting

Minutes of a great council meeting held at the date given below, in reference to the difficulties in regard to Sister Catherine Hummer.

Conestoga, May 28, 1763: The undersigned brethren assembled here from their different places of residence in the fear of the Lord in heartfelt and compassionate brotherly love, in order to see how we might advise our in-God-beloved brethren in reference to the many astonishing occurrences and various transgressions that have occurred since the exercises, visions, and actions in connection with Sister Catherine Hummer in the White Oak country have happened.

After hearing the accusations of the brethren against one another and their testimony — that they were not seeking any division, but were willing to hear our brotherly counsel of love — we have together listened with great conscientiousness to and considered the mind of each and every one of us. Each of us undersigned brethren has, one after the other, freely declared his mind and counsel and then, in the fear of the Lord, we agreed on this, that we would in unity counsel our brethren as follows.

First, we believe and find indeed, that Brother Hummer has brought too much of his human nature into those doings, out of which various fruits of disunity have grown. In the second place, we also believe that both sides have gone too far against each other in words and judgments. Hence it is our brotherly advice that Brother Peter Hummer should make acknowledgement where he might have transgressed in regard to brotherly obedience. And then, when there is acknowledgment on both sides, we advise out of brotherly love that on both sides all rumors and harsh expression be entirely renounced.

Although we have no consensus about the occurrence in question, those who believe in it are not to judge those who do not. Likewise, we shall not look down on those who derive some lesson and benefit from it. In general, we admonish you, beloved brethren, to receive one another as Christ has received us, and to forgive one another as Christ has forgiven us also. Let us altogether hold the opinion that all dispute, judging, and contempt has been and will remain completely laid aside. Let everyone leave to the other his own opinion in the fear of the Lord, that we might all spare our consciences. Moreover, it is our advice that all unnecessary and too-frequent visiting cease, and that all evil appearances be carefully avoided and that we practice truth and honesty in all things in order that truth may free us from everything that might still keep us in captivity and prevent us from attaining a unity of mind in Christ Jesus according to the will of God.

Now, if one or the other thinks that we have not sufficiently judged the occurrence, let him consider that we cannot in the least give cause for a separation for conscience' sake. Therefore we felt constrained not to criticize or judge this strange happening but rather urge everyone to a Godlike impartiality and patience, lest someone judge before the time when the Lord comes who will also reveal the hidden things of darkness and will make manifest the counsels of the heart. Then shall every man have his reward from God according to his faith and the fruits of his being.

Signed by our own hands on the date given above: Jacob Meyer, Martin Urner, Peter Dierdorf, Nicholas Martin, Lawrence Schrab, Henry Neff, Christopher Sauer, Jacob Stutzmann, Jacob Mohr, Henry Raudenbusch, Daniel Lettermann, Anthony Hartmann, Sander Mack, George Etter, George Schreiber, Joseph Reutsch, John Schleiffer, Matthew Schweitzer, Gideon Rausser, Daniel Arnold, Nicholas Lettermann, Stephen Ulrich.[80]

III. Relations

8. Brethren and Moravians

A movement closely akin to the Church of the Brethren in the eighteenth century was the *Unitas Fratrum* or Renewed Moravian Church. Known in Great Britain as the United Brethren (or, confusingly, sometimes as the Church of the Brethren) and in Germany as the *Brüdergemeine,* the denomination dates from a mid-fifteenth-century Hussite association of Christians. By Luther's time there were some four hundred congregations and two hundred thousand members in Bohemia and Moravia. Virtually blotted out by the harsh policies of the Catholic Counter Reformation, the Unity of the Brethren lived on in the period of the "Hidden Seed" in the hearts of some Moravian peasants and in the life of the great educator, philosopher, peacemaker, and author, John Amos Comenius (1592-1670), who in exile perpetuated in his person their apostolic succession of bishops, and published accounts of the Unity.[1]

The carpenter Christian David (1690-1744) learned of the Unity of the Brethren in secret talks with the Neisser family about 1717; his grandfather had declared before his death ten years previously: "I almost think that you will have to emigrate to another country where the Lord will prepare you a place, where you may serve him without fear, according to His holy word." A friend of David's was the Lutheran minister-elect in the Saxon village of Berthelsdorf, not far across the border in the Germanies from Catholic Moravia. In 1722, the first group of Moravians made the secret trek to freedom, in a manner not unlike escapes from Iron Curtain countries today.[2]

Nicholas Lewis, Count and Lord of Zinzendorf (1700-1760) — Lord of the Baronies of Freydeck, Shöneck, Thürnstein, and the Vale of Wachovia; Lord of the Manor of Upper, Middle, and Lower Berthelsdorf; Hereditary Warden of the Chase to His Imperial Roman Majesty in the Duchy of Austria below the Enns; Aulic and Justicial Counsellor to His Majesty, Augustus II of Poland, for the Electorate of Saxony — was the owner of the Berthelsdorf lands. He was prepared for his fateful encounter with the refugees from Moravia by his Pietistic education at Halle under August Herman Francke. Yet, it is clear that the count had little idea how his life would be changed when he first laid eyes on the rude log cabins erected on a hill called the "Watch of the Lord" — *Herrnhut*.

After much struggle and uncertainty among those who settled in the Herrnhut community, it was the count and the carpenter who led in the establishment of the Renewed Moravian Church in 1727. A deep and vital spiritual life empowered a tremendous expansion of missionary activity — a continuing characteristic which has earned for the Moravians a notable place in the history of Protestant missions. The gifted and energetic Count Zinzendorf threw himself into the movement and stamped it with his striking personality, which mingled, surprisingly, humility as a brother among religious equals with the customary presumptions of the nobility.

Many of the Radical Pietists in Germany and other European countries were won to the new movement. Zinzendorf visited the Wittgenstein area, which the Brethren had shortly before vacated, and attempted to organize the rugged religious individualists still there into a structured congregation, but met with little success. He had equal difficulties with the Inspirationists, despite close ties with their leader, Rock. These enterprises, and especially the outraged cries of orthodox Lutheran theologians, occupied the religious press of the day almost to the exclusion of other interests. The fame, and notoriety, of the Moravians under Count Zinzendorf was to impinge upon his plans for North America because many in Pennsylvania and elsewhere had already formed impressions of the count before his arrival in December 1741.[3]

EARLY CONTACTS WITH THE BRETHREN

Even before the coming of the count and his entourage to America, there was contact between the Moravians and the Brethren. (It is very likely that the Moravians knew about the Brethren quite early, of course, because of the Radical Pietist connections.) The first reports of the Brethren in America to come to Herrnhut were contained in letters from several Schwenkfelders who had formerly lived in Herrnhut.

These men were the followers of Kaspar von Schwenkfeld (1490-1561), a contemporary and critic of Luther, whose views have been characterized as Pietist before the advent of Pietism.[4] They also suffered persecution under Catholic authorities and were offered shelter by Zinzendorf on his estates, until the king of Saxony ordered their departure. The count aided them in their migration, and they naturally sent back detailed reports after their arrival in Pennsylvania in September 1734. The two principal figures were George Böhnisch (1695-1772), a Moravian who accompanied the Schwenkfelders, and Christopher Wiegner (1714-1777), a Silesian. They settled in Towamencin Township in Montgomery County, not far from Philadelphia (an area where the small Schwenkfelder denomination is still centered).[5]

Christopher Wiegner and George Böhnisch to Count Zinzendorf

Germantown, February 15, 1734

. . . The Brethren still show themselves brotherly and kindly toward us and, notwithstanding the fact that they know that we cannot be baptized if we continue in our calling, they asked us to come to their public meeting and gave us liberty to speak. . . . Afterwards we still had some questions about them and we inquired, whereupon the elders wrote a long letter in which they expressed themselves very openly about their whole cause — how it had its beginning and how one thing had grown out of another, and that according to the way they had been led they could act no differently than they do. Everything, as for example baptism and the Lord's Supper and brotherhood, they explained very beautifully. The elders extended a warm greeting to the congregation at Herrnhut. . . .[6]

Christopher Wiegner and George Böhnisch to Herrnhut

Towamencin Township, November 7, 1737

In Jesus dearly beloved brethren:

. . . in reference to what you wrote regarding the local Baptists, we think that you perhaps do not really know this kind of Baptist. They are so vastly different from others that once one of their leaders [*Lehrer*] himself said to me that he believed he would rather die than belong to some Baptist congregations. There are here four kinds: first, Mennonite Baptists, the English Baptists, and then those who are generally called Tumplers [Brethren]. From the latter originated the Sabbatarians. All of these live apart.

The Tumplers have here and in Georgia several congregations where more is to be found than with the others. The Sabbatarians believe that they have succeeded most in sanctification. They practice voluntary poverty and chastity. They have now built a large house for the single people. Whoever lives a life of celibacy among them is allowed to wear a long gown. At the dedication of this house they had a great love feast to which they invited all God-fearing people around the country. . . . [7]

SPANGENBERG'S REPORTS

As noted in Koch's letter (page 18), religious circles in Pennsylvania were impressed by August Gottlieb Spangenberg (1704-1792). The former professor at the universities of Jena and Halle joined the Renewed Moravian Church, much to the displeasure of his Lutheran friends including the noted Pietist leader, August Herman Francke. Spangenberg was called as the assistant of Count Zinzendorf in 1733, and lived out a full life as Moravian missionary, church leader, and finally, successor to Zinzendorf as head of the denomination.

First active in America in the attempted establishment of a Moravian colony in Georgia, Spangenberg came to Pennsylvania in 1736. Here he began by working on a farm, and quickly came into contact with religious figures of many different faiths. His humility and piety won him many admirers among the German sectarian and separatist groups, if not among the "church" folk, the German Lutheran and Reformed, who saw in the Moravians unwished-for rivals. Later, with the coming to America of the more aggressive and flamboyant Count Zinzendorf, the "low church" groups also came to be critical of the Moravians.[8]

Spangenberg wrote voluminous and diligent reports to Germany and The Netherlands of religious conditions in Pennsylvania, and, among many other items, provided informed and sympathetic appraisal of developments among the Germantown Brethren and the Ephrata community. Among the recipients of his reports were John Deknatel, David Nitsch-

mann, and Isaac Le Long. Deknatel (1698-1759) was an important
Mennonite leader in Amsterdam, who had met Spangenberg during his
visit to The Netherlands in 1734. The former became well known for his
Pietistic writings. Nitschmann (1696-1772), a native of Moravia, was the
first bishop of the Renewed Moravian Church. An intimate of Deknatel,
he made repeated trips to America. The third recipient, Isaac Le Long
(1683-1762), of German birth and Huguenot ancestry, had become a
publisher of books in Holland. His publications on the Moravians did
much to make them famous, if controversial. He was a leading figure in
a Dutch society for furthering Moravian missionary efforts in the New
World.[9]

Spangenberg to Deknatel

Towamencin Township, April 8, 1736

. . . In Germantown there is reportedly a congregation of the
Brethren, whose zeal and love has been praised to me by many brothers.
If the Lord so wills and I live, I shall visit them yet this week and
inquire about their foundation, for I like to hear everyone whom the
Lord allows me to meet. I am always happy when I encounter brethren, whether they are in this organization or that. At Conestoga there
is said to be a congregation which differs from these Brethren mainly
in this — that they observe Saturday instead of Sunday, for which reason
they are called Sabbatarians. About them, too, I can report only what
I have been told. [I] intend, however, to visit them also, if God be
willing. They are said to be very sincere and to show great power
[of the spirit]. . . . [10]

Spangenberg to the Congregation at Herrnhut

Towamencin, May 14, 1736

. . . I, along with Wiegner, visited the Brethren at Germantown.
There are souls among them who have experienced and suffered a
great deal for the sake of Christ. Even among the young there are
blessed instruments. They do not make exceptions among the commandments of Christ. The teaching in their congregations is done by
the oldest men [elders?], and there is liberty among them to speak.
Some time ago, when our [Moravian] brethren came into the country,
they [the Brethren] enjoyed great blessing. But the Enemy has done
damage to their brotherhood through marrying. They are becoming

in this like everybody else: they marry and are given in marriage, and they are not so strict about baptism and the Lord's Supper either.

I visited the Sabbatarians with our dear Nitschmann, and I returned only yesterday. They live forty miles from here. Two of them came to meet us, for we could not have found the way through the forest to them alone. When we arrived there, their elders and most important brothers called on us first. The next day they permitted us to speak individually with the brothers and sisters. In the evening they had the breaking of bread. If we had wanted it, they would have admitted us to it right away. The following day they took us to those who lived in the vicinity. In the evening they had a love feast, afterwards the breaking of bread and feetwashing. The third day they all accompanied us [on part of the homeward journey] with much love and many blessings.

In regard to their affairs, this is what we found. There are many unmarried persons among them, one by the name of Conrad Beissel. They gave the beginning to this gathering when they settled in the forest near a clear well and lived there very quietly. Later several unmarried sisters joined them. At first it was not their intention to expand very much, as it actually happened, for there are probably one hundred married and almost fifty unmarried persons in the congregation. The married ones have their households; the unmarried people live mostly alone but not all in one place. They are ruled by Gichtel's[11] principles.

In matters of the church they are like the Brethren. They do not agree [completely] with the Brethren, and in those matters in which they oppose them they are in the right. For example, they say that they [the Brethren] are not a congregation of Christ even though they believed that there were good souls among them, because they [the Brethren] had leaders who were ruled by the spirit of the world; they had no discipline, and did not sever the evil [ones]; they put greater emphasis on outward than on inward things; the spirit had left them; all it amounted to were clever words; when the good brothers, who were among them, ruled the congregation, it lay all in human hands.

They [the Ephrata Community] are Böhmist,[12] but they also use the Scriptures. They [the Brethren], however, consider the Scriptures to be an outward witness that one ought to hold just as the Scriptures say. A Reformed minister [Peter Miller] joined them, together with twelve of his people. He joined the unmarried brothers. He is very intelligent, almost like Steinhofer,[13] but not so [deeply] immersed in the blood of Christ, and assuredly seeks to save his soul. He also seeks to bring his former listeners to Christ.

Twenty among the unmarried are [living] just as in a monastery; they assemble at midnight, they eat, drink and sleep little, and are quite emaciated from fasting. They disdain the eating of meat and deny themselves various foods which they consider harmful. They love the narratives of the fathers of the church, but they are not content with a devout life only. Rather, they wish to attain rebirth. We talked at length with them and were with them not without blessing. However, we fear they might in part tire of the practices. . . .

A. G. Spangenberg[14]

Spangenberg to David Nitschmann

Towamencin, November 8, 1737

. . . c) I have had little dealings with the Sabbatarians since you left here, except that I have been visited by several of them three times and have written to Peter Miller twice. Their cause goes farther than I can comprehend, and I always fear there is even more to it. When Peter Miller was here last week, he explained it like this: there must always be a visible church on earth and in it would be such men, in whom the humble humanity of Christ resides and from whom the spirit is to be sought. Everyone who wants to be saved must come into this visible church, which may be recognized by its self-denial and suffering. When we asked him: "Where is this one [true] church? Do you perhaps think that it is the Sabbatarians?" he said: "Yes."

We asked further: "Do you then have those apostles who are here in Christ's stead, and from whom the gifts of the Spirit are to be sought?" He admitted this to be true. When we asked: "Who, then, are they?" he answered: "You know well on whom everything depends among us, namely, Conrad B[eissel] and Michael Wohlfahrt." We said: "How can it be seen that they are such men?" He answered: "If you will try, and will join us, you will find out, for such things cannot be easily explained to the mind." We continued: "So you do not believe that there is any other congregation on the earth than yours?" Answer: "If there is one and if [it] were to come to this country, where we are already established, then it would have to subordinate itself to

us: and if we went to them, then we would have to subordinate ourselves to them." "But do you not believe," we said, "that people
could be saved who are not in your fellowship?" Upon this he said:
"It might well be, that there is some one in the old country who did
not know of us and yet would be humbled [?] and saved from above."

What is to be done about this? We cannot separate ourselves
from these brethren, for they are very sincere and the Lord is with
them. Nevertheless, we cannot join them either, because they seem to
lean toward Gichtelianism. Besides, they use some unhealthy figures
of speech. For example, grace can be earned through works, such as
praying, fasting, and the like.

Today Michael Wohlfahrt and Welsh John were here to see me.
We parted in love and I asked them to be less narrow and rather
accept that which alone counts with Jesus Christ, namely, a new creation. There was no reason for us to separate ourselves from anyone
who did not agree with us in such matters that did not pertain to the
life of the new creation and to salvation. Otherwise, I had no objections
if those brethren and sisters, who were of one mind, way of life, and
guidance, adhered to certain rules and in doing so remained to themselves, as long as they did not attempt to force these upon others. Thus
this question remains: Is it necessary and profitable to seek a union
between the Moravians and the Sabbatarians? And upon what grounds
could such be established?

d) There is a new economy emerging among the Brethren at
Germantown. Several unmarried brethren have been very earnestly
and intimately united in the Spirit. They were tempted to leave the
congregation and join the Sabbatarians. However, they found it to be
better to confess the truth and either suffer for it or conquer through it,
and hoped for both at the same time. Meanwhile, several of the older
members who previously had possessed great [spiritual] strength which,
however, largely diminished later on, were mightily awakened and
humbled themselves before the Lord. Even among the Separatists, for
instance, [John Adam] Gruber, [John] Eckstein and others, there arose
a tendency for closer connection with other brethren, and there was a
secret prompting of the Spirit in them all.

But the sectarian spirit of the Brethren thwarted them, and they
could not join the Brethren congregation because they not only believed that too much emphasis was put on outward things like bap-

tism, breaking of bread, etc., but they also realized that discipline was lacking and that in marriage, marrying, the raising of children, etc., too much disorder prevailed. The matter was brought up and the Brethren began to insist more on discipline. But this disconcerted most of the older members, who cannot reconcile themselves to this, for they are not used to such things. The others, however, who are in favor of the matter, are supported by the Lord and are succeeding, although they must overcome many a difficulty.

The Separatists, especially Gruber, [Christopher] Sauer, Eckstein, have a separate meeting with the awakened Brethren, namely, [John Henry] Kalcklöser, [John] Hildebrand, Alexander Mack and his [spiritual] brother Stephen Koch, Dewald [Theobald] Endt and others. They attend the public meetings of the Brethren also and speak and pray there too, when they feel called to do so. What is to come of this, I do not know as yet. However, I would rejoice if the dead bones not only bestirred themselves but also united, and I do not doubt the Lord will clothe them with flesh and skin and call them to life through His Spirit.

e) The [Brethren] at Amwell are also split now. They, too, began to insist on discipline and agreed to curtail the socializing and pairing off of the young people. Now Naas' [daughter] was found guilty of sitting with a man who tried to force her to immorality [*Unzucht*], and of not removing herself from this person. Rather she remained in his lap for about an hour as if she were asleep. Therefore all of the Brethren found it necessary to exclude her from the breaking of bread and the kiss of love. However, her father thought, since she had not actually committed fornication, this would not do. He sided with her and accused all the Brethren of judging wrongly. Thus he separated himself, later attracted many to his side, and is now holding a separate meeting. I wrote to him urgently concerning this and faithfully admonishing him; however, it was to no avail. . . . [15]

Spangenberg to Isaac Le Long

Germantown, November 21, 1737

. . . 15) Please greet Brother Decknadel and give him in place of a letter the enclosure. It is a testimony dated March 5, 1724, by an old champion, John Naas, with whom I became acquainted here. It contains many good things. Perhaps he will know what he could do with it. But, I [now] notice, it has not been completely copied, and I do not know whether I will have sufficient time to do this before the ship sails. . . .[16]

September 25, 1738

. . . Messrs. [De] Koker at Rotterdam can give the best information on the ships which come here with Germans, for they are very faithful in taking care of those poor people.

. . . Just to mention another word about the conditions here, I must say that I have become acquainted with many dear and believing brethren here. However, they are either separated from others or they bear a sectarian yoke. . . . The congregations of the Brethren, who are called Dumplers because of their practice of immersion baptism, have caused a great stir in this country. There are among them old, experienced, and revered men who walk very simply in their Baptist life, and therefore have been warmly received by many people. But after several had come to the point where they thought that one ought to observe the seventh day even in the New Testament, this created the reason for them to separate into two different factions. Now they call the one group, which is the stock, the Old Baptists [Brethren] and the others the Sabbatarians. . . .

They, the Sabbatarians, are having a hymnal printed in Germantown, which is an extract from the so-called *Psalterspiel, Blumenkranz,* the Moravian and other hymnals.[17] Their congregation also is increasing very much, although they not so much seek those souls that have never heard of Christ as those who have already been awakened.

As regards the Old Brethren, whom I mentioned earlier, they are, for their part, separated into two factions. One insists on introducing a stricter discipline, and especially forbids young people to court and make love freely in the manner of the world; the other, however, thinks the matter should not be dealt with so strictly, for then too many would have to be rejected, [in fact] the matter would have to be begun with the children of the elders [*Vorsteher*]. They so completely disagreed on this point, that some of the latter were put in the ban by the former because they would not give in. Yet, I must admit that there are honorable people among them whom I hold very dearly and in high esteem. . . .[18]

Spangenberg to Count Zinzendorf

1738

. . . 9) The congregation of the Baptists who are called Dumplers (from [?] *imergendo*) at Germantown is completely split. The best of them left because they wanted to see the impurities punished that were prevailing in the congregation, which the majority would have tolerated. The others put something together again, which, however, can hardly be maintained before God (I think), because they do not wish to remove the evil and unclean from among them.

10) The Sabbatarians are now triumphing. Their affairs flourish. It is obvious to everybody that their outward practices are peculiar; for example, they neither sleep on straw nor in a bed, they eat no pork, and the unmarried brethren live on bread and water; they have unusual clothes that resemble monks' cowls; they do not engage in buying and selling nor in any trade by which to earn money; they diligently practice vigils and working and the like. If I did not know what Diogenes with his barrel amounted to, and what the Carthusian and the Franciscan monks are doing, I might also be almost beguiled. Yet I know from my own experience that outward practices and physical powers are neither the new creation nor do they bring about the second birth, but rather, that it all comes from grace through grace. Therefore I remain quiet and observe it, often with sadness, for the works are often made into righteousness, and grace is sought therefrom. O Lord, when shall my eyes and those of others properly be opened . . . !

Besides this, they adopt many things from the old covenant and try to lay them on the brethren's necks, as for example, that they should work on the first day, which is called Sunday, and observe the Sabbath, for it is said: "Six days you shall labor, and celebrate the seventh." Beards are not to be completely shaven, and the like. They have mightily endeavored to attract us to them, and when I consider individual brethren, I do find important people among them. But I have only fear of their [illegible] and their brotherhood as a whole, for I do believe or fear that it might become a new religion and sectarian business before many years have passed."[19]

Spangenberg to David Nitschmann

Skippack, March 7, 1739

. . . By now you will have received my letter in which I wrote you about the brethren from Georgia who are coming to this country. Since then nothing has taken place in regard to them except that Haberecht[20] was baptized by the Sabbatarians and lives among them. . . .

I have no longer anything to do with the Sabbatarians. Several weeks ago I visited them once again, but [I] must honestly admit that I cannot be happy about them, for I see quite clearly that false powers and not the Spirit of Christ are ruling the congregation. Besides, they not only baptize those who were baptized as infants, but even those who had previously been immersed by others. He, Conrad Beissel, himself, has engaged in water baptism four times. First [he was baptized] as an infant; later, he jumped into the water in order to baptize himself; third, he was baptized by Peter Becker; and finally by Michael Wohlfahrt. Moreover, they set themselves up too high and cast everything under their feet, trampling that which does not belong to them or does not bow to their yoke. I must say, I do not know whether the Papists or these Sabbatarians are the more sectarian.

Therefore we are minded not to quarrel and dispute with them, yet [at the same time] we cannot be in the same spirit with them. We offered them peace, but they insist that we be baptized into their brotherhood, or otherwise they want no peace. I esteem very highly the honest and simple souls among them, but I entreat God to free them from the yoke of man and the slavery of being under the spell of a foreign power. With many other souls, whatever their name might be, we find warm reception. . . .[21]

THE COMING OF COUNT ZINZENDORF
AND THE PENNSYLVANIA SYNODS

The Lutheran Count Zinzendorf, who had become the head of the Renewed Moravians, had from the beginning of his religious pilgrimage a broad outlook. Now considered to be one of the most important of the ecumenical pioneers, he had a vision of the reunification of the divided denominations into a "Congregation of God in the Spirit." He hoped to preserve the values of diversity in unity according to the motto: "In essentials unity, in nonessentials diversity, in all things charity."[22]

The plan articulated toward this end was the "Tropus" — from the Greek word for *way* (Philippians 1:18). Each denomination was thought of as a "school of wisdom" with its own merits and contribution:

Denominations (*Tropes*) are God's economy, machinery to bring truth and the love of His Son to men according to their capacity, and according to the temperature and atmosphere of the country. For England, Anglicanism is suitable; in the Spanish and Portuguese atmosphere, the Catholic; for the French temperament the last is not quite so fitting, hence the Gallican Church, a mixture of Catholic and Reformed with more freedom than in other Catholic countries. Protestantism suits Germany and still more the northern countries. The Savior has all the denominations under His protection and will not let them be destroyed.[23]

The Moravians, as an ancient Protestant church antedating the Reformation and possessing both Pietistic and Catholic elements, were well designed to serve as the vehicle for bringing the churches together in harmony and cooperation, thought the count.

It is not surprising that his attention turned to Pennsylvania as the place where the grand plan could be implemented. With freedom of religion as a basic pillar of the colony, he would not be faced with the combined weight of intolerant and vindictive state and church establishments which so plagued him in Europe. Also, the very multiplicity of separate religious parties presented a challenge. And further, he was apprised by the careful reports of his deputies (Spangenberg, Nitschmann) that the ground was prepared.

In 1736, stimulated by the appeal of John Adam Gruber, a group of men from several denominations and those adhering to none began meeting in the Perkiomen area. Henry Antes (1701-1755), a Reformed lay preacher, was giving leadership, as was Spangenberg himself. These "Associated Brethren of the Skippack" met every four weeks for mutual edification and exhortation. Zinzendorf saw the possibility of using this relatively unstructured but existing movement as a base for his new church form. Therefore, in the fall of 1741, he resigned his Moravian episcopate so that he "might be regarded in Pennsylvania as a free servant of the Church Universal," made his will, gave a series of farewell sermons to the congregations in Germany and The Netherlands, and sailed for Pennsylvania. One of his first actions upon arrival was a formal renunciation of his titles of nobility; he wished to be known simply as Herr von Thürnstein. Soon the egalitarian Pennsylvanians were calling him Brother or Friend Lewis.[24]

Spangenberg's Description of Pennsylvania in 1742

In the eight-volume life of Zinzendorf penned by Spangenberg, there is a brief statement introducing the various church groups with whom the count became involved, given for the better understanding of his European readers. The main attention of the visit was paid to the German-speaking groups, although Zinzendorf was eager to have the English denominations participate as well, which did happen to a limited degree.

Before I proceed to describe the actions of our count in North America, it would be helpful to give a brief introduction of the people whom he found there and with whom he was mainly concerned. These were first of all principally the many Germans living there, and secondly, the Indians who had owned this territory before the European settlers arrived.

According to a rather accurate estimate there were more than 100,000 Germans in Pennsylvania alone at that time. Many of them resided in the cities of Philadelphia, Germantown, and Lancaster. The others were scattered about on the land, and lived principally by farming.

The hope of full freedom of conscience denied them in Germany had motivated very many to take wives and children and leave for Pennsylvania. There were others who followed because they noticed that Pennsylvania was a land in which an industrious person could earn a good living. Those who came multiplied rapidly, and formed large families.

Many thousands of these people concerned themselves so little with religion that it became proverbial to say of a person who completely ignored God and His word that he had "the Pennsylvania religion." . . .

Besides the Lutherans and the Reformed there were found in Pennsylvania at that time, among others, the following religious denominations:

1) the so-called Quakers;

2) Mennonites, who oppose the baptism of infants, and baptize no one until he is able to formulate a confession of faith himself;

3) the so-called Dunkers (*Täufer*), who hold, in addition to the point of view of the Mennonites in regard to baptism that immersion is an essential part, and therefore they consider all those as unbaptized who have not been dipped under water during their baptism;

4) Sabbatarians (*Siebentäger*) who were one with the Dunkers, but in addition firmly maintain that one must celebrate the seventh day, not the first day, as the former is the true Sabbath;

5) the Schwenkfelders.

All of these have their separate congregations, and some of them their own unique doctrines and practices.

In addition there were also the

6) so-called Inspired, who came here from Germany but do not form their own congregation here;

7) Separatists, who once belonged partly to the Lutherans, partly to the Reformed, partly to the Mennonites, partly to other religious bodies, but now remain apart;

8) hermits, who see their cause in not only remaining single but also living completely alone and separated from all society;

9) the New Born (as they call themselves) who claim that if a man is reborn then everything which he does is good and right, for he cannot sin any more; indeed, they consider obvious acts of the flesh as good, according to this opinion.

These people were all, each for his own part, so convinced of their beliefs that they preferred their path to all others and judged those severely who did not join them. They especially despised the Lutherans and the Reformed, because not only was there so little vitality to be felt in their services, but also because so much of a disorderly and scandalous nature took place in their life and conduct. For this reason it came about that those Germans who were still concerned about religion would more likely be motivated to join one of the above mentioned religious factions than to attend the Lutheran and Reformed worship services.

(Note.) As far as the English residents of Pennsylvania and the bordering provinces are concerned, they were either members of the Episcopal Church or belonged to one of the groups which dissented from it. By Episcopalian I understand the Church of England which confesses the Thirty-Nine Articles and binds itself to certain forms found in the [Book of] Common Prayer. The main group among the dissenters was the Presbyterian, who did not permit bishops to have precedence but wished to have the church government served by a college of elders. This denomination was very strong at that time, and has expanded greatly. However, I will not take more time to describe them here than I did for the several small sects which I found there.[25]

Henry Antes Calls the First Synod

Shortly after the arrival of Count Zinzendorf in Pennsylvania, and evidently with his counsel, Henry Antes sent out a widespread appeal for the convening of a conference aimed at greater church unity. The Brethren were invited, and received letters identical with or similar to the following.

Frederick Township in Philadelphia County
December 15, 1741

In the name of Jesus. Amen.

Beloved [Friend and] Brother:

Frightful damage is wrought in the church of Christ among the souls that have been called by the Lamb to follow Christ, mainly through mistrust and suspicion toward one another and that often without reason whereby every purpose of good is continually thwarted although we have been commanded to love. It has therefore been under consideration for two years or more whether it would not be possible to call a general assembly, not to argue about opinions but to treat with one another in love on the most important articles of faith in order to ascertain how closely we can approach one another on fundamental issues, and for the rest bearing with one another in love on opinions which do not subvert the ground of salvation; in order that all judging and criticizing might be diminished and done away with among the aforesaid souls, by which they expose themselves before the world and give occasion for it to be said that those who preach peace and conversion are themselves at variance.

Therefore this very important matter has now been under advisement again by many brethren and God-seeking souls, and has been weighed before the Lord. It has been decided to meet on the coming New Year's Day in Germantown. Hence you are cordially invited to attend, together with several more of your brethren who have a foundation for their faith and can articulate it, if the Lord permits. It has been announced to nearly all of the others through letters similar to this one. There will probably be a large gathering, but do not let this deter you for all will be arranged without great commotion. May the Lord Jesus grant us His blessing thereto.

From your poor and unworthy, but sincere friend and brother, Henry Antes.[26]

Henry Antes to Count Zinzendorf

A few days later Antes wrote to the count describing his initiative.

December 18, 1741

My dear Brother Lewis Z[inzendorf]:

I greet you warmly and wish to inform you in our Emmanuel about the matter of the conference of brethren. As this appealed to us, I have not delayed further but announced it by messengers and letters throughout all of Pennsylvania, as far as I am known [to them] to the prominent leaders of the Brethren and the Sabbatarians, to the most outstanding leaders of the Mennonite ministers, Separatist souls, even as far as Germantown. It will probably be a large gathering, weather permitting, and I am asking you to plan to attend. The meeting is called for the coming New Year's Day according to our calendar used here in Pennsylvania. May the Lord Jesus grant that it be a blessing.

My dear brother, I must ask you to forgive my rudeness in writing in the familiar [du] form to you. Many simple souls have taken offense because the last time that you were in my home I addressed you in the third person [er] or by the formal [Ihr] form. I was able to give a reason for it for the time being by telling them that I was in the habit of using "er" or "Ihr" with persons whom I did not know very well.

The reason [for their complaint] was that I respected the person against the admonition of the apostle James and preferred the rich or great to the humble (according to their outward standing) and that that did not make any sense at all, especially since you desired to conceal your position as a count. I promised them therefore that since I now knew you better and considered you a brother I would henceforth treat you like any other brother. Therefore I must ask this favor of you and your other brethren whom I do not yet know, for the sake of the simple souls for whom, after all, the Savior died too.

Please greet all of the brethren and sisters with you on my behalf.

From your humble but sincere
Brother Henry Antes[27]

The Brethren and the Synods

Brethren leaders in attendance at the first three meetings of the synods held early in 1742 included Joseph Müller, John Peter von Laschet, Andrew Frey, Abraham Dubois, and George Adam Martin. Müller and Frey later joined the Moravians.[28]

The first synod (Germantown) set the framework for the further deliberations. When the Separatists protested the emphasis upon bringing the denominations more closely together, the conference, under the increasingly pervasive leadership of Zinzendorf, responded that the true church "is the Congregation of God in the Spirit throughout the whole world, constituting that spiritual body whose Head is Christ. But they also constitute a communion of saints who, though outwardly belonging to different denominations, agree in all essential points of doctrine pertaining to salvation." At the second synod (Falckner's Swamp) the main resolution passed also reveals the count's influence: "The proper object of this assembly of all evangelical denominations is that henceforth a poor inquirer for the way of life may not be directed into twelve different ways, but only in one, let him ask whom he will. But if any one should take a fancy to him who directed him in the way, and should wish to travel on this according to his method, he has full liberty to do so, provided he be as yet in no connection with any religious society."[29]

The next synod, held at Oley in February, saw the baptism of three Indians converted by Moravian missionaries. The form of baptism (which was not by immersion) was a stumbling block for the Brethren. For that matter, the other participants also became increasingly unhappy at the course of the synods, and dropped out one by one, leaving the Moravians standing alone by the seventh, held in Philadelphia in June, the last of the series. This synod was marked by summary statements about the participating bodies, which reflect the disappointment of the count in his hopes for closer union.

Ironically, the meetings had the effect of increasing denominational consciousness. The Lutherans and the Reformed soon received able pastoral leadership from abroad, sent by authorities who feared the loss of their co-religionists to the Moravians under the energetic Zinzendorf. The Mennonites and the Brethren evidently began at this time to hold yearly meetings and to publish materials to delineate more carefully their doctrinal positions. The Ephrata Community and the Separatists rivaled each other in writing denunciations of what they thought to be the duplicity of the Moravians in gathering members and of their doctrinal errors.[30] As a matter of fact, many of those who attended the synods did become Moravians. According to a Moravian scholar, "for the Moravians the synods were both gain and loss with respect to denominational growth, with the long range result being decisively the latter. Inasmuch as a significant number of the participants — including both Reformed and Lutherans, and an individual here and there of some of the lesser bodies — eventually joined the Moravian Church, the result was an accession of fine leadership for the church. Also, a handful of preaching places under the sponsorship of the synods became Moravian churches."[31]

The same writer has a good summary statement on the reasons for the failures of this early ecumenical venture in American church life:

> Admirers of Zinzendorf are among the first to admit that he was one of the reasons. He did not have a personality that made for peace among theologians. Apart from that, his rank was against him. The free spirit of Pennsylvania dislikes titles and grand airs. . . . Knowledge in America of the controversy surrounding him in Europe put him at a disadvantage from the outset. . . . The immigrant generation, with its first taste of freedom from the restrictions of the Old World, was still suspicious of anything that might hamper its individualism. Finally, the idea was difficult to understand. Zinzendorf's aim was neither organic merger nor simple federal union, but an attempt to make visible the invisible or true Church. Such a task neither theologians nor everyday Christians seemed as yet able to achieve.[32]

Here follow some excerpts on the Brethren from the minutes of the synods and from Zinzendorf's statements from that period.

Question 7. Zinzendorf. Each baptism, when it is being administered, is according to the ordinance of Christ. If I discarded infant baptism, I would be in accord with the Tumplers, etc.

Answer. We see from the way of life of the Tumplers that they live according to the ordinances of Christ. But we do not consider that they baptize after the ordinance of Christ.

Zinzendorf. I do not maintain that all Tumplers are Christians, but that their baptism is according to the ordinance of Christ. etc.[33]

. . . . .

My [Zinzendorf's] childlike declaration regarding infant or adult baptism in Pennsylvania.

. . . 5) In Pennsylvania the obvious ill success and curse which are resting upon the two Dunker denominations are an undeniable sign that the Lord is not with their witness, at least for this country. And even if [adult] baptism were introduced, all the Baptists [*Täufer*] would still have to be dismissed, who have up to now as thoughtlessly administered baptism as ever any pastor of religion has. For what greater claim to baptism (not to mention the partiality in baptizing the wife of Peter Wend and denying baptism to Schierwage) does a covetous Pennsylvanian have than a covetous or lascivious Lutheran does to holy communion? And if we are to speak in the presence of God, who is there in the country who has any chance not to be baptized by them if he desires baptism? What divine ordinances are we then to accept from people who have absolutely no common sense in [?] their hearts?[34]

. . . . .

Unanimous conclusion of the General Synod of Pennsylvania Concerning the Denominations.

. . . VII. The Dunker Church [*Täuffer Kirche*] failed to prove its origin and by this very fact demonstrated sufficiently that they have nothing at all to do with the Anabaptists who were condemned by the Augsburg Confession.[35] It is a congregation of God-fearing folk, who act after their conscience but without illumination, who are earnest and therefore appealing people. We would consider it only natural if they united with the Mennonites and came to an agreement about the method of baptism. That would make one sect less in the country. As long as children of God can make up their minds to live among them and be loyal to them, they are happy; as for us, let us only be concerned that Christ be proclaimed.

VIII. The congregation in Conestoga, which is inappropriately called Seventh-Dayers — because the Sabbath is not a thing for mockery — has, however, withdrawn from investigation as early as during the fourth conference. . . . The congregation of the Lord declares herewith that this sect organized in Conestoga with its two cloisters is merely a schismatic pack [*Rotte*] from the Dunkers, from whom they attempted to steal their baptism and calling. After they had accomplished this and had by and by alienated the loyalty of most of the sincere Dunkers with all kinds of pretense, they finally succeeded in seemingly creating an establishment. This, however, was in fact invented by the devil for the sole purpose of preventing in time the coming of the kingdom of Jesus Christ, to stir up violently the Separatists against anything that is called community, to plunge religious people by its horrible errors into suspicion and fear of the future reign of grace and, finally, to magically persuade those souls wishing to escape to a false doctrine and community so that when the gospel arrived no one would be there who hungered for it.

We have nothing to prescribe for their people because we do not know how they became involved with it — whether God's wrath has cast them there, or only because His infinite wisdom intended something good to come to them through it. We consider ourselves far too insignificant to interfere with this and would need to examine the case of each individual who suffers in their community, especially the imprisoned cloister-virgins of Kedar. May the Lamb crush this satan to death soon![26]

Brethren Reactions

A pointed statement about the synods is found in the autobiographical account of George Adam Martin. Although his tendency was always to magnify his own influence, there is reason to believe that his reaction to the synods was shared by other Brethren.

. . . it happened that Count Zinzendorf and many of his brethren came into the country and occasioned a great stir, especially by his synods. And because all denominations were invited to them, I too was delegated by my superintendent [Martin Urner] to attend them. When I arrived at the [third] synod, which was held at Oley, I found there some of our Brethren, Sabbatarians, Mennonites, and Separatists. The count himself was president and for three days I heard queer and wonderful things there. After my return home I went to my superintendent and said that I looked upon the count's conferences as snares, for the purpose of bringing simple-minded and inexperienced converts back to infant baptism and churchgoing and of erecting the old Babel again. We consulted with each other what to do, and agreed to get ahead of the danger, as some Brethren had already been smitten with this vain doctrine, and to hold a yearly conference, or, as we called it, a great meeting, and fixed at once the time and place. This is the beginning and foundation of the great meetings of the Brethren.[37]

In a three-volume work against the Moravians published by a well-known Lutheran pastor and theologian (Fresenius) in Frankfurt, Germany, there is a long description entitled "American Reports of Herrnhuter Matters," which contains detailed reports of the reactions of the Pennsylvania Separatists to Zinzendorf's visits. There are also many letters and pamphlets published in the collection, making it an excellent source. Christopher Sauer I and John Adam Gruber were the principal authors.

Several (Schwarzenau-) Brethren were quite taken in to the great regret of their fellow Brethren in other places who later, upon unanimous agreement, wrote very urgently to those (who had become involved in his [Zinzendorf's] cause) to renounce him again or they could not walk together. These things which happened to them and to the Conestoga group or Sabbatarians and their correspondence follow in separate appendices which they are having printed. The former especially had a much clearer perspective already at the first conference and would not become involved in this, and warned each other earnestly and faithfully. Yet they had to suffer some of their number, though not without opposition, to attach themselves to, yes, even join, the Moravians and finally in part even to leave the country with them, for example Andrew Frey and Joseph Müller. . . . [38]

These days two Mennonite ministers were also there to see him [Zinzendorf], and told him that they had once been Brethren [*Tuncktäufer*] and did not wish to have anything to do with infant baptism. He met them in a very friendly and modest way, and said that they were right, they [the Brethren] were a true congregation, and he would recommend them wherever he went. Andrew Eschenbach ought to join them; he had been baptized at Frankfurt on the Main. He [Zinzendorf] also intended to visit the great meeting which was to be held on May 16, [1742], etc. However, he was going to persecute the spirits of sectarianism as long as he lived. He did not actually go but instead sent them [the Brethren] a letter which he signed Lewis Siegfried.[39]

Zinzendorf's Letters to the Brethren

Count Zinzendorf was eager to bring the Brethren into his Congregation of God in the Spirit and hoped to speak to them personally at their conference on May 16, as noted above. Failing in this, he sent a letter to them which contained both encouragement and reproof. Prior to this he had written to Joseph Müller, a member of the Brethren who had become closely attached to his cause, advising him on how to proceed in approaching the Brethren to gain their closer cooperation.

Germantown, March 11, 1742

[To Joseph Müller]
My dear heart:
I cannot come to the conference on the fourteenth and fifteenth,

but on the evening of the sixteenth. Tell the sectarians the same things that I recently told Abraham [Dubois] and Peter Becker about the ordination of Brother Hollstein [who was made elder in the Reformed church at Germantown by Zinzendorf by the laying on of hands], namely, that if they think that they are a burden for the congregation, I renounce all friendship and association with them. They are a church who can hold their own love feasts like any other. Moreover, since they teach and live better, their church is better.

If, therefore, one of you wishes to hold a love feast with them, either with me in Philadelphia, or with Bechtel in Germantown, I would forbid it. I would just as little permit him that as I would Bechtel if he wanted to attend with Lutheran friends in Philadelphia. This means that each one should stick to his own denomination.

When, however, champions of Jesus from the Reformed, Lutheran, Quaker, Dunker, Sabbatarian, Mennonite, [or] Catholic churches observe the Lord's Supper, or elders gather at the body of Jesus, who belongs to no denomination, then all denominations must permit it.

One mocks those who like foolish virgins do not know what they want, and lets them go. The wise servants of the Lord among them are in part Protestants. That, tenderly beloved brother, is what I have to say to you!

[Count Zinzendorf][40]

* * * * *

Greetings in the name of the universal Christ, who shall not be divided in eternity! Beloved and honored Brethren-folk, under so many divisions and rending of the holy Head and Body in Pennsylvania more than other places:

I would gladly have come to you in person because of the following reasons. First, so that I could see your ordinances and practices, and could rejoice over the good, and learn something from you. Secondly, so that I could have fraternally discussed with you any reservations you have concerning my office and practice, in the hope that the Savior should have blessed it, and brought you to a toleration toward me and mine suitable to your religious form. Third, so that I could have informed myself thoroughly and clearly explained my views about the pack on the Cocalico [Ephrata] which had its origins among you. Like a faithful mother, I could have given you some suggestions how to deal mercifully and advantageously with these wayward children in order to save many of them, if not all.

Fourth, so that I could have advised you to maintain closer relationships with the several good souls in this land, who are especially good workers, for example, Andrew Eschenbach, Godfrey Haberecht, Theobald Endt, Frederick Ochs, Conrad Weiser, and others. This would bring the advantage that your church would not be divided again so soon, and in time be robbed of all power and flavor.

Fifth, so that I could have truly asked you to go further in tolerance, for you have a fine beginning therein, and not make your baptism and manner of baptism either the main thing or something infallible. As little as I desire to bring you over to my side, I must publicly witness to you, since you have compelled me, that neither your manner of baptism is correct, nor is adult baptism appropriate to the early church, except where people are converted only as adults. Despite this, I would not have the slightest reservation to use your manner of baptism nor would I advise your brethren against it, if they brought such ideas about infant baptism with them, but would rather respect their wishes in this. I consider it a deep mystery and believe that it is pearls cast before swine to dispute about the depths of infant baptism and the communion of flesh and blood of the elect souls, with some religious denominations and sectarian spirits. I defy all truly reborn and sanctified sinners to perceive anything about this!

Sixth, so that I could also have humbly brought you to speak respectfully instead of suspiciously about our brethren, Abraham Duboy, Peter Becker, Andrew and William Frey, Frederick Hollstein, Joseph Müller, and others, who have more or less connections with us. This is an honor for you, and the damage to you would be great if one or the other of these brethren were to be brought to the extremity by you that he had either to renounce you or Him who has arranged, according to His testament, that all are one, as the Father is in Him, and He in the Father.

Seventh, so that I could have implored you to make a real differentiation between the children of God, in so far as they are cast into the Greek, Catholic, Waldensian, Moravian, Evangelical, Reformed, Baptist, and Separatist molds, this in so far as they are one spirit with Christ, and members of that abundance of Him who fulfills all in all, and who gives them that which no religion can give them, that they are in Him, and have received this from His heart.

In case a Reformed brother wanted to attend when I administered the sacrament to some poor Lutheran sinners, I would certainly send him away and say: "Go to Bechtel in Germantown." Order is good in all things. However, if Bechtel himself wanted to partake of the Head and sought nourishment of His Body, His Corpse and His Blood, of which he is a member — as a champion of Jesus Christ in a company of such champions only — what should I do? If I sent him away, he would have the right to do the same to me. Therefore, let yourselves be made wise therein, beloved! Beware, dear friends and brethren, that you may not someday be accused of not being present at the first conference.

This matter rests before the Lord for better or for worse. Neither I nor any other servant of the Lord will mention a syllable about it. The conferences were arranged for your benefit and not for ours. The Lord, who is the Lord of my heart, had commanded me that I should heal Babel, and that I should seek salve for her wounds, as long as I can. This is so that Jesus might retain souls therein and not let them perish. Each sect should retain its good salt, lest it loses its savor. You are dealing with a person who will do this faithfully as long as it is possible.

After twenty years, I can say of the separatist Babel: "I have treated it, dear Lord, but it will not be healed. I hope now to gain permission to discard it." I think Pennsylvania will help me in this, if only I could come to a clear understanding on the Quaker matter!

I enclose you in Jesus' heart. For the sake of my brethren and friends, I wish you happiness, and for the sake of the household of the Lord, our God, I will seek your best.

Siegfried, the servant of the Lord

His symbols: Lord Jesus — in whom I live;
Lord Jesus — in whom I die;
Lord Jesus — in whom I am.[41]

ANDREW FREY AMONG THE MORAVIANS

As noted in the Frankfurt publication (page 288 of this chapter) two Brethren leaders — Müller and Frey — were so taken by Count Zinzendorf and his plans that they accompanied him back to Europe when he left in early 1743. A later comment in the same volume noted a specific reason for the count's interest in Andrew Frey.

An Excerpt from the American Reports of Herrnhuter Matters

. . . Count Lewis himself left Philadelphia on January 1, 1743, at nine o'clock in the evening. Among those who were taken along and went with him from this area was Andrew Frey. He had formerly been a Separatist, was later a Mennonite, was then a Sabbatarian but took offense at them and became a leader among the Brethren. He then became involved with this [Moravian] movement, and was made a leader. Count Zinzendorf had long recommended and urged that Frey travel with him, because of the other Brethren in Holland, as he himself admitted. As Frey was so weak physically, he did not want to agree to this at first, but finally he was convinced and strengthened in it through the drawing of lots.[42]

Frey's "Authentic Account"

In quite surprising fashion, Andrew Frey became involved in an international literary controversy about the Moravians. It happened that Frey's visit to the Moravian communities in Europe, principally Herrnhaag in the Wetterau, coincided with a critical period for the Moravians, referred to by their scholars as the "Sifting Time." One scholar finds its source in the one-sided emphasis which Zinzendorf introduced upon the subject of the atonement of Christ, possibly as a reaction to the various views on salvation he had encountered in Pennsylvania. It should also be mentioned that one wing of Radical Pietism also emphasized many of the themes which came to characterize the Moravians in Herrnhaag.[43]

The main element of the Sifting Time was "a morbid concentration and word-play upon the blood and wounds of the crucified Christ and a simulated irresponsibility of behavior supposed to be a demonstration of childlike faith." The excesses to which this led, although well documented, strain the credulity (and good taste) of modern readers. In the prolific hymns and poems produced in this era an excessive use of diminutives, sensual images, and playful phrases seems to border on the pathological. Small wonder that a sober Brethren influenced by the Mennonites and the Sabbatarians would feel critical.[44]

The early pages of the treatise written by Frey upon his return from Germany to Pennsylvania in 1747 explain the reasons for his publishing his unpleasant story. What he could not have foreseen was how the enemies of the Moravians would seize upon his narration as an eye-witness report which could be used to discredit the entire movement. This is the reason for the extensive publication of the simple account, which was reprinted in Germany in 1749, in Dutch translation in 1750, in English in 1753, and which was incorporated in other publications elsewhere. As recently as 1950 his story was utilized heavily in a book by a noted Roman Catholic scholar in England as an "honest witness . . . [whose] evidence cannot be set aside."[45]

The following narrative contains the occasion and motive of my becoming a member of the Society of Herrnhuters, and the reasons for my leaving them. [Because of my] having during my return here intimated to some persons of integrity what moved me to depart from the Community, they told me that upon my return to Pennsylvania my conscience would hardly let me be at peace if I did not expose the state in which I found it. . . . But hearing that some things had already appeared in print against this Community, I left the matter to the Lord, and gave myself no further concern about it; except when any questions were put to me, I spoke the plain truth according to my conscience.

But the Brotherhood at Bethlehem told the people that all I said of the Community was a heap of lies, I speaking out of mere resent-ment and malevolence, and that because Joseph Müller had married William Frey's daughter [Veronica], which never so much as once came into my thoughts. And as if that was not enough, a man in high esteem among them [Henry Antes] has given out that I myself had said to him: "Had the Community made me a bishop, I should have gladly stayed with them," which is another falsity coined to support their cause. . . . As to myself, I could freely have overlooked it without writing a single letter on such a foul subject, had they not gone about to wash their filthy hands and asperse me with a letter from Joseph Müller in Germany to his wife's parents in Pennsylvania, wherein he loads me with scandal, as behaving myself in an unbe-coming manner among them; and because they encourage the people with telling them that when Joseph Müller comes over I shall be set out in my proper colors. . . . Therefore in regard to my conscience I could not omit publishing Joseph Müller's letter with my commentary on it, leaving every one to judge according to his knowledge, and withal

heartily wishing that none would be offended or triumph at it, but
rather first examine themselves whether the tenor of their lives is
agreeable to an imitation of Christ before God who judges men according to the most intimate secrets of their hearts.

Andrew Frey

Copy of a Letter from Joseph Müller to William Frey

[Marienborn, 1747]

Dear and tenderly beloved Parents:

We often salute and kiss you from the Side-hole, and from the
Community of the Lamb, which He has purchased with His blood.
How blessed are we! We rest in His Side! The Side-hole and the
Lambkin fill the exulting heart with flame. And that is all which we
wish and can wish you, that you and our dear relations may from
the womb be brought into the little Side-hole, and there enjoy all the
felicity which the Lamb can impart to a justified sinner.

I thought to have been with you this summer, but it has proved
otherwise. Possibly I may come in 1748, if nothing intervenes. That
I earnestly long to see you soon I cannot deny. But to go away in
such a manner as Andrew has gone is what I will never do while I
have breath, as he went in great confusion. [He] had striven continually
to the utmost to conceal that wickedness which had first shown itself
in New York, until at last it broke from him as a stream which had
been dammed, so that during his four years stay here, without the least
good, he gave himself up to such a wicked course of life that I shudder
at the thought of it.

I'll give you one instance from which you may judge how it stands
with him. He once spoke to me these very words: "From the times of
the apostles there has not been in the world so profane a sect as the
Community. In every respect they are of a piece with the New Born
in Oley."⁴⁶ I hope you have so far experienced the contrary in your
hearts that it is needless for me to prove the horrible falsity of such
words.

It is now a year since he first showed an inclination to leave, which
for his sake filled my heart with grief, but that not mending the matter,
I said to him: "Andrew, there is one thing which on your account
goes very near my heart, and it is not your leaving us." He asked
what it was then. I answered: "It is that after being among the

Community for four years, you still know nothing of it." At this, turning up his nose he said that he knew them better than I did. "No," I retorted, "it is impossible that you should leave them if you knew them."

At length I persuaded him to go to Herrnhaag with me, upon which for a while he carried himself somewhat better, and being promised that he should be one of the next journey to Pennsylvania, it made him tolerably easy and steady. At last, hearing that the journey was postponed, so that there was room to conclude that it would not be this year, he threw aside the mask and resolved to depart immediately. Yet he was kindly furnished with a passport and money. Further, Brother Lewis [Zinzendorf], unwilling that he should go alone (as he was aged and weak), sent a brother along with him to attend on him to the end of his journey. But he . . . would travel by himself, and accordingly on May 5 [1747] he set out from here.

Many of us are concerned for Andrew. I am ready to believe that he has been treated by some of the brethren as a "Merry-Andrew" should be treated, at which afterwards they were displeased. They know no better way how to deal with an old Pennsylvania saint. They were ignorant that by often beating an old head so stuffed with *devotion* and *self-denial*, it falls to pieces.

I am sorry that I must send you such an account of this "Merry-Andrew." Yet is the information rather too short for a warning that you may know how to behave toward Andrew, he having said to his trusty brethren (one of whom by name of Sieberg has been expelled from the Community for his immorality and refractoriness), that when he set foot in Pennsylvania again, William Frey would not be long in Bethlehem, but he would have him back to live upon his land. He not only promises to alienate you from the Community, but also many more. But if your hearts through the Blood of Grace have experienced what I have, he is likely to come short of his aims.

He imagines he can overreach you and deal with you as formerly, when he was accounted a little god; but now you'll make a jest of him, being able to give him as good as he sends. For Andrew is no late acquaintance of yours, and if Andrew wishes to go on in his prating, tell him to forebear until I am part of the company. When he says anything, I'll be his interpreter, for he actually does not understand what he says to you.

Herewith we recommend you to the little bloody Side-hole, and ourselves to your affectionate thoughts, and remain, as in duty bound, your poor loving child,

Joseph Müller.

Salute in our names all your children and companions, Brother Spangenberg, Henry Antes, George Neuser. We heartily wish well to Brother Abraham and his children, together with the rest of the brethren, sisters, and children. [End of Müller's letter.]

Continuation of Frey's Authentic Account

... I am under the necessity of saying how and why I went among them [the Moravians], and how by the free grace of God without the intervention or assistance of men I was awakened, called, and brought to conversion. The merciful Savior imparted to me in some small measure the light and strength of that precious reconciliation which He so painfully obtained for me, by His blood and death on the cross, and caused me to feel it powerfully in my heart.

In the meantime, I became acquainted with Spangenberg, soon after his first coming into this country. The Lord was nigh unto us by His grace, and united us in love, so that he very often cordially discoursed of the mercy which the Savior had acquired by His death and sufferings. Likewise how gloriously the Herrnhuter Community in Germany lived and increased in the grace of reconciliation, and how affectionately they loved one another in a childlike temper and unblamable life. And from the love I bore him, I conceived a high opinion of the Community by such hearsay, being further persuaded that it ought to be so among God's children. . . .

Thus we lived together in entire harmony, and wished that well-disposed persons of all denominations would lay aside all grudges and cultivate complete love and confidence. Count Zinzendorf hearing of this our desire that a general love might prevail among persons of all parties, it was his advice to us that we should set up conferences for the promotion of universal love, and this was the origin of the synods. In the third synod, three brothers were chosen out of fifty, as presidents and directors of the conferences, and of these I happened to be one. And as I then believed in the Bible-lots, I could not object against it. I admit that self-love was somewhat flattered to be placed in such an office, though I understood nothing of the function. . . .

[Later] I was chosen by fifty votes and the usual lot to be elder over the unmarried brethren. This office was conferred upon me, and I was to move to Bethlehem, for which I was as little inclined as I was fit, knowing that were I to act according to my understanding and conscience, we should be continually at variance. To give up my understanding and my conscience to their method was what I determined not to do. Several of their proposals having a Lamblike appearance, and I lacking sagacity to distinguish between what proceeded from the real spirit of the Lamb, and what from the intrigues of man, I was at a loss how to act so as not to occasion fresh disturbances, which might be detrimental to myself or others.

I sank into the most distressing perplexity, lest I should sin against the Savior's interest, or be drawn in to be the tool of men, for I daily saw more and more things which displeased me. Perceiving that I could not be modeled to serve their turn, they let me know that I should go to Germany.

This at first I disapproved of, although I should have liked to get a thorough insight into the Community. On the one hand, I was taken with their friendliness and their doctrine of the merits of Christ's sufferings and death; on the other hand, I could not be reconciled to their monstrous grossness and extravagance of their imaginations. In this fluctuation of mind, destitute of counsel, I applied myself in earnest prayer to my God and Savior, that by His grace He would incline my heart to what was good in His sight, and recommended my outward and inward life to His will. Then I determined to proceed with them, begging with prayers and supplications that He would keep me from all the devices of man's self-will, and that He would preserve me from being scandalized at anything which by His grace was done among these people. . . .

Thus we proceeded on our voyage, and in five weeks reached London, a fortnight later we came to Amsterdam, and at the end of three weeks more arrived at Herrndijk; and wherever we came we found some awakened souls. Afterwards we came to Marienborn, from where, after a stay of four weeks, we proceeded into Saxony to Hirschberg, where we held conferences for nine days. From there we went to Herrnhut, and then to Silesia, dividing our time between traveling and daily conferences in order to establish societies in all areas. . . . In all places, however, we found some newly awakened souls, both high and low, sincerely disposed to follow the things which pertained to their salvation, that I was often filled with joy to see the divine grace calling and awakening people in many places to a real conversion. Indeed, I saw and heard of many glorious things, but there were others as bad, and although grace powerfully showed itself in many of the Community, yet when I looked for real conversion and change of life, I found myself among a worldly-wise sect, as I had before seen in Pennsylvania. As for myself, I endeavored with all my might to keep close to grace, by which also I was strongly assisted in comparing what I saw and heard of this people with the doctrine, life, and example of Christ and His apostles, and praying with many sighs that the Savior would lead me into all truth according to His good pleasure.

The other brethren and sisters who had come from Pennsylvania having once a love feast, the count told every one of them his thoughts of them, and when he came to me he said: "Brother Andrew has indeed an open countenance, but mark me, there is something amiss in his mind which hinders him from having any settled quiet." It was so indeed, and how could it be otherwise, hearing and seeing many things which grieved me. In the meantime I did as well as I could. . . . The count with his family . . .went to Holland . . . and the count's birthday falling in May, a letter came from Holland to Marienborn directing the houses to be illuminated on that day, which was accordingly done. They fetched wagons full of boughs, and with them covered the whole inside of the count's hall, which is a hundred feet long and forty wide . . . that it looked like an arbor, and also hung up three brass chandeliers. . . . Wooden letters above two feet high were made to form the name of Ludwig von Zinzendorf, and these, being gilded with gold, were fixed to the wall amidst a blaze of lights. . . . The outside of the court was adorned with festoons and foliage, and also with another representation of the name, not less illuminated than that within, so that in the hall and court there were not less than a thousand candles burning at once. . . . The panegyrics which were composed on this occasion were stuffed with high-flown praises that I could not have imagined should be lavished upon him who would admit of such encomiums and exaltations from men as happened at this festival, and many times afterwards. This was followed by the singing of hundreds of people and choice music, as if at some prince's court, of which I had indeed heard something before, but never had seen; nor was it ever seen among them who belong to Christ, and *have crucified the flesh with the lusts and affections thereof.* This jubilee came about no less seldom than eight times in the year, namely, for the count, the countess, the young count, the three young countesses, Ann Nitschmann, and John Langgut or von Wattenwille, the count's son-in-law.

This was a novelty to most and an abundance of other people flocked here to see this famous spectacle, this scene of gluttony, pride, and idolatrous profusion. An account of it being carried to Frankfurt and other neighboring places, it afforded abundant matter for ridicule and reproach, as it little agreed with the doctrine of Christ, that says: "Let your light so shine before men that they may see your good works, and glorify your father who is in heaven." But here a spirit of drunkenness and debauchery seemed to be broken loose among the Community. The young folks began to grow wanton, laughing, sporting, jesting, leaping, throwing one another on the floor, and struggling until they were quite spent and out of breath, besides many filthy, gross indecencies. . . . This is one of the fruits of the renowned church discipline, or rather of the licentious life of nature, tearing up all piety by the roots, as they have not hesitated more than once to say openly in their meetings that they would not cease until they had driven Pietism out of the Community, root and branch, and that the life of nature was what they would have or none.

The general elder over the unmarried brothers throughout the whole country, whose name is Rubusch, living at Marienborn, has been known to say: "All godliness, all devotion, all piety are no more than so many snares of the devil." At another time he said: "Things must be brought to this pass in the Community, that nothing shall be spoken of but Wounds, Wounds, Wounds; all other discourses, however scriptural and pious, must be spewed out and trampled under foot." . . .

A laborer among the unmarried brethren, whose name is Calic, has further said in the "Brethren's Quarter of an Hour": "It is a certain sign that a brother has not yet experienced the Savior's grace in his heart, if he meditates on the Bible, a thing so contemptible that it ought to be spat on, and is by no means deserving of the thoughts and attention of him to whom the Savior's wounds are known. For anyone having found lodging, bed, and board in the Lamb's wounds cannot be but merry, and live according to nature; so that when such a one plays any pranks that the godly ones cry out against them as sins, the Savior himself is so far from getting displeased therewith that He re-joices the more over the sportive little Wound-worms." . . .

If I offered to find fault I was so hooted and railed at that I was obliged to suppress my dislike, and recommend it to the Lord. I fully purposed, however, at the count's return, to talk the matter over with him, and hear how he relished such frantic wicked doings. He had been away since April, and it was November before he came back. In the meantime illuminations were not wanting on their birthdays, with such an increase of wantonness as drew from me sighs and tears beyond number, to see and hear the precious name, blood, and wounds of the holy Lamb made a cloak for all manner of licentiousness. . . .

When the count returned, Frey was unable to see him personally to make his complaints, and therefore wrote a letter. Part of the answer of the count, according to Frey's recollection, was as follows.

Dearly beloved little Brother:

I cannot but be displeased that matters went so amiss as I am in-formed; you by your small and great errors having caused great un-easiness to the brethren, which has alienated their respect from you. But no one is more offended than myself, because I cannot act in concert with you, and find you fall very short of the surname we had conferred on you of Andrew the Great. We are no Baptists [Dunkers] feeding people with legal coercions, though at the same time they are without regenerate hearts. A bear may be taught to dance, yet still remains a bear. . . . [Upon this, Frey determined to leave Herrnhaag.]

Frey Defends His Position

Two years after the publication of Andrew Frey's account in Ger-mantown, a rumor was abroad that he had retracted his criticism of the Moravians. Frey wrote a letter to be published in Sauer's newspaper in which he reaffirmed his writings.

Falckner's Swamp, April 20, 1750

William Frey was recently ministering in Great Swamp in the homes of several trustworthy people who earnestly asked him whether it was true that Andrew Frey had reunited with the Herrnhuters and whether he had retracted his booklet, *An Explanation*. They had heard this not as a rumor but from the so-called Herrnhuters themselves, who also said that Andrew Frey was their dear brother, that they loved him very much, etc. A leader of the Mennonites said to him [William Frey] that he had read my booklet and that they [the Herrnhuters] testified in their life and conduct that what I had written about them was true. But if I were to recant . . . he would consider me a changeable, wicked person; thus it would be impossible to know whom to believe. . . .

This was nothing new or strange to me at all, for far too often have I heard or seen them do such a thing. I know their love and that it is always mixed with lies and I have always considered it a trick of Satan's when a person speaks differently than he means. It is like the conversation between the old serpent and Eve when praising the forbidden fruit. In the very same way the Herrnhuters in Germany claimed (according to letters from trustworthy people) that I had recanted and was back within the Community again. In the very same way they claimed here that [Andrew] Gross [of Frankfurt] had recanted his writings and had joined the Community.[47] In the very same way they said in Cologne (where Gary B———l was known and loved) that he had become a member of the Community and was working with them for the Savior. On the other hand, others from their Community said (in order to extenuate the count) that Gary B———l had lied to Kiefer about the letter of excommunication.[48]

And thus they well know that in this way they can make me and my booklet suspect throughout the whole country. Thus they always have a deceitful way of making that suspect which is written in truthfulness against them. I say, however, in truthfulness before the Lord, that it has never entered my mind to retract what I have written. On the contrary, I testify openly about all men who have ever written the truth about them, no matter how learned or experienced they are, that they and I have fallen far short in describing this bottomless deceit and spiritual malice in its depth, height, length, and breadth. For since I realized what the foundation of these people is, nothing has seemed more repulsive to me than that they have changed the most precious expressions, such as Lamb, blood, and wounds to fit their sensuality as a false shield of faith, in order to fend off all Biblical truths and all testimonies from within and without, and to barricade their hearts to the disciplining spirit of grace, and also to make a mockery of conscience and, as it were, make it a cover for their lusts of eyes and flesh and their haughty lives.

This has been disclosed with many clear examples in the writings of other men. From this issues a false gospel, to preach a comfortable life for the flesh as a mockery of Christ and of all the faithful witnesses of all times. Indeed, with me there is the very opposite of recantation; instead, I would have much more to say. Spangenberg may be my witness, for when he asked me during my illness whether I did not regret having written the booklet I answered him: "Oh, no!" Rather, when I was at the worst point of my illness and I and all those standing about me thought that I was soon going to die, I felt a joyfulness in my heart that before my end I had made my testimony against this spiritual fraud.

This, then, is the account of my opinion of the angel of this Community [Zinzendorf] along with his great fellow-laborers who are at the helm.

Written by my own hand on April 20, 1750.

Andrew Frey[49]

JOSEPH MULLER AND THE BRETHREN

The other leading Brethren personality to join the Moravians was Joseph Müller (1707-1761) who, unlike Frey, remained with them for the rest of his life. As we have seen, he had no success in reconciling Frey to the Moravians in Germany. He was equally disappointed in his efforts to act as a middleman between his former fellows in the Brethren camp and his newly-found friends among the Moravians, despite repeated efforts.

Letter of a Brethren to Germany Concerning Zinzendorf and Müller

The Frankfurt publication contains a letter from an unidentified Brethren [*Taufgesinnten*] describing the often-cited incident during the Pennsylvania synods when Müller reproved Zinzendorf for his hot temper, and contains a further critical reaction to the count's efforts in Pennsylvania. (It is possible that the author was Mennonite instead of Brethren.)

Germantown, November 15, 1742

. . . [George] Stieffel is still living, and is now a Moravian. Lewis Zinzendorf came to us last fall, in 1741. He had great plans and thought that he would unite everyone under his leadership. . . . He wanted to be the head of the Separatists, Brethren, Sabbatarians, Mennonites, Schwenkfelders, Quakers, Reformed, and Lutherans. He has not been successful. He came too late and has achieved little. He has won some Brethren, Separatists, and Reformed, but the majority are from among the Lutherans.

Here in Pennsylvania he has found his master. He has met with people here who measure up to him. Rather than his being spared by them, he was well belabored. His anger and fiery spirit have betrayed him, so that he had to testify himself that in Europe he could get along but in Pennsylvania it was not possible.

A Dunker brother reminded him of this, and said that he had annoyed people at the synod by his anger and fiery spirit. "Oh," said Lewis, "if I only were a man like you, with such meekness. I would give anything for that." He said to the Dunker brother, whose name was Joseph Müller: "I believe that you could give me meekness if you laid your hand upon me and prayed over me." So this Dunker had to do this in the conference to the great man who tries to pose as our apostle. In order that the lesser be blessed by the greater, the greater must first be blessed by the lesser.

You wrote that they were very frivolous. We have found the same — that they are very impudent in their speech and laughter. Lewis tried in every way possible to bring our friend J. A. Gr[uber] into his fellowship. Gr., however, has always put him off. Count Lewis has spoken very harshly against the Separatists, and has assailed them with great zeal in the church at Germantown. He has betrayed himself far too much, and has revealed what he really is.

They have also baptized some Indians, or sprinkled them with a Kolabash (a plant like a gourd). These are, however, Indians who had learned to speak Dutch many years ago, and had been with the Reformed (as I was told). Lewis promised that that would be the last time that he baptized in that manner, but the promise was of no avail. On the second trip, they practiced it the same way on the Indians, so that [we could see that] Lewis and his people were not too careful in keeping their word.

We have ourselves experienced this, and some (who are conscientious people) say that they could accuse him of lies to his face.

He had received some unmarried German and English women into his fellowship. They were not there long before he gave them

husbands from among his young men. He also gave Andrew Eschenbach a wife, the daughter of Frederick [Ensler]'s sister. Her father is a
shoemaker; his name is Benedict. They are very dissatisfied that they
became so involved with Count Lewis; they had thought that all that
glittered was gold.

Lewis recommended Eschenbach to us with great cunning. He
said that we should accept Eschenbach into our fellowship. Abraham
[Duboy] said: "No, we do not want to have him. He believes in
infant baptism; he belongs in their fellowship." "No," said Lewis, "he
is a Baptist. He was baptized near Frankfurt on the Main [River]."
We said that he preached infant baptism. Answer: One should forbid
him that. We, however, saw through his cunning, as he is a poor
politician.

But, as was said above, the Pennsylvanians are too clever for him.
This is a free country. The people here are not much interested in
counts. That is enough about these matters. If one were to write
everything, it would keep one busy. I reported it only because when
Lewis returns he will try to exaggerate the work in Pennsylvania and
probably tell about the many congregations which he has here. He
would have very few people here if his followers from Europe (German
and English) had not come to Pennsylvania.[50]

Müller Decides to Leave Pennsylvania

The anonymous but well-informed author of the "American Reports on Herrnhuter Matters" provides some details concerning the
decision of Müller to accompany Count Zinzendorf to Germany in 1743.

From the place where he [Andrew Frey] lived [Frederick Town-
ship], two young women went along also, who had been incited and
enticed by Count Lewis. They made a great show of piety that they
were leaving their parents' house for the sake of the Savior and the
souls [to be saved], namely, Henry Antes' eldest daughter and the
daughter of William Frey, her companion, who had previously been
sought by Count Lewis from her father in marriage for one of the
count's men. When the father would not permit it, they got at it in
this way. Another was one of the Sabbatarians named Cässli, who
had just run away and had come here.

Furthermore, one who understood medicine, named Joseph Müller,
who had been quite renowned among the Brethren. He it was who

A portrait of Joseph Müller, taken from an oil painting preserved in the Archive of the Brüder-Unität, Herrnhut/Oberlausitz.

A

TRUE and AUTHENTIC

ACCOUNT

OF

ANDREW FREY.

CONTAINING

The Occasion of his coming among the HERRN-
HUTERS or MORAVIANS, his Observations on
their *Conferences, Casting Lots, Marriages, Festi-
vals, Merriments, Celebrations of Birth-Days, Impious Doctrines,* and *Fantastical Practices; Abuse
of Charitable Contributi , Linnen Images, Osten-
tatious Profuseness,* and *Rancour* against any who
in the least differ from them; and the Reasons
for which he left them; together with the Motive for publishing this Account.

Faithfully translated from the GERMAN.

---------------- Unitate *in illa*
Sæpe agunt ferri truculenta mente tyranni
Sæpe latro, larvaque vorax et fædus adulter.
Et simulatus amor, fallaxque modestiâ vultus,
Quæ tegit innumeras sub ovillo vellere fraudes.   BUCH.

LONDON,

Printed: and Sold by *J. Robinson* in *Ludgate-street, M. Keith* in
Grace-church-street, M. Cook at the *Royal Exchange,* and
J. Jolliff in St. *James's-street.* MDCCLIII.

[Price One Shilling.]

Title page of the London edition of Andrew Frey's account. Courtesy of
the library of the British Museum.

once tried to exorcise in the synod Count Lewis' wrathful spirit but because of it was himself deeply caught and imprisoned. He had kept his journey a secret, even from those closest to him and even from his own brother and sister; the latter had had a curious premonition, some time before this, about a child who was so horribly soiled that it could not be cleansed. This she told him with a clear interpretation, and among other things presented the most important and urgent appeals to change his mind, but he was so committed that he would not wait another day. . . .[51]

Joseph Müller's Autobiography

As was the Moravian custom, Joseph Müller penned his own life story, which has been preserved in the archive at Bethlehem. It is a particularly valuable document for its details of travels to meet Brethren in Europe in the 1740's. It may well be that Count Zinzendorf wished to establish contacts with the remaining elements of the Brethren movement who stayed in Europe through Müller, as mentioned above for Frey.

The storm at sea during the return trip to Europe was widely commented on in Moravian circles because of the count's accurate prediction that it would subside in two hours without causing a shipwreck, despite great fear on the part of the captain and the crew.

The language of the autobiography reflects some of the devotional quality of the Moravians which the Brethren found objectionable.

Joseph Müller in Bethlehem.

My brief and insignificant life history is as follows:

Born in Alsace near Werthe on October 23, 1707. My father and mother were natives of Switzerland and as Mennonites were expelled from there.[52]

From my childhood on I had a desire in my heart and wished very much to be saved. [I] often prayed to the dear God to have mercy on me and to be gracious unto me. I often resolved to live a very pious life. However, I was more likely to hit upon something bad than something good. This went on until the year '27, when we migrated to Pennsylvania. When we arrived in Holland I thought: "Now you are going on the great ocean and have not yet been baptized." Therefore I had myself baptized by a Reformed minister who happened to be going also to this country. Now, I thought, I will live up to my baptismal covenant; from this time on I will no longer do anything wicked. I did conduct myself very honorably on board the ship.

Upon arriving in this country I had to indenture myself to pay for the passage. Afterwards I associated with the young folk, amused myself in various ways and yet everyone considered me to be an honorable man. But I was not at rest in my heart. I often went into the woods and wept about it, until the year '30 when the Savior became close to me in my heart. I left all my previous companions and began to read diligently in the [New] Testament. In doing this the suffering and death of the Savior became amazingly important and great for me, especially the Gospel of John and his epistles. They tasted like honey to me, and for a time the Savior was so close to me by night and by day . . . that no man can be closer to his wife. At night I thought I was lying in His arms; when I awoke I thought I still had Him with me.

Gradually this great tenderness abated somewhat, about which I shed many tears and soon it [the tenderness] returned as to a mother who comforts and cares for her child. It did not remain, however, and I thought if only I knew one person who was converted [?]. I then happened to be hired by Baptists. I heard the people speak of beautiful things. I was very shy but I did begin to talk to the people and I told them how things had been going with me for a time, but that I no longer experienced such a continual pleasant feeling as at first. "Oh," they said, "you are on the right path; this is the right direction. Now the Lord has led you out of Egypt, now you are indeed delivered from Satan and sin, but now you still have to wander through the desert." They gave me books to read which described similar ways of providence. I then entered so far into the desert that I almost became a Christian, only I could not forget the tender feeling of the Savior which I had once felt and tasted in my heart. It was like an angel in my heart; I could not get over it and it lasted for about two years. Once I read the letter to the Romans and found that God had included everyone in unbelief so that He could have mercy upon all. From that hour on I was engulfed by streams of grace, which penetrated through bone and marrow.

After this I became acquainted with the Brethren and was baptized by them in the year '35 at Christmas, but upon my faith and not upon theirs. Later I became somewhat acquainted with Brother Joseph [Spangenberg], and when the brethren from Georgia came here I loved them, but I thought they still lacked a great deal. The same year Espinbach [Eschenbach] came into this country and after him his father and mother. I immediately felt extraordinary love toward them.

The following year the dear Papa [Zinzendorf] arrived here. I received him very well after my fashion at that time. In the year '43 I traveled with him to Europe, and was elected ship's elder at sea. The gracious preservation in the great storm and how He guided our little ship with His own hand through the cliffs is well known to the entire Community.

After being in London for about two weeks I was sent to Holland; from there I visited Friesland and Groningen and the Mennonites and Brethren there. After four weeks I returned to Heerendyck. After several days I traveled from there to visit Gernfeld; I visited Brethren and Mennonites, and also Pastor Hunge [Hencke] in Duisburg and [Gerhard] Tersteegen in Mühlheim on the Ruhr besides several other people like them. After our brethren and sisters had arrived from Holland by ship I traveled with them up the Rhine to Hanau and to Marienborn. In September I traveled to H[errn]hut, and to Gnadeneck to the Pilgrim Congregation, and from Gnadeneck we traveled to Silesia. We remained at Peilau [Peile] until Papa went to Riga. Then I returned to Herrnhut.

Soon afterwards when I was at Marienborn I came down with a high fever; they thought that I was going home [die]. Then I had a cold fever and was very ill. I did not want to go to the Lord's Supper for the sake of my brethren. After the Hirschberg Synod John Nitschman and Peistel [?] returned home. Then a Pilgrims' [Lord's] Supper was [celebrated], but no one told me anything about it. At night I lay under much tension and prayed to the Savior that if it were His will for me to participate in the partaking of His martyred body He might reveal it to me in my heart and grant me joyfulness thereto. Suddenly I felt in my heart that I ought to go along. I let John and Peistel know and they raised no objection. So I arose and went to the hall. I stood it from one o'clock until late at night. I began to feel surprisingly well and since I felt so well I no longer took any medicine, my fever left me, and the Savior made me well again through His martyred body.

I remained there for the winter and was installed as a single brother.

On April 29, in the year '44, I returned to Marienborn to the synod.

I also spent three months in the laboratory to assist the doctor.

On August 2 I was married to Veronica Frey [1723-1780] under the Heart's Supper along with four under-housefathers. (Veronica was born in Pennsylvania, in Fredericks Township, on May 1, 1723, Old Style. William Frey is her father, and in the year '43 she went with her mother to Europe. She does not know herself when she was received into membership.) We remained at Marienborn until the year '45.

On February 3, I went to Lindheim as the housefather for the children and my wife to the children in the orphanage at Herrnhaag. On August 9 I went to Herrnhaag as housefather for the children.

In the year '46 I visited Switzerland, including the Brethren in the Neuburg Mountains and returned home in December.

In the year '48, March 11, I visited the Mennonites in the Palatinate.

On March 29 I traveled with my wife and several married sisters to Herrnhut. I spent the summer at Hennersdorf, was servant [minister] to the Pilgrim Congregation, went along to the synod in Silesia, and was at the same time with the Royal Commission at Hennersdorf.

After August 13 I traveled with the [Ark?] and ten sisters again to Herrnhaag.

On October 1, I traveled with the single sisters to Frankfurt and by ship to Holland.

On November 11, I was sent to England and relieved Bundbusch at Meyoston [?]. I was housefather in the boys' home there.

In the year '49 I was recalled to London in order to travel along to Pennsylvania.

On February 20, 1749, we departed from London and arrived in New York on May 12, and on the 19th at Bethlehem.

On August 9 our first son was born and was christened Lewis.

On July 19 my affairs were driven into the little Side-hole.

On July 18 we were ordained as disciples by John Nitschman and Jule. My heart was so humbled and ashamed, and the streams from Jesus' wounds so penetrated me that I cannot describe it.

On [blank] I was ordained as deacon and my wife as deaconess.

In the year '52 [January 4] a son was born to us and was christened John.

Now here I am, a poor little worm, and wish in the end to be nothing but a blessed little mercy-gate enamored with the four little nails, and to hide in the split-open little side of Jesus and to be at home there forever. May the dear little mother help me thereto![53]

Joseph Müller Appeals to the Brethren

During his stay in Germany, Müller wrote several times to the Brethren in America to explain his reasons for associating with the Moravians. He emphasized that the Community "never seeks to bring a person from outside into their fellowship, but rather they much prefer each denomination to keep their children of God and witnesses of the Lamb themselves." At the same time he expressed sorrow at the news concerning their treatment of former members who now adhered to the Moravians: "I believe that they [Brethren] do not know what they do, for their conduct with my brother Abraham [Müller] and William Frey and others is irresponsible."

Furthermore, he assured them: "If the Savior had permitted it, immersion baptism would have been introduced. However, the Savior has never wished to allow this either in Pennsylvania or in Germany. The reason is none other than that we Dunkers place too much emphasis on this matter. . . . It displeases God when we adhere too much or cling to something if it is not Jesus and His death and wounds and bloody atonement. Everything else can become idolatrous for us, that is, baptism, Lord's Supper, feetwashing, going to meeting, vigils, praying, fasting, giving alms, and other deeds that can be performed." This reveals a basic difference in approach between the Moravians and the Brethren. To the Moravians, the Brethren seemed legalistic; to the Brethren, the Moravians seemed disobedient, if not antinomian.[54]

Upon his return to Pennsylvania in 1749, Müller addressed himself again to the Brethren. Explaining that his love for them was the reason for returning, he said that he wished to serve them, although he was hurt by their evident hostility to the Moravian Church to which he now adhered completely, after his earlier hesitation because of his Brethren affiliation.

November, 1749

Dearly beloved Friends:

After a period of seven years I have returned to this country under the gracious guidance of my good Lambkin, as you no doubt have already heard. I really cannot say that anything has moved me to leave Europe where all this time everything has been so pleasant and blessed for my heart and to return again but love and my loyal and sincere

heart toward all of you. I believed that I was bound upon my given
promise to serve you as the people from whom I went over to the
Moravian Community first and foremost with the gospel of peace of
our universal salvation in Jesus Christ through His perfect reconciliation
and redemption for all through His blood. In this sincere love to all
of you there has indeed been no change in me and I would still be
ready and willing to be used in my small way for the sake of all those
poor dear hearts who are truly concerned about nothing but this
Lambkin who was slain for us.

However, immediately upon my arrival in Pennsylvania I was
brought up short, was very discouraged, and began to have doubts —
and therefore took great offense — about associating with you after I
had learned and discovered with much disappointment that you and
your circumstances have greatly changed in this period, that you have
completely abandoned your old policy and no longer are what you
once were; but instead your hearts and minds are so possessed with
many prejudices and enmity against the [Moravian] brethren, and you
have associated with the other blasphemers and slanderers of our Community. Therefore it would be without any profit or purpose, perhaps
even cumbersome and unpleasant, for you if I were to come among
you. Also, under these circumstances I would hardly be able to produce
any results among you and would be a burden and nuisance for you
besides.

Lest you completely ignore how my heart still feels toward you and
why I have not yet come to you, I wished briefly to explain and witness
to it by these few lines. From the above you have sufficiently understood that up to now I have seen no purpose — neither for your sake
nor mine — in visiting you. I have been unable to imagine that it
would amount to anything but unnecessary and lengthy discourses
which would not serve our purpose at all, as well as quarreling, idle
talk, accusations, and justifications.

I am at this time no longer in the mood nor do I have any inclination for this sort of thing where everyone airs his own curious
ideas, questions, doubts, and accusations about the Moravian Community which they may have partly picked up from other disloyal and
libelous people, and partly brought forth from their own wicked, ruined,
evil hearts. I witness to you quite freely and without reserve out of my
own well-founded experience and the conviction of my heart, that I

belong with all my heart to this people, among whom I have lived
now for nearly seven years and from whom I have received during
this time so much love, loyalty, and care (although I was not yet an
affiliated member) and among whom my heart has found that for
which it had sought and striven for many years without success.

I do not necessarily consider them the only one but certainly the
best brotherhood and institution which is known to me at the present
time. This is by no means because of their beautiful outward order
and organization, which is commonly and mistakenly taken for the
thing itself, but rather because it rests simply and solely upon the
foundation of the prophets and apostles, which is Jesus Christ and His
blood, and which is separated by the word of the cross from any other
doctrine. If, however, despite all this, there exists among you one or
the other poor heart for whom it would be a blessing and a pleasure to
discuss this with me and to hear about his and my bleeding Lambkin
and His wounds for the benefit of his heart and soul, I shall be quite
willing to discuss this with any such poor little heart who is concerned
and perplexed. I would portray to him in few words the great love
which this same Lambkin has for sinners and His precious wounds
which He received for us as well as shall be given me in that hour
and minute by the best and universal proclaimer of the wounds of
Jesus, the dear Holy Spirit (to name it Mother would be quite fitting),
the Spirit who praises Jesus in His entire Bible.

Thus I greet all of you warmly and fraternally from our dear
Bethlehem on the Lecha [Lehigh River] where I am staying at the
present time. I expect [to hear from you] here about your reactions or
the one or other of you who is eager to speak with me. I am, as
always, filled with a warm love and fervent desire to meet you some
day in that place where the poor sinners stand quite humbled at the
great bliss and grace and where many a former enemy of the cross
lies prostrate at the wounded feet of the Lambkin.

Your faithful, loyal heart,
Joseph Müller[55]

The Brethren Reply to Müller

Müller's offer to serve them was hardly deemed tactful by the Brethren, who felt that he had wilfully left them to join an erring movement.
Of interest are their specific points of criticism upon Moravian doctrines

and practices. The letter amounts to an announcement of excommunication, closing with a sincere wish that Müller's eyes might be opened to his present state and that he might repent of his errors.

The number of signatures appended to the letter testifies to the seriousness of the communication, and gives an unexampled listing of the prominent Brethren leadership in the mid-eighteenth century.

Canantacken, February 12, 1750

Friend Joseph Müller:

We wish and hope for you all health and happiness in body and soul, and report at the same time that we have received your letter in good order and seen from it (and, as you write, have heard) that you have returned to this country under the gracious guidance of your Lambkin.

We can only say that what moved you to go to Europe and to leave it again and return was nothing but the universal spirit of deceit which motivates you and all others of your kind, and which makes you believe that in Europe things went so well and blessed for your heart. We can hardly believe that you were and still are in such bliss as you would like to think (that is, regarding the condition of your soul). As far as your outward motive, namely, that you fared well in regard to it — we will not take it up here. We can well believe you in this, namely, when we hear that it is completely bewildered, which did not seem to be your earlier understanding.

That you now offer to serve us with the gospel of peace (as you write) seems almost ridiculous to us, because we consider you to be quite incapable of this, and because you consider yourself, in your own estimation, so competent and wise (whereas we have read that when one sees a person who considers himself wise, there is more likelihood of his being a fool). [We are], on the other hand, very disappointed that you are seeking to associate with that in front of which you have spat out before, and not only that but that moreover you even offer to serve with your terrible great and small errors a people which from its heart abhors, flees, and shuns any such idol and calf-worship, as you know perfectly well.

The piety which you and your present congregation practice with fiddles, organs, flutes, oboes, bass-fiddles, bagpipes, and such nonsense, and infant baptism and your abominable leaders [?] (in the XIII appendix, second part, item, about your horrible matrimony)[56] — all of these are so suspicious to us that we consider the whole affair an abominable soup from which we do not wish to taste a single drop, whether it is you who brings it to us or someone else. But that you even intend to force your way in among us by virtue of the promise which you made at the great meeting on the Schuylkill was neither desired from you nor requested by those who knew you and your affairs. It did seem bad and despicable enough to us at that time that a person wanted so badly to be something for which he was incapable and for which he had no talent. It was just as the common saying goes and which an old man quoted at the time: volunteered services are seldom welcome.

You would have done better to remain silent about your sincerity, loyalty, and heritage, and then we might perhaps have held you in greater respect. It is only too well known to you as well as to us that you have been quite unfaithful and false with us; yes, indeed, you have even deceived the entire congregation inasmuch as you promised to serve them and their children and soon afterwards you ran away to Germany without a word. It seems that you are still the old simple and imprudent J. M. that you used to be, for you used to consider yourself wise, and still do so. Do you really think anyone is so simple as to desire such a servant of the gospel as you are now?

You also mention that you became very doubtful and even discouraged, immediately upon your arrival, and had to learn to your grief that we and our circumstances had changed so much and that we had completely abandoned our old system and were no longer what we used to be one time; but that instead, we had allowed our minds to be filled with many prejudices and enmity, and that we had associated with the old blasphemers and slanderers of your Community. This is something that cannot be proved, and is an obvious falsehood, not to say — for modesty's sake — a glaring lie. It astonishes us that the laws of reason allowed you to write such things inasmuch as you have neither seen us, much less talked to us, since your return. Therefore, the prejudice of which you accuse us is to be found in you and your letter.

In order that you, too, might not be in ignorance about us and our feelings toward you, you will undoubtedly have gathered from the above that you need not take the trouble to come to us, for you are looked upon by all of us as one who followed clever and foolish fables, and believed in and ran after all kinds of errors and perverted doctrines. It is therefore not worth our while to engage in a discourse or conversation with you, namely, in such a manner as to edify ourselves with you or to learn something from you, either small or great, much less to consider it a favor if you were to come. Of course, if you were penitent, contrite, and mournful in your heart, we would be obligated by the Savior of the world to offer you our handclasp again, because He has received gifts from the unfaithful.

However, inasmuch as you are still boasting of your present brotherhood, claiming that it is the best community with its institutions, and that you have found what your heart (although in vain) had been seeking and striving for, you are revealing once again that you have sought after something inferior. We are all the more astonished that you had sought this among the poor Brethren and striven after something like this among them, since you would never in your lifetime hear that among us are used fiddles, bass-fiddles, whistles, organs, harps, oboes, French horns, and bagpipes, that someone baptizes infants or that someone has "marriage-bands." If such things contain and carry within them such great salvation, they might after all be found in many a tavern.

J. M., for the sake of God and the salvation of your soul, remember the earlier days, when you became enlightened, how simply you respected the Word of God and how you have now completely strayed from that path, and how you have become a completely different person from what you used to be. And now on top of it you have the nerve to offer your service to us in your present condition! Be assured that if we desired and wanted to have servants of your make-up, we would not have waited for you because there are many of your kind who would like to serve us who would have much more talent for it than you. If we had sought such, why then did we go out of Babel of which we had indeed been a part? You have now really become a regular servant of Babel, who wants to help build another tower next to the great one.

We consider it almost unnecessary to add much more inasmuch as you will be able to gather sufficiently from the above that we regard your present affair as so bad, deplorable, miserable, blind, and bare, and, indeed, generally erring and perverse, that we do not wish to touch it, to say nothing of our allowing you to pass among us as a servant [minister]. We do not even wish to eat with you as long as you are going around in such an eccentric fanaticism and are dwelling among such a people (who are in their doctrine far worse and more perverted than Babel). Therefore we do not ignore [the fact] that you will induce several more Brethren to such a miserable wantonness and frivolity like yours.

We therefore renounce (and have done it a long time ago) [blank] all your perverted principles (however, if you reject them anew, you will be as we are), your "marriage-bands," "*Blauen* [?]" and chambers [?], your organs, whistles, flutes, oboes, French horns, bass-fiddles, small fiddles, and bagpipes, now and in eternity. Amen.

Therefore we do not greet you from our brotherhood, for we have read in the second epistle of John, verses ten to eleven: "If any one comes to you and does not bring this doctrine (that is, the teachings of Jesus Christ), do not . . . give him any greeting; for he who greets him shares his wicked work."

We do, however, wish you from our hearts that the Lord might give you a salve for your eyes, that you might realize your miserable condition in which you now stand, so that you might return and repent your idolatry, great and small errors, and clever and foolish fables. Then you would be dear to us as a brand plucked from the burning.

[Signed] Henry Jacobs, John Lehn, Joseph Latsche, John Dirdorff, Lewis Rothrock, Jacob Greif, Daniel Hinrichs, Rudolph Braun, Peter Knepper, John ————der, Philip Ehrhard; this I profess, John Jacob Peiterly, George Bäcker, Adam Sauer, John Leterman, John George Martin, Christopher Gusz, George Adam Martin, Henry Rundebusch, Alexander Mack, Matthew Schweitzer, Martin Urner, Peter Becker, John Schneider, Rudolph Harly, John Bechtelsheimer, Peter Greiling, John Preisz, John Mack, John Brecher, H. G.[57]

THE SAUER-ANTES CONTROVERSY

Although Christopher Sauer I printed the first American Moravian hymnal for Count Zinzendorf soon after the latter's arrival,[58] relationships between the two influential figures soon became strained. Sauer, a Separatist in religion and an ardent advocate of democracy, angered the count by opening the columns of his newspaper (a leading shaper of public opinion among the German settlers) to critics of the Moravians.

He was also in close touch with European Separatists who had previous unfriendly dealings with Count Zinzendorf. In the words of a German church historian, the count "met to his own surprise and occasional terror well-known acquaintances from castles of the Hessian nobility, and was astonished to find among them in the most isolated Pennsylvania woods the same gossip, the same defamation and allegations which he had hoped to evade by a six-week-long ocean voyage and week-long rides and canoe trips on the lakes and rivers of Pennsylvania." Sauer it was who provided a significant part of the communications between the two continents.[59]

Henry Antes, who had called the synods referred to earlier, took it upon himself to defend the count and his colleagues in a long manuscript which he took to Sauer to have printed. He was particularly aiming his comments at members of the Ephrata Community, who had published several pamphlets attacking the Moravians and what they considered the latter movement's overemphasis on marriage — an offensive point to the celibacy-proclaiming Sabbatarians.[60]

Excerpts From Antes' Manuscript Book, "Well-Founded Reminders"

. . . Finally, as far as the motivation for their [Ephrata's] writing and characterization, that there was not the least evidence of God among us, is concerned, because our movement cannot stand the slightest opposition, they can at the same time be in truth accused of a great imprudence. For otherwise they would have remembered that at the seventh and final conference with the churches, only a brief account was given as to how the various churches stood with whom there had been some contact. And on this occasion there was merely stated that they were nothing but a pack which had left the Brethren, whose baptism and calling they had sought to steal, and seduced their best members, and that this had been invented by the devil for certain reasons, to be found in the same conference on page 116.[61] There were only a few words, namely a "pack originated by the devil," and this enraged the intolerant Zion group to such a degree that they wrote an entire book against us and the Moravian Brethren.

. . . Not to mention others who remain rather quiet for the present as far as publication is concerned but who, at the same time, would like to see the Moravian Brethren along with the little church of Jesus from among all kinds of religions lose out and perish. We need only remember how very much the dear Brethren (whom one would gladly spare) were offended when the two cloisters of Ephrata and Zion were declared to be mere packs from the Brethren and invented by the devil; the dear Brethren were so disturbed about this and said (even to me personally) that [the synod] had gone too far with the Ephrata group. Now if one had asked them at the time when the Ephrata group split off from them and became a sect, whether the split was originated by God or by the devil, they would have promptly answered, by the devil. And if someone were to ask them now after they have accused us on this account, whether it was from God or the devil, they would be just as little able to answer (if they were in their right minds) as in former times the Pharisees and Sadducees could and would not [answer] concerning the baptism of John. . . . [62]

Excerpts From Sauer's Refusal

In a long letter, the Germantown printer described the reasons why he did not feel free to print Antes' book. There were errors and malicious statements in it, especially about the Brethren, according to Sauer.

[Germantown], September 6, 1743

Beloved Friend Henry Antes:

Our last agreement was that although I had several objections to your manuscript as far as I had read it, I would print it for you as something similar to my newspaper — where it often occurs that everyone describes his own actions as grand and well performed — but on the condition that it must not go against my convictions. However, as I continued to read it and in time finished it, I could no longer treat it like my newspaper. For if I object to some item in the newspapers that is either made up or which I consider to be harmful to someone, I omit it. And when I come across something of which I know for sure that it is impossible or sheer falsehood, I do not print it at all. Now I find in your manuscript various things in regard to which I am definitely convinced of the very opposite, but which you cannot possibly grasp in your present state of mind.

Other items, on the other hand, are so malicious that they would inevitably start another literary feud. At the present time it is contrary only to my convictions and I would have no objections if others were to print it, for thus the truth would plainly come to light, although I know that it will not remain hidden.

Let me remind you of a few passages from it, for I do believe that
you will be able to understand it. . . . Can you recall how disdainfully
you treat the Brethren when you repeat that the Ephrata group are a
pack invented by the devil, who originated among the Old Brethren
and took their best people with them? If the best people left the
Brethren and if the Sabbatarians are a pack invented by the devil, what
does that make the remaining ones, those who are the worst, who are
not as good as the pack? . . .

Your argument regarding the true sign as to which is the congregation of God, the one at Ephrata, Zion, or Bethlehem — namely, that
we would see which increases its numbers the most — was not well
chosen. For what congregation has grown more rapidly that
Mahomet's, if one were to call a party of men a congregation. This
congregation of the Brethren has increased its numbers by at least
fifty since the count left. That comes only from that loathsome pride
which always esteems itself higher than the other person and considers
him to be much inferior. . . .

John Christopher Sauer[63]

Antes Replies to Sauer

Here are excerpts from Antes' answer to Sauer's rejection of his
manuscript, with his brief comment on the Brethren expansion.

1743

Beloved Friend Christopher Sauer:

I received your letter as soon as I returned home after visiting you
recently and when I read it I found that it would perhaps be worthwhile to reply to it, especially because of your accusations, for I believe
that you are in the wrong. . . .

In the third place, concerning the Brethren, you are badly mistaken
and have drawn very incorrect conclusions [?]. I had not intended by
what I wrote to treat them disdainfully, but only to indicate to them
that they accuse us without reason of having gone too far by calling
the Zion group [Ephrata] a pack coming from them, and referred to
the other reasons as described in the seventh conference [synod]. . . .

There are no objections to the Brethren increasing their numbers.
As long as all of those whom they get are brought to Christ and

partake of His Spirit, we, on the contrary, rejoice in it. . . .

Your dutiful servant,

Henry Antes[64]

Antes and the Sauers

In a fragment of a letter of November 1743, there is a report by Antes of an encounter of his with the elder Christopher Sauer, and also with the son, Christopher Sauer II, who spoke on behalf of several Brethren. This passage seems to have ended the controversy. The manuscript remained unpublished.

November, 1743

. . . Therefore he [Sauer I] said that in the future he would take care not to print anything except what he could believe himself. I said: "That is good; I shall remember that and always keep it in mind and say: 'Whatever Sauer prints he also believes.'" Thus we parted from each other.

Then the younger Sauer said in the name of several Brethren members that he wanted to warn me in order to avoid future literary feuds, that, if my book were published, the Brethren would refute it. I said: "That is good; thus truth will come to light." He said: "Why did Count Zinzendorf separate from the Lutherans and become sectarian?" I said that, in the first place, this is not at all certain, and in the second place, I would let the Brethren pass judgment when they print their book.

Farewell.

[Henry Antes][65]

REPORTS OF MORAVIAN MISSIONARIES

In the voluminous manuscript travel diaries of the many Moravian missionaries, who were indefatigable in their efforts, are scattered references to the Brethren. One encounter was in Lancaster County between the Moravian George Hantsch, Sr. (d. 1754) and some Brethren.

Brother Hantsch Visits the Brethren, 1748

. . . on the 23rd [June 1748] Römer said to me that if I would visit his neighbor, he knew it would please him very much. His neighbor, Henry Küffer, a member of the Brethren and otherwise a tailor, was, however, not at home. But his wife was very pleased that I had come. She only wished that her husband had been home for it would have pleased him even more. She had also attended the synod at [Lancaster].

I visited Henry Kietzsch, for I had heard that he too was from Saxony and therefore a compatriot of mine. However, as he was a very zealous member of the Brethren he immediately wanted to argue with me about infant baptism. I said that it was not my business to become involved in this dispute and did not stay long with him.

. . . On July 18 . . . I set out early for Bethlehem and . . . went as far as the Cocalico to John Landes, a member of the Brethren. I stayed over night there. They were quite willing to take me in. I thought at first that he was a Mennonite; he said that he used to be a member. They were very friendly toward me. The dear Savior created an opportunity for me to speak to them about Him. They did always have a "but" to interject, that one must really in all things love in the way that the Lord Jesus had commanded. I said: "Yes, a believing child of God does not wish to live any other way even though it might be permitted."

On the 19th I left early and a young man accompanied me for five miles. He was going home; he had helped Landes with the harvest. He was also a member of the Brethren and had once been at Bethlehem. He asked me as we went along whether I was not bored traveling all alone. I said: "No; I am never alone; I always have Someone with me, with whom I can occupy myself and in this way I am never bored." He understood me very well and did not say much after that. We traveled together mostly in silence. At last he asked if I would come to his house for breakfast, but I did not feel so inclined and took a friendly leave of him. . . . [66]

A short and sincere DECLARATION,

To our *Honorable Assembly*, and all others in high or low Station of *Administration*, and to all Friends and Inhabitants of this Country, to whose Sight this may come, be they ENGLISH or GERMANS.

IN the first Place we acknowledge us indebted to the most high GOD, who created Heaven and Earth, the only good Being, to thank him for all his great Goodness and manifold Mercies and Love through our Saviour JESUS CHRIST, who is come to save the Souls of Men, having all Power in Heaven and on Earth.

Further we find ourselves indebted to be thankfull to our late worthy Assembly, for their giving so good an Advice in these troublesome Times to all Ranks of People in *Pennsylvania*, particularly in allowing those, who, by the Doctrine of our Saviour JESUS CHRIST, are persuaded in their Consciences to love their Enemies, and not to resist Evil, to enjoy the Liberty of their Conscience, for which, as also for all the good Things we enjoyed under their Care, we heartily thank that worthy Body of Assembly, and all high and low in Office, who have advised to such a peacefull Measure, hoping and confiding that they, and all others entrusted with Power in this hitherto blessed Province, may be moved by the same Spirit of Grace, which animated the first Founder of this Province, our late worthy Proprietor *William Penn*, to grant Liberty of Conscience to all its Inhabitants, that they may in the great and memorable Day of Judgment be put on the right Hand of the just Judge, who judgeth without Respect of Person, and hear of him these blessed Words, *Come, ye blessed of my Father, inherit the Kingdom prepared for you, &c. What ye have done unto one of the least of these my Brethren, ye have done unto me*, among which Number (the least of Christ's Brethren) we by his Grace hope to be ranked; and every Charity and Favour shewn to such tender conscienced, although weak Followers of this our blessed Saviour will not be forgotten by him in that great Day.

The Advice to those who do not find Freedom of Conscience to take up Arms, that they might be helpfull to those who are in Need and distressed Circumstances, we receive with Cheerfulness towards all Men of what Station they may be——it being our Principle to feed the Hungry and give the Thirsty Drink;—— have dedicated ourselves to serve all Men in every Thing that can be helpful to the Preservation of Men's Lives, but we find no Freedom in giving, or doing, or assisting in any ing by which Men's Lives are destroyed or hurt.——We beg the Patience of all those w believe we err in this Point.

We are always ready, according to CHRIST's Command to *Peter*, to pay the Tribute, that we may offend no Man, and so we are willing to pay Taxes, *and to render unto Caesar those Things that are Caesar's, and to God those Things that are God's*, although we think ourselves very weak to give GOD his due Honour, he being a Spirit and Life, and we only Dust and Ashes.

We are also willing to be subject to the higher Powers, and to give in the manner *Paul* directs us;——*for he beareth the Sword not in vain, for he is the Minister of God, a Revenger to execute Wrath upon him that doeth Evil.*

This Testimony we lay down before our worthy Assembly, and all other Persons in Government, letting them know, that we are thankfull as above-mentioned, and that we are not at Liberty in Conscience to take up Arms to conquer our Enemies, but rather to pray to GOD, who has Power in Heaven and on Earth, for US and THEM.

We also crave the Patience of all the Inhabitants of this Country,——what they think to see clearer in the Doctrine of the blessed JESUS CHRIST, we will leave to them and GOD, finding ourselves very poor; for Faith is to proceed out of the Word of GOD, which is Life and Spirit, and a Power of GOD, and our Conscience is to be instructed by the same, therefore we beg for Patience.

Our small Gift, which we have given, we give to those who have Power over us, that we may not offend them, as CHRIST taught us by the Tribute Penny.

We heartily pray that GOD would govern all Hearts of our Rulers, be they high or low, to meditate those good Things which will pertain to *OUR* and *THEIR* Happiness.

A part of the Mennonite-Brethren petition presented to the Pennsylvania Assembly on November 7, 1775. Courtesy of the Library Company of Philadelphia.

The cover of the almanac published by Christopher Sauer II for 1773 *(Der Hoch-Deutsch Americanische Calendar)*. The caption on the banner reads: "War and rumors of war."

9. Brethren and Universalists

As noted by observers such as Morgan Edwards (page 174) and Benjamin Rush (page 140), the early Brethren held the doctrine of universal restoration. This belief has been defined as the doctrine of "the final salvation of all men, in God's time and God's way."[1] The Greek term is *apokatastasis* and the German, *Wiederbringung.* It seems to have been first taught in developed form by the church fathers Origen and Clement of Alexandria of the early third century. It is based on the concept that a God of love would not permit His creatures to be punished forever for their sins, and the belief that in Christ "shall all be made alive" (1 Corinthians 15:22).[2]

The mainline Anabaptists did not emphasize this doctrine, but it was a marked characteristic of the Radical Pietist belief. Ensign comments: "On another major distinctive Radical Pietist doctrine, that of the restoration of all things (*Wiederbringung*), the early Brethren obviously fit into the Böhmist pattern. That they believed this is incontrovertible."[3] In the *Rights and Ordinances* of Mack, Sr. (1715), there is a clear statement of disbelief that punishment after death would last forever. However, he cautioned against a foolish dependence on universal restoration as making it unnecessary to live a disciplined life on earth: "It is much better to practice this simple truth, that one should try to become worthy in the time of grace to escape the wrath of God and the torments of hell, rather than deliberate how or when it would be possible to escape from it again."[4]

Although Brethren seem to have maintained this doctrine until well toward the end of the nineteenth century, it was never emphasized greatly in public.[5] The Baptist historian David Benedict (1779-1874) commented on it in 1820: "It is said, however, that they hold the doctrine of universal salvation, and hence they are often called Universalists; but this sentiment they are not forward to advance, nor strenuous to defend; and it is probable they maintain it with some peculiar qualifications."[6]

The Brethren made a clear distinction between the belief that God in His wisdom may redeem all men at some future time and the contention that there would be no future punishment at all, which they sharply rejected. This differentiation was not held to at all times by the Brethren, and led to cases of church discipline and, eventually, to the defection of several congregations to the Universalists.

Universalism in America

An anonymous critique of the Universalist movement, written in 1848 — *Universalism Tested by Reason and Revelation* — presented a concise history of the movement, its transplantation in America, and the shift in theological position in the last decade of the eighteenth century. Although the linking of the movement with infidelity has polemical motivation, the influence of liberal thought from France and England is known to have furthered the cause of liberal religious thinking at this time.[7]

The system of Universalism rose first in England. Its founder was James Relly (1720-1778), who commenced the promulgation of his doctrines about 1766. He taught that Christ as mediator was so united with mankind that His actions thus became theirs, and His obedience and suffering theirs; and, consequently, that He has as fully restored the whole human race to the divine favor as if all had obeyed and suffered in their own persons. He preached this doctrine in London, and succeeded in making John Murray (1741-1815) one of his converts. Mr. Murray first introduced this system into the United States.

He was a man who, according to his own confession, "had revolved through every sign of the sectarian zodiac, beginning with hyper-ultra Calvinism, and ending with the belief that the finally impenitent, after enduring punishment in hell for a limited period, will be converted and received into heaven, thenceforth to enjoy eternal happiness." This latter doctrine he consequently modified so as to exclude the idea of future suffering and commenced to preach it, but found very few who were willing to embrace the belief. So slowly did his cause gain in the public estimation that after laboring for a period of ten years, his followers consisted of only one small society in Gloucester, Massachusetts.

In 1780, he was joined by Rev. Elhanan Winchester, who before this time had been a Baptist minister in the city of Philadelphia. He was a man possessed of considerable talent, and calculated to render himself popular by his eloquence. He taught that men must render satisfaction for their sins by enduring punishment after death; that the duration of this punishment would be so great as to entitle it to be called eternal; but that they should finally be delivered and received into heaven. Notwithstanding this accession to the cause, it failed to progress and must have become extinct in a short time had it not been for an occurrence which more than anything else tended to establish Universalism in this country.

That occurrence was the extensive dissemination of infidel principles about the time of the French Revolution. The writings of Voltaire, D'Alembert, Rousseau, Volney, Diderot, and others of the French school of infidelity, together with those of Thomas Paine in the United States, exerted an important influence upon all classes. The studied arguments of D'Alembert and Diderot, the sparkling wit and polished shafts of Voltaire were calculated to excite the attention of the learnéd and more refined; while the low obscenity, and vulgar, ribald blasphemy of Paine were admirably suited for the lower classes. These writings became widely diffused and the minds of many having become poisoned by the pernicious doctrines which they contained, they were deterred only by the fear of public opinion from openly declaring themselves infidels.

At length, seeing this new system [Universalism] so nearly allied to it [their infidelity] in every feature, and essentially the same, they eagerly embraced it. A bolder stand was now taken. Heretofore they had taught that the wicked did suffer punishment for a limited period of time, but now embracing the opinions of their leaders, Balfour, [Hosea] Ballou, and others, they inscribed upon their banner the doctrine that there was no punishment of the wicked hereafter, that there was no hell, and with this emblazoned on it, boldly unfurled it to the breeze.

Infidelity, which had long been compelled to hide its odious head, dreading the severity of well-merited public censure, now threw around itself this newly made disguise, and boldly walked forth to proselyte all whom it could bring within the reach of its influence. The bark which until now had seemed unable to weather the storm, and appeared momentarily on the point of sinking, having thus been remanned and having its sails swelled with this new blast of infidelity, now rode over the waves and sped onward in her course with renewed and increasing speed. This coalition of Infidelity and Universalism, these two parts of a common system, proved eminently useful to the latter; for every convert to infidelity who shrank from an avowal of his sentiments joined the ranks of Universalism. Societies now sprang up in various places, and numerous individuals were added to its membership. . . . [8]

UNIVERSALIST AUTHORS ON THE BRETHREN

Richard Eddy

The best histories of the Universalist movement in America were written by the editor Richard Eddy (1828-1906) in the later nineteenth century. He based his work on original materials and achieved a considerable degree of accuracy. In the case of the Brethren contacts with Universalism, he was aided by information from his friend Abraham H. Cassel (1820-1908), the noted Brethren historian and antiquarian. In the early chapters of his two-volume history (1883-1885), Eddy devoted major attention to the Brethren.[9]

II. The Dunkers

The second channel through which Universalism came to us was the German Baptists, sometimes called Tunkers, more often Dunkers, and as they prefer to be called, Brethren. They originated at Schwarzenau, Germany, in 1708; but on account of persecution came to America in 1719, originally settled in Pennsylvania. They were from the first believers in universal restoration, but have, in the main, held it privately.

A division occurred in their ranks in 1725, led by Conrad Beissel, mainly on the question of the Sabbath, Beissel and his followers insisting on the observance of the seventh day. At first the seceders resorted to a hermit life, and subsequently they established a monastical society at Ephrata, Pennsylvania. Both branches held to the doctrine of the restoration of all souls. . . . [The author then quotes from an early account of Ephrata by the Swedish Lutheran pastor Israel Acrelius on Peter Miller's statements on restoration.][10] Elsewhere, in describing some of their peculiarities of belief, Acrelius says: "They believe in a purgatory, or purifying fire after death; on which account, also Father Friedsam [Beissel] at certain times offers prayers for the dead." . . . As late as 1793, James Bolton, one of their number, published a pamphlet, in which he severely censures the "Brethren" for not giving greater publicity to the doctrine of universal restoration, asserting that "the German Baptists all believe it." . . . [11]

James Bolton

In the pamphlet mentioned by Eddy, *James Bolton's Treatise, of the Universal Restoration, Preached and Commanded to be [P]reached by Jesus Christ,* likely printed in Ephrata in 1793, the author mentioned the Brethren in the context of proving that Universalism did not lead to moral excess:

> Those people that believe in the universal restoration live stricter than others who don't, in general: the German Baptists all believe it, yet no people live stricter or more moral than they do, and many hundreds beside them, yet it don't tend to make them licentious.[12]

Elhanan Winchester

The above-mentioned Universalist spokesman and theologian, Elhanan Winchester (1751-1795), a noted Baptist preacher in South Carolina and Philadelphia before he turned to Universalism, was intimately acquainted with the Brethren. In the preface of his important work *The Universal Restoration* (printed by Brethren as late as the 1850's) he described a visit to the Germantown Brethren during the critical year of 1781, when he was moving from a strict Calvinist to the more liberal restorationist position. Later in his book he included a glowing description of the Brethren, like Bolton's in arguing that belief in Universalism did not lead to a breakdown of morality.[13]

Eddy commented: "The other branch of the Dunker church also allowed the publication of books at Germantown, in defense of universal restoration. Both De Benneville and Elhanan Winchester were favorably received by them, and preached in their churches in several localities."[14] Dr. George De Benneville (1703-1793) is one of the fascinating figures of colonial Pennsylvania, and is generally credited with being the first Universalist preacher in America. Of Huguenot background, he was associated with the Separatists of Germany before coming to Pennsylvania in 1741. According to tradition, Christopher Sauer I gave hospitality to the immigrant, who was sick on arrival, and employed him for a time as an editor in his printing enterprise.[15]

Having heard that the German Baptists in Germantown, about eight miles from Philadelphia, held the doctrine of the Restoration, I had appointed to spend the first Sunday of April [1781] with them; . . . [I] took that opportunity to go and visit an ancient, venerable, and excellent man, Dr. George De Benneville, who received me in the most kind, open, and friendly manner; and his conversation was

most highly edifying to me. Afterwards I went to Germantown, and
lodged there all night, ready to preach the next day. . . .

But it is not only from reasoning, but [also] from facts, that I am
able to prove that the belief of the doctrine of the universal restoration does not lead men to sin. The Tunkers, or German Baptists, in
Pennsylvania and the states adjacent, who take the Scriptures as their
only guide in matters both of faith and of practice, have always (as
far as I know) received, and universally, at present, hold these sentiments. But such Christians I have never seen as they are; so averse
are they to all sin, and to many things that other Christians esteem
lawful, that they not only refuse to swear, go to war, etc., but are so
afraid of doing anything contrary to the commands of Christ that no
temptation would prevail upon them ever to sue any person at law,
for either name, character, estate, or any debt, be it ever so just.

They are industrious, sober, temperate, kind, charitable people;
envying not the great, nor despising the mean. They read much, they
sing and pray much, they are constant attendants upon the worship of
God. Their dwelling-houses are all houses of prayer. They walk in
the commandments and ordinances of the Lord blameless, both in
public and in private. They bring up their children in the nurture
and admonition of the Lord. No noise of rudeness, shameless mirth,
loud [or] vain laughter is heard within their doors. The law of
kindness is in their mouths. No sourness or moroseness disgraces their
religion; and whatsoever they believe their Savior commands, they
practice, without enquiring or regarding what others do.

I remember the Rev. Morgan Edwards, formerly minister of the
Baptist Church in Philadelphia, once said to me: "God always will
have a visible people on earth; and these are his people at present,
above any other in the world." And in his *History of the Baptists in
Pennsylvania,* speaking of these people, he says: "General redemption
they certainly hold, and withal, general salvation; which tenets (though
wrong) are consistent. In a word, they are meek and pious Christians;
and have justly acquired the character of the harmless Tunkers."[16]

NORTH CAROLINA

One area where the Brethren involvement in Universalism took a
more radical course was in the Carolinas. In both North and South
Carolina, many Brethren aligned themselves with the more aggressive

ideas of Universalism which achieved great popularity in America immediately after the Revolutionary War.

Eddy Comments on Developments in the South

About 1785, John Ham, an elder in one of their [Brethren] churches in North Carolina, began to preach the doctrine of no future punishment, and, being a man of great talents and of popular address, many converts were made to his views, chiefly in Virginia and the Carolinas. The church at large became alarmed, and at a council held about that time they decided against preaching or saying anything in public about the doctrine of Restoration. Subsequently, John Ham and his followers were cut off from the fellowship of the church.

This fact in the history of the Dunkers will explain what otherwise might seem to be contradictory, that while holding to the doctrine of universal restoration, they repel the charge of being Universalists. "If I were to say to my neighbors," said a Dunker preacher, whom the writer once visited, "I have a Universalist preacher stopping at my house, they would say: 'How do you dare to have such a character under your roof?' But if I should say: 'I have a friend with me who preaches universal restoration,' they would say: 'Have you? I am glad; I would like to come in and see him!' "[17]

The Brethren Reaction

The agitation led by John Ham was taken most seriously by the Brethren leadership, when reports reached them of the extent of the movement. The annual meeting of October 1794, held in the Shenandoah Valley, devoted most of its deliberations to this problem.

Annual Meeting of 1794: Article 2.

We hear that there arises a strange doctrine, or rather opinion, among the brethren in Carolina, and that some brethren are grieved about this matter, because some believe, say, and teach the following, i.e.:

1. That there is no other heaven but that in man.

2. That there is no other hell but that in man.

3. That God has no form or shape; and if a person would worship God, and would conceive in his mind God as in the human form; would imagine or believe that God had an appearance like a

man, such person would do the same as one who would worship a horse or any other beast.

4. That God is not wrathful, and would punish no person on account of his sins.

5. That the dead rise not; for out of the grave nothing would come forth.

6. That they will have nothing to do with the ban (or excommunication).

For this cause some brethren desire to hear the views or minds of the brethren (in general council), and therefore we inform the loving brethren that the view or doctrine of the old brethren is that we are to believe as the Scriptures say. For Christ says: "He who believes in me, as the scripture has said, 'Out of his heart shall flow rivers of living water'" (John 7:38). Again, we see that Christ in His whole life has looked upon the Scriptures, and has fulfilled them in all things. For when they came, and Peter struck with the sword, the Lord said: "Put your sword back into its place; for all who take the sword will perish by the sword. Do you think that I cannot appeal to my Father, and he will at once send me more than twelve legions of angels? But how then should the scriptures be fulfilled that it must be so?" (Matt. 26:50-54).

Now, to come to the before-mentioned points or propositions, our dear brethren will think ill of us because we believe as it is written, and believe also with David, that the word of the Lord is well refined, and a true doctrine, and that we also believe with Paul that it is our duty to bring into captivity every thought (all reason, says the German) to the obedience of Christ, etc.

1. Now, to come to the word about *heaven*. Moses says (Gen. 1:1): "In the beginning God created the heavens and the earth. The earth was without form and void." No man was created yet then and Moses calls something *heaven* that is not in man. And (Acts 1:9) we read: "And when he had said this, as they were looking on, he was lifted up, and a cloud took him out of their sight. And while they were gazing into heaven as he went, behold, two men stood by them in white robes, and said: 'Men of Galilee, why do you stand looking into heaven? This same Jesus, who was taken up from you into heaven, will come in the same way as you saw him go into heaven.'" Here we see there is a *heaven* up on high.

2. "That there be no other hell but that in man." We read (Luke 15 [16]:22ff.) about the rich man, that he died and that he also was buried. Now, it is without contradiction that when he died his soul and his spirit had departed from the body, and had found, it seems according to the Word, the hell in which he suffered torments. So we think it would be well for us, if we would on this point or word "hell" apply the doctrine of Paul, not to dispute about words; for we can notice in Holy Writ that the word hell is used for different things. But we believe, as it is written in many places mentioned, that there is a lake of fire or place of torment, which, according to the Word, is outside of man, as we read plainly (Matt. 25:41) where Christ says: "Depart from me, you cursed, into the eternal fire, prepared for the devil and his angels." Here we see clearly that the lake of fire is not in man, because men are sent into the lake of fire, and it says not that the fire should go into the men.

3. "That God has no shape or form; and if a person would worship God, and would conceive in his mind and believe God having a form like a man, such a person would do the same as if he worshiped a horse or any other beast." This, it seems to us, is speaking very derogatorily of God, or against God, though we believe, also from the heart that God is a Spirit, as Christ himself says, and that the true worshipers worship Him in spirit and in truth. But not at all contrary to this says John [1:1]: "In the beginning was the word, and the word was with God, and the word was God." And further on [1:14]: "And the word became flesh and dwelt among us, [and] we have beheld his glory." Here God has put on a visible form. Now, to be sure, in His worship man should not imagine a form or likeness of God; but if it should happen that a person or disciple would, in his worship in simplicity and sincerity toward God, look to God in the person or appearance of Christ, we consider it far less culpable than for a man to worship a horse or some other beast. We deem this a very unbecoming expression.

4. "That God is not wrathful, and punishes no person for his sins." Now, we believe also with John [1 John 4:16] that "God is love; and he who abides in love abides in God, and God abides in him," and that God is not angry like an unconverted man, but that penal judgments proceed from love to the human family. Yet notwithstanding, the Holy Scriptures or the men of God in Holy Writ call God's

judgment God's wrath, as Psalm 90:11: "Who considers the power of thine anger; and thy wrath according to the fear of thee?" Again, John the Baptist says (John 3:36): "He who believes in the Son has eternal life; he who does not obey the Son shall not see life, but the wrath of God rests upon him." And that the Lord would punish no man for his sin, we deem to be an error. Christ says himself: "Do you think that these Galileans were worse sinners than all the other Galileans, because they suffered thus? I tell you, no; but unless you repent, you will all likewise perish" (Luke 13:2, 3).

5. "That the dead rise not, for out of the grave nothing would come forth." We believe, as Christ says (John 5:28): "The hour is coming, when all who are in the tombs will hear his voice, and come forth," etc. So we read (Matt. 27:51, 52): "The earth shook and the rocks were split; the tombs also were opened, and many bodies of the saints who had fallen asleep were aroused, and came out of the tombs," etc.[18]

Maryland Elder Circulates the Conference Answer

A letter from Michael Pfautz to Brethren Martin Urner and Alexander Mack, Jr., underscored the seriousness of the issue. The "heads" and "pillars" of the congregations must be alert to stop the spread of this "perversion."

Pipe Creek, December 9, 1794

My very dearly beloved Brethren Martin Urner and Alexander Mack, along with a warm greeting of love; wishing you all health and happiness for body and soul; the God of peace may strengthen, sustain and bless you through Jesus Christ. Amen.

It occurred at the last great meeting held on October 10, 1794, in Virginia that Brother Stutzman from Carolina sent a letter with two brethren, namely Brother John Gerber and Brother John Burgert from Carolina, to the great meeting, because somewhat strange doctrines were cropping up among the southern brethren, and the brethren in North Carolina felt very uneasy about them, and therefore wanted to hear the opinion and judgment of the older brethren, etc. Thus it was done and a statement was prepared and our brethren brought a copy of it home with them, and when I heard it read it gave me much joy that the dear God had bestowed upon the brethren at the great meeting such a clear responsibility, insofar as I could judge.

Afterwards our brethren said that other brethren or congregations would also like to have a copy and therefore I copied it several times, and during the copying it occurred to me that it would be quite in keeping with faithfulness and love to send such a copy also to Brother Martin and Brother Sander. Inasmuch as I learned that the friend John Reinhard was said to be at the Pipe Creek, I thought that this might perhaps be the last opportunity this fall to send it to you.

But, dear brethren, you must try to understand the meaning of it, for I am such a poor writer, but yet I thought it necessary that you should for yourselves read and examine such perverted doctrines, because I think you will undoubtedly hear about it but perhaps not clearly enough in order to judge it. Besides, God installed you to be heads and bishops and pillars in the congregation so that if such perversion continues to spread, you would be informed about it, etc. I think that [Martin Urner] might pass it on to Brother Sander at a convenient opportunity. I will conclude and herewith commend you to the grace of God that He might sustain you in the discharge of all your responsibilities, etc.

One more thing I fervently desire of you, dear brethren, namely, that you might remember me before the Lord whenever the Lord gives you grace.

Written by me,

Michael Pfautz, your very humble fellow-brother.

This is to go to Brother Martin Urner on the Schuylkill and also to Brother Sander Mack in Germantown.[19]

Annual Meeting of 1798

Again four years later, the annual meeting of the Brethren (held at Little Conewago, Pennsylvania) found itself faced with the problem of Ham's heterodox beliefs. This time the action was one of disfellowshiping the Carolina leader and his adherents if they failed to cease proclaiming their erroneous views.

Article 1. It has been made known to us that last fall, at the great council meeting of the brethren in Virginia, there was some discussion on account of the different views of the brethren, especially those in Carolina, where a brother minister, by name John H[am], has defended himself in public, and brought to light many of his own sentiments. It is the case that the brethren who still hold fast to the word of truth, according to their best knowledge, could not break the bread of communion with said John H. [They] would, however, in such serious circumstances not lightly make a full conclusion without hearing first, also, the mind of their beloved old, and by many temptations, established brethren. Hence this is to inform our dear brethren in North Carolina that the case has been presented to the brotherhood by those brethren who have seen John H. himself, and have heard from him many of his (what can scarcely be called) doctrines, but rather perverse apprehensions of Holy Writ. We have quite unanimously concluded that we can not hold said John H. and all who are of his mind as brethren as long as they do not acknowledge the doctrine of Jesus and His apostles as a true doctrine sent from God unto salvation, and publicly confess, according to which doctrine we are to prove all the spirits and powers operating in us, and necessarily must. For we believe and confess, with David, that the Word of the Lord is a true doctrine and well refined. Therefore we can not acknowledge such as our brethren any more while they contradict the Holy Scripture in many points. This we, the undersigned brethren, confess and testify to hold them as strangers out of the church as long as they do not seek to and keep house according to the Scripture.

Signed by the brethren.

P.S. (Copy). This is to certify that I heard John H. say in his preaching that it would be no more sin to him to get up on the top of the barn that he was in and preaching in, and swear and blaspheme all the new-found oaths and curses, than to pray to God to forgive his sins, or to bless him in any respect. Furthermore, he said he had not served such a God that required the prayers of human creatures to forgive them their sins, or to bless them in any manner, these several years, nor never would. These are the words I heard, as near as I can remember.

Per me, Samuel Van Etten
John Keller[20]

Annual Meeting of 1800

Yet another Annual Meeting concerned itself with the Ham heresy, largely repeating the actions taken in 1794 and 1798. This closed the books on this particular episode, the result of which was to cost the Brethren a number of members in North Carolina.

Article 1. (Concerning two brethren in Carolina.) It has been made known to us that the brethren in Carolina desire to be informed more plainly about the conclusion made at the great meeting at Little Conewago, May 26, 1798, where it was concluded in union about Brother John H[am] and all who are of his mind that we could have no fellowship with him (and them) as long as they persisted in their erroneous doctrine contrary to Holy Scripture. And since it is requested to inform them why and for what reason it was done, we should specify by name the causes for which we can have no more fellowship with John H. and his sympathizers. This is to further inform them that the chief causes were already mentioned in a letter from the big meeting held at Shenandoah, Virginia, October 20, 1794, as follows, i.e. that there arises strange doctrine, or rather opinion, among the brethren in Carolina, and that other brethren are grieved by the same. (The six points are given in the Minutes of 1794.)

These six chief points have been specified in the above-mentioned letter of the great meeting with the answer as the old brethren have given their views and doctrine in refutation, which letter, as we presume, has been sent to the brethren in Carolina, and they are all desired to read the same at pleasure. Then again, at the great meeting which was held at Little Conewago, May 26, 1798, the same case was once more viewed by the old brethren. Also the Germantown brethren have sent their opinion by a letter from Brother Sander Mack, wherein it is sorrowfully lamented that among the little flock of the Dunkers [Taufs-Gesinnte] in America there should arise men who deny the resurrection of the dead, and that among brothers and sisters some had to have the misfortune to have their eyes smeared by that old, moldy, and horribly stinking leaven of the Sadducees. In addition a written testimony has come to hand about John H., that he is to have said in his preaching, which two truthful men have heard him say, and have testified to it. (See postscript, Minutes of 1798.)

Behold, much beloved brethren, in view of all the unscriptural doctrines and expression, we have been compelled to exclude from the fellowship and membership of the Lord Jesus at that great meeting of May 26, [1798], said John H. and all that are in union with him in such views, and we confirm again that conclusion unanimously in our great meeting of the brethren today, renouncing all fellowship with each and all such persons as hold such doctrines and views as are stated above, until they acknowledge their error and repent.

Still, we look upon this case with sadness and heartfelt grief, and wish them (grace) of God in Christ Jesus, whose mercy endureth forever, that they may earnestly reflect and consider what may make for their peace and everlasting salvation while yet it is the accepted time and the day of salvation. This we desire from the bottom of our hearts that the good God, through the tender mercy of Jesus Christ, would give and bestow to them and us for His merciful love's sake. Amen. So much from us, the undersigned brethren, assembled with one accord, and delivered to the hands of our loving brethren, who also will make it known to you orally in the name of the whole fraternity.[21]

SOUTH CAROLINA

The other Carolina colony also became deeply involved in Universalism. Here again, the result was the departure of numbers of Brethren and their incorporation into the Universalist denomination, which was taking rapid form at this time.

An article in a periodical devoted to German immigrants in the United States describes the general situation in which the South Carolina Brethren found themselves:

> More than one hundred years ago [*i.e.,* before 1783] a number of Germans settled themselves in the vicinity of Newberry, South Carolina in the triangle where the Saluda and the Broad Rivers converge. Some of them arrived there directly from Germany. The surroundings and the climate are exceptionally fine there and the German newcomers made themselves at home. They were particularly proud of their German language, and held to it firmly as long as it was at all possible to do so.[22]

Eddy Comments on South Carolina

In South Carolina the doctrine of universal restoration was preached among the Dunkers with great acceptance, as early as 1780. The circulation of the writings of Rev. William Law was the immediate incitement to energetic discourse on this view of human destiny. Rev. Mr. [David] Martin, a Dunker preacher, became convinced that he ought to preach the doctrine of universal salvation in its fullness. Giles Chapman, a Dunker preacher, followed his example in 1782, and soon the entire Dunker congregation became enthusiastic in the belief of universal restoration. It was the influence of their zeal, no doubt, which gave occasion for the inquiry of the Synod of the Carolinas to the Presbyterian General Assembly, in 1792 and 1794. . . . [23]

Judge O'Neal Describes the Dunkers

John Belton O'Neal, a Baptist judge and local historian of Newberry, South Carolina, has provided a warm description of the Brethren and their pastor, Giles Chapman, in his chronicle written in the years 1850-1858. The graveyard mentioned by the author is still intact, known locally as the "old Tunkard Cemetery."

Passing for a moment out of the immediate range of country through which we have been sweeping, and sliding within the bounds assigned . . . for the Quaker settlement, we meet with the only relics of the Dunkers or Dunkards, within my knowledge, in this state. Their settlement was mainly on the Palmetto Branch, north of Bush River. Of this persuasion were originally the Chapmans, Summers, Lynches, Prathers and Martins. David Martin, the father of the family here named, lived on Saluda, near Hewitt's ferry. . . .

The Dunkers are baptized by immersion: they kneel in the water, and are thus plunged three times under it; they neither shave their heads nor beards. Most of the leading Dunkers, in the settlement to which I have alluded, became Universalists, but not to the extent now held by that body of Christians. Many retained the long flowing beard. Often have I seen the patriarch of that settlement, the good old man, Joseph Summers, with his white beard extending to and resting on his breast. He was a native of Maryland. He introduced the wheat called the Yellow Lammas, by bringing as much as he could, in a stocking leg, from that state. It was perfectly white, when it was first brought. In a few years it became yellow, and was much valued. I fear in the many changes we have undergone, this valuable variety of wheat has been entirely lost.

My venerable friend, Giles Chapman, the great preacher of what was called Universalism, until within the last twenty years, certainly, always preached the Dunker faith. For I see "they deny the eternity of future punishment;" and such unquestionably was always his teaching. He, like his father-in-law, Joseph Summers, wore his beard.

Giles Chapman was a native of Virginia; he was born in 1748; his father, on immigrating to this state, first located himself for a season, at the place of our town. Giles Chapman was a saddler by trade. He married a daughter of Joseph Summers. From my earliest recollection, 1799 or 1800, he lived at the place where his worthy son, Samuel Chapman, Esq., now lives, and there he lived until his death, in, I presume, 1819.

He began to preach in 1782. Often have I heard his discourses. He was beyond all doubt an eloquent and gifted preacher; and seemed to me to be inspired with a full portion of that holy and divine spirit, which taught [that] "God is love." His education and means of information were limited, yet his mighty Master spoke by him, as He did by the fishermen "in words that burn, and thoughts which breathe." His ministry was much followed, and in recurring to his spotless life and conversation, his continual zeal to do good, his kind and benevolent intercourse with men, and the meek humility with which he bore the railing of the sects of Christians, who differed in opinion with him, I have never entertained a doubt, that whether right or wrong, in abstract matters of faith and theology, he was indeed a disciple of Him who came into the world to save sinners.

I can see him now as plainly in my mind's eye, as I have seen him hundreds of times, as well in all the various pursuits and intercourse of life as in the pulpit; and yet I find it difficult to give of him a life-like description. He was rather above the ordinary size; grey hair and beard, not very long, but worn; his dress very much that of Friends; a face of the most placid and benevolent expression.

He married more persons than any other clergyman; he never would have more than one dollar for his service. "That was as much as any woman was worth," was his laughing reply to the question: "How much do you charge?" This was his jest. For no man ever appreciated more highly woman, good, virtuous, suffering, feeble woman, than he did, and none had ever more cause to value her; for certainly none better as wife and mother was to be found than his "ain gude wife."

As a husband, father, master, neighbor and friend none was ever more justly beloved than Uncle Giles, as he was familiarly called by the country all around him.

The old Dunker meeting house stood near, and I think in the graveyard just at the edge of the Charleston road, a little north of east from Esquire Samuel Chapman's residence.[24]

Elijah Lynch Leads the Brethren to the Universalist Camp

Richard Eddy, again, is our source for the denouement of the developments in the Newberry area. The further history of the South Carolina Brethren is found in the annals of the Universalist denomination.

A new preacher, Rev. Elijah Lynch, entered the Universalist ministry in Newberry District, South Carolina, in 1805. He had been for some years a Dunker preacher, and when he decided to take the name of Universalist, the entire Dunker Church joined him in the change of name. [Eddy's note: *Universalist Magazine,* Vol. IX (1827), page 48.] For many years he officiated regularly in the meeting-house a few miles north of Newberry, and much of that time was the only Universalist preacher in the state. His death occurred August 10, 1842.

In an obituary furnished to *The Southern Universalist,* by Rev. L. F. W. Andrews, who officiated at Mr. Lynch's funeral, is the following: "During his last illness he dictated to his son what may be considered his dying testimony to the truth, from the passage in I Thess. 2:19. 'For what is our hope,' in which he has given evidence how sustaining was the *hope* which he possessed, on the near approach of death, and effectually rebuked the slanderous report already circulated that he had renounced his faith and burnt his books! His remains were committed to the tomb on Thursday, the 11th, in the burial ground where stood the church in which he received his first religious impressions of universal love, and where repose the remains of the venerated Chapman, from whose lips those sacred impressions were received."[25]

BRETHREN INVOLVEMENT WITH
UNIVERSALIST PUBLICATIONS

According to the Universalist historians, the Brethren in eighteenth-century America were quite active in the publication of pamphlets and books upholding the point of view of universal restoration. Although the picture is not altogether clear, there is some indication of Brethren involvement.

The Everlasting Gospel

One of the most influential works propounding the doctrine of universal restoration is *The Everlasting Gospel, Commanded to be Preached by Jesus Christ, Judge of the Living and Dead Unto all Creatures.*[26] Written under the pseudonym "Paul Siegvolck," the book's real author was a German pastor named George Klein-Nicolai. The book was first published as part of a three-volume work of the leading eighteenth-century restorationist theologian, John William Petersen (1649-1727).

There is considerable controversy as to the identity of the translator of the English edition of Klein-Nicolai's book, which was published by Christopher Sauer I in Germantown in 1753 — the first Universalist tract in America. Some claim that the translator, given as "John S." on the title page, was Sauer himself. Their reasoning is that Sauer's first name was actually "John," hence "John S." might be "John (Christopher) Sauer."[27] A recent scholar has proposed Dr. De Benneville as the translator.[28] However, the *Pennsylvania Gazette* for April 3, 1753, clearly states that it was "translated from the German by John S. Price." Inasmuch as John Price (Preisz) was the author of a book of poems published by Sauer in the same year, there seems little reason to doubt that he was the actual translator. Whether he was also the translator of the tract bound with *The Everlasting Gospel* entitled *The Fatal Consequences of the Unscriptural Doctrine of Predestination and Reprobation,* published the same year, is not known. Two more editions of *The Everlasting Gospel* were brought out by Christopher Sauer II in 1768 and 1769.[29]

A German Reformed Pastor on THE EVERLASTING GOSPEL

The Klein-Nicolai book had considerable effect in spreading Universalist ideas. It was the perusal of this book which started Elhanan Winchester on his restorationist pilgrimage. A German Reformed pastor, Nicholas Pomp (1744-1819) wrote an extensive critique of the book in 1774: *Brief Examination of the Doctrine of the Everlasting Gospel, by which it is clearly shown that the Restoration of all things is vainly sought in Holy Scripture.*[30]

[The belief] was never more widely spread than in the present century. . . . Yet nowhere has this doctrine been more successful and made greater progress than here in Pennsylvania. In Europe the industry of many learned and godly men has thrown insuperable obstacles in its way; but here the stream has been allowed free course, and the fire has burned as it would. There were already many copies of *The Everlasting Gospel,* which, not being privileged in Germany, were purchased at a cheap rate by money-making people and brought here. And they have also been industriously scattered by the press. The charming title, *The Everlasting Gospel,* induced many ignorant people to buy the book, and the doctrine it inculcates inclined many to believe.[31]

A recent study concludes: "There is . . . sufficient evidence that *The Everlasting Gospel* was an important link between the more generalized Universalism of the Pennsylvania mystics and the organized church of Winchester, Murray, and Ballou which came later."[32]

Later Relationships

There were important relationships of the Brethren and the Universalists after this period, especially in Pennsylvania, Kentucky, Illinois, and Missouri, but they took place in the nineteenth century and fall outside of the limits of this volume.

IV. Revolution

10. The Brethren Response

The outbreak of the American Revolution posed a severe problem for those churches which held to nonviolence. As the tensions sharpened, the revolutionary forces increasingly considered all those who did not actively join their cause to be against them. In the words of a contemporary Schwenkfelder chronicler: "The mad rabble said, 'If we must march to the field of battle, he who will not take up arms must first be treated as an enemy.' "[1]

Most of the German sectarians were Christian pacifists sharing a peace witness with the Quakers, who of course no longer directed the political affairs of the colony. Brethren, Mennonites, Moravians, Schwenkfelders — all are found in the records of the Revolution as conscientiously opposed to bearing arms.[2]

Added to the peace position was a generally conservative attitude of submission to the government. The scriptural admonitions of 1 Peter 2:13-14 ("Be subject for the Lord's sake to every human institution, whether it be to the emperor as supreme, or to governors as sent by him

to punish those who do wrong and to praise those who do right") and
Romans 13:1 ("Let every person be subject to the governing authorities.
For there is no authority except from God, and those that exist have
been instituted by God") were taken very seriously by the Biblically based
German groups. They had never developed a theology of armed resistance
to monarchs, such as marked the Calvinistic denominations.[3]

Moreover, they owed a debt of loyalty to the English kings to whom
they, or their fathers, had affirmed allegiance. Had not the English government allowed them to settle in the rich land of America and spared
them the harsh feudal exactions of the princes of Germany and the city
governments of Switzerland, which had caused them to migrate in the
first instance? Largely earning their living by farming, they did not
feel the economic pressure of the tightening English mercantile policies,
as did the townspeople of Philadelphia and Boston.

There seemed, then, reason enough for the German folk to distrust
the enthusiastic cries of rebellion by politicians and the anti-English indict-
ments of the Scotch-Irish frontiersmen.

It is easy to forget that the Revolutionary War had many of the
qualities of a bloody civil war. From the modern perspective, the doubtful
and desperate nature of the rebellion has long since been forgotten, covered over by patriotic sentiments and glorified history. But at the time,
hatred flared, neighbor rose up against neighbor, and it was truly a
time that "tried men's souls." It is estimated that about one third of the
population of America favored the Revolution, about one third remained
loyal to the English government, and the remaining third attempted an
uneasy neutrality.[4]

MORAVIAN ACCOUNTS OF THE REVOLUTION

Two contemporary writings by members of the Moravian Church may
serve as useful introductions to the story of the impact of the Revolution
upon the Brethren. By the nature of the case, the shift in governments, the
new laws and demands, the hazards of war, and the inflammation of
tempers affected the peace groups alike. Also, faced with a common threat,
they resorted from time to time to common measures enabling a united
front. For these reasons, it will be necessary, and helpful, to refer to the
other German sectarian groups as the Brethren relation to the Revolution is
considered.

Ettwein's Account of the Revolution

One of the most articulate and active of the Moravian Brethren leaders in the colonial period was John Ettwein (1721-1802).[5] Among his papers is an extensive account of the tribulations of the Moravians in the turbulence of the American revolt against England. Although not all Moravians held to a strict nonresistant position, the great majority of their members were Christian pacifists, and as such underwent the same difficulties as did the Brethren. Excerpts from Ettwein's manuscript story of the troubled period provide helpful background for understanding the legal and military burdens placed upon the German sectarians. The translation is by Professor Kenneth G. Hamilton.

A Short Account of the Disturbances in America and of the Moravian Brethren's Conduct and Suffering in this Connection.

With the conclusion of peace, in 1760 [1763], in which the French surrendered Canada to England and the Spaniards Florida, America entered upon a period of proud tranquility. It expanded and consolidated its position to an uncommon degree, and many people grew rich.

England labored under a heavy burden of debt and endeavored to persuade its colonies gradually to help carry the load. . . . Jealousy, fear, and suspicion of the government in England, reciprocated by it in its attitude towards the colonies, took root more and more and had unfortunate consequences on both sides. . . . [Ettwein discusses the events leading up to the outbreak of the Revolution.] In all provinces and counties, military associations were begun and a militia created. As a result, all who refused to bear arms or serve the cause had much to suffer; some were coated with tar on which feathers were then scattered, etc.

The articles of the first associations in the counties were: to defend their religious and civil rights with life and property and to organize companies of militia for this purpose, to elect officers, and to drill. No one was to be compelled to do this; each individual was to be free to volunteer for this, or not, to contribute towards the costs necessarily connected with this, or not. But this soon was changed, and many inclined to force all to cooperate with them. . . .

The town committees published on July 6, [17]75, a resolution of the Assembly [of Pennsylvania], dated June 30, together with a recommendation of Congress i.e.:

The House taking into consideration, that many of the good people of this province are conscientiously scrupulous of bearing arms, it is recommended to these conscientious people that they cheerfully assist in proportion to their abilities, such persons as cannot spend both time and substance in the service of their country, without great injury to themselves and families.

The communication from Congress read in part:

The Assembly, taking into consideration the situation of many conscientious people of this province, with respect to arms, have on the 30th day of June last, by their recommendation of that date given to them, as well as others, advice which we hope all persons will most cheerfully follow. The Congress, and your Assembly greatly to their honor, have taken means for the protection of America and this colony; and we would advise you, gentlemen, to carry into execution the plans recommended by them that this colony may unitedly act upon one and the same principle. [Note in the Herrnhut manuscript: That the rich Mennonites in Lancaster County and the Quakers in Philadelphia displayed so little inclination to follow this advice, gave the first occasion to the subsequent bitterness against them.]⁶ . . .

In October, [17]75, the committee in Philadelphia exerted pressure to have the Congressional mandate carried out and all able-bodied men between the ages of sixteen and fifty organized into militia companies. Non-Associators, who for conscience' sake could under no circumstances bear arms, were to be compelled to pay a sum which should coordinate their status with that of the Associators in respect to the danger, loss of time, and expenses of the latter. By means of frequent petitions and remonstrances, they succeeded in having a Militia Law passed, according to which the Associators were to drill twenty times annually, and the Non-Associators pay fifty shillings in lieu thereof. . . .

In March [1776], Congress ordered all Non-Associators to be disarmed immediately. . . .

In February and March, the Assembly again was importuned by the Associators to lay heavier fines upon the N[on]-A[ssociators]. By concerted action, petitions and remonstrances arrived from nearly all of the counties in the space of a few days. . . . In April, the tax was raised from fifty to seventy shillings to satisfy the Associators. The Assembly also urged well-meaning Non-Associators who had good guns to turn them over to designated collectors, and resolved to disarm all disaffected ones. . . .

In the meantime, Congress decreed that new governments should be constituted by the people; its tools in Philadelphia insisted that the Assembly could not do this but that a convention must be called for the purpose. . . . They sent people into the counties in order to win the committees to their view. In this connection, some did not hesitate to declare that whoever would so much as express himself as favoring the king should be hanged on the nearest tree. . . . The first business before the Convention was action to effect the complete disarmament of the N.-A.; and it was announced that drastic measures would be taken to equalize the burdens borne by the Associators, who were ready bravely to take the field, and the N.-A. who would remain at home in peace and safety. . . .

They voted that from September 14 on, the N.-A. should pay a monthly fine of twenty shillings in addition to a tax on their property of four shillings on the pound. . . .

In September, they declared that adherence to the king of Great Britain, and any support given him against the United States, constituted high treason.

They published on September 10 a Form of Government, allegedly for the consideration of the people. Therein it became evident that the Deists predominated in authority, if not in numbers: all who held credence in God and were outspoken enemies of the king became naturalized by this instrument; Jews, Turks, and heathen were authorized to sit in the Assembly and become counselors and presidents. In the entire Constitution, neither the Christian religion, nor the Bible, nor Christ [is] referred to by a single word. . . .

The Assembly, which had been superseded by the Convention, declared that the N.-A. need not pay the fine imposed by the Convention. However, the fine was collected by force. For various reasons, the [Moravian] Brethren unanimously resolved not to pay the fine willingly, but to wait until it was taken from them; and this was actually done. . . . [As the fighting grew heavier, some of the buildings at Bethlehem were requisitioned and turned into hospitals by the rebel forces.] . . .

The election of the new Assembly [1777], in accord with the decree of the Convention, was carried out in the greatest confusion. In some districts they held the election on the usual day in October, as specified in the Charter; in others they wanted to disregard the oath when balloting; in yet others no one was allowed to vote without taking the oath prescribed by the Convention. In the end, however, the Convention had its way, because their party was exceedingly active. They elected a majority of the Assembly and then did all in their power to reinforce the edifice they had built.

On June 13, 1777, a law was passed which decreed that all male, white inhabitants above eighteen years of age were required to take the following oath or affirmation prior to July 1, or August 1, in the case of the more remote counties:

I, N. N., do swear (or affirm) that I renounce and refuse all allegiance to George the Third, King of Great Britain, his heirs and successors; and that I will be faithful and bear true allegiance to the Commonwealth of Pennsylvania as a free and independent state; and that I will not at any time do or cause to be done any matter or thing that will be prejudicial or injurious to the freedom and independence thereof, as declared by Congress; and also, that I will discover and make known to some one justice of the peace of the said state, all treasons, or traitorous conspiracies, which I now know, or hereafter shall know, to be formed against this or any of the United States of America.

The justice of the peace shall give the person the following certificate. "I do hereby certify that N. N. hath voluntarily taken and subscribed the oath of affirmation, prescribed, etc."

The law read:

Whoever shall refuse or neglect to take or subscribe to the oath as herein stated, shall be ineligible to occupy any office or important post in this state, to serve on juries, to collect any debts by legal methods, to vote or be elected, to buy or sell or to bequeath to others any lands, houses, or legacies, and is to be disarmed.

Whoever shall leave the town or county wherein he resides, without such a certificate, may be considered a spy or one who fosters principles hostile to the United States, and may be arrested; should he refuse to take the oath before a justice of the peace, or to subscribe to it, he shall be thrown into a prison without bail until he shall take or subscribe to the oath.

Whoever shall issue a false certificate, shall pay a fine of fifty pounds. . . .

That winter [1777-1778], some seventeen thousand English troops were in and about Philadelphia. It was estimated that over twenty thousand people had fled from Philadelphia and twenty-three thousand had remained there. Washington's army built itself huts upon a hill some twenty miles away, headquarters being in Valley Forge.

Since very few people had conformed to the Test Act, a Supplement to it was passed on October 12. In it the age was fixed at sixteen years instead of eighteen. Moreover, should one or more witnesses denounce an individual as being hostile to the freedom and independence of the country, he was to be summoned by warrant before a justice and by him required to take the test; should he refuse, he was to be imprisoned, even though he had not left the county in which he resided. But when even this had little effect, it was proposed to confiscate the estates of all who would not take the test. . . .

Note. The Schwenkfelders, Separatists, and many others agreed, by means of deputies, in a gathering held at Oley, upon a protest against the test, which they planned to present to the Assembly. They sent it to the [Moravian] Brethren, also, asking them to subscribe to it. Since, in our opinion, it was both moderate and well-founded, we had no misgivings in adding our names to it, thus pleading for a change in the Test Act among a large group of others, without focusing attention upon ourselves. It was signed by about fifteen hundred people from Berks County, Northampton, and Philadelphia County. But just when it was to have been presented to the Assembly in Philadelphia, the latter was chased out of the city; the petition, or protest, lay in Germantown when the English came there and was not presented.[7]

In the last months of the year 1777, we had much to suffer on the score of militia, and substitutes. All male white persons, aged eighteen to fifty-three (judges, clergymen, and servants excepted), were inscribed and enrolled and divided into eight classes, which were to take the field in turn, as circumstances should direct. Should any refuse to go in person and fail to send a suitable man in his place within three days, after being notified, the county lieutenant (or *locum tenens,* as he was called) was to hire a man for him as cheaply as possible, notifying the culprit of the amount due plus expenses, and compel him to pay. For each day on which they failed to drill, they were to pay five shillings, ten days each year, and on two occasions seven shillings, sixpence. This gave opportunity for much corruption; the lieutenants said to the people: "This is your chance to make money; I need a man for .... and for ....; ask as much as you please, and they have to pay it," etc. The drill money has rigorously been collected. . . .

[The] Assembly passed a new law on April 1, [17]78, by means of which it sought to bolster up and support its unstable, violent rule. According to it, all male white persons above sixteen years were to abjure King G[eorge] III and all his heirs and successors prior to June 1, 1778, swearing allegiance to the Republic of Pennsylvania. Whoever should fail to do this, should be excluded from all the rights and privileges enjoyed by the freemen of the state and forfeit all legal rights; schoolmasters, merchants, apothecaries, doctors, surgeons were not to be allowed to carry on their professions. Non-jurors were to pay double taxes. After June 1, two or more justices of the peace could summon by any constable or officer any individual who had not taken the test and require the oath of him. Should he refuse to take the same, he could be imprisoned for three months or be bound over to the next [session of] court and fined, though not above ten pounds. The court could then again require such a prisoner, or one so bound to take the oath, record his refusal, and banish him from the country within the space of thirty days. This would entail the loss of his personal estate; his real estate, i. e. fixed goods and landed property, would pass to his nearest heir, provided the latter would take the oath. . . . This caused much consternation; and the knife was placed to the throat of many. . . .

In June, Mr. Limbach and Morey, two justices in Saucon, in Upper Milford, summoned a number of their neighbors to take the test, and since they refused, sent them to jail. Many did not appear; these got off successfully. But nine Mennonites and two others were harshly dealt with, in accordance with the latest Test Act. They were notified to leave the country within thirty days; all their movable property was taken from them and sold at public auction; their children's flour was taken out of the sack and even the women's spinning wheels. Siegfried, the sheriff, carried out his office with cruelty. . . . [Ettwein was delegated to take a petition on behalf of the Moravians to the Assembly.]

Toward the end of October, I went to Philadelphia with this petition. A long time passed, before the Assembly began its sessions. Two Quakers had been condemned to the gallows, Roberts and Carlisle, two old and otherwise highly respected and beloved men. Four thousand people had signed a petition to the Assembly to spare their lives, but the Presbyterians had contrived to prevent the House from assembling before they had been hanged. The president of Congress [Henry Laurens] had interceded for them in person; but Quakers were to be and had to be hung in Philadelphia. . . . [A revision of the Test Act was passed by the Assembly in December, 1778, with some of the harsher features removed.][8]

The Pacifist German Sectarians Defended

In response to an article in the Göttingen *Staats-Anzeiger* of 1783-1784 which accused the Mennonites of being dangerous and rebellious insurgents as demonstrated by their belligerence in the American Revolutionary War, an anonymous correspondent replied in a later issue from his firsthand knowledge of America that the report was totally erroneous.[9] The place of writing, Barby, and the information that the author had traveled to America in 1779 and returned in 1781 allows the identification to be made. The author was a Moravian, a member of the Unity Elders' Conference, Bishop John Frederick Reichel, who undertook an official visitation of the Moravian congregations in North America during that period. His statement, evidently never before published in English, is an important witness to the conduct of the Mennonites, the Brethren, and other German groups during the difficult Revolutionary era.[10]

A Defense of the Mennonites in N[orth] America directed against the [article] in Issue XX, p. 447[ff.]

At that place, lines 5-15, are these words: "The Mennonites — insurgents in America." Inasmuch as the author assures us that he has no other purpose than to spread light and truth, he will be all the less inclined to take offense at the correction of these last words, as in this matter also, nothing but the love of truth directs my pen.

Whoever might be reading that the insurgents in No. America are serving as proof that the Mennonites of our day are the most dangerous of all known religious sects in regard to the state, the civil constitution and the relationship of subjects to the authorities, and this because they, while they will not be persuaded to bear arms when the defense of it [the state etc.] is necessary, they arm themselves with the greatest zeal and an exceptional willingness for battle and preach war and the shedding of blood whenever the undertaking aims to overthrow the state, incite riot, break the bonds of society — can such a person think anything but that the Mennonites in America and those religious denominations who share the same doctrines in regard to the bearing of arms as the Mennonites, were the first to seize arms against Great Britain, who incited their neighbors to do the same, and set all wheels in motion in order to bring about the overthrow of the previous government?

The truth of the matter, however, is quite different.

Early in 1779 I went to New York with an English fleet. After receiving passes from the generals of both warring powers, I traveled in April to Pennsylvania by way of New Jersey. It was not until December, 1781, that I returned to England via New York. Thus, during a visit of nearly three years I spent mostly in Pennsylvania but also in North Carolina, Maryland and New Jersey, I had ample opportunity to learn who had been and still was the most effective in the instigation and continuation of the unrest at that time.

Pennsylvania is full of Quakers, also of various kinds of Baptists, [Tauf-Gesinnten] and other denominations who hold that they dare not bear arms with a good conscience. All of these groups have remained true to their principles from beginning until end. No Dunker [Täufer], no Quaker took up arms. What is more, all of these people were so sympathetic and loyal to the government of Great Britain that they could not be persuaded to abjure the king of Great Britain and his heirs in the required manner, even though the authorities would have been content with their conscientious affirmation, in the place of an oath. It is true that a number of Quakers did concede on this latter point of abjuration and separated themselves from the others. Yet even these, like their brethren and all the other denominations mentioned above, remained united in their conviction not to bear arms, and no one was forced to do so.

The Mennonites, who could not bring themselves at all to abjure the king of Great Britain, suffered severely during the year 1778, shortly before my arrival. They endured imprisonment, as did others of like mind. In several places even their property was seized and sold at public auction. They were often in danger of their lives among their neighbors who thought differently than they.

In October, 1778, the legislative authority made an end to the harsh practices of some of the lesser officials, by means of wise laws. Otherwise, the poor Mennonites as well as the other Non-Jurors would have suffered the most tragic experiences yet.

Now, then, do such people as these deserve to be pointed out as proof that those sects or religious denominations who refuse to bear arms are the most horrible hypocrites and traitors, who readily murder not only one another, but are also capable of preaching war and the shedding of blood when the intention is to overthrow the present government and create a new one? Of course not! The author of the above-mentioned article must have had completely false reports concerning the insurgents in America.

It is not to be denied that men there were in the American provinces who considered it their duty to incite the people to war against Great Britain, and that even from the pulpit. It is, however, quite unnecessary to indicate from which religious persuasion these men were, inasmuch as they are not ashamed of their conduct but rather believe that they have served their fatherland and their fellow-countrymen.

Just as little as it is my place to judge their conviction and manner of conduct, just as surely can I state that the Mennonites, Quakers and the other religious denominations who believe the bearing of arms to be against their consciences, are being done the greatest injustice by saying that they have changed their basic principles and have fought against Great Britain. Let their passiveness and suffering be interpreted as stubbornness or non-cooperation, or, what it really was, as a steadfast persistence in their conviction — in any case they ought to be given the same respect from the impartial public which is due even an erring conscience and which even that government which could not have been entirely satisfied by their point of view granted them during the last years of the war through a wise concession.

What I have said here applies only to what took place during the Revolution in No. America. I felt that I owed this much to the love of truth and to these my neighbors, though they are not closely connected with me in any way.

Barby, March 4, 1784   [John Frederick Reichel][11]

DECISIONS OF ANNUAL MEETING ON THE WAR ISSUE

Not surprisingly, the demands brought upon individual Brethren by the authorities (as cited in Ettwein's account) led to an airing of these problems in the Brethren yearly meetings. A consistent stance is revealed, which follows the nonresistant and pacifist principles of the historic peace churches, especially that developed historically by the Anabaptist movement.

Annual Meeting of 1778

This conference, held at the Pipe Creek congregation in Maryland, dealt with the problem of the oath of allegiance or "attest" required by the Pennsylvania government in June 1777, under stringent penalty for nonobservance. Evidently under this severe pressure, some Brethren, including ministers, did affirm their allegiance to the new government and renounce allegiance to the Crown.

After much reflection, in the fear of the Lord, it has been concluded in union, that the brethren who have taken the attest should recall it before a justice, and give up their certificate, and recall and apologize in their churches, and truly repent of the error. If they cannot do this, and instead justify themselves, the apostle exhorts us that we should withdraw ourselves from every brother who conducts himself wrongly, and such a brother will be deprived of the kiss of fellowship, of the council, and the breaking of bread, until he becomes obedient again. Ministers and elders who have taken the attest, and are sorry and grieved about it, who confessedly recall the matter before the justice of the peace and in the public church, counsel shall be held about them in their churches in the presence of one or more ministers or overseers to consider, in the fear of the Lord, whether he or such as before mentioned could serve again in their office. But if such minister or elder should stubbornly defend himself and justify his course, yes, even teach the same, then we cannot comprehend how he can be obedient to the spirit of truth, which teaches we shall not touch an unclean thing, nor be unequally yoked together with unbelievers, because Christ has no concord with Belial. Therefore, we decide that such laborers are unfit in the Lord's vineyard, and also unfit to be members in the church of the living God, until their minds are changed and they speak again with new tongues, or find their hearts with David. May God have mercy upon us![12]

Annual Meeting of 1779

The problem of the oath of allegiance, or attest, came before the church councils once more a year later at Conestoga, Pennsylvania. Steps in church discipline are outlined for those not obedient to the church's ruling against taking the oath. Ministers who took the attest are admonished not to exercise their offices until the matter is taken care of. A key sentence in revealing the Brethren attitude toward the state is found in the first part. Where a government did not have clear *de facto* power, it was obvious that God had not definitely spoken. Therefore, the prior allegiance should be maintained.

Regarding the taking of the attest, it has been concluded in union as follows: Inasmuch as it is the Lord our God who establishes kings and removes kings, and ordains rulers according to his own good pleasure, and we cannot know whether God has rejected the king and chosen the state, while the king had the government; therefore we could not, with a good conscience, repudiate the king and give allegiance to the state. And it seems to us that those who have done so have committed a fault, on account of which we could not break bread with them, but bear with them in love. But, if they would come moved by their own conviction, and would make acknowledgement, being truly repentant, then we will forgive them, and we believe God would also forgive them, and we will break bread with them. But in regard to the ministers, we think that they should stand still in their labor, and not baptize or administer the breaking of bread. Should they, however, become convinced in themselves that they have erred, and show contrition saying: "We are sorry," then we will forgive them and be in full fellowship with them, yet so that the churches to which they belong are satisfied with them when they should continue in their offices. But if such go still further in this matter, as holding office and so forth, show no sorrow, and rather continue in such course, then they should also be deprived of the church council and holy kiss, and *nota bene,* not only the ministers but all who have taken this course.[18]

Annual Meeting of 1781

A troublesome matter was faced by the Conferences of 1780 and 1781 held at Conestoga, Pennsylvania. Was a brother justified in hiring a substitute to do military duty in place of himself or a son? The ambivalence of the answer reveals that there was not a complete unity of mind on the matter. A further statement on the tax indicates that there were those who refused even to pay taxes to support the war, although most of the Brethren evidently did not go this far. Many Quakers took the position that they could not pay taxes levied directly for war purposes. They and those Brethren taking the same position underwent forcible seizure of property and sale at public auction to satisfy the demands of the rebel government.

Article 1. Inasmuch as at the great meeting at Conestoga last year, it was unanimously concluded that we should not pay the substitute money; but inasmuch as it has been overlooked here and there and some have not regarded it, therefore we, the assembled brethren, exhort in union all brethren everywhere to hold themselves guiltless and take no part in war or blood-shedding, which might take place if we would pay voluntarily for hiring men; or yet more if we become agents to collect such money. And inasmuch as some brethren have received written orders to tell their people and afterwards to collect (such money), accompanied by the threat of a heavy fine, we fervently exhort not to be afraid to do that which is right. Still, we exhort also that if a brother is fined, there should be provision made for such brethren, and assistance rendered as far as money is concerned. In case a brother or his son [is] drafted that he or his son should go to war, and he could buy himself or his son from it, such would not be deemed so sinful, yet it should not be given voluntarily without compulsion. But where this has been overlooked, and the substitute money has been voluntary, and (the brother) acknowledges his mistake from the heart and repents it, the church shall be satisfied with him.

If a brother bears his testimony that he cannot give his money on account of his conscience and would say to the collector: "If you must take it, then use your authority, I shall not be in your way" — with such a brother we should also be satisfied. But concerning the tax, it is considered that on account of the troublesome times and in order to avoid offense, we might follow the example of Christ (Matt. 17:24-27). Yet, if one does not see it so and thinks perhaps, he for his conscience sake could not pay it, but bear with others who pay in patience, we would willingly go along inasmuch as we deem the overruling of the conscience to be wrong."[14]

Annual Meetings of 1785 and 1790

The most thorough theological and Biblical statement concerning the Brethren position on war was issued at Big Conewago two years after the end of the Revolutionary conflict. It arose in connection with the teaching of a minister in western Virginia. Doubtless the memories of the war just ended and the concern for a clear enunciation of the church's position contributed to the decision to make such a full answer to the problem. There is no reason for feeling that this represented a new position for the church; rather, it is an elaboration of what was practiced during the difficult days of the war.

Valentine Power, the minister involved, was listed in 1772 as a property owner in the South Branch area of what is now West Virginia, near Petersburg. He was termed a "minister of the Duncard order" in the County of Hampshire, Virginia (the designation at that time), in 1783. According to J. M. Henry, Power and his brother Martin tended to favor the Tory position, and hence questioned the Brethren peace principle. Five years later the Annual Meeting (at Coventry?) found it necessary to call Valentine Power to account again for his variant teaching on war. It is thought that he left the Brethren and joined the Methodist church.[15]

Annual Meeting of 1785

Article 1. Our cordial and united wish and greeting of love and peace to the beloved members, brethren and sisters on South Branch, especially to the loving brethren, Valentine Power and Martin Power, and all the members in your vicinity. We wish you all much grace and peace from God the Father, through Jesus Christ, His dear Son, to be faithful to Him from the bottom of the heart, according to the guidance and direction of His holy and good Spirit, even unto a blessed and God-pleasing end. Amen.

We have in part seen, and also heard, that there has arisen some difference in several doctrines among some brethren of your church and others, and having also seen the letter of the loving brother, Valentine Power — who has written to the great meeting — and learned from it his views about "carrying on war," which are to be proved especially from the words of Peter (I Peter 2:13-14). We have considered and weighed the matter in union, and we trust in the fear of the Lord; but yet, for the sake of the word of God, we could not agree with such a view, because we do not see it thus, and do not understand the loving Peter thus in that same chapter, nor in his other discourses. But God grant that we may be directed according to His good pleasure.

First, we do not understand at all, from the words of Peter alluded to, that we can give ourselves up to do violence, or that we should submit to the higher powers in such a manner as to make ourselves their instruments to shed men's blood, however it might be done. It is indeed difficult to believe that Peter should have rejected in one place what he teaches in another; therefore we cannot understand him thus, but that his mind and admonition to "submit to every ordinance of man," etc., is something different. The question arises, how far or wherein are we to submit ourselves? And this question the loving Peter may answer himself.

We find (Acts 5:28) that the higher power to which Peter and John were subject had commanded them strictly that they should not teach in this name (the name of Jesus) any more, but they (the apostles) did not obey herein. And when they were asked again: "Did we not strictly charge you?" etc., then Peter and the apostles answered and said: "We must obey God rather than man." It will be well, when we always attend strictly to the meaning of Holy Writ; and in the very same chapter of Peter's alluded to, we see clearly that Peter exhorts for conscience toward God to endure grief and to suffer wrongfully, and says even that Christ became in this our example that we should follow His steps. Now we see that Christ always, in all His sufferings, endured them, and that with great patience, and never resisted or defended himself. Rather, as Peter says: "He committed himself to him that judges righteously."

We see furthermore that our loving Saviour, though innocent, was attacked in a murderous manner by just such men as Brother P[ower] has mentioned in his letter; but the Saviour stood fast in the covenant of faithfulness, as the brother stated. In a murderous manner He was attacked, and Peter was quick and ready to draw his sword according to the legal justice of God, and struck a servant and cut off his ear. But what says the Saviour: "Put your sword back into its place; for all who take the sword will perish by the sword." Here, indeed, was the greatest necessity (for self-defense), but all this time the Saviour resisted not; but He suffered patiently, and even healed the one whose ear was cut off, acting as it is written: "The righteous shall live by faith"; and again: "I believe, therefore I speak," etc. Thus our Saviour had said before, "That you resist not evil," for so He believed, and so He spoke, and so He died.

Furthermore the loving Saviour says: "He that believes in me, as the Scripture has said," etc. Now we will consider a little what even at His time the Scripture was teaching about Christ and His kingdom; so we see that the holy man of God, Isaiah, says of the time of Christ: "They shall beat their swords into plowshares and their spears into pruning hooks; nation shall not lift up sword against nation, neither shall they learn war any more" (Isa. 2:4). Again Isaiah (9:5), German version: "All war, with confused noise and garments rolled in blood, shall be burned with fire," etc. So we believe where that fire which Christ came to kindle, where that fire burns, there will be burned all war as predicted; for the love to God constrains to the obedience of this commandment, as John teaches, and as Christ requires and says: "If you love me, keep my commandments," and His commandments aim throughout at non-resistance.

So we hope the dear brethren will not take it amiss when we, from all these passages of Scripture, and especially from the words of Peter, cannot see or find any liberty to use any (carnal) sword, but only the sword of the Spirit, which is the word of God, by which we cast down imaginations and every high thing that exalts itself against the knowledge of God, and bring into captivity every thought as to the obedience of Christ, as Paul says (II Cor. 10:5). . . .

And as to the swearing of oaths, we believe the word of Christ, that in all things which we are to testify, we shall testify what is yea, or what is true, with yea, and what is nay, or not true, with nay; for whatsoever is more than these comes of evil. And herewith we will conclude for now.

This we intend to send you in writing with our dear brethren Daniel Leatherman, Jacob Danner, and Henry Danner.

Written May 15, 1785, at the great meeting on Big Conewago, from your brethren, united in love, Jacob Sauer, Valentine Pressel, Michael Bosserman, Martin Reinhart, David Studebaker, Peter Dierdorf, Martin Urner, Jacob Stoll, Christian Longenecker, Henry Neff, Lorenz Beckner, Philip Lewig.[16]

Annual Meeting of 1790

Article 2. At a great meeting of brethren on the Schuylkill at the home of Brother John Bach, May 22, 1790, the following was unanimously concluded by the brethren, that is: We wish and desire that the dear brother V[alentine] P[ower] would desist from his strange notion, because he has renounced with us before God, angels, and men everything which is contrary to wholesome doctrine, and because we believe and profess that Christ has prohibited His followers from swearing oaths and participating in war. Hence we must hold fast to His truth and word, and withdraw ourselves from every such brother who will justify swearing of oaths and warfare. It is impossible for us to break the bread of communion with such a brother, even if he would allege that the powers that be require us to do so. For our rulers could not do it, if they would, because we must obey God rather than men. But now, thanks be to God, we have such a government that will not require of us such action contrary to our consciences. But if there were one among us that had such a conscience that he could fight and swear oaths, such a person would not be one of us. . . .

Signed in the great meeting, in the name and with the consent of all the assembled brethren.

George Preisz, Martin Meyer, Michael Frantz, Daniel Bollinger, John Landes, Christian Lawshe, Justus Fuchs, Martin Gaby, Peter Keyser, Sander Mack, Nathaniel Schreiber, David Kuntze, Martin Urner, Peter Leibert, Jacob Boeshor, Jacob Danner, Abraham Lawshe.[17]

PENNSYLVANIA

Both of the Moravian accounts dealt heavily with the conditions in Pennsylvania, although taking the broader situation in the American colonies as their topics. For some further instances of the actions of the Pennsylvanian authorities and the Brethren response, the following material is presented.

Excerpts From the Pennsylvania Government Records

Included in Ettwein's report were the basic data on the several important Pennsylvania government actions regarding military service, the oath of allegiance, and taxes. Some additional excerpts from the published government records will supplement his account.

Assembly of Pennsylvania, November 24, 1775.

Resolved, that the said Committee be directed to make particular enquiry concerning the contributions made by the people called Mennonist, Omish [Amish] Mennonist, and Sunday Baptists [Brethren] in Lancaster County, in pursuance of the recommendation of the later House of Assembly on the thirtieth of June last, and report to this House at their next meeting, how much of the said contributions has been paid for the uses of any, and what battalion or company of Associators in that County. . . .

County Official to the President of the Executive Council
Hanover, November 12, 1777

. . . But on the whole I believe about one-half or some better is gone in these two classes, perhaps three parts or four. The great number of Quakers, Mennonists and Dunkers in this county occasions the company to be so hard filled up. The others in the upper end of the county which is mostly Irish people and Low Dutch goes pretty general. . . . So many scrupulous people as we have occasions much hiring and deters the business much. . . .

Lebanon, June 16, 1780

. . . Your Excellency will please to observe that many of the wealthy Mennonists and others who live in the neighborhood of Lancaster, Manheim and Conestoga, drive flocks of cattle over the mountains in the spring season, to the great distress of the poor inhabitants. Those men undoubtedly have them to spare, otherwise they would keep them on their own farms, and therefore, ought to be taken from them; but this cannot be done without the assistance of ten or twelve men to drive them together, which would be attended with extra charges. Therefore [we] wait your Excellency's particular instruction in the premises. . . .[18]

Correspondence on Military Matters

Two letters by Pennsylvania Brethren in 1775 reflect the problems brought on by the struggle. The first gives some indication how church discipline was brought to bear on a brother who did not follow the historic peace teaching of the church. The second reveals the perplexity faced by the denomination regarding taxes and forced contributions. The

Brethren generally came to take the position during the Revolution that money levied by taxes should be paid, as rendering to Caesar that which was his.

Krefeld, May 11, 1775

In Jesus the lover of our true life dearly beloved brother:

I received your dear little letter in good order. However, whether I can go to the next great meeting I do not know yet. I spoke with Brother Christopher Sauer whether he wanted to go. At the time he did not really intend to go, but if I can persuade him yet I would be glad to stay home this time, as far as my body is concerned. As regards my spirit, I would very much like to be present in warm love and well-wishing. If it should happen that he persists in his present intention not to go and if it were convenient for me to go there, I would nevertheless prefer to have permission from him and the brethren before I begin the journey. For this reason I cannot give a definite answer as to whether I will go or not.

As regards Brother Cornelius Nice, he has had his name put on the list for the drill. He seeks to remove himself from the congregation as much as possible and no longer likes to be called a brother. He refused the kiss to Brother Christopher Sauer when he spoke to him. When I learned of it and also spoke with him, I did not offer it to him. Thus he would be as good as expelled but we should gladly have more patience to see whether he might repent. I asked him whether he would be angry with me if I were to pray for him. He said no, he would like it. Then I advised him to try himself whether he could still pray.

As far as this present time is concerned, my impression is that this is the beginning of the time of troubles of which Christ said that while we should not be frightened, yet we ought to guard ourselves against men. However, I believe that the best guard consists in seeking to conduct ourselves in and with a good conscience, both toward God and toward every person and also in demonstrating our tenderness toward everyone, for the Lord is near.

It is true that the Lord, as the Scripture says, was not in the wind, nor in the earthquake, nor in the fire, yet near in the quiet gentle rustling. When that came, Elijah covered his face in his cloak and went out to meet the Lord. And especially because we cannot know the hour of our departure from this time, may the most gracious God grant that we might watch and pray in order to become worthy to escape everything that is to come and to stand before the Son of Man.

Indeed, the great blessedness of the latter times is close before the door. I do not, however, fully expect it in this life, which is subject to many a death, but rather hope for a better life which is eternal. The beginning of the time of troubles and the travail are in this life, and the hour of temptation ends and fulfills itself in the breaking of this life. Later in that other life we shall see what kind of child has been born to us. That is why Christ says that we are not to fear those that kill the body but cannot do anything after that. As far as I and mine are concerned otherwise, we are at present all rather well. After a warm greeting and kiss of love, I commend you to God and the word of His grace, He who has the power to edify us and to give us the inheritance, along with those who shall be saved in Christ Jesus. Amen.

Extend my friendly greetings to your dear parents and your brother and also to the dear members whom you might meet on your journey, if they happen to ask about me. (It may be that I shall write to my brother John tomorrow, but I do not know how it will suit.) My dear wife and children send their friendly greetings.

I remain your humble but faithful fellow brother,

Sander Mack.

To the beloved Brother John Preisz to be opened personally.[19]

Conestoga, September 21, 1775

First, my warm greeting of love to you, much beloved Brother Alexander Mack and your dear wife and children and to all of the members in Germantown:

I have received your dear letter to me and learned from it that a demand has been made upon you to give money and I further learned from it that you would like to know how we have given our money, [whether] "for protection money" or "for the needy." Let this serve as an answer that in part it has been given for both. There seemed to be no other alternative than to give something in order to be safe, for the *fire* was too much *ignited*. Therefore, we gave our money, and told the man to whom we gave it that we were giving our money for the needy as could be seen in the newspaper of July 27.

And as Congress had given Brother John Henrich and his traveling companion a statement in which was mentioned that the man was to turn it over to the *Committee Treasurer* and that the *Committee* was to use it accordingly, we therefore did as we were ordered and had no further scruples as to how the Committee used it. For we gave it in good faith for the needy and the man to whom we gave it gave us a receipt stating that the money would be used for that purpose. But as to how the fire began or how it originated in the first place, this I would rather tell you orally than in writing.

Concerning, however, what you have written about disunity among us, that I would also prefer to leave unwritten, for in that case I would also have to write that which I would rather tell orally. Besides, the disunity was not very great and only pertained to one single point on which we could not find complete unity.

As far as I am concerned, I am still fairly well and so also are the members with whom I live. They send you their greetings. Our dear Brother Daniel Hollinger has been called from time to eternity, right after the harvest.

In closing this thought yet:

"Unalloyed dove-like simplicity and love, in which we serve one another, is that which will exalt us; yes, even last in eternity and blossom in Paradise."

Be greeted from me once again; I remain your humble fellow pilgrim toward the peaceful eternity.

Jacob Stoll

To Alexander Mack near Germantown, to be opened personally.[20]

Petition of the Mennonites and the Brethren

A very significant document, often republished, is the memorial or petition of the Pennsylvania Mennonites and the German Baptists to the General Assembly submitted on November 7, 1775.[21] Its clear delineation of principle, irenic but firm tone, declaration of philanthropic concern, and theological clarity stamp it as a key source for understanding the church-state posture of the two groups. The fact that they could make common cause at such a critical juncture demonstrates an underlying unity despite differences over form of baptism and other relatively minor doctrinal points.

The background of the petition is the agitation by the Associators against the nonresistants after the outbreak of hostilities in April 1775. In Lancaster County the feeling against the Non-Associators grew so violent that the County Committee of Inspection and Observation felt called on to issue a broadside condemning mob action, containing the following sentence:

> The Committee, having received information that divers persons whose religious tenets forbid their forming themselves into military associations have been maltreated by some violent and ill disposed people in the county of Lancaster, notwithstanding their willingness to contribute cheerfully to the common cause otherwise than by bearing arms. . ., proceeds to discourage such mob spirit.[22]

The Quakers had submitted a memorial on October 27, 1775, and the other peace groups had also taken steps to have their views understood by the Assembly.

A Short and Sincere Declaration.

To our Honorable Assembly, and all others in high or low station of administration, and to all friends and inhabitants of this country, to whose sight this may come, be they English or German.

In the first place we acknowledge us indebted to the most high God, who created heaven and earth, the only good being, to thank Him for all His great goodness and manifold mercies and love through our Saviour Jesus Christ, who is come to save the souls of men, having all power in heaven and on earth.

Further we find ourselves indebted to be thankful to our late worthy Assembly, for their giving so good an advice in these troublesome times to all ranks of people in *Pennsylvania,* particularly in allowing those, who, by the doctrine of our Saviour Jesus Christ are persuaded in their conscience to love their enemies and not to resist evil, to enjoy the liberty of the conscience, for which, as also for all the good things we enjoyed under their care, we heartily thank that worthy body of assembly, and all high and low in office who have advised to such a peaceful measure, hoping and confiding that they, and all others entrusted with power in this hitherto blessed province, may be moved by the same spirit of grace which animated the first founder of this province, our late worthy proprietor *William Penn,* to grant liberty of conscience to all its inhabitants, that they may in the great and memorable day of judgment be put on the right hand of the just judge, who judges without respect of person, and hear of Him these blessed words: *Come, O blessed of my Father, inherit the kingdom prepared for you, . . . what you did to one of the least of these my brethren, you did it to me,* among which number (i.e. *the least of Christ's brethren*) we by His grace hope to be ranked; and every lenity and favour shown to such tender conscienced, although weak followers of this our blessed Saviour, will not be forgotten by Him in that great day.

The advice to those who do not find freedom of conscience to take up arms, that they ought to be helpful to those who are in need and distressed circumstances, we receive with cheerfulness toward all men of what station they may be — it being our principle to feed the hungry and give the thirsty drink. We have dedicated ourselves to serve all men in every thing that can be helpful to the preservation of men's lives, but we find no freedom in giving, or doing, or assisting in any thing by which men's lives are destroyed or hurt. We beg the patience of all those who believe we err in this point.

We are always ready, according to *Christ's* command to *Peter,* to pay the tribute, that we may offend no man, and so we are willing to pay taxes, *and to render unto Caesar those things that are Caesar's and to God those things that are God's,* although we think ourselves very weak to give God His due honor, He being a spirit and life, and we only dust and ashes.

We are also willing to be subject to the higher powers, and to give in the manner *Paul* directs us: *For he does not bear the sword in vain; he is the servant of God, to execute his wrath on the wrongdoer.*

This testimony we lay down before our worthy Assembly, and all other persons in government, letting them know that we are thankful as above mentioned, and that we are not at liberty in conscience to take up arms to conquer our enemies, but rather to pray to God, who has power in heaven and on earth, for *us* and *them*.

We also crave the patience of all the inhabitants of this country; what they think to see clearer in the doctrine of the blessed Jesus Christ, we will leave to them and God, finding ourselves very poor. For faith is to proceed out of the word of God, which is life and spirit, and a power of God, and our conscience is to be instructed by the same; therefore we beg for patience.

Our small gift, which we have given, we give to those who have power over us, that we may not offend them, as Christ taught us by the tribute penny.

We heartily pray that God would govern all hearts of our rulers, be they high or low, to mediate those good things which will pertain to our and their happiness.

The above declaration, signed by a number of elders and teachers of the Society of Mennonists, and some of the German Baptists, presented to the Honorable House of Assembly on the 7th day of November, 1775, was most graciously received.[23]

MARYLAND

The Brethren and the Mennonites also took joint action in the colony of Maryland in securing rights of conscience. The published accounts of the Proceedings of the Convention of the Province of Maryland refer to their petition. One of the results of the initiative was the establishment in the Maryland Constitution of the right of affirmation instead of the oath for the "people called Quakers and those called Dunkers, and those called Mennonists holding it unlawful to take an oath on any occasion."

On the point of fines in lieu of military service, the Convention took this action on July 6, 1776:

> Resolved that the several committees of observation may, in their discretion, prolong the time or take security for the payment of any fine by them imposed for not enrolling in the militia, and may remit the whole or any part of the fines by them assessed; and it is recommended to the committee to pay particular attention, and to make a difference between such persons as may refuse from religious principles, or other motives.[24]

This action, with its aura of tolerance, is said to have been "more liberal toward nonresistant people than the Acts of Pennsylvania." However, extant records of the application of the measure in two Maryland counties demonstrate that it could be applied rigorously. It was generally true in all of the colonies that the lesser levels of authority were culpable of excesses which were not in the intent of the higher authorities.

Proceedings of the Committee of Observation for the Elizabethtown District, Washington County

It appears to this Committee (from the representation of some of the members who have endeavored to get their neighbors to enroll in companies of militia) that the greatest number refuse in consequence of several religious sects being excepted by the resolves of the Convention.

Resolved, that this Committee is of opinion that its [sic] highly reasonable that every person who enjoys the benefit of their [sic] religion and protection of the laws of this free country ought to contribute either in money or military service towards the defence of these invaluable rights.

Resolved, that two shillings and six pence currency per week (for all those who are restrained by religious principles from contributing their proportion to military service) would be equal to mustering agreeable to the directions of the Convention.

Resolved, that a remonstrance is to be sent to the next Convention setting forth the cause and substance of the above resolve. . . .

[March 4, 1776]

Order that the captains of each hundred take an association paper, and present it to the inhabitants of their hundred for signing, and make an exact account of those that sign and those that refuse with their reasons for refusing. . . .

[May 7, 1776]

Resolved that this Committee do take into their consideration the summons issued last Committee for the appearance of sundry persons before them this day, to show cause why they do not enroll and associate, and deliver up their arms, in which the Committee concurred, and proceeded to examine the returns made thereon when it appeared the sundry persons following had due notice accordingly. They were called in turn and such as have appeared have not or are not able to give any satisfactory reasons to this Committee why they did not or do not enroll and associate and deliver up their arms according to the resolve of the late Convention in December last are fined and proceeded against as follows. . . .

[May 8, 1776]

Ordered that sundry persons to pay the sums annexed to their names in one month from the date hereof, and deliver up their fire arms immediately, if they have any, except pistols, to the several persons appointed to receive the same, viz. . . .

[December 18, 1776]

On motion resolved, that the Dunkards and the Mennonists be advertised, to pay their respective fines, to the Committee, on Tuesday next, otherwise, they may depend, that rigorous measures will be immediately taken to compel payment.

[December 22, 1767]

On motion of Col. Rench and seconded by J. Hughes, resolved unanimously that such of the young Dunkards and Mennonists as have not enrolled nor associated, shall immediately be requested to march with the militia, in order to give their assistance in intrenching and helping the sick and all such as will turn out voluntarily agreeably to the above request, shall have their fines remitted.

It is further unanimously resolved, that on the marching of the militia from the county, all they that are well affected to this state and not capable of marching with the militia, shall be formed into companies, with proper officers for the protection and relief of such families, as shall be left without assistance and that the officers of the companies so formed shall divide the settlement into certain circuits and ride round such circuits as shall be assigned them once a fortnight, and make particular enquiry into the distresses of the inhabitants, and order them such relief, as they shall think necessary, and should their companies not be sufficient for giving such relief; in that case, they are required to apply to the Dunkards and Mennonists residing nearest to give their assistance, and in case of refusal or neglect they shall take down their names, and return them to the committee, on the return of the militia, that proper notice be taken thereof.

A list of non-enrollers and non-associators residing in Capt. Baker's district were by him returned. . . .

A petition from the Mennonists and German Baptists was laid before the Committee praying their interposition with the Convention that they may be indulged with giving produce instead of cash for their fines. Ordered that Col. Beall and Capt. Chapline form a letter to that purpose. Col. Beall and Capt. Chapline brought in the following letter.

Upper District of Frederick County
July 3, 1776

Noble Sir:

Whereas the inclosed petition was laid before the Committee of this district praying their confirmation of the facts therein recited, and their interposition with your Honorable House, the Committee has therefore taken the liberty (being truly sensible of the justness thereof) to recommend the prayer to your consideration and that you will take order therein, and grant such relief as your Honorable House may think proper.

I am with due respect

Your most obedient servant
Signed by order of the Committee
Samuel Hughes, chairman

which is accordingly to be sent to the Convention.

[The Convention passed the resolution quoted on page 365.][25]

Journal of the Committee of Observation of the Middle District of Frederick County, Maryland, September 12, 1775 — October 24, 1776

[November 14, 1775]

Resolved that by the 28th instant every captain of the militia shall make a return of his muster roll, as it is hoped by that time that all effective freemen will be enrolled; but if there should be any so disaffected and obstinate as to refuse, it is desired that those persons formerly appointed to take an accounting of them bring in their lists, that they may be transmitted to the Convention which meets the fourth of next month; it is also resolved that those persons appointed to hand about the association papers bring in a list of all refusers, and that this resolve shall be fixed up in the public places of the district that every person may have an opportunity of complying with it.

[April 12, 1776]

Several lists of persons who had refused to enroll were returned, and they were fined as on the leaves preceding under their proper letters appear.

On motion resolved that persons be appointed in the several hundreds in this district to collect the fines imposed on those persons who refused to enroll and also to receive the arms of non-associators; after which the gentlemen mentioned in the preceding page were chosen. [List of twenty-three names of collectors for sixteen areas.][26]

NORTH CAROLINA

Specific attention was also paid to the pacifist groups in North Carolina in the wartime legislation. The same general pattern observed in Pennsylvania and Maryland also obtained here, that is, exemption from military service was granted but heavy financial obligations were exacted. Several of the pertinent laws are here given as an indication of how the groups were treated.

Requisition of Blankets

Friday, May 1, 1778

Mr. Speaker and Gentlemen of the Senate:

We herewith send for your concurrence a resolve of this House for supplying the army with clothing, etc.

T. Benbury, S. C.

At the same time received the resolve referred to in the above message, as follows:

Whereas, it is essentially necessary for the preservation of the health of the troops belonging to this state and to enable them to bear the rigor of a northern climate, that they be fully supplied with clothing and so as it is possible that supplies from abroad may fail hereafter.

Be it therefore resolved, that the several counties shall furnish clothing as follows. . . .

And the justices and field officers in every county at the first court after the Session of Assembly if convenient, or otherwise at the second court, are hereby authorized and required to proportion the clothing afore mentioned to the several companies and to the Quakers, Mennonists, Dunkers and Moravians where there shall be any such in the county. The several companies in the different counties being notified of their proportions by the justices and field officers shall agree among themselves what articles each person belonging to or living in the district of the company shall furnish and likewise the Quakers, Mennonists, Dunkers, and Moravians shall agree among themselves respectively. The captains of the companies and the head or leading men of the said persuasions shall return exact lists of the persons' names who are to furnish the different articles according to such agreement to the colonel or commanding officer of the militia in each respective county.

If any captain shall fail to return such lists it shall and may be lawful for the colonel or commanding officer aforesaid to issue his warrant against any one or more of the people belonging to the profession so failing, authorizing the person to whom the same shall be directed to seize and sell as much of the property of such person or persons as will purchase the quantity of clothing required and the colonel or commanding officer shall apply the money accordingly. If any person belonging to any company the captain of which shall have returned a proper list as aforesaid shall fail to furnish his or her proper quota the colonel or commanding officer may proceed in manner afore mentioned against the person so failing and apply the money in purchasing his or her quota of clothing provided that the colonel or commanding officer in any county shall not issue his warrant against any captain for not returning a list until twenty days after the court which shall apportion the clothing, nor against any individual of any company or society afore mentioned until the 20th day of September next.

The colonel or commanding officer in each and every county is hereby authorized and required to receive the clothing afore mentioned from the persons who shall furnish the same, and the said clothing shall be valued on oath by three indifferent freeholders or householders in the counties of Washington, Wilkes, Burke and Surry and in other counties by three freeholders, who shall certify the valuation. Such certificates with receipts endorsed thereon from the colonel or commanding officer of delivering thereof shall be received in payment of public taxes by the collectors in their respective districts. The colonels or commanding officers are impowered and required to hire wagons or carts and horses, and if necessary to press them to convey the clothing afore mentioned to Halifax Town as soon as may be, to be delivered to the commissary of stores or his deputy for the sole and particular use of the North Carolina troops. The colonel or commanding officers shall send one complete inventory of such clothing with the same to the commissary or his deputy, and another to the general assembly at their next session, together with an account of disbursements for conveying the said clothing to Halifax.

The House taking the said resolve into consideration, concurred therewith.

Ordered that the following message be sent to the House of Commons:

Mr. Speaker and Gentlemen of the House of Commons:

We have read and concurred with the resolve of your House for providing clothing for the Continental troops raised in this state.

W. Hill, S.S.

Draft Law
North Carolina Gazette, May 8, 1778

An act for raising men, to complete the Continental battalions belonging to this state.

Whereas it is absolutely necessary that the Continental battalions belonging to this state be completed, and it is found impracticable to obtain that end in the common mode of recruiting.

Be it therefore enacted by the General Assembly of the state of North Carolina, and it is hereby enacted by the authority of the same, that 2,648 men shall be raised and detached from the militia of this state towards completing the same, in the following proportion and manner, viz. . . .

And be it further enacted, that the Quakers, Dunkers, Moravians, and Mennonites shall furnish men in proportion to their respective numbers in each county, and in default thereof, the commanding officer of each and every county is hereby empowered to hire men instead of the men to be by them furnished, and by warrant under his hand, directed to the sheriff of the county, to levy the sum given for such man or men, on the goods and chattels, lands and tenements of any person belonging to such sect, as shall refuse or fail to find a man or men, agreeable to this act. . . .

An Act for Ascertaining what Property in this State shall be deemed Taxable Property, the Method of Assessing the same, and Collecting the Public Taxes and other Purposes
     . . . XXI. And be it further enacted by the authority aforesaid,

that the Moravians, Quakers, Mennonists, and Dunkers shall pay a three fold tax and all others who shall refuse to take an oath of allegiance as the law directs, shall also pay a three fold tax, and if any person coming within either of the aforesaid denominations, or refusing to take the oath as aforesaid, shall fail to return an inventory of his taxable property, according to law, the person so failing shall pay four times the tax which shall be assessed on persons in this state who comply in every respect with the laws thereof. . . .

An Act to prescribe the Affirmation of Allegiance and Fidelity to this State to be taken by the Unitas Fratrum, or Moravians, Quakers, Mennonists and Dunkards, and granting them certain indulgences therein mentioned, and other Purposes

I. In order to quiet the consciences and indulge the religious scruples of the sects called the Unitas Fratrum, or Moravians, Quakers, Mennonists, and Dunkards.

II. Be it enacted by the General Assembly of the state of North Carolina, and by and with the authority of the same, that the affirmation of allegiance and fidelity to this state shall hereafter be taken by all the above people in the form following, viz:

I, A. B., do solemnly and sincerely declare and affirm, in the presence of Almighty God, that I will truly and faithfully demean myself as a peaceable subject of the independent state of North Carolina, and will be subject to the powers and authorities that are or may be established for the good government thereof, not inconsistent with the Constitution, by yielding either an active or passive obedience thereto; and that I will not abet or join the subjects or forces of the King of Great Britain, or others, the enemies of this state, by any means, in any conspiracy whatsoever, against the said state or the United States of America; and that I will make known to the governor or some member of the council of state, judge of the superior court, or justice of the peace, all treasons, conspiracies, or attempts committed against the same, which shall come to my knowledge. Which said affirmation being taken before any justice of the peace in the county where they reside, at or before the first day of May next, shall entitle them to all those rights, privileges and immunities, they heretofore respectively enjoyed any law to the contrary notwithstanding; the assessment and payment of taxes only excepted.

III. And be it further enacted by the authority aforesaid, that all and every of the said people upon taking and subscribing the affirmation of allegiance and fidelity to this state as aforesaid, before the entry-taker of the county, may re-enter all their lands formerly made in Earl Granville's office, or Public Land Office, or any lands they, or either of them, have had the prior occupancy of, or may enter a caveat or claim against any person or persons who may have entered or surveyed the same; provided such entry, caveat or claim, be made at or before the first day of May next, after the passing of this act, and shall be entitled in preference of all others to obtain a grant for the same, according to the rules of the act of assembly for establishing offices for receiving entries of claims for lands, etc.

IV. And whereas, many ignorant, though good subjects of this state have not taken the oath of allegiance, owing to the neglect of the justices of the peace in many counties, be it therefore enacted by the authority aforesaid that all residents of this state, who have not been inimical, or heretofore refused to take the oath when particularly called on, and who shall take the oath of allegiance to this state prescribed by law before the first day of May next, or who have taken the said oath since the time prescribed by the said law, shall be admitted to all the rights, immunities and privileges of citizens, hereby granted to the Moravians and other people; any law to the contrary notwithstanding.

An Act for levying a Tax for the Year 1779; and other purposes

I. Whereas, it is necessary that the treasury should be as soon as possible supplied with money sufficient to defray the public expense.

II. Be it therefore enacted by the General Assembly of the state of North Carolina, and it is hereby enacted by the authority of the same, that for the year 1779 a tax of three pence shall be paid for every pound value of the taxable property within this state, and a proportionate poll tax on all such freemen as are subject to the payment of a poll tax, pursuant to an act passed this present session of Assembly, entitled "An Act for ascertaining what property in this state shall be deemed taxable property and the manner of assessing the same; and other purposes;" and that all such taxes be levied and accounted for pursuant to the directions of the said act.

III. And be it further enacted by the authority aforesaid, that a further tax of six pence over and above the aforesaid three pence in every pound value of taxable property belonging to Moravians, Quakers, Mennonists or Dunkards shall be paid for the year 1779 and shall be levied and accounted for in the manner above directed.

An Act to amend an Act, entitled, An Act for ascertaining what property in this state shall be deemed taxable property, the method of assessing the same, and collecting the public taxes, and other purposes

I. Whereas by the before recited act it is enacted that the Quakers, Moravians, Dunkards, and Mennonists, shall pay a threefold tax, without any exception, and it is found the said act will operate equally against all orphans estates, widows, and aged men of those societies, as well as those which heretofore were subject to militia duty: For remedy whereof.

II. Be it therefore enacted by the General Assembly of the state of North Carolina, and it is hereby enacted by the authority of the same, that anything contained in the before recited act shall not be construed to extend to any orphan under the age of sixteen years, or widow, or any person of fifty years and upwards, of said societies, to subject them to the payment of a threefold tax, unless such estate shall have been conveyed to them with intent to evade the operation of the assessment act aforesaid.

III. And be it further enacted by the authority aforesaid, that all and every persons of the people aforesaid, who shall fail or refuse to give in their taxable property according to the directions of the said act, shall pay three shillings in the pound for such their neglect or refusal, which shall be in lieu of their said tax. . . .

An Act for the relief of the people Called Moravians, Quakers, Mennonists and Dunkards, within this state [1780]

I. Whereas by an act of the General Assembly of this state entitled, "An Act to amend an Act for declaring what crimes and practices against the state shall be treason and what shall be misprision of treason, and providing punishments adequate to the crimes of both classes, and preventing the dangers which may arise from

persons disaffected to the state," all persons within this state are required to take an oath or affirmation to the state, and in case of refusal
are either to be sent out of the state or to be deprived of the benefit
and protection of the laws of said state, and disabled from prosecuting
or defending any suit either in law or equity; and whereas numbers
of persons under pretence that the people called Quakers, Moravians,
Mennonists and Dunkards, have not taken an affirmation to the state,
have entered and taken up the lands which the said denominations of
people have remained in quiet possession of for many years: For
remedy whereof, and to prevent such abuses for the future.

II. Be it enacted by the General Assembly of this state, and it is
hereby enacted by the authority of the same, that from and after the
passing of this act, when it shall appear that any of the people of any
of the said denominations within this state, who are in unity with
the people of their respective persuasions, shall have been lawfully
possessed of any lands within the said state, either by patent, deed or
otherwise, whereon any other person hath heretofore made entry and
under the abovesaid pretence, all such entries and the proceedings
thereon shall be deemed null and void; and in case any entries shall
hereafter be made on any of the lands of the said people, such entries
shall also be void and of no effect.

An Act to amend the Assessment Law, passed last Assembly at Hillsborough [1783]

I. Whereas, in a time of war it was necessary that all persons refusing from a conscientious motive to bear arms, should be taxed
heavier than those who actually performed military service, in consequence whereof the Moravians, Quakers, Mennonists and Dunkards,
were taxed in a threefold proportion; And, whereas, by divine providence peace and harmony are once more restored in the state, by
which means the cause for such unequal taxation is removed; and as
it is contrary to the spirit of our constitution that any citizen should
pay an extraordinary tax on account of religion,

II. Be it therefore enacted by the General Assembly of the state
of North Carolina, and it is hereby enacted by the authority of the
same, that so much of the assessment law, passed at Hillsborough in
the year 1782 as relates to the extraordinary taxation of the Moravians,

Quakers, Mennonists and Dunkards, be and is hereby repealed and made void.

III. And, whereas, many of the citizens of this state have hitherto refused and neglected to take the oath or affirmation of allegiance by law prescribed, and therefore have not any right or title to indulgence; Be it therefore enacted by the authority aforesaid, that all persons citizens of this state, who have not taken the oath of affirmation of allegiance by law prescribed, shall take the same within six months after passing this act, and all persons refusing or neglecting to take an oath or affirmation of allegiance as aforesaid, shall pay double the tax. . . .[27]

11. The Sauer Family

Particularly hard hit by the Revolution was the family of Christopher Sauer II (1721-1784), who, like his father, was looked to for counsel on political matters by many of the German element in America. The second Sauer also inherited from his father the long-standing enmity of the bloc of Pennsylvania politicians who opposed the Quaker preponderance in the colony. All students of the tangled political picture of the time agree that the Sauer press held a strategic position, in that its influence was long predominant in shaping the minds of the German voters who in turn often controlled the balance of electoral power.[1]

The basic policy of the Sauers was to uphold the Quakers, who guaranteed religious and civic freedom, and to oppose the Presbyterian-Anglican faction, who were known to support an aggressive policy and to favor a state church. Military and ecclesiastical establishments, therefore, were the chief targets of the Sauers' political activity.

The Lutheran leader, Henry Melchior Muhlenberg (who as an agent for the German Bibles sent to America from Halle had economic as well as religious motivation for opposing the German printer), wrote to Germany in 1748:

> The Quakers, who are the foremost party in this province, have on their side the German book publisher, Christopher Sauer, who controls the Mennonites, Separatists, Anabaptists [Brethren], and the like with his printed words and lines them up with the Quakers. All of these speak and write against the war and reject even the slightest defense as ungodly and contrary to the commands of Jesus Christ.

Again, writing in 1765, seven years after the death of the elder Sauer, he noted:

> . . . I have observed in this province that our German inhabitants have been previously prepared and instructed every year in the public newspaper by the German newspaper publisher, the late Mr. Christopher Sauer, as to how they should vote and whom they should elect, and the chief proposition of the exhortations and

instructions was always this: "Whatever you do, you German inhabitants, take care to elect assemblymen who will not relinquish one tittle, yea, one hairbreadth, of the ancient privileges, rights, and liberties granted by King Charles II to the proprietor, William Penn, and through him to the people." Accordingly the Germans would rather have given up their lives before they would have elected anybody but Quakers to the Assembly. The Germans had been so inculcated with the idea that if they failed to keep the Quakers in the government and elected in their place Englishmen from the Episcopal or Presbyterian churches, they would be deprived of their ancient rights and liberties and then they would be saddled with laws forcing them to engage in military drill to assist in defense against enemies, and also to pay a tithe to the ministers of the Episcopal church.[2]

To counter the influence of the Sauer press, in the words of a careful writer on the subject, "an almost continuous succession of short-lived opposition newspapers appeared [but] for a long time the ability of the Sauers enabled them to defeat all the efforts of their enemies." Benjamin Franklin, whose German-language newspaper effort had failed notably, was active in helping establish the rival journals.[3]

The same basic political position was held by Sauer II during the period from the death of his father (1758) to the outbreak of the Revolutionary War. During 1775-1777 he turned over his publishing interests to his like-named son Christopher Sauer (or Sower) III (1754-1799), and another son Peter (1759-1785). In the course of the Revolution the Loyalist tack of the sons combined with the nonresistant policy of the father to provide the opportunity for the long-time foes of the Sauers to crush the printing enterprise. Also involved was rivalry with another German-American printer, Henry Miller of Philadelphia.

THE POLICIES OF CHRISTOPHER SAUER II

Taking Up the Gauntlet

In a moving obituary written by Christopher Sauer II upon the death of his father in 1758, there is a clear statement of his intention to continue the publishing concern begun twenty years earlier along the lines set out by the founder. The same motto — "For the glory of God and my neighbor's good" — which had guided his father finds expression.

On September 24 [1758] the old and well-known printer Christopher Sauer departed this temporal life in the sixty-fourth year of his life, after living in this country for thirty-four years.

He was always kind and friendly to friend and foe. He boasted neither of his skilfulness nor of his mind, but rather remained humble. He at all times was concerned for the good and the freedom of this country, and he would neither by presents nor the flattery of the important be influenced to ignore this. For this reason he finally brought upon himself the hatred of those, both great and small, who would have been glad to see the country become subjected physically to bondage and slavery, and spiritually to darkness and shadow, so that they might fish in troubled waters. Yet, he feared their hatred as little as he sought their favor, and kept a watchful open eye and disclosed their plans wherever he noticed them.

In the meantime, their number has continually increased so that they now compose an entire society who call themselves "Watchmen." They are in truth watchmen, but of the type of which the prophet Isaiah speaks: " . . . [they] watch to do evil . . . " (29:20). These watchmen have long hoped for Sauer's death, for then they would have been sure of the game. Then they would gradually spread their poison and attain their goal. Yet, these people ought to remember that there is a God who sees how idle are the thoughts of the children of man and makes their counsel come to naught. Also [they ought to] consider that under the ashes there are sometimes hot coals hidden and ought therefore moderate their joy. Their godless watching will nevertheless turn out to be their own shame and disgrace.

In the meantime, I do feel myself compelled, out of love to God and for my neighbor, also to be a watchman and according to the ability which God will grant me to serve my neighbor with the gift which God has given me. It is true that I would rather, as heretofore, earn my humble bread by my bookbinding trade and be freed of the burden of the printshop, which would be much easier. Yet, as long as there is no one to whom I could entrust the printshop, I find myself obligated for the sake of God and my neighbor to continue until providence sees fit to give me an assistant, of whom I am certain that he is so founded in the fear of God that he would not be moved by money or flattery to print something which is against the honor of God and the well-being of this country. For it is to the honor of God and the well-being of this country that this printshop has been dedicated. And I will seek always to maintain this aim.

And just as I advised the enemies of the truth to moderate their joy, so I also advise the friends and well-wishers of the good to moderate their grief; for what is gone does not come again. In the meantime it will become evident that that which Sirach says (30:4-6) is also true ["When his father dies, it is as though he were not dead, for he leaves behind him one like himself. In his lifetime he sees him and rejoices, and in death he does not grieve. He has left one to avenge him upon his enemies, and to repay the kindness of his friends"]. Even though I have not received, nor probably ever will, such a rich measure of gifts [as he had], yet I shall faithfully serve with that which I will be given. And since I know that I, like my father and even much more than he, will have to pass through many good and bad judgments, I have already prepared myself even for that and neither one thing nor another will prevent me from doing what I believe is right and good. From this brief statement each discerning soul can easily see what he can expect of me, and what will be done in the future.

I remain, then, my dear readers' sincere and loyal friend,

Christopher Sauer.[4]

September 25, 1758

Election Advice

The way in which Christopher Sauer II carried out the legacy of his father can be discerned from the broadside he issued before the election for Assemblymen in 1765. The crisis brought on by the French and Indian War in 1755-1756 had resulted in the abdication of political power by many of the Quaker Assemblymen who could not square measures of military defense with their pacifist convictions. Thereafter, the policy of influential Quakers seemed to be one of preserving a minority in the Assembly conformable to the Friends' interests, while not seeking a majority position. This coincides with the suggestions of Sauer in this open letter. The criticism of the Stamp Act and support for united action of the colonies in protesting the tax to the Crown indicates a more pro-American position than Sauer has sometimes been credited with.

Germantown, September 18, 1765

Most Esteemed Countrymen, especially in Philadelphia, Bucks and Berks Counties:

This past year I have not infrequently been accused by several

among you that I conducted myself too quietly and impartially during
the last election, because a different posture was expected of me as a
printer, etc. Since there are again many questions as to what position
to take at the next election and because it would be too difficult to
answer everyone personally, I have finally decided to write my
thoughts in a very simple and honest manner and submit them to
everyone for his consideration, as follows:

First, for all those who think that they are certain to which
party they will give their votes in order to make the best choice next
October 1, I do not wish hereby to confuse them in their set opinion.
All those who have a religious opinion and wish to remain quiet in
faith and trust in God, well knowing that the sovereign hand and
providence of God does indeed govern all, need not be advised by me
either. Rather, I wish them perseverance in their faith. Whereas,
however, this faith is not given to every man, and most people do
feel that they must set to work upon what they think is right, yet
do not know how to untangle the matter — what is right or wrong
— to these I will address myself in the following manner:

It was undeniably a great blessing of God that for some eighty
years this land has had such a good, peace-loving government, and
that everyone has been able to worship God as he sees fit without any
coercion of conscience or prohibition. No other land in the entire
inhabited world is known that is as perfect as Pennsylvania has been
up to now, under our proprietary government.

That it has so far been the will of God that we should enjoy
this unmerited blessing is proved by experience. I have three convincing proofs of this: the first is that the otherwise quite godfearing
and most praiseworthy proprietor, William Penn, after bearing for
considerable time the discontented residents of his country and the
assemblies of the time (like Moses with the children of Israel in the
wilderness), who yet kept grumbling against him, became weary of
the burden and wished to hand the government over to Queen Anne.
God, however, who was not pleased by this counsel and had something better in store for this province, gave it a different turn and
caused the dear old father William Penn to be touched by a stroke
so that he became incapable of carrying out his intention and thus died.

Secondly, many years later, during the Spanish War which
started in 1740, a rather large number of inhabitants, mostly in

Philadelphia, would not depend on God, but, rather, fearing that the Spaniards would stage an invasion and rob them of their collected riches, decided to elect a new Assembly. (The then-existing old Assembly was too honest to risk such an important change.) The new Assembly was to seek to convert this province into a royal government. However, although they tried it several times, God destroyed their counsels every time and we continued to enjoy our old freedom.

Thirdly, our Assembly, upon which we depended to guard our freedoms most carefully, in the year 1764 was finally persuaded to call for a referendum on what the stand of the people of the province was on a change in the government. This was brought about by a selfish member [Franklin] and his consorts, who had presumably already offered for sale, if not having actually sold or given away, our privileges, so that he might secure himself greater favor and privileges in return (as can clearly be seen in reports from England). They finally secured as many as 3,500 for their lists, and even though they knew that this was not even a tenth of the population of this province, they still went ahead and sent to England a petition for a change of government. Although at the last election several of the most unfaithful members were removed, their party was still so strong that they had a vast majority of votes in the House.

The minority, which would have gladly seen our form of government remain unchanged on the old basis, were unable to accomplish anything. Instead, to the greatest displeasure of many thousands of good inhabitants of this province, that selfish F[ranklin], who has already cost this country so much money, was arbitrarily sent home at our cost, and he and another were given full power to dispose of our privileges as they thought best. And although he may have been diligent enough in carrying out his commission, it has still pleased God up to now to destroy also these faithless attempts and to preserve our old privileges for us.

Therefore I conclude that those act wisely who hold to the immeasurable privileges which God has preserved for us so far out of unmerited grace, and who will reject such thoughtless members at the next election, who so carelessly gambled with our privileges and who may treat them even more foolishly in the future (God might otherwise become weary and suffer us to be attacked by what we have not anticipated). At least in the above-mentioned three counties

[Philadelphia, Bucks, and Berks] such men ought to be elected of whom it is known for certain that they will not so despise our privileges as to leave them up to the arbitrary whims of several men, but rather recall that unprofitable and so-expensive hireling, or at least remove from his hands all power to dispose of our privileges. To [achieve] this it might be sufficient if a change occurred only in the above-mentioned three counties, for this would bring about a small majority of votes and our privileges would thus be assured.

I would not recommend the election of an entirely new Assembly throughout the province, because that might on the other hand bring about serious consequences. (This then is one reason why I do not print my counsel in the public newspaper because it is circulated throughout the entire province. If this balance is preserved in the Assembly, then I cannot see why we, dear countrymen, should fear at all these terrible monsters with which Mr. Franklin's adherents threaten us, for example, a burdensome militia law, the fortification of the city, a tyrannical Presbyterian government, becoming the serfs of the proprietor, and whatever other terrible prospects and pipe-dreams there are, with which these people seek to dazzle our eyes.

To speak quite plainly about the matter, most of the things with which they seek to deter the people from electing the men who would destroy their schemes, as well as many other burdens which we do not yet envision, are all the more likely to be feared if Mr. F[ranklin] and his followers achieve their triumph. If as many as nineteen or twenty Assemblymen are agreed upon doing away with the useless wastrels (for modesty's sake I shall not label them more bluntly) in these hard times, and seek to preserve the old institutions of this country, there will undoubtedly always be many among these twenty who will never agree to any of these frightful arrangements and so this fear may indeed be completely unnecessary.

Dear countrymen, should not still another question be considered, namely: What would our children say if we so disdained the immeasurable privileges which our fathers guarded so carefully that they came down to us? Can they not expect the same from us that we expected from our fathers? And even if it should seem to them that a real advantage could be expected from such a change, then that door will always be open to them; indeed we, too, if the need arises, will be free to elect such persons who will sacrifice our noble privileges to the Crown, and the latter will never be so ungracious as to reject such a splendid gift. It is quite easy to give something away, but to restore abandoned privileges is difficult, if not totally impossible. And then it will be said: "Why did you not keep the privileges which you had? We did not demand them of you; on the contrary, you offered them to us."

If we were to bring about a change in government without any need and it were not to the liking of our children, they would discontentedly ask us: "What kind of necessity caused you to desire such a change?" What else can we answer them with any foundation of truth than: "That which moved our first ancestors to eat good and evil from the tree of knowledge, namely, dear old folly [*Vorwitz*], and because they were no longer content with the state into which God had put them." If this answer satisfies their minds, then we shall soon be done. It is, however, to be feared that such an answer will hardly satisfy and scarcely convince them that we were as faithful to them as our fathers were to us. And how shall we appease our own hearts if through our own guilt burdens are laid on our shoulders? With what joy can we call to God for assistance in such temptations which we brought on ourselves? Shall we be able then to acquiesce in it as [we do] when such things are placed upon us without our own encouragement according to God's good counsel? That which God lays upon us He also helps us to bear, but self-imposed burdens are not accompanied by this comfort.

Furthermore, I wished to report this that several months ago the Boston Assembly sent a circular letter to all the assemblies and invited them to send delegates to New York in order to deliberate how and in what manner a petition to His Majesty, our gracious King, could be dispatched to ask him to relieve us from the all-too-heavy and unbearable burden of the Stamp Act and to hold counsel as to what might be offered to him in its place that would be more bearable. Who would have thought that there would be a single man in our Assembly who opposed such a most reasonable suggestion, since it is the most important part of their office, and the reason for their being elected by the country to alleviate the burdens of the country as much as possible. And as it was to be done by petition and not by rebellion, it could not have been displeasing even to the King. In the meantime, it became known that not a single one of the Assemblymen from Bucks County voted for this just matter. (Do such people deserve to be re-elected at all?) Several from the other counties also opposed it. It should be made public who was for or against it, so that the public might know who they are.

For the city and county of Philadelphia:
Thomas Willing, George Bryan, John Dickinson, Joseph Ritschertson, Amos Strettel, and Henry Kepple.

For Chester County:
Joseph Pearson, John Morton, Joseph Asch, John Fairlamb.

For Lancaster County:
Emanuel Zimmerman and Isaac Saunders.

For York County:
David McCanaughy.

For Northampton County:
George Taylor.

For Cumberland County:
William Allen.

The following voted against sending delegates:

For Philadelphia County:
John Hughes and Henry Pauling.

For Bucks County:
Gillis Knight, William Rodmann, Peter Schäffer, Samuel Faulk, Samuel Braun, William Schmitt, Henry Kreuser, and James Melvin.

For Chester County:
George Aschbridge, Charles Humphris, and John Jacobs.

For Lancaster County:
James Webb.

The others whose names are not listed here were presumably not in the House at the time the vote was taken.

Thus it was finally decided with a majority of one vote that the following members of the Assembly are to go to New York to attend the proposed congress, namely: Joseph Fox, John Dickinson, George Bryan, and John Morton.

In this essay I have throughout endeavored for brevity, so as not to burden my readers. Therefore it is likely that many will have criticism of this or that part of it. If I am challenged in such a manner that I deem it necessary, everything which is here reported briefly can be demonstrated in more detail. Yet, I will not answer in great length without necessity. Whoever does not like my counsel and has a better one for himself, or receives one from someone else, I shall not regard him with jealousy or disdain. I have written here nothing else than what I am obligated to answer everyone who inquires.

I remain, dear countrymen, your sincere German friend and well-wisher,

Christopher Sauer.[5]

THE IMPACT OF THE REVOLUTION

In the second half of the eighteenth century the Sauer printing establishment flourished as never before. The newspaper and the almanac had wide circulation up and down the seaboard, two more editions of the German Bible were completed (1763 and 1776), a religious magazine (considered by some authorities to be the first of its kind in America) was inaugurated for free distribution, the first American type foundry was established, and a host of books flowed from the active presses in Germantown. With the ceaseless effort and enterprise came prosperity, and Sauer came to be considered one of the wealthiest men in America. He could be counted on for generous and repeated gifts to educational and charitable endeavors such as the Germantown Academy (of whose board he was twice elected president) and the Philadelphia Hospital.[6]

The shock of the American Revolution shattered this pleasant picture. As an influential figure, and one who consistently opposed the more radical political ventures of the day, he was quickly singled out as an enemy of American liberty. His devotion to the English monarchy which had provided freedom and prosperity was bolstered by the natural conservatism of the propertied. But more important was his attachment to his religious faith, which taught nonresistance, submission to the powers-that-be, and nonlitigation. His steady adherence to these beliefs spelled tragedy. In a few years, the fruits of his entire life's work were seized. He was stripped of his estate, his possessions, his very clothes.

The Memorial of Christopher Sauer III

The events of the Revolution can best be followed in the account written after the war by Sauer's son, Christopher Sauer III. In a petition seeking compensation from the English government under a law promising financial aid to those Americans who had remained loyal to the Crown, the younger Sauer detailed the experiences he and his father had undergone. This memorial will be interspersed with contemporary documents which give more information on matters referred to summarily by Sauer.

No. 24 Charles Street
Matton Garden [London]
January 19, 1784

To the Lords Commissioners of His Majesty's Treasury.

The memorial of Christopher Sower, Jr., respectfully shows:

That your memorialist is a native of the province of Pennsylvania, in which he resided when the late Rebellion broke out. That his grandfather and [his] father emigrated from Germany to that province early in the present century and both of them carried on the business of printing and circulating a very extensive public [news]paper in the German language throughout the provinces, by which and by the introduction of various other useful arts into that, then young, colony, they gained the general esteem and confidence of the Germans and other inhabitants. That his father soon after the beginning of the Rebellion resigned the printing business to your memorialist, by which and [by] a correspondence with many of the principal Germans, he succeeded his father in their esteem and confidence.

That at the commencement of the late Rebellion, your memorialist and his father, from a sense of duty to their sovereign and attachment to the British government, opposed to the utmost of their power the rising sedition as well by frequent publications in his paper as otherwise, until at length the Council of Safety of Pennsylvania summoned your memorialist and his father before them, and forbade them to print a newspaper or any political piece whatever. That your memorialist for a short time suspended the publication, but being unchanged in his principles and anxious to prevent the mischiefs arising from the threatened Rebellion, at much hazard and without leave from the Rebel Council, again resumed his paper, and freely published many political pieces in favor of the British government, by which he trusts many were dissuaded from joining the Rebellion and preserved their allegiance to the British state.

That your memorialist and his father became so obnoxious to the rebel rulers that they were obliged several times to secret themselves from the fury of their mobs which were exerted to seize on their persons and threatened to tar and feather them and otherwise to treat them with the utmost indignity. At length they took refuge with the British army on its arrival in Germantown. . . .[7]

Summons by the Council of Safety

The summons by the Council of Safety mentioned by Sauer III has been preserved.

In Council of Safety, December 16, 1776
Sirs:

You are hereby ordered to attend this council at their chamber tomorrow morning at ten o'clock, and you are hereby forbidden to print in the meantime any political piece whatever, either as a newspaper or [a] handbill, or disperse any already printed until further orders.

By order of council
Thomas Wharton, Jr., President

To Messrs. Christopher Sower, Senior and Junior [II and III], printers at Germantown.[8]

A Subscription to the Germantown Militia

About this time, the Germantown residents were asked to contribute to the needs of the officers and men of the Germantown militia. The request and the response are here given. Noteworthy is the size of the elder Sauer's donation and the direction for its use. Several other members of the Germantown congregation also contributed.[9]

Memorial of the officers and others who compose the company formed in the lower district of Germantown, to the respectable inhabitants of the same in particular, shows:

That the said company have freely given much time and attention to learn their exercises, purely with a view to promote as far as depends on them the happiness of their country, their attachment to which has even engaged them in no small expense of money for suitable clothes and accoutrements with which they have the pleasure to assure you they are at length almost completely equipped. And although they have willingly applied what they could spare, it becomes necessary towards the current expenses for your memorialists to seek in the most decent manner, a small share of that countenance and assistance, which in your own just way of thinking is due to the virtuous cause we are all embarked in.

And your memorialists as in duty bound shall ever pray and to their utmost serve their country and you.

Signed by order and in behalf of the company,

Henry Hill, Capt.

Paid — Christopher Sower (for the poor women and children) £ 1-10-0
Paid — Christian Laaschet   0-10-0
Paid — Christopher Ming   7-6
Paid — William Miller, printer   0- 5-0
Paid — Christopher Sower, Jr.   0- 7-6
Paid — Jean Dedier   0- 5-0
         Frederick Flackenstine   7-6
         Henry Güterman   7-6
Paid — John Kime   5-0
Paid — William Kime   7-6
Paid — Justus Fox   0- 7-6
Paid — George Palmer   0-10-9

The Will of Christopher Sauer II

Doubtless the troubled times brought on by the Revolution turned Sauer's mind to an orderly disposition of his extensive estate. He was approaching sixty in 1777 and ready to turn over the active directing of his publishing interests to his sons. The will, although lengthy, is here given because of the information it gives on the Sauer family, the details of the family holdings, and the care with which Sauer attempted to dispose of his business.

In the Name of God, Amen!

I, Christopher Sower of Germantown in the County of Philadelphia, printer, being in good bodily health and of sound and disposing mind, memory, and understanding — praised be the Lord for the same — do hereby make my last will and testament in manner following. That is to say, first, I will that all my just debts and funeral expenses shall be duly paid and satisfied, for which and other purposes hereinafter declared, I do hereby nominate and appoint my two elder sons Christopher and Daniel executors of this my last will and testament.

Item, I do hereby declare and devise that the general plan of this my will and the chief end and intention of my own mind, to be pursued by my children and by all persons who by virtue hereof or otherwise shall have any matter to act, settle, or determine, respecting the execution thereof, is that my lands, tenements and hereditaments, and all my goods and chattels, rights and credits whatsoever, shall be equally divided among my seven children, to wit: Christopher, Daniel, Peter, Catherine, Esther, David and Samuel and by them held and enjoyed in severality and by their several and respective heirs, executors, and administrators, and that all the particular devises and bequests hereinafter contained upon any question or difficulty arising in the execution of this my will shall be reduced to and explained and determined by the rules of an equal division of the whole, so that respect be had to the true value of every part thereof.

Item, I do hereby constitute and appoint my respected friends Peter Keyser and Peter Leibert both of Germantown aforesaid, guardians of such of my children as shall be minors at the time of my decease. Item, I will and devise that the several estates hereinafter devised to my children shall be appraised or valued by seven discreet and reputable freeholders of the County of Philadelphia, each of my five elder children choosing one of the said appraisers and the said Peter Keyser and Peter Leibert to be the appraisers on behalf of my two youngest sons David and Samuel. And whatever the seven appraisers so appointed and to be chosen as aforesaid or any four of them shall under their hands and seals, certify to be the value of each particular tenement and lot or parcel of ground hereinafter specifically devised to any of my said children shall be deemed and taken to be the true value thereof and shall be charged accordingly to the equal share which the child to whom it is hereinafter devised is to take in my real and personal estate.

Provided nevertheless, that if any of my children, being at the time of such valuation of full age, shall within three months after, or being then under age shall at his or her arrival at the age of twenty-one years think him or herself aggrieved with the valuation of his or her own part (no dissatisfaction to be allowed in one of my children with the valuation of the estate of another of them) then he or she shall or may within the space of three months from the time of his or her arrival of the age aforesaid, by virtue of the devise hereinafter made, to him or her by public auction, of which at least four weeks public notice must be given in two English and one German newspaper, sell and dispose of the part and parcel of land to him or her specifically devised to the highest and best bidder and whatever price the premises shall sell for at such public auction, the same shall be charged to her or his equal distribution share in my real and personal estate.

Item, I give and devise unto my said son Christopher Sower all that my messuage, tenement and piece or parcel of land whereon I now live situate in Germantown aforesaid, joining the main street, and lands late of [John] Adam Gruber, now of Thomas Salter, a road leading to George Danhawer's mill, and John Wistar's land together with the appurtenances; to hold to him my said son Christopher, his heirs and assigns forever. Charged nevertheless and chargeable to his equal share in the division of my whole estate with the sum or sums of money which the premises shall be valued at or be sold for as aforesaid.

Item, I give and devise unto my said son Daniel Sower all that my messuage or tenement, paper mill, saw mill and two parcels of land near the falls of Schuylkill on both sides of the Wissahickon Road bounded by the said river and road and by lands of John Dickinson Esq. and wife, Jonathan Adams, and Doctor William Smith, together with the appurtenances . . . .

Item, I give and devise unto my daughter Esther Sower all that my lot or parcel of land situate in the township of Germantown on the south-easterly side of the great road leading to the falls of Schuylkill bounded by the same road and another which divides the townships of Germantown, Roxborough, and the Northern Liberties and by lands of Winard Nice, which I purchased partly of Theobald Endt and partly of George Herger, containing nearly seven acres together with the appurtenances . . . .

Item, I give and devise unto my daughter Catherine Sower, all that my lot or parcel of land situate at the upper end of Germantown aforesaid on the south-easterly side of a road commonly called Keysers Lane or Abingdon Road bounded by the same and by lands of Jacob Horter, John Engel, Benjamin Keyser and Joseph Keyser together with the buildings thereon erected and the appurtenances . . . .

Item, I give and devise unto my said son David Sower all that my messuage or tenement and lot of ground which I purchased of Thomas

Hyam and others, trustees of the London Company's lands situate in Roxborough aforesaid, bounded by the River Schuylkill, the great road leading from Philadelphia to Reading, and by lands of Samuel Powell and Christian Lashet containing eighty-three acres and three quarters of an acre together with the fishing place and all the other appurtenances . . . .

Item, I give and devise to my said son Samuel Sower all that my messuage or tenement and lot of ground in Germantown aforesaid which I purchased of the Sheriff Samuel Morris situate on the south-westerly side of the said Main Street and on the north-westerly side of the aforesaid road leading to the falls of Schuylkill, bounded by the said street and road and by lands of Justus Fox and of the said Christian Lashet. Also all that my other lot of ground, which I purchased of Hannah Rawlinson situate on the north-westerly side of the aforesaid road to Schuylkill, bounded by the same and lands of Henry Hill, Esq., John Keyser and William Tusten containing one acre and three quarters, be it more or less . . . .

Item, I will that my whole apparatus of the printing business shall be appraised by three master printers — one to be chosen by my said son Christopher, another by my said son Peter, and the third by the guardians of my younger children — and being so appraised I give and allow the same to my said two sons Christopher and Peter who shall as near[ly] equally as can be divided among themselves, every assortment of types, the presses, moulds and matrices for a letter foundry and all other tool, implements and materials to the printing business belonging, and shall be charged with, each of them one moiety of the sum found by the said appraisers.

Item, whereas I have not devised any part of my real estate to my said son Peter because he rather seems to decline settling in or near Germantown, so I will that his seventh part of my whole estate as near as can be guessed at shall as soon as possible be made up to him in cash, deducting the moiety of the value of the printing office in order to enable him to make any purchase of land elsewhere, whether he be then of age or not.

Item, whereas a considerable part of my personal estate consists in printed books and if either of my said two sons Christopher and Peter should for his own private advantage, undertake to reprint any of these books while a considerable number of the same sort belonging to my estate remains on hand, and unsold, the interest of all my children must be greatly affected thereby, for the preventing of which, I will and direct, that if either of my said sons should think proper to reprint any such sorts of books, although it was under the pretence of additions or improvements in matter and form he shall be obliged to take all such books of the same sort belonging to my estate to himself at the common price for which they are sold to stationers or bookbinders and the amount thereof shall be charged to his distributive share or seventh part of my estate and in case he should refuse to comply with the above directions he shall forfeit to my other children his full share and dividend in all the printed books that shall belong to my estate at the time of my decease and in the monies which shall from time to time arise by the sale thereof, anything in this my will before or after contained to the contrary thereof in any wise notwithstanding.

And for the better enforcing this direction I will that my son Daniel and the guardians of my younger children at the delivery or assignment of my printing office to my sons Christopher and Peter shall take bonds from them, for the performance thereof. And I further will and direct that the said stock of printed books shall be sold either at my said dwelling house by my son Christopher or elsewhere by any other person or persons whom my said executors and the guardians of my younger children shall intrust therewith. Keeping always the same price at which I usually have sold them or as near to it as can be. And the sale of these books shall in the same manner go on from time to time until they are all sold or until the 20th day of March, 1788, when my said son Samuel shall come to age. And then the whole stock remaining on hand shall be sold by public auction giving . . . notice . . . in the English and German newspapers.

And for as much as the keeping such large quantity of unbound books, the taking care thereof that they may not be destroyed or damaged by rain, snow or vermin, I will and direct that my son Christopher, or whoever shall be entrusted with the care and management thereof, shall from time to time be allowed a premium of ten per cent upon the amount of the sales thereof. For and in consideration of which premium he or they shall also answer to my estate such bad debts as shall happen by their selling books on trust, to indifferent persons.

Item, I will and desire that the said guardians of my younger children shall take care of and manage the interest and shares of them in my estate, and for that purpose inspect the accounts of my executors and provide that such of my children as have more than their equal seventh part of my estate in lands, and personal estate shall well and sufficiently secure the overplus in their hands to their younger brothers and sisters and in particular that the account of the sales of my printed books shall at least once a year be settled and the shares of the said children paid or secured to them respectively and in the year 1788 or sooner, if all my printed books shall be sold before that time, then a final settlement of all my estate shall be made between my said executors and the rest of my children. And I will that the aforesaid guardians Peter Keyser and Peter Leibert shall be handsomely allowed and paid for their trouble in the premises, but my executors who have received of me more benefits than their younger brothers and sisters can obtain shall in consideration of that equal share I have left them administer gratis on my estate.

Item, if any of my children shall die under age unmarried or without issue I will that the particular estate in land herein before given or assigned to him or her shall by my executors and the guardians of my children be sold at a public auction after a previous notice of at least four weeks given in the English and German newspapers. Peter Keyser, and Peter Leibert and the survivors and survivor of them upon receipt of the purchase money by proper deeds and assurances in the land to grant and convey the fee simple and inheritance of the premises to the purchaser or purchasers thereof. And the monies arising by the sale of such landed estate and all other such child's monies and effects part and share in my estate, in the hands of my executors or of the guardians of such child shall be equally divided among my surviving children and the issue of such of them as shall then be dead such issue taking such part as their deceased parent would have taken if living. Lastly, I do hereby revoke all other last wills by me heretofore made and published declaring this to be my last will and testament only. In witness whereof I have hereunto set my hand and seal the twenty-third day of March in the year of our Lord 1777.

Signed: Christopher Sower

Signed, sealed and declared by the testator Christopher Sower for and as his last will and testament in the presence of

Christian Laashet Thomas Longstroth Edmund Longstroth[10]

Sauer's Reaction to the War

The feelings of Christopher Sauer II found expression in a poem printed in his almanac for 1778 (issued in 1777).

Thou once so happy land, by God and nature blessed,
    and teeming with abundant joy,
But now alas, by sin and wrong and vice depressed,
    Thou seem'st to wither and to die.
O Land: what art thou now? A scene of dismal woes,
    To wake our pity and our tears;
Oppressed by rapine, murder and a thousand foes,
    Unknown in bygone years.
And desolation, hunger, want stalk in the wake
    Of the avenger's bloody steel.

Earth's pregnant fields lie waste, untouched by
    Who erst, full-peaceful turned the soil;
The unwilling sword he grasps and dashes in the fight;
    What tears will flow from this turmoil.[11]

TROUBLED EVENTS OF 1777 AND 1778

With the coming of the British to Philadelphia in September 1777, the war in all of its grimness was brought home to the Pennsylvania populace. Where before there had been sharp tensions between those fervently supporting the American Revolution and those who either retained their allegiance to the King of England or attempted to remain neutral, now the fronts became clear. Anyone not wholeheartedly on the American side was considered disloyal and traitorous by the rebels, and the opposite was true for the other side. The impassioned events involving the two Christopher Sauers illustrate this very well.

The Memorial of Sauer III Continued

The memorial of Christopher Sauer III of 1784, begun earlier, is now resumed. It reveals that he had definitely thrown in his lot with the British side. Some idea of his importance to them is seen by their willingness to exchange a maker of gunpowder for the American side to effect his release after capture.

. . . That your memorialist continuing with the [British] Army exerted his endeavors in His Majesty's service, by gaining intelligence for the commander-in-chief and serving as a guide, for which he received no reward whatever, and that he also served as a German printer and translator to the Royal Army without any salary.

That in the year 1777 [December 4], when the commander-in-chief marched to Chestnut Hill [above Germantown], your memorialist was required to serve as one of the guides to the army, when he was unfortunately taken prisoner by a rebel detachment and received an injury in his left arm, which has rendered it in a manner useless. That at the same time he was robbed of all his father's deeds, mortgages and many valuable papers of his own, and that being committed to the Rebel Provost he was there detained until he was exchanged for an artist [George Losch] in the making of [gun]powder employed by the Congress, then of great consequence to their service.

That in the year 1778 your memorialist's father and himself were attainted of high treason, and all their estates real and personal confiscated to the use of the rebel state and accordingly sold. . . . [12]

Sauer III as a Printer

Even before leaving Germantown, Christopher Sauer III, with his brother Peter, had done printing for the Quakers, who were eager to get their pacifist testimony before the public. In 1776 he printed Robert Barclay's *Apology* and also translated and began to print "The Ancient Testimony" issued first by the Society of Friends in Philadelphia on January 20, 1776. This testimony reiterated their loyalty to the Crown. The wife of one of the leading Philadelphia Quakers who were marched off as captives to Virginia by the rebel forces in 1777 referred in a letter to the publication:

> Sower did not go on with the German edition, being intimidated by his countrymen and his press removed out of his house. He tells he is like to set it up in this city, when I suppose he will be at liberty to go forward. [13]

That this was carried out is attested to by an entry in the minutes of the Quaker Monthly Meeting of Sufferings held on June 6, 1778:

> The treasurer when in cash is desired to pay unto Christopher Sower, Jr. [III], and Peter Sower the sum of forty-four pounds, sixteen shillings and three pence for translating, printing and

binding two thousand pamphlets in German, wrote [*sic*] by our
Friends lately banished from this city.[14]

The *Philadelphia Ledger* for November 19, 1777, had this announcement:

> Christopher Sower, Jr. [III], and Peter Sower have removed
> their printing office from Germantown to Second Street between
> Race and Arch Streets, in Philadelphia, where they carry on the
> printing business in its various branches as usual.[15]

In Philadelphia the young Sauer brothers published a newspaper,
Der Pennsylvanische Staats-Courier, which ardently advocated the Loyalist
viewpoint and issued German pamphlets intended to sway the opinions
of the numerous German-speaking residents of the province.

The rival German printer Henry Miller (1702-1782), who was
staunchly in favor of the Revolution, had fled the city when the English
entered. Upon his return he circulated a broadside which charged the
Sauers with partial guilt in seizing the printing effects which he left behind in the city. He also demanded that the Sauers' shop, left behind
when they in turn left in 1778 ahead of the returning American army, be
handed over to him as compensation for his loss.

Urgent Declaration to the Germans in Pennsylvania from Henry
Miller, the Printer in Philadelphia.

Philadelphia, July 22, 1778

Esteemed and worthy countrymen:

On the 25th of last September, when the bitter enemies of America
closed in on this city, I was forced suddenly to leave all that was mine
and turn my back on it in order to save my life and body from their
wrath by way of escape.

I had spent nine months and as many days as one driven into
misery, sorrow and want, when I returned to this city on July 4.
But to my great sorrow I discovered that I had been robbed of my
well-equipped printing shop which over many years and at great
expense I had brought together and built up with bitter effort and
sweat. [It was my intention] henceforth to dedicate it — impartially —
as long as the Lord would grant me life, to the upbuilding of the
kingdom of God and the virtue and advancement of the welfare of
this land, while [drawing from it] a needed income.

Since my arrival, wherever I am seen, in the city as well as in the
country, my former kind customers and friends keep asking me wheth-

er I will not soon begin to print again. Therefore I have found it necessary briefly to report to them truthfully by means of someone else's press this robbery which was planned and aimed at the ruin of the Germans and myself, as follows:

Christopher Sauer, Junior [III], of Germantown, who moved into the city with General Howe and was his German printer (after he had once led the enemy before Germantown and was there captured by our forces, but exchanged for Mr. Losch, the powder manufacturer), came to Mrs. Lehmann last January 29 (whom I had left upon her request in my house with her two children) and said to her that General Howe had made him a present of my printing shop to do with it as he pleased. However, he did not desire it, but only wished to take the keys to it to keep them for me to take possession of them again upon my return.

After some time he came and demanded to borrow or buy parts of [the print shop], which Mrs. Lehmann refused him. However, he later came at his own pleasure, opened the printing shop and did there what he wanted. During these events, the younger Sauer had gained a helper in his secret malice, named James Robertson, who was one of Howe's English printers. He came on June 4, before the enemy had left the city and asked Mrs. Lehmann whether she did not wish to sell him my printing shop. She answered, "No." He then demanded the key to it. He was told that Sauer had it. Robertson went and got the key from Sauer's wife, in Mr. John Morris' house where Sauer lived. He came and said that he had orders from headquarters to confiscate Henry Miller's printing shop because the Americans had taken his in Albany.

He had also brought with him a number of people, the king's wagons and carts, and loaded printed matter, the best press, letter cases, shelves, in sum, everything, and hurried with it as quickly as possible to the ship. The robbers Christopher Sauer, Junior, and company, took a part of the second press which was left behind and ruined it and what few printed materials had remained. A few days before the robbery, a strange woman was sent to Mrs. Lehmann to find out from her secretly whether Doctor Franklin had a large share in my printing shop. The same question was also put to her by Sir William Erskine at headquarters. However, she answered both times with "No" and assured them truthfully that the printing shop was completely and solely my property. The assumption that Doctor Franklin had a large share in my printing shop is probably owing to the fact that Sauer knew that I had worked for Mr. Franklin and had for many years enjoyed the esteem and favor of this very great and honest man.

In this way a useful citizen of this city, an honest man and a well-known and tested friend of America and her freedom was robbed of the means to support himself and his, and that by a premeditated and planned attack of two criminals, whose aim and purpose it was to deprive the Germans in this country of the opportunity of learning about public affairs so that they might be sure to remain in ignorance and many of them for want of better information and the insight derived from it might remain the blockheads of a party, which since the beginning of this conflict has already caused all-too-much misfortune in this country.

The income of the state is diminished by this robbery, for when a man cannot pursue his honest vocation, he is not in a position to contribute much to the needs of a state, etc. My loss is, as it were, irreplaceable, because there is no large quantity of type available in this part of the world.

As a large part of the younger Sauer's printing shop was left behind and has been discovered, it is submitted to the wisdom and justice of all the most respectful rulers of this state whether I do not deserve a compensation.

The authorities' especially, and the German public's generally, most loyal friend and servant,

Henry Miller. . . . [16]

The Sauers Proclaimed Traitors

On May 21, the American government issued proclamations which designated both Christopher Sauers as traitors, along with others.

Lancaster, May 21, 1778

On motion, the Council now took into consideration the issuing of a proclamation under the state seal, requiring divers persons, who, it is said, have joined the armies of the enemy, to render themselves, and abide their legal trial for such their treason, etc., according to law; and therefore, ordered:

That a proclamation be now issued under the state seal, requiring the following named persons: . . . Christopher Sauer, the elder, and Christopher Sauer, the younger . . . to render themselves respectively to same or one of the justices of the Supreme Court, or of the justices of peace of one of the counties within this state, on or before Monday the sixth day of July next ensuing, and also abide their legal trial for such their treason, on pain that every [one] of them not rendering himself as aforesaid and abiding the trial aforesaid, shall from and after the said sixth day of July next, stand and be attainted of high treason, to all intents and purposes, and shall suffer such pain and penalties and undergo all such forfeitures as persons attainted of high treason ought to do.[17]

Sauer II in the Hands of the Americans

When the British left Philadelphia for New York in June 1778, the younger Sauer went with them, as did other substantial residents of the city, becoming a Loyalist refugee. However, his father, who had not taken any active role in supporting the British, felt so sure of his innocence that he returned to Germantown on May 23. Here he was seized by a military detail, humiliated, and marched off to the American headquarters. He has left a moving account of his misfortunes and the later confiscation of his extensive estate at the hands of the civil government.

One historian has contended that Sauer had no one but himself to blame for his misfortune, in that he did not appear for the trial called for in the proclamation. However, Sauer was in the hands of the military at the time of the announcement. More importantly, his Brethren scruples against litigation would have prevented him from going to law to prevent the seizure of his property. Given the height of revolutionary sentiment at that time, the notoriety of the Loyalist position of his sons, the long-standing differences between Sauer and leading political figures, and, it should be said, the cupidity and the envy of certain local elements, there was little chance for a fair trial. One scholar concluded: "There is hardly any doubt that this confiscation of the older Sauer's property was unjust and probably illegal."[18]

The Lutheran minister, Henry Melchior Muhlenberg, who had once been on poor terms with Sauer I, had been in close connection with Sauer II through correspondence and visits. On June 12, 1778, he noted in his diary:

> A short time ago the German printer, Christopher Sauer, was taken prisoner in Philadelphia and brought to the American camp because his sons in Philadelphia have been treating the Americans

very unreasonably and abusively in the German newspapers. A
German general in the camp said a good word for him, which
brought about his release after he had sworn the oath of loyalty
to the state.[19]

It was the son of Pastor Muhlenberg, General Peter Muhlenberg,
who intervened for Sauer at the Provost. Sauer did not take the oath, as
mentioned incorrectly here, for one reason — that his conscience and his
Brethren teaching did not permit oath-taking.

A Quaker, John Pemberton, also noted the event; writing later (September 18, 1778):

> I visited Christopher Sauer, who had been taken prisoner by
> the Americans, stripped naked, and painted in different colors;
> confined at camp for some time, and at length released with a
> few rags given him. The man that painted him and had part
> of his clothes, was a few days afterward seized with a violent pain,
> and died in great misery, desiring that those clothes which he had
> taken from Christopher might be taken from his body; which
> being done he expired.[20]

The following is Sauer's own narration of his treatment at the hands of
the authorities.

Having heard how a number of Quakers were banished and carried away to Virginia and being informed that there [were] yet some
hundreds of substantial inhabitants on the list to be taken up and
secured among which my name also was put down and as there was
already a beginning made and some of the millers on [the] Wissahickon
were actually taken from their families, I considered what I could do,
knowing Germantown would always be a disturbed place. English
and Americans would continually march through it, forward and
backward. Having three of my children already living in Philadelphia
I bethought myself to go there to live in peace and accordingly went
to Philadelphia on the 19th day of October, 1777 (many months before
that act was made which forbade [me] to go to Philadelphia).

So I lived there quietly and peaceably till the 23rd day of May 1778
when I went back to Germantown and was in my house that night
and the next day till ten o'clock at night, when a strong party of Captain McClean's company surrounded my house and fetched me out of
my bed, it being a dark night. They led me through the Indian corn
fields. When I could not come along so fast as they wanted me to go

they frequently stuck me in the back with their bayonets. They brought me to Bastian Miller's barn where they kept me till next morning. Then they stripped me naked to the skin and gave me an old shirt and breeches so much torn that I could barely cover my nakedness. Then [they] cut my beard and hair and painted me with oil colors, red and black, and so led me along barefooted and bare-headed in a very hot sunshining day.

A friend of mine seeing me in that condition asked them whether they would not take the shoes from me if he would give me a pair. The officer gave his word they should not be taken from me if he would give me a pair, and so he took the shoes from his feet and the hat from his head and gave them to me but after we had marched six miles a soldier came and demanded my shoes and took them and gave me his old slabs which wounded my feet very much. On the 26th at nine o'clock I arrived at the camp and was sent to the Provo[st]. My accusation in the Mittimus was "an oppressor of the righteous and a spy." On the 27th in the morning God moved the heart of the most generous General Muhlenberg to come to me and inquire into my affairs. And promised that he would speak to General Washington, and procured for me a hearing and the next day sent me word that I should make a petition to General Washington, which I did. And through the good hand of providence and the faithful assistance of said General Muhlenberg I was permitted to go out of the Provo[st] on the 29th day of May. But I was not free, it being against my conscience to take the oath to the state, I was not permitted to go home to Germantown as appears by the following pass, viz: "Permit the bearer hereof, Mr. Sower, to pass from hence to Mathatchey, not to return to Germantown during the stay of the enemy in this state, he behaving as becometh. Given under my hand at the orderly office this 30th day of May 1778.

"Nicholas Gilman Asst. Adj't. Gen."

So I went to Methatchey and stayed there until the 23rd of June when I returned to Germantown and there lived quietly till the 27th of July when Colonel Smith and Colonel Thompson came to my house and asked me whether I had entered special bail at the Supreme Court at Lancaster. I told them "No." "Why not?" said they. "Because I had no notice." "That cannot be," said Thompson, "it was in the newspapers and handbills." I told them I had at that time been in the Provost and [at] Methatchey and had seen none of those papers and nobody had told me of it till after the time was expired. "Have you taken the oath to the state?" "No!" "Why not?" "Were you so attached to the king?" "No. It was not the attachment to the king but as you have in your act that they that do not take that oath shall not have the right to buy nor sell and as I find in the Book of Revelation that such a time will come when such a mark would be given, so I could not take that oath while it stood on that condition." "But you went to the English in Philadelphia," said Smith. I said: "Do you know why?" "No," said he, "nor do I want to know."

Then they told me that they were come to take an inventory of my personal estate and sell it, and to rent out my real estate. I told them I would submit to all that the Lord permitted them to do, and so Smith stood guard that I might not put anything out of the way. Thompson went out to get appraisers and a clerk and so they began to appraise. I then begged that they should let me keep my bed, but Smith gave for answer they had not right to let me have anything besides my clothes and provisions (which last they did not abide by, for when they found a barrel of beef they took it down although it was provision). I then begged for a few medicines which I had put by for my family's use as they were chiefly of my and my father's preparation and nobody else knew what they were. But Smith said: "Medicines are very valuable, they must be sold." Then I begged for nothing more but my spectacles which was granted.

On the 28th they told me that I must quit the house, for they must rent it out and so I moved out on the 30th of July. Then they proceeded to sell my effects, but before the sale came on my son Daniel endeavored to stop it. [He] applied to Thomas Mattock and asked him whether his father should not have a hearing. "Yes, but we must sell his effects first." He then applied to Mr. Lewis to stop the sale till next court, who endeavored to do it. But they had invented a lie that I or some of my people had secretly crept into the house and had destroyed all the New Testaments, and if the sale did not go on, all would be destroyed before the said court came on. And so they passed on with the sale of my personal estate and rented out my houses and lands for one year and then sold them also, contrary to the concession of the Convention in the case of Forfeited Estates that no estate could be sold before the youngest son is of age. And so they have not only broken the testamental rule in selling my estate, but have also published me in almost all newspapers as a traitor without any cause and without ever giving me a hearing or trial, although I never was gone a mile from my place of abode. Their own attorney, Mr. Bradford, has himself declared to a friend of mine that "if I had not forfeited my life I had also not forfeited my estate, for they had no more right to my estate than to my life."[21]

Notes and Queries by Sauer II

The details of the confiscation and sale of Sauer's property have been preserved in the official Pennsylvania records but are too lengthy to print here.[22] After the dispossession, Sauer and his four youngest children found temporary shelter in the home of Henry Sharpnack of Germantown, the brother of his wife, who had been spared the shock of the confiscation by her death on January 8, 1778. The once-wealthy Sauer returned to his first trade of bookbinding to earn a living, and faithfully repaid the loans considerate friends had tendered after his great loss. In April 1780, Sauer moved north of Philadelphia to Methacton, where he lived in a small building at Conrad Stamm's home. He continued his church work, visiting other congregations and preaching as late as two weeks before his death on August 26, 1784.[23] The only known reference he made to his misfortune of 1778 is found in the set of questions he submitted to the annual meeting of the Brethren held at Lancaster in 1780.

A list of that which was lent or provided me by various friends since the confiscation of my possessions, which I promise to repay honestly as soon as God places me in a position to do so. In case this should not be possible during my lifetime, they should be repaid out of my small estate as far as possible. I trust in God that He will richly reward for whatever I should be unable to repay.

Brother Henry Scharpnack lent 20 Congress dollars.
Brother William Hauschel [?] gave me 20 Congress dollars.
Friend Anthony Benezet gave me a guinea.
John Wiester gave me 8 dollars.
Reinhold gave me 1 lb. tea, 6 lbs. sugar, 3 lbs. coffee, makes 15 dollars.
Brother Haas gave me 6 dollars.
Friend Joseph Kratzer [?] in Lebanon gave me 8 Congress dollars.
The above have all been repaid.[24]

As there are debts yet due on bonds, notes and book debts, who has the best right to demand them of the people, or the State?

If a man is openly declared a traitor without a cause, without hearing or trial, when he was not absent and might have been heard, is it just to let him forever lie under that reproach?

Is it right that Colonel Smith be permitted to carry on a lawsuit against my son Daniel and to pocket 50 pounds in hard money to himself when he has paid the State (if he ever has) with a trifle of Continental?[25]

SAUER III IN NEW YORK

Christopher Sauer III did not sit idly in New York following his removal from Philadelphia but busied himself in mercantile and publishing pursuits. These were set aside, however, by his involvement as conveyor of intelligence to the British authorities. Because of his extensive contacts among the rural inhabitants of the middle colonies, he was able to transmit much information to army headquarters. A recent history of the under-cover operation of the British in the Revolutionary period assigns a considerable role to Sauer. The letters of recommendation which Sauer secured from the top British military leadership to support his later petition for assistance from the royal government also attest to his position.[26]

The Memorial of Sauer III Concluded

To provide a summary statement of his activities in New York after 1778, we return to the memorial of 1784.

. . . That upon the evacuation of the city of Philadelphia, your memorialist thus circumstanced, was obliged to leave his ancient father stripped of a very valuable estate in indigence and for safety to attend the British Army to New York. That when there he opened a correspondence with his friends in Pennsylvania, Maryland and the Delaware counties (some of whom had already agreed to arise in arms on the part of the Crown) to encourage them to persevere in their loyalty. That they in return appointed him to act between him and the commander-in-chief [General Clinton], which he did so effectually as to induce His Excellency to accept their services, and to communicate with them from time to time in the most confidential manner, as may appear from the several messages and orders which have been carefully preserved by your memorialist.

In these messages His Excellency gave them a watchword and directed them to increase the circle of their acquaintances, to furnish him with all important intelligence and to take every preparatory act for action when called upon, etc.

In the year 1780 your memorialist transmitted an address from them to . . . His Majesty through the hands of Joseph Galloway, Esq., and the Rev. Mr. Batwell, in which they represented their number to be greatly increased and offered to co-operate in the most effectual manner with a detachment of the king's forces, for the restoration of His Majesty's authority. That in consequence of this address as your memorialist has reason to believe, and the ruin which at that time hung over the Loyalists, the commander-in-chief was pleased to send your memorialist for the month of May, 1781, together with Colonel Rankin, who by this time had arrived in the British lines, with a private letter to General Philips, then commanding in Virginia, which letter was delivered to Lord Cornwallis, General Philips having died before they got there, and that in a few days after, they also tendered to His Lordship, the assistance of the said Associators, in reducing the three before mentioned provinces to His Majesty's government.

That in the year 1782 your memorialist presented [in England] a memorial in person to the Right Honorable Wellborn Ellisthen, then Secretary to the American Department, containing a repetition of the former offers and proposals of the associated Loyalists who had now so greatly increased in numbers, as not to leave them a doubt of success, and having also made a tender of his own further service, he was sent over to New York with His Excellency Sir Guy Carleton where he continued toward him all the services in his power.

That these and other incessant and disinterested services in behalf of the Crown were not only attended by a great expense and a variety of danger, but prevented your memorialist from pursuing with effect any line of business for his future support. And being thus reduced from a very respectable position to a state of indigence with a wife and one child and another which may be soon expected to support, your memorialist prays that Your Lordships will take his case into consideration and grant him such relief as his service and losses may appear to deserve.

Christopher Sower, Jr.[27]

Christian Musselman's Report

Among the papers sent on by Sauer to the British authorities was one based on a most interesting report submitted by Christian Musselman.[28] The name *Musselman* was current among Mennonite settlers in Bucks, Lancaster, and Lehigh counties. A Christian Musselman was among the founding settlers of a Mennonite congregation in Upper Milford Township, Lehigh County, about 1740. *Kauffman* and *Brenneman* were also well-known Mennonite names in eastern Pennsylvania. Philip Shoemaker was a member of the Conestoga congregation of the Brethren in 1764. The report, previously unknown, reaffirms the nonresistant policy of the peace churches.

That the Mennonists and German Baptists (the latter in derision called Dunckers) in the different parts of Pennsylvania, have long wished to know from authority how to conduct themselves during the present rebellion, that they might not give offence to His Majesty or his representative in America.

That at length some of the ministers and leading men of those two societies to wit: Michael Kauffmann, Senior and Junior, Philip Shoemaker, and Melchior Brennemann, all of Lancaster County, drew an address and petition to the king in behalf of those two societies (which Musselmann destroyed when taken by the rebels coming in) setting forth their happiness while under his government, their desire to be reinstated in the enjoyment of their former blessings, and their readiness to assist with their goods and chattels to bring about so desirable an event; and praying that a general line of conduct might be pointed out to them, to conduct themselves by, etc. whether their sowing grain, planting corn, etc. was not in some measure considered as aiding and abetting in the rebellion, and whether they would be suffered to enjoy their religious principles as heretofore. That he was directed to represent their request to the commander-in-chief and if he did not think himself authorized to answer it, he — Musselmann — was to forward the address to the throne.

I am well acquainted with almost all the leading men and with many of the laity of those two societies (it was my interest so to be) in Pennsylvania, and believe them to be the most loyal people in the world, and flatter myself that both the British and Hessian officers and soldiers, who were prisoners in the vicinity of those two sects will agree with me from experience. I judge the Mennonists in that province to consist of between two and three thousand families and from the Rev. Mr. Edwards' Journal it appears that the German Baptists consist of about three thousand members of their church, the women in the latter included. In political matters they are ignorant to an extreme and glory in being so. The aged of both societies profess to be conscientiously scrupulous of bearing arms, but the young men of the former, are not so much contracted. They have ever since the beginning of this rebellion excommunicated every person that took up arms against the king, or otherwise voluntarily assisted the rebels.

I have known them to be very anxious on the first commencement of this contest, to have a line of conduct pointed out unto them by the general. They have had several meetings on this occasion at one of which I was present and have heard of such an address being intended early last spring. I wish their request could (in part if not in the whole) be granted, and think I could safely and privately convey any message unto them without any particular expense to government.

[C. S., Jr.]

Major De Lancey[29]

Sauer's Appeal to His Countrymen

For part of his New York sojourn Sauer was active as a publisher, issuing the New York *Evening Post* for a time in 1782-1783.[30] His most important piece of writing was an open letter addressed to his fellow Germans in Pennsylvania and vicinity. He fervently called on them to resist the siren lures of the Revolution and to remain loyal to the British government. Of this pamphlet it has been said:

> This plea, while neither very well organized nor strikingly original, is by no means a weak composition. Sauer continually stressed the former prosperity of the Germans under British rule in contrast with their distress since the outbreak of the rebellion. He bitterly attacked Paine's *Common Sense,* the radical New Englanders, the German ministers who misled their congregations, the Continental Congress, and the foreign nations, France and Spain. Finally, with the fervor of an orator and an evangelist, he urged the Germans to refuse to obey the government and to unite to defeat the rebels. The whole address may be considered the valedictory of the Sauers as colonial printers.[31]

The pamphlet, unnoticed by bibliographers of this period, provides an excellent insight into Loyalist attitudes.

New York, April 14, 1780

Address to all Germans in Pennsylvania and neighboring provinces. Friends and countrymen:

The sorry situation into which you have been thrown by a pack of sly and selfish men calls me — yes, demands of every honest man who speaks or writes in liberty and needs not fear the unjust punishment of your tyrants (for I am, thank God, outside of their power) — to lead you out of the labyrinth in which you are wandering like knights-errant, and which finally leads to your complete destruction.

It is not unknown to me, my friends, that there are many among you who have long seen through the intrigues of the Congress and your other rulers, and who would have led the ignorant into the right path through public writings and warnings, except that the present slavery which the scepter of judgment wields is too horrible and the manifold penalties too harsh for anyone to expose himself to them. However, it is permitted me, as I am living under the protection of liberty, to speak the truth.

I was born and raised among you and lived happily. Our homes were our castles; without our permission no one could enter. By the fruits of our labors we were fed and given drink abundantly. We saw our friends near and far and found pleasure in one another in peace and unity. But alas! Those times have vanished!

Yet, dear countrymen, deep and festering as the wound is which has been made by the present rebellion, it can yet be healed by your own attitude. It is out of deep love for you, my fatherland, out of dutiful obedience to the king (the most gracious and most kind ruler in the world), and out of love of the truth, that I write to you the following lines. I wish that you may see the truths which are contained in this address. God is my witness that I have no other aim than through it to [cause you] to cast away all of the prejudices which you have allowed in the past six years, partly voluntarily and partly under compulsion, and to listen to reality; then it will be easy for you to judge for yourselves. You will find that truth shines with brilliance, even in the shabbiest dress. If you continue, do not be taken in by such an absurd prejudice *that all those are Tories* who warn you of complete downfall. Rather believe that he who depicts to you the impending ruin is your friend and a professor of the true freedom.

It occurs almost daily under your present tyrannical rulers, that

when a man innocently and truthfully thinks and speaks with favor
of the king and his previous government and justly despises the present
tyranny of Congress, he is thrown into the deepest dungeon and allowed to perish there without mercy, or may even be hanged. You
know of many who have met this fate.

The author of the notorious tract, *Common Sense* (an unruly
mind paid by the Congress) led you through this short treatise to the
pinnacle of the temple (if I may use this image) and showed you
the kingdoms of the world and their glory which were not in his
power. He made you believe pleasant tales, fabulous new joys and
new future governments, which can be brought about only by a pen
on paper. He made independence seem so glittering to you that the
brilliance dazzled you, just as one cannot immediately see the spots
in the sun because of its brightness. He portrayed for you the changing
of the form of government as being as easy as clearing a new piece of
land of trees, roots, etc. Yet, do make up your minds today to read
this marvel, *Common Sense,* weigh the author's counsels point by
point, examine for yourselves his various reasons why his new form of
government is better, compare his ridiculous predictions with the
events since that time; judge in how far his praised independence has
failed so far — then you will make a discovery which will astonish you.
You will find that the author is a bribed betrayer, and his tract a seed
of the evil spirit planted among you by the hand of Congress.

Read the so-call *Common Sense* more frequently than ever before,
and every time that you notice the leaders of this unjust revolution
declining lower and lower. As much as it misled you in the beginning,
it is now capable of opening your eyes. Now, friend, before you read
on, think back on those times, remember when you were judged by
the golden British laws in America, and compare them with the
present laws of Congress. I wager that the Congress will appear to
you like a monster and its members like so many tyrannical princes.
To the man who has common sense (and to my knowledge all of
you have good common sense) this will be as enlightening as daybreak.

Under the fictitious name of *Liberty* you have been brought to the
edge of the precipice (into which you must soon fall if you continue
your present path), and alas! you are becoming aware of it too late!
For the shortsighted among you, this path was embellished with a
thousand delights, for example, *liberty, no rulers, no taxes or duties,* in

short, *a golden era* was the doll which was given to you to play with. The trap was set many years ago with exceeding skill and care, and covered with so many enticements that one must admit that whoever wished to make the discovery had to be more cunning or just as clever as those who laid the trap with so much slyness.

You were still too new and unexperienced to examine the motives of your leaders in the rebellion. You were newcomers to the change of states and forms of governments. You were used to laws which can be comprehended by every common man. Alliances were unknown to you, because your king was able to protect you without them. You did not need to call on foreign and unknown nations for help. You knew your protector and were convinced that he would stand by you in all trials. But what can this powerful Congress do? Do they protect you against the savages? Do they protect you against the loss of your paper currency? It is easy for you to answer this yourself.

It was not the taxes on the tea or other duties to the king (which latter, after all, existed only in the imagination) that laid the foundation for the downfall of your previous benign government. No! Rather, it was many of your merchants who had squandered their wealth in debauchery that caused your misfortune. The debts which they had incurred with the merchants in England had become burdens to them, which they partly could not, and partly would not, repay. There was, of course, no other way out than to scheme for independence from Great Britain in order through it to cancel at the same time the debts from their books.

The sly New Englanders were unquestionably the first to wave a red flag. As rebels, they were driven out of their fatherland many years ago, and the poison of rebellion had perpetuated itself in their grandchildren. Before the outbreak of the rebellion they sent men of keen minds into all the provinces to investigate the feelings of the leading people. Indeed, they even sent out preachers (not as apostles of the truth in the name of the Lord, but rather in the name of the arch-rebel, Satan) to scatter from the pulpit the poison of rebellion to the innocent. And unfortunately, many of our German preachers defiled the pulpit with the poison of rebellion and washed their hands in innocent blood! All truths in foreign newspapers and other publications from England were suppressed, and the mouth of truth was thus stopped and a fountain of lies was opened instead.

The Congress submitted your complaints against the king which existed only in the imagination. You were told in the beginning that the Congress wished nothing else but the repeal of the latest acts of Parliament. Did not, however, the consequences soon prove that this was only an excuse to gain time in order to demand more?

The humble voice of Congress was at first the voice of a crocodile in order to attract the prey all the more easily into the net. How soon were they defiant and daring when they had the reins in their power! No, countrymen, their aim was not your welfare, but their own profit, pride and ambition, and partly a certain revenge on several members whose wishes had foundered in England. These men forged the present iron yoke upon you. Men of the foremost rank and ability in America who sat in the first Congress stole away, as soon as they discovered that the majority of votes sought to bring about independence from England. All news from England and speeches of several members of Parliament in your favor were kept from you (inasmuch as no printer, in consideration of the harshest penalties and persecutions, dared publish any truths and what would serve to your welfare without first asking for permission), or was so distorted that you were not able to recognize the truth in it.

The Congress repeatedly falsely assured you that the British Army could not penetrate into your land; that England would soon have to surrender, because their funds were already exhausted (1778); that the people of England were on the verge of rebellion against the king; that Ireland was ready to make itself independent of England — and all of the other unheard-of pipe dreams. Now you see that all of this was false. Can you then still be so foolish as to keep believing this pack of illegal possessors of all your property, yes, even your lives? If you still wish to do this, then "come now, you rich, weep and howl for the miseries that are coming upon you" (James 5:1).

It must create a disadvantageous image of you among Christian nations when they read that Congress proclaims days of penitence and fasting in order to entreat God for His assistance and blessing in the rebellion against their anointed ruler. Will not God despise them? And will not all civilized nations despise them and you as well?

The value of your Congress paper-currency is a circumstance which ought to cause you fear and trembling. How detestable is the deception! It goes, according to common sense, like this: *"Congress has bor-*

*rowed from you your property, that is your horses, cattle, wagons,
grain, straw, hay and the like, and has given you papers in return;
which will be worth nothing in six or eight years: for the company
is going bankrupt and you are cheated out of your property, and no
one will exchange the papers for ready cash, that is, Spanish mill'd
dollars."*

Congress plays with you like boys among themselves; now they
give you toys, and before you know it they want them back again.
Now they lead you to believe — *that they are now going to have a kind
of bill printed which are really good (the others must have been worthless!) for these are to be capable of exchange for hard money within
six years.* Only, who will give his good hard dollars for worthless
paper?

My friends, this is a new trap — watch out! The sum of the matter
is this: *you give paper in taxes and receive for your products a new
and freshly printed paper made by a new and fresh fraud.* This is the
truth about the money with which you must conduct a war and which
is nowhere of any value except where the Congress doles it out at the
point of a bayonet.

You have bound the rod with which they now whip you. *"These
dirty persons carouse on your alms without shame, looking after themselves; waterless clouds, carried along by winds; bare fruitless trees (in
late autumn) twice dead (uprooted), wild waves of the sea, casting
up the foam of their own shame"* (Jude 12).

How much has your prospect of a future American independence
been darkened recently! Does not the fortune of war begin to turn
against you and your allies? The French were not successful in land-
ing in England or Ireland, or in defeating the British fleet. It is going
even worse for the Spanish, who are not only forced to leave Gibraltar
but are losing a *fourth of their entire seapower to boot.* What does
the mighty Congress say now? I pity the poor [fools] for the time is
approaching when they must unanimously decide: *"We have no abiding place here."* Their intrigue is almost exhausted, they no longer
know how to keep you in bounds, for there are too many among you
who rather clearly see through their deception. This puts them into
fear and waiting. They know too well the unjustified quarrel with
their former protectors; they are convinced that it is a vice of the black-
est shade. But greed for power is too great a passion to be suppressed

through reasoning. They [would] rather risk their own as well as all of your lives than lose their power.

If you took a look at what is in the past, countrymen, how pleasant this memory must appear to you! You were free and happy. Every owner of a plantation was master on his own estate. The taxes to the government and the king were the lowest, in terms of your yearly income, of any kingdom in the world, notwithstanding it is the custom among all peoples and just that a subject who expects to be protected by his ruler should also contribute to this in fairness according to his ability.

But what would you gain if you really achieved your independence? Answer: *a shadow of happiness.* You would have to build and equip a fleet of warships, maintain a strong army, and pay many thousands of state officials, more than ever before. This fleet would have to be paid for, the army maintained, and the new officials would suck the marrow from your plantations. *"In those days there was no king in Israel; every man did what was right in his own eyes"* (Judges 21:25).

At the present time you have neither a fleet nor an army which is capable of fighting with the smallest power in the world, when you are taken out of the wilderness and from behind the trees. Your generals are not capable of holding a single fortification. And how could it be possible that your officers should understand the military arts? Two, three years of war make neither a good officer nor soldier. You have examples enough of this; for so far the American troops have always retreated where the British advanced with determination.

In our ranks your entire situation is known; little remains hidden. We know that your main army is not over five thousand men strong, poorly paid, poorly clothed and discontented. Over half of your Continental soldiers would desert within three months if our army had a position near yours; and difficult as deserting may be for them, they still escape by the droves.

I would have to be too expansive in an address if I were to describe to you your previous happiness in entirety in order to refresh your memory as much as I wished. And it would take a hundred pages if I were to relate to you all of the intrigues and knavish tricks of the Congress.

Many of you know from experience and the majority from history, that the king of France has always been one of the most treacherous powers in Europe. And who among you knows the actual treaties between the Congress and the king in France? Certainly no one except those who have power over you, and of which you will not become aware until you become subjects of *this most Christian king* (which God may spare you in His grace for a long time yet). For should Congress achieve its aim, they would doubtless (because of the many debts which they have made in France) surrender some of their *thirteen* so-called *states,* to France, so as to be able to make reparations quickly. Know then that none except fools lend their money without security. How is that, would you then be free subjects?

Perhaps there is now also an alliance concluded between the Congress and Spain. Then you would even be exposed to the Holy Inquisition; for you need not believe that the king of Spain would be your friend without selfish purpose. This nation would put you (according to its unbearable pride) in fear and trembling through a thousand cruelties in order to prepare you for slavery.

Oh, countrymen! How can you look upon this tragedy so long! How can your common sense allow all of this to rule over you! It astonishes us in the British lines that you let yourselves be led to your deaths as patiently as sheep to be slaughtered. If you would only consider that it was England who placed you into this country with a generous and gentle hand, made easy the beginning of your agriculture and protected you against all your enemies — will you not appear in the eyes of the entire world as an ungrateful nation?

Assume, for once, the following and draw the conclusions in reference to your entire present conduct toward Great Britain: "A young traveling man arrived toward evening at the plantation of a rich man in the county of ———————— in Pennsylvania (1745); the farmer invited the man, who was a stranger to him, with great kindness into his house, and offered him shelter for the night, which the traveler accepted with many thanks. The farmer entertained him with all that was in his possession to give. During the evening, asking each other all kinds of questions, they became acquainted (better than is usual between strangers). The next morning as the traveler wished to leave, the farmer said: 'My friend! It is true, I do not know you very well, but you seem to be a diligent and honest man, your face and your speech seem to witness to that; do you wish to stay here with me?

The harvest is coming soon and you could help me harvest my crops; you shall earn a great deal of money and besides I will treat you like one of my sons.'

"The traveler was happy to have found such an honest and friendly man and proved himself during the harvest to be a diligent worker. After the autumn season the farmer said: 'Friend, you have won my love and confidence through your good conduct. Stay this winter with me; in the spring I will accept you as one of my children, for I have many thousand acres in ——————— County, from which I will have a large plantation measured off for you, and also give you an advance in livestock and money of which you need not pay any tariff during the first ten years. You can become as wealthy as I am. But you must promise that after ten years you will deliver to me a six-year-old ox. Apart from this the land is to be your and your grandchildren's property.'

"The traveler occupied the plantation, according to the promise, cleared it and built it up to great profit. Shortly thereafter he married a daughter of the farmer. As the time had come for the agreed-upon rent to be paid, the farmer (now a father-in-law to the once traveler, now son) came, rejoiced in his good circumstances and reminded him of the agreement. The son-in-law answered him impetuously: 'Father-in-law, I am now a completely different man than I was when I spent the first night and the harvest with you, and now I will no longer have anything to do with you and your family. I can look out for myself. I cannot give you anything.' He took him by the arm to throw him out of the house. 'Stop, friend,' began the father-in-law, 'is that the thanks for my friendly simplicity? I have, as you know, a large household to provide for, and have given you a large share of my wealth without cost, wherewith you have been able to achieve your present prosperity. And now you will not even pay me this small rent?'

"The impetuous son-in-law however (without even giving him an answer) gripped him by his arm, led him out of the door with the threat that if he did not immediately get out of the yard he would put his dogs on him. The father-in-law was dumb with astonishment and wished to explain further his just cause. But no, the now arrogant man said: 'I shall and will hear nothing from you,' and whistled for his dogs, which sprang viciously upon the good old father-in-law, dragged him to the gate, ripped the clothes from his body but did not hurt him very much. The farmer then sent one of his friends to his son-in-law to admonish him and to reprove him for his deed, and also to remind him of his debt. Yet this person fared just like the old man — the dogs chased him here and there and his life was in danger. The son-in-law went further in his wickedness. He attacked with his servants the plantation of his father-in-law, killed all the livestock, and would have become dangerous to the old man and his family if the old man had not known of his arrival. How the conflict between these two ended is unknown."

From this you can draw a parallel to the present rebellion. There is still time, countrymen, to throw off this iron yoke! Enough friends will join you who are tired of the burden of a contrary government which imposes upon them a pack of dictatorial men, in order to rid themselves of the same. The burden is already so heavy on some of you that it will seem unbearable in the future.

Your future condition will be a three-fold slavery: the French will give you *wooden shoes* for your tanned or untanned hides; the Spanish will erect *monasteries for priests* in your best area, whose inhabitants you would have to support as *useless members of human society;* and the Congress will treat you as renters, to whom you would have to deliver two-thirds of your harvest annually.

The offers of England are after your own desire, that is: "You are to be reinstated into all of your former rights, and in still more than you had in 1763." Is not this generous? After you have rebelled against this kingdom and caused so much waste of blood and wealth? Nevertheless, you are to be reinstated into all of your former rights. Tell me of another nation capable of such generosity toward a people who had caused so much unrest.

The scarcity of food is increasing daily among you (even though your land is very rich) but we cannot consider this in any other light than as a just punishment from heaven. Your conditions are truly bad! One is aware in the British lines of all your needs better than you are yourselves, because you never learn the truth from your own rulers and their adherents.

Now then, countrymen! Do not be discouraged. Begin to improve your fate, as is in your power. Refuse to pay your taxes to the Congress, because they are too unjust and too high. Refuse to join the militia who are to march into battle without knowing for what they are fighting. Refuse obedience to your present tyrannical judges (whatever their names may be). Refuse to have the new paper money printed in your name and with your permission because it is not the property of the Congress but yours. You must redeem it, not Congress. Refuse the paper money for your grain which you have to give to the commissaries for the army; an army which will so quickly lead you to ruin as you can scarcely imagine.

Gather on your commons, deliberate with one another, listen to the opinions of each neighbor, consider the motivations of each, whether he speaks out of selfishness, ambition — inasmuch as he perhaps represents an office under the power of the Congress — then unite as one man and demand an accounting from your present rulers. You need no arms and weapons. Merely your number (if it is large) must tip the balance.

There is not the slightest doubt that if you do this, you will be, so to speak, the key to the opening and restoration of the previous peaceful government. All of North America will owe you gratitude for your efforts for generations to come, for such a great work which you were able to perform without any bloodshed. Fifteen hundred of you are already a sufficient number to dictate laws to the Congress. Lose no time in founding this good work for the glory and honor of all of you! This is the opinion of all your friends and countrymen here.

The time has come; your salvation is nigh. Should you now begin this good work, and in the course of it have need of assistance in completing it, then you may know without any further assurance that the British general and commander-in-chief will proffer you every assistance which has been given him by the king for this purpose. As swiftly as you have been swept along in the present rebellion, just as swiftly you can wrest yourselves from it, if you will consult your own common sense, and if you consider your own benefit.

Now is the time; your misery is at its zenith! The question arises: will you use the means which are herewith put into your hands for your deliverance or will you let yourselves be led like patient sheep to the slaughter as sacrifices of the Spanish and the French? "Who among you still stands [in solid intention to remain a loyal subject of the king] let him take care lest he fall."

I close herewith, and assure you of my and of your friends' wishes for your early deliverance.

[Christopher Sauer III][32]

SAUER III IN ENGLAND

As noted in his memorial, Sauer traveled to London during the Revolution in order to "forward a petition to the foot of the throne." Following the close of hostilities, Sauer was an exile in London for nearly two years, during which time he sought compensation from the Crown for his services during the war.

Testimony of Abraham Pastorius

Of the many statements and recommendations supporting Sauer's memorial to the British government, from British officers and fellow Pennsylvanian Loyalists, one is here reproduced. Abraham Pastorius, the descendant of one of Germantown's founders, appeared at the hearing of the commissioners in England to testify on Sauer's behalf.[33]

Says he knew the claimant from the time he went to school with him. So far as he has seen he has conducted himself as a man attached to this country. He was avowedly so and remembers once or twice a mob being raised with an intention to use him ill, but being informed of it he got out of the way.

Says the claimant was an overseer of the poor and raised money by subscription among the Loyalists for them, rather than go to a rebel magistrate to get the duplicate signed.

Says he knows the printing office. In 1775 he understood the father had given up the business to his two sons, the claimant and a younger brother [Peter], but lived in the house himself. Cannot pretend to set a value on it. . . .

Says he knows the old man's estate was sold after they left Philadelphia. He was esteemed a Loyalist and thought to be worth between sixty to seventy thousand pounds currency.

Says he knew but one instance of any of the Society of the Dunkards taking part against the government and he was on that account excluded.

They were (father and sons) in great business as printers.[34]

The Decision of the Commissioners

On April 29, 1784, the commissioners in London made their summation of the evidence concerning the loyalty of Sauer to the king and his services and losses during the Revolution. Their decision was largely favorable. In addition to the annuity and some indemnity for the property loss, Sauer was also made deputy postmaster of St. John, New Brunswick, and printer of the province for the king. It was this province which provided shelter for thousands of Loyalists who chose or were forced to leave their former homes. Soon after his arrival in 1785 he began publishing a newspaper, the *Royal Gazetter and Weekly Advertiser,* continued until 1792.[35]

April 29, 1784

Sower, Christopher:

Is a native of Pennsylvania. When the troubles commenced he was [a] very young man and he was with his father in the printing business. He was partner with his father. In 1776 the rebels stopped his press and he believed they would have confined him if he had not known a circumstance which would have hurt the American cause. The governor offered him a bribe, provided he would espouse the cause. He was [a] German printer and was born of German parents and lived in Germantown. He joined the army in 1777 when they came to Germantown. He went with the army but he never bore arms; he only printed for the army. He had no property but a printing office which his father gave to him and which cost him fifteen hundred pounds of that money and he promised to settle the house in which he lived upon this young man after his death. His brother who was in partnership with him was by his father's directions to have the use of the printing press until he came of age which would have been in the year 1780.

There are very strong certificates to Mr. Sower's loyalty and services from Sir William Howe, Sir Henry Clinton and several other officers to confidential services on many occasions, and says himself that he has frequently risked his life in the services and he has almost lost the use of one arm.

The certificates being so full no further certificates or attendance required.

He has a wife and one child here and no support.

£ 40 per Annum from
April 5, 1784

Decision.

This man appears to have behaved extremely well and to have shown great zeal in the cause of Great Britain. He joined the British army very early and probably would have borne arms if he had not been more useful in another way, but being a printer and a German printer he was of great use to the army as appears by the certificates which are signed by almost all the general officers. He had no great property but he lost it all with the employment of his trade.

In addition to his being thrown upon the wide world without support, he has received a very material injury in the service. He has almost lost the use of one arm from a blow with a musket. This is a circumstance which always has great weight in our decision.

Under these circumstances, therefore, notwithstanding his property was not large or his family numerous we think ourselves justified in recommending an allowance of forty pounds a year and that it should commence from the 25th of March 1784.[36]

Christopher Sauer III to Samuel Sauer

A letter has been preserved which was written by Sauer from London to his brother Samuel (1767-1820) upon learning of the death of their father. It was to Samuel's home in Baltimore that Christopher Sauer III went in the first part of 1799. He died there of a stroke on July 3 of the same year. Another brother, and former partner in printing, Peter Sauer, mentioned in the letter as a practicing physician in the West Indies, died there of yellow fever later in 1785.[37]

London, February 2, 1785

My dear Brother:

I received your letter of September 1, last, and was much affected at the information it contained. The father, then, who raised us with tenderness, in whose lap and from whose lips we have received so much and such salutary instructions, as must appertain to life everlasting if practiced by us, is no more. I never was more unmanned than when I received this news. All my philosophy forsook me at once, which is the more extraordinary as my soul wished him well, and I am convinced that his change is for the better. He lived the Christian and died the death of the righteous. Oh, may our latter end be like his! He is numbered among the children of God and his lot is among the saints; he has fought a good fight, has finished his course, has kept the faith. He knew his Redeemer lived. Merciful men are taken away. The righteous are taken away from the evil to come. They have no continuing city here. They enter into peace and rest in their beds. And although I am sensible of all this I grieved and sorrowed as if I was ignorant concerning them that are asleep — even as others which have no hope. Forgive me, dear brother, this digression, forgive me this burst of sorrow.

I cannot say that I am pleased with the manner in which you have deposited his remains. [Neither] our dear mother nor one of the family was ever buried in a walnut coffin, nor do I believe it would have been agreeable to him if he had known it in his life time. I note what you have said of your intention of erecting to his memory ornamental tomb stones, and am fully persuaded that it would be a much greater ornament to his memory to have his virtues engraved on the hearts of his children, of which number I am one. I shall not however oppose you in showing him this mark of your affection and respect and if you put your design into execution you will send me the inscription on them.

Our parents being now transplanted into a world where the clock does not strike and from whence no one returns, it becomes my duty as an elder brother to enjoin you never to lose sight of those instructions you have from time to time received from them. Put them in practice and you will be benefited by them. You will find them an ample compensation for one's terrestrial hope and disappointments. Let your spare time be spent in reading books on religious, moral and historical subjects; they will enlarge your mind, disclose the wiles of Satan and lead you to the knowledge of man. In the first must be your delight, and the others you will consider as only secondary things. Make piety, industry and honesty the undeviable rule of your whole life. Make yourself master of your trade or the profession you are now learning and do not for any paltry reason change it for another.

It gives me singular satisfaction to reflect that you live in the neighborhood with Brother Urner and let me earnestly recommend to you [to] consult him on all occasions and take his advice as that of a father. Salute him and his family most cordially from me and [my wife] Hannah and assure him that, although at this great distance, I am open to both instruction and reproof. And, finally, dear brother, remember what I have said unto you I say unto you all. In your next you will give me further particulars of daddy's latter end, his last sayings, who those three persons were he baptized last, and from whence Brother Urner and Samuel Hopkins took the subject of their admonition at his funeral. The most trivial circumstances will be a treasure to me.

Within these few days I have received a letter from brother Peter, dated Nassau near Providence, November 25, in which he tells me little more of himself than [that] he is a practitioner of physics at that place and hopes to do well. I have this day written a long letter to uncle [Henry Sharpnack] in which I gave him a full, and I trust a satisfactory account of William Piper's receipts.

About seven months ago divine providence favored us with a young son who still remains nameless [later named Brook Watson Sauer]. Hannah has never been right well since; but is now entirely laid up. I have had an inflammation in the pleura but am now much better of it. The children are in perfect health. Priscilla desires her love to you and all her uncles and aunts.

I have not yet had a hearing before the Commissioners of American Claims about father's estate; but expect it will come on in the course of this month or the beginning of the next, when I shall send you such accounts as I may be able to give. I shall go with my family to Nova Scotia the ensuing spring, perhaps in the month of April. The king has appointed me his printer and deputy postmaster general of that place. This latter appointment gives me in so far pleasure as it affords me an opportunity of corresponding more safely and freely with my relations in Pennsylvania. On my arrival there I shall send you my address. As so many of my letters have miscarried I have written this in English that in case it should be intercepted [the remainder is lost].[38]

V. Publications

12. Doctrinal Writings

A recent tabulation of publications of the Brethren lists some fifty items between the arrival in America and the turn of the century.[1] This number does not include the many issues of the press at Ephrata or the voluminous output of the Germantown press of the Sauer family, except where individual books or pamphlets were clearly authored by Brethren or printed on behalf of the Brotherhood.

The earliest publication in America was a tract by Alexander Mack, Sr., against the sabbatarian view of Beissel and his group. No known copy exists today, but there were contemporary references to it. John Adam Gruber wrote to Germany in 1731 (see page 118) that "Al[exander] Mack is involved . . . in a published argument about the observance of the Sabbath." A German Radical Pietist wrote about "the oral and published argument inflamed by this [sabbatarianism] among the New Baptists."[2]

With the exception of fragments published in English translation in the books of Martin G. Brumbaugh (1899), John S. Flory (1908), and Samuel B. Heckman (1912) very little notice has been taken of this literary activity. This has been largely owing to two reasons. First, the writing was done in German; increasingly in the nineteenth century, and almost completely thereafter, knowledge of German was lost among the Brethren. Secondly, very few copies of these publications exist. If it had not been for the collecting zeal of Abraham Harley Cassel, whose extensive private library is now dispersed primarily among institutions in Pennsylvania, Virginia, and Illinois, many of the publications would have been lost.[3]

These writings can be divided into two groups: those which are mainly doctrinal in quality, and those which are mainly devotional, although the categories often overlap. In the following are given in translation what is considered to be a representative selection from the doctrinal writings, both published and unpublished. Not all could be included, not even all of each individual selection.

FRAGMENTS FROM THE BIBLE OF MACK, SR.

The personal Bible of Alexander Mack, Sr., has been preserved, and is now located at Bridgewater College, Virginia. A notice in an early page of the Bible, written by Henry Kurtz, important Brethren publisher of the nineteenth century, reads:

> This hand-Bible, formerly the property of Brother Alexander Mack, Sr., who died as early as 1735, and of Alexander Mack, Jr., who lived to be very old and lived to see the present century [died in 1803], came as a present from the congregation of Germantown through Brother Philip Rothenberg into my hands in 1841.

Besides notations on family data by Mack, Jr., it contains several pages of barely legible manuscript notes by the father. Portions of these fragments were published by Henry Kurtz in his church periodical, *The Gospel Visitor* (1852).[4] Some of Mack's notes are given here.

The first operation of grace in the soul is a true awakening from the carefree slumber in sin and separation from God, and a recognition of our poverty and revelation of the divine life. Out of this arises in the soul the hunger and desire for help, sanctification, forgiveness of sins, and righteousness. Then grace shows how sanctification and forgiveness, indeed everything, can be received from Jesus alone. Then grace effects obedience to Jesus and, prior to this, the true faith out of which obedience issues.

. . . . .

The following passages demonstrate to us the kind of tongues of the old man of sin: Sirach, chapter 28; Psalms 5 and 140; James 3; Proverbs 18.

Now follow the passages which demonstrate the manner of new tongues of the newborn children and heirs of the kingdom: Proverbs, chapters 12 and 15; Song of Solomon 4; Isaiah 35 and 52; Acts 2, 10, and 19; Zephaniah 3:13; Revelation 14.

.　.　.　.　.

St. Dionysius was a bishop of Ascalon in the Holy Land, and at his time it was said that Clement asserted that the Lord Jesus had baptized the apostle Peter, and Peter had baptized James and John and Andrew, and these in turn had baptized all [the] apostles (page 755 in the book called "The First Temple of God in Christ").

.　.　.　.　.

It is Almighty God who created all nature, human beings as well as beasts, and when nature suffers want, God, its Creator, has mercy and comes to its assistance. Therefore David says that the Lord gives to the beast his food and to the young ravens which cry. Yes, in Psalm 104[:27] David says: "These all look to thee, to give them their food in due season. When thou givest to them, they gather it up; when thou openest thy hand, they are filled with good things. When thou hidest thy face, they are dismayed; when thou takest away their breath, they die and return to their dust." Oh, wonderful, eternal, and almighty Creator and Sustainer of all angels, men, and all creatures! Hallelujah!

.　.　.　.　.

In the Book of Concord of the Augsburg Confession, printed in 1580, page 221, there is said to be a reference to more than seven thousand Lutheran theologians who speak about immersion baptism as follows [in Dutch]: That they immerse us in the water which closes in above us, and then pull us out again; this immersing and pulling out again makes up the power of baptism. Also, Zwingli in his book written against the Catabaptists, page 17, states that the Zürich authorities ordered that whoever was or would be baptized by immersion was to be drowned by immersion. This was directed against the Anabaptists.

.　.　.　.　.

A scholar named Coccejus thoroughly discusses in his *Thesaurus Catolica,* volume 2, book 5, article 16, that no other baptism was generally practiced in the church from 100 A.D. until 1600 A.D. than immersion baptism. He proves this in every century from the writings of learnéd authors who have written on baptism, that thus sprinkling, also of children, did not become completely predominant before the year 1600, even though it had already begun with Luther. However, Luther himself wrote sharply against this [practice]. Indeed, in the entire Russian empire to this day they still baptize children by immersion and consider sprinkling not a valid form of baptism because they belong to the Greek [Orthodox] Church.

.   .   .   .   .

The learnéd astronomers write that the sun is 166 times larger than the entire earth and that the sun is 187,000 miles in distance above the earth and that the planet Mercury is twenty-two times larger than the earth and is seven thousand miles in distance above the earth. The planet Jupiter is ninety-five times larger than the earth and is many thousands of miles in distance above the earth. Oh, what a wonderfully great and incomprehensible Creator must He be who has created and sustained such creations!

God has thus placed man in this world as in a foreign garden, in which he is to live and eat of all its fruits, but he is not allowed to take anything away with him. Rather, he must leave everything in the world just as God commanded in the law in the book of Deuteronomy, chapter 23[:24]: "When you go into your neighbor's vineyard, you may eat your fill of grapes, as many as you wish, but you shall not put any in your vessel" to carry out. It is the same with the riches of this world, with eating, drinking and clothing. But when man wants or has to leave [the world] again, he is not allowed to take anything along even if he had been a king. That is why Jesus teaches the renunciation of the riches of this world, even of one's life. Has it not been very wonderfully and wisely ordained by God that men have the best things in common such as life and body? Now Jesus says that life is more than eating and the body is more than clothing. Thus the wealthiest people in this world have a small advantage only in the lowliest things, such as in food and clothing.[5]

BRETHREN ANSWER TO A QUAKER TREATISE

In 1747 the Society of Friends had Christopher Sauer I print a German translation of a booklet written by the Quaker Benjamin Holmes. The writing, entitled *A Serious Call in Christian Love,* was first printed in

London in 1725, and had been translated in 1744. It is thought that one purpose of the publication was to spread Quaker beliefs among the growing population of German-speaking residents in Pennsylvania.[6]

Because Holmes criticized in the book those who considered outward baptism important, emphasized the operation of the Holy Spirit according to Quaker fashion, and seemed to interpret the Scriptures incorrectly, it was felt by the Brethren that a response was indicated. One of their number penned the same year a brief reply, calling it *A Humble Gleam;* this was also printed by Sauer. Vernard Eller suggests that Alexander Mack, Jr., might have been the author. Although he had but shortly before returned from his sojourn in the wilderness with the Eckerlins, which would speak against his authorship, Mack had reestablished himself in the Germantown congregation sufficiently that by 1748 he was called to the ministry. Another scholar suggests that John Adam Gruber wrote it, but this is unlikely.[7]

Both the Holmes writing and the Brethren response were taken to task by a separatist writing published by the Sauer press a year later. Here it is conjectured by Eller that Sauer I himself was the author. The viewpoints expressed in the third booklet do coincide with the known religious posture of the Germantown printer, but it is impossible to say with certainty who actually wrote either of the two later tracts.[8]

A Humble Gleam of the Despised Little Light of the Truth which is in Christ; illuminating several reasons, which have recently come to light afresh in a small tract called *A Serious Call in Christian Love to all People,* etc. And in order that the reader of that tract might read it with even greater benefit, here in this *Humble Gleam* a scriptural witness on three points is submitted to him: I. On the Holy Scriptures; II. On the True Conversion; III. On the Baptism of Christ. Published by a lover of the truth, with the approval and at the cost of the Brotherhood which bears this witness. 1 John 4:1: "Beloved, do not believe every spirit," etc. Germantown, [Christopher Sauer], printed in the year 1747.

1 Corinthians 1:20: "Where is the wise man? Where is the scribe? Where is the debater of this age? Has not God made foolish the wisdom of the world?" 1 Corinthians 1:23: " . . . but we preach Christ crucified, a stumbling block to Jews and folly to Gentiles. . . . "

Preface

That a little tract has appeared under the title: *A Serious Call in Christian Love to all People, to Turn to the Spirit of Christ in Them,* etc. (along with some observations on seven points which are listed in the title of the same booklet) was first of all reason to rejoice over an intention which wishes that all people might be converted. Secondly, in reading through this booklet many beautiful and glorious scriptural passages were found which could be contemplated with great benefit, especially if the reader took enough trouble to look these up in the Holy Scriptures, where they are all in their proper context, so that every well-disposed, sincere soul can easily find the correct meaning from what precedes and follows.

Also it has been thought necessary to remind somewhat — which can give an encouragement — to obey in the fear of the Lord the important Scripture verse which is in the title of the above-mentioned booklet, namely: "Test everything; hold fast to what is good" (1 Thessalonians 5:21).

The dear friends have undertaken to set forth their understanding and opinion on seven points. If it is really their concern that all people be converted to the spirit of Jesus Christ and be baptized by the same Holy Spirit, according to Joel 3:1, they cannot expect that their opinion be accepted without examination, but rather they will examine in Christian love the following three necessary reminders: I. *On the Holy Scriptures;* II. *On the True Conversion;* III. *On the Baptism of Christ.*

First, there is a brief exposition so that everyone can easily understand it. Next, the objections which the friends made against baptism in the above-mentioned booklet are dealt with.

That which reveals is light. One must read and consider in the fear of God, and examine the Scriptures to see if these things be true (Acts 17:11). May God, who abounds in mercy and does not wish that anyone be lost, but rather that all may come to the knowledge of the truth, add His blessing to this through Jesus Christ our Lord. Amen.

I. *On the Holy Scriptures*[9]

The Holy Scriptures is a letter of God which He has written to the human race through the operation of His Eternal Spirit, etc.

That which stands written in the New Testament is especially directed to all those who hope to become heirs of those blessings which are willed in the New Testament to the children of the new covenant. Whoever is one of those has reason to look upon the New

Testament as a letter written to him by the eternal God, and to prefer it by far to all other books, publications, letters, and opinions, and especially his own thoughts. Just as even among men every will is confirmed through the death of him who made it, in order that one might know that it is the very last will of the one who made it, and that later nothing may ever be changed (Hebrews 9:17); likewise Christ, through His death confirmed and sealed the New Testament.

Therefore the necessity of Christendom requires that all the words of Christ and His Spirit be so read, considered and believed, that they are taken in and accepted with such tears, sighs, and prayers crying to God with deeply contrite hearts that they shall all gradually change into the reader himself. This is so that the entire New Testament is written into the heart of the reader by the finger of God until the entire life of the reader becomes a living letter of God in which one can read all of the commandments of Jesus Christ (2 Corinthians 3:3). It is not nearly enough to consider the New Testament as a book which does contain truths although they do not concern us very much, or do not commit us to the carrying out of Christ's commandments.

II. *On the True Conversion*

The necessity of conversion, the way to conversion, as well as the benefit of true conversion — all these are thoroughly described in the above-mentioned letter of God. Let no one imagine that he is converted if he has neither love for the New Testament nor for the commandments of Jesus Christ established therein. He who is converted has indeed experienced that all the words of Jesus Christ are spirit and life. No beginning of true conversion occurs without the finger of God appearing and breaking the stubborn selfishness of man so that the words of God may penetrate the heart. Such a person loses all desire and boldness to pervert the Holy Scriptures and to interpret it according to his own opinion. Rather, he considers all of his knowledge to be simply idle foolishness and much less than unknowing ignorance. Such a person can cry out with Saul in fear and trembling: "Lord, what wilt thou that I do?" (Acts 9:6).

If someone wishes to know what he was answered, let him but continue to read as far as verse twenty. Such a person can, according to the nature of the circumstances, say together with the convinced Jews at Jerusalem: "Men and brethren, what shall we do?" (Acts

2:37). What they were answered is found in the following verse, namely, "Repent and be baptized every one of you in the name of Jesus Christ for the forgiveness of your sins; and you shall receive the gift of the Holy Spirit," etc. What do you think, dear friends? Was that not the Spirit of Jesus Christ which gave this answer through the apostle Peter to the men moved to conversion? Or if someone were to come to your meeting (congregation) and were to be moved and compelled by the Word to call out, "Men and brethren, what shall I do?" would you be able to give him the same answer?

Thus it is the beginning of a true conversion when a man does no longer know what he is to do, or when he can perhaps say with Zaccheus: "Behold, Lord, half of my goods I give to the poor; and if I have defrauded anyone of anything, I restore it fourfold" (Luke 19:8). Or with Cornelius: "I have fasted, I have prayed, and a man stood before me in bright apparel saying: 'Your prayer has been heard and your alms have been remembered before God. Send therefore to Joppa and have called,' etc. He will say to you when he comes, etc.: 'So I sent to you at once,' etc. Now therefore we are all here present in the sight of God, to hear all that you have been commanded by the Lord" (Acts 10). These verses can be looked up and considered word for word, since, for brevity's sake, not all of the words are given here.

Likewise, it is not meant that he who is not in the same circumstances should use these words. Rather, this much can be seen in both examples, that a beginner in a true conversion does not twist the meaning of the Scriptures nor is he concerned with advanced scholarship. Instead, he finds himself moved by repentance to change his life and conduct. He hungers and thirsts after righteousness, loves fasting and giving alms in secret, and continues in prayer until it comes before God. Finally, he is being prepared and made willing to hear everything that God commanded a poor sinner to be told. The complete death sentence will be pronounced upon all his works until he falls before the feet of God and cries from the bottom of his heart: "Lord, what wilt thou that I do?"

Now someone might say, however, that Cornelius boasted of his works. Notice, however, how diligently he listened to the words of God out of Peter's mouth, and consider especially the last verses of Peter's sermon, namely the forty-second and forty-third, which read thus: "And he commanded us to preach to the people, and to testify that he is the one ordained by God to be judge of the living and the dead. To him all the prophets bear witness that through his name, all who believe in him receive forgiveness of sins."

We will then realize that his good works notwithstanding, Cornelius stood in no righteousness of his own; rather, his soul was as it were crushed by the desire to receive forgiveness of sins in the name of Jesus. That is why, for his assurance, he received the seal of the inheritance of the saints in the light, that is the gift of the Holy Spirit before the water baptism. Therefore, Peter said in verse forty-seven: "Can anyone forbid water for baptizing these people who have received the Holy Spirit just as we have?" And in verse forty-eight he commanded them to be baptized in the name of the Lord. Thus it can be seen of what great importance in the work of conversion Peter considered baptism to be, so that he did not consider those who had been baptized in his presence with the Holy Spirit too holy to be again baptized with water. As it were, he says rather: They are well prepared for it. Or, if we and others have partaken of this blessing before we were baptized with the Holy Spirit, who will forbid them the water, with whom Jesus, the baptizer, has already made the beginning with the Holy Spirit?

What, however, would many of the conceited and wise of our time have said if they had been present? Would they not have burst out in alarm: "What kind of an astounding affair is this, that one should baptize with water men who have already received the Holy Spirit?"

In the above a true conversion has been described to some extent. Yet, the complete and perfect conversion consists mainly in this — that all the works of the devil in us are destroyed (1 John 3:8). Secondly, that we are completely cleansed by the blood of Jesus Christ from all sins and vices (1 John 1:19[9]), and made holy (Romans 1:4); and therefore reconciled with God (2 Corinthians 5:20). And thirdly, that we turn away from the world and from ourselves through repentance (Acts 20:21), and that through faith we come to God in Christ and become new creatures through the rebirth (John 3:3), as those who were created in Christ Jesus for good works (Ephesians 2:10). So that consequently it can be said of a totally converted person: "The old has passed away, behold, the new has come!" (2 Corinthians 5:17).

III. *On the Baptism of Christ*

The baptism of Christ is exactly the same with which Christ our Lord was baptized. This baptism had its beginning in the Jordan and was completed on the hill of Golgotha on the cross. That is, His body was baptized with water by John in the Jordan; His Spirit was baptized even at the same hour by His heavenly father with the Holy Spirit, who descended upon Him from heaven in the form of a dove and rested upon Him (Matthew 3:16). His soul, however, was baptized with suffering, pain, and sorrow unto death (Matthew 26:38) in which baptism of suffering He finally poured out all His blood (John 19:34). We therefore can say: We believe in no other Christ than Him who himself was baptized with water and with spirit and with blood. These are the three witnesses on earth, the spirit and the water and the blood, of which John speaks in his first epistle in the fifth chapter in the eighth verse: "And these three agree." Furthermore, he says, verse nine: "If we receive the testimony of men, the testimony of God is greater; for this is the testimony of God that he has borne witness to his Son. He who believes in the Son of God will receive such testimony from him, etc."

You see, dear friends, whoever has such a witness with him has the one baptism of which Paul writes to the Ephesians (4:5). Just as there is but one Lord who was baptized with water by John in the Jordan (Matthew 3:16) and who baptized with the Holy Spirit (Acts 2:2-3) and cried out on the cross: "My God, my God, why hast thou forsaken me?" (Matthew 27:46), so also the baptism of the water and the baptism of the spirit and the baptism of the blood are but one and the same baptism, especially when they are together as John says in his first epistle (5:8). Likewise, spirit, soul, and body make only one man, so that even in a living person none can be without the other. Even if one saw the spirit of a man without his body, one would at least have to have certain characteristics before one could believe that it was really he.

In the same manner, if someone claims to have the spirit of Jesus Christ and yet is not reminded by Him (John 14:26) of all that Jesus said and commanded in the days when He had lowered himself to us, one is not required to believe such a spirit. That, however, suffering in Christ may also justly be called a baptism, is taught by Christ himself when He says: "I came to cast fire upon the earth; and would that it were already kindled! I have a baptism to be baptized with; and how I am constrained until it is accomplished!" (Luke 12:49-50). He also spoke of this to His disciples (Matthew 20:23): "You shall be baptized with the baptism of which I shall be baptized." The disciples of Christ were baptized with this threefold and yet single baptism of Christ just as their Master had been baptized with it. They were baptized with water as their dear Lord and Master made them disciples (John 3:26; 4:1).

They were baptized with the Holy Spirit at Pentecost after the ascension of Christ (Acts 2:2-4). As to how the baptism of suffering or blood was fulfilled upon the disciples of Jesus, this Paul taught us in the fourth chapter [of the first epistle] to the Corinthians, verse nine, when he says: "For I think that God has exhibited us apostles as last of all, like men sentenced to death; because we have become a spectacle to the world, to angels and to men," etc. Still more clearly, however, and more universally he explains this in 2 Corinthians 4:10-11 when he says: "And always carrying in the body the death of Jesus, so that the life of Jesus may also be manifested in our bodies. For while we live we are always being given up to death for Jesus' sake, so that the life of Jesus may be manifested in our mortal flesh."

The baptism of blood and suffering was fulfilled in many of the early Christians through the shedding of their blood; those, however, who did not achieve the outward crown of martyrdom yet carried about with them the death of Jesus in their bodies and thus had shared the baptism of blood through an inward martyrdom by the crucifixion of their desires (Galatians 5:24).

(There now follows a discussion of those objections which the dear friends have made in their booklet against baptism in water.)

The first of these is that Simon the magician was also baptized and despite this was found in the bond of iniquity and the gall of bitterness even after his baptism. Answer: Simon the magician did not achieve the essence of the outward water-baptism because he did not become subject to the righteousness which has validity before God; rather, he remained bound in his own iniquity, for his heart was not upright before God and he had not repented ([Acts] 8:21-22). Whoever, therefore, even up to the present day, has not repented because his heart is not upright before God in that he harbors perverted designs and still has himself baptized, he does this to his own judgment just as did Simon the magician and many others. However, he who would be baptized out of love to Christ and His commandment, let him hear what John writes in his third epistle, verse eleven: "Beloved, do not imitate evil but imitate good."

Christ was indeed baptized himself. Therefore it is not necessary to imitate the magician for he was wicked, but, rather, one need only imitate Christ, like a sheep the good and faithful shepherd (John 10:27), who said at His baptism: "For it is fitting for us to fulfill all righteousness" [Matthew 3:15]. Let no one be afraid of baptism because Simon the magician was also baptized. Otherwise one would have to be afraid of believing that there is only one God for "even the demons believe — and shudder" (James 2:19).

The second objection is taken from the statement of Peter in his first epistle (5:20-21), where he testifies that in baptism it is not the removal of dirt from the body which saves us but the covenant of a good conscience with God. This by no means contradicts baptism in water, but, rather, as can be seen from many places in the New Testament, the first Christians made the covenant of their good conscience with God in the water. It likewise becomes very evident from this [above verse of] scripture. Secondly, one need only read these verses to realize that here Peter could not possibly have meant the baptism of spirit without the baptism of water, for the Flood is far more a prefiguration of the baptism of water than of the baptism of the spirit. The Flood has special significance in respect to the death and burying of the old creature, which significance is reflected in the baptism in water of which Paul so beautifully writes in Romans 6. This does not save us, as Peter says, but rather the covenant of a good conscience with God saves us, and that only in the resurrection of Jesus Christ. That is, we are not only buried with Christ by the baptism but are also resurrected with him and walk in a new life; then are we saved (Romans 6:4).

Of course, this does not happen by cleansing the body of dirt, just as the Jews with their many baptisms achieved merely bodily cleanness. Rather, one is saved through the covenant of a good conscience with God which was made in the water.

The third objection is taken from the commandment itself (Matthew 28:19), where it is asked whether there is not just as good reason to believe that if our dear Savior had wanted them to baptize with water He would have expressly made reference to it. Answer: That was completely unnecessary. He only needed to say: "Baptize them," and they already knew what was meant. [This means] that they had already baptized more with water and had seen it done as can be seen in John 4[:1-2]. There would be more reason to say that if He had wanted them to baptize with the Holy Spirit, it would have been necessary to give an express reference to that. For that would have been something new, inasmuch as they themselves had not really been baptized with the Holy Spirit by the time they received the commandment (Luke 24:29), and yet the commandment mentions the Holy Spirit as little as the water. If we really wish to know what the Master commanded them, we need only refer to the New Testament to see what they did. Since they were so faithful that Christ was able to say: "He who hears you hears me" (Luke 10:16), likewise in this matter they did, or commanded to do, nothing that they were not commanded by Christ to do and to teach.

The fourth objection is taken from the words of Paul (1 Corinthians 1:14-17) where he says: "I am thankful that I baptized none of you except Crispus and Gaius; lest anyone should say that you were baptized in my name. (I did baptize also the household of Stephanus. Beyond that, I do not know whether I baptized anyone else.) For Christ did not send me to baptize but to preach the gospel." Answer: Christ was not sent to the lost sheep of the house of Israel only (Matthew 15:24) and nevertheless He was ordained to be the salvation of God until the ends of the earth (Isaiah 49:6). It was He upon whom the Gentiles were to hope (Matthew 12:21). I hope the friends will not deny that Christ was really sent into the world for the salvation of all men. Because He was first sent to the Jews and from there only to the Gentiles, He was able to say as long as His mission to the Jews was not completed: "I am only sent to the lost sheep of the house of Israel." When, however, His mission to the Jews was finished, it was directed specifically to the Gentiles. Therefore, Paul was sent to preach the gospel and in the preaching of the gospel baptism was included.

Where the people did not completely believe in the gospel, but rather were carnal, as were the Corinthians (where one called himself belonging to Paul, the second to Apollos, the third to Cephas, and the fourth to Christ), Paul could justly say: "Christ did not send me to baptize but to preach the gospel." However, where the people repented and believed in the gospel from their hearts, the gospel brought about baptism quite by itself. If anyone is under the delusion that Paul preached a different gospel, without a baptism, let him look up the scriptures which we will here indicate to him. First, Acts 18:8 reads: "Crispus, the ruler of the synagogue, believed in the Lord, together with all his household; and many of the Corinthians hearing Paul believed and were baptized." The very same gospel he preached to the jailer, Acts 16:30-33, for it is written in verse thirty-three that he was baptized in the very same night. Furthermore, it was this gospel which Paul preached that convinced Lydia so that she was baptized together with her entire household (Acts 16:13-15). The very thing that Paul was able to say of the institution of the Lord's Supper: "I received from the Lord what I also delivered unto you" (1 Corinthians 11:23), he could well have said about baptism. One need only read Acts 9:6-19 and Acts 22:16 to see that he [Ananias] to whom the voice of heaven had sent him [Paul], who in turn, had been sent by the Lord to him [Ananias] to preach baptism to him.

In summary, if one examines thoroughly all the verses of the New Testament one will not find that a single person became a believer with all his heart through the preaching of the gospel whom the apostles or Jesus Christ or otherwise disciples of Christ did not either baptize or command to be baptized. Therefore, even though it may not always be specifically stated that the apostles or other disciples preached baptism, yet the context of the narrative always shows that baptism was bound to the gospel just as the commandment of Jesus reads in Matthew 28. For example, Philip preached the gospel to the eunuch in the chariot and as they followed the road they came to some water and the eunuch said: " 'See, here is water! What is to prevent my being baptized?' And Philip said: 'If you believe with all your heart, you may.' And he replied: 'I believe that Jesus Christ is the Son of God.' And he commanded the chariot to stop, and they both went down into the water, Philip and the eunuch, and he baptized him" (Acts 8:35-38).

The fact that Paul thanked God that he had not baptized many of the carnal Corinthians does not make baptism insignificant; on the contrary, it witnesses to its noble character, for he says: "I thank God that I baptized none of *you* except Crispus and Gaius, etc." One must take notice of the word *you* and then one will realize that his speech had an aim. He did not thank God that he had not baptized many others in other places; rather, it says, of *you,* that is, among those who quarreled about the instruments [*Werkzeuge*] so that one said: "I belong to Paul;" the other, "I belong to Apollos," etc. (11-12). Therefore he also says in verse thirteen: "Is Christ divided? Was Paul crucified for you? Or were you baptized in the name of Paul?" Of course, Paul would have preferred to baptize no one by his own hand than to have Christ divided, in that the people clung to the instrument and might well have said: "Paul is the man on whom I depend, for he preached the gospel to me and also baptized me with his own hand." Therefore Paul himself ends the matter and says: " . . . lest anyone should say that you were baptized in my name" (verse 15).

It is true, Paul had emphatically preached the gospel with baptism at Corinth so that many Corinthians who heard it believed and were baptized (Acts 18:8). But because they did not wish to give Christ alone the glory, but, rather, in a sinful way quarreled over the instruments, Paul withdraws again from there and shows them Christ, the true Man, who was crucified for them and in whose name they were baptized. If one reads the eleventh and twelfth verses of the third chapter of the Acts of the Apostles, one will realize that Peter and John were also such men who did not wish that the people should look to them, as if they had made the lame man walk. That is why in the eighteenth verse [sixteenth] they expressly witness who was the Man who had performed the act and in whose name it had been done. For the apostles were faithful to Him who had sent them and always sought to give Him alone the glory, lest anyone be diverted from Christ and be led into carnal loyalties.

It is hoped that whoever considers this in the fear of the Lord will realize that the gospel which Paul preached included baptism just as was the case with the other apostles. Therefore if anyone preaches to us a gospel which does not include this, and, at the same time, tries to make us believe that Paul, too, preached such a gospel, we will gladly leave him uncorrected before his master, as a foreign servant. But he must not think ill of us if we are unable to believe anything without examination, especially when we read what Paul says in Galatians 1:8-9.

The fifth objection is taken from the baptism of the Holy Spirit, where the friends would like to prove that Christ sent His apostles to baptize with the Holy Spirit, and that especially with the words of Peter (Acts 11:15, 16): "As I began to speak," says Peter, "the Holy Spirit fell on them just as on us at the beginning. And I remembered the word of the Lord, how he said: 'John baptized with water, but you shall be baptized with the Holy Spirit.'" One needs only to look at the scripture and the meaning is clear. It does not say: "*You shall baptize with the Holy Spirit,*" but rather it says: "*You shall be baptized with the Holy Spirit.*" Likewise, Peter does not say: "I baptized the people with the Holy Spirit." Rather, he says: "The Holy Spirit fell on them just as on us at the beginning." Undoubtedly he means thereby the pouring out of the Holy Spirit at Pentecost which all those before whom he was justifying himself were able to remember. Who, then, was the baptizer when the time was fulfilled on the day of Pentecost, as they were all together in peace, [when] suddenly a roaring sound came from heaven like a mighty wind, and filled all the house where they were sitting? (Acts 2:1-2). Was it not the same who said to them: "And behold, I send the promise of my father upon you; but stay you in the city, until you are clothed with power from on high" (Luke 24:49). And in the same manner, Peter says, the Holy Spirit had fallen upon those who were gathered in the house of Cornelius. For this reason he could not have thought of a baptism which men can perform but, rather, he thought of the [event of] being baptized which Christ, the true baptizer, had promised them with the Holy Spirit as His own words expressly state.

Later, when He commanded them to baptize, He specifically mentions the water. However, if one is still determined to insist that Peter baptized them with the Holy Spirit because the Holy Spirit came upon them in his presence, then it would be just as fair to say that John the Baptist baptized Christ himself with the Holy Spirit, for after John had baptized Christ in the Jordan the heavens were opened and John saw the Spirit of God descending like a dove, and alighting upon Him (Matthew 3:16).

Yet I maintain that we would do better by simply believing what John says (John 1:33): "He who sent me to baptize with water said to me: 'He on whom you see the Spirit descend and remain, this is he who baptizes with the Holy Spirit.'" You see, dear friends, He is the same. (Note: He it is, and who will take it from Him, that

He should not remain so?) Exactly for this did He prophesy to His own that He would remain with them until the end of the world, so that He could do himself [those things] which surpass the strength which they received from Him but are yet part of preaching of the gospel (see John 14:13): "Whatever you ask in my name, I will do it. . . ." That which He says in the previous verse: "Truly, truly, I say to you, he who believes in me will also do the works that I do; and greater works than these he will do," He explains himself and says: "Because I go to the Father." That which Jesus did before His death His disciples did also. Of the Holy Spirit He himself says (John 16:7): "Nevertheless I tell you the truth: it is to your advantage that I go away, for if I do not go away, the Counselor will not come to you; but if I go, I will send him to you."

Here we see that Christ himself had first to be crucified, killed, and buried, and raised again from the dead and thus completely cast off His mortality, before He baptized His disciples with the Holy Spirit. The works of Christ, therefore, which He performed in the days of His flesh or humility on earth, were imitated by His disciples through faith; however, that which the Son of God performed before His advent in the flesh and after His ascension cannot be repeated by any man. That which the friends go on to say, namely, that one cannot prove infant baptism from the commandment in Matthew 28, is praiseworthy. For baptism is not meant for natural children but for repentant sinners.

In the sixth place, however, the friends compare the baptism of Christ to the circumcision of Christ performed in His infancy — as if one had as little reason to be baptized after the example of Christ as to be circumcised after His example — this justly merits astonishment about the fact that people who so pride themselves on the Spirit have not learned to make a better distinction. Have, perhaps, the dear friends never read what Christ says: "The law and the prophets were until John; since then the good news of the kingdom of God is preached . . . " (Luke 16:16)? One need only glance at this verse to understand readily that the circumcision of Christ which took place long before the preaching of John in the desert belongs to the prophecies of the law and the prophets; the baptism, however, of John belongs to the preaching of the gospel. Should this, however, not prove clear enough, they will perhaps be able to distinguish between commandment and prohibition [*Gebot und Verbot*]. For we read of the circumcision of the apostles in the fifteenth chapter of Acts that it seemed good to the Holy Spirit and the apostles not to lay this as a burden upon the Gentiles. (Read the chapter from the beginning as far as verse twenty-eight: also Galatians 5:2 as well.) Of the commandments of Christ, however, which occur in the preaching of the gospel, Christ himself says (Matthew 28:20): "Teaching them to observe all that I have commanded you."

The seventh objection the friends take from Matthew 3:11 and mean to say that John distinguished right there between the baptism of water and the baptism of the spirit. Such differentiation is, actually, partially true provided that one adheres to the intention which John had, namely, to humble himself and to glorify Christ. If, however, one deducts the opposite from it, and seeks to exalt oneself above Christ and all His apostles as if one no longer needed that to which Christ had subjected himself, and which His apostles did and taught in His name, then the scripture is indeed all too miserably perverted and it is necessary to look at it more closely and really contemplate it. To this end one must be sure to read the three verses together, namely ten through twelve; then the first and the last can very neatly explain the middle one. In verse ten he says: "Every tree therefore that does not bear good fruit is cut down and thrown into the fire." And in [verse] twelve he says: "His winnowing fork is in his hand and he will clear his threshing floor and gather his wheat into the granary, but the chaff he will burn with unquenchable fire."

Now let us consider the middle verse, which reads: "I baptize you with water for repentance, but he who is coming after me is mightier than I, whose sandals I am not worthy to carry; he will baptize you with the Holy Spirit and with fire." What is said here? Can anyone find a reason to read there another meaning than this, namely: I am a man and baptize you with water for repentance; He, however, who comes after me is God; He will baptize the repentant with the Holy Spirit and the unrepentant with fire, and that with the very fire into which the tree is thrown that does not bear good fruit (according to verse ten) which is the very fire in which the chaff is burned (according to verse twelve).

The eighth objection against the one baptism, according to Ephesians 4:5, has already been sufficiently discussed in our third point of reminder on the baptism of Christ. The further wish of our friends, namely, that all might come to the one baptism of which Paul writes (1 Corinthians 12:13; Galatians 3:27) is our wish too, but with this difference that just as the friends wish that men might be led past the water baptism and thus seek in every place to part them from the baptism of Christ, so we wish that men — through the obedience of faith which the apostles of Jesus Christ sought to establish among all Gentiles (Romans 1:5; 16:26) — might be saved from the wrath to come, that is, from the baptism of fire (Mark 9:47-48).

Furthermore, as to feetwashing, of this the friends wrote quite correctly that in consideration of John 13, from the first to the fourteenth verse, both example and commandment are found together. But they had better read also what Christ says in conclusion in the seventeenth verse, namely: "If you know these things, blessed are you if you do them." And then the fourteenth verse of chapter fifteen: "You are my friends if you do what I command you." You could thus examine yourselves whether you are of a mind to be proved Christ's friends. To the friends' further statement, namely, that they do not think that our Savior ever observed water baptism, we would only say this much in brief: Water baptism was very highly esteemed not only by Christ himself but also by the Holy Spirit and by the Eternal Father himself.

Inasmuch as the friends cannot accept this they must be shown the place where it is to be found, namely Matthew 3:16-17. "And when Jesus was baptized, he went up immediately from the water, and behold, the heavens were opened and John saw the Spirit of God descending like a dove, and alighting upon him; and lo, a voice from heaven, saying: 'This is my beloved Son, with whom I am well pleased.'" They may further look up Mark 1:10-11 and Luke 3:21-23 and they will find a threefold witness to this truth.

Further, since the friends themselves admit in their booklet, page forty-four, that they can find in respect to feetwashing both example and commandment, yet at the same time they are of the opinion that those who have attained the spiritual duty [feetwashing] which is there pointed out have achieved the ultimate [purpose] of the outward visible sign, one must confront them with a simple question, namely: Have all of your friends progressed farther than did Peter, to whom Christ said (John 13:8): "If I do not wash you, you have no part in me"? For

all of them say that feetwashing is not necessary. And if they have
truly progressed farther, upon what path did you lead them? You
have never washed their feet and, according to your own confession,
you would have had to wash their feet at least until they had attained
the spiritual duty, which is expressed by it, thereby progressing farther
than the disciples of Christ ever had when Christ, their Lord and
Master, washed their feet. Or have you perhaps never been willing to
humble yourselves so far as to wash your disciples' feet? Take care;
you might have climbed over the wall (of the commandments of Jesus
Christ, which in your eyes seem to be insignificant indeed) and seated
yourselves prematurely in the sanctuary. For Christ says: "I am the
door; if anyone enters by me, he will be saved," etc. (John 10:9).

Conclusion

After some objections have been briefly discussed, we turn again
to the matter itself, and wish to illuminate a bit the three points proposed in this little tract, yet in as short a compass as possible, lest anyone come to the conclusion that he is to be lectured to, which is ill
received in any case these days, where so many claim to have received
the Holy Spirit. On the other hand, very few can be found who possess
that wisdom which is welcomed, because one generally thinks much
less of one's neighbor than of oneself, which ought not to be so. Far
be it from us to impose our opinion on a single person; rather, it was
only our desire to witness in childlike simplicity to that which we are
being taught under the guidance of Jesus Christ, the initiator and ful-
filler of our faith in the days of our pilgrimage through real experience.
Otherwise, although we cannot deny that in regards to the things of
which we speak we have been taught by a real experience, we cannot
and will not pretend that our experience is higher than it is in itself.

We do not wish to call the beginning of the way of Christian
teaching the end, because possibly we have not yet reached its end.
Meanwhile no one can in truth deny that even this beginning experience ought to teach us more about the end of the way than our mere
imagination could, if one had never experienced the beginning of the
way. Therefore, we ask everyone who has not yet reached the beginning of a Christian life and conduct, through the true repentance
of the heart and conversion to God, for the sake of his own salvation
not to do violence with his merely carnal understanding of these
things which as a natural man he cannot understand, if one thing or

another seems absurd to him. Rather, he should faithfully ask God to grant him repentance, that he might be made free from all the bounds of error upon the paths of the true conversion through the eternal truth which is Christ himself, in a real knowledge of God and His Son Jesus Christ through experience. Then he will soon recognize that a very humble experience upon the path which is Christ himself is better than a grand imagination of the way which is Christ himself.

To those, however, who perhaps have progressed further in a real knowledge of God and His Son Jesus Christ through experience than the knowledge out of experience given to us has been able to instruct us so far, we wish to present this which we have written so far, and shall write in conclusion, to faithful examination in the fear of the Lord. For the Spirit of Jesus Christ is but one Spirit and creates unity, peace, and love among those who are filled with Him. He also gives to those who do not grieve Him grace that each can be instructed and advised by the other, and submit to one another in love. It is indeed of little importance to us that we are being judged as men who seek to preserve their salvation in outward things, and do not think highly of the essence of the things with which they are dealing, as long as our conscience witnesses to us that we are not of those who hope for the visible, but rather for the invisible.

To those, however, who perhaps in the sincerity of their hearts wish to demand the foundation of the hope that is within us, we herewith witness in all simplicity and sincerity of the spirit, before the countenance of Jesus Christ, the judge of the living and the dead.

In the first place, on the Holy Scriptures: even though we hold them in high respect and esteem for the sake of Him who gave them, and by whose spirit they were dictated so that we therefore recommend them to all people, whose salvation is dear to them, to read them diligently in all fear of the Lord, yet we do not believe that reading as well as not reading the Holy Scriptures will serve to the judgment of all those who are not converted to God with all their hearts.

In the second place, on the true conversion: even though we indeed firmly maintain out of love to Christ and His true words that no professor of Christ has a right to omit water baptism and to separate it from the work of conversion, still we do not consider water baptism alone the seal of the true conversion, [but] rather the gift of the Holy Spirit (Acts 2:36) which is the guarantee and seal of our inheritance

(Ephesians 1:13-14; 2 Corinthians 1:21-22). And if God had separated the baptism of water and spirit from each other, and had given us the choice of the one we wished, then we would not act wisely if we stretched out both our arms for the baptism of the Holy Spirit, neglecting the other. Especially even now when we realize with open eyes that the baptism of Christ was arranged by God himself, yet we are not baptized in water for the sake of the water but rather for the sake of the Holy Spirit, because we know that the Spirit of God, through which we seek to be baptized, has commanded the water baptism, and therefore does not disdain water as do those who boast of Him in vain. He would [otherwise] not have been seen so kindly upon the water on two different occasions. To be true, the first time at the work of the first creation the Spirit of God only hovered above the face of the waters (Genesis 1:2). The second time, at the work of the second creation, the Holy Spirit descended from heaven in the form of a dove to the water of the Jordan (Matthew 3:16) in order to bless the baptism of Christ begun in the water.

If, however, someone receives the water baptism and does not also receive a gift of the Holy Spirit, and is in addition very content with his unblessed water baptism, such a one is in a bad condition. Even where Spirit and water are together the water cannot bless the Spirit but the Spirit must bless the water. How then could the water replace the lack of the Spirit? This is impossible. Likewise, nowhere is it written that whoever is baptized in water is a child of God; rather, it says they who are driven by the Spirit of God are children of God. Since then so much, yes, as it were, everything, rests upon the baptism of the Holy Spirit, we admonish everyone who reads this (if he values his soul) not to deceive himself in this important matter by a foolish imagination, in that he thinks that he has already received the Holy Spirit even though it is evident that the opposite is the case with him.

When Jesus promised His disciples that He would send the Comforter, the Holy Spirit, He said: "He will . . . bring to your remembrance all that I have said to you" (John 14:26). Therefore, if someone receives a spirit which convinces him inwardly of being the promised Spirit of God that was promised in the prophecy of Joel, and it does not remind him of all that which Jesus of Nazareth taught His disciples seventeen hundred years ago, such a spirit quite obviously denies that Christ came into the flesh. For if the things which Jesus did and taught are not worth enough to be called to memory by the Spirit of God to the children of the new creation, then Jesus told His disciples an untruth when He said that the Spirit promised by God would remind those who received Him of everything that He had said to them. If then Jesus had spoken an untruth, He is not the Christ of God and therefore Christ has not yet come into the flesh. About such a spirit John witnesses: "It is not of God" (1 John 4:3).

For example: Jesus said ([Note] Matthew 6:19ff.): "Do not lay up for yourselves treasure on earth etc. . . . For where your treasure is, there will your heart be also." Therefore if someone receives a spirit which tells him inwardly that he could lay up treasures on earth, [because] his heart could still be apart from it and in heaven, then such a spirit obviously denies that Christ came into the flesh. For if Jesus did not know what He was saying, whether it was lies or the truth, then He was not the Christ of God.

After this one single test, each can now examine himself in all other matters of which Jesus spoke. To this end it is good and very beneficial to read diligently and to meditate upon the New Testament, so that one would at least learn whether one believes in Christ or not. For it is much better to consider oneself a still completely unbelieving and unconverted person, if one is actually such a one, than to pretend to oneself and foolishly to make believe that one has already received the Holy Spirit while one does not yet know and much less has experienced to what the Holy Spirit of God drives a man who is filled with it. Jesus came into the world for judgment so that those who are blind should see, and those who think that they see should become even more blind.

To the feet of Him, the true Shepherd of His lambs, this simple witness of His truth be laid and warmly recommended. May He work in us through His Spirit and in all His sheep that which can be pleasing before Him and His heavenly Father. Amen.[10]

THE DOCTRINAL TREATISE OF MICHAEL FRANTZ

One of the strong early leaders of the colonial Brethren in Pennsylvania was Michael Frantz (1687-1748).[11] Born in Switzerland, he settled in Lancaster County, not far from the site of the Ephrata Community. He was the leader of that part of the Conestoga congregation which remained loyal to the Brethren. In 1747 the Germantown congregation asked for his judgment on a problem of church polity.[12] More than twenty years after his death, some of his writing, in both prose and poetry, was published by the Sauer press in Germantown (1770).[13] A few pages were published in English translation in 1940-1941.[14] Because of the length of the publication, here is given only the prose section dealing with the outward and inward communion.

Simple Doctrinal Considerations and Brief Confession of Faith of the Pious Teacher, Michael Frantz, Late Elder of the Brethren Congregation in Conestoga. Now published for the general good. Germantown: Printed by Christopher Sau[e]r, 1770.

1 Corinthians 1:18, 21-23: "For the word of the cross is folly to those who are perishing, but to us who are being saved it is the power of God. . . . For since, in the wisdom of God, the world did not know God through wisdom, it pleased God through the folly of what we preach to save those who believe. For Jews demand signs and Greeks seek wisdom, but we preach Christ crucified, a stumbling block to Jews and folly to Gentiles."

Chapter 2:4-6: "And my speech and my message were not in plausible words of wisdom, but in demonstration of the Spirit and power, that your faith might not rest in the wisdom of men but in the power of God. Yet among the mature we do impart wisdom, although it is not a wisdom of this age nor of the rulers of this age, who are doomed to pass away."

[*Some thirty pages of poetry are omitted.*]

To the Congregation
On the inward communion with God

The communion of the believers is with the Father and with His Son Jesus Christ (1 John 1). The communion of the Father [is] with His children who are born of Him; [they] receive also from their heavenly father the heavenly inheritance and possessions, which they inherit through Jesus Christ if they also die with Him. In turn they return to the Father everything that they received from Him, and they keep nothing for themselves, and are as those who have nothing and yet possess everything (2 Corinthians 6). And as the Father has given them everything through Jesus Christ, they have everything if they are poor in spirit. All good gifts come from above, from the Father of the light, which they received from Him as His children of the light, and through the good gift from above. They also bring the Father spiritual fruits through the Holy Spirit. He gives them spiritual water from above and this turns into a wellspring of water in them which flows into eternal life (John 4).

That is the true living wellspring of faith, which is driven by the Holy Spirit and rising flows upward into the eternal life; this, then, is a wellspring of love from above, which returns to where the wellspring of love originates. They move upward who are driving the spiritual water upward. Receiving love out of a pure heart and a good conscience and sincere faith (1 Timothy 1) and also a broken heart overflowing with tears, and for this grace and comfort and through grace, they shine forth love and mercy through the divine brilliance of righteousness which they show toward the old creature, so that in return they receive again grace for such grace, love for love, and mercy for mercy (John 1).

That is communion with the Father and with His Son Jesus Christ, because the Father gave them the divine nature and the entire holy life of virtue of Jesus Christ, and because He gave them everything, they in turn give Him everything out of love, yes, their whole heart. If He comes and knocks on the door of their hearts, they open it for Him, and He will eat the [Lord's] Supper with them and they with Him. Oh, it is a truly pleasing communal Love Feast and Supper which such true, faithful, united bearers of the love-cross of Jesus will have, who are also united with Jesus in suffering and in the death of the entire old creature, and are resurrected with Christ and ascend with Him to Heaven. That is setting one's mind on that which is above — where Jesus is, sitting at the right hand of God.

Setting one's mind on things that are above (Colossians 3)

There is also a divine communion of believers when they eat and drink for the sake of their outward bodies. They have invited Jesus and remember Him, with thanksgiving and praising for His goodness, and in the same way they remain in the Lord in their outward life and conduct, in working, in waking and sleeping. Their thinking and speaking is in the Lord, and they then have communion with one another. They admonish, edify and stimulate one another together to cling to the Lord and to follow after Him to love Him from their whole hearts. They sing hymns of praise and thanksgiving to the Lord.

When they come together in the meetings they display among themselves a childlike, simple, humble reverence in order to appear before their great majestic king, Lord and God Sabaoth, and to be taught by Him and not by men. It is Christ who speaks through them; therefore it is not the word of man but rather the word of God. They also accept it as God's word and the Word grows in them as a seed sowed by God in a well prepared field of the heart. Because it is the same kind of seed, it therefore grows to the same knowledge of the Son of God to be one heart and one soul with one another because then they have one heart, soul and knowledge, and recognize together one evangelical foundation according to the truth. Thus one serves the other with the gift which he has received, they are subject one to the other in the fear of God, and hold fast to humility (1 Peter 4).

Thus they as living members of Jesus perform acts of service to one another according to the task of each member in proportion, and cause the body to grow for its own improvement and all of that in love (Ephesians 4). This is the way the members act: none despises the other, rather they bear with one another; they are altogether of a like mind, sympathetic, loving, brotherly, friendly, preferring one another in honor (2 Peter 3). If one member suffers, all the members suffer with him; if one member is honored, all rejoice with him (1 Corinthians 12 [26]). Such then are members of the head, Jesus, adhering [to Him], pure, holy members of Christ. Whoever despises, rejects, denies, or harms one of the least of these members, he does it all to the Lord as the Lord himself says (Matthew 25).

Therefore, the Lord will not have any prostitute members on His body, that is, in His congregation. If a member has an idol in his heart, he will be called a whoring member, be it covetousness of money or honor or worldly pleasures, or fleshly lusts, or anything that belongs to the realm of the prince of the world, all that does not belong among the community of the members of Christ. Therefore, if one of the pure members becomes impure, and does not purify himself again or will not let himself be purified, then such a member must be cut off with the sword of the divine word. To do this then causes the pure members of Christ great pain when a member must be cut off from the body. Thus the members of Christ do as they were taught by their Lord and Master. If they transgress and do not remain in the teachings of Christ, they have no God. If, however, they remain in the teachings of Christ, then they have both the Father and the Son (2 John). Therefore they remain constant in the teachings of the apostles and in communion and in the breaking of bread, and in prayer (Acts 2).

They are also called to keep steadfastly the harmony of the spirit, through the ties of peace, because they are one body. They have but one spirit, and likewise but one hope of their calling. Also they have but one Lord, one faith, one baptism, one God and Father of us all, who is above you all and through you all (Ephesians 4). And because the Father is above them all and through them all and in them all, with the smallest as well as the greatest, therefore each esteems the other higher than himself in humility (Philippians 2). They have one mind and one spirit among themselves, and everyone who is born of God is minded as was Jesus Christ (Philippians 2). And since they all have but one heavenly Father, they are all children of the same God, and are of one mind in the inward divine communion.

As long as they remain children of God, there is no partisanship among themselves, nor division nor scholarly disputes, but, rather, just as a man and a wife are not two but one flesh, the children born of God become one Spirit with Christ, for they are all baptized by one Spirit into the body (1 Corinthians 12). The children born of God are children of light, for God is a light; whoever says that he has communion with Him and walks in darkness is a liar (1 John 1). The children born of God are children of love, for God is love (1 John 4). God is holy and pure, therefore the children of God must be holy in all of their conduct (1 Peter 1). The children of God are unworldly children without money, greed and idols, unchastity, pride, anger and strife. In sum, the children of God, who have communion with God, are free of all vices and sins, and are no longer bound to anything if they have renounced all (Luke 14).

Therefore, the children of God have no communion with the darkness if they have communion with God. What is darkness? Just that, when the sun of love has lost its light, when mercy no longer shines, when humility, meekness, patience and forbearing toward one's brother no longer shine, that is already in part a great darkness. This does not come from God. That is why He will have nothing to do with it. For whatever does not come *from* God can likewise not come *to* God; therefore all good gifts and all perfect gifts come from above, from the father of light (James 1). Thus the Father gives His gifts to all His children together. He gives them of His love, pure love. In the same manner He gives them mercy and patience; the entire virtuous life of Jesus Christ He gives to them for nothing, and the dear children of the Father return it freely to the Father, without any coercion or pressure. Rather, they are obedient to Him in all things, and subject as obedient children, and that is called communion with the Father and with His Son Jesus Christ. Amen. That is the inward communion.

On the outward communion with God

Out of the inward communion is born the outward communion, for as the Father in heaven is merciful and perfect, so are His children (Matthew 5; Luke 6). The children of the heavenly Father have indeed a splendid portion and a great name, because they are called children of God (1 John 3), children of the heavenly Father (Matthew 6), children of the highest (Luke 6), children of the light (1 Thessalonians 5; James 1). Besides, they are not only children but they themselves have been made kings and priests by their high King, who is a King of Kings (Revelation 1). Also, this King of Kings and Lord of Lords, namely Jesus Christ, is the Lord and Master of all the children of God (John 13), their brother (John 20), their advocate (1 John 2), and reconciler, their wisdom, righteousness, salvation and redemption (1 Corinthians 1). In short, He has become everything for them that serves for a divine and blessed way of life, and for the praise of the great God in eternity. Amen.

Now because He has become everything to them, He has given them everything including himself, and since He has given them everything, they are minded as Jesus Christ was also (Philippians 2). And when they are so minded, they have become sharers of the divine nature (2 Peter 1). If they have Christ and the divine nature, which indeed all must have who wish to inherit the eternal life with Christ, they are merciful among each other, just as their heavenly Father is merciful (Luke 6). Furthermore, they are also compassionate, of like mind, brotherly, loving, friendly (1 Peter 3). If one member suffers, all members suffer with him; if one member is glorified, all rejoice with him (1 Corinthians 12). Whoever is a true member of Christ, he will be compelled by the love of Christ to do so and to walk as He walked (1 John 2).

Likewise [they do] as He commanded to reward where there is no hope for receiving in return (Luke 6). He who does not do this is no doer of the word (Matthew 6; Luke 6; James 1). Also, they are to give gladly, be united, be helpful, not be proud nor hopeful for uncertain wealth but for the living God (1 Timothy 6). Whoever does not do so is no doer of the word (James 1). They also love their neighbors as themselves, even if it be their enemies (Matthew 22; Luke 6). And whatever they wish that other people do to them, they do the same to them (Matthew 7). And whoever does not do this, he does not remain in the teachings of Christ, and he who does not remain in the doctrine of Christ, has no God (2 John, verse 9). And he who has no God is no member of Christ. When He has no union with His members he can be no member adhering to Christ. If he has the riches of this world, and sees his brother in need, yet closes his heart against him, how does God's love abide in him (1 John 3)? But there will be an unmerciful judgment upon him who did not show mercy and mercy triumphs over judgment (James 2).

If the inward communion with God has been truly realized, it will issue in outward communion as described above, with all kinds of virtues of love, for when the name of the word of congregation or communion is spoken in truth, then the words "mine" and "yours" must no longer be heard. That is to say [that] no one is to own or possess anything by himself any longer. To this extent "mine" and "yours" may be spoken on this basis, that this is mine and that is yours to administer and keep until a time of need for the poor and suffering in and outside of the congregation. To love one's neighbor as one's self shows clearly what communion is. Thus it behooves him who has two coats to give to him who has none, and he who has food, let him do the same (Luke 3). From this it is to be understood that he who has two portions, be it food or clothing, house, property, livestock, money or whatever his neighbor needs for his life's necessity, then love should compel him to give to his brother and to his neighbor and to do as he can for their need.

Love has no aim or measure as to how much one should give. Rather, it helps and gives gladly of its own volition as long as it has something and is able to help. Yet, whoever has two of something, whatever it may be, and gives one of the two to him who has none and needs one, he has done nothing more than did Zacchaeus, and what one is obliged to do (Luke 19). This is then called communion and loving your neighbor as yourself, [in] being so moved out of love to do as one is obliged to and as one is also obliged to give to him who asks (Luke 6).

But he who will not give to him who asks of him and who will not help in need, when he is indeed able to help, he will remain a debtor before God until he pays with love and mercy what he owes. Otherwise, he will be measured with the measure of harshness with which he measured (Luke 6). Therefore man is told what is good and what the Lord demands of you, namely to preserve God's word, to do justice, and to love kindness, and to walk humbly before your God (Micah 6[:8]). God demands back from us that which He has given us through Jesus Christ, namely, His whole gospel, to give it to Him with interest when He shall come on the great day of judgment. That which He demands of us through His word we are obliged to pay Him out of love and not by force.

The whole gospel is based on freedom, through the movement of the Spirit, for those whom the Spirit moves are God's children (Romans 8). Thus the Spirit of God moves to love, and love cannot help but move to loving, and love is the fulfilment of the law (Romans 13). Love is subject to love in love, and obedient in all things. God is love and whoever abides in love, he abides in God and God in him (1 John 4).

It is the manner and property of love to do everything gladly and voluntarily whatever love, i.e., God, has commanded. He who has love will be moved by love to help gladly in case of need as he can, to give gladly to him who asks, to give gladly to him who wishes to borrow from him, to lend gladly where there is no hope [of repayment], to love his enemy gladly, gladly to let him do injustice, gladly to feed his enemy if he is hungry and to give him drink if he is thirsty (Matthew 5; Luke 6; Romans 13). For as God demands all this of men, as mentioned above, then all those who are born out of the love of God will perform and pay their required duties here in this time of grace and free themselves completely, and owe nothing to anyone and only love one another (Romans 13).

Just as a wicked man can outwardly be reduced to great poverty and debts, and, if he will not pay or cannot pay, must expect to be thrown into prison by the power of the authorities and, if he cannot pay, be even sold; in the same way, if we do not pay our debts, namely, give alms which we owe, then we shall also be sold and shackled under the servile yoke of sins. Then we need not be so serious about the debts which we are to pay the poor in his need. He could be accused of being a frivolous or a lay or a wicked man. Yet Christ says that the heavenly Father is gracious to the ungrateful and wicked, therefore be merciful as your Father is merciful (Luke 6).

Even if it were possible that a brother or [a] sister could justly be accused of having run up — through his or her disorderly conduct and life — such debts, that is, outwardly, and he himself could not longer help him or her, then one ought to remove oneself in spirit from him but love ought not to grow weary of helping him. However, if a person will not work either out of laziness or impudence, he ought to eat his own bread as Paul says (2 Thessalonians 3). He also says there that he who will not work ought not to eat. This applies especially to those who teach a perverted doctrine or a false foundation and act with impudence, and claim that one need not work at all but live only by faith. To such ought to be commanded in the name of our Lord Jesus Christ that they work with a quiet manner and eat their own bread, and if they are not obedient, one should have nothing to do with them (2 Thessalonians 3).

Whoever will not work because of laziness and at the same time conducts himself frivolously and disorderly, runs up debts while realizing that he cannot repay them, and still promises to pay them at a certain time, which he is unable to keep, and if this is done without the knowledge and approval of the congregation and outside of the congregation, where he is to let his light shine but where, on the contrary, he represents a darkness and an offense, and makes debts in this way and is therefore impoverished, that is a great debt of sin before God and man.

As he has cheated others out of their money or possessions, and as he did not seek aid or counsel from the congregation, one can no longer treat such a person in a brotherly and intimate way according to the spiritual and inward communion because he was unfaithful to the outward community. Yet one ought not to turn darkness on him, but, rather, let the light shine upon him. If he is hungry, feed him; if thirsty, give him drink; if naked, clothe him, etc. If, however, he continues in dissolute worldly quarrel, then there is no obligation to him, to his unrighteous bonds, with which he has chained himself in sin and cannot help himself any more. Whoever loves the world and seeks only the world, let him be helped by the world. If he does not scorn or disdain the congregation, let him be admonished as a brother and not treated as an enemy (2 Thessalonians 3). If he accepts brotherly admonition, then one must show the brotherly love to him which he has need of.

The same applies to the entire congregation. Do not give more than needed, nor ask to receive, and let no one desire to receive but rather gladly give, because to give is more blessed than to receive (Acts of the Apostles 20). It is better to give alms than to lay up treasures of gold (Tobit 12). If it is taken from the poor box of the loving heart, then it can also be put into the holy poor box of heaven and be preserved unto the life eternal; but if it is kept in the pride box of the heart, then a treasure of the wrath of God will be gathered and preserved which will come upon the children of unbelief (Romans 2; Colossians 3). Therefore one should measure it with the omer of love so that it be fair, as Paul teaches about the children of Israel: he who gathers much has not abundance, and he who gathers little has no want (Exodus 16; 1 [2] Corinthians 8). For as long as there is abundance and want, there is no pure genuine communion, for communion equalizes everything with the measure of love and balance of love. As the Lord said to the children of Israel there is never to be any poor man among you, and the poor will never cease out of the land, and the poor will always be with you (Deuteronomy 15; John 12).

Thus the outward communion as well as the inner communion rests on the same love. Let each look not upon his profit but rather upon the profit of another, and let no one seek his own profit but rather the profit of another and each be minded as was Jesus Christ (Philippians 2; 1 Corinthians 10). He who will inherit with Jesus Christ must be minded as He was, live as He lived (1 John 2), love as He loved (John 14), become poor as He became for our sake, so that you should become rich through His poverty (2 Corinthians 8). Even though He was such a powerful King of all Kings and a Lord of all Lords (1 Timothy 1), who was so rich as no king in the whole world ever was even if he had thousands and thousands of worlds with all of their glory and splendor, our King Jesus Christ still left behind him an innumerable, and immeasurable and much more unfathomable glory, and [yet] became the poorest among all who are in heaven and on earth. Whoever wishes to follow him must also deny everything that he has; otherwise he cannot be His disciple (Luke 14). And he who cannot become poor if need be for the sake of his brother and neighbor" (Sirach 29[:10]), how will he give his life for Him, even unto death? For Christ our dear Savior gave His most precious life up into death for us, likewise we ought to lose our lives for our brothers. But he who sees his brother suffer want and need and does not help him according to his need, how then can he lose his life for him (1 John 3)?

The inner and outward communion exists in a brotherly warm compassion, cooperation, sharing what is needed. He who has received aid is to accept it with gratitude as given by God and show himself brotherly and harmoniously in return of love toward God and man. Wherever he can, he is to repay or otherwise serve with the gift which he has received, be it much or little, as long as it is done with a true heart. The giver ought to put it cheerfully into the poor box as if he gave it to God himself, and the needy ought to receive it as the love of God and fervently thank God for it.

The communion of the saints is of one heart and soul, if only they were all one body, one soul and one heart, because God wants such a community and no other (Acts 4:1; 1 Corinthians 12). Thus, in truth, there is but one God and Father, who makes out of the hearts of all believing children one heart, one soul, the same knowledge of the Son of God, the same evangelical foundations of faith. From this comes the same love, the same spiritual children, the same temporal fruits, which are still part of the inner communion.

If the foundations of faith are (communally) understood by all together and immediately practiced, then the inner and outward communion can exist. For this reason the bride of Christ is of the same mind as her dearest Bridegroom (Romans 12). He had earnestly and powerfully prayed for them, that they might all be one, even as "thou, Father, art in me, and I in thee, so that they may be one in us: I in them and thou in me, so that they may be perfectly in one" (John 17). For the same reason Paul admonishes us and says: "I appeal to you, brethren, by the name of our Lord Jesus Christ, that all of you agree and that there be no dissensions among you, but that you be united in the same mind and the same judgment" (1 Corinthians 1[:10]). "May

the God of steadfastness and comfort grant you to live in . . . harmony
with one another, in accord with Christ Jesus" (Romans 15[:5];
Philippians 1:2; 1 Peter 3). For if a congregation does not speak with
one voice, or the same language, it will be confused and will be called
Babel. Every kingdom which is disunited within itself will be laid
waste, etc. (Matthew 12).

The inner and outward communion cannot exist, then, if they are
not diligent to preserve unity in the spirit (Ephesians 4). [Each] must
also be diligent and united in working, so that he may have to share
with the needy. Let each one be minded to want to give and not to
want to receive, because to give is indeed more blessed than to receive
(Acts of the Apostles 20). For if each person prefers to give rather
than to receive, the poor as well as the rich, then there is union and
all is well and quite equal. Upon the love-balance all will be equal
and one.

The poor must not wish to become rich (1 Timothy 6) and the
rich [man], if he is rich in God, cannot remain rich in the world, for
he is forbidden to lay up treasures in his heart which are temporal.
Yes, all men are forbidden the laying up of treasures, as well as whoredom and idolatry. If the rich man loves God and His word and his
brethren and all mankind more than his property and money, he cannot remain rich. If he only has food and clothing then he should let
that be enough (1 Timothy 6). Therefore the rich and the poor shall
have but one heart, one soul, one spirit, one body and one love. Then
the inner and the outward will untiringly commune with each other.

Even if it were the case that outwardly one could not live together
but rather be quite scattered, one here, another there, yet pure love will
not be parted or scattered, but rather through the wind of the Spirit
blow the fire of love quickly to all places where there is need and do
everything together. And although one lives here and the other there,
if it cannot be otherwise and although one has much, the other little,
yet pure love calls nothing its own, nothing to leave to children or
children's children, or a treasure to leave to his relatives. Instead, he
lays it at the apostles' feet, for the apostles followed in the footsteps of
Jesus. Whoever wishes to be a disciple of Christ and the apostles must
not call his property and whatever he has his own. As part of the community he can indeed own it as far as is known. If I had three hundred
acres of land and much other property and money besides, I would be

able to be its steward or custodian until need became evident in the community. Then if the need demanded it, no more of the above would be mine but what were my necessities of life.

Who is thus minded, and acts in this manner, indeed lays it at the apostles' feet and therefore remains constant in the teaching of the apostles and in the communion and in the breaking of bread and in prayer. Then no one will say of his possessions that they are his, but at that point they hold all in common (Acts of the Apostles, chapters 2 and 4). This is our communion with the Father and with the Son Jesus Christ. Amen.[15]

THE WRITINGS OF ALEXANDER MACK, JR., ON DOCTRINAL ISSUES

As mentioned earlier, it was Alexander Mack, Jr. (1721-1803), who was the most active literary figure among the colonial Brethren. A previous chapter was devoted to his extensive personal correspondence. The following chapter will feature some of his many poems, virtually all of which were published both in the original German and in English prose translation by Samuel B. Heckman as *The Religious Poetry of Alexander Mack, Jr.* (1912).[16]

Here will be given in translation two of his more significant shorter doctrinal productions. The remaining part of the chapter will be taken up by his theological disputation with a Lutheran author.

An Exercise for Youth

This undated manuscript catechism is found in the Cassel Collection at Juniata College, Huntingdon, Pennsylvania, the repository for the important early Brethren documents. Abraham H. Cassel tentatively attributed its authorship to Alexander Mack, Sr., but the manuscript is in the younger Mack's handwriting. It seems more likely that he is the actual author.

In light of the Brethren involvement with Universalism (see chapter nine), the strong emphasis here upon punishment of sinners seems to strike a Calvinistic note. The Brethren held to the Biblical teaching of judgment, but at the same time would not deny the possibility of a universal restoration at some future date.

An Exercise for youth.

1st Question: What does the godless man lose when he is cast into the fiery pit?

Answer: Presumably, himself, his soul, his life and the good which he received disappears and that for which the godless hopes is lost.

2nd Question: What does the godless man find in the fiery pit which burns with fire and brimstone?

Answer: Presumably, the terrible judgment of the fury of fire, which will consume the adversaries (Hebrews 10:27).

3rd Question: What will seem terrible to him there?

Answer: Presumably, falling into the hands of the living God (Hebrews 10:31).

4th Question: Why will this be terrible for the godless man?

Answer: Because he has always fled from these hands, although he has received everything good from them. Yet they are the hands which have always threatened him with the unbearable wrath which God has promised in His word to sinners if they do not cease their scandalous flight. Now, however, they cling to Him as they are filled with flames of fire which take revenge on all those who do not honor God and who are not obedient to the gospel of His Son.

5th Question: Will the sinner even there find God, whom he has always denied with all of his evil works?

Answer: Presumably, yes, because God is everywhere present.

6th Question: What of God is it that the sinner will find there?

Answer: Presumably, the devouring fire and the everlasting burnings (Isaiah 33:34).

7th Question: What will the devouring fire there consume?

Answer: Presumably, the tree that does not bear good fruit and all sinful chaff (Matthew 3:10-12).

8th Question: What then might the worm be like that does not die there according to the testimony of the judge of all the world (Mark 9:44ff.)?

Answer: Presumably, the immortal spirit will probably seek Death there, with whom he voluntarily made a covenant, but he [Death] will flee from him from eternity to eternity.

9th Question: How long might Death flee?

Answer: Until the word of the Eternal, One and Almighty God

has become his ultimate poison, so that he is completely swallowed up in the victory (Isaiah 25:8).

10th Question: What is the cry of triumph for this victory?

Answer: Presumably, "Death, where is thy sting? Hell, where is thy victory?"

11th Question: To whom belongs the honor? And whose is the unspeakable joy of the eternal triumph over all His enemies, of whom it is testified that Death will be the last?

Answer: God and the Lamb!

12th Question: Do not the Scriptures say that God is love? How then can He hate or how can He be angry? Or how can He do any of the things that are written in the Bible?

Answer: God is indeed love: and out of pure and genuine love He certainly made and created all things. But because He is what He is, and desires for His creation all that is best, all that is blessed, and all that is joy, it is likewise entirely impossible that a single one of His creatures could make himself independent of God. Therefore Christ says: "And this is eternal life, that they know thee the only true God, and Jesus Christ whom thou hast sent" (John 17:3).

13th Question: Will then the only good God ever fulfill all the punishments that are in the Bible?

Answer: Everything will finally be so accurately fulfilled with the devil and his angels and the true children of the devil that it will be said that not one thing is lacking, everything has been done.

14th Question: Where does God, who is love, keep His wrath with which He can fulfill such terrible things?

Answer: Presumably, with Him it is sealed up in His treasures (Deuteronomy 32:34-35).

15th Question: Why does God threaten so long and [still] demonstrate His love to us?

Answer: Because He is patient with us and does not wish for anyone to be lost.

16th Question: Why then do still so many become lost?

Answer: Because they do not believe that God can be that angry and do not fear such wrath, according to Psalm 90:11.

17th Question: But what kind of fear is it about which John speaks: "There is no fear in love . . . " (I John 4:18)?

Answer: Presumably, it is that fear which arises from unbelief and distrust of God: one doubts if God will ever fulfill His promise to His people. Or whether He will even give His servants the promised wages, or justly distribute the promised glorious inheritance among His children. Therefore, one secretly hopes that He would also fail to fulfill His threats. This kind of fear has "pain" and leaves people mired in their sins.

18th Question: What then is the fear of the Lord which is so praised in the Holy Scriptures? And what are its fruits?

Answer: It is the beginning of wisdom. It wards off all sins! It also helps to get out of sin; and leads the sinner so to God that He must have mercy upon him as upon a beloved child. As David said: "I am in great distress; let us fall into the hand of the Lord, for his mercy is great; but let me not fall into the hand of man" [2 Samuel 24:14]. Thus the fear of the Lord gave him light and insight so that he could say: "Lo, I have sinned . . . but these sheep, what have they done?" [2 Samuel 24:17]. Then the punishment came to an end, and a place was shown to him where he was to build the altar and offer sacrifice thereupon, so that the plague might cease completely and reconciliation be brought about.

19th Question: Do you perhaps have something more to say about this fear of the Lord?

Answer: Yes.

20th Question: What is it then, or what else do you have to say?

Answer: First, everything that the prophet Isaiah wrote about in his eleventh chapter, especially in the second and third verses; and secondly, that which Jesus taught His disciples (Matthew 10:28); thirdly, what Peter writes in his first epistle, 1:17; and finally, the sermon of the angel who was responsible to proclaim the eternal gospel to those who dwell on earth, to all nations and tribes and tongues and peoples, and spoke with a loud voice: "Fear God and give Him glory, for the hour of his judgment has come; and worship him who made heaven and earth, the sea and the fountains of water" [Revelation 14:6-7]. Also let us not despise the warning spoken by Paul, the apostle of the Gentiles, in Romans eleven, namely in the twentieth verse: " . . . you stand fast only through faith. So do not become proud, but stand in awe."

21st Question: Inasmuch as Christ has died for us, who overcame the devil and death and the world through His own blood, death and resurrection, and who has taken for himself the keys to Hell — why must we still fear defeated enemies?

Answer: Do not be mistaken. God is not mocked. What a man sows, so shall he reap. Whosoever sows carnally will be ruined in the flesh.

22nd Question: By what then can one test the Spirit which teaches us the fear of the Lord in the New Covenant? And, how can one know that it is the consoling comforter which Jesus promised to His disciples?

Answer: The Spirit of Jesus does not teach us to be afraid of defeated enemies. On the contrary, it confirms for us the great joy of the victory which the gospel has proclaimed to us, namely, that our heavenly David has defeated the satanic Goliath. He proclaims to us also that all Philistines will flee before us because Immanuel is our ally! But he also reminds us through the words of Christ that we are not to fear defeated enemies, but rather the unconquerable Friend, and therefore we must not free the man banned in the death of Christ, namely the old Adam who was buried through baptism, from his grave, nor call him our brother again, as King Ahab did, when he shared the joy of the glorious victory with Benhadad the outcast. Instead, like the children of Israel, we must pursue the fleeing enemy and not make any alliance with them even though their champion was dead. [The manuscript breaks off here.][17]

A Letter Concerning Feetwashing

As an appendix to the 1774 (second) edition of the writings of Alexander Mack, Sr., *Rights and Ordinances* and *Basic Questions,* there was printed an open letter by Mack, Jr., on the subject of feetwashing.[18] More interesting than the information this provides on that particular ordinance are the principles of Scriptural interpretation and the insight into ways of solving problems revealed in it.[19]

These might be summed up in these phrases. First, the Brethren were concerned to remain open to new revelations of God's truth communicated through the agency of the Holy Spirit. Second, such revelation would of necessity be in harmony with the Scripture. Third, the agreement of the Brotherhood would be brought into play in establishing new understandings. The early Brethren, therefore, were characterized by openness to new insights, devotion to the Bible, and consensus among the community of believers.

The letter was first translated in the Kurtz-Quinter edition of 1860, often reprinted.[20] The following has been newly translated.

May grace and peace from God the Father through Jesus Christ increase in you all. Amen.

Beloved Brethren:

We have learned that some brethren have some difficulty concerning the feetwashing which Jesus commanded of His followers, as if this took place between the supper and the breaking of bread; they are of the opinion that it is not right to wash feet before the supper. Therefore I have been moved in my spirit out of simple love to write concerning the reason why we wash feet before the supper. At the same time I want to say this, that if a brother or some other person can in love and humility demonstrate by the word of the Lord something other than what is now done, we are willing to accept it, and not only on this point of the feetwashing but also in other things. Indeed, we do not intend to rest upon old practice but the word of the Lord alone is to be our rule and guideline.

First of all, we see how the ancient devout fathers practiced feetwashing after the Law (Genesis 18:4; 24:32; and 19:2). One sees here quite clearly that the devout fathers performed feetwashing before the meal. It can be seen that under the Law in the image worship Moses had to make a large laver and fill it with water, and Aaron and his sons, yes, the succeeding priests, had first to wash hands and feet when they were to serve in the Temple, as can be seen in Exodus 40:31-32. Indeed, one can see that under the Law feetwashing was customary, as is seen in First Samuel in the twenty-fifth chapter, forty-first verse.

At the time of the Lord Jesus, when he himself preached the gospel, feetwashing was still a customary practice when friends wished to render a service of love to one another. This custom was always practiced before the meal, as may be seen in the Gospel According to Luke, 7:44. In that instance, Jesus chided the Pharisee during the meal that when He had come into his house he had not offered Him any water for washing His feet.

Now, to come to the matter itself, one realizes, in the first place, that when the feast of the Passover was approaching, the Lord Jesus sent two disciples, namely Peter and John (the very disciple who describes the feetwashing, John 13). He it was who was sent by the Lord Jesus to prepare the Passover lamb. According to the evangelist Luke (22:8) [14], when it was evening the Lord Jesus came with the disciples and sat down. The evangelists Mark (14:17) and Matthew (26:20) report the same. Now the other evangelists record nothing of the feetwashing, but the evangelist John describes it in chapter 13, according to the Greek text as Reitz, the Dutch translator, yes, and even Felbinger, rendered it.

In the second verse, John (who himself had prepared the supper) says: "When the supper was done . . . , " according to the Dutch. Felbinger puts it this way: "When the supper was over." Reitz expresses it even more clearly and adds "was prepared." Others translate it following the Greek, as it also reads in the Greek dictionary: "when the supper was made," or "when the supper had been brought about." The wording used by Luther, "after the supper," does not appear like this in the Greek. Rather, John writes thus (13:2): "when the supper was done," that is, "everything was ready," Jesus rose from the prepared supper, as is continued in verse four, "he rose from supper, and washed his disciples' feet." It further states that they also are to wash one another's feet in lowliness, humility, and love.

That Jesus sat down with the disciples after the feetwashing is recorded not only by John [who wrote] that he ate, as can clearly be seen in the twenty-sixth verse, where He dipped the morsel of the Passover lamb and gave it to Judas, but it is also recorded by the evangelist Matthew (26:23) that Jesus said: "He who is dipping his hand into the dish with me, he will betray me." Mark also writes (14:20): "He who is dipping in the dish with me." Here can be seen that when John writes "for whom I dip the morsel," it occurred during the eating of the Passover lamb. That the feet had already been washed can also be seen from John in the twenty-first verse: "Truly, truly, I say to you, one of you will betray me." Now at the time when Jesus said that, the feet had already been washed and Judas was still there.

Now referring again to Matthew 26:21 and Mark 14:18, the two evangelists testify that Jesus said this during the meal as they ate. Now the other evangelists say nothing about the feetwashing, whereas John writes nothing about the institution of the breaking of bread. Therefore the Scriptures must necessarily be read and understood with a spiritual eye of love and tranquility. Even if all the translators had written, as Luther did, "after the supper," one must properly understand it, "after the supper was done, or prepared." However, they make it very clear that Jesus, when the supper was ready (or made, or done, or prepared) rose from the prepared supper and when washing the feet washed also those of Judas. For as soon as Jesus continued and said during the meal, "One among you will betray me," there was no peace or stopping until Judas had left the room.

Now, three evangelists state that Jesus revealed the traitor Judas during the meal. The evangelist Luke, however, adds this statement at the end, after the breaking of bread, when he places it in 22:21 following the breaking of the bread: "But behold the hand of him who betrays me is with me on the table." Now this word, according to the other three evangelists, belongs not after the breaking of the bread but rather during the eating of the Passover lamb. For this, Judas was clean, according to the Law, of clean physical body, and therefore Jesus could wash his feet also, namely, before the supper. But if Jesus had wished to make a special preparation for the breaking of bread through feetwashing, and washed also the feet of Judas and broke bread even with the traitor Judas (whom Jesus indeed knew), then it would be permissible to offer and break the bread of fellowship with an open sinner.

That is to say, if one knew that a person had already announced to a gang of thieves or murderers that he was going to steal or murder that same evening, one could still, despite the knowledge of it, break bread with him in fellowship, because Jesus himself had done the same. However, this must be far from all true believers. Indeed, for my part, I would rather not break bread any more than [break it] with persons of that ilk. Now the blind scribes say that Judas broke the bread of fellowship with Jesus and stubbornly insist on the letter, because Luke states that Jesus said only after the breaking of bread: "The hand of my betrayer is with me over the table." They will not use the other evangelists on this point.

True lovers of wisdom must not be of such a mind. Rather, the true wisdom and its lovers must be so fashioned as James teaches (3:17) and says: "But the wisdom from above is first pure, then peaceable, gentle, open to reason." It is a common fact that when a person discerns some insight on his own and then pursues it according to his own will, he will not be open to reason. Man through his own wisdom disputes about the shell and forfeits the essence.

Therefore, dear brethren, let us all be wise, and especially in regard to feetwashing. Let us pay attention as to how one should be minded; in love and peace and humility we are to submit to one another. Indeed, Christ gave us no certain command as to when such should be done, whether before or after the meal, but He commanded that we should do it and also love one another. For Christ did not say that one should recognize His disciples by the feetwashing or the breaking of bread, but He said that by this shall every man know that you are my disciples, that you have love for one another. Oh, how Satan could mock us if we were to quarrel with one another about the time when the feet should be washed, and love would be destroyed — indeed, even the feetwashing and the breaking of bread would be completely abolished and peace destroyed. That would suit Satan just fine and the teachings of Jesus would be mocked by the other people.

Therefore, it is of the highest necessity that one compose oneself in love and peace, and think to oneself that one should pray to the dear God for more and more wisdom. I am able to write this in truth out of experience, namely, when we were in the beginning of our baptism, we washed one another's feet in blessing and in the awakening of love after the meal and after the breaking of bread. Later we saw more clearly and, with blessing, washed one another's feet after the meal and before the breaking of bread. Later, after Reitz had published his New Testament [translation], and a brother joined us who knew Greek and properly explained to us that Jesus washed the feet before supper, then we were humble and did it always before the meal. Now no brother will think ill of us if we do not wish to begin all over again, but, rather, until someone can advise us better no one will take it amiss if we do as we understand it.

Yet I say this, that if I came to a brotherhood which wished to have breaking of bread and the elders of that brotherhood did not acknowledge other than that the feetwashing should be after the supper, I would participate quite simply in love and peace and would nevertheless explain it to them according to the Scriptures. I would wait in love and have patience with them until they too gained this insight, for I am certain that when the matter is considered quite impartially and one remains in love and peace, it will be easy to realize and see that it is just as above demonstrated, that Jesus rose from the made or prepared supper and washed the feet of His disciples and then sat down and ate, and [that] during the meal Jesus revealed the betrayer, who then went out, and [that] only then did Jesus institute the breaking of bread. In this way the Scriptures harmonize.

The prefiguration of the devout fathers prior to the Law and under the Law coincide exactly. Therefore, one will be able to face God and man with a good, calm conscience. If, however, one were of the opinion that one ought to wash the feet only after the meal, I would not have the courage to claim this with an intelligent understanding of the Scriptures. It would be difficult for anyone to do, for if one considers only the two evangelists Matthew and Mark, both of them write, first Matthew 26:26: "Now as they were eating, Jesus took bread, and blessed, and broke it. . . ," and the evangelist Mark writes also (14:22): "And as they were eating, he took bread, and blessed . . . and said, 'Take, eat; this is my body.'" Now it is very obvious that no change had taken place between the eating of the Passover lamb and the breaking of bread, for if the feetwashing had taken place in between, they would certainly have recorded it. However, because it took place before the meal, they did not write about it but rather left it out. John, however, described it — the feetwashing — and, on the other hand, omitted the breaking of bread.

Therefore the Scriptures require spiritual eyes, mind, and understanding, for otherwise, through the letter, one would achieve but misery and division, if without true enlightenment one intended to cling to the letter in one place and act against and disregard it in another.

Therefore, dear brethren, let us watch and be careful, and above all preserve love, for thus one preserves light. The spirit of truth testifies in 1 John 2:10: "He who loves his brother abides in the light, and in him there is no cause for stumbling." The good God, who is the pure impartial love, can and will supply gradually where insight is lacking here or there. I now close and ask again all brethren to allow and to consider this in love with a calm spirit.

I am your weak brother,

Alexander Mack.[21]

THE APOLOGIA BY MACK, JR.

In 1788 Alexander Mack, Jr., published at Ephrata a seventy-one-page *Apologia or Scriptural Vindication* which has been called "undoubtedly the ablest defense of the doctrines of the church that appeared before the beginning of the nineteenth century." The fact that the Brotherhood bore the expense of printing indicates that Mack's views were "fully endorsed by that body as a sound exposition of her principles."[22]

The format of this disputation is unusual and somewhat complicated. A manuscript discussion upholding the correctness of infant baptism, set in dialogue form between a "Churchman" and an "Anabaptist," which had been written by a leading Lutheran theologian, came into Mack's hands. He considered this a challenge to Scriptural truth which needed rebuttal. The method he chose was to publish the manuscript, interpolating his own comments and arguments under the pen name *Theophilus.* The printing was done on the press of the Ephrata Community, which gave Peter Miller (1710-1786), the successor to Conrad Beissel as spiritual leader, the opportunity to add some of his own commentary in footnotes.

Though unnamed in the *Apologia,* the original author of the manuscript (who wrote the material of both the "Churchman" and the "Anabaptist") was the Reverend Dr. John Christopher Kunze (1744-1807). This Lutheran clergyman and professor had been educated at the Halle Orphanage and the University of Leipzig. He came to America in 1770 and married a daughter of Henry Melchior Muhlenberg the following year. In 1779 he became the head pastor of the Zion Lutheran congregation in Philadelphia, where he was also active in efforts, with varying degrees of success, at education in theology and German in connection with the University of Pennsylvania.

Five years later he moved to New York as pastor of the Lutheran Christ Church there, and became a professor of Oriental languages at Columbia College, although he failed to attract enough students to function as a teacher. His dream was the establishment of a high-quality seminary for the training, in America, of Lutheran pastors. The archives at Halle bulge with his many proposals and pleas for the support needed for such an undertaking. According to his biographer, "as a scholar Kunze had few equals in the United States, and in his own denomination his influence was second only to Muhlenberg's. . . . He had a minute knowledge of Greek, Latin, Hebrew, Arabic, and Italian literature. . . ."[23]

The writing used by Mack, "The Refuted Anabaptist," was, according to Kunze, an exercise he had composed as a young man. About 1782 he had loaned it to a friend who placed it into circulation. In 1781 Kunze had published a book entitled *Something Concerning the Correct Paths of Life*, in which he devoted more than seventy pages to a discussion of the correct understanding of baptism. In his words: "I write these proofs of the validity of infant baptism for the sake of my dear congregation. They have for some time now had numerous opportunities here near the city to observe adults being baptized by Anabaptists. Some of them find this attractive."[24]

The commentary added by Mack and by Peter Miller will be italicized for the sake of greater clarity.

Apologia, or Scriptural Vindication of Several Truths. Called Forth by a Recently Composed Writing Under the Name of "The Refuted Anabaptist," in a Dialogue Written for the Common Man. This entire dialogue is here communicated verbatim in these pages, and the apology as a vindication of the offended truths is added thereto by Theophilus. Ephrata, printed at the cost of the Brethren, in the year 1788.

. . . . .

The following pages are dedicated to the cornerstone laid in Zion, chosen, precious and well preserved — According to the guideline of eternal truth — For complete judgment of the faithful and truthful witness by the truth — Before whom no thing is invisible, but rather all things are laid bare and disclosed before his eyes, he it is of whom his poor speck of dust, Theophilus, speaks. "But in your hearts, reverence Christ as Lord. Always be prepared to make a defense to any one who calls you to account for the hope that is in you" (1 Peter 3:15).

. . . . .

Churchman: Now then, bring on everything you know against infant baptism, for I am convinced that it can be sufficiently proved and justified.

Theophilus: I feel compelled for sufficient reasons, as a soul who loves and honors God and His truth, to be the third man in this discussion so that everything may be based on the testimonies of two or three witnesses and so that the common man (for whom this work was composed) might recognize what truth is. I shall patiently listen to the arguments of the so-called Anabaptist and then to whatever defense the so-called Churchman will be pleased to make, and then I shall in modesty give my comments according to the truth.

Anabaptist: Good, let us make the trial. The Savior commanded us specifically in Matthew 28:19 first to teach and then to baptize; but how can this be done with children?

Churchman: The Savior does not say one syllable of all that. The cited scripture is incorrectly translated, and should read: "Make disciples of all nations, baptizing them." As a matter of fact this is quite obvious, for the Savior says in the following passage: "teaching them to observe all that I have commanded you." What is it that one should teach them first? Perhaps something which the Savior did not command, for He purposely uses two different words: first He says *"matheteysate"* — make disciples; but afterwards, *"didascontes"* — teaching them. Does He not indeed perhaps seek to prevent your opinion, which in any case could not be proved, even if the words in the German Bible were translated correctly, which they truly are not. The fact that a matter is named or mentioned first is far from being a proof that it existed or must be practiced first. Otherwise John would have first had to baptize rather than preach, but who will believe this? Indeed, even the infant Jesus would have had to be before Mary, His mother, because several times He takes precedence before her. In His existence as God, He was, of course, prior; however, how could He have been first a child? Indeed, God the Father would have to be before His eternal Son and Spirit, because in the Bible He is always named first.

But why should one talk of this at such length? Providence has refuted you long ago. It always allows the deaf and dumb, who are incapable of being taught, and who cannot be instructed in the teachings of Jesus in any manner, to be born. In the Old Testament such were cared for because they were circumcised in infancy. Is then the New less merciful? Are then these poor ones not to belong to the congregation of Jesus, to the people of God, who are cleansed through the water bath in the Word? Do they have less right than all others in Christ? Where do you find a command to exclude them? Once they have become adults it is impossible to be convinced by all of them that they are in communion with the Spirit of Jesus. But since the children of the Christians are promised this Spirit, who is to prevent the water from baptizing all infants? Lest one or the other poor creature be kept from and robbed of the grace of the holy baptism and the right of the firstborn inherent in it, Luther wrote in a certain instance to the king: "Crack this little nut for me, Hal of England." This is what we intend to say on this occasion to you, dear friends!

Theophilus: It seems that this discussion is to be begun with many harsh complaints and accusations, which are impossible to prove: for in the first place, all Baptist-minded [Taufsgesinnete] are accused who say, believe and teach; that Christ commanded in Matthew 29:19 first to teach and then to baptize. Of all of this, he [Churchman] says, the Savior did not say one syllable. Which is to say, the Baptist-minded are all gross and shameless liars. But how can this be proved? He says: the cited scripture is incorrectly translated. This, of course, makes a harsh accusation against Doctor Luther that he did such violence to this very important text and did such poor work that because of it many thousands have become liars in that they say of the dear Savior that one must first teach and then baptize, because He commanded this, whereas He did not say one syllable of it.

Yet, the One who bade Luther faithfully to translate the New Testament from the original language into our German mother tongue for the sake of the common man has also taken care lest his work be in vain, and awakened for him an entire cloud of witnesses, all of whom as brave men, out of love for the general benefit also translated the New Testament. What I have read of these, so far, in German, Dutch, French and English, all agree with Luther, namely that Christ in Matthew 28:19 placed the teaching before the baptism. However, it seems that he [Churchman] does not require of one thoroughly to investigate this grave main accusation, and therefore he points us to another direction and says that it is obvious, for the Savior speaks in the following [passage]: "Teaching them to observe all that I have commanded you."

What is it that one should teach them first? Perhaps something that He did not command? To whom is this mocking question direct-ed? Is it directed to Christ himself because He commanded to teach and to baptize all nations, and yet supposedly has not commanded what to teach them before the baptism? Or is it directed only to the

Baptist-minded who, according to Christ's commandment wish to teach first and then to baptize and yet are supposedly unable to discover what actually Christ commanded to teach before the baptism? Be this mocking question directed against Christ himself or against His disciples, I nevertheless find myself compelled to answer it thoroughly and honestly. It says in Luke 24:46-47 that Christ spoke to his disciples: "Thus it is written, that the Christ should suffer and on the third day rise from the dead, and that repentance and forgiveness of sins should be preached in his name to all nations, beginning in Jerusalem." This the apostles and faithful servants of Christ have always earnestly taught before baptism, and have even after baptism taught to observe and to keep it along with everything else that Christ had taught them, or what else He commanded them.

Now the friend here introduces to the common man two Greek words and explains how they are to be understood in our language, namely: that Christ first said "make disciples," and, afterwards "teaching them." Now if these words are translated correctly, which may be left to his own judgment, it does not at all detract from the opinion of the Baptist-minded — on the contrary, it supports it. For if Christ, who had given His holy apostles power to perform miracles, even to raise the dead, nevertheless gave them such a commandment that they are indeed to make disciples for Him, but to do this by teaching, what then is the origin of the new commandment to make disciples of those whom one cannot tell a single word about the teaching? Is it not true that it is written: "You shall not tempt the Lord your God" [Matthew 4:7]?

Further, it was said that the fact that something is named or mentioned first is far from being a proof that it also existed or is to be practiced first, for otherwise John would have first had to baptize before he preached. But who would believe this? Such an argument and such a conclusion in order to pervert the Holy Word of God on the holy baptism is better suited for a fool than for a reasonable man.

If an honest farmer were to say to his servant, "Today go and mow a little wheat and thresh it so that the children may have bread," and the servant went, took the flail and began to thresh before it were mowed, and a friend of the farmer passed by and said, "What are you doing there? Your master said that you should mow and thresh; but you are threshing it and who is to mow it then?" And if the servant answered, "The fact that some thing is mentioned first is far from being proof that it is also to be done first," would this make sense?

If this conclusion is not valid as regards the commandment of a mortal man, how much less valid must it be as regards the commandment of the Highest? What Luke 3:3 says of John: "And he went . . . preaching a baptism of repentance for the forgiveness of sins" makes sense. And Mark 1:4: "John was baptizing in the wilderness, preaching a baptism of repentance for the forgiveness of sins" also makes sense, for this is only a narration of that which happened. Nonetheless it is not completely without reason that in the narration, baptism in some measure precedes the preaching, for the repentance and the faith in Christ were to follow the baptism of John, whereas at the baptism of Christ the repentance and faith in Christ must precede, and then they are to baptize.

And that the child Jesus is several times set over His mother has likewise nothing irregular about it but, rather, shows the most beautiful correctness. The wise men came from the East and sought the child and found the child and His mother. It was the child whom they were seeking; therefore it is only correct that He is set over His mother. If they had not found the child they would have been deceived. Thus even Herod, as an enemy of the child, sought the child, and as he did not find him, he was deceived. Therefore, it states [Matthew 2:14] that Joseph took the child and His mother to himself, etc.

What then, in consideration of holy baptism, are we to conclude in this matter? Perhaps in the end something more profound will be achieved if we consider it in the fear of the Lord. God asks for faith; He commanded all men to repent. Christ sends His disciples into all the world to preach repentance and forgiveness of sins in His name (Luke 24:47). And in Mark 16:15-16, He says: "Go into all the world and preach the gospel to the whole creation. He who believes and is baptized will be saved but he who does not believe will be condemned." What else is this than that God wants repentance and faith, and that He wishes to add baptism to it as a sign of the covenant and of the peace between God and man, or the repentant sinner? The world will have nothing to do with repentance and worries little about faith, but it does want to have some kind

*of baptism so that it might have the appearance of a congregation of
Jesus Christ cleansed in the water bath of the Word, wherewith it
can hold off all the disciples of Christ and preachers of repentance.*

*What will finally result from this affair? Who will be deceived,
God or the world? Whoever is at one with His God, repents, and is
baptized, to him God gives the gift of the Holy Spirit, as a certain
guarantee of the inheritance which is prepared for him in heaven.
But whoever does not repent and does not believe in the gospel, he
remains a child of this world and cannot receive the spirit of truth
and is therefore deceived.*

*It is curious that although in the Bible God the Father is al-
ways set over His eternal Son still He is also most criticized for it;
for, after all, all so-called Baptists [Täufer] on the entire earth acknowledge this in the baptismal ceremony and pronounce very deliberately: "You are baptized in the name of the Father and of the
Son and of the Holy Spirit." If they then recognize this order in the
ceremony to be correct, why not let the entire order of God take its
course? And let repentance and faith come before the baptism; that
would be correct!*

*As far as the deaf and the dumb are concerned, who, as you say,
cannot be instructed in the teaching of Christ in any manner, the
Baptist-minded would be well advised to believe in the words of their
Master, who said: "That which is impossible with men is not impossible with God." And whenever and whoever God commanded to
baptize one must be obedient. But whoever is not commanded [to do
it] and still does it, he is meddling and unable to help either the
deaf and the dumb or himself. Otherwise one might in all humility
and love assume that even though the word cannot be discerned in
their mouths and ears, it may yet after God's purpose still be in their
hearts. And even though the faith cannot be directly shown to them,
still it can be shown to them inwardly and indirectly (because, as the
Scriptures say, it is shown to all mankind). If they believe in their
hearts, they will be justified. But to insist on guiding men directly,
whom the hand of eternal Providence has intended to guide indirectly,
seems to me to be meddling, if not tempting God, which is forbidden.*

Anabaptist: One should not consult so much with reason. I must
reject infant baptism until you can give me examples of baptized chil-

dren or a command for it. But where does it say so? On which page am I to find it?

Churchman: Certainly in more places than there are examples or commandments for administering the Last Supper to women. The one has at least as many and just as good reasons as does the other. Otherwise, I have long since noticed that your doctrines shy away from reason, and cannot stand critical investigation.

Theophilus 2: The question whether the sisters should also participate in the Communion or not was answered perfectly by Jesus himself, the faithful and truthful Witness himself, in Matthew 28:20. There He commanded, with all the power that was given Him, His disciples to teach (those to whom they had preached repentance and forgiveness of sins, according to Luke 24:47, and whom they thereupon, after they had believed, baptized, according to Mark 16:16, and of whom by teaching and baptizing they had made disciples) all things which He had commanded them. And upon giving this commandment He then testified and said to them: "And lo, I am with you always, to the close of the age." Therefore faithful disciples of Christ had no doubts whether faithful sisters of Christ (who together with them wished to do the will of the heavenly Father) should be admitted to the Last Supper or not. For they had preached to them the gospel of Christ and had baptized them (Acts 16:14-15). And now they were commanded to teach them to keep not only several things according to their own wishes, but rather all things, that is, all that He had commanded them. If an equally solid basis could ever be given for infant baptism, as this reason shown by Christ himself for the partaking of the Supper by the sisters, then the Baptist-minded would soon change their minds.

Anabaptist: Those may well be fine reasons; but how can a child be baptized with benefit and blessing when it knows nothing of the entire service?

Churchman: What does it know about the blood of Jesus? Just as much as about baptism. But is it not beneficial to him [just] because he knows nothing of it? [If not,] then the sun be darkened when a child dies!

Theophilus 3: That the blood of Jesus benefits children even before they know anything about it is a precious and dear word. For, since

Jesus Christ came into the world to save sinners, children could not possibly be excluded. For if He saves those who have actually committed sins if they repent them, should He not wish to save those who are only sinners by birth and have not yet committed any real sins? I say, could it be that He did not want or was not able to save them? Far from it! However, that such children, whom God in His wise counsel decided to take to himself out of this evil world into His heavenly Kingdom in their state of innocence, do not know any more of the blood of Jesus than of a weak action, which is practiced upon them according to man's own opinion without God's commandment, this will convince no lover of Jesus.

Anabaptist: Children are in a state of such uncommon innocence that it is safest to leave them to God, and believe that they have no need of baptism.

Churchman: They are indeed innocent before men but not before God. "Before you," says the psalmist, "no living thing is righteous." Do the children not also belong to the living? If you deny this, I will count you as a brother of that Anabaptist who once insisted to me that children were not people but only creatures.

Theophilus 4: It is true that under certain circumstances it can sometimes be said that children are innocent before man but not before God. Especially when parents or friends look upon their own flesh and blood all too selfishly, they can sometimes justify even the small movements of the seed of the serpent and declare them innocent, to the encouragement of the same and to the great harm of their children. But that is no reason for assuming it of all children in general as a general truth. The true innocence of children in general is seen and recognized by God much better than by poor men. All innocence given or preserved in children is of God and for God. Although Jonah was a faithful prophet before God, he was a man, and hence he did not see the innocence of the children in the great city of Nineveh until God revealed it to him.

What should we say? Men do not readily see the innocence of children, but God sees it and even the small movements of the noble seed of the woman in the children are often hated and declared most guilty. How did it go with the dear Joseph in his innocence among men, wherein the noble seed of woman moved from his childhood on, and brought forth perfectly innocent words and deeds. Was not his innocence oppressed, accused, persecuted, and tormented until the Almighty placed his innocence on the candlestick? It was the same with David. Jeremiah was chosen a prophet in his mother's womb and also lived in innocence until an advanced old age. Yet he was almost continually accused by men. We would not do ill if we say that in the true innocence and for the sake of the one Mediator, Jesus Christ, children are innocent before God, but not before all men.

As regards the false innocence which the poor men see in their own flesh and blood, that is all guilt before God, for a "man looks on the outward appearance, but the Lord looks on the heart" (1 Samuel 16:7). However, the fact that despite this no living person is righteous before God, and that children as long as they live are also [to be counted] among the living, is beyond dispute. But if they die in that innocence which God gives them, they are, then, when they are dead, no longer among the living nor any longer unrighteous, but are made righteous through the blood of Christ. To insist that children are not persons seems to me quite unreasonable.

Anabaptist: Indeed, I do not wish to keep what little understanding I have captured to that extent. Yet, to return to the previous statement, baptism is called a covenant. Is it not, however, a godless thing to bind someone without his consent and knowledge? This is what [Whiston] taught us. [25]

Churchman: What is one to think of people who practice other than they teach? Many of your servants were bound [indentured] to you in their infancy without their knowledge and consent. Why did you not let them go free long since? For if a father has no right to bind his child to God, then he has still less right to bind [him] to some other man. God himself has bound us to godliness, and we as His property and subjects are under obligation to keep a good conscience as soon as we come into the world. Baptism does not lay a new or heavy yoke upon us and could rather be called a stipulation of our obligation. [Whiston] was a very learnéd Englishman. Yet the fact that he was forced to resort to such arguments makes it clear that neither wit nor erudition can aid your lost cause.

Theophilus 5: As far as the learnéd Englishman, of whose statement you spoke, is concerned, I will neither praise nor criticize him, be-

cause I do not know what preceded and what followed the statement, inasmuch as the name of the man and his writings are unknown to me. Yet, as regards the use which you were pleased to make of this statement, it seems to me that devout parents who bind their children to the fear of God and the keeping of His commandments do well. Unconverted parents, however, who despise God's counsel for them through an unrepentant life, and yet bind their children to it so that they, when they grow up, likewise despise God's counsel for them — these parents are doing a great wrong.

Anabaptist: What if I present the matter in a different way? Baptism is called a covenant. A covenant requires consent and sufficient understanding. Yet, are these things which are appropriate for children? Who can prove this to me? Should I not write on the margin, "Here fell the infant-baptizers"?

Churchman: No, not so fast! Baptism seems to be a covenant and testament of God with man rather than of man with God. For that reason it is not called a covenant of a good conscience because one promises this [good conscience] to Him, but rather because in it God bestows this by forgiving sins, and expects the exercise of a good conscience from the baptized. This can be proved by many reasons and can even be used to support infant baptism, especially since the words do not say "the covenant of a man," but rather "of a good conscience with God."

Yet, even if we do grant your concept, we will still win on every side. Consent of a child is unnecessary as long as others have the right to bind it. Next to God, our parents possess this right also. Abraham subjected himself to Melchisedek long before Levi was born; yet, this became one of the reasons why the levitical order of priests was less than that of Melchisedek. Joshua and the leaders of Israel bound the entire people and their descendants by a covenant which they made with the Gibeonites and God punished these descendants many hundred years later when this covenant was violated by Saul, whose children in turn had to be hanged to satisfy the Gibeonites. If the father were able to commit, in the political sense, so many thousands, the majority of whom were not even born, who then will deny us the right to dedicate and commit to God our already-born infants?

Hannah dedicated her son to the service of God in a special understanding and bound him even to the detail that he was to be a Nazarite and was not to allow a razor to touch his head. If this was not binding for him, then her vow was error and folly. If, however, it was [binding], then who will prevent us from doing the same? Do we perhaps have less right with our children than she had with hers? Now hear your cause receive the mortal blow: we have the right to bind our children to godliness, that is, to the practice of a good conscience, and with baptism He demands such a conscience. Therefore we can, will, and may baptize our children. What can you say against it? Yet, to ward off all [attacks] it is to be noted that such binding must not be done according to our opinion but rather in the way and manner which God himself ordained, that is, through baptism. For in this the covenant of a good conscience (Ephesians 5: 26) begins, and the cleansing of the congregation.

Theophilus 6: The covenant of God is to be considered with more importance than merely to say: it seems that it is a covenant of God with man rather than of man with God. For what sort of human covenant could the poor sinner make with his Creator? Or what does this mean? God has always made His covenant himself with His poor creation, and that for important and incontestable reasons. When God made a covenant through Noah with His descendants He said: "I establish my covenant with you, etc." (Genesis 9:11). He placed the sign of this covenant in the heavens, verse 11 [13]. When God made His covenant with Abraham (Genesis 17[:2]), He said: "I will make my covenant between me and you." But he commanded him [to practice] circumcision, and said (verse 11): "You shall be circumcised in the flesh of your foreskins, and it shall be a sign of the covenant between me and you."

In Jeremiah 11:10, God says: "The house of Israel and the house of Judah have broken the covenant." And in Jeremiah 31:31: "Behold the days are coming . . . when I will make a new covenant with the house of Israel and the house of Judah, not like the covenant which I made with their father . . . my covenant which they broke, so that I had to reject them, says the Lord." And Ezekiel 16:61 [and 62]: "Then you will . . . be ashamed when I take your sisters, both your elder and your younger, and give them to you as daughters, but not on account of the covenant with you. I will establish my covenant with you, and you shall know that I am the Lord."

It is unnecessary to list further testimonies. Since God himself says that it is His covenant which He has always established with His creation and that also the New Covenant, which He wishes to establish with poor sinners according to His promise, is likewise His covenant, I do not know who could contradict Him in this. Yet this remains a puzzle that, while it is God's covenant, God's counsel is to be of such little account. God's counsel is sincere, honest, and certain. Repentance and forgiveness of sins are to be preached to all nations and every one is to repent and be baptized. His promise accompanies His counsel. He who believes and is baptized shall be saved. What can a poor man object to this?

Men bring many arguments why they should be able and permitted to bind their children to godliness as soon as they are born. This is, it seems to me, completely unnecessary; God has never yet forbidden or commanded it. But whoever wishes to bind a small innocent child and then, as [he] grows up and as God gives him understanding and ability and opportunity to read and hear the word of his God, does not permit him to keep everything which Jesus has commanded (who, after all, has shed His blood for us) — that is wicked. And if the whole world united and tried to make it valid before men and prove it, in the end one would still have to account for this before Him who has said: "For whoever is ashamed of me and of my words . . . of him will the Son of man also be ashamed."

Anabaptist: Yet, one reads that the men who were baptized at the time of John and the apostles acknowledged God, heard His word and repented of their sins. These we consider to be the conditions for baptism: but how can these be fulfilled with children?

Churchman: You must first prove them before you make so much dependent upon them. I can read nowhere that God specified them as conditions. Rather, one can remove the entire objection with four letters, namely, by the little word "only." Where does it state that *only* such were baptized? Nor is that enough. It must also be proved that only such may be baptized. Even if one could prove that only such were baptized it is far from being proof that only such are to be baptized.

Have you ever read that the Savior washed the feet of women? Why then do you do it? In the future, then, practice it only among the men, however, not until you can prove the way you practice it. If we live until this can be done, we are likely to live forever. Do not think unkindly of me, my friend, but your objections all seem to be confessions of sin. Everything that you demand at the baptism can be done by a five-year-old child. Why do you allow yours to run around so long without instruction and baptism and [let them] sow their wild oats until their twentieth or thirtieth year? Do you dare cast accusations of Babel, while having so much confusion before your own door?

Theophilus 7: That the little word "only" consists of four letters and that it is besides a small word — in this he [Churchman] counted correctly and also judged correctly. It could, however, become much greater for him by a wicked use than he might wish. Are the Baptist-minded to be accused of baptizing only those to whom they believe the counsel of God is directed, according to the Scriptures, and that therefore Jesus had commanded that they be baptized? In that case would not the Baptist-minded be much more justified to accuse you and say: "Since you are so clever and so often accuse other people, why then do you baptize only those of whom you know that they are not commanded to be baptized? Could you, in so many years, point to even a single person to whom you have preached repentance and forgiveness of sins who subsequently acknowledged God, was converted, and thereupon was baptized by you?" Certainly as long as you lack this witness you should not beat and accuse your fellow servants: the Lord might come in the hour when He is not expected, etc.

That the Baptist-minded have never read that the Savior washed the feet of women is true too. That, however, he [Churchman] asks, why then do we do it, is a foolish question. You cannot prove that they do it or ever did it. In the meantime, let me ask you: Have you never read that the women washed the Savior's feet? Or have you not also read that Paul, upon the election of a widow, counted it among the good works if she had washed the feet of the saints [1 Timothy 5:10]? When you have read it, then remind yourselves that the apostles of Jesus Christ were faithful servants of Him who sent them, and did not forget that they must teach those men and women whom they had made disciples, to keep all that He had commanded them.

In answer to his [Churchman's] opinion that also the brothers ought no longer to wash one another's feet until they could prove their administering of this ordinance, let me say this: he who wishes to do what Jesus commanded need not obtain his manner of administering from a sleeping servant, for the love of Christ gives much better instruction.

That the Baptist-minded do not baptize their children before they are five years old may well be excused if one remembers that they firmly believe that the covenant of God under the economy of the New Testament demands only voluntary lovers of God and of His truth. Indeed, not even the devout mother of Augustine was able to convince her son to be baptized until he had attained the years of manhood. Secondly, your baptized children give in general the unbaptized children of the Baptist-minded an extremely bad example, who, after all, according to your opinion, are supposed already to have been sealed with the seal of the Holy Spirit.

Anabaptist: I must not praise this myself; yet, to return to the previous [questions], faith comes from preaching, which children cannot understand. Consequently, they have no faith and must not be baptized.

Churchman: Far too much is made of the matter when one claims that faith (Romans 10:17) stems only from preaching; especially [when concluding] from this passage which is perhaps even an objection of the Jews against Paul which he answers in the eighteenth verse. Nothing further can be concluded from it than that the Word is a means of effecting faith, but certainly not that it is the only means. It [faith] is a certain result of uniting with the spirit of Jesus; and that child who does not stand in it lives in a state of condemnation. One need only consider here that this spirit is a living, continually acting spirit, and that part of spiritual-mindedness is primarily faith, and that from faith the appropriate concepts are made in order to realize this. Faith and believing [*Glaube und Glauben haben*] are distinctly different just as life and efficacy: for the one is the basis of the other, or its result.

It may be said better in English: "There is a difference between faith and believing." To the latter belongs the practice of reason, but not to the former, otherwise a sleeping apostle could not have had faith. Therefore a child who has the Holy Spirit would immediately practice faith which is active through love, if, through a miracle, it could receive all of those capabilities and insights which it can gain in twenty years. Moreover, faith is demanded as much for salvation as for baptism, and if they are not to be baptized because of lack of faith, then they will be condemned for the same reason. Without faith it is impossible to please God. Yet, what is the point of all this? I could indeed dispute with you in your own manner: Prove [to me] that children have no faith. Where is this written?

Theophilus 8: Paul says that faith comes from preaching, and preaching from the word of God; that it should come only from preaching, Paul did not say, of course. It will not do to conclude more from one word than the meaning of the word implies. But if a child, who is not in union with the spirit of Jesus, lives in a state of condemnation, how much more [is that true for] an adult?

That faith and believing are distinctly different, as life is from efficacy, as the friend wisely noted, may be accepted. However, lest from this one arrive at an erroneous conclusion, one must carefully consider that there is a still greater difference between a child who cannot yet believe and an adult who does not wish to believe. The fact that a child, if it has the Holy Spirit, could immediately practice faith, as the friend notes, if it (namely by a miracle) received all those capabilities and insights which it may gain in twenty years, is not proof at all for infant baptism. You might as well say to the farmer or countryman after he has sowed his wheat: "Suppose that by a miracle your wheat had received the qualities which it would have received by the next harvest, then you could already mow it." Would he not say: "That might well be, in the meantime, however, I must be patient as the Scripture says, and await the early and late rains, so that when the proper time comes I can be pleased with my work, so that if God blesses my work and my fields, I can finally mow it. But you can well see that I cannot mow it yet." Therefore, the Son of man well understood the mystery of faith and yet commanded nowhere to baptize infants. And because He was also the

Son of God and the true sower of the seed of the Kingdom, one does well not to anticipate Him.

That a child, however, if it should not be baptized because of lack of faith, should be condemned for the very same reason is a very unchristian and unreasonable conclusion. When Christ says: "He who does not believe should be damned," He speaks of those who do not wish to believe after they have heard the gospel, and certainly not of the children who do not hear the gospel and consequently cannot believe in it. Whether it is written that children have no faith, I cannot remember either.

Anabaptist: But where [does it say] that they have [faith]? Show this to me and I will give in. Indeed, I will have all of my children baptized. Here is my hand on it.

Churchman: Done! It shall be binding. David says: "For thou, O Lord, art my hope, my trust, O Lord, from my youth. Upon thee I have leaned from birth" [Psalm 71:5-6]. Well, then, an honest man is as good as his word! Is it not so? I am to call the pastor tomorrow! I once brought this forth against a Baptist preacher and he became very quiet. A bystander, however, who was not exactly sparkling with wit, continued by making this objection: David did not write this when he was a child of eight days. Answer: Whenever he may have written it, it was either true or false. If he did not depend on God from birth, then the Bible contains untruths. Yet, he continued: David was a remarkable person. Answer: But David himself says the opposite of himself. Yes, he continued, that happened in the Old Testament. Answer: All the more so in the New, where God with His grace comes so much closer to the human race. You see, my friend, such heroes are the Anabaptists. How easily they can be trapped here, anyone can guess: for whoever believes, he should also be baptized.

Theophilus 9: Whoever can elevate his ideas so high above the ideas of his neighbor before he has even examined whether his own ideas are indeed better than the ideas of his neighbor, he gives [us] to understand that he has too high an estimate of himself. David in his conversion realized his misery of sin so deeply that he speaks so convincingly of it that it could be very beneficial to anyone who would really examine his conscience. Should he, I say, therefore not have been a remarkable man? [*If that were so*] *then the good God did not stop to think when He said:* "*I have found a man after my own heart.*" *True gratitude is a good sign of a remarkable man. Whoever is still very ungrateful is not yet a remarkable man.*

One might also mention that if David had not been a remarkable man and this word ("*I have leaned upon thee from my birth*"*) could indisputably be thus applied to all children, and it would then further be concluded that the children believe, and whoever believes should be baptized! If one then were to say: If all who will depend upon God have such faith that they should be baptized, then one should baptize even the young ravens, for David says of them that they call upon the Lord (Psalm 147:9). I say, if one were to conclude thus, would this not be absurd?*

What should one say to this? Should one not say: "*If infant baptism must be defended with such miserable conclusions, one would do better to ignore it . . .*"*? Should one not say in the words of the remarkable man:* "*How long shall my honor be violated? How much you love the idle and lies so gladly. Selah.*" *Did not the dear friend so wisely remark above that there is a difference between believing and faith, as* [*there is*] *between life and efficacy? But, of course, just for the purpose that he might prove that the children have faith. No sooner does he think he has proved it than he triumphs and forgets all such difference and gives himself airs as if it were an undeniable fact that if but a spark of faith were in a child, the capability for faith were there already.* [*It would be*] *just as if one were to say that once it is certain that there is life in a child before birth, then the efficacy is already there to perform an excellent handwork. Or else one ought to baptize people in their sleep: for a sleeping apostle undoubtedly also has faith.*

Christ never said [*that*] *whoever has a tiny spark of faith in him and is baptized shall be saved. Rather, He said most deliberately,* "*Whoever believes. . . .*" *Note: whoever believes, not where faith sleeps without efficacy, as a spark of fire in the ashes. Rather, where it is efficacious, in such a way that he who has heard the gospel also accepts and believes it. Note, he who believes and is baptized shall be saved. However, he who (namely, when the gospel is preached to him) does not believe, what is this other than one who wantonly refuses to believe? He will be damned.*

I well know that this sentence will seem harsh to many. One certainly does not stand in need of damning small infants who, even though there may be a little spark of faith dormant within them, nevertheless cannot yet hear the preaching nor even believe, and therefore according to the counsel of God cannot yet be baptized.

Anabaptist: Yet, can you be quite certain of your baptism? We say no! Is it not more advisable to baptize no one in infancy?

Churchman: Did you see Jesus crucified? No! Therefore on the main point we must depend upon witnesses. Why not then on the lesser? For truth is said to consist of the testimony of two or three witnesses. If, however, it were better not to take any minors into the covenant, God would not have done this in the Old Testament. For He does the best at all times.

Theophilus 10: What would it have availed a poor man in Israel if he had only been able to hear of a brass serpent which was set up for salvation? He had to see the serpent; yes, he had to see it himself, and no other for him! Therefore this important matter must not depend on witnesses. If we wish to be thoroughly healed of our deep defect, then we must look upon Jesus the crucified himself. Why does he [Churchman] answer so quickly with no to the very important question which he poses to himself? Has he perhaps never read how David in Psalm 22 actually saw Jesus the crucified and yet it was still long before the Son of man was to be so miraculously raised and exalted? Even though he had not yet seen Jesus crucified, he will nonetheless, I hope, agree with that person who says to him that David was a remarkable man.

It is a fact that truth is said to consist of the testimony of two or three witnesses. But this does not mean that untruth can exist even if it has many witnesses. There were many witnesses who testified of the calf which Aaron made, who said: "See, these are your gods, etc." [Exodus 32:4]. But they all perished. That God included minors in the covenant at the time of Moses is true. He also did it at the time of Abraham and also at Noah's, and has also done it in Christ. And it is true that He does the best at all times. That men, however, who, after all, are dust, wish to anticipate God through many and varied conclusions, find fault with His wisdom and despise God's counsel toward them, that is a pity to be deplored.

Anabaptist: This is all very strange to me. I have become very eager to listen to the proofs for infant baptism. At the same time I am gaining some confidence in you because you are not a scholar, for we are taught many prejudices against the latter from our childhood on.

Churchman: The Savior commanded: "Go into all the world and make disciples of all nations, baptizing them, that is, in that you baptize them." Here is a sufficient command. Baptism is the means to make disciples and is or will be given to all nations in the world. By this I can understand nothing less than the entire human race. Children, however, make up a great majority of mankind, and that among all nations, and are specifically counted by God among the nations. Who will then deny them baptism? Are they not to belong to Jesus' congregation? And since children were included in the Old Testament, why not also in the New?

Theophilus 11: If he [Churchman] is really no scholar, as his eager disciple claims, it is even less fitting for him to despise the important work of Luther and so many other scholars and to claim to do better teaching himself than the words of the divine commandment in Matthew 28:19 read in our German mother tongue, for he does not understand himself the original language. Yet we will look at what contribution this brand-new translation will make for infant baptism. Thus the divine commandment is to read as follows, namely, "Go into all the world, and make disciples of all nations, baptizing them." In this translation the bed is still too narrow for infant baptism, because the making of disciples still preceded the baptizing. Therefore he has to explain the word "baptizing them" and says: "That is, in that you baptize them." That is to say that baptism must be set ahead of the teaching, otherwise it does not fit infant baptism.

Even if the [order of the] words [is] reversed, in practice it still does not work well. For in this way the apostles would have been able to make few disciples if they had baptized them before teaching. This he [Churchman] finds out in making his disciples. How many words he must teach until he can persuade his disciples to have their children baptized. Thus, for all that, Luther's translation is or can be at the very least just as good as this newfangled one, let one interpret it as one will. Yet on the basis of this new translation he ventures upon a mighty jump and says: "Here is sufficient command!"

Question: Why? Answer: Baptism is a means for making disciples. Question: How has it now become the only means on the basis of this new translation? If one assumes that it is a means, then it cannot be the only means.

Christ and His apostles always considered the teaching of repentance the most powerful means and always pursued it before baptism. He [Churchman] continues and says: It is or shall be given to all nations in the entire world. But how shall it be given — according to the will of God or the will of man? The Holy Spirit says: "Repent, and be baptized every one of you" (Acts 2:38). The infant baptizers say that one must baptize young infants, who are unable to repent. And when they are grown, and are able to repent through the grace of God and wish to be baptized according to God's commandment, then one must tell them: "You are baptized." If, however, all of this is of no avail, and the promptings of the Father on the poor sinner become too strong, in such a way that he really repents, and is baptized according to God's commandment, then the infant baptizers say: "That person is an Anabaptist, etc." Through this arrangement it has happened and still does happen that many thousands are robbed of repentance.

That under the words "all nations" even children are understood is an incontestable truth. Likewise, that they deserve the covenant, the gift of grace, and the promise, has been sealed by Christ with His own blood. Yet, to insist on giving infants more than one is able to, and then to prevent them when they are adults from coming to Christ and receiving the gift from Him, that is certainly playing fast and loose.

Anabaptist: However, what I understand by a disciple is a person who has attained much knowledge and sanctification. But does this character fit children?

Churchman: The Savior must have understood what He said, when He commanded making disciples of all nations by baptism. When we speak of the enslaved black or Indian nations, do we mean thereby only the adults or also the women and children? Certainly also the latter! How could the apostles have understood Jesus differently than that He meant by all nations and that in all the world, indeed the sum of them, namely, men, women and children? Were they perhaps made to think that God speaks with two tongues and, in order to cause confusion, speaks one way in the Old and another way in the New Testament? You, of course, keep yelling, "The Old Testament is null and void; it has no authority." Yet, if you are so ignorant of the Scriptures as to see no difference between the Law and the Old Testament, one ought to shed tears of blood for those who have fallen in with you.

Since then this word of the Old Testament to which Jesus and Peter referred counts the children among the nations, and [since] all nations have been bound to baptism, as a means by which they are to become disciples, and [since] every means of grace works powerfully where man does not willfully resist, we may draw the irrefutable conclusion that all the baptized who do not resist the spirit of Jesus Christ are truly His disciples. Or did Jesus not know the purpose of baptism to make disciples, and merely spoke without thinking? Who dares think thus of the great God incarnate? Yes, indeed, He can work through each one that for which He has intended him. He can even destine children for disciples, that is such persons who are to be sanctified, sealed, taught, and saved by Him with the Holy Spirit.

In everyday language a person who is bound in the intention of learning a craft is called an apprentice, that is, a disciple [*Lehrjünger*] [as he is] called in his indenture, even if he were only one day old. Why then should this not also apply to those who are bound to Jesus? The following remark places the matter in complete certainty: Whoever does not have Jesus' spirit is not His; therefore, whoever has it is His. Whoever is His, is so in every respect, namely, His disciple, His child, His bride, or however else the Bible might term it. I see no reason to doubt this, for the Holy Spirit is called the earnest and seal of our inheritance. If I am an heir, who will deny me the name of the heirs? This Spirit, however, is also promised to the children, and is given in baptism, and consequently children can indeed be made disciples through baptism. What can you say against this?

Theophilus 12: The precious Savior indeed well understood and knew what kind of commandment He gave His apostles for all nations, and undoubtedly He still remembers well what He commanded the holy evangelist Luke to write of this important commandment (Luke 24:47), of the preaching of repentance and forgiveness of sins, and what He commanded the holy evangelist Mark to write of the preaching of the gospel, of faith and of baptism (Mark 16:15-16). Likewise He doubtless still remembers very well what He commanded the holy evangelist Matthew to write (Matthew 28) about the making of disciples. Yet, what does my friend think, should then the Son of God, who has eyes like flames of fire, not also see the forwardness of the children of men? How they pervert His faithful words and perhaps through a new translation and a great many absurd conclusions seek to obscure the faithful and good counsel of God so that the common man is not to know how the pure counsel of the Highest is to be understood? It is true, they boast of knowing that the counsel and commandment of God are directed to the children as well as the adults, and yet they deprive them of the opportunity of subjecting themselves to it according to divine order.

They know from the Scriptures that the Holy Spirit has been promised to the children as well and endeavor to convince them that they have already received it before they thought about asking for it. They could easily realize, if they but wanted to, that the testimony of the Holy Scriptures does not show us one single example that the Holy Spirit was given to a single baptized person who had not done repentance. However, we do see the contrary, namely, that the Holy Spirit was abundantly given to those who repented and believed in Christ (Acts 10:44) and that before they were baptized. But the fact that baptism, as a sign of the covenant, was given them later does by no means indicate that baptism is the only means to receive the Holy Spirit.

Certainly, whoever will see can conclude with certainty that the baptism is much rather dependent upon obedience of faith than that the Holy Spirit should be dependent upon baptism. Those who became believers through Philip's preaching of the Kingdom of God and the name of Jesus Christ were baptized and yet did not immediately receive the Holy Spirit (Acts 8:16-17) until the apostles came down and prayed over them, or laid their hands upon them. Therefore if the Holy Spirit is not directly dependent at all times on the baptism which Christ commanded, how then can it be dependent on the baptism of small infants which Christ never commanded?

The apostles understood Christ correctly and if He had commanded them to baptize infants they would indeed have done it, even though they did not know anything of his [Churchman's] new translation. God is not double-tongued and His holy counsel of love does not really cause confusion even if clever unreasonableness is accustomed to take offense with His ordinances and therefore causes much confusion. Nevertheless the only wise God has never yet wished to depend upon human thinking. It is true that He always included children along with their parents in His faithful covenant, not only those born but also those yet unborn, throughout all generations until the end of the world. But He has never yet asked any man's advice concerning the decree where the sign of His covenant was to be placed. With Noah, He placed it in the heavens. With Abraham and Moses, in the flesh of the Jewish male infants. In Christ and through Christ, the holy man of the covenant of the New Testament, He commanded to baptize repentant sinners who had come to believe in Him. He promised to give His Holy Spirit to all those who did not despise His counsel but accepted it in the right manner.

Is it not absurd for a man who even styles himself a churchman to pose such a question to the Baptist-minded who will have nothing to do with any other kind of baptism than that commanded by Christ and practiced by His apostles? I say again, "Is it not absurd to ask such people such a question, namely, did Jesus not know the purpose of baptism, etc.?" Yet, this question does not concern a true Baptist-minded person in the least; let him [Churchman] answer it himself. A true Baptist-minded person does not expect to improve the counsel of His creator in any way. That which he further asserts, namely, that the great God incarnate can bring about through each of His commandments that for which He had especially ordained it, so that He could even make disciples of children, is not being contested. After all, He was able to ordain even Paul from his mother's womb to be not only a disciple but even to proclaim the gospel and He did not need a single commandment of man therefor.

To that which he [Churchman] further remarks about an indenture, by which a child one day old is to be called an apprentice, I say this, that the name is far from being the thing itself, because it is a fact that there are many who are called Christians, but that does not necessarily make them Christians.

Finally, he seeks to give this dubious matter complete certainty all at once by a single remark: Whoever does not have Jesus' spirit is

not His; but whoever has it, he is His. Whoever is His, is so in every
respect. And because he has read in Acts 2 that in the divine order
the children are also promised the Holy Spirit, he dreams: The
spirit of Jesus is so inseparably bound to the uncommanded infant
baptism that He can attribute to a baptized infant all the privileges
that belong to a true Christian. I must confess that I am happy for
every innocent child, be it baptized or not, to share in the happiness
which Christ and His death have earned him; but that the infant
baptism supposedly contributes much to it is an error. Yet he
[Churchman] asks his disciple: "What objections do you raise against
it?"

Anabaptist: I do not wish merely to prattle and I can think of nothing
profound. But I know you; a good opinion never counts with you,
only reason and proof for everything. This is not especially in vogue
with us. In the meantime I would still like to hear something specific
to your objection, that there was no commandment given for it.

Churchman: There you confessed the truth for once. If your people
in their writings but pour out a long broth then this is commonly
accepted as gospel even if it were no more coherent than the feet
which Nebuchadnezzar saw in his dream. One only need to read the
booklet which Alexander Mack [Sr.] published under the title: *Ex-*
position of the Outward Yet Sacred Rights and Ordinances of the
House of God[26] and one will demand no [further] proof for this.

However, to return to your suggestion, let me say this: if infant
baptism is wrong, then God forbid, it is possible to conclude from
this that Jesus Christ is not the true witness. For when He worded
the commandment in such general terms He ought to have forbidden
it lest He gave cause for error. I would rather have a thousand infants baptized than think thus of Jesus. Indeed, the same judgment
would fall upon the apostles, for when they taught that baptism was
taking the place of circumcision then they certainly would have had
to indicate it if the one did not belong to the children as well as the
other. Indeed, who would ever believe that so many thousand Jews
were baptized without inquiring about their little ones? [Who would
even believe] that their enemies have never accused them of this
preference of the Old Testament over the New? If the Bible is
silent on this point then this proves more than you like [to admit].

Yet I could never accept this with a good conscience.

Theophilus 13: As far as your judgment is concerned about the mentioned booklet, the author of which passed away in the Lord more than fifty-one years ago, it seems to me that the Baptist-minded would do well to leave this up to Him who judges rightly. But as regards the teaching of the commandment for infant baptism, which he [Churchman] immediately gave to his eager disciples I would only say this much in heartfelt love, namely: if there were anyone who had carefully read what a serious farewell the great God incarnate bade His disciples (in the body) and how He then emphatically promised that He would remain with them until the end of time (in the spirit), and had also read and understood how He chose three witnesses, namely, Mark, Luke, and Matthew, to make God's counsel known to us as it was to be proclaimed to all nations — he ought to have understood at least this much from it, that Jesus as the true man of the covenant included all children until the end of the world in His great covenant of grace, and that for the same reason it is His wish that one wait with the baptism of infants until the counsel of God can be carried out upon them according to His will, lest one prevent them to come to Him through the promptings of His Father. Precisely for this reason He gave but one commandment for fathers, mothers and children, because He confirmed them the same promise through His Holy Spirit, namely: repent and each one be baptized, and then you will receive the gift of the Holy Spirit (Acts 2). Whoever has understood this through careful reading and meditating and still concludes that if the baptism of infants is not correct then Jesus Christ is not the faithful and true witness, this person in doing so would reveal nothing but an irresponsible horror of the devastation of his poor heart.

Friend Printer! Be so good as to include these remarks in your work as soon as possible. The so-called Churchman borrows a lame analogy from the natural kingdom on page twenty-eight when he opines that a one-day-old child could be bound through an indenture to a trade. In this connection it would be useful to consider the following: all members of the new covenant must be volunteers, who after taking everything into account have made the confession of their submission to the household of Christ themselves (and not through their god-parents). This is the strongest argument against infant baptism because at the time of their baptism they do not understand the least about the importance of this contract upon which our eternal salvation rests and which is, of course, demanded by the new covenant. Here, God dare not use coercion, but rather as they approach the household they are accepted into that filiation which will last until the new covenant has delivered all the volunteers who[se names] were written into the book. But that such a union is required upon entering into the covenant of grace can easily be guessed by anyone who knows human faithlessness. The covenant is two-fold and leads men to salvation or to damnation. Infant baptism can effect neither; they can all excuse themselves by pleading ignorance. No father has the right to bind his child to his religion, for the new covenant dissolves all natural bonds. However, he can be of greater use to him by keeping him in strict discipline, for the Law is our taskmaster to Christ.

P[eter] M[iller]

Should, however, my dear friend be unable to understand this, it would be much better for him [Churchman] to lament with all his heart his own ignorance than to pretend that one ought to shed tears of blood over the ignorance of those Baptist-minded who cannot distinguish sufficiently between the Law and the Old Testament. Even if there were really someone among them who would say out of ignorance: the Old Testament is worthless, it would still be much easier to instruct him as to how and where the Old Testament and the old law are still valid and how and where the Old Testament and the old law are fulfilled by the New, I say, it would be easier to convince him of this in love and also more beneficial than to weep tears of blood over him.

Yet in these days there is no great danger of tears of blood being shed. For many thousands of nominal Christians it is easier to shed blood than to weep blood, because most of them so lack the spirit of Jesus that they would rather laugh uproariously and foolishly ten times a day than to shed one single honest tear of repentance.

The dear friend further remarks that this same judgment should be passed on the apostles because they did not testify or indicate why small infants should not also be circumcised by baptism in the New

Covenant as they were by circumcision of all Israelite male infants in the Old Covenant. Thus, this gives reason to consider in the fear of the Lord the following.

When Christ before His ascension laid His hands upon the apostles and blessed them after He had given them the express commandment to proclaim the counsel of God in all the world, making disciples of all nations through preaching, baptizing, and teaching, this commission had to be considered a humanly impossible task, and therefore He gave them another separate commandment which had to undergird, guide, and accompany them in everything which He had commanded them, namely, that they were to wait for the promise of the Father (Acts 1:4). Through this they were clothed with power from on high, and under this guidance of this spirit of grace they honestly fulfilled their office and everything took place at its appointed time. Whether the apostles at Jerusalem taught that baptism was taking the place of circumcision has hardly been proved, for they suffered many thousands of converted Jewish Christians to circumcise their children after the fathers had already been baptized. From this it could much rather be concluded that nothing at all was said of infant baptism because even at the council not one word about it appears. This total silence proves, of course, more than he [Churchman] likes.

Anabaptist: I remember another argument that you use which I have often heard ridiculed: one must baptize children because they were under original sin. It seems inconceivable to our people that a child should be able to commit sin.

Churchman: We certainly do not say that they commit sin but rather that they have sin, and this we were taught by the Bible. The condemnation in Romans 5:18 has come for all humans. Are not children also humans? Can God condemn the innocent? No, but children are not innocent, for no living person is righteous before Him, and death is the wages of sin. Do not children die too? Is God justified in paying them such wages, if they have no sin? The apostle does not call it a gift of grace but rather the wages of sin. We argue this way: baptism is a means to forgiveness; children are not righteous before God, and are therefore in need of it; consequently they shall and must be baptized. Is this then something ridiculous? Or are you like the Deists, who are much better at laughing than at thinking reasonably? That is the way it was with the wretched Mr. Edelmann.[27] Otherwise it should be noted that according to Origen (a teacher of the early Christians) it was because of the above reasons that the church had received the apostolic practice of baptizing infants.[28]

Theophilus 14: Whoever can laugh about original sin is vain and not thoroughly converted; let him profess whatever he may. Yet, the quoted verse, Romans 5:18, reads thus: "Then as one man's trespass led to condemnation for all men, so one man's act of righteousness leads to acquittal and life for all men." Just as this text proves that condemnation included even all children because they too are human, it also proves on the other hand that the justification of life will also include children because they too are human. That infant baptism is necessary for this cannot as easily be concluded.

The passage which he [Churchman] quotes from Origen that the church received the practice of baptizing infants from the apostles is very uncertain and doubtful, because no mention can be found in the entire New Testament that the Christians were ever told to baptize their infants. Rather, it appears that the apostles said absolutely nothing of infant baptism to the Jewish Christians in Jerusalem because since they were permitted to circumcise their infants, they insisted so emphatically that even the gentiles be circumcised. And yet in all this not a single word was said about infant baptism. Likewise in the writings of Paul one reads not one word of infant baptism when he professes that he has not withheld anything that was beneficial but rather has proclaimed the entire counsel of God so that he would be innocent of their blood (Acts 20:20, 26, 27).

It may be clearly concluded that, if the apostles had wished to recommend infant baptism to the baptized Jews, it would not have been necessary for them to permit circumcision. Yet it seems that they would have rather left them to do something which God, after all, had commanded rather than give them something in return which God had not commanded.

Anabaptist: This thing about Edelmann is a sore point with me; we will leave him to the rational animals. No one else will have anything to do with him. But to stay on the topic, what convinced you personally most of infant baptism?

Churchman: The word of the Savior: "Unless one is born [anew] of water and the Spirit, he cannot enter the Kingdom of God. That which is born of the flesh is flesh" [John 3:5-6]. I had enough [command of] German to know that the little word "one" [*jemand*] means the same as "anyone" and also enough [knowledge of the] Bible [to know] that children are also flesh born of flesh, that is, they are highly corrupted and wretched. Therefore, since the Savior pronounces to everyone, because of this innate corruption, that the rebirth out of the water and the Spirit is so extremely necessary, why should I exclude children instead of recognizing their baptism as necessary and divine? Certainly, my doubts vanished through this like fog in the sun.

Theophilus 15: That rebirth is highly necessary for all men is quite right according to the Savior's words. But whoever wishes to prove that a child — provided it has received the outward ceremony of baptism — is therefore reborn and that a child who has not received it is in greater danger of being lost, demonstrates clearly that he, like the Athenians, is all too superstitious in every respect. Are all the male infants lost who shed their blood at Bethlehem for Jesus' sake? Did not the thief on the cross enter Paradise according to the words of Christ? It is far better to believe in Christian love that God who alone is wise and with whom nothing is impossible can very easily cause a child to be reborn when He wishes to take it to himself from this wicked world into His heavenly Kingdom. Such is much closer to the Christian faith than to trust in an inadequate commandment of men.

If it were not that so much more harm has been caused by infant baptism than it has brought benefit, one might perhaps consider it an intermediate thing [Mittelsache] and remember that it will disappear by itself just as child communion disappeared. This latter was proved by the same reasons as infant baptism and since the time of Cyprian was held in the same esteem as infant baptism for several hundred years. Above and beyond all of this it is very doubtful, for I have never read that human blood was ever shed over child communion, whereas so many thousand devout souls were mercilessly killed because they would not respect the superstition which accompanies infant baptism. Yet he [Churchman] thinks that all of his doubts evaporated before this superstition like fog in the sun.

Anabaptist: I would like to stir up more of those [doubts]. In what way were then all of them baptized among you reborn, which they indeed deny by their lives? Besides, some say that water signifies here tears of repentance.

Churchman: The answer is already found. The majority, unfortunately, drop out of their baptismal covenant and must be reborn if they are to be saved, because misuse does not nullify correct use. Tears never signify water in the entire Bible, unless it says weeping tears or the like. Since no such description appears here, then nothing other than common water is understood. Is one then to condemn those who cannot even cry out of anguish of soul, or even the children who do not weep tears of repentance?

Theophilus 16: A hasty answer to an important question of course demonstrates a ready wit. But a matter which is in itself incorrect is not made correct even if one adorns it with all evidences of honor due a sound matter. If the baptism of infants were commanded by God, and if it were then also carried out as commanded by God, it would, of course, be a correct use. But since God did not command it, then it is in itself already misuse. Inasmuch as one pretends to make by this a world full of reborn men and thus to plant Christ's garden with trees of righteousness, the Spirit of Christ has a perfect right to say to these gardeners: "Either plant a good tree, and then its fruit will be good; or plant a rotten tree, and its fruit will be rotten, for the tree is known by its fruit" (Matthew 12:33).

One should also take to heart what is contained in the next two verses, namely: "The good man out of his good treasure brings forth good, and the evil man out of his evil treasure brings forth evil. For out of the abundance of the heart the mouth speaks" [Matthew 12:35, 34]. And since so many of these children (reborn in this manner), before they are even able to choose the good and to reject the evil, bring forth from their little hearts the evil treasure of their poor parents and wretched god-parents when the little mouth, which ought to praise its Creator, curses, swears, and profanes the name of God, who can then say that such a child is reborn? Who will then perhaps object [by saying] that the poor child has broken its baptismal covenant when it does not possess the ability yet to choose or to reject for itself? Who would dare to say that such a child received the Holy

Spirit at its baptism and this Holy Spirit had now departed from the child when after all, the poor child has not yet consciously sinned against [Him]?

Or who would say that the Holy Spirit is there to be true, but that He is not powerful enough to govern the little tongue in the presence of its wicked parents? Indeed, the small children in the Temple could shout a lovely hosannah to the King of glory so that the proud Pharisees and priests had to listen, to their great displeasure, and yet they [the children] were not baptized. Who can say that such children should not be more deeply rooted and included in the new covenant of grace of Jesus Christ, who even today praise the Lord in their tender childhood and from whose mouths one hears not one curse or wicked word, even though they are not baptized, than the baptized [children] who show the very opposite?

Anabaptist: I wish to hear the rest of the story. How can you use Ephesians 5:26 as a proof? As far as I can see, there is no infant baptism to be seen there.

Churchman: Note: ordinarily, no one sees more poorly than he who does not wish to see. You have not yet been able to find one example of baptized children in the Bible, whereas we shall soon prove that many thousands were baptized. Regarding the words mentioned, it must be remembered that the word of the New Testament speaks of no other water bath and specifically calls baptism a bath of rebirth. In this the cleansing of the church is done which is spoken of as an accomplished matter. The little word *has* appears in the past sense (in the *praeteritum*). This is done in order to show that whoever is unbaptized does not yet belong to the church and has no part in her privileges. If this was punishment in the Old Testament, what would it be in the New Testament? The church is due [the right of] the first-born and she is the bride and queen. If then the children are to belong to the church, they must be baptized. If they die unbaptized, then they will not attain the salvation of the first-born despite all the salvation which they find, because during their lives on earth they do not belong to the church of the first-born. This conclusion is so great that a father had better lose his life than permit his child to remain unbaptized.

Theophilus 17: Weighty people can, of course, make weighty con-

clusions. Still, small people have often learned this much from the Bible, that weighty people also make mistakes and now, perhaps, even this, that God alone is Almighty. Now let them consider that Jesus Christ the Head commanded His church that repentance and forgiveness of sins should be preached to all nations and that those who receive this in faith should be baptized, yet [He] did not exclude those who perhaps cannot be baptized. He excluded from His church only those who will not believe, and consequently also from the privileges of the church.

Note: Two important conclusions appear here in broad daylight: God excludes all unbelievers who (note) despise the counsel of God for them. Weighty people have a different conclusion: They exclude all unbaptized. The unbelievers, however, who despise the counsel of God for them cannot be excluded by them, for these are in the majority and have gotten the upper hand. This, it seems to me, is one of the main reasons why friends of God often have graced such a church with the name of Babel, which, namely, either could or perhaps even would not exclude unbelievers and despisers of the Divine Word. Especially where the responsible shepherds themselves were unbelievers and impious persons.

Please note further that if the little word "has" — because it appears in the past sense — excludes the children, who have depended on the Lord from their mothers' wombs and thus have faith, only because they have not yet been capable of being baptized according to divine order, the little word ("has") also excludes him [Churchman] for indeed he was not there yet when Paul said of the Lord: "He cleansed his church," for the little word "has" occurred in the past sense and he and all of us were yet to be. I must admit, this little word ("has") has never seemed to me exclusive, but rather on the contrary as a quite prophetic inclusive word, in which past and present are the same, as can be seen in Isaiah 9:6: "For to us a child is born, to us a son is given." There the word "is born" occurs, to be sure, in both [the] past and [the] present sense, yet, according to the principal circumstances, is doubtless to be understood also in the future sense.

As, however, the little word "us" might be regarded an exclusive little word it can exclude no one else than the unbelievers who exclude themselves according to Mark 16ff. Why? Note: Because of the great and incontestible inclusive word in John 3:16: "For God so loved the world that He gave his only son, that all — note: all — who believe in him should not perish but have eternal life." One can confidently conclude from this that no one — from among men, women, and children, yes, from all people — no one is excluded, until the last day, except he who does not believe and thus excludes himself. That Paul says: "He cleansed her by the washing of the water with the word," shows that the Word is the most powerful cleansing agent, just as Christ said to His disciples: "You are already made clean by the word which I have spoken to you" [John 15:3]. Therefore, the powerful cleansing agent is and remains the Word and not the water. That is why no other water bath can cleanse, than the water bath in the Word. All water or water bath which is not found in the Word does not cleanse the soul.

Anabaptist: It is believed that the Savior gave to His church the Holy Spirit. Can the children also receive this if they are included in it?

Churchman: The apostle says: "Repent, and be baptized every one of you in the name of Jesus Christ for the forgiveness of your sins; and you shall receive the gift of the Holy Spirit. For the promise is to you and to your children" [Acts 2:38-39]. Children have not done dead works and therefore do not stand in need of repenting dead works. There is no obstacle on that side in their way of attaining forgiveness and such a gift. According to these words, baptism is the means thereto, hence, they [the children] must be baptized.

Theophilus 18: To comment in the most impartial manner upon these matters: there appear here two different covenants. The New Testament covenant of grace of our God calls together God-fearing people by the voice of the Holy Spirit from all nations under the heavens, preaches to them the gospel of Christ so emphatically that it penetrates to the bottom of their hearts so that they exclaim, saying: "Men and brethren, what shall we do?" The answer is as stated above, and to be read in Acts 2:38-39. Yet most people will not fear God, nor be righteous before God, and thus will not be called out of their distance by the voice of God so that the evangelical voice of grace might penetrate their hearts and so that they might also learn to ask about God. For that reason repentance cannot be proclaimed to them in such a manner that they should know what it is.

Nonetheless, the world would like to be saved. What is to be done? Clever, wise, and understanding men arrive at a different counsel, namely, that children have done no dead works and therefore do not need the repentance of dead works, and therefore from this side there is no obstacle in their way to attain forgiveness and such a gift. According to these words baptism is the means to it, and consequently they [the children] should and must be baptized. Now if this human counsel were found in the New Testament, which Christ sealed with His blood, it would not be human but divine, and could be considered an addition to the new covenant of grace. Since, however, there is absolutely nothing at all in God's word to be found about it, it remains human counsel and human word according to which the poor creation wants to make a human covenant with its Creator; God does not feel obligated to add His Holy Spirit to it. Yet the question is whether they will receive it before they are adult.

Churchman: The matter must rest with these words "to you and your children is the promise." Thus this promise is for my child as soon as it is my child, and this is true when it is one day old as well as when it is twenty years old. I see in John that God can give them the Holy Spirit. The promise, however, says that He wants to. But baptism is the means. Who will then forbid the water to baptize them?

Theophilus 19: To say and to pretend that baptism is the means, and under this pretense to practice baptism and recommend it as the only means whereby forgiveness of sins and the Holy Spirit may be given, sound exceedingly superstitious and idolatrous beyond measure.

It is true that we see in John that God gave the Holy Spirit to an unbaptized child. Yet, where is it written that He gave a baptized child the Holy Spirit? Does this not demonstrate as clearly as the sun that water baptism is not given in the sense that we should become idolators and seek our salvation in a handful of water, while it is to be found in the blood of Jesus Christ?

Anabaptist: The Kingdom of God belongs to the children in any case. Why then should baptism be necessary for them? To be true, one reads that the Savior blessed them, but not that He baptized them. Such being the case, who will believe that they need forgiveness? Are they not saved in any case?

Churchman: Of which children does Jesus speak? Of children of
the covenant. For none were born before a certain period and by the
eighth day they had to be circumcised. Those who were not circumcised were saved by sacrifice. Now prove that others are also to receive
this promise. Yet, it is here as with the Quakers. John promised the
baptism of the Spirit to those whom he baptized with water. But they
[the Quakers] make a leap and wish to attain it without the water
baptism. Were the children whom Paul called holy unbaptized? Who
can prove this to me? For what reason are they called holy? Because of their own perfection, or because of the gift of the merit of
Jesus? Certainly because of the latter. Who will deny them the
baptism through which this merit is valued and the Holy Spirit is
given?

Yes, we can even reverse it. For if the Kingdom belongs to the
children, who will deny them the means to it? If the land is mine,
do not the deed and the seals on it also belong to me? Do look at
the words quite carefully. The Savior says: "The Kingdom of God
is of them," and despite this He blesses them. If they had need of
that, then certainly also of baptism through which the Savior's highest
blessing, namely, the Holy Spirit, is given. No one will be so ignorant
as to think that because Jesus blessed one, six, or ten, it was as good
as if He had blessed all, or that our children are less in need of it
than those children. Indeed, He wishes that they be brought to Him.

Now this can happen only through baptism, inasmuch as no one
can come directly to Him, because He himself did not indicate any
other means, and because in it we are putting Him on and are buried
with Him in death, consequently are brought into His church. As
regarding forgiveness, it is easy to see one's way clearly on it: Jesus
said to His disciples: "Blessed are you who are poor in spirit, for
yours is the kingdom of heaven," and yet taught them afterward to
pray for forgiveness. Otherwise it is to be noted that the Savior baptized no one: But does that mean that baptism is therefore of no
account?

*Theophilus 20: This is no reason to disdain baptism, although it is
written: "Although Jesus himself did not baptize, but only his disciples"
(John 4:2). If some wish on this account to skip water baptism and
grasp the baptism of the Spirit, it must not be commended. However,*

he who on the other hand wishes to skip faith in Christ and repentance (it being the testimonial of the living God) and to grasp water baptism risks a much more dangerous jump.

That Christ said (Matthew 5:3): "Blessed are the poor in spirit, for theirs is the kingdom of heaven" indicates for what reason He promised the Kingdom of heaven to the small infants, namely, because He saw that they were poor and because He himself had become such a poor child for their sake. Besides, He even intended to give His life for them according to His Father's will, and to redeem them through His blood from all those who envied them or contended their promised inheritance. But that circumcision or sacrifice [is] to have contributed much to this is not even probable, much less certain. Rather, on the other hand it is certain that the Eternal Word through which all things are created, both the visible and the invisible, will faithfully keep His promise to each poor soul, as long as he [the latter] does not allow himself to be bewitched by the treachery of the devil and to be put into such pride that such a formerly poor man or woman rejects the Kingdom of God by his own volition and therefore considers himself unworthy of eternal life.

Besides it is to be noted that Jesus did not say: "Bring the children to me," rather, "Let the children come to me" [Matthew 19:14]. And in John 6:44 He testified and said: "No one can come to me unless the Father who sent me draws him; and I will raise him up at the last day." Whoever considers this in the fear of the Lord needs nothing but faith in the Son of God; then he can well see from Christ's own words whose is the Kingdom of God, namely, all those small and poor [souls] who are prompted by the urging of the Father, and therefore allow a fervent desire to come to Jesus to reign in them. Yes, for all such is the Kingdom of heaven.

This promise continues as long as Christ promised to be with His disciples, that is, until the end of the age, or until the day of the last judgment. Then He will prove it and will raise them by authority of His indisputable Word, even if all gates of hell must be broken in the process. Otherwise, it is to be noted (John 3:25-26) that baptism was called a cleansing by the disciples. If the apostles had believed that one could also cleanse the infants in that manner, they would not have rebuked those who carried the children, but, rather, baptized the little children and themselves lifted those little lambs from the water and carried them to the arms of their good Shepherd. But as this custom was foreign to them, and they did not yet thoroughly understand the cleansing in the blood of Jesus, they rebuked those who carried them. On this occasion Christ could have instructed both His disciples as well as us about infant baptism very easily with but few words, if it had been His and His Father's will that the infants so dear to Him and young should be received into the covenant of grace in that way.

That our little ones stand just as much in need of the blessing of Jesus as those who were brought to Him at that time is a precious truth. The question is only this: whether a single human commandment under all the heavens could in the least contribute to this? Therefore I judge that it is much safer to believe the faithful words of Christ, who says: "If two of you agree on earth about anything they ask, it will be done for them by my Father in heaven. For where two or three are gathered in my name, there am I in the midst of them" [Matthew 18:19-20]. In every fellowship where Jesus is in the midst of them according to His word, children can be brought to Him that He might bless them.

As to the other gracious reminder of the beloved friend, namely, that if the land is mine, then the deed and the seals are mine also — that is a well-founded fact. In the meantime one certainly does not blame an executor of a will for his similarly well-founded caution when he waits with the transmission of the deed until the time set by the father. That the children of the believers (1 Corinthians 7) must have been sanctified through infant baptism may not readily be concluded. Otherwise one could conclude that the believing wife had baptized her unbelieving husband.

Anabaptist: You also take your arguments from circumcision. I would be glad to accept it if it had been something universal and not imposed upon the one sex only.

Churchman: This has various reasons, and perhaps also this: Eve sinned first, and this was to be especially distinguished. Therefore shame fell upon the daughters which lasted until Christ was born of a woman and reconciled the world. Now, Paul says of baptism and of the claim to Christ: "There is neither male nor female" [Galatians 3:28]. However, this could have been no special advantage of the New Testament if it had been thus in the Old Testament also. Otherwise only the sign was lacking. For they also had to be reconciled and consecrated as a people of the covenant. Otherwise, how could Moses have been able to say in the mentioned place, "All of the people of the church," if the little girls had been excluded? Therefore, our arguments on circumcision are based on an eternal fact, and baptism is not for nothing called the circumcision of Christ (Colossians 2:11). How could it be called thus if there was no connection with the same? Yet, how could it be even similar to it if the children were excluded? In short: whoever wishes to know the mysteries of this matter need only read the letter to the Galatians in prayer and supplication. In conclusion: [give an] answer to this only: Have you ever seen a trait or a flaw in a shadow which was not also to be found in the original?

Theophilus 21: That the Israelite girls were not excluded from the covenant of God even though they did not have the outward sign of the covenant, the beloved friend himself has thoroughly proved. However, this is still to be noted, namely, that even the male infants of the Israelites who were born in the wilderness were not circumcised in their infancy and were undoubtedly not excluded from the covenant either, but they did not receive the sign of the covenant until their mature years at Gilgal under Joshua, after they had seen the mighty works of their God and the great unfaithfulness of their fathers, and how these had not remained in the covenant of God the sign of which they had received in their youth in Egypt. It is likewise noteworthy that these children of the covenant, who had grown up without the sign and who had not received the sign of the covenant with total consent of their healthy judgment until [they had] a living faith aroused through God's mercy, turned out much better for God than the others. These are the ones to whom the promised land was given.

Now since the Lord himself spoke (Jeremiah 31:31) that He was going to make a new covenant not like the one which they did not keep, when He had to force them etc., who then will remonstrate with God for failing to command to baptize young infants? That which the friend refers to in Colossians 2:11 is certainly worth considering! Paul shows that the circumcision of Christ was done without hands, partly in Christ himself, and partly in that one is buried with Him through baptism. If this circumcision of Christ is done in Him and without hands, who will then be so unreasonable as to conclude that

*this could be done without Christ's commandment through infant
baptism? The counsel of the beloved friend to read the epistle to the
Galatians in prayer and supplication is good, and to be accepted with
gratitude. In the third [second] chapter Paul says: "Let me ask you
only this: Did you receive the Spirit by works of the law or by hearing with faith?" Now the poor little infants are to receive the Spirit
through a work which clever people attempt to prove out of the
shadow of the Law, because the small and tiny infants cannot yet
understand the preaching of faith. I will listen in patience to the
answer of the Anabaptist to his closing question and to his subsequent
interpretation of it.*

Anabaptist: No, in the original I find everything down to the smallest
detail; anyone can convince himself of this who will look at a tree
and its shadow with some attention.

Churchman: What? And you [claim that you] have not yet been
able to find an example of baptized children in the Bible! Do you
not know, Paul says that our fathers were all baptized under Moses
in the sea and under the cloud. Were they all adults? Did they not
bring any children out of Egypt or beget any in the wilderness? Indeed, if so many thousand were baptized in the prefiguration or
shadow why not also in the essence? Especially as the Old Testament
portrays Jesus and His people? Certainly for conscientious people this
is enough and for the unscrupulous we do not write except that we
would only add in love for those who perhaps desecrated their first
baptism for the sake of a beautiful wife or a valuable plantation:
such scoundrels will have their share in the pit which burns with fire
and sulfur, unless they truly repent.

*Theophilus 22: The shadow of the Law had various baptisms (He-
brews 9:10). The essence of the new covenant cleanses us (John 13:
10) by one baptism (Ephesians 4:5). Whosoever abandons the essence
and grasps the shadow might easily grasp in vain. Paul says (1
Corinthians 10:1-2): "I want you to know, brethren, that our fathers
were all under the cloud, and all passed through the sea, and all were
baptized under Moses in the cloud and in the sea." St. Paul tells the
dear Corinthians the fact that the fathers of the Israelites were baptized
under Moses as a secret, but as regarding infant baptism the holy word
of the Bible retains its usual silence even here. Despite this the friend*

*will seriously prove here infant baptism and how does he do it?
Answer: He says: "Did they not bring any children out of Egypt
or beget any in the wilderness?"*

The first question gives an opportunity to consider that certainly
there were children along although Paul says nothing of their baptism.
But what is the purpose of the second question, whether none were
begotten in the wilderness? Is that perhaps so as to complete the
promised number since he [Churchman] promised to show that so
many thousand were baptized? When they went through the Red
Sea they were still in the beginning of their journey and could not
possibly have begotten children yet. Later, of course, during the forty
years of their journey they begot many children. Yet, how could
these increase the number of children who were supposed to be
baptized at that very point? They were not there, of course, and were
at that time yet to be. If he could prove that those children who were
there at that time were baptized along with their fathers, the matter
might make a better impression. The Baptist-minded want to have
facts and cannot content themselves with such unscrupulous suppositions. When you baptize infants in your churches who can say that
you baptize fathers? When God baptized fathers, why do you say
He baptized children? The fact that a person was present when people were baptized is far from being proof that he was therefore also
baptized.

From that, however, which he [Churchman] mentions about those
who perhaps desecrated their first baptism for the sake of a beautiful
wife or a valuable plantation, nothing certain can so easily be concluded, because it is difficult to guess against what he is agitating or
who it really is whom he is threatening with the pit of fire. However,
a true conversion will not harm anyone. But if he thinks when someone wants to become converted to God and is baptized upon his faith
according to the commandment of Christ, that this person is such a
scoundrel because he did not sufficiently honor the baptism received
in his infancy so that he now has the right to threaten him with the
fiery pit, then I would not care to share in the judgment which he
would be thus bringing upon himself.

Anabaptist: Yes, there would be something in that if you also had
the right baptism. Yet you are ashamed of immersion. Jesus our great

Forerunner was baptized in this manner and even the word "to baptize" is supposed to be Old German for "to dip."

Churchman: In what way was Jesus our Forerunner? In His virtues, but not in His actions. Otherwise we would not be allowed to own anything of our own, carry any money, speak German; [we would be allowed to] ride donkeys only, and so on. Or do you want to follow Him only where it costs no self-denial? If the one deed binds us then all the others do likewise.

Yet He was not so in the baptism. For His [baptism] and that of the disciples were not the same. Is He perhaps supposed to have been baptized in His own name for the forgiveness of sins and for sanctification? Who will solve this difficulty for me? This baptism was indeed the consecration*) to His office of mediator, and as this had been portrayed by the ordination of the priests of the Old Testament, it explains the words when He says: "It is fitting for us to fulfill all righteousness" [Matthew 3:15].

---

*) *It is true that the baptism of Jesus Christ was, as the so-called Churchman says, an ordination to His office of mediator. As He became the guarantor for all of humanity, it was necessary that between His Father and himself a contract be made in which the Father left Him the heathen as an inheritance and the end of the world as His property with the condition that He was to pay the debts which Adam had made. This contract had to be confirmed in the water and it so pleased the Father and the Holy Spirit that He appeared in the form of a dove above Him and gave His consent.*

But when the Churchman pretends that the baptism of Jesus and that of His disciples were not the same, he has revealed his ignorance. Just as the Chief High Priest pledged himself to the Father through His baptism to make the entire rebelling creation subject to Him, so all of His followers with their baptism have pledged themselves by oath to Him to assist Him in this important task. That is why Peter calls them a royal priesthood (1 Peter 2:9).

That he thinks that the words "for thus it is fitting for us to fulfill all righteousness" are binding only for Christ but not [for] His followers, in this he reveals once again his ignorance in divine matters. Adam, when he revolted against God, came under the law of nature, and from that he was later reduced to lawlessness. In order to help him the household of Moses was established, in which the debts which Adam and his race had made had to be repaid. For without this no one could become a follower of Christ, because he was still debtor before the Law. For this reason the Law is called a taskmaster for Christ. However, as through this legal righteousness no soul could be humbled, the counsel of God demanded that the household of the New Covenant be established in which obedience is rendered not by the lesser to the greater (as in the household of Moses) but by the greater to the lesser. The foundation of this household was laid by Christ when He was baptized in the Jordan by John, who was lesser than He. And this is what is meant by "to fulfill all righteousness."

Now when the Churchman teaches that this was not written for us for the purpose of discipleship and that it was not necessary for us to fulfill all that, he makes Christ a servant of sin, who pays the bill for so many undisciplined and lawless men in order that they might sin the more freely at His cost, and that this attained righteousness of Christ could be made available for whores and criminals without their having to follow Christ in fulfillment of righteousness, which would open a door to all unrighteousness. P[eter] M[iller]

That He was indeed supposed to have been immersed*) thank you very much, if you can prove it. Yet from these words: "He went up out of the water," it can certainly not be done [*i.e.*, proved] for this was said of Moses, who had not even been in, let alone under, the water. Otherwise it is to be noted that the apostles did not write in Old German but in Greek, and there "to baptize" also means "to wash" and "to sprinkle."

---

*) That Christ was immersed under the water is a matter which (as far as I know) no scholar has yet denied. When God wished to establish the ceremonial service among the Jewish people He first revealed everything to Moses in a vision on Mount Sinai and later spoke to him: "And see that you make them after the pattern for them which is being shown you on the mountain" (Exodus 25:40). The patterns of heavenly matters had to coincide most exactly with the originals.

And since the household of the New Covenant has more important objectives than that of the Old Testament, it is only fair for me to ask the so-called Churchman: "Who gave them [the church-people] the right to corrupt the household of the New Covenant in such a way that it can no longer represent what it should? You have made a sprinkling out of baptism, changed the Supper into a daytime meal, even abolished the feetwashing, etc., etc., which was instituted just as well as baptism." They thereby show how they pervert the counsel of God, because baptism portrays our burial (Romans 6:3-4). If they can prove that the holy apostles sprinkled or only baptized in and not under the water, then we shall consider him [Churchman] a master in Israel.

Let him show us in the dictionaries where "baptizo" is used for "sprinkle." Homer, in his description of the Trojan Wars, uses the word "baptizein" when he says that the Greeks tempered their battle-axes in water.

"Baptizo" actually means "immerse" and that is why it is also used for washing.

"Bapto" means "dip," which is used with Lazarus (Luke 16), and with the morsel (John 13:26). But nothing is more curious than that the Churchman is so absurd as to drag in the word "sprinkle" (which, as you know, is called "rantizein" in Greek) and wants to make it baptism. In this he reveals that he is a superb perverter of Christ.

P[eter] M[iller]

Theophilus 23: The deeds of Jesus were all virtues, and His virtues were the sources of His deeds. Whosoever hates His virtues also hates His deeds; and whosoever loves His virtues loves also His deeds. When Jesus rode on the donkey and the children shouted Hosannah, these were similar deeds. The Son of God honored His Father and the children honored Him also. The shepherd went ahead and the lambs followed him, and that did not seem hard for them. When Jesus was baptized by John in the Jordan, and poor sinners were also baptized, these were similar deeds. The Son obeyed His Father, and the poor sinners were also obedient to God, and the angels in Heaven rejoiced over both. Whether Jesus was completely immersed under the water serves to establish the truth that Jesus himself stated that in His church all things should be valid through the testimony of two or three witnesses (Matthew 18:16).

Now the beloved friend reports that the apostles did not write Old German, but rather Greek and there, he says, "baptize" also means wash and sprinkle. We were not entirely unaware of this. Despite this, in order to be fair, we will accept it here for what it is worth, especially as it gives us the opportunity to investigate the nature of this matter according to the counsel of Jesus.

Luther is the first witness*) who testified to us upon God's commandment that the Greek word could best be interpreted by the Old German word "taufen" [to baptize] according to its true sense and meaning. For, he says, "taufen" means "tiefen" [to lower], "vertiefen" [to submerge], or "tief einsenken" [to sink (something) in deeply].

---

*) Doctor Martin Luther, Volume 6, in the sermon on the sacrament of baptism, folio 131, 6, writes thus:

Baptism [die Taufe] is "baptismos" in Greek, and "mersio" in Latin, and means to plunge something completely into the water, so that the water covers it. Although in many places it is no longer customary to thrust and dip infants into the font, but only with the hand to pour the baptismal water upon them into the font, nevertheless the former is what should be done. It would be proper, according to the word "Taufe," that the infant, or whoever is to be baptized, should be put in and sunk completely into the water and then drawn out again. For even in the German tongue the word "Taufe" comes undoubtedly from the word "tief" [deep] and means that which is baptized is sunk deeply into the water. This usage is also demanded by the significance of baptism itself. For baptism, as we shall hear, signifies that the old man and the sinful birth of flesh and blood are to be wholly drowned by the grace of God. We should therefore do justice to its meaning and make baptism a true and complete sign of the thing it signifies. . . .

The sign consists in this, that we are thrust into the water in the name of the Father and of the Son and of the Holy Spirit; however, we are not left there but are drawn out again. This accounts for

the expression: "aus der Taufe gehoben" [raised up from baptism].[29]
(See also Luther's sermon, in "The History of Baptism," page 924.)
We also wished to include what Augustine (in "The History of
Baptism," page 712) and Jerome (page 324) say about the mystery of
the threefold immersion, etc.; but space does not permit it here.[30]

Jeremiah Felbinger,[31] *a faithful servant of the Word, is the second*
witness whom the Lord has called to translate the New Testament
into our mother tongue. He renders the word somewhat more accord-
ing to New [High] German usage saying: "Jesus came to John to the
Jordan, in order to be immersed by him and after He had been
immersed, He came out of the water, etc." The third witness is John
Henry Reitz,[32] *a God-fearing scholar, whom the Lord has also called*
to translate faithfully the New Testament from the Greek into our
mother tongue. Although he uses the word "taufen" [baptize] as a
testimony that Luther was a faithful witness, yet in order that the
common man, who cannot quite understand the Old German word,
might be able to grasp the full meaning of the word "taufen", he adds
in his work "eintauchen" [immerse]. Herewith he testifies that Jere-
miah Felbinger is also a faithful witness.

Now whether or not many learnéd and unlearnéd content them-
selves with the opinion of our friend and say: "The Greek word could
also mean to wash or to sprinkle," yet that Daniel is not yet born
who can prove that these three witnesses have borne false testimony.
On the contrary, the truth compels them that in the baptismal cer-
emony of the Germans the Old German word "Taufe" must be used.
If they were thoroughly convinced that the word "to wash" better
expressed the intention of God, why then do they not say: "I wash
you"? Or if they were thoroughly convinced that "to sprinkle" could
better express what the actual intention of the divine commandment
is (which is composed in the Greek language), why then do they not
say: "I sprinkle you"? On the contrary, when they name the three
highest names, then imagination must stand back and the power of
the truth compels them to say: "I baptize you," or "You are baptized,"
even though they do not stop to think whether they are doing what
they say.

Although it is true that the English nation preserved almost the entire Greek word in the baptismal ceremony, however, the High Church in England especially is so prepossessed in favor of the truth of these three witnesses that when they ordain or confirm a bishop, he promises that if a person were to desire to be immersed after the example of the first Christians, he would consider it his duty to baptize the person in this way.

Anabaptist: Yet He was baptized by John of whom it is certain that he immersed, for the word says specifically: "John also was baptizing at Aenon near Salim, because there was much water there" (John 3:23).

Churchman: Because he baptized where there was much water, how does that prove that he also baptized *in* much water? By the same token Job must have done a great deal of riding, because we read that he had many camels and donkeys. Yet, instead of being certain [that John immersed], it is not even true, because he was no Samson, nor [made of] steel and iron. He certainly would have had to be both, if he were going to stand constantly in water and baptize so many thousand in that manner. We have no right to assume miracles where the Bible indicates none, especially because we read that John performed none.

Theophilus 24: My beloved friend! I have been listening with pleasure, and it seems to me it was a happy idea when he [Churchman] thought of Job's riding. I must admit that I have read the Bible several times through and yet have never wondered whether Job rode or not. Yet I must admit to my simplicity, that if I had once read in the Bible: "Job often went riding, because he had many camels," you could have hardly convinced me that he did not often mount camels. And when it says about John that he "was baptizing at Aenon near Salim, because there was much water there," you will have a hard time convincing me that the Spirit of God did not for this very reason wish to testify to us through the little word "because" that John needed much water for his baptism.

As far as the riding of Job is concerned, the Holy Scriptures maintain the same silence that they do about infant baptism. Therefore, whether he rode or did not ride rests on suppositions, just as with infant baptism, where some speculate that also children were baptized at the time of the apostles. But upon thorough investigation there appears to be a complete lack and lamentable poverty of proof. As to what the friend notes further about John not being a Samson, that gives opportunity to consider that he — just like Samson — was dedicated to God from his mother's womb on, and, moreover, never became unfaithful as did Samson. Why would he not have had the capability to do that which the Lord had sent him to do? Christ says of him that "among those born of women there has been no one greater than John the Baptist" [Matthew 11:11]. Moreover, his baptism was not of man but from heaven.

What our God commands a man to do, that he can do. If Samson was able to catch three hundred foxes and do with them as is written, then John was much more able to baptize three hundred poor sinners in one day in the water of the Jordan and other waters according to opportunity, for He who had commanded him to do it was able to strengthen him. Besides, John had early quite a few disciples who followed him and were able to help him according to the will of God. In the light of all this it appears how very miserable and vain are all the arguments that are raised against the truth.

Anabaptist: Yet did not Philip and the eunuch go down into the water? What is this supposed to say?

Churchman: Not immersion: or else your ministers will have to be sure to go under the water with the person being baptized, for the words say: "They both went down into the water [Acts 8:36].

Theophilus 25: That they went down into the water means only what they intended to do. But this is not all; it also says, "and he baptized him," and Jeremiah Felbinger says, "he immersed him," and Reitz testifies that this is the truth.

Anabaptist: One is to be buried in the baptism. Is this also possible in another fashion?

Churchman: Yes, for Paul says with Christ into death. Is the water death?

Theophilus 26: Of course, water is not death, nor is the earth death, with which one buries a natural dead man. And yet one completely covers the dead with the earth. In the same manner also water covers those who are buried through baptism into the death of Christ.

Anabaptist: In the great flood water covered the whole earth. In the same manner, we say, it must cover the whole man in baptism.

Churchman: But to prove this is more honest. Did it [the flood] not also cover the children? Why do you not baptize them? Yet the prefiguration does not point to the drowning of the world, but rather to the deliverance of the Noahites. Were then they also under water? No, my friend, you have no proof, and that the one or the other was baptized in water is far from binding us, because we are never pointed to examples without commandments. Otherwise, all women would have to find their husbands as Ruth did. Besides, you have not yet been able to differentiate between "in" the water and "under" the water.

Theophilus 27: How busy the shrewd mind is to despise the counsel of God for himself and is not aware where it is mocking itself! We are known never to point to examples without commandment and he [Churchman] proves this in a very mocking way with Ruth. Despite this, one looks for an example for infant baptism among the children of those who were drowned because of their unbelief, while one knows very well that Paul did not derive the meaning of baptism from the drowned but from the eight souls who were in the ark. And then one will even make a mockery of baptism asking: "Were then these also under water?" Answer: Yes, of course! In fact, forty days and forty nights until the rain from heaven ceased.

Anabaptist: Well, then justify sprinkling to me. That you should be able to do. Do you have as much [proof] for it as we do for immersion?

Churchman: God himself calls the sprinkling which the old Israelites received under the cloud a baptism. As they walked through the sea the cloud was not above but behind them, which does away with your common misunderstanding. And it is also known that a cloud only sprinkles both when it rains as well as when dew falls. Since then God himself calls sprinkling baptizing, and commands us to baptize, who will prevent us from baptizing in this manner? Especially since He let us know that He was not concerned with the cleansing of the filth from the body. Of what use then would immersion be?

Theophilus 28: Whether the cloud of which St. Paul speaks in those forty years (during which the children of Israel were under its direction and guidance) precipitated on a single occasion enough water by rain or dew that a person could be sprinkled with it, remains an unanswered question. But that it — at the time when it was not above the children of Israel but behind them and ahead of the Egyptians as the children of Israel went through the sea — supposedly sprinkled the entire multitude of Israel, this could hardly survive as a clever legend, much less be accepted as a truth. St. Paul says: "They were baptized in the cloud and in the sea." Why then does he [Churchman] leave out the sea? I shall submit my thoughts [on this] for his examination.

This baptism occurred in the shadow of the Law under Moses and represents the baptism of water and [that] of the Spirit which appear under Christ as part of the New Covenant. Just as one can go through the shadow of a fire without being burned, so they went through the sea without getting wet. The cloud, however, illuminated the night for them and baptized them with light. Just as the night, when it is completely without light, covers man entirely with darkness and, as it were, baptizes him with it, in the same manner the cloud baptizes the children of Israel with its bright light. The angel of the covenant who was present in the cloud and the pillar of fire was, as it were, the true baptizer who led them through the fear of death and through the Red Sea. He rescued them and overthrew their enemies with violence so that they perished in the mighty waters.

Now when they had been delivered and saw their enemies floating dead on the shore, they were rescued and baptized by a mighty hand. However, he who is to baptize according to the commandment of Jesus and who would do the will of the heavenly Father, he is indeed taught by Moses himself (Deuteronomy 15:18) to heed Christ the great prophet. Christ has never pointed the Baptist-minded back to learn from Moses at the Red Sea as to how one must baptize. What then is the use of all these foolish legends? Nothing else, of course, but perhaps to cause a fictional Anabaptist to speak in confusion when he says as follows:

Anabaptist: Their [immerson is] of [no use]. I shall no longer resist the truth. Why do you not talk with your preacher about baptizing my children? I shall no longer rage against my own flesh and blood.

Churchman: You are doing right. Now you can easily see that our doctrines are founded in the Bible and those of your people partly in imagination. In many things they dispute like Separatists. Many of them say: "Away with outward baptism; one must receive it inwardly." "What?" said a good friend, whom I told of this. "What? Are we first to cut the people in two before baptizing them?" My friend's answer seems a bit flippant. Yet it is to be noted that he did not speak against what is inward in a healthy mind, let alone against the inner baptism. But many of these people make of their inner being a hiding place for their ignorance, many also for their wickedness. No tender conscience dares play thus with the word, especially when it has experienced that Peter immediately ordered water baptism for those who had received the Spirit baptism in the fullest measure.

Theophilus 29: That the beloved friend has sought with great pains to base through various doctrines his favored opinion about the baptism of young infants on the Bible, can, of course, easily be seen in this entire dialogue and has justly awakened in me a holy reverence for the holy words of the Lord our God. In the meantime the lovers of Jesus honor the true and narrow path which their Master himself has trod. The laws of their God are dear and precious to them, for they know above all that the Lord himself has founded them eternally (Psalm 119:152). Even though clever people seek to base other customs and laws on the Bible, yet they do not find any room where they could put them. Even though they skim with their keen minds through the testimonies of the Bible, still no trace remains there of such an endeavor. If one wishes to read something about the baptism of infants, one must open the works of clever people. As soon as one closes them and turns to the Bible, there is nothing there. And even if someone quotes half a Bible verse in order to give his opinion a good appearance, the Baptist-minded have Bibles and open them themselves and usually find the opposite from that which he had endeavored to wrest from it. This, then, appears quite unreasonable to a truthful man to treat God's word in this way, and even if one so-called Anabaptist said, "The baptism of Christ is of no avail," then they [the Baptist-minded] think that this person has become a blasphemer. May the good God have mercy upon him and his teacher that they be converted in order that they might be helped.

Refuted Accusations
First: The Baptist-minded are accused that they rage against their own

flesh and blood because they do not baptize their young children. The Baptist-minded firmly believe that a human commandment is of no benefit to a dying infant. But they believe that it is extremely harmful to a child whom the Lord grants to live and to recognize His will, because commonly God's commandments are annulled by man's commandments. Whoever calls this concern raging, is greatly mistaken.

Second: The Baptist-minded are accused that their doctrines are based on imagination, whereas they seek to maintain no other doctrine than the will of their heavenly Father as it is revealed through Jesus Christ in the Holy Scriptures, before which doctrine all imagination disappears as the frost before the brilliance and heat of the sun.

Third: The Baptist-minded are accused that their doctrines shy away from reason . . . and could not stand close investigation. And yet the Baptist-minded wish to have no other doctrines than the words of their Savior as they are written in the New Testament, which words have never yet avoided reason. They can not only stand the closest investigation like a highly purified gold, but will also remain when heaven and earth must pass away.

Fourth: [This is] that a lover of the truth is accused of doing injustice to reason by imprisoning it under the obedience of truth; whereas there is indeed no greater honor below all the heavens for our little reason than when it may glory in the bonds and shackles of the heavenly wisdom; and whereas, when it is found outside of this captivity, outside of its place of refuge, it cannot be considered other than an outlawed harlot, who for her punishment must suffer herself to be tormented, weakened, and destroyed by the terrible monster of unreasonableness.

Fifth: [This is] that the Baptist-minded are accused of being "Anti-Baptists" [Widertäufer]; whereas they have upheld the true baptismal order of Jesus Christ for all nations on earth, and therefore are not against, but rather for, baptism. That, however, the Anabaptist in the dialogue still rightly deserves this name [of Anti-Baptist] is proved by his last statement in which he declares the baptism practiced by Christ and His apostles to be entirely unnecessary, wherewith he, of course, proves that he is against baptism. But because Christ himself says: "Whoever is not against us is for us" [Mark 9:40], the honest Baptist-minded are not Anti-Baptists.

Finally, to come to the conclusion of this dialogue, the beloved friend noted . . . that some say: "Away with the outward baptism, we must receive it inwardly." This he said once to one of his friends, who said: "What? Must one first cut the people in two before baptizing them?"

To make a helpful observation on this, the wise instruction which the beloved friend has given in this dialogue comes in very handy, namely, that faith and believing are to be distinguished just as life and efficacy. To use this now in its correct sense, the illuminating state‑ment of the faithful and true witness serves well, who testifies and says: "Behold, the kingdom of God is within you" (Luke 17:21). Now there where the Kingdom of God is within man, there is also faith, yet with very great differences. In some it is so dead and buried like the fire in a cold stone, with others it is like a spark in the ashes, and again with others like a rather large piece of coal. But with all of them something essential must take place, inwardly or outwardly, most generally inwardly and outwardly at the same time, that is to say, something essential must take place for man to receive the ability to believe or to indicate that faith is not for him but rather that un‑belief is the element in which he has chosen to live and to die. There‑fore Paul testifies (Acts 17:31) that God offers faith to all men, and therefore the apostles and servants of Christ have at all times endeav‑ored to pierce the hearts of people with the two-edged sword of the Word and to cut apart the hiding places of their ignorance and malice and through the preaching of the Kingdom of God to make room for the inward Kingdom of God and to destroy the kingdom of Satan.

There where this divine work is received in man, Christ himself is received in His rightful property (John 1:12). To them He did give the power to become children of God. Note: Those children who believe in His name deserve the bath of rebirth. With them even the water baptism makes its beginning inwardly and is outwardly performed as it pleases God. Christ says: "Every one who looks at a woman lustfully has already committed adultery with her in his heart" [Matthew 5:28]. If then the kingdom of Satan has such power over man, who lets himself be captured by the net of shameful lusts, how much more power does the Kingdom of God have over a man who lets himself be captured by the net of the holy gospel, which was spun and woven by the heavenly wisdom.

Therefore, when the eunuch said to Philip: "See, here is water! What is to prevent my being baptized?" (Acts 8:36), he had already accepted the water baptism inwardly in faith. Yet Philip wanted him to put on Christ inwardly through faith before he stepped into the water, therefore he said: "If you believe with all your heart, it may be." He answered: "I believe that Jesus Christ is the Son of God." Paul speaks in this sense (Galatians 3:27): "For as many of you as were baptized into Christ have put on Christ." Of such a man it can in truth be said that he is baptized. But he will mock neither the outward nor the inward baptism. Rather, I believe that whoever puts on Christ at the same time puts on the entire counsel of God and says from the bottom of his heart and mind with the converted Saul: "What shall I do, Lord?" [Acts 22:10].

Finally, it must be considered that just as faith and believing must be distinguished, there is also a great difference between a healthy and a sickly faith. Therefore St. Paul admonishes Titus, his righteous son, to punish some of them severely that they might be sound in the faith (Titus 1:13). Just as a sick person cannot do what is often easy for a well man, so a sick faith cannot believe everything that otherwise is easy for a healthy faith to believe. Therefore it cannot be the victory which overcomes the world.

I must, therefore, freely confess that in the entire dialogue about baptism, I have perceived a very great sickness of faith in our beloved Churchman. Especially where he himself testifies that he cannot believe that John the Baptist could have baptized all the people by immersion. For, he says, he was no Samson, nor made of steel or iron, so that he could have constantly stood in water. It seems to me that a healthy mind could almost without faith have judged the matter better. Yet, I have often perceived that a sick faith can also cause a sickness in mind, just as a healthy faith alone is capable of healing a sick mind and of preserving it in good health. A healthy faith clings to God's Word, which heals everything, even where otherwise neither herbs nor plasters can heal.

If we consider the matter merely with natural understanding, it is known that natural fishermen spend almost night and day for months at a time mostly in water, just for the sake of their temporal nourishment. Some have such constitutions that it does not harm them in the least, even though in these Occidental lands the water in the winter is much more penetrated by cold than in the warm Orient. I find therefore not the slightest reason to doubt that John, in the time that he had had, could have baptized as many people here in Pennsylvania as he did in the East. But to believe that he could not have done it in those warm lands is believing in far-too-sickly a manner through an all-too-great unreasonable rationalization. I therefore find myself compelled in ardent love to oppose a bit this sickness of faith. In the first place, it is certain that the commandment of God is the eternal life, and the secret of godliness is beneficial in all things, and that it has the promise of life here and hereafter. God-fearing men live herein in daily experience.

In the second place, I must testify here before God that in these cold Western lands, during the brief time of my pilgrimage, over one thousand people of various constitutions have been baptized in this manner by immersion and many in cold winter at that. I have not heard of a single one who has suffered the slightest harm or discomfort in the health of his body by this. On the contrary, there are conscientious people who will testify that they had periods of illness which were cured in the water bath through the Word. I would like to relate just one single example among many.

Some sixty-six years ago in Europe in the Palatinate, there was in Rheinderken, a small village near the Rhine River not far from Mannheim, a sister who had long been ill and bedfast, so that her friends despaired of her recovery. It pleased Providence to happen that a minister of the Baptist-minded, named John Naas, came there to visit the friends. He was accustomed to edify with divine conversation the friends gathered there at the place where the sick sister was and could listen. On this occasion the sick sister also spoke and testified that she had a fervent desire to be baptized upon her faith according to the manner of the first Christians.

The friends who were present objected and voiced their concern that it was not advisable to attempt this, because she was so weak that one could not very well take her to the Rhine River, and if she were to be brought there with great effort she might then even die in the hands of the baptizer, which would immediately cause great blaspheming. However, John Naas went to the bedside of the sick sister and spoke with her and said: "Do you have faith that this work of the Lord can be carried out on your sick body?" She an-

swered: "Yes!" Thereupon he said: "Then I also have faith to per-
form it on you."

Hereupon the friends dropped their objections and got ready to
satisfy the sister and her faith. They took her, dressed her for baptism
and carried her on both arms with great trouble into the Rhine.
There she knelt down in the name of Jesus and was immersed by
John Naas in the name of the Father and the Son and the Holy Spirit.
Thereupon hands were laid upon her, and she was prayed over. All
at once she was well, came up out of the water and with great rejoicing
preceded the others and when she returned home she served them.[33]

Further evidences of the assistance of grace and the power of God
sensed in administering holy baptism could easily be cited. Yet my
purpose here is merely to testify that among a thousand not one ex-
ample is to be found where the water of baptism has caused the
slightest harm to someone's health. And herewith I think best to
conclude my Apology.

.   .   .   .   .   .

Kind Reader:
There is another work at the [same] printer's who did this, in which
all the main points of Theophilus are listed and refuted and, as it
were, answered by Theophilus. If the interested parties [Liebhaber]
find no [!] pleasure in this and desire that it too be published, they
may subscribe for it.
Note: This booklet can also be had at Justus Fuchs' in Germantown,
at Jacob Karch's in Lebanon, at John Morris', clerk in York town, at
Henry Danner's, Daniel Fahnstock's and others in York County.[34]

RESPONSES TO THE APOLOGIA

An early reaction to Mack's publication came from John Baumann,
whose property adjoined the Ephrata Community. He is said to have taken
over the Ephrata press at the close of the century, and was likely related to
the Brother Benjamin Baumann who printed for Mack. Judging from his
letter, he could be classified as a Separatist in his religious views.[35]

John Baumann to Alexander Mack, Jr.

[Ephrata, 1788]

Dear and kind friend:
I read in the recent pamphlet that the element of water is credited

with such great power, namely, making spiritual children of God and reborn ones (page twenty-seven). There are hardly two among twenty who can say this about themselves in truth, and even then it would not be because of this natural water. No wonder that simple people or children upon reading such think that it is a very easy thing to become a child of God. Especially, when they have not been able to read a chapter in the [New] Testament with understanding, for whoever is under eighteen [years of age] is counted as a child. Thus, the last time you baptized, [you were baptizing] children, against which you so often protested.

I cannot think that you believe so naively that it is the natural water which is meant in John 3:5. Without question, that water is meant about which Jesus spoke to the woman of Samaria. It is possible that all outward commandments and ordinances in the Old and New Testaments which were misused by the unfaithfulness of men and the scheming of the enemy were counted as idolatries.

God commanded that the serpent of brass be raised; later the Jews burnt incense to it. Hezekiah was not afraid to destroy it [2 Kings 18:4] (see the commentary about this in the Berleburg Bible).[36] How much the Jews boasted and bragged about their circumcision, Temple, and sacrifices; you know well what came of it.

Thus, my dear friend, it is very probable that the majority of those who make so much of the water, depend upon it as if now they were better [than others] etc., so that they burn incense to the water or practice idolatry with it, which is amply evidenced in their disputes about it with others. Yes, they make a shibboleth of it. For most of them it serves as nothing else but to condemn other sects, and they would like to be regarded the only church of the Lord.

Such people are very similar to the Roman [Catholic] sect, which in its sectarian zeal condemns all others. When one clings so much to the outward ceremonies and shadows, and esteems them so highly, the main things are passed over. The Quakers had a tract printed in 1747. To refute it, the Brethren printed one in great haste.[37] There it says (page fifteen): "Him we shall gladly allow to stand uncondemned before his Lord as a strange servant." And (page sixteen) already the text from Galatians 1:8-9 is quoted. Can this be understood any other way than that he who does not preach the outward baptism along with the gospel is condemned? Is that not a scandalous, inconsistent way of writing, [and] so close together [at that]!

It cannot be proved that Jesus or the apostles pronounced this curse on those who neglected water baptism. Another sectarian judgment is on page twenty-six [namely] that the Quakers prided themselves in vain of possessing the Spirit of God. It is credible that the Lord will have His own even among them, as well as among the Brethren and all other sects. The basis of their sect is more spiritual than that of the Brethren. Our Savior says, John 6, verse 63: "The flesh is of no avail."

It seems as if the Brethren seek their salvation and life in outward ceremonies, because they want to place the curse on all others. They should rather take the Jews as an example who, it seems, had more faith in the ark of the covenant than in the almighty God, for they sent for the ark instead of turning to the Lord as they should have done (Isaiah 34:22 [?]). However, their idolatrous attachment to the ark had a miserable result as they had lost only four thousand before but afterwards lost thirty thousand men plus their idols. Thus a person reveals what spirit's child he is, like the disciples who wanted to cause fire to fall from heaven. An answer on page six of the *Forty Questions:*[38] Is it not probable that if many faithful souls had been compelled through the inward voice they would not have rendered obedience immediately; but rather they have gained insight into what shall come out of the outward ceremony.

You have made a decision that no one should take interest. Yet one of you has taken sixty pounds in rent where the building was scarcely worth sixty pounds. If you wish to ask me, I can name the man. Concerning usury see Deuteronomy 23:18. It seems that the profit from interests is too small for you. The merchants say the same, etc.

I remain your debtor-in-love, well-intentioned friend,

John Baumann.

P.S. In the second vision of the booklet about the condition of souls after death, printed in Germantown in 1755,[39] something is reported which all preachers and listeners ought to take as an example. The answer to the tenth question deals with renunciation: What things must the Brethren in this country renounce more than other sects? Some are more fashionable than other people. I have had a bedstead made for my daughter. It was not tall enough for the fine sisters. There had to be pieces put on top. Some of them waste their precious time by calling at their sisters' to have — as they call it — "tea with them." They spend their time libeling their own people, and others, and when they return they are less than when they went.

A booklet was printed at Hall's in Philadelphia in 1759, written by William Zell.[40] I would like to see how you or those of your opinion could refute it. He did not pronounce the curse of Galatians often over all those who were not of his opinion. Many could learn from him to restrain their sectarian zeal (Acts 10:35).

To be delivered to Alexander Mack.

Kunze's Rebuttal

The *Apologia* brought an immediate printed reply from John Christopher Kunze. His ninety-two-page rejoinder, again presented in the form of a dialogue between a Churchman and an Anabaptist, was printed somewhat later in 1788 in Lancaster, Pennsylvania, although Kunze was at this time living in New York.[41] The length of this publication precludes its incorporation here, but the translated title page and preface will give some indication of the sharpness of his retort.

One of his Philadelphia colleagues, J. H. Christian Helmuth (1745-1825), writing on baptism in 1793, had this comment:

But we are forced to break off here, because time and space do not allow this point to be further emphasized. Besides, the teaching on infant baptism has been so thoroughly demonstrated in various tracts, even here in America, that it would be superfluous to say another word about it. [Note.] See Dr. Kunze's *Something Concerning the Correct Path of Life* and his anonymous but well-known *Conquered Anabaptist. . . .*[42]

The Conquered Anabaptist, in Conversations about Infant Baptism and Immersion; Written in Contradiction of Theophilus, for the Benefit of the Common Man, by a Seducer who is Yet Sincere.

"Hold firm to the word . . . to confute those who contradict it" (Paul to Titus, Chapter 1:9).

Lancaster: Printed by Albrecht and Lahn, 1788.

The Author's Preface

This little book owes its existence to no sectarian partisanship. I

am bound to believe and confess that which is true; in this I know
no indifference. Yet, at the same time, I covet from my heart the
very freedom of conscience for all men which God has also granted
to me. I am bound in love and justice to treat all persons alike and
to consider as a friend and brother everyone who has the true faith
and who conducts himself rightly, no matter what his religious affiliation is. This is, of course, not the impartiality which a certain contemporary gang [*Haufe*] preaches, but it is the Biblical one and therefore I
shall remain in it. The other kind is poison wrapped in gold foil.

No! It is rather because of the malice of my opponents that I
have been forced and compelled to write. In my youth I wrote as
a personal exercise the dialogue which they have made public property
by printing. Six years ago a friend of mine borrowed it, and that for
his own personal use. I neglected to forbid him to circulate it further,
and, unintentionally, the writing came into the hands of the Anabaptists.

They immediately flew into a passion and buried me under a
load of intended refutations. I answered, and the matter would have
rested there, if the spirit of contention and proud imprudence had
not spurred them to publication. They, of course, say on their title
page that they were challenged to it by my dialogue, yet I know
nothing of this. Also, our dispute would have remained a private
matter forever, and no one would have suffered any harm from it,
for Solomon says: "One knife whets another, and one man the other."

I really have good reason to complain that they have treated me
against all principles of Christian fairness. In a most unfair way they
have made a public uproar out of the private dispute which we had
with each other. In equally unfair manner they have had my composition printed without taking counsel with me, or securing my
permission.

Still, if they had not distorted it, I might have remained content.
But, various Scriptural citations which were in my manuscript were
omitted, and words were exchanged for others in order to make my
speech bare and ridiculous. For example: on page twenty-five, line
eight (in their book) I had added Genesis 17:14, and on page forty-
one, line two, I had written "loss" instead of "conclusion." As many
as six years ago I protested in writing against the distortion of this
work, but in vain.

The Mennonites have no part in our dispute. They are for the most part peaceful and patient people who leave their fellowmen in peace. They also have many honest and well-meaning souls among them, to whom I wish all health and happiness from the abundance of Jesus.

My opponents profess themselves to be immersionists. I possess, besides their little book, various manuscripts from them. Everything important which appears herein I have collected and attributed to my "Anabaptist." Their objections are for the most part so shallow that I am almost ashamed to present them. Yet, I was forced to work with the materials which they laid before me. Even if they may seem insignificant to us, nevertheless, they appear to them to be important, and therefore have to be taken into consideration.

[John Christopher Kunze][43]

A FINAL WORD BY MACK, JR.

A final word in the printed disputation between Mack, Jr., and Kunze is found in the *Appendix to the Conquered Anabaptist,* published in late 1788 by the Brethren author. Again cast in dialogue form, the pedobaptist position is given by the "Children's Friend," the "Opponent," and the "Churchman." Mack's point of view is articulated by the "Child."

Of particular interest in this polemic are the historical data and the repetition of Peter Miller's involvement (given in italics). The latter indicates a degree of cooperation between the two sister groups in the later eighteenth century which has not previously been taken into account to any degree.

Appendix to the Conquered Anabaptist, containing two dialogues, and the final farewell of Theophilus.
"Always be prepared to make a defense to anyone who calls you to account for the hope that is in you" (1 Peter 3:15).

. . . . .

Ephrata: 1788

The Churchman complains in his preface that his manuscript was printed without his consent. Answer: After all, he says on his title page that it was "written for the common man." We know no better way to make a manuscript useful to the common man than by publishing it.

. . . . .

The First Dialogue

Children's Friend: The translation (Luther's Matthew 28:19) is incorrect or else Jesus spoke unintelligibly.

Child: This, it seems to me, is not only a quite awkward but even a sinful conclusion. It is true, I too have heard that learnéd men like to draw conclusions; but why does one not rather draw conclusions that can stand before God and men? In fact, Theophilus admitted in his *Apologia* that the last translation was also correct. Luther's translation says: "Teaching all nations, and baptizing them, etc." The others say: "Make disciples of all nations, baptizing them." Does then a better conclusion belong here? If Luther's translation were incorrect, then the others would also be incorrect. For all of them attest to but one and the same truth, although in somewhat different words. For certainly, to teach and to make disciples do not contradict each other; nor does to baptize and baptizing them. On the contrary it shows the most beautiful harmony.

It almost seems to me that Wesley and the Children's Friend himself must be convinced in their hearts that this my conclusion is much better than that which the Children's Friend made earlier. For if a marked difference could be extorted from the two translations whereby Luther's translation could be rejected, what need would there be to say: "The fact that something was written first is far from proof that it must also be done first." Yet, my esteemed Children's Friend, let us for this time disregard with due respect Luther's translation, namely, the translation of the commission in Matthew 28, and let us pretend that it does not exist in the world, and let us go by the translation of Wesley and other learnéd men. However, not in the sense in which you envision it as if one were to fell you with your own sword. For this would not be Christian and is not at all our vocation. We are to be only the aides of the truth and show the path to the erring. If, after this, he [Children's Friend] will still err, we have at least done our part and can take leave in peace from this present wicked world.

And now my esteemed Children's Friend! Christ said to His disciples, "Make disciples of all nations, baptizing them etc." These very disciples of His, He himself had made disciples, baptizing them. Just as He had had mercy upon them, they, too (according to the measure of grace which He had given them and was yet to give them) were to have mercy upon all nations and, according to occasion and opportunity, they were to perform upon these [nations] what He had performed on them. How then did He make them disciples, baptizing them? Had He not taught them anything before the baptism? That, the Children's Friend himself cannot believe. On the contrary, He first taught them, and then, baptizing them, made them disciples. He later, after they had surrendered themselves to Him through baptism, continued to teach everything that the Father had commanded Him and sent them the Spirit of truth, which was to remind them of everything that He had told them before and after baptism.

Now the dear disciples could hardly have misunderstood their Master: for example, word and deed together make a complete teaching. Now when the disciples of Christ, according to the specific commandment of their Master, had waited in Jerusalem until they were filled with power from above, and received on the Day of Pentecost the promise of the Father, God gave them an opportunity to fulfill the commandment of their Master and baptized them in order to make disciples. And that they did. But how did they do it? Answer: They gave them as much instruction about the mystery of the cross as was needed, and because Peter was the spokesman, it says (Acts 2: 41) [that] "those who received his word were baptized" etc., and (verse 42): "They devoted themselves to the apostles' teaching and fellowship, to the breaking of bread and the prayers." Here was evidenced for the first time by the apostles total obedience to the commandments of Jesus Christ, as He spoke (Matthew 28): "Make disciples of all men, baptizing them, and teach them to keep all things which I have commanded you."

However, because it says those who gladly received His word were baptized, children cannot understand the word, and therefore cannot receive it either. There is consequently no basis to be found here to draw a conclusion about the baptism of infants. But the fact that Peter said: "For the promise is to you and to your children and to all that are yet to be . . . whom the Lord our God will call to Him" indicates that to them and to their children only one promise is given, namely, that if they receive the word of the cross, repent, are baptized, they will receive the gift of the Holy Spirit.

Children's Friend: The persons of whom they were to make disciples are all nations, the majority of whom are children. The majority of them die in infancy. Therefore, if one had to first teach everyone, it would not even be possible to make disciples of all nations, or even half of them.

Child: I have thoroughly studied this statement in the fear of the Lord, and find no other way to come out of this labyrinth and be blessed than simply to believe that God is faithful. He can indeed place upon His creatures whatever obligation He wishes. But when He lays upon us an obligation, He first works [in us] the willingness. If one accepts it in such a way that one wills as He wills, He also effects and grants the completion according to His good pleasure, and then all is well; God is satisfied and man is blessed.

This statement is certain and upholds the entire mystery of salvation and, of course, also in the commandment (Matthew 28). Christ said here to twelve apostles: "Go into all the world etc." He made them willing to do this. He, however, permitted James to be beheaded by Herod, who therefore did not go to all the world. And yet he entered into his rest as a loyal servant who had done His Master's will. But the thing that this brings even more to the fore is: Christ commanded His apostles to make disciples of all nations, and that by baptizing them and also teaching them to keep everything that He had commanded them, saying: "Lo, I am with you always, to the close of the age."

This shows clearly that He meant with the words "all nations" even us as well. Of course, they were unable to teach us orally, therefore they had to teach us in writing, and hand down to us the counsel of God collected in writings. In this teaching or making of disciples by baptizing them, He is and remains with them all days until the close of the age. If Christ had commanded infant baptism, they would obviously not have taught most of the nations [all that He had commanded them], namely, all those whom they could not reach orally, but had to teach in writing. Yet, they could have done it quite easily with a verse of three or four lines.

For almost sixteen hundred years, the dear Messrs. Infant-baptizers have now been seeking in the Bible a well-founded proof for infant baptism and have not yet found it. Therefore the Baptist-minded still insist on this one point and say: "Show us one single commandment or example for infant baptism in the Holy Scriptures and we shall be in harmony with you!" But as long as this does not happen, you must not take it amiss that we believe the history of baptism which reports that infant baptism was instituted by the popes and that it was a commandment of the Roman Catholic emperors. The learnéd among the Roman Church admit quite freely that infant baptism is not based on the New Testament, but is rather a statute of their church.

Children's Friend: Many a one begins with us in the spirit and ends up with you in the flesh. You put your baptism into his head and then he is supposed to have followed the prompting of the Father. Instead of running after salvation he lets them dip him into the water, the poor wretch! He is to seek Christ in the river whom we are not to seek in more comfortable places, as in the desert or in one's chamber, etc.

Child: This severe accusation sounds indeed abusive enough, yet why do you not name a single one by name who did that in Germany or here in Pennsylvania? You have enough courage to say it of many a one but why do you not show us a single name? I, for one, am not one of them. I did not receive baptism in my infancy, but only when I was seventeen years of age. Besides at that time I was not in America but in Friesland. Since you give us no name, I would like to tell you a bit about a brother, Partel Jürgen Peterson, who lived in Altona, [Germany].[44] He, too, was honored in his infancy with sprinkling, but his parents and sponsors did not have enough love for him even to let him learn to read. He was also brought up very roughly.

In his youth he pursued the fishing trade and when he was grown up he became a soldier. However, when the promptings of the Father drew him inwardly to repentance, he applied for his release. This was most difficult at first, but finally the Lord ordained it that after all he was given his freedom. As soon as he was free, he returned to Altona and was fully determined to lead a different life. Therefore he attended church diligently.

Once when he heard a preacher preach very sharply about the future punishment of the godless, Jürgen went away sadly. However, he returned for a second and third time to this preacher and requested him to please show him the way to heaven. But the preacher always answered him: "I do not have the time."

"Yet," (he said at last), "there is a book, which is called the New Testament. You buy that and read it. The way to heaven is described correctly and infallibly therein." Jürgen asked whether it would be possible to obtain this book in Altona. The preacher said: "Oh, yes! You can secure it in several bookstores." The poor man bought himself a Testament and made friends with the school children so that they instructed him outside of school hours in the primer [*Namenbuch*]. Within fourteen days he had learned to read.

Philadelphia, September 10, 1788.

Worthy Brother Benjamin [Baumann]:[45]

I received safely your letter of August first, and read it with pleasure. I also gave it to Brother P[eter] L[eibert] to read, and your opinion pleases both of us very well (namely that you will delete the numerous digressions). Yet, it seems to me that if the conversation about the immersion and the feetwashing is to be printed, then the conclusion of the entire dissertation should not be forgotten. For in it I bade a final farewell, and I do not intend to become involved in any written dispute, rather, insofar as it depends on me, [I would] have peace with all men. May the Lord grant us His grace to pray from our hearts for the so-called Children's Friend!

Dear Brother! You will best know how to interpret my simple letter. As far as the circumstances of my life are concerned, my strength is fading daily, for I am old and tired of living; the time of my departure is at hand and I am longing, as a broken vessel of divine mercy, for the complete release from this body of death. Herewith I remain your warmly disposed brother,

Theophilus.

Churchman: I have nothing for nor anything against immersion; it is for me neither more nor less valid than sprinkling. God did not prescribe a manner of baptism for us, etc.

N. S. If you had said this earlier, we could have been spared much. For the Baptist-minded do not find fault with whoever justifies and

*practices sprinkling but at the same time admits that immersion is just
as good. However, we do not go by what the Anabaptists do. You
are so bold as to call your shadow an Anabaptist, and give him such
a whipping that he breaks out in cold sweat as can be seen in your
book — and then we have to bear the blame and you are the man
who claims he does not wish to dispute.*

*Churchman: Theophilus has been trying to appeal to my conscience
by saying that blood has been shed because of infant baptism, the
poor wretch! The same is true of adult baptism at Münster. My
conscience is clear!*

*N. S. If your conscience is clear regarding the falsification of The-
ophilus' manuscript, then it must be very dull. However, I am surprised that you do not spare your reputation. Anyone who reads the
Apologia can see that Theophilus writes (page fifty-six): "The deeds
of Jesus were all virtues, and His virtues were the sources of His
deeds etc." Why then do you attempt to persuade the common man
to believe that Theophilus knows no difference between virtues and
deeds? If you could refute his statement, then why did you quote
him falsely? Theophilus rightly distinguishes between the two words:
a virtue can exist as little without a deed as a fire without heat. You
yourself count love among the virtues. Why then does Theophilus'
speech seem strange to you? The teaching and deeds of Jesus flowed
from this noble virtue (love); they all are also lovely, good, and beneficial. To Him be praise and honor in eternity. Amen.*

*That to which he [Churchman] refers about Münster does not
concern Theophilus. The church used to ascribe this evil (but un-
justly) to the Mennonites. Yet you praise them in your preface. Therefore you will listen patiently to Menno's explanation about infant
baptism, as follows:*

*"Before I had ever heard of the existence of the brethren, [I
heard] that a God-fearing, pious hero named Sicke Snijder was beheaded at Leeuwarden for being rebaptized. It sounded very strange
to me to hear of a second baptism. I examined the Scriptures diligently
and pondered them earnestly, but could find no report of infant
baptism.*

*"After I had noticed this I discussed it with my pastor and after
much talk he had to admit that there was no basis for infant baptism*

in Scripture. Still I dared not trust my own understanding but consulted several ancient authors. They taught me that children are by baptism cleansed from their original sin. I compared this idea with the Scriptures and found that it did violence to the blood of Christ.

"Afterwards I consulted Luther. For I sought for the basis of baptism. He taught me that children were to be baptized on account of their own faith. I perceived that this also was not in accordance with the Word of God.

"Thirdly I consulted Bucer. He taught that infants are to be baptized so that they might be the more carefully nurtured in the way of the Lord. I perceived that this doctrine was also without foundation.

"Fourthly I consulted Bullinger. He pointed to the covenant and to circumcision. This I found likewise to be incapable of Scriptural proof.

"Then I noticed from all these that writers varied so greatly among themselves, each following his own wisdom; then I realized that we were deceived in regard to infant baptism.

"[Despite this, I continued] led by covetousness and the desire to obtain a great name. . . . I spoke much concerning the Word of the Lord, without spirituality or love, as all hypocrites do . . . [until] after about nine months or so, the gracious Lord granted me His fatherly Spirit, help, and hand. Then I, without constraint, of a sudden, renounced all my worldly reputation, name and fame, my unchristlike abominations, my masses, infant baptism, and my early life. . . ."[46]

He [Jürgen Petersen] read his Testament with great eagerness, and learned the way to salvation. He also learned therein how the first Christians baptized, and asked whether there were still any people who baptized as the first Christians did. He was then told that there were such people in Krefeld under the King of Prussia. As soon as Jürgen heard this he set out and went to Krefeld to the house of a brother. He told him how things had gone with him and that he desired to be baptized. The brother wanted him to stay with him, [as] he would present it to the brethren on Sunday. Jürgen, however, said: "No, it must be done today."

He persisted until he persuaded the brother. It was winter, however, and the ice was very thick on the water, so that it had to be chopped open with an axe. The onlookers stood upon the ice. He was baptized, went home happily, and led a devout life until his natural death. He lived to be almost ninety years of age. This man often visited us in Friesland, and therefore I learned to know him very well. I loved him dearly and he [loved] me. But I am certain that the brother sought nothing in the water than in obedience of the faith to subject himself to the divine command. Whoever seeks something else in the water is in error.

Children's Friend: You should first have proved that Jesus was immersed and that now everyone is obligated to do the same.

Child: Doctor Luther says (*T[auf] H[istorie],* page 924): "Baptism is *baptismos* in Greek, and *mersio* in Latin, and means to plunge something completely into the water, so that the water covers it."[47] And since Jesus was baptized by John in the Jordan, there remains for a truthful soul no doubt concerning the immersion of Jesus. As far as the other question is concerned, whether everyone is obligated to do the same, listen to what Augustine says to the newly converted [*Junggepflanzte*]: "Before we immersed your whole body in the holy baptismal water, we asked you: 'Do you believe in God?' etc. Then each of you answered: 'I believe.' This we did according to the commandment of Jesus Christ, our Savior, who commanded His apostles: 'Go therefore, teach all nations, baptizing them etc.'" (*T[auf] H[istorie],* [page] 712).

Children's Friend: But since the word *baptizein* actually means . . . with water, no translator has a right to render it otherwise.

Child: That the word *baptizein* also means washing cannot detract in the slightest from the matter. It is sufficient that the word *baptismus* (not only signifies but also) means immersion. Otherwise, baptism would signify a burial; Christ, however, did not command us to bury or wash off in baptism, but rather to be immersed. The burying and the washing off still occur in baptism, if it is done properly. But that is done through a more powerful hand than through the hand of a mortal baptizer. I have already presented to you the testimonies of Luther and Augustine on immersion. If this should not be enough, hear also the testimony of Jerome as it is written in the *History of*

Baptism [*Tauf-Historie*], page 324. Jerome in [commentary on] chapter four of Ephesians also agrees: "One faith, one baptism, etc. It is said 'one faith' because we believe at once in the Father and in the Son and in the Holy Spirit: for we are baptized in the same way in the Father, in the Son and in the Holy Spirit and immersed three times, so that the mystery of the Trinity should be demonstrated, etc."

Now, whoever wants to see, can see as clearly as the sun that Jesus was immersed, and that He commanded to immerse. That this practice remained in the church for over thirteen hundred years is testified to by your own writings. Why then does anyone want to distort the word "immersion" and make "washing" out of it? As a matter of fact, it would be much more troublesome to wash the person. Yet, immerse they will not nor wash; so they sprinkle a little water on the forehead. And since they cannot well make themselves believe that this is right, they force a disputation on those who practice it correctly. If God is satisfied with you, why do you not remain quiet and let those be in peace of whom you know, and in your heart must be convinced, that they practice it rightly? After all, they do you no harm; rather, they pray for you.

Many a man has taken great pains to differentiate between the baptism of John and the baptism of Jesus in order completely to do away with water baptism. This is, of course, not your intention, for you only wish to do away with immersion. But even when you have made three baptisms out of it, you will still find in each case the Greek word which means immersion, and therefore despite all your effort, you have done nothing. As to what he [Children's Friend] further mentions, that one should baptize the people into Christ and not into water, this reminds me of the words of Luther: "When we say 'a little water' [*klein Wasser*] then the fanatics say 'no water' [*kein Wasser*]."[48] I am amazed that a scholar should so completely forget the beginning of his question. The question was whether Jesus, when He was in the Jordan, was immersed by John or not? Theophilus cited three witnesses for this, in his *Apologia*. Of those you thoroughly denounced one and later admitted that he gave a true witness. Nevertheless, you still wish to win and [therefore] you are teaching us that we should be immersed into Christ.

Did then John immerse Jesus into Christ, or did he immerse Him into the water of the Jordan? Even though the opponent struck an empty blow, he was not aware of it, and therefore the precious words of Paul (Romans 6:3) must serve him as a sword to deny and to revile that very baptism of which he is, after all, convinced in his own conscience that even Paul and Peter and the believers of their time received it in all sincerity according to the will of God.

That which the learnéd opponent would have liked to say in conclusion, [namely], that God himself called sprinkling baptism (1 Corinthians 10:2) belongs among the untruths, for nothing of this is found in the place mentioned. That the cloud of which St. Paul speaks rained, rests on supposition . . . that cannot be proved, and has been sufficiently refuted in the *Apologia* (page sixty-three). That Peter is supposed to have taught that the washing off of filth from the body was nothing, that the Children's Friend himself cannot believe. For if the filth were not washed from the body, then we could not succeed in this world which is so full of filth. Peter, by teaching us that the washing off of the filth of the body does not save us, directs us to the covenant of a good conscience and to the resurrection from the dead, in order that we might not seek in vain our happiness and salvation in this world and in this life (1 Corinthians 15:19).

The Second Dialogue:

Opponent: Your feetwashing is a murder knife with which innocent souls are slaughtered.

Child: I do believe that Jesus, the great friend of children, commanded the holy feetwashing in the last night when He was betrayed.

Opponent: All this cannot be proved and it is still questionable whether it happened at the Last Supper. The ancients called the evening meal supper and all the events which are recorded in John 13 seem to have happened several days before the night in which He was betrayed.

Child: I have already heard this at length that several have written thus. Yet one cannot blame a child if it trusts and believes more in the Great Children's Friend who gave His life for us than in all others. Jesus said to Peter (John 13:38): "Truly, truly, I say to you, the cock will not crow, till you have denied me three times." Whoever then insists that this took place several days earlier seems to contradict the

Great Children's Friend. In that case one would have to pretend a miracle here if the cock was not supposed to have crowed for several nights. Yet, as the Scripture here says nothing of such a miracle, the children do not presuppose one.

Opponent: And even if I believed it, what would it prove? It does not follow from this that one should wash feet before the [Lord's] supper. Otherwise one would also have to recline at the supper, because Jesus and His disciples, like all Near Easterners of that time, did so. Where is it that the Savior said that we should do this just before the supper?

Child: Jesus says (John 13:15): "For I have given you an example, that you should also do as I have done to you." He, however, did not say that you should recline at the tables at supper. Rather, He says: "If I then, your Lord and Teacher, have washed your feet, you also ought to wash one another's feet." Thus the Master gave His disciples an example that they should do as He did. Therefore, this example is nowhere more fitting than where the good Master put it, that is, before the supper.

Opponent: But since the true feetwashing people are saved men, then the true feetwashing must not be practiced by any vicious person in its nature and extent. Yet many among you wash the feet of others, who could not think less of anything than of salvation. According to the Bible, these are not blessed; consequently your [feetwashing] must not be the true one.

Child: That many among us wash the feet of others who could not think less of anything than of salvation we children would like to know who told him [Opponent] that. We, for our part, know nothing of it, and he is, after all, no searcher of the hearts that he should know what our brethren think when they wash one another's feet. Or has perhaps our Opponent in his judging spirit raised himself over our brethren? Has he perhaps forgotten what the true Feetwasher says: "Judge not lest you be judged"?

That, however, it should be concluded that our feetwashing is not the true one even if there were really one individual present who did not think of salvation is far too weak an empty blow to knock the holy feetwashing out of the hands of the Baptist-minded. When Jesus himself washed with His own hands the feet of His disciples, Judas was one of the Twelve. He was neither saved nor clean. And yet that was the one true and most [nearly] perfect feetwashing that ever was on earth.

Opponent: You have, however, made of that which the Savior designated as a work of servanthood a religious service. This, of course, would be the easiest way to glorify the old Adam. Of course, he [the old Adam] would not like to demean himself to wash perhaps the dusty legs of a Negro, or the dirty rags of a beggar. Yet to wait upon a clean company and on top of that so falsely to appropriate the promise at the Lord's supper, that is what gives him life.

Child: It seems indeed that my Opponent has never yet rightly understood the holy feetwashing of Christ, because he so exclusively considers it to be an outward washing off of the filth from the body. Has he read what Jesus said to Peter: "If I do not wash you, you have no part in me" (John 13:8)? Up to that point, however, Peter himself had had no real concept of it, but this key opened his heart so that he said: "Lord, not my feet only but also my hands and my head!" Jesus said to him: "He who has bathed does not need to wash, except for his feet, but he is clean all over; and you are clean, but not all of you." From this conversation between Christ and Peter the exact relationship that exists between the holy baptism and the holy feetwashing emerges very clearly.

For just as a poor sinner who repents according to God's counsel, and believes in the gospel, has his sins washed away in the holy baptism (Acts 22:16), so also for a brother or [a] sister of Christ (Matthew 12:50) the word of Christ becomes powerful and effective for a thorough cleansing of the feet of his or her faith after each false step that he or she truly repents. This is brought about by his having his feet washed and washing the others' feet in obedience of the faith and genuine gratitude. However, his gratitude must be a true one so that he might be willing and ready from the bottom of his heart to be reminded and disciplined by a fellow-member in respect to anything that might be contrary to the saving doctrine. But just as in holy baptism, the washing away of the filth of the body does not save us; rather, the covenant of a good conscience with God, the very same applies to the feetwashing of the saints.

Opponent: The Savior wanted to prevent such lack of love among His own and since the disciples had walked with Him that day He humbled himself thereto. In so doing He left us an example of love and humility and established the teaching that a Christian should conduct himself as the servant of all his brethren. No one would practice this unless grace ruled in him. That is why Jesus says: "If you know these things, blessed are you if you do them" (John 13:17). The word "are" has a beautiful emphasis here; He does not say that they will be so only in the future, but that they are blessed even now if they do so. No one, however, can be blessed already now in this time, except those who belong to Christ. Those, however, without exception, who belong to Him crucify their flesh along with their lusts and desires.

Child: This witness honors the feetwashing to such an extent that all true children of God must affirm it. For you not only admit it, but also know that feetwashing belongs of right to those who belong to Christ and who crucify their flesh along with their lusts and desires. These, then, are blessed even now, in the deed of their believing obedience, and will also be blessed in eternity, for obedience is the essence of all virtue (1 Samuel 15:22). Such was the Son of God to His Father and the eleven disciples to their Master, and it was to them that He commanded the holy feetwashing. It is true, he also washed the feet of Judas, but yet did not command him to do it. For after He had said: "If you know these things, blessed are you if you do them!" He immediately said: "I am not speaking of you all; I know whom I have chosen; that the scripture may be fulfilled, 'He who ate my bread has lifted his heel against me.'"

The assumption that on that day they had walked so far on their physical feet that they therefore had need of washing their feet as an outward work, is not at all probable. According to all evidence, Jesus did not come any farther with His disciples than from Bethany, which was only a short walk.

Opponent: There have always been people who trifled with this matter. To wash clean and already-washed feet over again I cannot help but call precisely that. The popes, the emperor, and the kings of France have also always had the practice of washing the feet of some paupers on Maundy Thursday. Yet, how humble or blessed do you think they were? The true feetwashing is not only a work of love but also a work of servanthood. One must wash the dirty and dusty feet of a poor traveler if he has need of it, etc. One might perhaps inquire of you: when have you done this to a traveler or a poor man?

Child: I rejoice from the bottom of my heart that our Great Children's Friend is such a king that even emperors and kings had to confess that even His seemingly humble commands are nevertheless sacred. But how blessed they were in doing so can be best determined by our Great Children's Friend. Have they not by the very fact that they performed it on Maundy Thursday (that is during Holy Week) professed that it does not belong to the vanity of the world but rather to the crucifixion of the flesh?

That you, however, say [that] one must wash the dirty and dusty feet of a poor traveler, if he has need of it, etc., is also good and was very common at the time of Christ (Luke 7:44: compare Genesis 18:4, 19:2, 43:24). That you say, however, in reference to Theophilus [that] one might perhaps inquire of you: when have you done this to a traveler or a poor man? Then I must indeed do my Opponent justice and answer him according to the truth. As many as forty-five years ago [at Ephrata], Theophilus washed the feet of many poor travelers and not only of brethren but also others. However, it is true that out of carelessness he has neglected to do it many a time, even with brethren, which he regrets. For it is a mistake which does great harm always to let it go until the need is greatest, especially in the good deeds to the poor. Our life is short and once it is over, we can no longer make up for neglect.

Opponent: Regardless of the fact that I myself accept feetwashing as a work of love and servanthood, I still do not dare to render it to any one. For the apostles received many special commandments which do not apply to anyone else, as the example in Luke 10:4 shows. Thus the question is really this: Did not this concern only them, especially since the apostles afterwards did not burden anyone with it or introduce it into the church?

Child: "Truly, truly, I say to you, a servant is not greater than his master, nor the apostle greater than He who sent him. If you know these things, blessed are you if you do them" (John 13:16-17). Because our Great Children's Friend said this, it was not necessary to burden anyone with it, for the love of Christ made it a light burden and one preferred the other in reverence. Yet, it should not remain hidden who was an idle or a diligent washer of feet, otherwise Paul would not have said (1 Timothy 5:10): "As one . . . who washed the feet of the saints, relieved the afflicted and devoted herself to doing good in every way." Yet no one dare conclude from this that the first Christians were such unfaithful fellows as to burden only the women with the feetwashing. Oh, no, no one is being burdened. Rather, the love of Christ taught it to every one, and also gave him the power thereto, so that he at once and in fact was capable of being blessed.

Note

I hope that from that which I have written so far it will be sufficiently evident that the truth in and of itself is strong and not to be refuted, and that even Theophilus in his old age does not intend to deny it. Rather, he is still ready to make a defense [to] anyone who calls him to account for the hope that is in him. Meanwhile it is my only intention to maintain peace, in the first place with God and with His dear truth, and secondly, with all men who fear the Lord and desire to do right, and thirdly, even with all other men. Therefore I herewith bid a friendly farewell to my learnéd Opponent. I cannot look upon the dear Children's Friend as an opponent only, even though he calls himself that, for we are pilgrims and travel toward a long eternity.

The fervent wish of my heart is that both Theophilus and the Children's Friend might be received there by the Eternal Love as friends of God and His truth, which certainly will happen if we are but truly washed from all the filth of the Opponent, by which we shall become truly acquainted with the free open well of Israel. As the Children's Friend wishes, so am I wishing and praying most warmly.

Theophilus

Another Churchman's Report to N. S. About the Origin of This Writing

Several years ago a certain person [Kunze] began a quarrel with his own shadow: he called the latter "Anabaptist"; himself, however, he called "Churchman." When, however, this poor Anabaptist referred to the passage (Matthew 29:19) to teach first and then to baptize, the so-called Churchman said: "The Savior says of all that not one syllable; the quoted passage is incorrectly translated." The poor Anabaptist allowed himself to be persuaded that Luther had lied. (At this point he recalls in my mind the words of Christ: "If they have called the master of the house Beelzebul, how much more will they malign those of his household" (Matthew 10:25). If the Churchman calls Luther a liar and falsifier of scripture, why should he not attack Theophilus and P[eter] M[iller] in the same way?) After a long conversation he brought the Anabaptist to the point where he promised to have his children baptized. The Churchman praised him for this and thought that he now had felled a hero. He also circulated a communication among all the Anabaptists and sent it especially to P[eter] M[iller], in which he challenged them to a disputation of all points and said: "In the name of God, whoever has courage and heart, let him stand up!" This conversation was later printed word by word in the year 1788 at Ephrata and the *Apologia* of the offended truth was added thereto by Theophilus and several annotations by P[eter] M[iller]. Whereupon the so-called Churchman now calls P. M. an uninvited guest, despite the fact that he himself invited him with his own hand.

I saw in his manuscript before his *Conquered Anabaptist* was printed that he treated Theophilus, P. M., etc., very offensively and with scorn. When I had the opportunity I asked P. M. whether he would not defend himself if the so-called Churchman were to print something against him. Thereupon he said, that is *P[eter] M[iller]*: "Defend myself? Do you think that I would read his book? I am far from it. A written dispute is as harmful to pilgrims as a defeated Asahel to the soldiers of David (2 Samuel 2:23)."

Churchman: If I had that in mind, I would not have made any annotations, etc.

P. M.: In this you are right. However, with me it is different. I have sprinkled many a child and convinced the parents that it was baptized and consecrated it to God, while I was convinced in my conscience that such was not the counsel of God, but rather an old custom. There are still many heads whom I sprinkled in their infancy, who still comfort themselves with it and say: "P. M. baptized them," etc. It would not have been good if I had remained completely silent on such an occasion. He dare not deny to me or various scholars that Christ and His apostles were baptized under the water.

When God desired to institute His ceremonial service among the Jewish people, He first showed Moses everything on Mount Sinai and then said to him: "And see that you make them after the pattern for them, which is being shown you on the mountain" (Exodus 25: 40). The pattern for heavenly things had to coincide precisely with their originals. And since now the household of the New Covenant has more important patterns than that of the Old Testament, it is only fair for me to ask the so-called Churchman: "Who gave you the right to distort the household of the New Covenant in such a way that it no longer represents what it should?"

They have made a sprinkling out of baptism. They have changed the supper into a daytime meal. Feetwashing, which has been instituted just as clearly as baptism, they have completely abandoned, etc. In so doing they demonstrate that they distort the counsel of God. While baptism portrays our burial, the sprinkling portrays the reconciliation of the old Adam, etc. If you can prove to us that the holy apostles sprinkled the people or baptized them only in but not under water, then we will consider him a master in Israel.

Let him show us the dictionaries where *baptizo* or *baptismus* is used for sprinkling. *Baptizo* or *baptismus* means actually "immersing" and therefore it is also used for washing. *Bapto* means "dip," which is used with Lazarus (Luke 16) and with the morsel (John 13:26). But nothing is more amazing than that the Churchman so inappropriately applies the word *sprinkling,* which, as you know, means *rantizein* in Greek, and tries to make it into baptism. In doing this he brings into daylight what a splendid distorter of Scripture he is.

Churchman: I do not understand much Greek and have to get the grammar from the dictionaries. I have looked in several for the explanation of this word (*baptism*) and found every time that it means immersion. However, nothing is said of sprinkling. Our pastor himself admits in his book that the word *baptism* means immersion, and explains at great length how one ought to be baptized into Jesus. Yet in doing so he advances so far into Quaker territory that I must say: "Let us either receive the water baptism according to the apostolic order or not at all."

N. S. I have also said it already, nevertheless, the Lord God of truth mercifully save us from this last statement of yours. Should we, for the sake of a man, whoever he may be, disregard the ordinances which the Son of God has brought from heaven and commanded us to do? Far from it! If the baptism of the Spirit alone were sufficient for salvation then Peter would not have found it necessary to recommend water baptism for those who believed his preaching and had already received the baptism of the Spirit in rich measure (Acts 10:48). God is not bound to these means, but rather we are bound to them to demonstrate our obedience; the children, however, can excuse themselves with their lack of knowledge.

I am very grateful for the report of the conversation which you had with P. M., and wish you and him that which I wish for myself, namely, the peace of God, through Jesus Christ.

Amen.

The Other Churchman's Further Report to the Reader

I deliberately write the "other Churchman" lest anyone come to the incorrect conclusion that I am he who calls himself (1) Churchman, (2) Anabaptist, (3) Children's Friend, (4) Opponent, (5) Seducer who is yet sincere, etc., and who by these secret names has begun so much dispute over words with himself and with others. No, I am not he. Rather, I am a lover of peace, and am herewith telling you that all that has so far been printed in Ephrata and Lancaster under the name of Anabaptist and Churchman was only one person. The Children's Friend and the Opponent in this booklet are likewise only one and the same person.[49]

13. Devotional Writings

It would be possible to gather the impression from the preceding chapter that, for the Brethren, literary endeavor was equated with doctrinal or controversial writing. This would be an error. Even more striking than the Brethren zeal in contending for the faith as they knew it was their activity in composing devotional materials. This effort might be considered part of the heritage of their Pietist background, inasmuch as that movement has been known for emphasizing the writing of hymns and edifying works.

For the size of the Brethren membership, the number of those whose poetry has been preserved is rather large. A recent anthology of American poems written in the German language includes works from no fewer than eleven Brethren.[1] An early hymnal published by the Brotherhood, the *Small Davidic Psalter,* was reprinted eight times during the eighteenth century, and at least five times during the early nineteenth century before going into stereotyped plates and innumerable printings. This hymnal was used by other German religious groups as well as by the Brethren.[2]

One of the problems in presenting poetry written originally in another language is that a straightforward translation, acceptable with prose materials, fails to do justice to the very qualities which make poems moving and beautiful. Fortunately, several of the poems have been put into modern English verse by contemporary Brethren poets. Recognition of them is given in connection with the individual items. Titles in parentheses have been added by the translators.

ALEXANDER MACK, SR.

Two of the hymns of the first minister of the Brethren, Alexander Mack, Sr., were included in the preceding source book, *European Origins of the Brethren.*[3] The following was found in the notes in his personal Bible.

(The Martyr's Role)

The martyr's role is wholly gain
In contrast to hell's frightful pain;
That role is brief, whereas 'tis sure

That hell forever will endure.
He who holds Jesus in his heart,
Though troubles be his earthly part,
To heaven's joys goes happily
To live through all eternity.
This truth, O Christian, keep in sight
And contemplate it day and night;
Of this marked difference be aware:
In sorrow here; in joy there.
That life on sinful pleasure spent
Will suffer there in great torment.

— Translated by Ora W. Garber[4]

PETER BECKER

According to Martin G. Brumbaugh, Peter Becker (1687-1758) was "perhaps the most gifted singer and the most eloquent man in prayer in the colonial church."[5] One of his hymns has been preserved. It was included in several of the hymnals published by the Brethren in the later eighteenth century. The translator, John S. Flory (1866-1960), produced the first comprehensive study of the literature of the colonial Brethren in his dissertation, "Literary Activity of the German Baptist Brethren" (1908).

Patience

Thou, poor pilgrim, wander'st here
    In this vale of gloom,
Seeking, longing ever more
    For that joyous home;
Yet many friends oppose thee here
So that now thou weepest sore, —
        Patience.

Go thou forth, on faith rely,
    Be only undismayed;
Cling to thy God, his love apply
    If thee the world upbraid;
This course through life will lead thee safe,
Though under it thy flesh shall chafe, —
        Patience.

If upon the narrow way
      Thou suffer scoffings here,
Just go on in the path of right,
      But shun the broad way's snare;
Though men may look at thee askance
And thou must often grieve perchance, —
      Patience.

Believe me true the time will be
      All this shall pass away;
Contests and strifes shall finally
      Pass from the mind away
Of him who here in faith contends
And all his enemies overcomes, —
      Patience.

Truly wonderful's the strife
      We engage in day by day,
Yet many perils we ne'er see
      That lie along our way;
Constant watchfulness we need
With prayer and efforts to succeed, —
      Patience.

Lead'st thou the strife against the flesh
      And thinkest thou hast won,
Before thou know, it breaks its leash —
      Again thou'rt overcome.
Therefore watch, entreat and pray
And at thy post remain alway, —
      Patience.

If at times thy faith is weak
      And thou art full of care,
Be not by this dismayed, but seek
      Thy God's help everywhere.
When no other help is found,
God will compass thee around, —
      Patience.

Thy God leads thee most wondrously
    In this bleak desert wide,
That he may bring to light of day
    What in thy heart doth hide,
That how thou mayest understand
Thyself to God to recommend, —
      Patience.

And if the way seem still so hard
    Before thy thoughtful mind,
Look to thy Savior, trust his word,
    And vict'ry thou wilt find.
He chose the way of sorrow free
And died upon the bloody tree, —
      Patience.

Patient was the love of Christ,
    Throughout his blessed life;
This in sincerity he showed
    In every hostile strife.
As patient as a lamb was He
That died upon the sacred tree, —
      Patience.

In this mirror thou may'st see
    Thyself, thy form, thy face,
But think how small thou still must be;
    Forget thou never this:
Thy Savior's likeness thou shoulds't gain,
And suffer gladly every pain, —
      Patience.

In this view thou comest short,
    Thou my poor, poor soul;
Therefore must thou still resort
    Within this gloomy vale.
Oft dost thou thyself survey
To find thyself in sorrow's way, —
      Patience.

And when thou seem'st deserted quite
     And thy poor heart hast proved,
Then thou bewailest thy poor plight,
     To pain and anguish moved.
Help in thyself thou canst not get,
Submit then gently to thy lot, —
         Patience.

Ah, precious soul, take courage new,
     All this shall have an end;
The cross's load will grace renew;
     Soon blissful rest thou'lt find.
The sorrow of this fleeting time
Is worthy of the joy divine, —
         Patience.

         — Translated by John S. Flory[6]

JOHN PREISZ

On the authority of Abraham H. Cassel, bibliographers have attributed an undated booklet of religious poetry written by John Preisz to the Sauer press in the year 1753. John Preisz (c.1702-1725?) was the only son of John Jacob Preisz, who migrated to Pennsylvania in 1719 with the Peter Becker party, settling along Indian Creek in Montgomery County. According to the history of Lower Salford Township, young Preisz "was a minister at an early age. He became noted for his aptness in writing poetry. In 1753, Christopher Sauer, of Germantown, published a collection of his hymns, but in spite of his talents he became so weakly that his father feared that he would not live to have issue, and, so anxious was the parent to leave a name and posterity behind him that he encouraged his son to marry while still very young. He did so and was blessed with two sons."[7] Local lore has it that the wife was an Indian maiden who had been befriended by the Preisz family.

Man, Like a Flower

Man, like a flower, may have a name
Which carries both prestige and fame.
The flower oft quickly wastes away,
As mankind's image also may.

And many a man conceited is
Because of all the wealth that's his.
Therein he does not think aright;
Acts disappear as does a light,

For when the wind against it blows
The light goes out, no longer glows.
And everyone can clearly see
That thus must man's condition be.

— Translated by Ora W. Garber[8]

THE SMALL DAVIDIC PSALTER

In 1744 Christopher Sauer I printed for the Brethren *The Small Davidic Psalter (Das kleine Davidische Psalterspiel der Kinder Zions).* According to the preface, which is translated below, there was a shortage of hymnals in the congregations, and a problem with using two or three different ones. The hope was to create an "impartial" or nonsectarian hymnbook by choosing hymns from several sources. Many were taken from the bulky European hymnbook of the Community of True Inspiration known as the *Davidisches Psalterspiel,* first printed in 1718. Some texts were taken from manuscript. It has already been indicated that the smaller Psalter proved to be very popular, which occasioned repeated reprinting.

Preface

In Jesus, the crucified head of His church, whom He redeemed and bought by His blood and death for His own in time and eternity. May the Father of all spirits give His blessing, salvation, and grace through this true Son of God to this simple work of love.

Most beloved friends and brethren, yes, all lovers of divine truth, who are interested in this *Psalterspiel,* the spirit of truth and true praise and thanksgiving wishes that as the mouth outwardly lets the voice sound forth, so also the heart may sound in unison before the Lord. To God the sacrifice of the lips alone is not proper, as in times past the Lord so often had to complain about His old Israel: "This people honors me with their lips, but their heart is far from me; in vain do they worship me, teaching as doctrines the precepts of men" (Matthew 15:8). To such a people speaks the Lord: "Take away from me the noise of your songs; to the melody of your harps I will not listen" (Amos 5:23).

If God demanded in the Old Covenant that He be served with heart and mouth, how much more in the New Covenant, where God is to be served and worshiped in spirit and in truth? And since the world is so full of these lip-servants, in singing, in beautiful melodies of hymns, and even in praying and speaking, the souls who value their salvation should conduct their worship service, be it in singing, praying, or speaking, in such a way that it flows from the bottom of their hearts. It should be done to the honor and glorification of God with girded loins, so that the hurrying senses may be kept within bounds, in order that everything that is done is done in the name of Jesus Christ to the honor of the Father.

The reason for publishing this small Davidic Psalter was the fact that in the meetings of the membership there was often a great lack of hymnals, and that in some meetings there were two, yes, even three, different hymnals used. Therefore it was agreed to have a hymnal printed. It was also unanimously agreed to select the majority and best known of the hymns from the well-known large *Psalterspiel,* the melodies of which are the most widely known, and to put them into the present format. Great pains were taken also to act in the most impartial manner, inasmuch as hymns have been selected from the hymnals of other authors also, along with some hymns which were found in manuscript. Thus, it can really be said that this is an entirely nonsectarian hymnal — a simple little flower-garden of all kinds of blossoms or hymns, for all those lovers who praise the Lord with heart and mind.

And as it is not the intention to speak in very high terms of this hymnal in the preface (although this is done by other authors), this work will be left to praise itself, because we well know that on earth everything is in the state of imperfection. Therefore even all hymnals are to be counted among the imperfections. For this reason a perfect hymnal has never been published but rather each lacks something and must be judged accordingly. Therefore this hymnal is turned over to be judged and is simply called by the name, The Small Davidic Psalter, just as the most precious teachings of Jesus are simply called with a humble title, the New Testament.

But as every good thing which the Spirit of God works, be it in speaking, praying, or in the flowing of hymns, originates in the perfect ocean of divinity, therefore everything hastens back to its origin where it can regain in perfection before the throne of God the perfect praise. Thus the believers on earth still ought to edify one another according to the counsel of the holy apostle Paul, when he speaks: "Address one another in psalms and hymns and spiritual songs, singing and making melody to the Lord with all your heart" (Ephesians 5:6[19]). Therefore the praise of the believers will persist on earth until the perfect praise will be revealed. Therefore let us now sacrifice to God the sacrifice of praise through Him at all times, that is, the fruit of the lips that acknowledge His name (Hebrews 13:15).

The time will yet come when this will come to pass of which the prophet Isaiah speaks: "From the ends of the earth we hear songs of praise, of glory to the Righteous One" (24:16); but now we still hear so often: "Oh, how lean I am."

Now, may the Lord fulfill His prophecy soon to the comfort of all expectant souls who believe in the hope of Zion, and that the Spirit and the Bride speak: "Come, and he who hears it let him say come, and whoever will, let him take the water of life without price."

Hallelujah, Salvation and Praise, Honor and Power be to God our Lord, in eternity. Amen!⁹

JACOB DANNER

Besides his efforts at defense of Brethren doctrines, Jacob Danner was known as a strong minister and facile hymnwriter. The following hymn was included in the *Small Harp*, an addition to later editions of the *Davidic Psalter*.

(Friends, Good Night)

Friends, good night to you, my truest;
Cherished friends, good night to you;
Mourners, too, good night, my dearest,
You who weep for one so true;
Though I soon shall leave this vale,
And you lay me in this dale,
I shall see a glorious dawning
As we hail that blessed morning.

O! how I shall then embrace you
And with heartfelt clasp you greet;
Though time summons from his purlieu,
Which was here indeed not sweet,
Yet a day 'twill surely bring
When our hearts with joy shall sing;
Nor shall we grim care bemoan there
But sing hallelujahs most rare.

O! how transient time runs onward,
Term of life for man designed;
God in heaven be our soul's guard
That we be not so entwined
With the pleasures of this world,
Which at man are ever hurled,
And which man must ere be shunning
As his life its race is running.

When my mind was not expecting,
Came the fatal arrow death,
Soul, heart, body straight dissecting
Took away in haste my breath;
While ye loved ones watch and pray
Be to you good night alway;
God grant you in death salvation
And high heaven's approbation.

Time of joyous, tender youth years,
And the pleasures of past days —
Gone are they with many felt tears.
What a riddle all these ways!
Life without complaint or need
Doth to death in few days speed.
Soul from body's cut asunder;
Stare we at the corpse in wonder!

Yet my soul hopes to discover
Comfort in my Savior's death,

Who will soon my soul recover
From the curse of Satan's breath
And deliver me from pain,
That I may in heaven's train
Praise my God with angels winging,
Hallelujahs ever singing.

Be ye comforted, my brethren;
Sisters, comfort be to you;
Members, comfort be your Sovereign.
Know God's Word is ever true
Saying: "In God's kingdom there
Shall the just no preference share,
Like the clear sun will be shining.
O that soon we be arriving!"

Though your parents loved me dearly,
And for me they prayed to God,
Though I know I've grieved you yearly,
Grant to me a parting nod.
What I've left to you undone
Grieves me at each rising sun.
God will grant you boundless blessing,
And I'll find in Him caressing.

Now adieu! there comes a parting
And my body nears the grave.
If in death I must feel smarting,
May my Lord my anguish lave.
Through His kindness, grace, and love
And His patience from above,
May I from my sins be shriven
And eternal life be given.

Now a fond good night, my children.
Dearest wife, good night once more.
Let us love but not the less then
As one heart and soul of yore.

God is love and us repays
When in love we walk His ways;
What is found in Him abiding
Will not see in death a parting.

— TRANSLATED BY RALPH W. SCHLOSSER[10]

HENRY DANNER

Little is known of Henry Danner, other than that he was a brother of the above Jacob Danner.

A Journey Song

What is it that has led us
Away from Germany?
The love of God has sped us
To that community
Which God, the Lord, has founded
In this, a strange new land.
With faith in Him unbounded,
Our lives are in His hand.

Adverse though the beginning,
With storms along the way,
Our goal we yet were winning
With every passing day.
Good things now satisfy us
In this our present life
Because the Lord stood by us
Throughout that time of strife.

Up, then, belovéd brothers,
Give praise to God, who fed,
Through the ministry of others,
Our souls with heavenly bread,
The heart's true wish fulfilling
With manna from on high.
O God, may I be willing
With Thee to live and die.

O God, hear Thou our crying,
Grant us the soul's new dawn,
Thy glory multiplying
As we shall journey on,
Thy glory multiplying
By every kind of man.
O God, hear Thou our crying
And bring us home again.

The time will soon be breaking,
Dear comrades of the way,
When, parted, we'll be taking
Our leave of earth's short day.
Here is a life of sorrow;
Not long will it endure.
Submit to God's tomorrow;
Eternal bliss is sure.

Beloved, you must arise now,
For your journey's needs prepare;
In faith you must devise how
To give them needed care.
Here have we no remaining;
No enduring home have we.
God's grace our souls sustaining,
His church our home shall be.

God wishes to uphold us
In joy and in despair,
That He may yet enfold us
Both here and over there.
He guides the openhearted
Through angels sent to man,
Lest we from Him be parted,
And brings us home again.

Heartfelt felicitations,
Dear comrades, and adieu.

Again come separations,
With the journey's end in view —
That goal which we selected,
Our chosen destiny.
Farewell, beloved, respected,
Until eternity.
— TRANSLATED BY ORA W. GARBER[11]

WILLIAM KNEPPER

One of the so-called Solingen Brethren, imprisoned in Germany for nearly four years at hard labor for adhering to the Brethren faith, was William Knepper (d.1755). During the early part of the captivity, while awaiting sentence, Knepper wrote more than four hundred hymns. Some of these were printed in the European Brethren hymnal, *Spiritual Hymnal for All Lovers of Truth* (1720).[12]

On his deathbed in Pennsylvania, Knepper wrote a final communication to his family, which has been preserved by descendants and printed in an English translation. The following is the text of the 1880 edition.

The Testament of William Knepper

The testament of William Knepper now resting in God, a brother and witness of the truth; having been imprisoned in Germany for the testimony of Jesus, [who] ended his life among the Baptists [Brethren] in Pennsylvania.

To the Brethren, and his children. Composed on his death-bed.

[May] Jesus Christ, the bright-shining morning star, the root and offspring of David, enlighten and penetrate the foundation of your hearts, that we may be a light in the Lord, and be filled with the spirit. Amen.

Beloved brethren and sisters, a hearty salutation to you all. My desire is that Christ, the true new life, might live, rule and reign in you, that your heart might be the temple wherein His holy Spirit may dwell that we could sing and make melody to God. For in this manner God will be praised and sanctified in us, when we are heavenly-minded, and have our conversation in heaven. This is to know God in the spirit, and in truth to serve and worship Him. For here begins the daily dying in the flesh, that the spirit may have free course; for they that are carnally minded cannot please God, inasmuch as to be carnally minded is death, but to be spiritually minded is life and peace for he that has suffered in the flesh has ceased from sin. Therefore our souls should always exercise in a constant cleaving to Jesus the true vine, that we might always gain, out of His living root and fullness of grace, [and] receive grace for grace to take root and increase according to the inner man.

Yes, brethren, that we might once become the true people of God, as those who flee from the perishable lusts of the world, riches, and all evil with covetousness. Oh, how we should feel and experience in ourselves the power and presence of the living God. Yes, we should rejoice in Him, and again be encouraged through the spirit, and exclaim, in the Lord is our victory, and all our help and beginning consists in the name of the Lord. Blessed is he who earnestly strives to be a living member in Jesus, who is his chief head, that he may be animated and ruled by Him, as his king. Then will the king with His countenance disperse every evil from his heart. And he that will be heavenly and spiritually minded cannot attain better thereunto than by keeping Jesus the crucified continually in remembrance. For, the world and the devil must give way to the word of the cross.

And if the subtility of reason, human or devilish wisdom, or spirit and world are coupled together, meaning to serve two masters at once, so that he [Satan] intends also to sit in the mental heavens, then must Satan fall as lightning from heaven in all those that are upright and pious, because the word of the cross will not suffer him to reign or dwell by His side, as also the ark of the covenant and Dagon could not stand together. Oh, what a noble and precious thing it is in an honest soul, that is ever diligently watching, and always examines well what it is that moves, affects and disturbs it! The true and well-beloved bride of Jesus, the soul that belongs to Him, should not suffer itself to be stirred up, moved or led by any thing but alone through the voice of the bridegroom, its kind friend, who loves it so highly, that the hairs of his head are full of the drops of the night.

Yes, our souls have cost His blood. Ah, whose heart should not be softened, who remembers the great love of this friend! Whoever contemplates His descent from the Father, His humility and coming to us in flesh. Oh, [for] whom should not mild tears flow over the cheeks because of this ardent love, who moved Him to come to poor sinners, to call them to repentance, and to receive them through grace. But alas! one that is blind does not see it; and one that is deaf in the spirit feels and hears it not. For, although Jesus wept over the wickedness of man, and over Jerusalem, that even His tears rolled down from His sanctified head, over His pure and innocent cheeks, yet in that time they remained obdurate and hard. Alas! if the heart is not in anguish, and the spirit not bruised, the word of God will have no hold on poor mankind; for that reason, brethren, let us always mourn, hunger and thirst, then He will ever be in our midst; as will be seen in the disciples that went to Emmaus and the shepherds in the field, when Christ was born, as also in the wise men of the east, whose desire for salvation was so great.

Oh, brethren, and all beloved members, who are called with me, God grant that we may never cease to hunger after Jesus and His word, until in [the] future we may fully awake in His likeness! Oh, that we may not be members of the Laodicean church, which is now so very great, so that it is spread throughout all Europe, and has also extended itself here; and is yet daily spreading itself among the brethren of our community! Ah, many, alas, how many, I fear, the mouth of God will spew out. Oh, brethren, let no one tolerate anything of such a rich mind; otherwise the first birthright will be forfeited. Let us rather always learn to feel our poverty and imperfections, and thereby have much confidence in Jesus. Oh, how deceitful is the heart, and how full of selfishness is this poor life, in words and in works, poisoned and corrupted!

He that will earnestly deny himself and do good will experience how the evil will cleave to him. Here the contest will begin, and a constant penitence and contrition. Here through temptation we take heed to the word, which is given us for consolation, exhortation, doctrine and chastisement. Here is always hunger and thirst after the righteousness of Jesus, who of God is made unto us widom and righteousness, and sanctification and redemption; for which my soul longs, and is desirous, with all those who sigh, and long for the manifestation of the children of God.

. . . . .

To my children, P. K. and the remaining:

My heart's beloved children, whom I love, embrace and kiss: and have many hundred times from their birth laid before the feet of Jesus in my inward and public prayers and sighing, and in the spirit presented them before His hand of blessing, who is the only redeemer and restorer of the fallen and ruined image of God; that He might bless them and restore in them the image of God which was lost through sin and disobedience; and renew them again unto eternal life, and give them to comprehend the wickedness in flesh and blood inherited through sinful seed, and that they may learn to give themselves unto Him, and through repentance, faith, and baptism of water and spirit be entirely born again unto a living hope and a new creature.

Yes, this living hope in us is the life of Christ Jesus, whereunto I was also by Him inwardly called, awakened and quickened: so are the children of believers, who continually offer them up to God in faith, also holy with them, while they have the blessed life and example of Christ and their parents continually before them. For they, as believing parents teach them also as much as possible, to keep the commandments of God, and to walk in them: even as believing Abraham also has done, by reason of which he was also called out and separated, and was called the father of all believing. Therefore, as my condition now is such that it seems as if my pilgrimage here would soon come to an end, I would exhort you, my children, and put you in mind through this letter what will be for your good, concerning manifold doctrines and opinions. I will then express to you something of my sense and inward knowledge and confession of faith, for an everlasting remembrance: that you may know that it is the best only to look to Jesus in simplicity and sincerity.

Pray without ceasing to Him for His good and Holy Spirit, who will lead you into all truth. Always strive against your selfishness, open and secret anger, rage, concealed and open malice of the heart and the flesh; the youthful and ruinous enjoyments of the world, covetousness and the desire of riches. Let your behavior — inward and outward — be meek and lowly. Be content whether you have much or little; wish others much, and be simple and sincere toward all men; love especially the brethren; follow gladly the counsel of the pious, yea, more than your own will. Learn diligently the good counsel of God for your souls, especially that which Jesus the Son of God Himself has brought from Heaven, in doctrine and life, and also revealed through His ambassadors. Oh, [may] the passive and patient Lamb reveal Himself with His spirit and mind in your hearts and entire life; follow Him patiently who, when He was reviled, reviled not again, and threatened not once when He suffered: much more He prayed for His enemies, and also taught us the same.

Judge no one rashly or thoughtlessly. Keep what you have, believe and know, and leave others over to God the righteous judge and King of kings; whether they do well or ill, it is all for themselves and also for yourselves what you do. Remember that God, who sees and hears all things, will also bring all before the judgment, also the hidden counsels of the heart and the thoughts. Meditate often thereon, and on what Jesus has said, that, of every idle word that men shall speak, they shall give account thereof. Therefore let your words be few and learn to bridle your tongue, otherwise all your religion will be vain. For that reason, my beloved little lambs, always and daily remember the end. Follow the truth, and not falsehood nor cunning fables of the present nominal Christianity, which has perverted and changed nearly the whole doctrine of Christ by adding and taking away.

Therefore, I am often greatly concerned for you, lest you might come upon ways of error, against God and His holy gospel, should they even be highly adorned and appear beautiful and holy. Choose, and hold fast to the word of truth. Strive for the narrow way, and a meek and lowly life. Seek ardently for that which few seek and desire. Neither fear nor shun the reproach of Christ, which will follow his poor life. Love all the brethren, and look chiefly to those who in the most pure and simple manner seek to exemplify the life of Christ. Guard against the spirit of offence as against the devil himself. Ask little of others, and yourselves manifest much, and always be inwardly grieved because you cannot exhibit more perfect fidelity. When you are despised for doing that which is good, learn to bear it patiently; and do not become weary, for all things must be tested, and that which is done in the Lord will endure, though it may here remain concealed. For there are always wicked and disorderly people, who are lurking for us like lions in their dens, sparing themselves, and often bringing the lambs of Christ upon the slaughter bench. These are they who strain at a gnat and swallow a camel: secret tale-bearers and infernal slanderers; from these we cannot entirely escape. Here we must be patient, as Christ also has taught us by doctrine and example, that it may not vex us or make us weary. There are such among brethren who are false, having crept in privily, from whom faithful souls must often suffer much more than even from the wicked world itself, for they are very ready to judge others, but shun and forget themselves. But all this will have its time. They will not prosper long. For through their subtility, which this spirit will operate in them, they will at last come into such things which will foreshow that they are bringing themselves into a snare.

Commit those to God who will not suffer themselves to be admonished, and let them go where they will, and pray diligently for all men, as well for the offensive, forward, and wicked, as for them that are mild and good; as also for the government, especially that under which liberty of conscience may still be enjoyed. I, your father, have believed in the living God, who created the heaven and the earth, the sea and the fountains of water, the wet and the dry, the light and the darkness, and have perceived through His light that He has formed an eternal, deep and inexhaustible decree, in and through His only begotten son before the foundation of the world, to create man in His image, and when He had done this it was all very good. If they had then remained in that state and image, they would not have experienced the difference between good and evil.

But now, the Father, Son and Holy Spirit, or that high Being of all Beings, the Lord Jehovah, foundation and life of all things, has permitted it to be so; otherwise He would have been highly honored of them and their offspring, in the highest simplicity. But as this has not yet come to pass, a wonderful providence, or I may say, God's secret counsel of permission has over-ruled the miserable fall of sin; else how could God be all in all? For the devil can do nothing of importance except by permission; for he was at that time already cast out, and bound in chains of darkness like a chained dog. Thus I consider and believe, that, although the devil believed that he had already and forever succeeded, he has, nevertheless, forever lost, and will lose all. And also in this transgression itself, he is completely vanquished; but not through Adam, no! but through the secret and hidden wisdom of God. For, like as Pharaoh, through the hardness of his heart, was the cause of the manifold wonders of God being made manifest in Egypt.

So also, through the devil's boldness with Adam and Eve, the patience and long suffering of God, our eternal Savior, was in the highest degree made known and manifest; as also His inscrutable wisdom, mercy, gentleness, love, faithfulness; in short, all the attributes in the depths of God were called forth through the fall of sin. The devil also will fare no better than Pharaoh did, who, when he thought to destroy Israel, plunged himself and his host into the sea. Much might be said at large concerning these things, but I will only yet say this, that God will be much more and higher honored, glorified and praised, when He will have brought all things again into its proper order. For He has concluded all in unbelief, that He might have mercy upon all: and he that is awakened in the faith will give Him all the honor and glory in all endless eternity: therefore He will also be forever glorified above all things.

If then the first fruit is holy, the lump of the whole creation will also at last be holy again. For God designed that in the creation He should be revealed in His unspeakable and manifold attributes of righteousness as well as in the deep foundation of His love, mercy, and manifold powers of His wisdom and wonders, through which He at first created all things, and will also again bring all under subjection unto Himself; for of Him, and through Him, and in Him are all things. Hallelujah! To God and the Lamb be all the honor forever! Amen.

I, your father, have believed that there is but one living faith, and only one baptism in water, which Jesus Christ Himself has commanded when He was about to depart from His disciples; as it is known that I thus believe and have believed through the grace of God and His light, which has shined in me, that I must truly repent, as all must do who will come to God. And that I also should, according to my faith, after my three parts, spirit, soul and body, which I now design to withdraw from the world, suffer myself to be three times immersed in the name of the Father, and of the Son, and of the Holy Spirit, according to the original word. He that will thus change his mind, and will exercise in the spirit, to live according to the same, will surely be saved in His faith and genuine baptism, because he has put on Christ, Who is become his only Redeemer, Saviour and Mediator. For, if we walk in the light, we have fellowship with God, and the blood of Jesus Christ will cleanse us from all sin.

Now, such as have offered and given themselves unto God in the true faith, because they have been baptized into one body by one spirit, and have been made to drink into one spirit, should also, according to the command and out of love, break the bread of communion in remembrance of the death of Christ, because the apostle had also received it of the Lord. Therefore, as often as we eat of this bread, and drink of the cup of the Lord, we shall show the Lord's death. It was also my belief that when and where this can be done it should be practiced, whether with many or few brethren; but if it cannot be, it is still the truth, and my practice, to keep Christ the crucified always in remembrance.

I have likewise believed that God's children, if they truly love one another, should also, according to the example of their Master, gladly and willingly wash one another's feet, which signifies inward humility, that one should bow and humble himself before the other. See John 13. Although this seems outwardly mean and suspicious in the eyes of carnal reason, yet, he who will practice it in faith and love, and in an inward, fervent obedience, will feel an inward blessing, and will experience that these precepts are of God. But without faith it is impossible to please God, and will benefit no man, only him that believes and is obedient.

I have also perceived very sensibly that the subtle serpent, as, in the beginning he deceived our first parents, is yet eager to do the same, and is seeking to lead us away from the simplicity which is in Christ Jesus. I have experienced much within myself, that all things are so miserably subverted; the true baptism, the real supper or breaking of bread, and feetwashing put away, or in all these the opposite introduced. So there are also many among pious souls who are fallen into this folly, so that they deem it unnecessary, or carry it to such a high degree that no one should be permitted to baptize who has not established his mission by signs and miracles: one is a deceit of the old serpent as well as the other; trust neither of the two: for if it were not necessary, ah! why has the Lord Jesus done it Himself? Why did He suffer Himself to be baptized? Why did He wash His disciples' feet? Why did He eat the supper with them? All human reason is here taken captive.

Therefore, always take your understanding, will, and imagination captive under the obedience of the gospel; and always exercise and associate with those that love peace, and pursue it. Always consider yourselves low and small in your own eyes, and if you love peace and follow after it, the spirit of peace will be with you. And there will always be such brethren that will be like-minded with you. Keep yourselves always with them that love peace and consider themselves small, and that do not exalt themselves above others, but are reconcilable and forgiving; for they that walk most upright can best forgive, and bear with others. For I have often experienced that those who conduct themselves the meanest are the most ready to judge others: and I have often suffered severe persecution from such hypocrites when I was in prisons in the midst of babel for the sake of the word of truth.

But they will not endure long, their pride and condemning judgment will at last fall upon their own heads; therefore be not associated with them: be ready to forgive, [be] reconcilable, and inclined to peace; for, as we do to our neighbors it will be done to us again; as we forgive our neighbor, it will be forgiven us. Oh, how close it searches when we are about to die; this I now feel in my wearisome disease! Oh, how the word of God cuts down the high cedars of Lebanon! Oh, how the voice of God shakes the wilderness of Kadesh — that is, the unconverted heart! Oh, how consoling is a good conscience! Here the saying is true, "The righteous has hope in his death." Therefore, my heart's beloved children, keep this my last will and letter well in remembrance, and when you come to years of understanding, be diligent in good works, and strive to make your calling and election sure. Be not ashamed of the doctrine of my Saviour and yours, to unite yourselves forever with Him, through repentance, faith, baptism, [Lord's] supper, feetwashing, and breaking of bread. Then when the chief shepherd and bishop of our souls will appear, He will not be ashamed of you.

Now, my beloved children, what I have written shall speak to you when you are grown up and have come to your understanding, because you can, as yet, conceive or comprehend but little of what I say unto you; therefore I have written it. Then when I am dead, and shall speak no more with you, I may speak to you through writing when you are grown up. Through this you can also know my sentiment, my faith, my baptism, and my doctrine, for all this has caused me much sorrow from the days of my youth; whereas, the God of love has called me powerfully, early in my youth, when I was seventeen years of age, and revealed to me the vain life of sin, that I was overwhelmed with such anguish of hell that my tongue cannot express it. And, although I have never been a very gross sinner, yet, so powerfully has the inward and outward abomination of desolation been revealed to me that I was made to seek God through heartfelt repentance, Who also suffered Himself to be found of me. And, because of my seeking God, I was compelled, as a malefactor, to endure bonds and imprisonment three years and three fourths, for which I yet praise God with all my heart. Two years after I was released from prison I married your mother, and we lived twenty years peaceably together in matrimony, and have endured love and grief with patience. And now, take to heart what I say for I now consider my end, and write with great consideration of heart because I know that this will be my last writing in this world, and with this I leave you over to God, and hope to see you again forever in Heaven.[13]

CHRISTOPHER SAUER II

Two examples of the poetic efforts of Christopher Sauer II are given below. The first is an acrostic composed on his sixtieth birthday, September 26, 1781. The thoughts expressed take on added poignancy as reflections on the loss of his worldly goods and the turbulence of the time. The translator was connected with the Snow Hill Nunnery, at Quincy, Pennsylvania, north of Waynesboro. The second is taken from the 1761 edition of Sauer's almanac, published in 1760; it comments on the contemporary struggle of the Seven Years' War, known in American history as the French and Indian War. The seizure of the French fortress at Quebec by General James Wolfe was decisive in the eventual British victory.

An Acrostic

C hristians here must suit themselves,
    In the cross's narrow path;
    Here by patience and by stooping,
    We must rise to heaven-wards.
    He who hopes with Christ to dwell,
    Must the cross remember well:
    Those who there will be rewarded,
    Crowns of thorns here too will carry.

H ere we must in sorrow labor,
    And with trials often meet;

If we would the kingdom enter,
And with saints be clothed in white.
And will wear a starry crown
While they here have overcome.
Those who here in tears have sown
Shall appear before the throne.

R ightful calling, seeking, praying,
Open us the way to God;
Calling on him in distresses,
Comfort brings in time of need.
None have been forsaken yet,
Who on God their trust have set.
They who by faith to him look,
Truly build upon a rock.

I was always wrongly going,
Since my wisdom was but small;
Now I trust my shepherd's leading,
Who has power over all.
His protection will provide,
Under crosses that betide,
So that I His care can trace,
In the times of deep distress.

S uch love is beyond a measure,
Which around me He has thrown.
Thou my soul be not forgetful,
Of the mercies He has shown.
Thou art in His debt indeed,
Patiently to give Him heed;
Him to serve and Him to love,
While here in this world you move.

T o be true was my intention,
But too often I have failed,
Year for year, thou hast been waiting,
And thy patience did extend;
Till my strength was weakened down,
And with self-will I was done;
And resolved henceforth to live,

As the Lord did wisdom give.
O selfishness, thou wretched folly,
    Ofttimes dost thou bring distress;
    Could I overcome thee wholly,
    Always feel that blessedness;
    Of that strong redeeming love,
    And the power from above;
    Me to lead in all His ways,
    Ever living to His praise.

P rove me Lord and search me wholly,
    Thou canst know my inner life;
    Guard my heart from ev'ry folly,
    Let me conquer in the strife.
    Oh let winds that trouble blow,
    Teach me better thee to know:
    That upon a trial's day,
    I may bear the crown away.

H ere there is yet time for working,
    Sternly still, the right pursue;
    Very soon there will be given,
    Great rewards to all the true,
    Who with courage ventured on,
    And could say, vain world be gone:
    With thy tempting pleasures all,
    Seeking us to bring to fall.

S ixty years have now been fleeting,
    Of my timely staying here;
    As an arrow shot off quickly,
    Idleness does disappear.
    Oft does it our time consume,
    That we do not hurry on;
    And complain when 'tis too late,
    That we did not change our state.

A las I must feel very lowly,
    Many times lament the loss;
    That so much of worldly trouble,
    Found much place within my breast;

And my heart did so confuse,
That of love I oft did lose:
And the work which most was needed,
Often times was unattended.

U nder many storms of trouble,
And temptations great and small,
God still knew how to protect me,
That I did not come to fall.
Love to me did still extend,
Wonderful and without end,
Without Him I must have perished,
In the times of great distresses.

R ejoice my soul and give thou praises,
For the patience of thy God;
Since He has by many wonders,
Kept for thee an open path.
May His great and sovereign will,
Keep me in His statutes still;
May His care me still befriend
Till my last expiring end.

— TRANSLATED BY OBED SNOWBERGER[14]

Reflections Concerning General Wolfe
O Wolfe, you were a faithful one
While in the service of the king.
Who can exceed what you have done?
With courage you risked everything.
Undaunted was your diligence
By peril or insecurity.
You scorned all safe convenience
That you might strike the enemy,
Devoured them as if they were bread,
And by the thousands struck them dead.

Would that all Christian men might see
Your brave example, in their strife,

And to our King as faithful be
In holy warfare in this life.
Would that our love of worldly ease
Might be completely laid aside
And that, against our enemies,
Nought save Christ's valor were applied.
While others in death's ruin lie,
Who serves the Lord can never die.

The earthly warrior's fame no permanence
    secures;
The heavenly warrior's fame eternally
    endures.
— Translated by Ora W. Garber[15]

Here follow the prefaces written by Sauer II to the two volumes of his religious magazine (*Geistliches Magazien*), which was distributed without cost. It has been called by the foremost American bibliographer the first magazine of a spiritual nature (with one possible exception) to be printed in the American colonies. The periodical, issued at irregular intervals between 1764 and 1770, has also interested scholars of American printing because number twelve of the second volume was printed with "the first type ever cast in America."[16] Of more interest in the present context is the motivation and spirit displayed by the Germantown printer. The Bible referred to was his second edition of the Bible in German, printed in 1763.

Preface to Geistliches Magazien (1764)

Kind reader:

I have often considered, with a heart and soul moved by the love of God and neighbor, what great ignorance and carelessness in divine matters may be observed with very many people in this country. This usually derives from the fact that they either have little interest or opportunity to hear godly and edifying conversation or to read writings of the same kind. If a man ever does hear an edifying admonition or sermon, more often than not the spirit is so poorly prepared to receive that which he hears that most has been forgotten by the time he arrives home; and then there is no one there to repeat it, if one were at all concerned to try to remember better what he had heard. Religious books are also seldom found in people's possession. Either the people are too poor or they always know something else to spend their money on than books. If someone ever does buy a fine religious book, he will be bored before he has read even a few pages and sometimes he puts it away for a whole year before it is half read.

The consideration of these things I sometimes took so much to heart that I became very deeply grieved about them and wondered how this lack might be filled somewhat. It did often occur to me that if one were occasionally to put into people's hands something that was brief and to the point, and without any cost, many might perhaps take enough time to read carefully half a signature through and could perhaps find something which would move their hearts to meditate on it further. And if they found something to their taste in it, they would perhaps peruse it again sometime, and would find still more good in it than at the first reading. If after a time a similar testimony were to come into the home, they might do the same.

These, then, have been my thoughts for some time already; but as all good intentions under heaven have always had their obstacles, so it has also happened to this one and it has been prevented from time to time. Now, however, as I have so happily completed the great work of printing the Bible under special divine assistance, it seems to me that it is my deepest obligation out of gratitude to God not to delay this good undertaking any longer, the more so when I remember that the foundation of this printshop was laid to the glory of God and my neighbor's good, and that God has created me like all men and has kept me alive to no other purpose than to advance His glory and to serve my neighbor with all that lies in my power.

Thus I now begin the publication of a small magazine of that kind, which at first shall consist of an entire signature because of the preface. In this undertaking I shall not commit myself to a certain time or number but rather proceed as materials come to my hand, and as time and circumstances permit. That I seek no temporal profit in this undertaking will be believed by all because I am giving them away. And that I am not driven to it by any vain ambition will be illuminated by the fact that I shall not put my own works on the market therein (although I will not suppress the grace if it imparts even to me something for the good of my neighbor, for I will take the same freedom which I grant others), but rather make an effort to make such excerpts from all kinds of old and modern writings,

English as well as German, which can be useful and would not offend any religious denomination. Yet, it is sometimes impossible to avoid, without mutilating a man's work, that some things are stated which perhaps contradict this or that catechism. The kind reader must not be disturbed by such, as long as they do not contradict the Book of all Books — the Holy Bible.

I begin this new undertaking with the first chapter from the blessed English preacher William Law's *A Serious Call to a Reverent and Holy Life,* translated from the English. In the future more half-signatures will be filled with extracts from this splendid book, which is still unknown among the Germans. Should perhaps in this piece some expression seem to my reader to be too strong, he should not be annoyed; others will perhaps not find it so. The truth always bears salt with it, and where it finds wounds of sin, it stings. But it also heals him who uses it correctly.

Otherwise, this undertaking is a magazine in which various kinds of things will be found: admonitions, reprimands, edifying letters, biographies of pious individuals, edifying events, and what otherwise serves to the glory of God and the good of the neighbor. Everyone is free to send in something, with or without his name [attached], which will be included as soon as it is possible, but it must not be longer than can be printed on a half-signature, and it must be free of all harsh judgments of persons. Otherwise it would be against the purpose of this impartial undertaking, which has for its purpose not the advancement of salvation in one but in all religious denominations. Controversies will not be accepted, except where they are free from the above-mentioned harsh expressions, and are directed only against certain errors and not against persons or to serve to the illumination of certain obscure sayings.

When they are folded, these half-signatures may be bound together with a few stitches, cut at the top, and thus read and preserved neatly until enough are together that they may be bound into a book. Thus a person collects quite without any expense a beautiful house-magazine out of which his descendants can still read much that is good.

That the kind reader may use this work to the glory of God and to the good of his soul is the wish of his loyal friend and well-wisher,

Christopher Sauer.

Preface to the Second (Volume or) Part (1770)

Kind reader:

When I began to publish the *Geistliches Magazien* in 1764, I did not dream that such an impartial undertaking could also be regarded with jealousy inasmuch as it was not intended to treat the differences between religious opinions or to dispute with any one, but rather to advance and to encourage in everyone what is so necessary for all men, namely, fear of the Lord, conversion, belief in Christ through whom the heart is cleansed, along with a pious conduct and the true salvation without which no one may see the Lord. Yet, I have had to experience that even this undertaking, as with all pious men and writings, has had to undergo both good and bad judgments.

Some suspected it of being bent on introducing a special religious opinion and despising others; others feared, and not without reason, that it would disturb them in their sinful carnal security if they read it and considered the matter. Such people are like the deaf adder about which David speaks in Psalm 58:4-6, which stops its ears to the voice of the charmer. They are determined to be ignorant and take care that nothing should come before their eyes or ears which might disturb them in their carnal rest and sinful life. Small wonder that such burn the pages of the *Geistliches Magazien* or make sacks out of them, as unfortunately too many have done. This will certainly not help them, for whoever can know the truth and deliberately ignores it will not be accounted among those who did not know the will of the Lord and will therefore suffer but few lashes. Rather, in addition, they will also be held to account for this "not-caring" (Matthew 24:39) and will be punished for it.

This is to say nothing of those who attack in a malicious way that which they do not understand or know nothing of. As do all other religious writings or talks, it will bring about even greater judgment for them because for them even the saving gospel which Christ and His holy apostles proclaimed will be but a smell of death to death (2 Corinthians 2:15-16 and 2 Peter 3:16). They would not be worth all the effort and paper if there were not so many people in the country who have indeed evidenced such great pleasure both in writing and orally in these simple testimonies of divine truth which have been made public in these pages from time to time. For their sake and that of all others who are concerned about the salvation of their souls, and who, as diligent little bees like to sip honey from every noble little blossom and wish to collect for themselves a good contribution to their spiritual strengthening, I will nevertheless continue, as long as God grants me life and ability, to publish a second volume of this *Geistliches Magazien*. Several fine pieces have already been sent in for it, and I hope that God may accompany my unselfish undertaking with His blessing to all dear readers, who are concerned with their eternal salvation and are not too filled with prejudices against it. If this is accomplished my work and paper are well repaid.

Therefore, I begin this time with a piece which a God-seeking friend wrote and included sealed [in his will and] addressed to the printer, to be sent to him after his death that it might be included in these pages. This, then, was sent after his death. Now, I would wish that everyone who reads this testimony might read it and ponder it in the same earnestness out of which it flowed in love for them. They may be assured that the deceased sought only the benefit of their souls by it. If he had sought honor or esteem he would have put his name and address on it. May then all who receive these simple pages remain not only readers and hearers of the truths contained therein, but become true doers of the same: this is the sincere wish of the friend of all of you,

Christopher Sauer.[17]

ALEXANDER MACK, JR.

It has already been seen that Alexander Mack, Jr., was the foremost Brethren literary figure in the eighteenth century. Most of his poetic compositions were published in the previously noted study by Heckman. Among them were several lengthy poems contributed to Sauer's religious magazine. Two shorter poems have been prepared in English from one of them, and are given below. Another Mack composition, written as a series of ten poems, has been translated in its entirety. It was dedicated by the poet to the "beloved young people."

(Redemption)

1 (1)

Up! Let us give consideration
Unto that widening abyss

Which, threat'ning, lies between damnation
And that eternal state of bliss,
In order that we may avail
Ourselves of God's help without fail.

2 (6)

False hopes that life is what it's seeming
From this most foul abyss upwell;
And many on its brink are dreaming,
Not knowing it's the brink of hell.
Ah, vain their groundless, foolish zest —
'Tis hell that burns the sinner's breast.

3 (7)

Oft beaten, but to no real gaining,
A fool's foul mouth can find no rest.
Itself and others often paining,
It seems to count it all a jest.
Good men are sorely, deeply stirred
When wicked men ignore God's Word.

4 (10)

With God's power in men's hearts resounding,
The power of evil must abate.
Christ's reconciling blood abounding,
Man enters through the narrow gate.
By love his faith will strengthened be
In practice of true chivalry.

5 (11)

Within us then the hope can flourish
For life that's promised in God's Word.
This hope in turn our souls will nourish
As they with love divine are stirred.
The body and the soul rejoice
To hear love's kindly, gracious voice.

— Translated by Ora W. Garber[18]

(Scene of Judgment)

1 (52)

When God, by throngs of saints surrounded,
Appears among the sons of men,
All evil ones shall be confounded
As He exalts the faithful. Then
The miracle of Jesus here
With His believers will be clear.

2 (54)

Among the hosts of angels holy
Our eyes shall clearly, rightly trace
God's favor toward His children lowly
As manifested by His grace.
In contrast to the base and mean,
God's kindness shall be fully seen.

3 (55)

All people shall be separated
(Like flocks by shepherds set apart)
On either side as designated
By the demands of His pure heart,
Sheep at the right of His great throne,
Goats at the left — as is well known.

4 (56)

And when, the judgment throne appearing,
The righteous Judge shall elevate
Those who on earth have been God-fearing
Unto a joyous new estate,
How harsh these words to some shall be:
"You cursed ones, depart from me"!

5 (59)

What then shall say the King of Glory?
"You who in brief mortality
Have, from the dawn of ages hoary,
Been blest of God consistently,

Take now the Kingdom He prepared
For you who in His love have shared.

6 (60)

"When I was hungry you provided
In love that I might nourished be.
And oftentimes my thirst subsided
As you brought soothing drink to me.
When you observed my nakedness
You ministered to my distress.

7 (61)

"When I was ill, in prison lying,
You kindly visited me there;
None your inheritance denying,
The fruits of love you now may share:
God's realm, prepared for righteous man
Since time and this our world began."

8 (62)

The saints, with grateful agitation,
Shall ask: "Lord Jesus, when did we,
That we now have Thy commendation,
Administer relief to Thee?
Was it not just the other way:
Thou didst sustain us day by day?"

9 (63)

Then shall the King, His words explaining,
Say unto them: "What you have done
Unto another, life sustaining,
Yes, even to the humblest one,
In truth my body nourishes,
Wherein my mystery flourishes."

10 (64)

To those, then, at His left side standing,

The King shall point and sternly say:
"Your fate is of your own commanding.
When I sought food you turned away
And gave me none; when I sought drink
You could but of your own needs think.

11 (65)

"Ill and unclothed, in destitution,
From you I have received no aid.
You merit now full retribution
In that no helpful move was made.
Because you have ignored me so,
Your happiness can never grow."

12 (68)

They then shall speak to Him, inquiring:
"Lord, when in times gone by have we
E'er known that Thou wert food desiring
And have not given it to Thee?
Great Prince, when did we scorn Thy thirst,
That we should now become accursed?

13 (69)

"When did we see Thee naked going
And fail to meet Thy urgent need?
And when have we ignored Thee, knowing
We ought to do some kindly deed
And minister to Thee? Lord, how
Comes this harsh judgment on us now?"

14 (70)

Then shall the King, to them replying,
Speak thus: "Whenever you disdained
These faithful ones, not even trying
To give them help, I have maintained
A deep concern. You scorned my Bride
Who stands near by, at my right side."

15 (71)

And then into that realm infernal,
Away from Christ, the lost shall go.
The saved, consigned to life eternal,
The joys of heaven with Him shall know.
For heaven their godly hearts have yearned;
Toward it their steps have long been turned.

16 (79)

Our God, through His divine persistence,
His holy purpose will attain
Though Satan offer fierce resistance.
Acknowledging God's righteous reign,
The saints, on bended knee, shall call
On Him who is their All in All.

     — TRANSLATED BY ORA W. GARBER[19]

The Excellencies of Jesus
1. ON BEAUTY

Amongst the beauteous human children
   Jesus' beauty ranks supreme;
None more lovely can affect one
   Even when he all hath seen.

Every charm of flower passeth;
   Human beauty fails in death;
But my true friend's beauty lasteth;
   It will never grow the less.

God's dear angels are more beauteous
   Than mere man can ever be;
But the loveliest son of Nazareth
   Dimmeth even their beauty.

Many thousand stars shine brightly
   In the glory of the night,

But when the sun arises blithely,
   Their fine splendor fades from sight.

Also thus the hosts of glory,
   Even God's own seraphim,
Fall down, honor, and adore Thee,
   Lovely Jesus, without end.

What shall human beauty count for,
   Here in this dark vale of death,
'Gainst th' eternal praises offered
   Him whom angels count the best?

If once human beauty flourisheth
   As though it wore a crown of gold,
Yet, O so quickly then it perisheth,
   A chastened spirit bare and cold.

O how soon that heart sinks under
   Which, through desire, itself
      doth spend!
Its whole being falls asunder
   Through trusting flesh which
      time must rend.

But love of Jesus elevates us
   To the angels' high desire;
Other love inevitably passes,
   Meriting nothing but the fire.

In summation, Jesus only
   All true beauty typifies;
Any other sort of beauty,
   Like a dead bloom, is despised.

2. On Love

Amongst the love of human children
   My Jesus' love is pure and strong;

None more loving can impress one
  Even of the angelic throng.

Jesus' love imparts the true life
  Which other love can but disturb.
Jesus' love all things supplieth
  To him who doth believe His word.

Jesus' love will stand the trial;
  Other love can but deceive.
Jesus' love is my recital,
  For it doth every want relieve.

Jesus' love a hot fire burneth
  Which can cause our hearts to melt;
Jesus' love so rare and precious
  Takes our misery to itself.

Jesus' very love sinks under,
  Deep into our deepest need,
And brings forth unexpected wonder,
  Out of death, new life indeed.

Carnal love so many thousands
  Has betrayed with shame and loss;
Jesus' love its share has touched and
  Brought back to God through the
    cross.

Whoso would love rightly value
  Must be filled with love for Christ —
Evidencing it as is due,
  'Tis but mere show otherwise.

Yet might e'en the greatest sinner,
  If he would for love make place,
Enable love to be the winner

And give himself life's highest
   grace.

Jesus' love is then the bright sun
   Shining in that man's new sky,
That joy always to be chosen,
   A delight that will not die.

In short, true love must be grounded
   Upon Jesus, God's dear Son,
And in consequence is granted
   The crown of life which love has
won.

3. On Wisdom

More than all the human children
   Is my Jesus sage and wise;
Aye! It is a poor befooled one
   Who will not give Him the prize.

If indeed man's knowledge groweth
   While not submitted unto Christ,
It on him a weight bestoweth,
   Bringing him to earth despised.

Truly good and truly wise men
   To Jesus quickly grant the prize,
For they know that only from Him
   Comes the good that in them lies.

Only Jesus' wisdom offers
   Base and scope for wisdom true;
It eternal is and spotless;
   It is God's own right and due.

Willingly the very angels
   From Him their instruction take;

Pious men obey Him as well
    And His commands their duty make.

Jesus' wisdom shines more brightly
    Than the brightness of the sun,
And it goes its way more lightly
    Than the quickest spirits run.

Jesus' wisdom indeed leads us
    Into heaven's banquet hall;
Human wisdom makes us worthless,
    Brings us under misery's thrall.

If His wisdom is to teach me
    I must childlike be and small,
Me, from me, unto Him turning,
    Listening to Him above all.

Any sort of worldly wisdom
    Cannot Jesus' wisdom know;
Thus to foolishness it must come
    When that Light itself doth show.

Jesus — next the Father only —
    Doth true wisdom truly own;
Other wisdom ultimately
    Must its splendor then disown.

4. ON HONOR

Honor those to whom you owe it;
    Yet the honor Jesus claims
In triumph over all things goeth,
    For pure and godly is its frame.

Human honor itself consumeth,
    For to its object it is fixed;
Jesus' honor aye continueth,
    For it is holy and unmixed.

Carnal honor comes to nothing,
    As the wind blows smoke away;
Who honors God will, in his seeking,
    To true honor find the way.

Pride and arrogance to humble,
    Honor's King bore shame and scorn
As He carried of His own will
    All our need and hopes forlorn.

Thus true honor He has possessed
    Since He, on Golgotha's rise,
Suffered in our stead sin's duress
    As the Lamb of Sacrifice.

He God's glory manifested
    Throughout His brief span of life,
Honoring the Name most blessed
    In the mis'ry of death's strife.

Yea, it was the King of Honor,
    Lord indeed from eternity,
Now o'er all things made the ruler
    By God for His humility.

Whoever, then, would look for honor
    Must with Christ bear scorn and shame;
He will wear 'midst heaven's splendor
    The golden crown of honor's fame.

But whoso sinful body honoreth
    Rather will find sore disgrace
To be that which he garnereth
    At the great King's honoring-place.

To God alone belongs the honor
    In all places near and far,

And Jesus' honor grows the greater
Both now and also evermore.

5. On Riches

Among the wealthy human children
    Jesus is and remains rich;
There's no wealth that can come to one
    Which will Jesus' riches match.

Riches which by thieves are stolen
    Can be guarded through great pain,
But the riches that my soul owns
    Must be of a different strain.

All the wealth of Solomon's kingdom
    Afforded for him, nonetheless,
Not so much of satisfaction
    As would one hour of blessedness.

Croesus' wealth all wealth exceeded;
    Yet his wealth, if truth were known,
Was by him not as much needed
    As the words poor Solon loaned.

Solon said: "I cannot count one
    Happy until he is dead."
Through this word God saved the rich man
    From an execution dread.

Yet had Croesus failed to admit
    The valid thrust of Solon's speech
Until he was forced to face it
    When his life was in the breach.

Jesus' riches are kept hidden,
    Thus they do no one deceive

But through the sea of trouble lead
    one
And one's sense of fear relieve.

Jesus' gold is clear and lovely,
    In the fire so well refined;
Other gold, though bright it may be,
    Can't display so true a shine.

Jesus' gold has better virtue
    Than the virtue of this time;
With eternal youth it breaks through
    And will last in heaven's clime.

Jesus' gold in truth will make rich
    Those who are in spirit poor;
Therefore God the Father doth wish
    To prize this gold forevermore.

6. On Nobility

Only to our Christ's nobility
    Is all honor always due;
In spite appearance, man's nobility —
    Since 'tis mortal — must fall through.

Christ's nobility I will honor
    And devotedly confess,
Because He has proved with power
    That He can ennoble us.

We are dust from dust created
    And corrupted through our sin;
Eternally would we be degraded
    Had not God's Son entered in,

Looked upon us in His kindness,
    And then through His healing blood,

Taken His stand in the breach for us,
   Venturing there with courage bold.

In these times of grief and trouble
   Here within this foreign land
I consider in my sorrow
   Only Jesus' noble stand.

Then doth life itself soon quicken,
   Burgeoning forth e'en out of death
If it now the praise gives to Him
   Who us with God reconcileth.

Christ himself was thus born noble,
   God of God from eternity,
That He might bring us, so ignoble,
   Back again to nobility.

That we who are of dust and ashes
   Should again, through his noble
      blood,
Become the heirs of God's own
      promise —
   This thought also makes me bold.

Those who are to Christ related
   Inwardly this quality know
Which in days to trouble fated
   Ever nobler doth grow,

Until they from earth awaken,
   Joyful now and satisfied;
Then how noble God can make one
   Will by all men be descried.

7. ON FAITHFULNESS
Far beyond all human children
   Is my Jesus good and true;

Who can find a faithful person
   If he gives not Christ this due?

Faithful men are most praiseworthy;
   Yet we all know how it goes —
When a real test comes then hardly
   Anyone steadfastness shows.

Blessed is the man who knoweth
   Jesus' good and faithful heart
Which faithfulness on him bestoweth
   And turns his yearning heavenward.

Heavenward is one attracted
   When he, close that faithful breast,
Truly one time has partaken of
   God's fast faith and angels' fest.

Out of heaven has come Jesus,
   He who is our faithful knight,
To take up His just cause for us
   And in the gates establish right.

Faithful He himself has shown us,
   And His faithful shepherd blood
On the cross forever floweth —
   Oh! the crimson of that flood!

Hell and death He now doth conquer
   As a true, victorious knight,
And our justice He has paid for
   Through that faithful ransom-rite.

Come thou here and help us tell men
   Where true faithfulness is found:
In man's heart Christ's blood trans-
      fusion
   Makes the greatest sinner sound.

No untrueness can be seen in
　　Him who cannot tell a lie;
Our untrueness then must weaken
　　When on Him we fix our eye.

In summation, pure fidelity
　　Springs from Jesus' heart and breast,
And Jerusalem the Heav'nly
　　Increases faithful spirits' zest.

8. On Power

Great and mighty we must call those
　　Who are rulers of the earth;
Therefore I the power propose
　　Of Him who brought this world to birth.

Human power knows a boundary
　　And so soon comes to its term;
In the grave it has no memory —
　　Death shows no one much concern.

Jesus' grave bears silent witness
　　To what omnipotence can do;
That which the abyss would suppress
　　Heaven has exposed to view.

If a king takes his leave from us
　　He cannot his power retain;
Christ along our streets still cometh
　　With an everlasting gain.

Human help is insufficient
　　In the hour of death's night,
But Jesus' death is the denouement
　　Of God the Father's perfect might.

Jesus' death and life now reigneth
　　Over Death and over Life

Till He at His feet detaineth
All that doth against Him strive.

Wheresoever Jesus goeth,
There the Fiend stands in dis-
grace;
Where the Father His might showeth,
There the Fiend's might must
give place.

Therefore I will praise that power
Which can always me defend;
Though before hard trials I cower,
Jesus makes himself my friend.

Though I am so weak and so small,
Strong and great my enemy,
Jesus hears as oft as I call
And to His care taketh me.

Thus there is no power can steal me
Out of that almighty hand;
Through faith, Christ's blood makes
me mighty;
On His Spirit's pledge I stand.

9. On Splendors

Of splendors big and splendors little
This earth produces not a few,
Yet 'tis heav'n alone has title
To what I can call splendor true.

Human splendor and its pleasure
Here in this brief shadow-world
'Neath the sun soon bloom and wither
As a field with flowers furled.

Rain and dew and bright, warm sunshine
  In the lovely month of May
Through the wealth of heaven's design
  Give the world its splendor-day;

But then heat and hail and windstorm,
  Autumn's chill and winter's freeze,
Straightway devastate and deform
  Garden, field, and stand of trees.

Likewise too for the poor sinner
  With his splendors of this life
In the ice of death's cold winter
  Naught but *finis* is in sight.

But that soul has greater splendor
  Which with spiritual eyes can see,
In the dark that faith was meant for,
  Hope of heaven blooming free.

Where the glorious Lord of Glories
  In a cattle stall was born,
There one sees that the vainglories
  Of this world deserve but scorn.

Splendors one indeed will look on
  When the winter of this time
One day finally will be gone
  In eternity's warm clime,

There where heaven's springtime
    bloometh,
  Where God's worthy host divine
Through the Holy City moveth,
  Godly, glorious, line on line.

Whoso now becometh lowly
  Here within this time of grace

There on the new earth will surely
    Blossom splendors forth apace.

10. ON CROWNS

Crowns which on high heads are carried
    In this world of omens full
Can to us speak truth more varied
    Than a dolt dreams possible;

For what before us is presented
    In this preparatory school
There divinely is recited
    In front the Lamb's headmaster-stool.

Yea, all kingly crowns bring honor
    To the New Jerusalem
Which He, of all things the Author,
    Founded on twelve precious gems.

Therein David's crown will prosper
    Upon Zion's mount with joy,
A thousand crowns used for its luster
    Along with all else God employs.

Caesars' crowns show up as sordid
    Seen against our monarch's crown
Which the Maker of the world did
    Set on his beloved Son,

Who a crown of thorns accepted
    In this world of spite and hate
And who, when we were dejected,
    'Stablished God's right in the gate.

Thus, to live with crown upon Him
    Is Jesus' wont eternally,
For that head bears many of them
    Which bowed itself so humbly.

He has crowns, too, to distribute
  To each soul who doth Him know,
Lets His blood new health contribute;
  On such, life's crown He doth
    bestow.

Four and twenty crowns shall be cast
  Down before the Godhead's throne
When the Father's pleasure at last
  Is revealed through the Son.

O Lord Jesus! Thine own behest —
  Would it were now my heart's crown,
That I might Thy praises invest
  Though I am only dust and ground.

— TRANSLATED BY VERNARD ELLER[20]

Appendixes

I. List of Deaths (Alexander Mack, Jr.)

Register of the dear brethren and sisters especially known to me who have passed from time to eternity up to the present during my brief life-span.[1]

1 A single brother, in Schwarzenau, whose family name was Hirsch
2 Ernest Christopher Hochmann von Hagenau [Hochenau] expired in Schwarzenau[2]
3 Daniel Fritz, a brother in Schwarzenau and
4 his wife, Sister Elizabeth
5 Bro. Hoecker in Krefeld and
6 his wife
7 Bro. John George Schmidt in Krefeld and
8 the sister, his wife
9 Bro. William Grau [Grahe] in Krefeld and
10 his wife, the daughter of Bro. Naas and
11 her mother, his [Naas'] first wife
12 Bro. John Lobach in Krefeld
13 Christina, an unmarried sister from the area of Findelheim [or a foundlings' home] who died triumphantly in Schwarzenau
14 Bro. Stetzius [crossed out]
15 Bro. Stetzius in Krefeld
16 Bro. Augustin in Surhuisterveen
17 Bro. Jacob Schneider and
18 his wife, the first woman elder [Altistin] of the congregation at Schwarzenau; after her husband's death she lived and served the congregation for seven years
19 Bro. George Graebi [Grebi] and

20 his wife, a sister
21 Bro. Alexander Mack and
22 his wife, Sister Anna Margaretha
23 Bro. John Henry Kalckloeser and
24 his mother, the old sister and
25 his two wives, the dear sisters
26
27 Bro. John Naas and
28 his two wives, the dear sisters
29
30 Bro. Abraham Duboy
31 Bro. Peter Backer [Becker] and
32 his wife, Sister Dorothea
33 Bro. Stritzka, a nobleman from Koeln [*ein Colischer Edelman*][3]
34 Sister Charitas
35 Bro. John Henry Traut who expired unmarried
36 Bro. Holtzapfel and
37 his wife, Sister Lena Holtzapfel
38 Bro. George Balzer Traut and
39 his two wives, the dear sisters
40
41 Bro. Jeremias Traut, also unmarried
42 Bro. Emmanuel Kalckloeser and
43 his wife, Sister Catharina
44 Bro. Jacob Bossert, Sr. and
45 his two wives, the sisters
46
47 Bro. Christian Martin and
48 his wife, the sister and
49 his mother
50 Andreas Bony and
51 his wife, the former [Widow] Nediger [Noethiger]
52 Bro. Lucas Fetter [Vetter] and
53 his wife, the sister
54 Bro. John Flickinger, unmarried
55 Bro. Christopher Kalckgloezer and
56 his wife, the sister
57 Bro. John Gomri [Gumre] and
58 his wife, the sister
59 Bro. John Kipinger and
60 his wife, Sister Johana
61 Bro. John George Koch and
62 his wife, the sister
63 Bro. John Valentine Mack and
64 his wife, the sister

65 Bro. John Mack and
66 his wife, the sister
67 Bro. Stephen Koch, unmarried
68 Sister Sophie
69 Bro. Christian Liebe
70 Bro. Michael Frantz and
71 his wife, the sister
72 and his daughter, the sister
73 Bro. Martin Urner and
74 his wife, the sister and
75 his daughter, the sister
76 Bro. Michael Eckerling [Eckerlin] and
77 his wife, the sister
78 Bro. Daniel Eckerling
79 Bro. Hoheim in Altona
80 Bro. Samuel Eckerling
81 Bro. Israel Eckerling
82 Bro. Immanuel Eckerling
83 Bro. Gabriel Eckerling
84 Bro. Pardolt Petersen in Altona
85 Bro. John Fischer in Altona
86 Bro. Phillip Zettel and
87 the sister, his wife
88 Bro. Lawrence Schweitzer and
89 the sister, his wife
90 Bro. Daniel Eicher and
91 his wife, the sister and
92 his daughter, the sister
93 Bro. Phillip Ruland and
94 his wife (with daughter)
95 Bro. Michael Pfautz, Sr. and
96 the sister, his wife
97 Bro. Peter Hummer and
98 his wife, the sister
99 Bro. Henry Schneider in Conestoga
100 Bro. Henry Schneider in Germantown
101 Bro. [John Jacob] Preisz, Sr. and
102 his wife, the sister
103 Bro. John Preisz and
104 his son and the son's wife, the sister
105
106 Bro. Anthony Dierdorf and
107 his wife, the sister
108 Bro. Rudolph Herli [Harley] and
109 his wife, the sister

110 Bro. John von Lashet and
111 his wife, the sister
112 Bro. Dietrich Fahnestock and
113 his wife, the sister
114 Bro. Jacob Mohr and
115 his wife, the sister
116 Bro. Matthew Schmidt and
117 his wife, the sister
118 Bro. John Mohr and
119 his wife, the sister
120 Bro. John Theobald End[t] and
121 his wife, the sister, the elder
122 Bro. Doctor Jacob Mo[h]r
123 Bro. Frederick Ochs and
124 his wife, the old sister
125 Bro. Henry Schlingluff and
126 his wife, the melancholy sister
127 Bro. Peter Schilbert and
128 his wife, the sister
129 Bro. Henry Schlingluff's oldest daughter
130 Bro. Jacob Weis and
131 his daughter, Sister Sophia
132 Bro. John Brecht and
133 his son, a brother
134 Bro. John Schleifer and
135 his wife, the sister
136 Bro. Rothrock and
137 his wife, the sister
138 Bro. John Frick and
139 his wife, the sister
140 Bro. Joseph Mueller
141 the mother of the still-living Martin Urner
142 Bro. John Hildebrandt and [number repeated]
142 his wife, the sister
143 Bro. Henry Hoecker
144 Bro. Lewis Hoecker and
145 his wife, the sister
146 Bro. Christian Eckstein
147 Sister Elizabeth Eckstein
148 Bro. Riszman
149 Bro. Nerwick and
150 his wife, the sister
151 Bro.   Grumbacker and
152 his wife, Sister Elizabeth
153 old Brother Matthew Schweizer

154 dear Bro. Uhli Reinhart
155 dear Bro. John Kaempfer, Sr. and
156 his wife, the sister
157 the beloved Brother Daniel Ritter and
158 his wife, the sister
159 dear brother George Balzer Gantz and
160 his wife, Sister Agenes
161 Bro. Phillip Kuester
162 dear Sister Juliana Rubickam
163 dear Bro. George Schreiber
164 Sister Anna Schreiber
165 dear Sister Hannah Keyser
166 Bro. William Nice and his wife
167 Anna Maria Nice
168 beloved Brother Christopher Saur and
169 his wife, Sister Catharina
170 dear Sister Margaretha Gorgias
171 Sister Fend
172 dear Sister Philipine Hertzback, the elder
173 beloved Sister Margaret Bayer, the elder
174 dearly beloved Bro. Phillip Weber and
175 his wife, Sister Louisa
176 much respected Bro. Stephen Ulrich
177 Bro. Nicholas Martin
178 Bro. George Adam Martin
179 Bro. David Martin
180 Bro. Ernest Stoll
181 Bro. [Jacob] Sontag
182 Bro.   Mohler
183 Bro. Henry Neff and
184 his wife, the sister
185 Brother Kinsing
186 Bro. Jacob Stutzman
187 old Sister Schreiber
188 Sister Philipine Schreiber
189 Bro. Peter Wertz
190 Bro. Peter Dierdorf
191 Bro. John Bechtelsheim, Sr.
192 Bro. Jacob Mohr, Jr.
193 Bro. Henry Dierdorf and
194 his wife, the sister
195 Bro. William Wertz
196 Brother Gideon
197 Brother Aller
198 Bro. Keim and

199 his wife, the sister
200 Bro. Schwartz and
201 his wife, the sister
202 Bro. Eichenberg, Sr.
203 Bro. Valentine End[t]
204 Bro. Paul Leibgeb and
205 Christina, his wife, the sister
206 Bro. Godfrey Liebgeb and
207 his wife, the sister
208 Sister Regine
209 Bro. Jacob Bossert, Jr. and
210 his wife, the sister
211 Brother Gusz
212 Brother Ephrem
213 Bro. Godfrey Geyer
214 Bro. Carl Harlacker
215 Bro. Peter Jaeger and
216 his wife, the sister
217 Bro. Jacob Koch and
218 his wife, the sister (Anna Elizabeth)
219 and their daughter, Sister Catharina
220 Bro. Peter Schneider
221 Bro. Peter Grumbacher
222 Bro. Uli Grumbacher
223 Brother Hartman, Sr. and
224 his wife, the sister
225 Sister Rousefeler
226 Brother Demuth and
227 his wife, the sister
228 Brother Andrew Frey
229 Brother William Frey
230 Brother Lichte, Sr. and
231 his wife, the sister
232 Brother Kaempfer, Jr.
233 Bro. Julian Stump
234 Bro. Jacob Stump and
235 his wife, Sister Betty, daughter of P. Becker
236 the wife of Jacob Lichte, Brecht's daughter
237 Bro. Jacob Schneider and
238 his wife, the sister
239 the first wife of Friend Graff (Groff), Bro. Rudolph Herly's daughter
240 old Sister Hellerlis
241 Brother Hecker who married in Krefeld and
242 Brother Gotze Goiin [Gossen Goyen], his father-in-law
243 Bro. John Bechtelsheim and

244 his wife, the sister and
245 the wife of his brother, the sister
246 Bro. Henry Weber, an unmarried brother
247 Bro. Anthony Schneiter
248 Brother William, an unmarried brother
249 Bro. Andrew Gesell, unmarried
250 Bro. John Gesell, unmarried
251 Bro. Abraham Latscha
252 Bro. Eisbert Bender and
253 the sister, his wife
254 Bro. Carl Lewis Bender
255 Bro. Peter Lesle
256 Sister Petikoffer
257 Bro. Andrew Feit and
258 his wife, the sister
259 old Brother Friedli Steiner and
260 his wife, the sister
261 Bro. John Steiner, Jr.
262 Bro. John Steiner, Sr.
263 young Brother   Dock
264 young Brother Friedli Steiner
265 Bro. Anthony Miller and
266 his wife, the sister
267 Bro. Abraham Paul and
268 Sister Sophia, his wife
269 old Brother Albert Engelhard and
270 his son Englehard, passed away in Germantown
271 old Brother   Grumbacher at Pipe Creek
272 Brother Grauling
273 Sister Leibert
274 Brother   Boebel and
275 the sister, his wife
276 old single Sister Gertrude
277 old sickly Sister Magdalena
278 Bro. John Keim
279 especially beloved Bro. William Knepper and
280 his beloved wife, Froni, the sister
281 Bro. John Henckels and
282 his wife, the sister
283 Bro. Lewie Boinon and
284 his two wives, the sisters
285
286 beloved friend Simon Siron and
287 his sister-like wife
288 the very sister-like friend, Poel

289 dear brother Wagner who was baptized at Amwell with the sister Engel
290 dear Bro. Phillip Diel and
291 his brother's first wife, the sister
292 dear Brother Christopher Saur's mother (the sister)
293 fraternal friend John Wuester and
294 his last wife, Sister Anastasia
295 bosom-friend and Brother Conrad Mattheus
296 beloved friend John Seelig
297 much respected friend Dr. Benewell (aged 90 years)
298 my especial friend Rosh (Rush)
299 my faithful Brother William Butzmueller in Krefeld
300 Brother Dubs baptized with Sister Longenecker
301 Brother Clemens at Great Conewago [*grossen Canawaken*]
302 Bro. Richard Roob and
303 his wife, the sister
304 Bro. Edmond Lonsthroth
305 Brother Holstein at Falckner Swamp
306 Bro. John Schlingluff and
307 his wife, the sister
308 the unmarried Sister Robin
309 Bro. Caspar Engel, the second husband of Sister Lis
310 Bro. John Ley
311 Bro. John Peter, or John Peterson at Pipe Creek
312 Bro. Peter Zuk, at Great Swamp
313 Sister Stober
314 old Brother Rincker at Great Swamp
315 Brother Stout and
316 his wife, the sister
317 Brother Dascher
318 Sister Bach
319 Brother Kaempel in Amwell, N. J.
320 Mrs. Landes, the daughter of Bro. Naas
321 Sister Ruth
322 old Brother Conrad Stam and
323 his wife, the sister
324 Brother Hoecker in Amwell
325 old Brother x who had so many bees along the Schuylkill
326 Bro. George Reyer, the tanner
327 much beloved Brother Reyer who wanted to marry old Sister Baeyer
328 beloved Sister Susanna Weber and
329 beloved Bro. Phillip Weber, her husband
330 Alexander Weber
331 beloved Sister Anna Barbara van Lasche; she departed on January 10, 1796
A. D., her natural age being 71 years, 5 months, and 9 days
332 dear Sister Reiter, the daughter of Brother Gomri

333 beloved Bro. Jacob Bauman
334 Sister Hertzbach
335 Sister Rose
336 daughter of Bro. Bauman
337 very faithful and esteemed Bro. Daniel Letterman in Maryland
338 dear Sister Maria Hops
339 upright and dear old Sister Babi, the second wife of Bro. Martin Urner
340 dear Bro. Gerrit Clemens, in his 63rd year (1799)
341 much beloved Bro. Martin Urner in his 74th year. He was the cousin of the older Bro. Martin Urner and his successor in the office of elder in the congregation on the Schuylkill; he passed away in May, 1797.
342 Bro. Christopher Sauer, Jr., died on July 3, 1799 in Baltimore, aged 45 years
343 In the spring of 1801 the well-beloved Johnny Landes passed away at an advanced age on the Cocalico, in Lancaster County. After he had waited for his release a long time, with much patience and with great shortness of breath, his spirit was finally called home, and his body was committed to the earth or laid in the lap of the mother of our bodies, until the seventh trump will be blown.

In West Friesland many Dutch friends joined the congregation, of whom the following were especially known to me, and have also departed this life.[4]
1 Bro. Jacob Dircks Huisinga
2 Bro. Albert Jans
3 Bro. Levi Rose
4 Bro. Den Cate
5 Bro. Dirk Hendricksen
6 Bro. Peter De Kocker
7 Bro. Jellis De Kocker
8 Bro. Michael De Kocker
9 Bro. Peter Arian
10 Bro. Adrian Pfau, the wonderful almoner, called by God and most faithful, who annually contributed in Amsterdam 100,000 Dutch guilders from his personal fortune

Well-known brethren who passed away in Ephrata.[5]
1 Bro. Michael Wohlfahrt
2 Bro. **Conrad Beis[s]el or Friedsam Gottrecht**
3 Bro. Martin Bremer
4 Bro. Joel
5 Bro. Risman or Philemon
6 Bro. Benedict Jugtli [Juchlie]
7 Bro. Jacob Gasz
8 Bro. Aleaser
9 Bro. Peter Geer
10 Bro. John Maili

11 Bro. Hans Meili
12 Bro. Frederick Falsz
13 Bro. Nehemia
14 Bro. Sealthiel
15 Bro. David Schaefer
16 Bro. Joseph Schaeffer
17 Bro. Nathaniel, Bro. Eicher's son
18 Bro. Hasuel
19 Bro. Rudolph Naegli
20 Bro. Jemini
21 Bro. Reb or Rufinus
22 Bro. Isai or David Lesle
23 Bro. Daniel Eicher
24 Bro. Peter Miller, September 25, 1796, aged 87 years 5 months
25 Bro. Simon Koenig

II. List of Deaths (Christopher Sauer II)

Register of some well-known persons and when they died.[6]

1741	May 12	Bro. John Naas died
	[May 20]	Michael Wohlfahrt died in his 55th year
	June 15	Bro. Julian Stump was buried
	Oct.	Bro. Andrew Bony died
	Nov. 2	Bro. Peter Schneider died
1744	Mar. 20	Elizabeth Wentz died
	Dec. 4	Bro. Grumbacher was buried
1745	April 26	John Selig died
	May 16	Bro. Schilbert died
1746	May 27	Christ. Wiegner died
1747		around Christmas Michael Frantz died
1748	Mar. 20	Jacob Stump died
	Mar. 21	Abraham Duboy died
	Feb. 29	Henry Kalckloeser died
	Aug. 26	John Roeszer died
	Aug. 30	Conrad Matthai died
1749	Sept. 21	Godfrey Geiger died
	Nov. 1	Peter Wentz was buried
	Nov. 23	Jacob Weisz died
1751	Jan. 16	Bro. Brecht died
1752	June 13	Sister Schilbert died
	Dec. 14	my dear mother passed away in the Lord
1753	Aug. 13	my daughter Maria Christiana died
1756	Feb. 14	Sister Brecht died
1757	Oct. 18	Bro. Gundy died
	Dec. 26	Bro. Liebe died
1758	Mar. 19	Bro. Peter Becker died

	May 12	Bro. Caspar Feith died
	Aug. 27	Sister Charitas died
	Sept. 25	at noon my dear father passed away in the Lord
1761	Jan. 13	my mother-in-law passed away
1765	Jan. 14	Bro. Henry Weber died
	Aug. 30	Sister Gertrude Demuth died
1766	July 7	Conrad Beissel died
1769	May 21	Michael Pfautz died
1773	Feb. 1	Bro. Daniel Eicher died
1774	June 3	John Cowl[?] died
1775	Aug. 19	Sister Hannah Keyser died, aged 38 years, 1 month, and 1 day
1777	Jan. 8	my dear wife Catherine passed away in the Lord
1779	June 21	Bro. Richard Roob died, in his 70th year
	Sept. 20	Sister Anna Maria Neisz died, 76 years old
	Dec. 13	Bro. Henry Schlingluff died, 84 years old
1780	Feb. 23	Bro. Conrad Guth died
	July 10	Nanny Leibert died
1783	May 26	Bro. George Schreiber died
	Nov. 23	William Neisz died
1784	Jan. 8	Lydia Sauer died
	Aug. 26	at two o'clock in the morning, my dear father Christopher Sauer passed away in the Lord and was buried on the 27th. [Entry likely made by his daughter Catherine, who cared for him during his last years.][7]

Notes

Introduction

1. Winthrop S. Hudson, *Religion in America* (New York: Charles Scribner's Sons, 1965), p. 4.
2. Franklin H. Littell, *From State Church to Pluralism* (Garden City, N. Y.: Anchor Books, 1962), p. 3.
3. Sidney E. Mead, *The Lively Experiment: The Shaping of Christianity in America* (New York: Harper and Row, 1963), p. 2.
4. Quoted in Carl Bridenbaugh, *Mitre and Sceptre* (New York: Oxford University Press, 1962), pp. 133-135 from the *New York Mercury* (July 23, 1753); the quotation is modernized in spelling.
5. Quoted in Clifton E. Olmstead, *History of Religion in the United States* (Englewood Cliffs, N. J.: Prentice-Hall, Inc., 1960), p. 73; the quotation is modernized.
6. For details on state-church arrangements, see William Warren Sweet, *Religion in Colonial America* (New York: Charles Scribner's Sons, 1942). The early legal penalties are printed at length in H. Shelton Smith *et al.,* eds., *American Christianity* (New York: Charles Scribner's Sons, 1960), I: 41-44.
7. This section is largely dependent upon Sweet, *op. cit.,* pp. 313-339 and Mead, *op. cit.,* pp. 1-37. The latter plays down the effect of the left-wing movements, highlighted by Sweet. The quotation is from Mead, *op. cit.,* p. 29.
8. The quotation is from Philip Schaff, printed in Mead, *op. cit.,* p. 3.
9. For a discussion of Samuel Smith, see Roger E. Sappington, "Eighteenth Century Non-Brethren Sources of Brethren History, IV," *Brethren Life and Thought,* II (1957), 4: 65-75. The journal will hereafter be cited as "BLT."
10. Anthony Benezet to Samuel Smith, 17th of 8th month, 1765, A.L.S., Historical Society of Pennsylvania, Philadelphia. The archive will hereafter be cited as "HSP Philadelphia."
11. Robert Proud, *The History of Pennsylvania . . .* (Philadelphia: Zachariah Poulson, Jr., 1798), II: 345-348.
12. William M. Mervine, ed., *History of the Province of Pennsylvania by Samuel Smith* (Philadelphia: The Colonial Society of Pennsylvania, 1913), p. vii.

13. For another account of the baptism, see pages 523-524.
14. These incidents are discussed in Donald F. Durnbaugh, "Brethren Beginnings: The Origins of the Church of the Brethren in Early Eighteenth-Century Europe," (unpub. Ph.D. dissertation, University of Pennsylvania, 1960), pp. 113-115.
15. Smith, *op. cit.,* pp. 181-183 and 188-190.

I. TRANSPLANTATION

1. ARRIVAL AND SETTLEMENT

1. For a listing of contemporary publications which both encouraged and warned against migration to America, see Emil Meynen, ed., *Bibliography on German Settlements in Colonial North America* (Leipzig: Otto Harrassowitz, 1937), pp. 23-28. Also note Samuel W. Pennypacker, *The Settlement of Germantown, Pennsylvania and the Beginning of German Immigration to North America* (Lancaster, Pa.: Pennsylvania German Society, 1899).
2. Chapter V, "Emigration," in Donald F. Durnbaugh, ed., *European Origins of the Brethren* (Elgin, Ill.: The Brethren Press, 1958), pp. 281-320. See also Friedrich Nieper, *Die ersten deutschen Auswanderer von Krefeld nach Pennsylvanien* (Neukirchen, Kr. Moers: Buchhandlung des Erziehungsverein, 1940).
3. Durnbaugh, *Origins,* pp. 301-312, and Andrew S. Berkey, ed., *The Journals and Papers of David Schultze* (Pennsburg, Pa.: The Schwenkfelder Library, 1952-1953).
4. The Käsebier and Sauer letters were originally published in the writer's translation in "Two Early Letters from Germantown," *The Pennsylvania Magazine of History and Biography,* LXXXIV (1960), 220-233, with detailed notes. The magazine is hereafter cited as "PMHB." A reference to Käsebier's early occupation is found in *Verschiedene alte und neuere Geschichten von Erscheinigungen der Geister* (Germantown, Pa.: Christopher Sauer I, 1744), p. 91ff.
5. The best source on Count Casimir is Friedrich W. Winckel, *Aus dem Leben Casimirs, weiland Grafen zu Sayn-Wittgenstein-Berleburg* (Frankfurt/Main: Heinrich Ludwig Brönner, 1842). See also Karl Hartnack, "Schwarzenau," *Wittgenstein,* XLV (1956), Vol. 20, 83-93.
6. K 36, Fürstliche Sayn-Wittgenstein-Berleburgisches Archiv, Berleburg. The archive is hereafter cited as "FSA Berleburg."
7. J. Christopher Sauer to [Gov. R. H. Morris], March 15, 1755, Cassel Collection MS 95, Juniata College library, Huntingdon, Pennsylvania. The collection, which will be used extensively in this book, will hereafter be cited as "Cassel Coll." The passage is quoted in Dietmar Rothermund, *The Layman's Progress* (Philadelphia: University of Pennsylvania Press, 1961), p. 91, and in Martin G. Brumbaugh, *History of the German Baptist Brethren in Europe and America* (Mt. Morris, Ill.: Brethren Publishing House, 1899), p. 377 (incorrectly listing Gov. William Denny as the recipient).
8. "Das Leben des Herrn Charles Hector Marquis St. George de Marsay," fol. 294ff., a bound manuscript in the private collection of Dr. J. F. Gerhard Goeters, Bonn/Rhine. For a discussion of Sauer's influence, see Donald F. Durnbaugh, "Christopher Sauer, Pennsylvania-German Printer," *PMHB,* LXXXII (1958), 316-340.
9. Published in English translation by R. W. Kelsey, "An Early Description of Pennsylvania. Letter of Christopher Sower, written in 1724, Describing Conditions in Philadelphia and Vicinity, and the Sea Voyage from Europe," *PMHB,* XLV (1921), 243-254.

10. K 36, FSA Berleburg.
11. On the De Kokers and the Brethren, see Durnbaugh, *Origins,* pp. 263-264. Biographical information is in J. C. van Slee, *De Rijnsburger Collegianten* (Haarlem: der Erven F. Bohn, 1895).
12. Fasz. 9897, fol. 18, Abt. 74, Baden Generalia, Badisches Generallandesarchiv, Karlsruhe.
13. *Glaubhafftes Send-Schreiben aus Pensylvania in America . . . welchem noch beygefüget ein anderer merckwürdiger Brieff aus bemeldten Landen . . .* (Frankfurt/Main: Just. Heinr. Wigand, 1739). The only known copy is in the private collection of Dr. Martha Haeberlin, Bad Nauheim.
14. For information on Dr. Luther, see Gustav Mori, *Die Egenolff-Luthersche Schriftgiesserei in Frankfurt am Main . . .* (Frankfurt/Main: Stempel, 1926) and Bernhard Mueller, *Frankfurt/Amerika* (Frankfurt/Main: 1926), pp. 23, 28.
15. Edward W. Hocker, *Germantown, 1683-1933* (Philadelphia: the author, 1933) contains information on several of the signers.
16. On Goyen, see Nieper, *op. cit.,* p. 31ff.; Otto Schowalter, "Goyen, Gosen," *Mennonitisches Lexikon,* II: 151-152; and Dirk Cattepoel, "Das religiöse Leben in der Krefelder Mennonitengemeinde des 17. und 18. Jahrhunderts," *Beiträge zur Geschichte rheinischer Mennoniten* (Weierhof/Pfalz: Mennonitischen Geschichtsverein, 1939), pp. 5-28.
17. Mappe 34/2, Mennonitisches Gemeinde Archiv, Krefeld. The archive is hereafter cited as "MGA Krefeld."
18. Mappe 34/1, MGA Krefeld.

2. EXPANSION AND SCHISM

1. According to the Chroniclers, " . . . on the ocean they had lost their love for one another, and . . . had even become scattered over the country." In another place, George Adam Martin wrote in the *Chronicle* that "the spirit of discord also moved with them, and so wounded and corrupted them on the other side of the ocean, that they could hardly be cured in America." The quotations are from the English translation by J. Max Hark, *Chronicon Ephratense: A History of the Community of Seventh Day Baptists at Ephrata, Lancaster County, Penn'a,* by "Lamech and Agrippa" (Lancaster, Pa.: S. H. Zahm and Co., 1899), pp. 15, 249. This is hereafter cited as "Chronicon." For a recent discussion, see Floyd E. Mallott, *Studies in Brethren History* (Elgin, Ill.: Brethren Publishing House, 1954), pp. 48-49.
2. William J. Hull, *William Penn and the Dutch Quaker Migration to Pennsylvania* (Philadelphia: Swarthmore College, 1935), pp. 219-220.
3. On the great awakening, see Hudson, *op. cit.,* pp. 59-82, and William Warren Sweet, *The Story of Religion in America,* rev. ed. (New York: Harper and Bros., 1950), pp. 138-154.
4. Julius F. Sachse, *The German Sectarians of Pennsylvania, 1708-1800: A Critical and Legendary History of the Ephrata Cloister and the Dunkers* (Philadelphia: the author, 1899-1900), two volumes. Although these books and Sachse's other writings on this subject contain very valuable material, they must be used with caution because of the author's proclivities for the esoteric and dramatic. The "legendary" in the title sometimes indicates oral tradition of early history and sometimes Sachse's idea of what should have happened.
5. The learnéd John Kelpius (1673-1708) of Transylvania led a group of Pietist mystics to Pennsylvania, where they established a hermitage on the Wissahickon

near Germantown. Following the death of their leader, the group broke up, some finding their way into the Ephrata Community later. See Julius F. Sachse, *The German Pietists of Provincial Pennsylvania, 1694-1708* (Philadelphia: the author, 1895) and Oswald Seidensticker, "The Hermits of the Wissahickon," *PMHB*, XI (1887), 427-441.

6. Brumbaugh, *op. cit.*, pp. 155-160.

7. [Henry Sangmeister], *Leben und Wandel des in Gottruhenden und seligen Bruders Ezechiel Sangmeister, weiland ein Einwohner von Ephrata von ihm selbst beschrieben* (Ephrata, Pa.: Joseph Baumann, 1825-1827), four volumes. H. W. Kriebel, "Henry Sangmeister, the Ephrata Chronicler," Lancaster [Pa.] County Historical Society *Papers*, XVI (1912), 5: 127-232, defends Sangmeister's account. A critical review was written by Felix Reichmann, "Ezechiel Sangmeister's Diary," *PMHB*, LXVIII (1944), 292-313. Reichmann considers the diary to be a partial forgery of limited historical value. Sangmeister's opinion of the Chroniclers' bias is found on pages 7-8 of volume one.

Despite a voluminous literature on Ephrata and Conrad Beissel — see Eugene E. Doll and Annaliese M. Funke, comps., *The Ephrata Cloisters: An Annotated Bibliography* (Philadelphia: Carl Shurz Memorial Foundation, 1944) — there is no fully satisfactory treatment. The latest full-scale history of the Community, by James E. Ernst, *Ephrata: A History* (Allentown, Pa.: Pennsylvania German Folklore Society, 1963), although improved by the editorial notes of John Joseph Stoudt, is largely a collation of the *Chronicle* and Sangmeister's diary. The biography of Beissel by Walter C. Klein, *Johann Conrad Beissel: Mystic and Martinet* (Philadelphia: University of Pennsylvania Press, 1942), is marred by the lack of sympathetic understanding displayed by the author. His own account of his research was: "Despite the slender prospect of success, I have plodded through the material, without shirking the boredom of many a somnolent afternoon passed in the society of some of the weakest minds of the eighteenth century, not to mention the defectives of subsequent generations" (p. 207). The most adequate appraisals are still to be found in the works of Oswald Seidensticker, especially *Ephrata, eine amerikanische Klostergeschichte* (Cincinnati: Mecklenborg and Rosenthal, 1883).

8. *Chronicon*, pp. 24-27. In this and following quotations from the Hark translation, there have been slight changes in the text based upon the original German. Sangmeister, *op. cit.*, I: 12.

9. *Chronicon*, pp. 27-29; Sangmeister, *op. cit.*, I: 12-13.

10. *Chronicon*, pp. 31-33; Sangmeister, *op. cit.*, I: 13.

11. *Chronicon*, pp. 33-37; Sangmeister, *op. cit.*, I: 15-17.

12. Sangmeister, *op. cit.*, I: 17-20.

13. *Chronicon*, p. 48; Sangmeister, *op. cit.*, I: 20-22.

14. For a discussion of these differences, see Donald F. Durnbaugh, "The Genius of the Brethren," *BLT*, IV (1959), 1: 4-34 and 2: 4-18.

15. *Chronicon*, pp. 48-51; Sangmeister, *op. cit.*, I: 22-24.

16. Sangmeister, *op. cit.*, I: 24.

17. *Chronicon*, p. 95. An early MS copy of the Koch vision is found in the MGA Krefeld, Mappe 35/6. This vision was printed in the *Geistliche Fama*, II (1736), xx, 65-72; the Sauer publication of it was in the previously cited *Verschiedene . . . Geschichten* (1744). The Krefeld copy was published in Cattepoel, *loc. cit.*, pp. 25-28. It is given in English translation in Brumbaugh, *op. cit.*, pp. 133-143. See also John S. Flory, *Literary Activity of the German Baptist Brethren*

in the Eighteenth Century (Elgin, Ill.: Brethren Publishing House, 1908), pp. 228-233.

18. Sangmeister, *op. cit.*, II: 123.
19. *Chronicon*, pp. 95-101.
20. On Lobach's life and leadership, see Durnbaugh, *Origins*, pp. 190-204.
21. August Gottlieb Spangenberg, Moravian leader; see pages 207-281.
22. Gerhard Tersteegen (1697-1769) was an outstanding figure among mystically inclined German Pietists. He lived a retired life near Solingen.
23. Hubert Rahr (1678-1746), a Reformed industrialist in Krefeld and intimate of the Brethren and the Mennonites, had befriended the Solingen Brethren after their release from captivity.
24. Koch's letter was published in a rare booklet titled *Lebens-Beschreibung von Conrad von Beuningen, Gewesenen Bürgermeister in Amsterdam; Als auch eine Ernstliche Ermahnung an Junge und Alte. . . . Nebst einem Anmercklichen Brieff ausz Pensylvanien in America . . .* (Krefeld: 1739), pp. 34-46; in the Haeberlin Collection. Two other letters from Koch to Lobach are mentioned and partly quoted in Max Goebel, *Geschichte des christlichen Lebens in der rheinisch-westphälischen evangelischen Kirche* (Coblenz: Karl Bädecker, 1860), III: 264-266.
25. *Chronicon*, pp. 122-125.
26. Letterbook of Conrad Beissel, fols. 19-27, HSP Philadelphia, Ac. 1923. An excerpt from the letter is found in Brumbaugh, *op. cit.*, pp. 125-126.
27. Brumbaugh, *op. cit.*, p. 208. Sachse, *Sectarians*, II: 397-398, takes Brumbaugh to task for this interpretation, commenting: "Now, as a matter of fact, there is not a single word of apology by Beissel in either the introduction or the epistle itself; nor was it intended to be any letter of vindication of anyone. If anything, it is a justification of Beissel's course, wherein he sets forth at length his position and teachings."
28. Letterbook of Conrad Beissel, fols. 126-129, HSP Philadelphia. See Sachse, *Sectarians*, II: 396-397.
29. Letterbook of Conrad Beissel, fols. 61-64, HSP Philadelphia. See Brumbaugh, *op. cit.*, 202-208, for a partial English translation.

3. CONTEMPORARY ACCOUNTS

1. Felix Reichmann and Eugene E. Doll, eds., *Ephrata, As Seen by Contemporaries* (Allentown, Pa.: Pennsylvania German Folklore Society, 1952).
2. George Keith (1638-1716) led a schismatic group within the Society of Friends about 1690. Although he later joined the Episcopalian Church (Anglican), many of his followers became Baptists, some holding to the Sabbatarian branch. See Rufus Jones, *The Quakers in the American Colonies* (New York: Russell and Russell, 1962), pp. 437-458.
3. *Materials Towards a History of the Baptists in Pennsylvania both British and German . . . Vol. I* (Philadelphia: Crukshank and Collins, 1770), pp. 74-79.
4. "Americanische Nachrichten von Herrnhutischen Sachen," in Johann Philip Fresenius, *Bewährte Nachrichten von Herrnhutischen Sachen . . .* (Frankfurt/Main and Leipzig; 1747-1748), III, 3: 87-872.
5. For information on Gruber's contacts with Europe, see Donald F. Durnbaugh, "Johann Adam Gruber: Pennsylvania-German Prophet and Poet," *PMHB*, LXXXIII (1959), 382-408.
6. "Extract-Schreiben aus J. A. Gr[uber's] Brief aus Germantown," *Geistliche Fama*,

I (1731), iii, 4: 50-52. Published in English translation in Sachse, *Sectarians,* I: 204-206, and partially in Reichmann and Doll, *op. cit.,* pp. 3-4.

7. Besides the writings of Mori, *op. cit.,* and Durnbaugh, "Sauer," previously mentioned, see also Edward W. Hocker, "The Founding of the Sower Press," *Germantown History,* II (1938), 6: 137-155, for information on Sauer's contacts with Europe.

8. The bibliographies of the Sauer press list no publications by John Hildebrand for 1750.

9. "Copey eines merkwürdigen Schreibens des Herrn Sauers in America . . . ," *Acta historico-ecclesiastica* (Weimar: 1751), XV, 3: 210-226; published also in English translation in Reichmann and Doll, *op. cit.,* pp. 45-48.

10. Sangmeister, *op. cit.,* II: 112-113.

11. *Der durch Europa und America aufmerksame Reisende* (Altona: Johann L. F. Richter, 1777); *Anonimus' Travels throu' Europe and America* (Ephrata: 1793).

12. *Reisende,* pp. 8-9.

13. The most convenient edition of the Halle Reports is W. J. Mann *et al.,* eds., *Nachrichten von den vereinigten deutschen Evangelisch-Lutherischen Gemeinen in Nord-Amerika, absonderlich in Pennsylvanien* (Allentown: Brobst, Diehl, and Co., 1881-1895), two volumes, also available in translated form (1880-1881).

14. *Kurtze Nachricht von einigen Evangelischen Gemeinen in America,* 2nd ed. (Halle: Waysenhaus Verlag, 1750), pp. 145, 216-217.

15. *Ibid.,* pp. 374-376.

16. Mann, *op. cit.,* II: 193-195.

17. *Ibid.,* II: 354-356.

18. Theodore G. Tappert and John W. Doberstein, trans., *The Journals of Henry Melchior Muhlenberg* (Philadelphia: The Muhlenberg Press, 1952-1958), I: 86, 144, 204, 213, 396, 627; II: 114. Excerpts are slightly altered.

19. Mann, *op. cit.,* II: 73-74, 75, 77-78, 79, 268.

20. The basic material for the history of the German Reformed Church in America is found in William J. Hinke *et al.,* eds., *Minutes and Letters of the Coetus of the German Reformed Congregations in Pennsylvania, 1747-1792* (Philadelphia: Reformed Church Publication Board, 1903); Joseph Henry Dubbs, *Historic Manual of the Reformed Church in the United States* (Lancaster, Pa.: Inquirer Printing Co., 1885); William J. Hinke, ed., *Life and Letters of the Rev. John Philip Boehm . . . , 1683-1749* (Philadelphia: Publication and Sunday School Board of the Reformed Church in the United States, 1916).

21. Hinke, *Boehm,* pp. 200-203; adapted.

22. Hinke, *Boehm,* pp. 234-249; adapted.

23. Hinke, *Boehm,* pp. 386-395; adapted.

24. Synodal Archive of the Reformed Church, The Hague; the archive is hereafter cited as "SAR The Hague."

25. SAR The Hague.

26. The Duché writing is listed in Eugene E. Doll, comp., "Sources for the History of the Ephrata Cloisters," in Doll and Funke, *op. cit.,* p. 54.

27. Du Simitière Papers, No. 17, The Library Company of Philadelphia.

28. [Benjamin Rush], "An Account of the Manners of the German Inhabitants of Pennsylvania," in *The Columbian Magazine or Monthly Miscellany . . . for January 1789* (Philadelphia: 1789), III: 22-30; the article was reprinted by I. D. Rupp (Philadelphia: Samuel P. Town, 1875) and by Theodore E. Schmauk (Lancaster, Pa.: New Era Printing Co., 1910).

4. On the Frontier

1. On the Danner family, see J. Maurice Henry, *History of the Church of the Brethren in Maryland* (Elgin, Ill.: Brethren Publishing House, 1936), pp. 34-44. According to Ira D. Landis, "York County, Pa.," *Mennonite Encyclopedia,* IV: 1008, Danner was an early member of the Mellinger Mennonite congregation of Lancaster County, and crossed the Susquehanna by 1719.

2. A biography of Cresap is Kenneth P. Bailey, *Thomas Cresap: Maryland Frontiersman* . . . (Boston: Christopher Publishing House, 1944).

3. John Gibson, *History of York County, Pa.* (Chicago: F. A. Battey Publishing Co., 1886), quoted in Henry, *op. cit.,* p. 38.

4. Samuel Hazard, ed., *Colonial Records of Pennsylvania* (Harrisburg and Philadelphia: 1838-1853), IV: 56ff.; see also Henry, *op. cit.,* p. 36.

5. *Ibid.,* IV: 64; see also Henry, *op. cit.,* pp. 36-37.

6. *Ibid.,* IV: 67; see also Henry, *op. cit.,* p. 37.

7. Quoted in Galen B. Royer, ed., *A History of the Church of the Brethren in the Middle District of Pennsylvania* (n.p.: Middle District of Pennsylvania, [1925]), p. 19.

8. E. Howard Blackburn and William H. Welfley, *History of Bedford and Somerset Counties* (New York and Chicago: The Lewis Publishing Company, 1906), I: 68-69.

9. Quoted in Blackburn and Welfley, *op. cit.,* I: 69 and Royer, *op. cit.,* p. 20.

10. U. J. Jones, *History of the Early Settlement of the Juniata Valley,* ed. by Floyd G. Hoenstine (Harrisburg, Pa.: The Telegraph Press, 1940), originally published in 1889.

11. *Ibid.,* pp. 192-193, 196, 199-200.

12. Royer, *op. cit.,* pp. 23-24. See also *Collections of the Historical Society of Pennsylvania* (Philadelphia: 1853), I: 44.

13. Martin G. Brumbaugh, "An Outline for Historical Romance," the Pennsylvania German Society *Proceedings and Addresses,* XXXIX (1928), published in 1930.

14. For the early history of the Eckerlin family, see Durnbaugh, *Origins,* p. 81ff.

15. Sangmeister, *op. cit.,* I: 152-158. This account makes clear what is misleading in the English translation of the *Chronicon* — that the person baptized with Eckerlin was not Christopher Sauer I but Henry Miller.

16. The most careful treatment of the early history of the New River settlements is in Frederick B. Kegley, *Kegley's Virginia Frontier* (Roanoke, Va.: 1938), pp. 116-131. A chapter in E. S. Smith *et al.,* eds., *The Pennsylvania Germans of the Shenandoah Valley* (Allentown: Pennsylvania German Folklore Society, 1964), pp. 83-100, is devoted to the Eckerlin migration and associated developments.

17. It has been suggested that the physician was Dr. George De Benneville.

18. *Chronicon,* pp. 184-185, 187-189.

19. *Der Hoch-Deutsch Pensylvanische Geschichtschreiber,* No. 63 (October 16, 1745).

20. *Der Hoch-Deutsche Pensylvanische Berichte,* No. 70 (May 16, 1746). See Sachse, *Sectarians,* II: 220, and Reichmann and Doll, *op. cit.,* for other English translations of the original.

21. As pacifists and vegetarians, the Ephrata Community members frowned on hunting.

22. *Chronicon,* pp. 224-225.

23. Cassel Coll., MS 67; published in translation in Brumbaugh, *History,* pp. 220, 225-226.

24. The reference to the Dunkers and road work is found in Lyman Chalkley, "Before the Gates of the Wilderness," *The Virginia Magazine of History and Biography,* XXX (1922), 2: 183-202. The journal is hereafter cited as "VMHB." See also

Kegley, *op. cit.*, p. 117. For the Schnell and Brandmueller note, see William J. Hinke and C. E. Kemper, eds., "Moravian Diaries of Travel Through Virginia," *VMHB,* XI (1903), 2: 125. John W. Wayland protested the identification of the group as Dunkers in the annotation — "The Dunkers and the Sieben-Taeger," *VMHB,* XII (1905), 3: 313-317.

25. The Walker journal has often been published. It is available in Lewis P. Summers, *Annals of Southwest Virginia, 1769-1800* (Abingdon, Va.: the author, 1929); the reference to the "Duncards" is on pp. 10-11 of this edition. A thorough study of Walker is found in Archibald Henderson, "Dr. Thomas Walker and the Loyal Company of Virginia," *Proceedings* of the American Antiquarian Society, N.S., XLI (1932), 77-178. This journal is hereafter cited as "AAS Proceedings." This passage is also printed in Klaus Wust, "German Mystics and Sabbatarians in Virginia," *VMHB,* LXXII (1964), 330-347, the best treatment on the Eckerlins in Virginia.

26. An early reference to the Eckerlins on Dunkard Creek is taken from the *National Intelligencer,* Washington, D. C., and reprinted in Sherman Day, *Historical Collections of the State of Pennsylvania* (Philadelphia: George W. Gorton, 1843), pp. 359-360. The Indian agent George Croghan noted in his report of May 25, 1751, that "a Dunkar from the colony of Virginia came to Logstown and requested liberty of the Six Nations chiefs to make a settlement of the River Yough-yo-gaine, a branch of the Ohio" — *Colonial Records,* V: 531. This is discussed in Alvin G. Faust, "Some Aspects of the Social History of Somerset County," *The Western Pennsylvania Historical Magazine,* XXI (1938), 197-198, and in Solon Buck, *The Planting of Civilization in Western Pennsylvania* (Pittsburgh: University of Pittsburgh Press, 1939), p. 139. The settlement also figured in history as the original terminus of the Mason and Dixon line of 1763; see A. H. Mason and W. Swindler, "Mason and Dixon: Their Line and Its Legend," *American Heritage,* XV (1964), 2: 22-29, 93-96.

27. The most complete account of the Cheat River settlement of the Eckerlins is by Felix Robinson, "The Wilderness Monks," *Tableland Trails,* I (1954), 4: 38-59. The local history by Oren Morton, *A History of Preston County, West Virginia* (Kingwood, W. Va.: The Journal Printing Company, 1914), pp. 46-49, has considerable detail. Foster M. Bittinger, *A History of the Church of the Brethren in the First District of West Virginia* (Elgin, Ill.: Brethren Publishing House, 1945), pp. 21-29, contains valuable material but confuses the several distinct settlements.

28. See Wust, *loc. cit.,* p. 339.

29. Probably with "Traut" John Henry Traut is meant; he was a leader among the Brethren in Germany; see Durnbaugh, *Origins,* p. 151ff. John Tennhardt was a maker of wigs at Nuremberg, who died in 1720; he wrote beginning in 1710 literally hundreds of letters urging repentance upon the royalty and nobility of Europe.

30. *Chronicon,* pp. 225-226, 229-231.

31. See Wust, *loc. cit.,* pp. 341-347.

32. Sangmeister, *op. cit.,* II: 46-47.

33. Adelaide L. Fries, *Records of the Moravians in North Carolina* (Raleigh, N. C.: 1922), I: 133-134. See also John H. Clewell, *History of Wachovia in North Carolina* (New York: Doubleday, Page and Company, 1902), p. 33.

34. Sachse, *Sectarians,* II: 331-359, has an elaborate account.

35. *Chronicon,* pp. 231-233.

36. Sangmeister, *op. cit.,* II: 79-81.

37. M. I. Hays, ed., *Calendar of the Papers of Benjamin Franklin in the Library of the American Philosophical Society* (Philadelphia: American Philosophical Society, 1908), I: 33. Printed also in Sachse, *Sectarians*, II: 335 in facsimile. The account of the captivity is corroborated by French sources. The aide-de-camp of Marquis de Montcalm wrote in his diary, under the date September 1-10, 1757: "Some Ottawas at thirty or forty leagues from Fort Duquesne seized three hermits of some kind, whom they have sent to Montreal. For eleven years they had lived alone in these mountains, having left a monastery established in Virginia forty [*sic*] years ago. These are probably some Anabaptists chased out of Alsace, where they had taken refuge." The excerpt is from Edward P. Hamilton, ed. and trans., *Adventure in the Wilderness: The American Journals of Louis Antoine de Bougainville, 1756-1760* (Norman, Okla.: University of Oklahoma Press, c.1964), pp. 180-181.

38. Cassel Coll., MS 67.

II. CONGREGATIONS

5. COLONIAL CONGREGATIONS

1. *A Short and Plain View of the Outward, Yet Sacred Rights and Ordinances of the House of God* (Philadelphia: John Binns, 1810), pp. 15-16.

2. Moses Coit Tyler, *The Literary History of the American Revolution* (New York: 1897), II: 387, provided the critical estimate of Edwards.

3. William Rogers preached a memorial discourse after Edward's death which provides basic biographical material; it is published in John Rippon, ed., *Baptist Annual Register* (London: 1796), pp. 308-314. See also William H. Allison, "Edwards, Morgan," *Dictionary of American Biography* (New York: Charles Scribner's Sons, 1943), VI: 40-41. The full title of the first volume of his history was *Materials Towards a History of the Baptists in Pennsylvania both British and German, Distinguished into Firstday Baptists, Keithian Baptists, Seventhday Baptists, Tuncker Baptists, Mennonist Baptists. Vol. I.* (Philadelphia: Crukshank and Collins, 1770). The comments on his intentions and methods are found on pages i-ii.

4. Others dispute this explanation; see pages 193-199.

5. On Becker's early life, see Durnbaugh, *Origins*, p. 151ff.; in America, see Brumbaugh, *History*, pp. 191-211.

6. On Mack, Sr., see Hermann Brunn, *Schriesheimer Mühlen in Vergangenheit und Gegenwart* (Mannheim: Verlag Wilhelm Burger, 1947), pp. 111-113; Durnbaugh, *Origins*, pp. 38-56, 107-148, 159-177, and elsewhere; Brumbaugh, *History*, pp. 71-100 and elsewhere.

7. On Mack, Jr., see Brumbaugh, *History*, pp. 211-273; Samuel B. Heckman, *The Religious Poetry of Alexander Mack, Jr.* (Elgin, Ill.: Brethren Publishing House, 1912); and chapters 5-7, 10, and 12-13 of this book.

8. On Sauer II, whose name is also spelled *Saur, Sower,* and even *Sowr,* see Brumbaugh, *History*, pp. 387-437; John S. Flory, *op. cit.,* p. 100ff.; Edward H. Hocker, "Founding," pp. 66-110; Oswald Seidensticker, "Die beiden Christoph Saur in Germantown," *Der Deutsche Pionier*, XII (1880-1881), 10ff.; XIII: 63ff.; and many other sources.

9. On Duboy (Dubois), see Durnbaugh, *Origins*, pp. 151, 301; Brumbaugh, *History*, pp. 144-145.

10. On Urner, see Brumbaugh, *History*, pp. 273-279; Isaac N. Urner, *A History of*

the *Coventry Brethren Church in Chester County, Pennsylvania* (Philadelphia: the author, 1898); S. R. Zug *et al.*, eds., *History of the Church of the Brethren of the Eastern District of Pennsylvania* (Lancaster, Pa.: 1915), p. 17ff.

11. On the younger, see Brumbaugh, *History*, pp. 279-288, and Urner, *op. cit., passim;* and Zug, *op. cit.*, p. 211ff.
12. On Sonday (Sonntag), see Brumbaugh, *History*, pp. 306-307; Zug, *op. cit.*, pp. 82-85.
13. On Frantz, see Brumbaugh, *History*, pp. 300-303; Zug, *op. cit.*, p. 78ff.
14. On Pfautz, see Brumbaugh, *History*, pp. 303-305; Zug, *op. cit.*, p. 78ff.
15. On Klein(e), see Brumbaugh, *History*, pp. 320-321; Zug, *op. cit.*, p. 78ff.
16. Martin was one of the most controversial figures among the colonial Brethren. See Brumbaugh, *History*, p. 290ff; H. Austin Cooper, *Two Centuries of Brothersvalley Church of the Brethren* (Westminster, Md.: The Times, Inc., 1962), pp. 115-143 and elsewhere; Mallott, *op. cit.*, p. 83ff.; Zug, *op. cit.*, p. 73ff. Martin's autobiography is found in the *Chronicon*, pp. 242-256 (partially reprinted in Mallott, *op. cit.*, pp. 327-340).
17. Edwards, *op. cit.*, I: 64-90.
18. Morgan Edwards, *Materials Towards a History of the Baptists in [New] Jersey.* . . . Vol. II (Philadelphia: Thomas Dobson, 1792), pp. 144-146.
19. Edwards' references are to William Douglas, *A Summary, Historical and Political, of the First Planting, Progressive Improvements, and Present State of the British Settlements in North-America* (Boston: Rogers and Foule, 1749-1753), II: 150, 335-336; and to Jedidiah Morse, *The American Geography* (Elizabethtown, [Mass.]: Shephard Kollock, 1789), pp. 324-325.
20. For information on Naas, see Durnbaugh, *Origins*, p. 151ff.; Brumbaugh, *History*, pp. 100-130.
21. "Materials Towards a History of the Baptists in the Province of Maryland," pp. 8-10, in the library of Crozer Theological Seminary, Chester, Pa. A microfilm of this and the other Edwards volumes is available from the Historical Commission, Southern Baptist Convention, Nashville, Tenn.
22. Martin is not listed among Brethren ministers in Henry, *op. cit.;* see Brumbaugh, *History*, pp. 280, 326-327.
23. On Letterman (Leatherman), see Henry, *op. cit.*, pp. 57-66.
24. Tanner's name is usually spelled "Danner." See Brumbaugh, *History*, pp. 321-326; Henry, *op. cit.*, pp. 30-44.
25. On Stober (Stover), see J. Linwood Eisenberg, ed., *A History of the Church of the Brethren in [the] Southern District of Pennsylvania* (Quincy, Pa.: Quincy Orphanage Press, [1941]), pp. 7-8, 431.
26. Likely Ulrich Crumpacker; not mentioned in Henry, *op. cit.*
27. "Materials Towards a History of the Baptists in the Province of Virginia," pp. 103-104; MS in the Crozer library.
28. These names are not mentioned in histories of the Brethren in Virginia. A Christopher Gusz (Geisz?) signed a Brethren document in 1756; see page 315.
29. G. W. Paschal, ed., "Materials Towards a History of the Baptists in the Province of North Carolina," *The North Carolina Historical Review*, VII (1930), 3: 365-389; taken from the MS volume. The paragraphs on the Brethren are found on page 393 (pages 41-43 in the original). The editor notes: "There is no further reference to these Tunker Baptists. Probably they were soon merged with the Separates [Separate Baptists] of Sandy Creek. Probably the three churches named were in the counties of Stanley, Anson, and Montgomery and

their membership was soon absorbed by the Separatist Baptist churches in that section" (p. 393).

30. Brethren literature does not mention a minister of this name.

31. The Kearn family name reappears in connection with the Brethren in Kentucky.

32. A letter of 1794 mentions a "Brother Stutzman from Carolina" who is perhaps identical with the "Studeman" mentioned by Edwards; see page 330.

33. "Materials Towards a History of the Baptists in the Province of South Carolina," pp. 68-71; MS copy in the Crozer library. See also Joe M. King, *A History of South Carolina Baptists* (Columbia, S. C.: General Board of the South Carolina Baptist Convention, 1964), pp. 86-89.

34. For a quotation from a letter of Pearson to his son, see King, *op. cit.,* p. 89.

(Broad River, May 5, 1764) As God [h]as Allowed me this Oppertunity by Mr John Green one of Your Companions Acquaintance I am to Inform you that our Redeemer has preserved us in Health and in the unity of the Spirit, and as God through his sparing mercy Allows us the Oppertunity to meat before him morning and Evening to Celebrate his praise, and Offer up prayers and Thanksgivings to his Dreadfull Majesty who Measures out the Heavens with A Span and weighs the Mountains in A Ballance and Contains the Great Waters as in the Hollow of his Hands and who is of purer Eyes than to behold iniquity in any of his Creatures here below he being so pure & Holy y^t he Charges his Angles with folly and the very Heavens are not Clean in his Sight, much more such poor polluted Creatures as wee are who were born in sin and brought forth in Iniquity and by our Actual Transgretions against the mighty God have incured his Displeasure but as JESUS the Saviour of the World hath delighted himself Amoungst the sons of men our Hope is in Him. . . .

35. Cooper, *op. cit.,* pp. 115-117, has some information on the Martin family. David Martin died in mid-May 1817.

36. See page 270.

6. GERMANTOWN

1. George N. Falkenstein, *The German Baptist Brethren or Dunkers* (Lancaster, Pa.: Pennsylvania German Society, 1900), p. 109.

2. See Brumbaugh, *History,* pp. 155-190; Abraham H. Cassel, "A Short Sketch of the Brethren's First Organization, Meeting House, and Graveyard in Germantown, Pa.," *The Germantown Independent* (Sept. 22, 1883), typescript in the University of Pennsylvania library; Falkenstein, *op. cit.,* pp. 109-136; Falkenstein, "A History of the Brethren Church at Germantown," *The Brethren's Family Almanac* (Mt. Morris, Ill.: Brethren Publishing Co., 1895), p. 3ff.; N. H. Keyser *et al., History of Old Germantown* (Philadelphia: McCann, 1907), pp. 68-70; Silas Thomas, "The Brethren of the Past in Germantown and Philadelphia," *The Brethren's Family Almanac* (Huntingdon, Pa.: Quinter and Brumbaugh Bros., 1880).

3. Christian Lehman was an active citizen and notary of Germantown in the later eighteenth century.

4. Lehman Papers, D 61, HSP Philadelphia.

5. Brumbaugh, *History,* pp. 166-169.

6. Falkenstein, *Dunkers,* pp. 113-115. This and the other original deeds are now deposited in the Brethren Historical Library, Elgin, Illinois.

7. *Ibid.,* pp. 117-119.

8. *Ibid.,* pp. 120-121.

9. *Ibid.,* pp. 121-123.

10. Cassel Coll., MS 16.

11. Revised from Henry Kurtz, ed., *The Brethren's Encyclopedia* (Columbiana, Ohio: the author, 1867), p. 135.

12. Cassel Coll., MS 67.

13. Cassel Coll., MS 13. Printed in "Ein beinahe hundertjähriger gemeinschaftlicher Brief, an den Bruder Christoph Saur," *Der Evangelische Besuch,* IV (1856), 3: 33-35, (hereafter cited as "EB") and in English translation in Kurtz, *op. cit.,* pp. 137-140.

14. Cassel Coll., MS 91.

15. C. Henry Smith, *The Story of the Mennonites,* 3rd ed., revised by C. Krahn (Newton, Kans.: Mennonite Publication Office, 1950), p. 534; Thomas E. Drake, *Quakers and Slavery in America* (New Haven: Yale University Press, 1950), pp. 5-13. The text is found in *PMHB,* XIII (1899), 265-270.

16. Quoted in Brumbaugh, *History,* p. 420.

17. Hocker, Sower, p. 31.

18. Cassel Coll., MS 13.

19. [H. D. Davy and J. Quinter, eds.], *Minutes of the Annual Meetings of the Brethren* (Dayton, Ohio: Christian Publishing Association, 1876), p. 8. This and other minutes utilized later in this book have been slightly revised.

20. From a copy made by Abraham H. Cassel of the original, Cassel Coll., MS 18.

21. Cassel Coll., MS 18.

22. Cassel Coll., MS 66.

23. Cassel Coll., MS 18.

24. For biographical information on Sauer II, see note 8, chapter 5.

25. See chapter 11.

26. Descriptions of Sauer II and his publishing concern are found in Isaiah Thomas, *The History of Printing in America,* 2nd ed. (Albany: 1874), p. 270ff., and in William McCulloch, "Additions to Thomas' History of Printing," in *A.A.S. Proceedings* N.S., XXXI (1921), part 1, 146.

27. The mother of Sauer II had left her family to join the Ephrata Community, where she was given the name "Sister Marcella" and acted as "sub-prioress." See the note introducing Sauer's letter to Germany on page 120.

28. The arrangement between Longenecker and Zug had its problems, which were attended to by the Annual Meetings of 1803 and 1804 — Davy and Quinter, *op. cit.,* pp. 31-32, 36-37.

29. Sauer's journal, from which the excerpt is taken, formerly part of the Cassel Collection, is now located in the Schwenkfelder Library, Pennsburg, Pa. See Abraham H. Cassel, "Brother Christopher Saur's Journal," *The Brethren's Family Almanac* (Huntingdon, Pa.: Quinter and Brumbaugh Bros., 1881), pp. 17-18.

30. With the above.

31. There are seven letters by Justus Henry Fuchs (Fox) in the Cassel Coll., MS 38. See Charles L. Nichols, "Justus Fox," *A.A.S. Proceedings* N. S., XXV (1915), 55-69, based on McCulloch, *loc. cit.*

32. Cassel Coll., MS 91.

33. Cassel Coll., MS 91.

34. For information on Mack, see note 7, chapter 5.

35. See chapter 13.

36. Cassel Coll., MS 66.

37. Cassel Coll., MS 66.

38. Cassel Coll., MS 13.
39. Cassel Coll., MS 66.
40. See Brumbaugh, *History,* pp. 267-268.
41. Cassel Coll., MS 13.

7. MACK CORRESPONDENCE

1. Brumbaugh, *History,* p. 228.
2. Zug, *op. cit.,* pp. 291-296. See also George F. P. Wanger, comp., *A Genealogy of the Descendants of Rev. Jacob Price, Evangelist-Pioneer* (Harrisburg, Pa.: The Evangelical Press, 1926). There are manuscripts dealing with the Price family in the Cassel Coll., MS 85.
3. Cassel Coll., MS 67.
4. Cassel Coll., MS 67; printed in English translation in Brumbaugh, *History,* pp. 237-238.
5. Cassel Coll., MS 67; printed in English translation in Brumbaugh, *History,* pp. 239-240, 243.
6. Cassel Coll., MS 67; printed in English translation in Freeman Ankrum, *Alexander Mack, the Tunker and Descendants* (Scottdale, Pa.: the author, 1943), pp. 39-40.
7. Brumbaugh, *History,* pp. 250-251; Ankrum, *op. cit.,* pp. 31-32, from which it was taken for publication in Don Yoder, "A Letter from Sander Mack," *The Pennsylvania Dutchman,* I (1949), 4: 5. The periodical is hereafter cited as "PD."
8. Cassel Coll., MS 67.
9. This letter may have some connection with the discussion on baptism between Mack, Jr., and a Lutheran theologian (see chapter 12).
10. Cassel Coll., MS 67; printed in English translation in Ankrum, *op. cit.,* pp. 36-37.
11. Cassel Coll., MS 67; printed in English translation in Ankrum, *op. cit.,* p. 39.
12. Cassel Coll., MS 67; printed in English translation in Brumbaugh, *History,* pp. 249-250.
13. Edwards, *Materials II,* p. 144.
14. This corrects a mistaken date given in Charles G. Sower, *Genealogical Chart of the Descendants of Christopher Sower, Printer of Germantown* (Philadelphia: C. G. Sower, 1887); see Brumbaugh, *History,* p. 431.
15. Cassel Coll., MS 67.
16. Cassel Coll., MS 67.
17. Cassel Coll., MS 67.
18. On Urner, see note 11, chapter 5.
19. Cassel Coll., MS 67. Portions of the letter are published in Brumbaugh, *History,* p. 283.
20. Cassel Coll., MS 67. See Brumbaugh, *History,* p. 284.
21. On William Mack, see Ankrum, *op. cit.,* pp. 53-59. Cassel Coll., MS 67.
22. See page 188.
23. Cassel Coll., MS 67; see the note in Brumbaugh, *History,* p. 280.
24. Cassel Coll., MS 67.
25. See chapter 13 for one of Danner's poems; Henry, *op. cit.,* pp. 39-44.
26. Cassel Coll., MS 67; printed in English translation in Brumbaugh, *History,* pp. 323-326.
27. Abschriften von des lieben Bruder Grubers Letzt angekommen Briefen an die Brüder und Mitverbundenen in Teutschland, April 19, 1763, HSP Philadelphia, Am. 173.
28. *Chronicon,* pp. 268-271, 276.

29. Cassel Coll., MS 67, partially given in Brumbaugh, *History,* pp. 522-523. See also Zug, *op. cit.,* pp. 370-373.
30. The minutes are printed in "Brüderlichen Rath vor bald Hundert Jahren," *EB,* III (1855), 9: 107-108.

III. RELATIONS

8. BRETHREN AND MORAVIANS

1. The general history of the Moravians is told in Edward Langton, *History of the Moravian Church: The Story of the First International Protestant Church* (London: 1956) and J. Taylor Hamilton, *A History of the Unitas Fratrum, or Moravian Church, in the United States of America* (New York: The Christian Literature Col., 1895). On Comenius, see also the section by Matthew Spinka in R. Rouse and S. C. Neill, eds., *A History of the Ecumenical Movement* (London: SPCK, 1954), pp. 88-91, as well as his *John Amos Comenius* (Chicago: 1943).
2. Hamilton, *op. cit.,* p. 433.
3. There is an awakening interest in the fascinating personality of Zinzendorf. His writings have recently been reissued in seventeen volumes, edited by Erich Beyreuther and Gerhard Meyer (Hildesheim: George Olms Verlagsbuchhandlung, 1962ff.). Three recent biographies are Erich Beyreuther, *Zinzendorf* (Marburg: Francke Buchhandlung, 1957-1961), three volumes; A. J. Lewis, *Zinzendorf: The Ecumenical Pioneer* (Philadelphia: Westminster Press, 1962); and John R. Weinlick, *Count Zinzendorf* (New York and Nashville: Abingdon, 1956). The standard biography was written by Zinzendorf's colleague and successor, August Gottlieb Spangenberg, *Leben des Herrn Nicolaus Ludwig Grafen und Herrn von Zinzendorf und Pottendorf* (Barby: 1772-1775), eight volumes, translated in a one-volume edition by Samuel Jackson (London: Samuel Holdsworth, 1838).
4. Howard Wiegner Kriebel, *The Schwenkfelders in Pennsylvania* (Lancaster, Pa.: Pennsylvania German Society, 1904).
5. The Schwenkfelder movement maintains an excellent historical library at Pennsburg.
6. Rep. 14 A, 21/3, Archiv der Brüder-Unität, Herrnhut/Oberlausitz. The archive is hereafter cited as "ABU Herrnhut." Photostats of these documents are available in the Library of Congress, Manuscript Division.
7. Rep. 14 A, 21/4, ABU Herrnhut.
8. Levin T. Reichel, *The Early History of the Church of the United Brethren in North America* (Nazareth, Pa.: Moravian Historical Society, 1888) and W. A. Schwarze and Samuel H. Gapp, eds., *A History of the Beginnings of the Moravian Work in America* (Bethlehem, Pa.: The Archives of the Moravian Church, 1955).
9. On Deknatel, see C. Neff's article in *Mennonitisches Lexikon* (1913), I: 398-399. The Moravian histories have extensive coverage of Nitschmann. The role of LeLong is portrayed in Wilhelm Lutjeharms, *Het Philadelphisch-oecumenisch Streven der Herrnhutters in de Nederlanden in de achttiende Eeuw* (Zeist: 1935).
10. Rep. 14 A, 18/2, ABU Herrnhut.
11. Johann George Gichtel (1638-1710) was a German follower of Jakob Boehme and spent many years in Amsterdam as head of a group of mystics.
12. Böhmist — that is, followers of Jakob Boehme (1575-1624) of Görlitz, **Germany,** the leading European mystical theologian, whose thinking influenced all of those groups classified as Radical Pietists. The best recent discussions of Boehme are by Emanuel Hirsch, *Geschichte der neuern evangelischen Theologie* (Gütersloh:

Gerd Mohn, 1960), II: 208-255, and Ernst Benz, *Der Prophet Jakob Boehme* (Wiesbaden: Franz Steiner Verlag, 1959).

13. Friedrich Christoph Steinhofer (1706-1761) was a leading Pietist pastor in Württemberg with close connections with Spangenberg and the Moravians.
14. Rep. 14 A, 18/1 (9-12), ABU Herrnhut.
15. Rep. 14 A, 18/1 (20-21), ABU Herrnhut.
16. Rep. 14 A, 18/1 (26-27), ABU Herrnhut.
17. The hymnal was *Zionitischer Weyrauchs-Hügel* (Germantown: Christopher Sauer, 1739). It is referred to as the first book printed with German type in North America.
18. Rep. 14 A, 18/1 (36-44), ABU Herrnhut.
19. Rep. 14 A, 18/1 (51-55), ABU Herrnhut.
20. Rep. 14 A, 18/1 (49-50), ABU Herrnhut.
21. Godfrey Haberecht (1700-1767) had come to America with Spangenberg and became one of the Solitary at Ephrata in November 1738. He returned to the Moravians in 1741.
22. See Lewis, *op. cit.,* pp. 138-160.
23. Quoted in Lewis, *op. cit.,* p. 140.
24. See the comments about the association in Don Yoder, "Christian Unity in the Nineteenth Century," Rouse and Neill, *op. cit.,* pp. 228-230.
25. Spangenberg, *op. cit.,* V: 1379-1383.
26. H. Antes Varia, Personalia Pa., Archives of the Moravian Church, Bethlehem, Pa. The archive will hereafter be cited as "AMC Bethlehem." Records from the Moravian Church Archives, Bethlehem, Pennsylvania, are reproduced by permission of the Provincial Archives Committee of the Moravian Church. Further reproduction is not permitted except by the written permission of the Archives Committee.
27. H. Antes Varia, Personalia Pa., AMC Bethlehem. Reichel, *op. cit.,* pp. 92ff., contains the text of the important invitation in English translation. This has recently been published in Richard C. Wolf, *Documents of Lutheran Unity in America* (Philadelphia: Fortress Press, 1966), pp. 3-4.
28. The full reports of the synods were printed in English and German by Benjamin Franklin; these are noted in Oswald Seidensticker, *First Century of German Printing in America* (Philadelphia: Schaefer and Koradi, 1893), pp. 16-19. Brumbaugh, *History,* pp. 471-488, has an account of the conferences; see also Reichel, *op. cit.,* pp. 96-112.
29. Quoted in Lewis, *op. cit.,* p. 145.
30. The polemics are listed in Seidensticker, *Century,* pp. 14-23.
31. Weinlick, *op. cit.,* p. 165.
32. *Ibid.,* p. 167.
33. Quoted in Fresenius, *op. cit.,* III, iii, 2: 253.
34. *Ibid.,* 14: 400-401.
35. The Anabaptists are condemned on five points in the Lutheran confession drawn up at Augsburg in 1530; see Theodore G. Tappert, ed., *The Book of Concord* (Philadelphia: Muhlenberg Press, 1959), pp. 31, 33, 35, 37, 38.
36. *Die Büdingsche Sammlung einiger in die Kirchen Historie einschlagender sonderlich neuerer Schriften* (Büdingen: J. C. Stohr, 1742-1745), II, xii, 715.
37. *Chronicon,* p. 245.
38. Fresenius, *op. cit.,* III, iii, 1: 155.
39. *Ibid.,* IV, iii, 1: 190.

40. *Ibid.*, III, iii, 14: 400-401.
41. *Ibid.*, III, iii, 15: 401-410; *Büdingsche Sammlung*, III, xv, 16: 326-330.
42. Fresenius, *op. cit.*, III, iii, 1: 227.
43. Weinlick, *op. cit.*, p. 202. See also the evaluation of another Moravian scholar, Edwin Albert Sawyer, *The Religious Experience of the Colonial American Moravians* (Nazareth, Pa.: Moravian Historical Society, 1961), pp. 89-107.
44. The definition is by Weinlick, *op. cit.*, p. 198; his chapter is entitled "Costly Enthusiasm." A much less friendly account is the study by Jacob John Sessler, *Communal Pietism Among Early American Moravians* (New York: Henry Holt and Company, 1933), pp. 156-181.
45. "A Brethren Bibliography, 1713-1963," *BLT*, IX (1964), I and 2: 1-177, contains references to the Frey publications. The Roman Catholic comment is in Ronald A. Knox, *Enthusiasm: A Chapter in the History of Religion* (Oxford: Clarendon Press, 1950), pp. 408-416. Knox discounts to a degree the report of Frey, stating: "He strikes the reader as something of a prig, and something of an eccentric himself: easily shocked, and of a credulous nature which invited his [Moravian] Brethren to play pranks on him" (p. 414). The editors of *Beginnings of Moravian Work* say of Frey: "As an eye-witness of the 'Sifting Period nonsense' (Zinzendorf's own word) when it was at its worst in Herrnhaag, his testimony has been widely quoted and believed and still is hashed up by some writers as 'Moravianism.' But 'Wetteravianism' is Wetteravianism — and not Moravianism" (p. 130).
46. Andreas Frey, *A True and Authentic Account . . .* (London: 1753), pp. 3-25. See "A Brethren Bibliography," No. 13, for the full title.
47. *Pensylvanische Berichte* (May 1750?).
48. Fresenius, *op. cit.*, III, iii, 52: 785-788.
49. *Ibid.*, III, iii, 1: 227.
50. Delbert Gratz, *Bernese Anabaptists and Their American Descendants* (Scottdale, Pa.: The Herald Press, 1953), pp. 38-39, lists a Müller family as migrants from the state of Bern to Alsace between 1671 and 1711.
51. Nothing definite is known about this group, although there are other early references to Brethren in Switzerland.
52. Memoralia, Box II, AMC Bethlehem.
53. J. Müller to A. Dubois, [Marienborn, June 23, 1744], and J. Müller to the Brethren, Marienborn, May 21, 1744, Religious Controversies, AMC Bethlehem.
54. Religions-Sachen, No. 50, Pennsylvania Controversies, AMC Bethlehem.
55. The reference is evidently to the *Büdingsche Sammlung*, III, xiii, no. 2.
56. Religious Controversies, AMC Bethlehem.
57. *Hirten Lieder von Bethlehem* (Germantown: Christopher Sauer, 1742); Seidensticker, *Century*, p. 15.
58. See Durnbaugh, "Sauer," pp. 330-340.
59. *Chronicon*, pp. 145-156.
60. The reference is to the printed minutes.
61. H. Antes, Personalia Pa., AMC Bethlehem.
62. H. Antes, Personalia Pa., AMC Bethlehem.
63. H. Antes, Personalia Pa., AMC Bethlehem.
64. H. Antes, Personalia Pa., AMC Bethlehem.
65. Br. Georg Hantsch Gen. Bericht von seinen gethanen Mennonisten Besuch, Folder JB II, 1 D, AMC Bethlehem. See Don Yoder, "Brother Hantsch Visits the Mennonites: A Moravian Missionary Diary of 1748," *PD*, III (1951), 11: 1, 5-6.

9. Brethren and Universalists

1. Thomas Whittemore, *The Modern History of Universalism* (Boston, Mass.: Abel Tompkins, 1860), p. 30.

2. For a convenient summary on early teaching on this doctrine, consult Richard Eddy, *History of Universalism* (New York: The Christian Literature Col., 1894), pp. 255-305.

3. C. David Ensign, "Radical German Pietism (c.1675-c.1760)" (unpub. Ph.D. dissertation, Boston University Graduate School, 1955), pp. 285-286.

4. Durnbaugh, *Origins,* pp. 399-400.

5. A recent study is Michael L. Hodson, "The Church of the Brethren and Universalism" (unpub. independent study, Bethany Theological Seminary, 1965). Note the extended debate at the Annual Meeting of 1878, quoted on pp. 35-37.

6. David Benedict, *A General History of the Baptist Denomination in America and Other Parts of the World* (Boston: Lincoln and Edmonds, 1813), II: 552.

7. The best studies of the rise of liberal theology in the period are by G. Adolph Koch, *Republican Religion: The American Revolution and the Cult of Reason* (New York: Henry Holt and Co., 1933), and Herbert M. Morais, *Deism in Eighteenth Century America* (New York: Columbia University Press, 1934).

8. *Universalism Tested by Reason and Revelation* (Philadelphia: H. M. Clayton, 1848), pp. 8-11.

9. The Cassel Collection contains correspondence with Richard Eddy; Hodson, *op. cit.,* pp. 10-11, contains some excerpts.

10. Israel Acrelius, "A History of New Sweden; Or the Settlements on the Delaware River," trans. Wm. M. Reynolds, in *Memoirs* of the Historical Society of Pennsylvania, XI (1874).

11. Richard Eddy, *Universalism in America* (Boston: Universalist Publishing House, 1884-1886), I: 35-41.

12. The quotation is from page 7. According to Funke, *op. cit.,* pp. 124-125: "Refers to the German Baptists and their belief in universal restoration; treatise regarded by Richard Eddy as evidence that their creed was one of the channels through which Universalism entered. Possibly printed by Solomon Mayer in Ephrata."

13. This is discussed in Roger E. Sappington, "Eighteenth-Century Non-Brethren Sources of Brethren History, II," *BLT,* II (1957), 2: 69-72.

14. Eddy, *America,* I: 37.

15. A recent biography of De Benneville is Albert D. Bell, *The Life and Times of Dr. George de Benneville: 1703-1793* (Boston: The Universalist Church of America, 1953). His autobiography was published by Elhanan Winchester, *Der merkwürdige Lebenslauf . . . des ohnlängst . . . verstorbenen Dr. Benneville* (Baltimore: Samuel Saur, 1798). An English translation was published by N. Bertholet Grubb, *Life and Trance of Dr. George de Benneville of Germantown, Pa.* (Schwenksville, Pa.: 1882), and most recently in the *Annual Journal of the Universalist Society,* II (1960-1961), 71-87. Clinton Lee Scott, *The Universalist Church of America, a Short History* (Boston: Universalist Historical Society, [1957]), p. 7, refers to Sauer as a "Universalist Quaker."

16. Elhanan Winchester, *Universal Restoration, Exhibited in Four Dialogues Between a Minister and His Friend* (Worcester, Mass.: Isaiah Thomas, Jr., 1803), pp. xiv, 154-155.

17. Eddy, *America,* I: 37-38.

18. Davy and Quinter, *op. cit.,* pp. 20-24.

19. Cassel Coll., MS 67.

20. Davy and Quinter, *op. cit.*, pp. 26-27.
21. *Ibid.*, pp. 29-31.
22. "Deutsche Ansiedlungen in Nord- und Sud-Carolina in letzter Jahrhundert," *Der Deutsche Pionier*, XV (1883-1884), 253.
23. Eddy, *America*, I: 38.
24. John Belton O'Neall, *The Annals of Newberry* (Newberry, S. C.: Aulla and Houseal, 1892), pp. 65-67. The inscriptions on the tombstones of the cemetery are given in George L. Summer, *Newberry County, South Carolina, Historical and Genealogical* (Newberry, S. C.: the author, 1950), pp. 101, 442. The family names are Chapman, Lynch, Summer, Paysinger, Kepler, Elsmore, Donner, and Sheppard.
25. Eddy, *America*, II: 86-87.
26. Seidensticker, *Century*, p. 41; Eddy, *Universalists*, pp. 328-329.
27. Whittemore, *op. cit.*, I: 225, in commenting that the book was first published in English by Sauer, wrote that it was " 'translated into English by John S.' — perhaps a son or brother of the printer."
28. Bell, *op. cit.*, p. 43.
29. See Seidensticker, *Century*, pp. 41, 78, 80. The latter two editions were in German.
30. N. Pomp, *Kurzgefaszte Prüfungen der Lehre des Ewigen Evangeliums* (Philadelphia: Henry Miller, 1774). See James I. Good, *History of the Reformed Church in the United States* (Reading, Pa.: Daniel Miller, 1899), pp. 548-549.
31. Pomp, *op. cit.*, p. 2.
32. Scott, *op. cit.*, p. 8.

IV. REVOLUTION

10. THE BRETHREN RESPONSE

1. Howard W. Kriebel, *op. cit.*, p. 151.
2. See Wilbur J. Bender, "Pacifism among the Mennonites, Amish Mennonites, and Schwenkfelders of Pennsylvania to 1783," *Mennonite Quarterly Review*, I (1927), 3: 23-40 and 4: 21-48.
3. The differing positions may be traced in Roland H. Bainton, *Christian Attitudes Toward War and Peace* (New York and Nashville: Abingdon Press, 1960), pp. 143-172.
4. The estimate was made by the patriot leader John Adams; cited in Wesley M. Gewehr *et al.*, eds., *The United States: A History of a Democracy* (New York: McGraw-Hill Book Company, 1960), p. 71.
5. Kenneth G. Hamilton, *John Ettwein and the Moravian Church During the Revolutionary Period* (Bethlehem, Pa.: Times Publishing Co., 1940).
6. The original Ettwein MS was taken to Herrnhut in 1781, and a copy left in Bethlehem. The two MSS differ in details, which are indicated in Hamilton's annotations.
7. There had been an earlier meeting of the nonresistants. "A respectable number of inhabitants of Berks County, who were conscientiously opposed to bearing arms held a meeting at Reading, September 1, 1775. In a letter transmitting the resolutions adopted by the meeting to the Committee of Safety in Philadelphia . . . [were] these words: 'Inclosed is a copy of the resolves entered into by the deputies of a considerable number of inhabitants of this county as are conscientiously scrupulous of taking up arms, though at the same time fully sensible of the justice of our cause and willing as afar as in them lies to contribute to their support" (Kriebel, *op. cit.*, p. 151).

8. Hamilton, *op. cit.*, pp. 225-306 (excerpts).
9. "Mennonisten in Holland. Aus einem Schrieben aus ——, vom 18. Nov. 1783," *Staats-Anzeigen*, A. L. Schlözer, ed. (Göttingen: 1738), V, 20: 445-449.
10. Hamilton, *op. cit.*, pp. 167n, 215n.
11. "Verteidigung der Mennonisten in N. America," *Staats-Anzeigen*, A. L. Schlözer, ed. (Göttingen: 1783), IV, 15: 373-376.
12. Davy and Quinter, *op. cit.*, pp. 5-6.
13. *Ibid.*, p. 6.
14. *Ibid.*, pp. 7-8.
15. The quotation from J. M. Henry is found in the section on Powers in F. Bittinger, *op. cit.*, pp. 30-32. For the early reference to "Felty Powers" see Boyd B. Stutler, "The Kennan Massacre," *West Virginia History*, I (1939), 1: 30-48.
16. Davy and Quinter, *op. cit.*, pp. 10-12.
17. *Ibid.*, pp. 17-18.
18. *Pennsylvania Archives*, 8th Series, VIII: 7365; 1st Series, V: 767-768; 1st Series, VIII: 328-329.
19. Cassel Coll., MS 67; printed in English translation in Brumbaugh, *History*, pp. 228, 235-237.
20. Cassel Coll., MS 67.
21. Portions of or the entire text of the petition are found in the following: Bender, *loc. cit.*, 4: 38-40; Rufus Bowman, *The Church of the Brethren and War: 1708-1941* (Elgin, Ill.: Brethren Publishing House, 1944), pp. 79-81 taken from the official publication in the *Votes of the House of Representatives of the Province of Pennsylvania*, 1767-1776, VI: 645; *The Monthly Gospel Visitor*, XXI (1871), 243-245; *Penn-Germania*, N.S., XI (1913), 111-113; C. H. Smith, *The Mennonites of America* (Goshen, Ind.: 1909), pp. 370-372.
22. Bender, *loc. cit.*, 4: 23.
23. For bibliographical description, see Harold S. Bender, *Two Centuries of American Mennonite Literature* (Goshen, Ind.: Mennonite Historical Society, 1929), pp. 6-7, and *A Brethren Bibliography*, No. 27-28.
24. Bowman, *op. cit.*, pp. 85-86.
25. "Proceedings of the Committee of Observation for Elizabethtown District (Washington County)," *Maryland Historical Magazine*, XII (1917), 142-163, 261-275, 324-347; XIII (1918), 28-53, 227-248.
26. "Journal of the Committee of Observation of the Middle District of Frederick County, Maryland, September 12, 1775 — October 24, 1776," *Maryland Historical Magazine*, X (1915), 301-321; XI (1916), 50-66, 157-175, 237-260, 304-321.
27. *North Carolina State Records*, XII: 638-641; XIII: 411-417; XXIV: 200-204, 219, 221-222, 281-282, 329, 492-493.

11. The Sauer Family

1. For general orientation on the subject, see Arthur D. Graeff, *The Relations Between the Pennsylvania Germans and the British Authorities: 1750-1776* (Norristown, Pa.: Pennsylvania German Society, 1939) and James O. Knauss, *Social Conditions among the Pennsylvania Germans in the Eighteenth Century* (Lancaster, Pa.: Pennsylvania German Society, 1942). The best study on the religious and political interaction is Dietmar Rothermund, *op. cit.* A detailed study of the role of Christopher Sauer I is in William R. Steckel, "Pietist in Colonial Pennsylvania: Christopher Sauer, Printer, 1738-1758" (unpub. Ph.D. dissertation, Stanford University, 1949). See also Bowman, *op. cit.*, p. 68ff. and Donald F. Durnbaugh,

"Relationships of the Brethren with the Mennonites and Quakers, 1708-1865," *Church History*, XXXV (1966), 1: 35-59.

2. Tappert and Doberstein, *op. cit.*, I: 212 and II: 191.

3. James O. Knauss, *Christopher Saur the Third* (Worcester, Mass.: American Antiquarian Society, 1931), an offprint from *AAS Proceedings*, N.S., XLI (1931), part 1, 235-253.

4. *Pensylvanische Berichte* (September 30, 1758).

5. *Wertheste Landes-Leute, Sonderlich in Philadelphia, Bucks und Berks-Caunty!* (Germantown: Christopher Sauer II, 1765), in HSP Philadelphia.

6. Edward W. Hocker, *Sower*, p. 84; M. G. Brumbaugh, "The Two Christopher Sowers," *History*, pp. 338-437; James P. Wickersham, *A History of Education in Pennsylvania* (Lancaster, Pa.: the author, 1886), pp. 171-172, 235-237.

7. Bundle 72/I/111-117, Class 13, Audit Office Records, Public Records Office, London. The archive is hereafter cited as "PRO London." There are copies of this material in the Loyalist Transcripts, New York Public Library.

8. Bundle 102/882, Class 13, Audit Office Records, PRO London.

9. Ashmead Scrapbook, p. 18, HSP Philadelphia, Am. 009. This is referred to in Bowman, *op. cit.*, pp. 84-85.

10. Taken from a copy in the Cassel Coll., MS 91. The original is preserved in the archive of the Society for the History of the Germans in Maryland, Baltimore. Two publications from the original have been made: Dieter Cunz, ed., "Two Christopher Sower Documents," *PMHB*, LXIX (1945), 60-70; [Klaus Wust, ed.], "The Last Will of Germantown Printer Christopher Sower of March 23, 1777," Society for the History of the Germans in Maryland, *Thirty-Second Report* (Baltimore, Md.: 1966), 61-64.

11. *Der Hoch-Deutsch Americanische Calendar* (Germantown: Christopher Sauer II, 1777); the translation is taken from Bowman, *op. cit.*, p. 85.

12. Bundle 72/I/111-117, Class 13, Audit Office Records, PRO London. A contemporary diarist noted the capture of young Sauer: "The Continentals at Frankford, not hearing of the British advancing till 12 o'clock, moved off to Germantown, when they took Christ'r Sower, Jun., who went with a division of the Army to that place" — "The Diary of Robert Morton, Kept in Philadelphia while that City was Occupied by the British Army in 1777," *PMHB*, I (1877), 1-39.

13. The letter by Mary Pemberton is in the HSP Philadelphia; it is published in Hocker, *Sower*, p. 92.

14. Allen C. Thomas, ed., "A Bundle of Old Bills and What They Tell," *Bulletin* of the Friends Historical Society of Philadelphia, V (1913), 2: 52-58.

15. For information on the publications of the young printers during this era, see Seidensticker, *Century*, p. 99ff.

16. *Heinrich Millers, des Buchdruckers in Philadelphia, nöthige Vorstellung an die Deutschen in Pennsylvanien, etc.* (Philadelphia: 1778), a broadside in HSP Philadelphia. For a detailed description of the dispute from Miller's point of view, see Charles F. Dapp, *The Evolution of an American Patriot* (Lancaster, Pa.: Pennsylvania German Society, 1924). Miller's attack on Sauer III was circulated in the press in the *Pennsylvania Evening Post* (July 28, 1778).

17. Samuel Hazard, ed., *Colonial Records*, XI: 493-494, 745.

18. Hocker, *Sower*, pp. 98-99; Knauss, *Saur*, p. 9n.

19. Tappert and Doberstein, *op. cit.*, III: 163.

20. "Life of John Pemberton," *The Friends Library* (Philadelphia: Jos. Rakestraw, 1842), VI: 297.

21. Cassel Coll., MS 97. Published also in Bowman, *op. cit.*, pp. 94-97 and Brumbaugh, *History*, 415-419.

22. *Pennsylvania Archives*, 6th Series, XII and XIII, *passim*.

23. Daniel M. Anders, "Last Years of Christopher Sower," *Historical Sketches*. A Collection of Papers prepared for the Historical Society of Montgomery County, V (1925), 162.

24. Cassel Coll., MS 97; published also in Brumbaugh, *History*, pp. 421-422.

25. Cassel Coll., MS 97; published also in Bowman, *op. cit.*, p. 98.

26. Carl van Doren, *Secret History of the American Revolution* (New York: The Viking Press, 1941), 129ff.; Knauss, *Saur, passim*.

27. Bundle 72/I/111-117, Class 13, Audit Office Records, PRO London.

28. The correspondence of Sauer III with the British authorities has been preserved in great part in the William L. Clements Library, University of Michigan, Ann Arbor, among the Sir Henry Clinton Papers. This holding is hereafter cited as "CLUM, Ann Arbor."

29. Christian Musselmann's Report, September 1, 1780, Clinton Papers, CLUM, Ann Arbor. See Knauss, *Saur*, p. 16. Information on the Mennonites named is found in John C. Wenger, *History of the Mennonites of the Franconia [Pa.] Conference* (Scottdale, Pa.: Mennonite Publishing House, 1938).

30. McCulloch, *loc. cit.*, pp. 89-247, has information on Sauer III derived from Brook Watson Sower, a son. See also Lorenzo Sabine, *Biographical Sketches of Loyalists* (Boston: 1864), II: 323.

31. Knauss, *Saur*, pp. 14-15. To call the pamphlet the "valedictory" is misleading in that Sauer III was an active printer in Canada and three of his brothers carried on the printing trade in Pennsylvania and Maryland.

32. *Zuschrift an die Teutschen in Pennsylvanien, und benachbarten Provinzen* (New York: 1780). This is not listed in the major bibliographies. Bundle 102/882, Class 13, Audit Office Records, PRO London.

33. Knauss, *Saur*, p. 20.

34. Bundle 38/301-302, Class 12. Audit Office Records, PRO London.

35. For information on the Loyalists in Canada, see W. S. McNutt, *New Brunswick: A History, 1784-1867* (Toronto: Macmillan of Canada, 1863). A thorough description of Sauer's publishing enterprise there is in Marie Tremaine, *A Bibliography of Canadian Imprints, 1751-1800* (Toronto: University of Toronto Press, 1952), p. 207ff.

36. Bundle 100/228, Class 12, Audit Office Records, PRO London.

37. Charles G. Sower, *op. cit.*

38. Cassel Coll., MS 91. This was also published in Cunz, *loc. cit.*, and Brumbaugh, *History*, pp. 426-429 (partial).

V. PUBLICATIONS

12. DOCTRINAL WRITINGS

1. *A Brethren Bibliography*, pp. 11-22. See also Earl F. Robacher, *Pennsylvania German Literature* (Philadelphia: University of Pennsylvania Press, 1943), p. 20ff.

2. *Geistliche Fama*, I (1731-1732), 3: 51 and 10: 87; *A Brethren Bibliography, No. 5.*

3. Brumbaugh, *History;* John S. Flory, *Literary Activity of the German Baptist Brethren in the Eighteenth Century* (Elgin, Ill.: Brethren Publishing House, 1908); Samuel B. Heckman, *The Religious Poetry of Alexander Mack, Jr.* (Elgin, Ill.: Brethren Publishing House, 1912). Recent articles on Cassel are: Donald F.

Durnbaugh, "Abraham Harley Cassel and His Collection," *Pennsylvania History*, XXVI (1959), 4: 332-347; and "Abraham Harley Cassel (1820-1908)," *History of the Church of the Brethren — Eastern Pennsylvania, 1915-1965* (Lancaster, Pa.: Forry and Hacker, 1965), pp. 292-301.

4. [Henry Kurtz, ed.], "The Operation of Grace in the Heart of the Sinner," *The Gospel Visitor*, II (1852), 143-144; this is reprinted in J. E. Miller, *Stories from Brethren Life* (Elgin, Ill.: Brethren Publishing House, 1942), pp. 37-38. See also John S. Flory, "Alexander Mack's Bible," *Gospel Messenger* (1911), 7: 99-100, 8: 114.

5. The Bible is a Luther translation printed in Lemgo, Germany, in 1723, now in the Mack Library, Bridgewater College, Bridgewater, Virginia.

6. Benjamin Holme, *Ein Ernstlicher Ruff in Christlicher Liebe an alles Volck . . .* (Germantown: [Christopher Sauer], 1747). See Seidensticker, *Century*, p. 28. The booklet is discussed in Durnbaugh, "Relationships," p. 41.

7. Vernard Eller, "Friends, Brethren, Separatists," *BLT*, VII (1962), 4: 47-56; John J. Stoudt, review of *A Brethren Bibliography*, *PMHB*, LXXXVIII (1964), 4: 489-490.

8. The third pamphlet was *Eine Kurtze Vermittelungs-Schrift, in sich haltende, eine Ansprache an alle Menschen . . .* (Germantown: [Christopher Sauer], 1748); Seidensticker, *Century*, p. 31.

9. For a discussion of this interpretation of scripture see Chalmer E. Faw, "The Brethren and the Book of Books," in Paul H. Bowman, ed., *The Adventurous Future* (Elgin, Ill.: The Brethren Press, 1959), pp. 103-116.

10. *Ein Geringer Schein des Verachteten Lichtleins, der Wahrheit die in Christo ist . . .* (Germantown: [Christopher Sauer], 1747); Seidensticker, *Century*, p. 28; *A Brethren Bibliography*, No. 9.

11. See chapter 5, note 13.

12. This is based on an unpublished letter in the Cassel Collection, MS 67.

13. *Einfältige Lehr-Betrachtungen, und kurtzgefasztes Glaubens-Bekäntnisz des gottseligen Lehrers, Michael Frantzen* (Germantown: Christopher Sauer, 1770); Seidensticker, *Century*, p. 81; *A Brethren Bibliography*, No. 24.

14. Helen Harjes Muller, trans., "Writings of Michael Frantz," *Schwarzenau*, II (1941), 2: 78-82.

15. The book is discussed in Brumbaugh, *History*, pp. 300-303, and Flory, *Activity*, pp. 206-213.

16. See note 3 of this chapter. Heckman was aided in his work by M. G. Brumbaugh, who then held possession of the Cassel Collection (containing the Mack manuscripts) prior to his depositing of it at Juniata College.

17. Cassel Coll., MS 66.

18. "Beylage. Ein Brief wegen dem Fuszwaschen," in . . . *Grundforschende Fragen . . .* (Germantown: Christopher Sauer, 1774); a third edition was printed by Samuel Sauer in Baltimore in 1799.

19. The letter is discussed in detail as indicative of Brethren epistemology in Vernard Eller, "A Protestant's Protestant" (unpub. Ph.D. dissertation, Pacific School of Religion, 1964), pp. 102-106.

20. Henry Kurtz and John Quinter, eds., *Rights and Ordinances . . . also Ground Searching Questions . . .* (Columbiana, Ohio: 1860).

21. Alexander Mack, Jr., "Beylage;" the passage is discussed also in Donald F. Durnbaugh, "Brethren and Schism," *BLT*, XII (1967), 3: 24-33.

22. Brumbaugh, *History*, pp. 251-256; Flory, *Activity*, pp. 252-254.

23. Biographical information on Kunze is found in George H. Genzmer, "Kunze,

John Christopher," *Dictionary of American Biography*, X: 512-513; Henry E. Jacobs, *A History of the Evangelical Lutheran Church in the United States* (New York: The Christian Literature Co., 1893), p. 285ff.; H. M. M. Richards, *Descendants of Henry Melchior Muhlenberg* (Lancaster, Pa.: Pennsylvania German Society, 1900), p. 39. See also Mann, *Nachrichten*, for letters by Kunze to Germany.

24. *Etwas vom rechten Lebenswege* (Philadelphia: Melchior Steiner, 1781), p. 141; some copies have the title, *Ein Wort für den Verstand und das Herz vom rechten und gebanten Lebenswege* (Seidensticker, *Century*, p. 108).

25. William Whiston (1667-1752) was a learnéd British mathematician and theologian, successor to Isaac Newton as professor of mathematics in Cambridge. Expelled from the university in 1710 because of his non-orthodox views on Christology, he wrote extensively on biblical and theological topics, including a multivolume *Primitive Christianity Revived* (1711). In 1747 he left the Church of England and joined the General Baptists.

26. *Kurtze und einfältige Vorstellung der äuszeren aber doch heiligen Rechten und Ordnungen desz Hauses Gottes . . .* ([Berleburg?]: 1715); *A Brethren Bibliography*, No. 2.

27. Johann Christian Edelmann (1698-1767), a leading Radical Pietist and separatist in Germany, was connected with many of the religious currents of the eighteenth century before moving into a rationalist position. His autobiography (1752) is a basic source for nonchurchly religion of his time.

28. Origen (c.182-c.251), of Alexandria, was the first systematic theologian of Christianity and an important apologist, although later pronounced a heretic by the Fifth Ecumenical Council in 553.

29. The latest translation of Luther's comments on baptism is W. Theodore Bachmann, ed., *Word and Sacrament I*, Vol. 35, *Luther's Works*, H. T. Lehman, gen. ed. (Philadelphia: Muhlenberg Press, 1960), pp. 29-30.

30. The reference is to Jakob Mehrning, *S. Baptismi Historia: Das ist, Heilige Tauff-Historia . . .* (Dortmund: 1646-1647). This book, which contains more than eleven hundred pages, was published by the Dompelaar movement and stresses the importance of immersion baptism. See Otto Schowalter, "Mehrning, Jakob," *Mennonitisches Lexikon*, III: 65. A copy is in the Mennonite Historical Library, Goshen, Ind.

31. Jeremias Felbinger (1616-c.1690), a Lutheran scholar in Silesia and Pomerania, was expelled from Germany because of his religious views, and spent the last part of his life in The Netherlands. He is known for his linguistic labors, especially biblical translations, and his doctrinal book, *Christliches Hand-Buchlein* (1661), reprinted by Samuel Sauer in 1799 along with the two Alexander Mack, Sr., treatises. See *A Brethren Bibliography*, No. 53.

32. Johann Heinrich Reitz (1655-1720), a Reformed theologian and linguist, was a church official in the Palatinate in the late 17th century before driven out by the French invasion. After an uncertain life in central Germany as a Radical Pietist, he ended his life as teacher of a Latin school in Wesel, having made his peace with the established church. He is best known for his compilation of edifying biographies, *Historie der Wiedergebohrnen* (1717).

33. See the account of this event on page 18.

34. *Apologie, oder schriftmäsige Verantwortung etlicher Wahrheiten . . .* (Ephrata: 1788), 71, [1]pp.; *A Brethren Bibliography*, No. 37.

35. Cassel Coll., MS 67. Information on the Baumanns is found in H. A. Rattermann,

"Der alte Ephrata Press," *Der Deutsche Pionier*, VIII (1876), 2: 45-48; Felix Reichmann, "Ezechiel Sangmeister's Diary," *PMHB*, LXVIII (1944), 3: 292-313; and Alfred L. Shoemaker, "The Ephrata Printers," *PD*, IV (1953), 9: 11-12.

36. The Berleburg Bible (1726-1742) was produced by Radical Pietists in Germany.

37. The reference is to *Ein Geringer Schein;* see note 10 of this chapter.

38. Alexander Mack, Sr., . . . *Grundforschende Fragen* . . . (1713), reprinted in America in 1774 and 1799.

39. *Verschiedene alte und neuere Geschichten von Erscheinungen der Geister* (Germantown: Christopher Sauer, 1755); Seidensticker, *Century,* p. 44.

40. William Dell, *The Doctrine of Baptisms, Reduced from Its Ancient and Modern Corruptions* . . . , 5th ed. (Philadelphia: B. Franklin and D. Hall, 1759); listed in Charles Evans, *American Bibliography* (Chicago: 1903-1933), No. 8338.

41. Kunze explained that the numerous typographical errors in his book were unavoidable because of his distance from the printshop (p. 92).

42. Justus H. C. Helmuth, *Betrachtung der Evangelischen Lehre von der Heiligen Taufe* . . . (Germantown: Michael Billmeyer, 1793), p. 282.

43. *Der Besiegte Wiedertäuffer, in Unterredungen über Kindertaufe und Untertauchung* . . . (Lancaster, Pa.: Albrecht and Lahn, 1788), [3], 92 pp. A copy is in the library of the American Philosophical Society, Philadelphia. The book is not mentioned in the pertinent bibliographies.

44. This incident is discussed in Durnbaugh, "Beginnings," pp. 84-85.

45. From the context, it seems that "Brother Benjamin" was the printer of the treatise. It may be that he was one of the Baumanns who were printing at Ephrata during these years.

46. The most recent translation is found in John C. Wenger, ed., *The Complete Writings of Menno Simons*, L. Verduin, trans. (Scottdale, Pa.: 1956), pp. 668-672.

47. The reference here and in following passages is to the Mehrning history of baptism; see note 30.

48. For a typical statement of Luther's views on baptism versus the Anabaptists, see Conrad Bergendorf, ed., *Church and Ministry II*, Vol. 40, *Luther's Works,* H. T. Lehman, gen. ed. (Philadelphia: Muhlenberg Press, 1958), pp. 229-262.

49. *Anhang zum Widerlegten Wiedertäufer. Enthält Zwey Unterredungen, und den gäntzlichen Abschied Theophili* . . . (Ephrata: 1788), 25, [1]pp.; *A Brethren Bibliography,* No. 38.

13. DEVOTIONAL WRITINGS

1. John J. Stoudt, *Pennsylvania German Poetry, 1685-1830* (Norristown, Pa.: Pennsylvania German Folklore Society, 1956).

2. *A Brethren Bibliography,* No. 7.

3. Durnbaugh, *Origins,* pp. 404-405.

4. See chapter 12, note 5.

5. Brumbaugh, *History,* p. 208.

6. Flory, *Activity,* pp. 204-206. Published in German in Stoudt, *Poetry,* pp. 25-27.

7. James Y. Heckler, *History of Lower Salford Township, in Sketches* . . . (Harleysville, Pa.: Weekly News Office, 1888), cited in George F. P. Wanger, comp., *A Genealogy of the Descendants of Rev. Jacob Price, Evangelist-Pioneer* (Harrisburg, Pa.: The Evangelical Press, 1929), pp. 2ff.

8. *Geistliche u. andächtige Lieder aufgesetzt von Br. Johannes Preisz, einem in den Leidens-Wegen sehr geübten Creutz-Träger* ([Germantown: 1753]; Stoudt, *Poetry,* pp. 172-173.

9. *Das Kleine Davidische Psalterspiel der Kinder Zions* . . . (Germantown: Christopher Sauer, 1744), [6], 530, [28]pp.
10. *Die Kleine Harfe, gestimmet von unterschiedlichen Lieblichen Liedern oder Lob-Gesängen* . . . (Chestnut Hill, Pa.: Samuel Sauer, 1799), pp. 47-49; Stoudt, *Poetry,* pp. 20-22.
11. "Ein Reise Lied," *Die Kleine Lieder Sammlung* . . . , 2nd ed. (Ephrata: Joseph Baumann, 1827), pp. 200-201; Stoudt, *Poetry,* pp. 18-20.
12. See Durnbaugh, *Origins,* pp. 250, 405-407.
13. *The Testament of William Knepper* ([n.p.]:1880); *A Brethren Bibliography,* No. 285. See the unpublished genealogy of the Knepper family compiled by Grace E. Smith, in the Bethany Theological Seminary library.
14. *Christopher Sower. First German Printer in America* (Quincy, Pa.: Obed Snowberger, 1889), broadside. See also Brumbaugh, *History,* pp. 434-437; *Die Kleine Harfe,* pp. 9-11; Stoudt, *Poetry,* pp. 182-184.
15. "Gedanken über den General Wolff," in *Der Hoch-Deutsch Americanische Calendar, auf das Jahr 1761* (Germantown: Christopher Sauer, 1760); Stoudt, *Poetry,* pp. 184-185.
16. "With the exception of 'The Christian History,' periodically published by Thomas Prince, junior, from 1743 to 1745, this is the first distinctively religious magazine printed in the United States" — Evans, *American Bibliography,* No. 9676; "First religious journal published in America" — Karl J. R. Arndt and May E. Olson, *German-American Newspapers and Periodicals, 1732-1955* (Heidelberg: 1961), p. 522.
17. *Ein Geistliches Magazien* (Germantown: Christopher Sauer, 1760-1764), 2 vols.; *A Brethren Bibliography,* No. 21.
18. *Ibid.,* II, No. 10, stanzas 1, 6, 7, 10, 11; published in German and a literal English translation in Heckman, pp. 200-205. The present version was first published in *BLT,* III (1958), 3: 2.
19. *Ibid.,* II, No. 10, stanzas 52, 54-56, 59-65, 68-71, 79; Heckman, pp. 220-233. The present version was first published in *BLT,* VI (1961), 2: 32-35.
20. *Ibid.,* II, No. 12; Heckman, pp. 233-267.

APPENDIXES

1. Cassel Collection, MS 66. Translated from a copy made by Abraham H. Cassel from the diary or common-place book of Alexander Mack, Jr. This was drawn upon for the list of "members who joined the church in Europe" found in Brumbaugh, *History,* pp. 54-70.
2. So far as is known, Hochmann never became a member of the Brethren. They were ordinarily careful to apply the designation "brother" only to members. It is therefore significant that this appellation is lacking in this case.
3. Brumbaugh reads this as "a Polish nobleman" — *History,* p. 68.
4. See the discussion in Durnbaugh, "Beginnings," pp. 152-158.
5. A rather complete listing of Ephrata deaths is found in Julius F. Sachse, "The Registers of the Ephrata Community," *PMHB,* XIV (1890), 297-312; also separately printed (Philadelphia: 1891).
6. Sauer's journal, Schwenkfelder Library.
7. Charles G. Sower, *Genealogical Chart of the Descendants of Christopher Sower, Printer of Germantown* . . . (Philadelphia: the author, 1887).

Index

Achenbach, Barnett, 184
Acrelius, Israel, Swedish Lutheran pastor, 324
Adams, Charles, 215
Adams, Jonathan, 391
Affirmation, 346, 365, 376. *See also* Oaths.
Africa, slave trade in, 207
Agabus, Brother. *See* Koch, Stephen.
Agonius, Brother. *See* Wohlfahrt, Michael.
Agrippa, Brother. *See* Miller, John Peter.
Albach, ———, a brother from New Jersey, 188
Albertus, Brother, of Falckner's Swamp, 65
Albright congregation (Pa.), 144
Aleaser, Brother. *See* Eicher, Jacob Christian.
Allegheny Mountains, 141
Aller, Brother, 601
Alsace, 305
Altona (Germany), 122, 533
Amana Community (Iowa), 65. *See also* Community of True Inspiration.
Amish, 151, 359
Amos, Brother. *See* Meyle, John.
Amsterdam, 271, 297
Amwell (N. J.), 55, 100-104, 134-135, 186-187
Amwell congregation, 100-104, 186-187, 275
Amwell Presbytery, 134-135
Anabaptists, 125, 128-129, 135, 286, 321, 352, 377, 427, 470-547
Anastasia, Sister, last wife of John Wuester, 604
Andrews, L. F. W., 337
Anguis, James, 114
Anne of England, 381
Annual Meeting, 200, 208-209, 265-266, 287, 313, 327-334, 352-358
Antes, Henry, Moravian leader in Pennsylvania, 282-283, 293, 296, 304, 316-319
Antietam (Md.), 186, 252-255
Antietam congregation, 188
Arian, Peter, Dutch member, 605
Arnold, Daniel, of Redstone, 246, 266
Arnold, Gottfried, German Radical Pietist, 249
Arnold, Samuel, 184
Ascalon, 427
Associated Brethren of the Skippack, 279
Associators, 406
Augsburg Confession, 286, 427
Augustin, 597
Augustine, Bishop of Hippo, 514, 537

B———, Gary, 301
Bach, John, 358. *See also* Buch.
Bach, Sister, 604
Bäcker, George, 315. *See also* Becker.
Bäcker, Susanna, 216
Bacon, Henry, 142
Bakener, Lawrence, 184

Bakener, Nicholas, 184
Bakener, Nicholas, Jr., 184
Baker, Daniel, 184
Baker, Jacob, of Little Swatara, 182
Baker, Jacob, of Oley, 179
Baker, Margaret, 210
Baker, Marilis, 184
Baker, Mary, 175
Baker, Sarah, 211
Baker, Susan, 212
Baker, Susannah, 175
Baker, Wendel, 183
Ballinger, Daniel, 180. See also Bollinger.
Ballou, Hosea, Universalist leader, 323, 339
Balshbach, George, 181
Baltimore (Md.) congregation, 247
Ban, 78, 276, 328, 358. See also Exclusion.
Baptism, 17-18, 66, 77-80, 91, 124, 127, 140, 174-175, 203-204, 211-218, 240-241, 245-246, 269, 276, 278, 284, 290, 309, 427-428, 434-447, 470-547
Baptist (Brethren), 17, 115, 199
Baptists, 129, 172-173, 186, 290, 322, 325, 350; American Baptists, 172, 193; Dutch Baptists, 197-198; English Baptists, 175, 247, 270; General Baptists, 174; German Baptists, 211ff.; Keithian Baptists, 113; Seventh Day Baptists, 176, 185, 190-191.
Bär, Barbara, 183. See also Bear, Behr.
Barby (Germany), 349, 351
Basel, 18, 40
Bashor. See Beasher, Beshor.
Bassenman, Michael, 184
Baumann (Bowman), Benjamin, 114, 534
Baumann, Catharine, 213
Baumann, Jacob, of Germantown, 53, 175, 211, 605
Baumann, John, 114, 524-527
Baumann, Jr., Brother, of Germantown, 219
Bayer, Widow, of Germantown, 210-211, 256, 601, 604. See also Beyer, Boyer.
Bear, Henry, 178
Bearing, Liss, 183
Beary, George, 183
Beaver Creek (S. C.) congregation, 190
Beaver, King, Indian chieftain, 145
Bechleshammer. See Bechtelsheimer.

Bechtel, John, German Reformed pastor, 53, 289, 291
Bechtelsheimer, John, Amwell minister, 100, 187, 315, 602, 603
Bechtelsheimer, John, Jr., 601
Bechtelsheimer, Margaret, married Abraham Laushe, 187
Becker (Baker, Bäcker), Anna Dorothea Partmann, wife of Peter, 107, 111, 176, 210, 598
Becker, Catherine, wife of George, 213
Becker, Christopher, 180
Becker, Elizabeth, 176
Becker, George, 213
Becker, Mary, 176
Becker, Nancy, daughter of George, 213
Becker, Peter, Germantown minister, 61-62, 65-68, 70, 76, 79, 85, 87, 88, 90, 95, 98, 114, 161, 173, 177-179, 185, 193, 244, 278, 289, 290, 315, 598, 606; letters to from Beissel, 104-111; biography of, 176; poem by, 549-552
Becker, Widow, 180
Beckner, Lawrence, 357
Bedford County (Pa.), 144ff., 185
Beggarstown, 175, 176, 193. See also Germantown.
Behr, Mrs., 180. See also Bär, Bear.
Beightley, Catherine, 183
Beissel, Conrad, Superintendent of the Ephrata Community, 185, 278, 324, 605, 607; relations with Brethren, 64-89; letters of to J. Mohr, 102-104; letters of to P. Becker, 104-111; mentioned by contemporary writers, 112-120; relations with the Eckerlins, 149-157, 161; mentioned by Spangenberg, 272-273
Beissel, Louisa, 114
Beldhausen (Boldhausen), Conrad, 101, 114
Bellenger, Magdalena, 180
Bence, John, 185
Bender, Carl Lewis, 603
Bender, Eisbert, 603
Bender, Lod., 114
Bender, Peter, 185
Bendle, Henry, 114
Benedict, ———, 304
Benedict, David, 321
Benedict, Elizabeth, 182

Benedict, Widow, 182
Benezet, Anthony, American Quaker, 15, 53, 207, 404
Benezet, Philip, Philadelphia merchant, 56-59
Benneville, Dr. George de, 325, 338, 604
Berkeley County (S. C.), 190-191
Berkey, Michael, 183
Berks County (Pa.), 179, 182, 347, 380, 385
Berleburg (Wittgenstein), 24, 117
Berleburg Bible, 25
Bern Township (Pa.), 182
Bernard, Anthony, 178
Bersh, Philip, 181
Berthelsdorf (Saxony), 267-268
Beshor (Beasher, Büszhaar), George, 182, 222
Beshor, Jacob, 182, 358
Bethany (Bethania), Ephrata building, 113
Bethel Township (Pa.), 182
Bethlehem (Pa.), 155, 293, 295, 297, 304, 308, 320, 345
Beussel, Peter, 185. See also Beissel.
Beussel, Philip, 185
Bickel, Elizabeth, wife of Henry, 129
Bickel, Henry, 129
Bickel, Mr., 129
Big Conewago, 355-357
Bigler, _____, 184
Bingeman family, 154
Bitner, Catherine, 180
Blansh, _____, 179
Blunston, Samuel, Pennsylvania official, 142
Böbel, Christopher Adam, 201-202, 603
Boch, Abraham, 178. See also Bach.
Boch, Catherine, 178
Boehm, John Philip, German Reformed pastor, 131-134
Boehme, Jacob, German mystic, 137, 260, 272, 321
Bohemia, 267
Bohni, Jacob, Swiss migrant to South Carolina, 40. See also Boni.
Böhnisch, George, Moravian, 269-270
Boinon, Lewie, 603
Boldhausen. See Beldhausen.
Bollinger, Daniel, 358. See also Ballinger.
Bolton, James, Universalist author, 324-325
Boni (Bhoney, Bonney, Bony), Andrew,

Brethren leader, 173, 195, 598, 606; letter of to Europe, 39-41
Boni, Joanna Noethiger, wife of Andrew, 598
Bonser, Matthew, 184
Book of Concord, 427
Boquet, Col. Henry, Pennsylvania military figure, 144-145
Borghart, Salome, 181
Bosserman, Michael, 357
Bossert, Jacob, Jr., 602
Bossert, Jacob, Sr., 598
Bossert, Mary, 175
Boston (Mass.), 115, 384
Bowman. See Baumann.
Bowman, Elizabeth Painter, 213
Bowser. See Powser.
Boyer, Elizabeth, 175. See also Bayer.
Boyer, Margaret, 175
Brandel, Elizabeth, 182
Brandmueller, John, Moravian missionary, 159
Branser, Christopher, 181
Breaking of bread, 216-217, 272, 275, 353, 358
Bream, Barbara, 114
Brech, John, 177
Brecher, John, 315
Brecht, John, 600, 606
Brecht, Sister, 606
Bremer, Martin, 605
Breneisen, Jacob, 182
Brennemann, Melchior, 407
Brethren, description of in Europe, 16-20, 90-91; persecution of in Europe, 18-20; groups remaining in Europe, 20, 292, 307-308; migration to America, 19, 21, 23-60; contemporary accounts of, 36, 112-140; renewal and expansion of in America, 61-67; schism within, 68-111; in Germantown, 30, 85, 116, 160-161, 192-231, 270-282; as pioneers, 141-169; congregations, 173-191; doctrines, 174-175, 425-547; membership lists, 175-191, 211-217, 219-220, 597-607; discipline, 200-209, 238-239, 265-266, 272, 275, 277, 311-315, 352-358, 360, 450ff.; relations with Moravians, 269-320; relations with Universalists, 321-339; involvement in the Revolution, 341-423;

writings, 425-596. *See also* Dippers, Dumplers, Duncards, Dunkards, Dunkers, Eighth-day Tumplers, New Baptists, Old Brethren, Schwarzenau Brethren, Sunday Baptists, Täuffer-Gemeinde, Tauffs-Gesinnte, Tumblers, Tumplers, Tunker Baptists, Tunkers.
Bridgewater College, 426
Bright, _____, wife of Edward, 213
Bright, Edmond, 213
Bright, Edward, 213
Bright, Elizabeth, wife of Edmond, 213
Brilharth, John, 183
Brilharth, Peter, 183
Brissel, David, 184. *See also* Pressel.
Brissel, Henry, 184
Brissel, Michael, 184
Brissel, Sarah, 184
Brissel, Velte, 184
Broad River (S. C.), 334
Brown, George, Pennsylvania minister, 184
Brown, Rudolph, of Conewago, 184, 315
Brown, Rudy, of Little Conewago, 183
Bruch, Manass, 184
Brüdergemeine, 267. *See also* Moravians.
Brüderthal, 185
Brumbaugh, Martin G., Brethren historian, 62-63, 149-150, 193, 229, 232-233, 425, 549
Bucer, Martin, Protestant reformer, 536
Bucher, Peter (Brother Joel), 84-85, 605
Buck, John, 181
Bucks County (Pa.), 177, 380, 385, 407
Büdingen (Germany), 17, 65
Bullinger, Henry, Swiss reformer, 536
Burckhart. *See* Borghart.
Burgert, John, 330
Burial ground, in Germantown, 217-220, 228
Burkholter, John, 184
Büszhaar. *See* Beshor.
Butzmueller, William, 604

Calic, Brother, 299
Calvinism, 16, 140, 176, 322, 325, 342, 459
Canomore, Jacob, 190
Carlisle, Abraham, Philadelphia Quaker, 349

Carter, Eve, 216
Carver, John, Maryland minister, 188. *See also* Garber, Garver.
Casimir, Count of Sayn-Wittgenstein-Berleburg, 24ff.
Caspipina. See Duché, Jacob.
Cass, Friny, 181
Cassel, Abraham Harley, Brethren collector, 211, 232, 324, 426, 459
Cassli, _____, 304
Catawba congregation (N. C.), 189
Cate, Brother den, Dutch member, 605
Catechism, 459-463
Caufmann, David, 74
Chapman, Giles, South Carolina minister, 335-337
Chapman, Samuel, son of Giles, 336
Charitas, Sister, 598, 607
Charles II, King of England, 378
Cheat River (W. Va.), 160-162, 165-167
Cherokees, 167
Chester County (Pa.), 178, 385
Chestnut Hill, 396
Chiefly, Joh., Virginia minister, 189
Christian, Egite, 177
Christian, Lodowick, 177
Christian, Mary, 177
Christina, Sister, 71, 597
Chronicon Ephratense. See Ephrata Chronicle.
Church and state, 341, 352-358, 362-365
Church discipline, 200-209, 238-239, 265-266, 272, 275, 277, 311-315, 353-358, 360, 450ff.
Church establishment, 12-14, 377
Church fathers, 273, 321, 427, 497, 514, 537
Church government, 175, 187, 272
Church of England, 279, 281, 377-378
Clemens, Brother, of Great Conewago, 604
Clemens, Catherine, 214
Clemens, Gerhard (Geret, Garehart), 212, 219, 227, 605
Clemens, Gertrude, wife of Gerhard, 212
Clemens, John, 215
Clement of Alexandria, 321, 427
Clinton, Sir Henry, British officer, 405, 420
Clouds Creek (S. C.) congregation, 190-191

Clover Creek (Pa.) congregation, 144
Coccejus, Dutch theologian, 427
Cocalico. *See also* Cocolico.
Cocolico (Pa.), 112, 179, 289, 320
Cocolico (Pa.) congregation, 179-180
Codorus (Pa.) congregation, 183
Codorus Township (Pa.), 183, 262
Cologne (Germany), 301
Columbia College, 469
Colvill, Col. Thomas, 137
Comenius, John Amos, Moravian scholar, 267
Committee of Observation (Md.), 366-369
Community of True Inspiration, 65, 117, 126, 553. *See also* Amana.
Concord, ship bringing Mennonite-Quakers, 23
Conestoga (Pa.), site of Ephrata Community, 65-111, 117, 132, 173, 190, 265, 271, 286, 353, 354, 359
Conestoga (Pa.) congregation, 44, 68ff.
Congress of the United States, 343-349, 409ff.
Conscientious objection, 343, 364, 375-376. *See also* non-resistance.
Conversion, 431-433, 445
Cook, John, 185
Corbitt, Michael, 212
Council of Safety (Pa.), 387-388
Coventry (Pa.), 250-252
Coventry (Pa.) congregation, 62-68, 128, 178-179
Cowl, John, 607
Craven County (S. C.), 190
Crayling, Widow, 177
Crefelt, Jos., Virginia minister, 189
Croghan, George, Pennsylvania frontiersman, 145
Cumberland County (Pa.), 385
Cyder, Mrs., 182. *See also* Seyder.

Dänckel, Barbara, 217
Däschler, David, Philadelphia merchant, 53, 55
D'Alembert, John, French deist, 323
Danfelser, Wendle, 178
Danhawer, George, 391
Daniel, Brother, of Amwell, 103
Danner, Elizabeth, wife of Jacob, 259

Danner, Henry, 142, 183, 201, 248, 357, 524; poem by, 558.
Danner, Jacob, Brethren minister, 142, 183, 188, 232, 255, 357-358; letter of to Mack, Jr., 257-259; poem by, 555-558.
Danner, Michael, early York County resident, 141-144, 183, 257
Dascher, Brother, 604
Dasker, Henry, 178
David, Christian, Moravian leader, 267-268
Deacons, in Germantown, 220
Deal, Frederick, 177. *See also* Diehl.
Deal, John, 182
Dedier, Jean, 389
Deism, 322, 345
Deknatel, John, Dutch Mennonite, 270-271, 275
Delaware Indians, 160-161, 164-165
Demuth, Gertrude, 607
Demuth (Demud), John, 177, 602
Denny, Gov. William, 142-143
Deschler. *See* Däschler.
Dessau, Prince of, 20
Dettery, Elizabeth, 213
Devotional writings, 548-596
Dick, Adam, 184. *See also* Duick, Duke.
Dickinson, John, 391
Diderot, Denis, French deist, 323
Diehl, Philip, 177, 201, 604
Dierdorff (Deerdorf, Dirdorf), Anthony, 184, 186, 599
Dierdorff, Henry, 184, 601
Dierdorff, John, 184, 315
Dierdorff, Peter, 184, 266, 357, 601
Dilsheim (Düdelsheim, Germany), 176
Dippers, 173, 186. *See also* Brethren.
Dock, Brother, 604
Doctrinal writings, 425-547
Donner. *See* Danner.
Double (Duble), Lawrence, 114
Douglas, Dr. William, writer, 186
Dover (England), 25
Dress, 124, 174, 336. *See also* Joseph Müller portrait.
Drukel, Barbara, 215
Dubois (Duboy), Abraham, Brethren minister, 150-151, 178, 284, 289, 290, 304, 598, 606
Dubs, Brother, 604

Duché, Jacob, Anglican curate, 136-137
Düsseldorf (Germany), 19
Duick (Duck), Betty, 211
Duick, Margaret, 215
Duick, Sibilla, 214
Duick, Thomas, 223
Duke, George, 213
Dull, Elizabeth, 215. See also Diehl.
Dumplers, 135, 173, 276, 277. See also Brethren.
Duncards, 159-160. See also Brethren.
Dunkard Creek (Pa.), 160
Dunkards, 16-21, 145-148, 164-165, 186, 193, 419. See also Brethren.
Dunkers, 127, 135, 140, 159, 173, 280, 285-286, 303, 324-325, 335ff., 350. See also Brethren.
Duschong, William, 227
Dutch, in Pennsylvania, 43

Eberbach/Neckar (Germany), 65, 115
Eby, Andrew, 181
Eby, Barbara, 181
Eby, Christian, 183
Eckerlin family, 120-121, 149-169, 224
Eckerlin, Ann, wife of Michael, 149-151, 599
Eckerlin(g), Daniel, 599
Eckerlin, Emanuel (Brother Elimelech), 101, 149, 153, 599
Eckerlin, Gabriel (Brother Jotham), 121, 149-169, 599
Eckerlin, Israel (Brother Onesimus), 81, 116, 119-121, 144-169, 599
Eckerlin, Michael, Strasbourg Pietist, 149, 599
Eckerlin, Samuel (Brother Jephune), 121, 149-169, 599
Eckstein, Christian, 600
Eckstein, John, of Germantown, 53, 274-275
Eckstone, Elizabeth, 114, 599. See also Eckstein.
Eddy, Richard, Universalist historian, 324-325, 337
Edelmann, John Christopher, German Separatist, 497
Edesto (S. C.) congregation, 191
Edis family, 179
Edwards, Morgan, Baptist historian, on

Ephrata, 112-116; on Brethren, 172-191, 193, 243, 254, 326.
Ehrhard, Philip, 315. See also Erhard.
Eichelberger. See Eychelberger.
Eichenberg, Sr., 602
Eicher (Eiker), Anna, daughter of Daniel 75, 78, 84
Eicher, Daniel, Brethren leader, 75, 78-79, 81, 84, 178, 599, 606, 607
Eicher, Jacob Christian (Brother Eleaser), 114, 605
Eicher, John, 178
Eicher, Maria, daughter of Daniel, 75, 78, 84, 114
Eicher, Nathaniel, 162, 606
Eighth-day Tumplers, 134. See also Brethren.
Eldrick, _____, 184
Eleaser, Brother. See Eicher, Jacob Christian.
Elimelech, Brother. See Eckerlin, Emanuel.
Elizabeth, Sister, 71
Eller, Vernard, 429, 582-596
Ellis, Liss, 179
Endt (End, Ent), John Theobald, Germantown merchant, 196, 197, 275, 290, 391, 600; letters of to Krefeld, 53-60
Endt, Syblla, 175
Endt, Valentine, 602
Engel, Caspar, 604
Engel, John, 391
Engel, Sister, wife of Caspar, 604
Engelhard, Albert, 603
Engelhard, Lewis, 255
Engelhard, son of Albert, 603
England, 308, 322, 342ff.
English, in Pennsylvania, 43, 281
Ensler, Frederick, 304
Ephraim, Brother. See Höhnly, Jacob.
Ephrata Chronicle, 62ff., 193, 247, 259-263; bias of, 64. See also illustrations.
Ephrata Community, beginnings of, 64ff.; relations with Brethren, 89-90; visit of in New Jersey, 100-104; contemporary descriptions of, 97-98, 112-140; relations of with Eckerlins, 149-169; congregations connected with, 185, 189, 192-193; relations of with Moravians, 270-282, 316-319; relations of with Universalists, 324. See also illustrations.

Ephrata press, 138, 469ff., 524ff.
Episcopalian Church, 281
Epstein (Germany), 174
Erb, Widow, 220
Erboch, Lawrence, 177
Erhard, David, 184. *See also* Ehrhard.
Erskine, Sir William, British officer, 398
Ertzstone, Peter, 181
Eschenbach, Andrew, Moravian, 288, 290, 304, 305
Ethics, 207-209
Etten, Samuel van, 332
Etter (Eter, Etor), Christian, 183
Etter, George, 183, 266
Etter, Henry, 181
Etter, Jacob, 181
Etter, John, 181
Ettwein, John, Moravian chronicler, 342-349
Euphrates. *See* Ephrata.
Europe, religious heritage of, 11-12
Evans, Joseph, 142
Ewarry (N. C.) congregation, 189
Exclusion, 333-334, 419, 455ff. *See also* Ban.
Eychelberger, Peter, 180
Ezekiel, Brother. *See* Sangmeister, Henry.

Fahnestock (Fahnstock, Fahnstick), Armella, 101
Fahnestock, Daniel, 185, 524
Fahnestock, Dietrich, 101, 185, 600
Fahnestock, John, 114
Fahnestock, Peter, 114
Falckner's Swamp (Pa.), 65, 79ff., 87-88, 132, 284
Falkenstein, George N., Brethren historian, 192-193
Falz, Frederick, 606. *See also* Foltz.
Feetwashing, 18, 62, 140, 233, 272, 443-444, 463-469, 482-483, 539-544
Feit, Andrew, 603
Feith, Caspar, 607
Felbinger, Jeremiah, German scholar, 465, 514
Fendt (Fend), Mary, 175, 312, 216, 601
Fetter, Lucas, 173, 598
Fischer, John, 20, 599
Fischer, Sophia, 210-211
Fith, Eve, 175

Flackenstine, Frederick, 389
Flickinger, John, 598
Flohry (Flory), Abraham, 180
Flory, John S., Brethren historian, 425, 549-552
Foltz, Elizabeth, 185
Fornication, 275
Fort Duquesne (Pa.), 166-167
Fox, Anna Margaret Mack, wife of Emanuel, 214, 244. *See also* Fuchs.
Fox, Dorothea, 211
Fox, Emanuel, 214, 219, 244
Fox, Peter, 184
Fraktur, 115, 119, 121
Francke, August Herman, German Pietist, 268
Frankfurt/Main (Germany), 41-42, 116, 118, 154, 287, 288, 301, 304
Franklin, Benjamin, 169, 382, 398, 399
Frantz, Barbara, 180
Frantz, Christian, 182
Frantz, John, of White Oak, 180, 181
Frantz, John, of Little Swatara, 182
Frantz, Mary, 180
Frantz, Michael, Brethren minister and author, 180, 220, 222, 358, 599, 606; writing of, 447-459
Frantz, Michael, of Cocolico, 180
Frantz, Michael, of Little Swatara, 182
Franzina, Sister, 71
Fray, Christian, 184. *See also* Free, Frey.
Frederick County (Md.), 188, 244-250, 257ff., 368-369
Frederick, Isaac, 66, 67
Frederick, Veronica, wife of Isaac, 66, 114
Free, Joseph, 223
Free, Lawrence, 190
French, 162, 166-169
French and Indian War, 146-148, 380, 569
Fresenius, John Philip, Lutheran theologian, 287
Frey, Andrew, 79-80, 82, 602; writings on Moravians, 284, 288, 290-302, 304. *See also* illustration.
Frey, Veronica, daughter of William, 293, 307
Frey, William, 81-82, 602; relations with Moravians, 290, 293, 300, 301, 304, 307, 309
Frick, _____, 185

Frick, John, Brethren minister, 177, 178, 600

Friedsam, Father. *See* Beissel, Conrad.

Friesland, Brethren residing in, 20, 24, 174, 307

Fritz, Daniel, 597

Fritz, Elizabeth, 597

Fuchs (Fox), Justus, Germantown type-maker, 175, 199, 201, 203, 219-220, 223-224, 259, 358, 389, 392, 524

Funk, Christina, 114

Funk, Jacob, 114

Funk, Martin (Brother Manasse), 162

Funk, Samuel, 114

Funk, Veronica, 114

G———, H., 315

Gabel. *See* Gebel.

Gaby, Martin, 179, 222, 358

Gallican Church, 279

Galliond, Stephen, 66

Gantz, Agnes, second wife of George B., 601

Gantz, George Balzer, 63, 161, 173, 601

Gantz (Gans), Johanna, wife of George B., 63, 176

Garber, John, 114. *See also* Carber, Ger-ber.

Garber, Ora W., 548-549, 552-553, 572-573, 577-582

Gardner, Catherine, 114

Gasz (Gass), Jacob (Brother Lamech?), 73, 85, 605

Gaube. *See* Gaby.

Gebel, Abraham, 185

Gebel, Benjamin, 185

Gebel, Philip, 185

Geer (Gehr), Peter, 605

Geib, Margaret, 180

Geiger, Conrad, 606

Geiny, Henry, 183

Geiny, John, 183

George III, King of England, 345-346, 348, 372, 395, 403

Georgia, 191, 270, 278, 305

Georgia congregations, 191, 270

Gerber, John, 330. *See also* Garber.

German Baptists, 324-325, 365, 407-408. *See also* Brethren.

Germans, in Pennsylvania, 43, 125-226, 139, 280-281, 377ff., 409ff.

Germantown (Pa.), 23, 33-39, 53-60, 96-99, 117-118, 171, 173, 270-282, 347-361, 400. *See also* illustration.

Germantown Academy, 386

Germantown congregation (Pa.), organiza-tion and expansion of, 61-111; descrip-tion of, 175-177, 192-231; records of, 209-220; burial ground of, 217-220, 228; church government, 447-448. *See also* illustrations.

Germany, 16ff., 193, 267ff., 342

Gerst, Nicholas, 182

Gertrude, Sister, 603

Gesell, Andrew, 603

Gesell, John, 603

Geyer, Godfrey, 602

Gibble. *See* Giebel.

Gichtel, John George, German Radical Pietist, 272, 274

Gideon, Brother, 601

Giebel, Henry, 181

Gilman, Nicholas, 402

Gingle, Conrad, 180

Gish, Catherine, 181

Gitter, Bernhard, 101

Gitter, Magdalena, 114

Glades (Pa.), 248

Gmähle, David, 87

Gnadeneck (Germany), 307

Gomory. *See* Gumre.

Good (Guth), Conrad, 175, 607

Good, Daniel, 114

Good, Rosina, 114

Good, Samuel, 180

Goodman, Philip, 177

Gorgas, Benjamin, 215, 219

Gorgas, Jacob, 114

Gorgas, Julia, wife of Benjamin, 215

Gorgas, Margaret, 215, 601

Gorgas, Rachel, 216

Gorgas, Sarah, 215-216

Goyen, Arnold, son of Gossen, 53-60

Goyen, Gossen, Krefeld resident, 54, 602

Grace, 426

Graff, Friend, 602

Graff, Henry, of Amwell, 53

Graff, Jacob, 114

Graff, John, 66

Graff, Joseph, 114
Graff, Maria, 114
Graff, Mark, 113
Gramar, Anna Maria, 114
Grau (Grahe), William, one of the Solingen Brethren, 597
Grauling, Brother, 603
Great Awakening, 14, 61
Great Cove (Pa.), 145
Great Swamp (Pa.) congregation, 177-178
Great Swatara (Pa.) congregation, 222
Grebi (Gräbe), George, 173, 597-598
Grebielein, Claus, 246
Greek Orthodox Church, 290, 428
Greif, Jacob, 315
Greiling, Peter, 315
Grevy, George, 173. See also Grebi.
Gripe, ———, 184
Groningen (Netherlands), 307
Gross, Andrew, Frankfurt bookdealer, 118, 301
Grove, John, 182
Grub, Abraham, 178
Gruber, Eberhard Lewis, Inspirationist leader, 117
Gruber, John Adam, Pennsylvania religious leader, 53, 117-118, 259-260, 391, 425; relations of with Moravians, 274-275, 279, 287, 303
Gruber, son of John Adam, 122
Grumbacker, Brother, 600, 606
Grumbacker, Brother, of Pipe Creek, 603
Grumbacker (Crumpacker, Grumbacher), Catherine, 178
Grumbacker, Elizabeth, 600
Grumbacker, Peter, 602
Grumbacker, Ulrich (Uli, Wollery), Maryland minister, 188, 602
Gülte (Güldin), Samuel, 34
Gumre, Anna, wife of John, 63, 99, 176
Gumre (Gomorry, Gomri, Gomry), influential Germantown member, 24, 30-31, 61-63, 99, 151, 173, 176, 598, 604. See also illustration.
Gundy, Brother, 606
Gusz (Guss), Christopher, Virginia minister, 189, 315, 602
Güterman, Henry, 389
Guth. See Good.
Guthmann, a cousin of Martin Urner, 251

Haas, Brother, 404
Haas, Christian, 180
Haas, Frederick, 215, 217, 219
Haas, Widow, 220
Haberecht, Godfrey, Moravian, 278, 290
Hackman, John, 181
Hageman, Henry (Brother Nehemiah), 81, 606
Hahn, Mrs., 114. See also Höhn.
Hall (Germany), 17, 20
Halle (Germany), 98, 125, 268, 270, 377, 469
Ham, John, Brethren Universalist, 327-334
Hammaker (Hammacher), Adam, Pennsylvania minister, 181
Hampshire County (Va.), 355
Handschuh, John Frederick, Lutheran pastor, 130-131
Hanover Township (Pa.), 183
Hantsch, George Sr., Moravian missionary, 319
Harburg (Germany), 17
Harlacher (Horlacker), Catherine, 180
Harlacher, Charles, 232, 252-254, 602
Harlacher, Salome, 180
Harley family, 176
Harley (Harli, Heerli), Barbara, wife of Rudolph, Jr., 212
Harley, Maria, wife of Rudolph, 242
Harley, Rudolph, 175, 186, 232, 242, 252, 315, 599, 602
Harley, Rudolph, Jr., 212
Harnly, Jacob, 180
Harold, John, 183
Harpine, Margaret, 179
Hartenburg Castle (Germany), 19
Hartman, Anthony, Maryland minister, 188, 266, 602
Hartman, Regina, 150
Hartman, Susanna, 114
Harwick, Nicholas, 178
Hassert, Arent, Krefeld resident, 58
Hasuel, Brother, 606
Hauschel, William, 404
Hausser, Conrad, 181
Heafly (Höffle), Elizabeth, 114. See also Heffly.
Heafly, John, 114
Heafly, Joseph, 114
Heaven, 327-329

Heckman, Jacob, 182
Heckman, Peter, Pennsylvania minister, 182
Heckman, Samuel B., Brethren historian, 425, 459
Heffly, Peter, 178. *See also* Heafley.
Hegeman, Catharine, 114. *See also* Hageman.
Heidelberg (Germany), 115
Heidelberg Catechism, 202-205
Heidelberg Confession, 16
Heiner, John, 184
Heisler, Mary, 214
Heisler, William, 213
Hell, 327-330
Heller, Jacob, 180
Hellerlis, Sister, 602
Helmuth, J. H. Christian, Lutheran pastor, 527
Hencke, pastor, in Duisburg, 307
Henckels, John, one of the Solingen Brethren, 603
Hendricks, Daniel, 164
Hendricks, Henry, 143
Hendricks, James, 141-143
Hendricks, John, 143
Hendricksen, Dirk, Dutch member, 605
Henkle, Susanna, 213
Hennersdorf (Germany), 308
Henrick (Henrich), Adam, 182
Henrick, Catherine, 114
Henrick, James, Pennsylvania minister, 183
Henrick, John, 362
Henrick, Maria, 114
Henry Albert, Count of Wittgenstein, 25
Henry, Barbara, 181
Henry, George, 181
Henry, J. Maurice, Brethren historian, 355
Henry, Peter, 185
Herger, George, 391
Hermits, 281
Herrndijk (Netherlands), 297, 307
Herrnhaag (Germany), 292-300, 308
Herrnhut (Germany), 268-271, 297, 307-308
Herrnhutters, 82, 116, 119, 293, 296, 300-301. *See also* Moravians.
Hershy, Jacob, 180. *See also* Hirsch.
Hertzbach (Hertzback), Margaret, 175, 211, 605

Hertzbach, Philipine, 601
Heuple, Henry, 114
Heuple, Mrs., 114
Hildebrand, John, 63, 77-80, 84-85, 121-122, 151, 176, 275, 600
Hildebrand, Maria, wife of John, 63, 176, 600
Hill, Capt. Henry, 389, 392
Hinrichs, Daniel, 315
Hirsch, ———, 597
Histant, Mrs., 180
Hochmann, von Hochenau, Ernest Christopher, 597
Höcker, Henry (Brother Jonadab), 71, 81, 94, 96, 597, 600, 602
Höcker, Lewis (Brother Obed), 96, 114, 169, 232, 600
Hoech, Bastian, 196
Hoech, Johanna, wife of Bastian, 196
Hoecker, Brother, of Amwell, 604
Hoecker, Maria, 114
Hoeff, Henry, 183
Höffle. *See* Heafly, Heffly.
Hoffman, John, 114
Hoheim, Brother, 599
Höhn, Henry, 66, 67, 71, 78, 81, 85
Höhnly, Jacob (Brother Ephraim), 156, 602
Holderman, Elizabeth, 178
Holland, 20, 137, 174, 193, 298, 307. *See also* Friesland.
Höllenthal, Anthony, 162
Hollinger, Daniel, 180, 362
Hollstein, Frederick, 289, 290
Holmes, Benjamin, Quaker author, 428
Holstein, Brother, of Falckner's Swamp, 604
Holtzapfel (Holsapple), Henry, 63, 176, 598
Holtzapfel, Lena, wife of Henry, 598
Hook, Andrew, 114
Hopkins, Samuel, Philadelphia Quaker, 423
Hopp, Zacharias, Rotterdam merchant, 57
Hops, Maria, 605
Horter, Jacob, 391
House meetings, 188
Housel, William, New Jersey minister, 187
Housteter, Christian, 183

Housteter, Nicholas, 183
Howe, Sir William, British general, 398, 420
Hubbs, Charles, 214, 219, 220
Hubbs, Mary, wife of Charles, 214
Huber, Ann, 181
Huber, John, 114
Huber, Widow, 180
Huft, Elizabeth, 180
Huguenots, 271, 325
Huisinga, Jacob Dircks, Dutch member, 605
Hummer, Catherine, visionary, 232, 259-266
Hummer, Peter, father of Catherine, 259, 262, 264-266, 599
Hunterdon County (N. J.), 186
Huntzman (Huntsman), Hezekiah, 216
Huple, John, 113
Hyam, Thomas, 391-392
Hymen, Great, 183
Hymnals, Brethren, 553-555, 560; Ephrata, 276; Moravian, 276

Indian Commissioners, 137
Indian Creek (Pa.), 233-243
Indian Creek (Pa.) congregation, 232, 552. See also illustrations.
Indians, 145-149, 154, 156, 160-162, 163-169, 280, 284, 303
Infant baptism, 124, 203-204, 278, 280, 285, 290, 303, 320, 470-547
Ingles, Caspar, 179
Ingles, Elizabeth, 178
Inspired, 259, 268, 281. See also Community of True Inspiration.
Irish, in Pennsylvania, 43
Iroquois, 165
Isaiah, Brother. See Lesle, David.

Jacobs, Henry, 315
Jacobs, Philip, 228-229
Jaebez, Brother. See Miller, John Peter.
Jaeger, Peter, 602
James, Owen, American Quaker, 15
Jans, Albert, Dutch member, 605
Jansin, Catherine, 114
Jemini, Brother, 606
Jena (Germany), 270
Jephune, Brother. See Eckerlin, Samuel.

Jerome, church father, 514, 537
Jethro, Brother, 152
Joder, Jacob, Pennsylvania minister, 179
Joder, John, 179
Joel, Brother. See Bucher, Peter.
Jonadab, Brother. See Höcker, Henry.
Joner, Jonas, 180
Jones, Charles, 142
Jones, U. J., Pennsylvania historian, 145-148
Joseph, Brother. See Spangenberg.
Jotham, Brother. See Eckerlin, Gabriel.
Judaizers. See Weidner, Adam, and Cauffmann, David.
Judgment, 459-463, 579-582
Jugtle (Juchlie), Benedict, 605
Juniata College, 459

Kagi. See Kögie.
Kaiserslautern (Germany), 115
Kalcklöser (Kalkloesser, Kalckglasser), Catherine, 598
Kalcklöser, Christopher, 598
Kalcklöser, Emanuel, 598
Kalcklöser, John Henry, Germantown minister, 53, 70, 94-95, 275, 598, 606
Kämpel, Brother, of Amwell, 604
Kämpfer (Kempfer, Kemper), John, 63, 69, 176, 212, 222, 601, 602
Karchs, Jacob, 524
Käsebier, John George, Wittgenstein Pietist, 24-32, 37-38
Kauffmann, Michael, Jr., 407
Kauffmann, Michael, Sr., 407
Kearn, Conrad, North Carolina minister, 189
Kearn, Hans, North Carolina minister, 189
Kedar, Ephrata building, 119, 155, 287
Keim, Brother, 601-602
Keim (Kime), John, 175, 389, 603
Keisser, Elizabeth Rincker, life of John, 244-246
Keisser, John, 245-246
Keithian Baptists, 113
Keller, Frederick, 114
Keller (Kellar), Jacob, 114
Keller, John, 332
Keller, Joseph, 114
Keller, Sebastian, 114

Kempfer. *See* Kämpfer.
Kenickmaker, Adam, 114
Kentucky, 172
Kentzel, Liss, 182
Keyser, Barbara, wife of William, 214
Keyser, Benjamin, 391
Keyser, Catherine, wife of Michael, 214, 244
Keyser, Dirck, 212, 214, 216, 219, 223
Keyser, Elizabeth, wife of Dirck, 214
Keyser, Hannah, daughter of Dirck, 214
Keyser, Hannah, wife of Peter, 212, 216, 601, 607
Keyser, John, 392
Keyser, Joseph, 391
Keyser, Lydia, 213
Keyser, Mary, wife of Peter, 216
Keyser, Michael, 175, 212, 214, 216, 219, 244
Keyser, Peter, 175, 212, 216, 219, 220, 227, 257, 358, 390, 394
Keyser, Peter, Jr., 214, 216, 219
Keyser, Rachel, wife of Dirck, 212, 216
Keyser, Thomas, 215
Keyser, William, 214, 219
Kiefer, ———, 301
Kietzch, Henry, 320
Kime, William, 389
Kimmel, Barbara, 114
Kimmel, Jacob, 114
Kimmel, Philip, 185
Kinsey, Christian, 179
Kinsey (Kintzey), David, 179, 222
Kinsing, Brother, 601. *See also* Kuensing.
Kipping. *See* Kippinger.
Kippinger, Johanna, 173, 598
Kippinger, John, 173, 598
Kirkland, Snowden, 190
Kish, Sophy, 182
Kiss, fraternal, 360
Klein-Nicolai, George, writer on Universalism, 338-339
Kleine, Daniel, 179
Kleine, David, 182
Kleine, George, Pennsylvania minister, 179, 181, 182
Kleine, Peter, 179
Kling, Anna Margaret, 176
Knepper family, 185
Knepper, Peter, 315

Knepper, Veronica, 603
Knepper, William, Brethren author, 560-569, 603
Knodel, Jacob, 180
Knorr, Hannah, married C. Sauer III, 213
Knorr, Susanna, 213
Koch, Anna Elizabeth, wife of Jacob, 602
Koch, Barbara, 180
Koch, Catherine, daughter of Jacob, 602
Koch, Jacob, 62, 63
Koch, John George, 598
Koch, Mary, 180
Koch, Stephen, Brethren and Ephrata leader, 63, 78, 90-99, 176, 275, 599
Kögie, Brother, 248
König, Simon, 67, 110, 606
Königmacher. *See* Kenickmaker.
Koker, de, family, 276
Koker, Jellis de, Dutch member, 605
Koker, Michael de, Dutch member, 605
Koker, Peter de, Dutch member, 39-40, 605
Kolb, Dielman, 228, 244
Kolb, Elizabeth, 216
Kolb, Lydia Mack, wife of Dielman, 244
Krabiel, Christian, 180
Krafft, George, 246
Kratzer, Joseph, 404
Krefeld (Germany), 17, 20, 24, 40, 53-60, 174, 184, 536
Krefeld (Pa.), 225, 233-243
Kuensing, Henry, 180
Kuensing, Jacob, 180
Kuester, Philip, 601
Küffer, Henry, 319
Kulp, Lydia, 214. *See also* Kolb.
Kun, Henry, 177
Kuntz, Henry, 426
Kuntze, Daniel, 358
Kuntze, Dr. John Christopher, Lutheran theologian, 469-547

Laasphe (Wittgenstein), 221
Lamech, Brother. *See* Gasz, Jacob.
Lancaster County (Pa.), 112, 115, 138, 143, 179ff., 280, 319-320, 344, 359, 363, 385, 407, 447
Landert, Mary, wife of Sigmund, 67, 114
Landert, Sigmund (Brother Sealthiel), 67, 71, 72, 606

Landes (Landis), Catherine, 180
Landes, David, 180
Landes, Henry, uncle of Maria Naas, 55, 62, 75-76, 178, 210
Landes, Jacob, 180, 213
Landes, John, Pennsylvania minister, 73, 84-85, 179-180, 320, 358, 605
Landes, Johnny, 73
Landes, Magdalena, 180
Landes, Margaret, 180
Landes, Maria, wife of Jacob, 213
Landes, Mary, 179-180
Landes, Susannah, 180
Landstuhl (Germany), 185
Lang, Charles, 211
Lang, Frederick, 62
Lang, Valentine, 182
Langanecker (Longanecker, Longanacre), Christian, Pennsylvania minister, 180, 357, 222
Langanecker, Elizabeth, 181
Langanecker, Henry, 181
Langanecker, John, 180
Langanecker, Owen, 178
Langanecker, Peter, 177
Langanecker, Sister, 604
Langanecker, Ulrich, 181
Langstroth (Longstroth), Catherine, wife of Thomas, 212
Langstroth, Edmond, 213, 257, 395, 604
Langstroth, Thomas, 212, 395
Lap, Rudolph, 211
Laschet, Abraham, Jr., 187
Laschet (Laaschet, Laasche, Lashet, Lausche, Laushe, etc.), Abraham van, New Jersey minister, 187, 215, 358, 603
Laschet, Anna Barbara van, 187, 211, 604
Laschet, Christian van, 60, 175, 199, 215, 219, 220, 358, 389, 392, 395
Laschet, Henry (Herman), of Krefeld, 60, 187
Laschet, Jacob, 187
Laschet, John van, 187, 208-209, 600
Laschet, John Peter van, 186, 283, 284
Laschet, Joseph, 184, 315
Laschet, Margaret, 187
Laschet, Mary, 184
Laskin, Sister von, 104
Lautermilch, Brother, 181
Law, William, author, 334, 575

Lawrence, Thomas, mayor of Philadelphia, 59
Leatherman. See Letterman.
Lebrecht, William, 114
Lehigh County (Pa.), 407
Lehman, Benjamin, 193, 214, 216, 219
Lehman, Christian, Germantown surveyor, 193
Lehman, Elizabeth, 214
Lehman, Mrs., 398
Lehman, Sibilla, 216
Lehn, John, 185, 315
Leibert, Anna, wife of John (?), 213
Leibert, Elizabeth, wife of John, 216
Leibert, John, Germantown member, 213; list of, 211-216
Leibert, Nancy, 607
Leibert, Peter, Germantown trustee, 175, 196-199, 211, 214-215, 219, 220, 257, 258, 358, 390, 394
Leibert, Sister, 603
Leibert, William, 212, 216, 219, 220
Leibgeb, Christian, wife of Paul, 602
Leibgeb, Paul, 602
Leighty, Hannah, 114. See also Lichty.
Leip, Elizabeth, 183
Lentz, Jacob, son-in-law of Mack, Jr., 228
Leshar, Magdalena, 114
Les(s)le, David (Brother Isaiah), 606
Les(s)le, Peter, 603
Les(s)lie, Valentine, 87
Lessley, Ann, 114, 190
Lessley Christina, 114
Lessley, Elizabeth, 180
Letterman (Leatherman), Daniel, Maryland minister, 184, 186-187, 189-190, 232, 243-250, 255, 258, 266, 357, 405
Letterman, John, 315
Letterman, Nicholas, 266
Levy. See Liebe, Christian.
Lewig, Philip, 357
Lichte, Daniel, 219
Lichte, Sr., 602
Liebe, Arnold, son of Christian, 57-58
Liebe, Christian, European leader, 39-40, 54, 59, 61, 63, 174, 199, 606
Liebgeb, Godfrey, 602
Ley, John, 604
Light family, 179
Light, Jacob, 178

Light, John, 178
Linganore (Frederick County, Md.), 257
Little Conewago (Pa.) congregation, 183-185, 244, 254-255, 331, 333
Little Swatara (Pa.), congregation, 181-182, 222
Lobach, John, one of the Solingen Brethren, 19, 96-99, 597
London (England), 297, 308, 322, 387ff.
London Company, 393
Long, Isaac le, Dutch publisher, 271ff.
Longanecker. *See* Langanecker.
Longstroth. *See* Langstroth.
Lord's Supper, 18, 62-63, 233-235, 269, 476. *See also* Love feast.
Losch, George, powdermaker, 396, 398
Lots, drawing, 296-297
Love feast, 76-77, 186, 217, 272, 449, 464-469
Lower Salford Township (Pa.), 235, 552
Lowman, Henry, Pennsylvania minister, 185
Loyalists, 378, 400, 405-422. *See also* Tories.
Luis, 84. *See also* Luy.
Luther, Dr. Henry Ehrenfried, Frankfurt merchant, 41, 154
Luther, Dr. Martin, Protestant reformer, 428, 472, 488, 513-514, 530, 536, 537, 538
Lutherans, German, 125-131, 133, 139-140, 173, 267-268, 270, 280, 281, 284, 286, 290, 291, 303, 319, 377, 427, 469-547
Luy, ——, 150-151
Lynch, Elijah, South Carolina minister, 335, 337
Lynd, Catherine, 216
Lynd, James, 216

Maastrich (Belgium), 55
Mack family, 236, 238-239
Mack, Alexander, Jr. (Sander), son of Alexander, Sr., 90, 315, 358, 426; and S. Koch, 93-96; and the Eckerlins, 121, 152-158, 169; in Germantown, 175-177, 192, 193, 196-199, 201-206, 211-221, 275; biography of, 177, 224-231; correspondence of, 232-266, 330-331, 333, 359-362; writings of, 429, 459-547, 577-596

Mack, Alexander, Sr., first Brethren minister, 24, 63, 171-174, 178, 193, 321, 598; in America, 86-90; biography of, 176; writings, 89, 118, 425-428, 463, 493-494, 548-549
Mack, Anna Margaretha Kling, wife of Alexander, Sr., 176, 598
Mack, Elizabeth, daughter of Alexander, Jr., 177
Mack, Elizabeth, daughter of Valentine, 114
Mack, Elizabeth Neisz, wife of Alexander, Jr., 228-229, 236
Mack, Hannah, daughter of Alexander, Jr., 177, 212, 238-239
Mack, Jacob, 232, 256
Mack, John, son of Alexander, Sr., 176, 195-196, 254, 315, 599. *See also* Mock.
Mack, Lydia, daughter of Alexander, Jr., 177, 227, 228, 243
Mack, Margaret, daughter of Alexander, Jr., 177
Mack, Margaret, wife of John, 195-196
Mack, Sarah, daughter of Alexander, Jr., 177, 212, 216, 238-239
Mack, Valentine, son of Alexander, Sr., 94-95, 157-158, 176, 598
Mack, William, son of Alexander, Jr., 177, **252, 254, 256**
Mackinet, Blasius Daniel, Germantown merchant, 53
Mackley, Susanna, 182
Magdalena, Sister, 603
Mahanaim (Va.), 152, 156
Manasse, Brother. *See* Funk, Martin.
Manheim (Pa.), 359
Manumission of slaves, 208-209
Marge, David, 182
Maria, Sister, 71
Marienborn (Germany), 17, 174, 244, 297-300, 307-308
Marriage, Brethren views on, 75-76, 91-92, 271-272, 275-276; Ephrata views on, 84
Marsay, Count de, Wittgenstein Pietist, 32-33, 38
Martin, Catherine, 190
Martin, Christian, 598
Martin, David, South Carolina minister, 190-191, 248, **334-335, 601**

Martin, David, Jr., 190

Martin, Esther, 190

Martin, George Adam, Brethren and Ephrata minister, 184-185, 190, 247, 284, 287, 315, 601

Martin, Jacob, 114

Martin, John, 144-145

Martin, John George, 315

Martin, Maria, 114

Martin, Nicholas, Brethren minister, 184, 188, 190, 246, 254-255, 266, 601

Martsch, Mrs., 184

Maryland, 44, 135-136, 141-143, 172, 189, 257, 330-331, 350, 365-369

Maryland congregations, 187-188

Matthe (Matthai), Conrad, 151, 604, 606

Mattock, Thomas, 403

Mayer. See Meyer, Moyer.

Mayle. See Meyle.

McClean, Capt. Joseph (?), 401

Meetinghouses, 192-199, 212, 218, 337. See also illustrations.

Meinzinger, Andrew, 177

Meng (Ming), Christopher, of Germantown, 53, 389

Mellinger, Gertrude, 114

Mellinger (Millinger), Magdalena, 175, 180

Menich, Simon, 182

Mennonites, 15, 23, 36, 66, 76, 124, 126, 127, 133, 134, 138, 140, 151, 172, 173, 177, 207, 239-240, 244-245, 270, 271, 280, 281, 283, 284, 286-289, 292, 301, 303, 305, 307, 308, 320, 341, 344, 348-351, 359, 362-376, 379, 407-408, 529, 535-536

Meredith, David, 213

Messerbach, John, 185

Methacton (Pa.), 210, 221, 222, 402-404

Methodists, 137, 247, 355, 530

Metsgar, Jacob, 181

Meyer, Jacob, 222, 266

Meyer, Martin, 180, 358

Meyle (Maili, Mayle, Meili, Moyly), John, Ephrata leader (Brother Amos), 62, 68, 73, 82-84, 113, 114, 150, 605, 606

Middle Creek (Md.) congregation, 188

Migration, from Europe to America, 20, 24, 41-53, 171-172

Migtonia, Sister, 71

Militia, 343ff., 347, 359-363, 366-368, 378, 383, 388-389

Mill Creek (Conestoga), 65, 221

Miller, Abraham, 296, 309

Miller, Anthony, 603

Miller, Barbara, 178

Miller, Bastian, 402

Miller, Elon, 114

Miller, George, of Ephrata, 114

Miller, George, Pennsylvania minister, of Great Swatara, 181

Miller, Henry, mason, 151-152, 158

Miller, Henry, Philadelphia printer, 378, 397-399

Miller, Jacob, 184

Miller, Jeremiah, 114

Miller, John, of Bermudian, 185

Miller, John, of Ephrata, 114

Miller, John Peter, Ephrata leader (Brother Jaebez, Agrippa), 113, 115-116, 138, 185, 272-273, 324, 469, 470, 484-495, 510-511, 545-547, 606

Miller, Joseph, 177

Miller, Maria, 114

Miller, Michael, 190, 255

Miller, Salome, 177

Miller, Tobias, 180

Miller, William, 389

Ministry, 221

Minnich. See Menich.

Mock, John, 195. See also Mack.

Mohawks, 166

Mohler, Ann, 180

Mohler, George, 180

Mohler, Henry, 180, 601

Mohr, Christina, wife of Jacob, Jr., 103

Mohr, Dr. Jacob, 600

Mohr, Jacob, Jr., 103, 266, 601

Mohr, Jacob, Sr., of Amwell, 186, 600; letter to from Beissel, 102-104

Mohr, John, 101, 600

Monocacy (Md.), 135, 183, 188

Monocacy congregation, 188

Monshour, Dorothy, 114

Monsieur, Christian, 178

Montgomery County (Pa.), 269, 552

Montreal (Canada), 166-168

Moravia, 267-268, 271

Moravians, 12, 15, 82, 116, 140, 155, 159, 164-165, 191; relations with

Brethren, 267-320; in Revolution, 342-351, 369-376. *See also Herrnhutters, Unitas Fratrum,* United Brethren, Unity of Brethren.
Morris, John, of Philadelphia, 398
Morris, John, of York, 524
Morrison's Cove (Pa.), 144-149, 248
Morse, Jedidiah, author, 186
Moser, Mrs., 180
Mount Joy Township (Pa.), 181
Moyer, Barbara, 114. *See also* Mayer, Meyer.
Moyer, Frederick, 182
Moyer, Jacob, of Ephrata, 113
Moyer, Jacob, of Northkill, 182
Moyer, Jacob, Pennsylvania minister, of Little Conewago, 183
Moyer, John, of Ephrata, 66, 76, 114, 180
Moyer, John, of Little Conewago, 183
Moyer, Joseph, 183
Moyer, Mrs., 183
Moyer, Nicholas, 184
Mueller, Joseph, 600
Muhlenberg, Gen. Peter, son of Henry Melchior, 401
Muhlenberg, Henry Melchior, German Lutheran pastor, 125-131, 377, 400-402, 469, 470
Müller, Bastian, 250
Müller, George, 222
Müller, Joseph, Brethren and Moravian leader, 283, 284, 288-289, 290, 291, 293-296, 302-315, 600. *See also* portrait.
Mummard (Mummert), Ann, 184
Münster (Germany), 535
Müntz, John Benedict, 53
Murray, John, Universalist, 322, 339
Music, Ephrata, 115, 121, 138; Moravian, 312, 315
Musselman, Christian, report on Loyalists, 407-408

Naas, Jacob William, son of John, 53-60
Naas, John, Brethren minister, 18, 24, 54, 60, 63, 98, 116, 174, 177, 182, 186-187, 275, 523-524, 598, 606
Naas, Margaret, wife of John, 193-104, 210, 597
Naas, Maria, wife of Jacob William, 53-60

Nägele (Neagley), Jacob, 114
Nägele, John, 184
Nägele, Rudolph (Brother Zephania), Ephrata leader, 66, 73, 75, 114, 606
Nathaniel, Brother. *See* Eicher, Nathaniel.
Naturalism, 118
Neave, Richard, London merchant, 57-59
Neave, Samuel, Philadelphia merchant, 57
Neff, Henry, Pennsylvania minister, 183, 266, 357, 601
Neff, Jacob, 147-149
Negroes, 191, 207-209
Nehemiah, Brother. *See* Hageman, Henry.
Neiper, Peter, 184. *See also* Knepper.
Neisser family, 267
Neiswanger, Ann, 183
Neiswanger, Jacob, 183
Neisz (Nice), Anna Maria, 601, 607
Neisz, Cornelius, 213, 360
Neisz, Elizabeth, 177
Neisz, George, 185
Neisz (Myse), Mary, 175
Neisz, William, 601, 607
Neisz, Winard, 391
Nerwick, Brother, 600
Netherlands, 270ff.
Nethigeim, Widow. *See* Boni, Joanna.
Neusner, George, 296
Neuwied (Germany), 187
New Baptists, 132, 425. *See also* Brethren.
New Born, 281, 294
New Hannover (Pa.), 128-129, 179
New Jersey, 55ff., 100-104, 134-135, 172, 186-187, 350
New River (Va.), 152-165, 224
New York, 40, 469
Newberry (S. C.), 334-337
Newlanders (shipping agents), 23, 42, 45-46, 49
Newmoyer, George, 185
Nice. *See* Neisz.
Niederer, Jacob, 255
Nitschmann, Ann, Moravian leader, 299
Nitschmann, David, Moravian leader, 270-275, 277-279
Nitschmann, John, Moravian, 307-308
Noble, Abel, 113
Noethiger. *See* Boni, Joanna.
Non-Associators, 344ff., 352-355
Nonlitigation, 400

Nonresistance, 140, 144-149, 174, 341ff., 352-358, 378ff. *See also* Conscientious objection.

Northampton County (Pa.), 347, 385

North America, religious movements in, 11

North Carolina, 172, 178, 326-334, 350, 369-376; Universalism in, 326-334

North Carolina congregations, 189ff., 326ff.

Northkill congregation (Pa.), 182-183

Oath of allegiance, 352-353, 372, 376

Oaths, 138, 140, 204, 346ff., 358, 403. *See also* Affirmation.

Obed, Brother. *See* Höcker, Lewis.

Ochs (Ox), Betty, 227

Ochs, Frederick, 290, 600

Ohio, 144, 172

Old Brethren, 121, 151, 247, 276, 318. *See also* Brethren.

Oley (Pa.), 65, 79, 173, 284, 294, 347

Oley (Pa.) congregation, 179, 222

Olinger, Widow, 177

Oliver, Nicholas, 214, 216, 219

O'Neal, John Belton, judge and author, 335-337

Onesimus, Brother. *See* Eckerlin, Israel.

Ordination, 221

Origen, of Alexandria, 321, 497

Original sin, 75-76

Oswald, Philip, 185

Overseer of the poor, 221

Pacifism, 341ff.

Paine, Thomas, Revolutionary author, 323, 410

Palatinate (Germany), 17, 141, 308

Palatines, migration of, 25ff., 37

Palmer, George, 389

Partmann, Dorothy, married Peter Becker, 176

Passover, 233

Pastorius, Abraham, Philadelphia Loyalist, 419

Pastorius, Elizabeth, 215

Patchet, Elijah, South Carolina minister, 191

Paul, Abraham, 603

Paul, Sophia, wife of Abraham, 603

Pearson, John, assistant minister in South Carolina, 190; letter from, 619

Peedee River (N. C.), 189

Peiterly, John Jacob, 315

Pemberton, Israel, Philadelphia Quaker, 56-57

Pemberton, James, Philadelphia Quaker, 15

Pemberton, John, 401

Peniel, Ephrata building, 155

Penn, William, 363, 378

Pennsylvania Assembly, 343-349, 359, 362-365. *See also* illustration.

Pennsylvania Synods, 278ff., 282-291, 296

Pennsylvania, focus of migration, 23-24; conditions in, 30-31, 34-38, 40, 43-45; frontier of, 141-149; Scotch-Irish in, 43, 144, 342, 359; Brethren congregations in, 173-186, 192-231; Germans in, 280-281; English in, 281; Moravians in, 269-320; Universalists in, 322-324; Revolution in, 341-365, 377-423; university, 469

Pequea stream (Pa.), 66, 114

Perkiomen (Pa.), 279

Peter, Brother, 200-201

Peter, George, 183

Peter, Stephen, 183

Petersen, John William, writer on Universalism, 338

Peterson, John, of Pipe Creek, 604

Peterson, Partel Jürgen, German member, 533-534, 536-537, 599

Pettikoffer (Pethkoffer, Pettenkoven, etc.), Ann Elizabeth, wife of John, 114, 195

Pettikoffer, Isaac, 114

Pettikoffer, John, 114, 175, 193-195, 603

Pfau, Adrian, Dutch member, 605

Pfautz (Pfauts), Jacob, 178

Pfautz, John, 180

Pfautz, Michael, Jr., 232, 251, 607

Pfautz, Michael, Sr., Pennsylvania minister, 180-182, 599

Philadelphia (Pa.), 29ff., 34-36, 122ff., 192-193, 280, 282, 284, 322, 344, 347, 380, 385, 390, 401

Philadelphia Hospital, 386

Philemon, Brother. *See* Reisman.

Pietism, 14, 15, 24-25

Pink, Nicholas, 135

Plank, Catherine, 179

Poel, _____, 603
Powell, Samuel, 392
Power, Martin, Virginia minister, 355-359
Power, Valentine, Virginia minister, 355-358
Powser, Maude, 183
Powser, Mrs., 183
Prather family, 335
Preisz (Price), Conrad, 179
Preisz, Daniel, son of John, 233
Preisz, David, 179
Preisz, George, 358
Preisz, John Jacob, 63, 176, 233, 552, 599
Preisz, John, son of Daniel, 206-207, 213, 233-243, 338, 360-361
Preisz, John, son of John Jacob, 233, 315, 509; poem by, 552-553
Preisz, William, 213
Presbyterians, German, 115, 173, 176-178, 185; English, 135, 281, 335, 377-378, 383. See also Reformed.
Pressel, Valentine, 357. See also Brissel.
Protestantism, 278-279
Proud, Robert, American Quaker, 15
Providence (Pa.), 128-130
Provost Marshal, 221, 402
Prussia, King of, 19-20, 536
Publishing, 202-208

Quakers, 11-12, 14-16, 23-24, 36, 118, 122, 125-126, 129, 138, 140-143, 174, 207, 280, 289, 303, 336, 341, 344, 348-351, 359, 365-376, 377ff., 380, 396, 401, 428-447, 504, 525-526, 546
Quebec (Canada), 166, 169

Raab, Elizabeth, 212. See also Roob.
Raab, Jacob, 213.
Radical Pietism, 25, 86, 117, 122-125, 268-269, 292, 321, 425
Radical Reformation, 13-14
Raffo Township (Pa.), 180
Rahr, Hubert, Krefeld resident, 99
Rank, Michael, 222
Raudenbusch (Rundebusch), Henry, 184, 266, 315
Rausser (Rouser), Gideon, New Jersey minister, 187, 266
Rawlinson, Hannah, 392
Reading Township (Pa.), 184

Reb, Christian, 113-114
Reb, Rufinus, 606
Redemption, 577-578
Redemption system, 48, 51
Redroch, John, 177
Redstone congregation (Pa.), 246, 248
Reesop, George, 184
Reformed, Dutch, 131-135, 305; German, 16, 115, 131-136, 139-140, 202, 270, 272, 280, 281, 284, 285, 289-291, 303, 338. See also Presbyterian.
Regine, Sister, 602
Reichel, John Frederick, Moravian bishop, 349-351
Reicker, Philip, 181
Reiller, Elizabeth, 182
Rein, Elizabeth, 180
Reinhard (Reinhart), Frederick, 178
Reinhard, John, 331
Reinhard, Martin, 357
Reinhard, Maud, 178
Reinhard, Owen, 178
Reinhard, Peter, Brethren minister, 178, 222
Reinhard, Ulrich, 227, 601
Reinhold, 404
Reinsel, Ustace, 184
Reiss, George, 185
Reist, Catherine, 178
Reiszman, John (Brother Philemon), 96, 113, 600, 605
Reiter (Righter), George, 215, 219
Reiter, Sister, 604
Reiter, Widow, 215
Reitz, Henry, Pietist author, 465, 467, 514
Religious liberty, 13, 14, 19, 35, 280, 354ff., 364ff.
Relly, James, Universalist leader, 322
Renewed Moravian Church, 267ff., 271. See also Moravians.
Repman (Rebman), Dorothy, 182
Resurrection, 328-330
Reubey, Apolonia, 216. See also Roberly.
Reubey, Julius, 216
Reusz, Count of Vogtland, 24
Reuter, Frederick, 185. See also Reiter.
Reutsch, Joseph, 266
Revolution, American, 146-148, 341-423
Reyer (Royer), Catherine, of Cocolico, 180
Reyer, Catherine, of White Oak, 181
Reyer, Christopher, 180

Reyer, Daniel, 180
Reyer, Emich, 180
Reyer, George, of Cocolico, 180
Reyer, George, of White Oak, 181, 604
Reyer, John, 180
Reyer, Peter, 180
Rheinderken (Germany), 523-524
Rhine River (Germany), 18, 45-46
Rhode, Peter, 177
Rhodes. See Rotts.
Righter. See Reiter.
Rincker, Brother, of Great Swamp, 604
Rincker (Rinker), Catherine, 177
Rincker, Henry, 214
Rincker, Regina, 244-245
Rincker, Widow, 177
Ritter, Daniel, 63, 179, 601
Roaring Spring (Pa.), 148
Roberly, Appollonia, 212, 216. See also
  Reubey.
Roberly, Julius, 212, 216
Roberts, John, American Quaker, 349
Robertson, James, 398
Robin, Sister, 604
Rochelle (France), 169
Rock, John Frederick, Inspirationist leader,
  268
Roemer, Philip, 181
Roesler, John, 606
Rohrer, Jacob, 114
Roland, ———, 84. See also Rouland.
Roman Catholic Church, 166, 279, 289,
  290, 292
Ronneburg Castle (Germany), 17
Roob, Elizabeth, 175
Roob, Richard, 175, 604, 607
Rorback, Barbara, 114
Rose, Ann, 215
Rose, Levi, Dutch member, 605
Rose, Sister, 605
Rosh, John, 180, 604
Roth (Rotts), Henry, 135, 185
Roth, Henry, Jr., 185
Roth, Sister, 604
Rothenberg, Philip, 426
Rothrock, Brother, 600
Rothrock, Lewis, 315
Rotterdam (Netherlands), 25, 39-41
Rouland, Philip, 180, 599. See also Ro-
  land.

Rousefeler, Sister, 602
Roxborough (Pa.), 25
Royer. See Reyer.
Royer, Brother, 222
Rubickam, Juliana, 601
Rubusch, 299
Ruebel, Pastor, 19
Rünckel, Widow, 210
Rush, Benjamin, 139-140
Rutemburg Mountain (Germany), 19
Rutter, Rev. Thomas, 113

S., J. B., 122
Sabbatarians, 69ff., 82, 113, 118, 119, 133-
  134, 159, 190-191, 270-282, 303-304,
  425. See also Ephrata Community.
Sachse, Julius, historian, 62
St. Dionysius, 427
St. John, New Brunswick, 420-421
St. Peter's (Philadelphia), 136
Salter, Thomas, 391
Saluda River (S. C.), 334
Sandhills (Sandbergen, Md.), 244ff.
Sangmeister, Henry (Brother Ezekiel),
  Ephrata critic, 64ff., 90, 122, 150-152,
  162-164, 169
Sarets, Widow, 216
Sauer press, 90, 221, 300, 338, 425, 428-
  429, 448
Sauer, Adam, 184, 315
Sauer (Sower), Brooks Watson, son of
  Christopher III, 423
Sauer, Catherine Scharpnack, wife of
  Christopher II, 175, 177, 221, 244, 404,
  601, 607
Sauer, Catherine, daughter of Christopher
  II, 177, 222, 226, 390-391
Sauer (Saur, Sower, Sowr), Christopher
  I, Germantown printer, 26ff., 55, 117,
  207, 259, 275, 607; letter of to Germany, 32-39; influence of, 32-33; signer
  of pamphlet on migration, 41-53; report by on Ephrata, 118-122; on Mack
  and the Eckerlins, 155-156; relations of
  with the Moravians, 287, 315-319; relations of with Universalists, 325, 338;
  politics of, 377-378; obituary of, 378-
  380; possible writing of, 429. See also
  illustration.
Sauer, Christopher II, Germantown printer

and Brethren minister, 38-39, 192, 196-199, 201, 244, 245, 266, 319, 360, 400, 601, 605; biography of, 177; and church discipline, 202-207; on slavery, 207-208; baptizer, 212-214; journal information, 220-227; during Revolution, 377-423; will of, 389-395; as publisher, 202-207, 552, 553, 569-577

Sauer, Christopher III, printer and Loyalist, 177, 212, 222, 605; and Revolution, 378, 386-390, 392, 393, 395-400, 405-421; letter of from London, 421-423

Sauer, Daniel, son of Christopher II, 177, 222, 226, 389-391, 393, 405

Sauer, David, son of Christopher II, 177, 213, 222-223, 226, 390-391

Sauer, Esther, daughter of Christopher II, 177, 213, 222, 226, 390-391

Sauer, Hannah Knorr, wife of Christopher III, 422

Sauer, Jacob, 357

Sauer, Juliane, sister of Christopher I, 38

Sauer, Lydia, 607

Sauer, Maria Christina, daughter of Sauer II, 222, 226, 606

Sauer, Maria Christina, wife of Christopher I, 33, 37-38, 120, 221, 604, 606

Sauer, Peter, son of Christopher II, 177, 222, 378, 390, 392-393, 396, 421, 423

Sauer, Samuel, son of Christopher II, 177, 222, 226, 248, 390, 392-393, 421-423

Saunder, Samuel, North Carolina minister, 189

Saxony (Germany), 17, 267-269, 297

Sayn-Wittgenstein-Berleburg, 24

Schäffer (Shafer), David, 606

Schäffer, George, 223

Schäffer, Joseph, 66, 71, 114, 606

Scharpnack (Sharpnack, Sharpneck), Catherine, married Christopher II, 177, 222

Scharpnack, Henry, 175, 199, 212, 216, 222, 404, 423

Scharpnack, Sarah, wife of Henry, 212, 216

Schierwage, ———, 286

Schilbert (Shilbert), Abraham, brother of Peter, 196

Schilbert, Brother, 606

Schilbert, Peter, 175, 179, 195-196, 199, 218, 600

Schilbert, Sister, 606

Schilling (Shilling), John, 164, 167-168

Schlatter, Michael, German Reformed pastor, 135-136

Schlauch, Catherine, 181

Schleiffer (Sleifer), John, 177, 266, 600

Schlingluff (Slingluff), Anna Barbara, married Jacob Baumann, 211

Schlingluff, Catherine, 211

Schlingluff, Christian, Jr., 211

Schlingluff, Elizabeth, 211

Schlingluff, Henry, 175, 196, 201-206, 211, 221, 252, 254, 600, 607

Schlingluff, John, 175, 212, 216, 604

Schlosser, Ralph W., 555-558

Schmidt, John George, 597. See also Smith.

Schmidt, Matthew, 600

Schnables, Rose, 182

Schneider family, 176

Schneider (Snyder, Schneiter), Anthony, 175, 201, 205, 603

Schneider, Barbara, 183

Schneider, Catherine, 219

Schneider, Hans Adam, 183

Schneider, Henry, of Conestoga, 180, 599

Schneider, Henry, of Germantown, 599

Schneider, Henry, Jr., 180

Schneider, Jacob, 255, 597, 602

Schneider, John, 315

Schneider, Peter, 602, 606

Schneider, ——— Mack, mother of Jacob, 256

Schnell, Leonard, Moravian missionary, 159

Schob, Barbara, 180

Schrab, Lawrence, 266

Schreiber (Shriber), Anna, 601

Schreiber, George, 175, 196-198, 201-206, 221, 255, 256, 266, 601, 607

Schreiber, Katherine, 175

Schreiber, Nathaniel, 175, 211, 358

Schreid, Mrs., 114

Schriber, Philipine, 601

Schriesheim (Germany), 176

Schuh, Martin, 180

Schuylkill Brethren. See Coventry congregation.

Schuylkill River (Pa.), 222, 313, 358

Schwartz, Brother, 602

Schwartz, George, of Cocolico, 180

Schwartz, George, of Germantown, 200-201

Schwartz, John, 183

Schwarzenau (Wittgenstein), 17, 20, 24-25, 65, 70, 89, 173-174, 176-177, 186, 235

Schwarzenau Brethren, 118, 288. *See also* Brethren.

Schweitzer (Sweitser, Switzer), Barbara, 179

Schweitzer, Esther, 178

Schweitzer, Jacob, 178

Schweitzer, Lawrence, 53, 201, 599

Schweitzer, Matthew, 266, 315, 600

Schwenkfeld, Kaspar von, Protestant reformer, 269

Schwenkfelders, 15, 127, 140, 269, 281, 303, 341, 347

Scotch-Irish, in Pennsylvania, 43, 144, 342, 359

Scriptures, 272, 328, 430-443, 445, 468

Scusinger, Godfried, 114

Sealthiel, Brother. *See* Landert, Sigmund.

Sebalt, Leonard, 182

Seebach, Christopher, Wittgenstein Pietist, 38

Seelig, John, 604, 606

Seibers, Jacob, 114

Sell, Andrew, 178

Sell, James, Brethren historian, 144, 148-149

Senseman, Jacob, 114

Senseman, John, 87-88

Separatists, 66, 89, 117, 127, 130, 133, 140, 154, 259, 274, 281, 287, 290, 291, 292, 303, 315-316, 325, 347, 377, 524

Service, 450ff.

Severens, John, married Maria Naas, 57-58

Seyder, Jacob, 213. *See also* Cyder.

Shalles, Sebastian, 185

S(h)aron, Ephrata building, 113, 155

Sharpnack. *See* Scharpnack.

Shenandoah River (Va.), 189

Shilbert. *See* Schilbert.

Shingas, Indian chieftain, 145

Shoemaker, Margaret, wife of Peter, 194

Shoemaker, Peter, 194-195

Shoemaker, Philip, 407

Siebenberg(er), John Christian, 295

Siegfried, Lewis, pseud. of Count Zinzendorf, 288, 291

"Sifting Time," 292-293

Silence, Ruth, 213

Silesia (Germany), 17, 297, 307

Simeon, Martha, 114

Siron, Simon, 603

Skippack (Pa.), 65, 173, 176, 220, 222, 233, 244, 277, 279

Slavery, 207-209

Slingluff. *See* Schlingluff.

Smith, Belzar, 185

Smith, George, of Germantown, 216

Smith, Col. George, 402-403, 405

Smith, Henry, 142

Smith, Jacob, 182

Smith, Samuel, Quaker historian, account of Brethren by, 14-21

Smith, Susanne, wife of George, 216

Smith, William, Anglican divine, 12, 391

Snell, Philip, 184

Snow Hill Nunnery, branch of Ephrata, 569

Society of Friends. *See* Quakers.

Socinianism, 118, 174

Solenberger, Sarah, 182

Solingen Brethren, 19, 560

Somerset County (Pa.), 144

Sontag (Sonday), Jacob, Pennsylvania minister, 179-180, 601

Sontag, Mary Landes, 179

Sophie, Sister, 599

Souder, Jacob, 183

South Branch (W. Va.), 355

South Carolina, 40, 325-327; Universalism in, 334-337

South Carolina congregations, 190-191

Sower. *See* Sauer.

Spangenberg, August Gottlieb (Brother Joseph), Moravian leader, 98, 270-282, 296, 302, 305

Spanish war, 381

Sperry, Mary, 215. *See also* Spyra.

Spiritualism, 121

Spitler, Jacob, 183

Spitler, William, 183

Sponhauer, Jacob, 180

Spregle, Jacob, 114

Spyra, William, 175

Stahlnecker family, 164
Stamm, Catherine, daughter of Frederick, 214
Stamm, Conrad, 175, 212, 216, 404, 604
Stamm, Frederick, 214
Stamm, Hannah, wife of Ulrich, 175, 211, 212
Stamp Act, 380, 384
State, 362-365
Stauffer, Abraham, 184. See also Stober, Stover.
Stauffer, Ulrich, 212
Stauffer, ———, 185
Staut (Stout), Jacob, 177
Stedman, Charles, ship captain, 50
Stedman, John, ship captain, 50
Stedtler, Susanna, 114
Steiffer, ———, 115
Steiner, Barbara, 180. See also Stoner.
Steiner, David, 254
Steiner, Frederick, 603
Steiner, Friedli, 603
Steiner, John, 201, 603
Steiner, John, Jr., 603
Steinhofer, Friedrich Christoph, 273
Stetius, Luther, one of the Solingen Brethren, 597
Stewardship, 453ff.
Stieffel, George, 302
Stierli, Widow, 229-231
Stiler, Matthew, 183
Stillen im Lande, die, 122-125
Stober, Sister, 218, 604
Stober, William, Maryland minister, 188
Stohler, George, 181
Stohler, Hans, 182
Stohner, Henry, 181
Stohner, John, 182
Stohner, Mary, 182
Stoll, Ernest, 601
Stoll, Jacob, Brethren minister and author, 232, 357, 361-362
Stoner. See Stohner.
Stony Creek congregation (Pa.), 185
Stoudt. See Staut.
Strasbourg (France), 17, 149
Strasbourg (Va.), 163
Strickler, Conrad, 142
Stritzka, Brother, 598
Studebaker (Studybaker), Catherine, 184

Studebaker, David, 357
Studeman, Jacob, North Carolina minister, 189
Stumpf family, 176
Stumpf (Stump), Betty Becker, wife of Jacob, 182, 602
Stumpf, Jacob, 602, 606
Stumpf, John, 75, 78, 82
Stumpf, Julian, 602, 606
Stuntz, ———, 115
Stutzman (Studsman), Jacob, 184, 255, 266, 330, 601
Substitutes, military, 353-354
Summer, Joseph, 335
Sunday Baptists, 127, 359. See also Brethren.
Superintendent. See Beissel, Conrad.
Surhuisterveen (Friesland), 174. See also map.
Susquehanna River (Pa.), 141ff.
Swedes Spring (Pa.), 115
Sweigard, Jacob, 184
Sweitzer. See Schweitzer.
Switzerland, 17, 18, 305, 342, 447
Sychrist, Eva, 180

Tanner. See Danner.
Täuffer-Gemeinde, 30. See also Brethren.
Tauffs-gesinnte, 199. See also Brethren.
Taxes, 354, 359-362, 364, 371-376
Taylor, Thomas, 191
Teeter. See Titer.
Tennhard, John, Radical Pietist, 161
Tersteegen Gerhard, German Pietist, 90, 98-99, 307
Theophilus, pseud. for Mack, Jr., 469
Thomas, Henry, 181
Thomas, Margaret, 181
Thommin, An., 114
Thompson, Col. William, 402-403
Thürnstein, Herr von, pseud. for Count Zinzendorf, 279
Tillman, Jacob, 183
Timotheus, Brother. See Mack, Alexander, Jr.
Titer, John, Maryland minister, 187
Tories, 220, 355, 409ff. See also Loyalists.
Towamencin Township (Pa.), 269
Transatlantic passage, 34, 41-53, 99
Traub, Paul, 185

Traut, George Balser, 63, 173, 176, 598
Traut, Jeremiah, 63, 176, 598
Traut, John Henry, 30, 63, 68, 78, 92, 161, 173, 176, 598
Traut, Magdalena, wife of George Balser, 63, 176
Triffel, Triny, 177
Trimmer, Andrew, 184
Tropus (denomination), 278
Trustees, of Germantown, 220ff.
Tulpehocken Township (Pa.), 182
Tumblers, 173. See also Brethren.
Tumplers, 130-134, 191, 270, 285. See also Brethren.
Tumplers, Seventh-Day, 134. See also Brethren.
Tunker Baptists, 189-191, 186-187. See also Brethren.
Tunkers, 173, 186-187, 189, 324, 326. See also Brethren.
Tunkerstown, 113, 114. See also Ephrata.
Tusten, William, 392
Typecasting, 224
Tysen, Elizabeth, 215
Tysen, William, 215

Ullery, Daniel, 148
Ulrich, Stephen, 266, 601
Unitas Fratrum, 267. See also Moravians.
United Brethren, 267. See also Moravians.
Unity of Brethren, 267. See also Moravians.
Universal restoration, 321
Universalism, 127, 140, 174, 321-339
Universalists, 322-330, 459
Upper Milford Township (Pa.), 177, 348, 407
Urner, Barbara Sweitser, wife of the younger Martin, 178, 179, 251, 252, 605
Urner, Catherine Reist, wife of the older Martin, 62
Urner, Elizabeth, daughter of the younger Martin, 179
Urner, Jacob, son of the older Martin, 178
Urner, Jonas, 216
Urner, Joseph, son of the younger Martin, 179
Urner, Martin, Brethren minister (d.1755), 62, 76-77, 177-179, 182, 287, 315, 599

Urner, Martin, Brethren minister, nephew (cousin) of the older Martin, 178-179, 213-214, 222, 232, 250-252, 255, 266, 330-331, 357, 358, 422-423, 600, 605
Urner, Martin, son of the older Martin, 178
Urner, Martin, son of the younger Martin, 179
Urner, Mary, daughter of the older Martin, 178
Urner, Mary, daughter of the younger Martin, 179

Veronica, Sister, 71, 210
Vetter. See Fetter.
Virginia, 44, 149-165, 172, 178, 327ff., 401
Virginia congregations, 189
Visions, 92-93, 259-266
Voht, Nathaniel, London merchant, 57
Voltaire, French deist, 112, 323
Volzin, Catherine, 114

Wachovia (N. C.), 164-165
Waggoner (Wagner), George, 184
Waggoner, Hans, 190
Waggoner, Philip, 178
Wagner, Brother, 604
Waldensians, 290
Walker, Dr. Thomas, surveyor, 159-160
Waller, Stephen, Maryland minister, 188, 254-255
Walter, Caspar, 75
Ward, Nathaniel, Puritan divine, 13
Warren, James, 190
Warrington Township (Pa.), 184
Washington County (Md.), 366-368
Washington, George, 347, 402
"Watchmen," 379
Wattenwille, John von, 299
Weaver. See Weber.
Weber (Weaver, Weaber), Adam, 214, 219, 238-239, 244
Weber, Alexander, 604
Weber, Daniel, 257
Weber, Elizabeth, wife of John, 215
Weber, Hannah Mack, wife of Adam, 244
Weber, Henry, 221, 227, 602, 607
Weber, Jacob, 66
Weber, John, 212, 214, 215, 216, 219, 244, 245

Weber, John Peter, of Little Conewago, 183

Weber, Laura, wife of Philip, 601

Weber, Melchior, 185

Weber, Philip, 175, 198-199, 201-206, 219-221, 244, 601, 604

Weber, Susan, daughter of Philip, 214

Weber, Susanna, wife of John, 214

Weber, Susanna, wife of Philip, 604

Weidner, Adam, 74

Weidner, Lazarus, 239-240

Weise, Hesther, 183

Weiser, Conrad, 290

Weisz, Jacob, 87-88, 600, 606

Weisz, Sophia, daughter of Jacob, 600

Welfare. *See* Wohlfahrt, Michael.

Welsh, John, 274

Welshaver, Jacob, 142

Weltner, Susanna, 183

Welty, Barbara, 178

Wentz, Elizabeth, 606

Wentz, Peter, 286, 606

Werner, Phillippina, 213

Wertz (Werds, Wirtz), Peter, 103, 184, 220, 601

Wertz, William, 601

Wesley, John, Methodist leader, 530

West Virginia, 355ff.

Westenberger, Christopher, 180

Wetterau (Germany), 292

Weyley, Adam, 185

Wheat, 335

Whiston, William, British scholar, 478-479

White Oak congregation (Pa.), 180-181, 222, 259ff., 265

Widdenbarger, Mr., 185

Widder, Christopher, 180

Wiederbringung, universal restoration, 321

Wiegener, Christopher, Schwenkfelder, 269-271, 606

William, Brother, 603

Winchester, Elhanan, Universalist author, 322, 325-326, 338-339

Wine, George, 183

Wirtz. *See* Wertz.

Wissahickon Creek, site of the first American baptism of the Brethren, 62, 218. *See also* illustration.

Wistar (Wiester, Wüster), John, Philadelphia merchant, 53, 55-56, 391, 404, 604

Wister, Sarah, Philadelphia chronicler, 227

Wittgenstein, County of, 17, 32, 177, 221, 268

Wohlfahrt, Michael (Brother Agonius), Ephrata leader, 65, 66-67, 73-75, 79-80, 84, 87-88, 151, 273-274, 278, 605, 606

Wolf (Woolf), Andrew, 178, 251

Wolfe, Gen. James, 572-573

Wolff, Nicholas, Wittgenstein Pietist, 30, 32, 33, 37

Wood, Catherine, 215

Wood, John, 215

Woods, Daniel, 183

Woolf family, 179

Woolf, Jeremiah, 180

Woolf, Jeremiah, Jr., 180

Woolf, Rant, 180

Woolman, John, American Quaker, 12, 207

Württemberg, Duchy of, 17

Wüster. *See* Wister.

Yadkin River (N. C.), 189

Yellow fever, 217-220

Yoder. *See* Joder.

York County (Pa.), 141ff., 183-184, 262, 385, 524

Yount. *See* Yunt.

Ysenberg, County of, 17

Yunt, Rudy, 183

Zeigler, Jacob, 214

Zeigler, Philip, 182

Zellers, John, 215

Zephaniah, Brother. *See* Nägele, Rudolph.

Zettel, Philip, 559

Ziegler, Elizabeth, wife of William, 215

Ziegler, Jacob, 219, 244

Ziegler, Sarah Mack, 244

Ziegler, William, 215, 219

Zimmerman, Henry, 72

Zinn, Elizabeth, 114

Zinn, Garret, 160

Zinn, George, 114

Zinn, Henry, 154

Zinn, Herman, 114

Zinzendorf, Count Lewis von, 117, 119, 134, 177, 268ff., 278-305

Zion, Ephrata building, 113, 155

Zionitic Brotherhood, 118. *See also* Ephrata Community.
Zittels, Widow, 21
Zuck. *See* Zug, Zuk.
Zug, Christian, 180
Zug, Jacob, 180
Zug, John, 180, 222
Zug, Hans, 177
Zuk, Peter, 604
Zweibrücken (Germany), 182
Zwingli, Huldreich, Protestant reformer, 427